𝐏𝐏 PARAGRAPH PUBLISHING

Paragraph Publishing, St Faiths House,
Mountergate, Norwich, Norfolk, NR1 1PY.
Tel: 01603 633 808 Fax: 01603 632 808 Email:
info@daysoutatlas.co.uk
Web site: www.daysoutatlas.co.uk

First Paragraph Publishing edition: May 2002

British Library Cataloguing-in-Publication
Data. A catalogue record for this book is
available from the British Library.

ISBN 0-9537771-8-9

Reprographics by Anglia Colour, Norwich.
Printed and bound by Heron Print, UK.
Distributed by MDL, Houndmills,
Basingstoke, Hampshire RG21 6XS.
9 8 7 6 5 4 3 2 1

EDITOR & PUBLISHER   Damian Riley-Smith
PRODUCT MANAGER   Michelle Smith
DESIGN   Stephen Bird
                      Ron Keenes
                      Lorna Crosbie-Smith
RESEARCH & SALES   Colin Willsher
                      Ben Weaver
                      Joanne Morley
PRODUCTION MANAGER   Rubyna Sheikh
SOFTWARE   Kingswood
FINANCE   Trudi Foster

Photographs: © Great Scot, © Dumfries &
Galloway Tourist Board, © Bristol Tourism
Conference Bureau, © Greater Glasgow & Clyde
Valley Tourist Board, © Perthshire Tourist Board,
© Edinburgh & Lothians Tourist Board, © Gus
Campbell, © Aberdeen & Grampians Tourist Board,
© Highlands of Scotland Tourist Board, © Scottish
Borders Tourist Board, © North West Tourist
Board, © South East England Tourist Board,
© Orkney Tourist Board, © National Trust
Photographic Library, © Chester Zoo, © Corbis
Corp, Northumberland Tourist Board, © Graeme
Peacock, © Bicton Park, © Alnwick Castle
Publications, © British Tourist Authority,
© Poundhill Gardens, © Farmer Giles Farmstead,
© Scarborough Sealife Centre, © Wolterton Hall,
© Donkey Sanctuary, © Longleat, © Harewood
House, © Mannington Hall, © Michelle Smith,
© Historic Scotland, © Bank of England Museum,
© Wimbledon Tours, © Argyll, the Isles, Loch
Lomond, Stirling & the Trossachs Tourist Board.

DAYS OUT ATLAS

2002-2003

FIND YOUR WAY TO BRITAIN'S

- Animal attractions • Heritage & culture
- Indoor activities • Outdoor activities
- Outdoor attractions • Water activities

THE MAPS

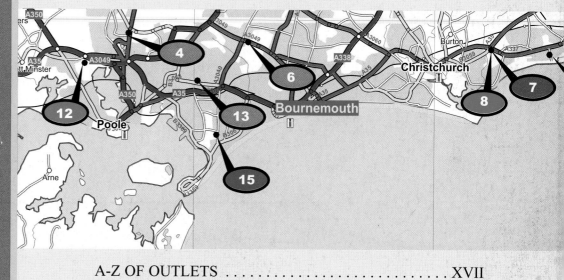

DAYS OUT ATLAS

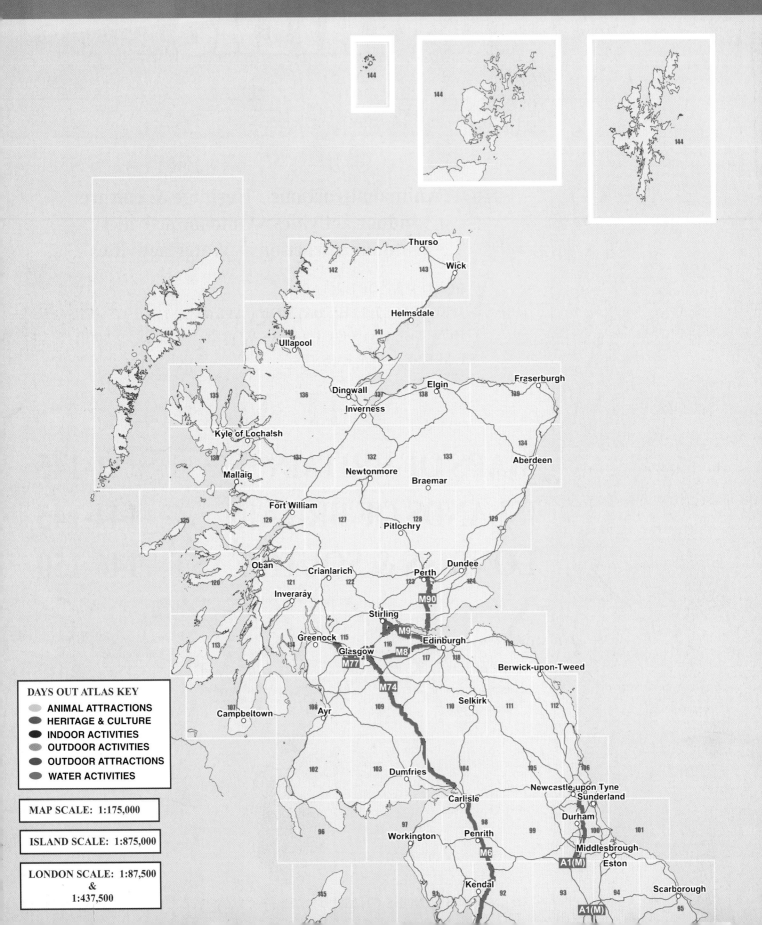

144

144

144

144

Thurso
Wick
142 143
Helmsdale
141
140 Ullapool
Fraserburgh
Elgin
Dingwall 137 138 139
136
Inverness
135
134
Kyle of Lochalsh
138 131 132 133 Aberdeen
Mallaig
Newtonmore
Braemar
Fort William
125 126 127 128 129
Pitlochry
Oban
Dundee
Crianlarich Perth
120 122 123 124
Inveraray M90

Stirling
M9
Greenock 115 Edinburgh
113 114 116 M8 119
Glasgow 117 118
M77
Berwick-upon-Tweed
M74

Selkirk
107 108 109 110 111 112
Campbeltown Ayr

Newcastle upon Tyne
102 103 Dumfries 104 105 106 Sunderland
Carlisle
Durham
98 100 101
97 99
Workington Penrith
96 Middlesbrough
A1(M) Eston
M6
145 Kendal Scarborough
91 92 93 94 95
A1(M)

DAYS OUT ATLAS KEY
- ANIMAL ATTRACTIONS
- HERITAGE & CULTURE
- INDOOR ACTIVITIES
- OUTDOOR ACTIVITIES
- OUTDOOR ATTRACTIONS
- WATER ACTIVITIES

MAP SCALE: 1:175,000

ISLAND SCALE: 1:875,000

LONDON SCALE: 1:87,500
&
1:437,500

MAP NUMBERS & KEY

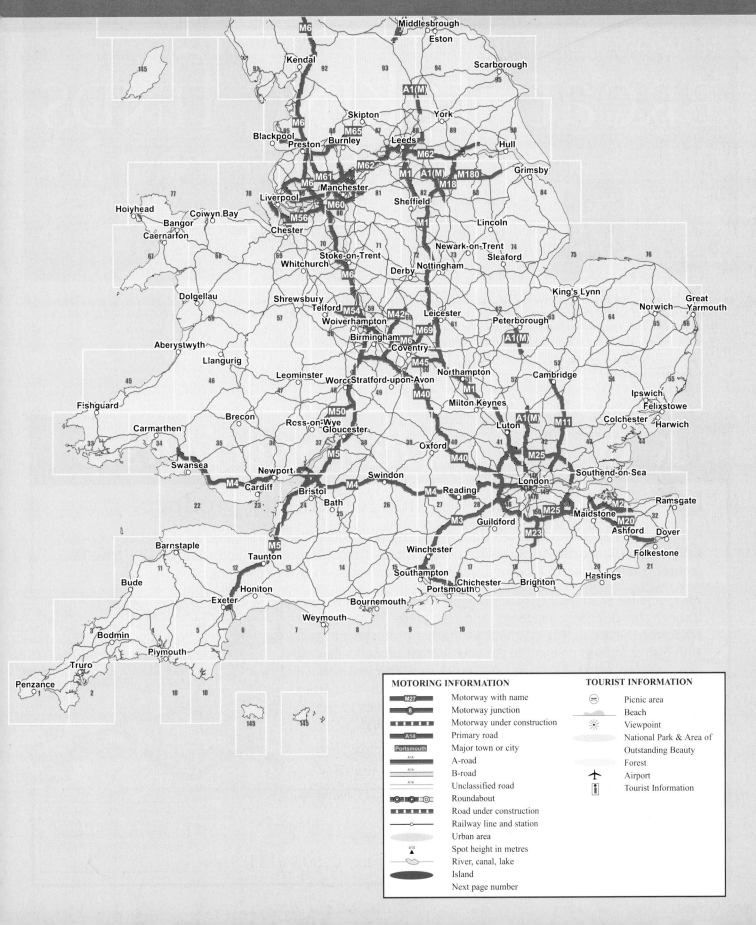

MOTORING INFORMATION

- M27 — Motorway with name
- 8 — Motorway junction
- Motorway under construction
- A14 — Primary road
- Portsmouth — Major town or city
- A14 — A-road
- A14 — B-road
- A14 — Unclassified road
- Roundabout
- Road under construction
- Railway line and station
- Urban area
- ▲410 — Spot height in metres
- River, canal, lake
- Island
- Next page number

TOURIST INFORMATION

- Picnic area
- Beach
- Viewpoint
- National Park & Area of Outstanding Beauty
- Forest
- Airport
- Tourist Information

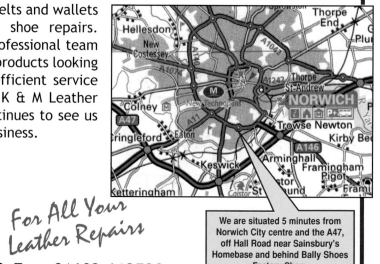

How many times have you run out of ideas for things to do at the weekend? Or found yourself far from home with the family to entertain? Or been caught by the weather with a car full of 'enthusiastic' children at half-term?

We have created the **Days Out Atlas** so these challenges become a thing of the past. More importantly, we wanted to create a publication to help you plan your trip before you set out.

Where is the nearest zoo? Can I find three interesting places to visit within ten miles of my parents' home? If I want to spend a cultural day out, how do I find all the suitable places. The **Days Out Atlas** answers these questions by letting you know what is available and where it is - essential when you're out and about on Britain's busy roads. Space does not allow detailed listings on every attraction, but half the fun of a day out is exploring - and exploring with knowledge. We have tried to identify every attraction that may be on your route so you can drop in, give them a call or - at the very least - ensure you don't drive past and say "if only I'd known".

As with any first edition I am sure not every relevant attraction has been identified, so please let us know of any omissions or places you feel we should consider. As a guide the **Days Out Atlas** cannot answer all your questions - but it does answer that key question that has always vexed me - what are the great days out within easy reach of where I am or where I am going?

We recommend you call before you visit any of the attractions, and if you mention the **Days Out Atlas** you will be assured of the very best attention.

Have many great days out!

Damian Riley-Smith

The *Days Out Atlas* shows the way to thousands of attractions in England, Scotland and Wales. When planning a day out to a particular part of the country our aim is to help you find all the locations of interest to you, through easy to use maps and information.

The *Days Out Atlas* is small enough to fit in the glove box of your car and when you find yourself passing through a particular area of the country, you can use the *Days Out Atlas* to find all the fun things to do in your chosen area.

We have tried to include every animal attraction, outdoor attraction, indoor activity, outdoor activity, water activity and heritage & culture site that welcomes visitors for at least five months of the year, five days a week and at least five hours a day.

Each of the six different types of attraction has a different colour lozenge. You will find a guide to each lozenge colour throughout the Atlas pages. Each attraction is identified by its own unique number. This number is shown on the map, in the listing box and in the index at the back. London has a different map scale because the density of attractions is so great.

Many properties are owned or managed by a group, such as the National Trust or English Heritage, and where this is the case we have identified this with initials after the name, as outlined below. Telephone numbers may connect to a central location, and for ease we have listed the head office numbers here. There are also regional offices which you can ask for from the head office.

NT = *National Trust 020 7222 9251*

NTS = *National Trust for Scotland 0131 243 9300*

EH = *English Heritage 020 7973 3000*

HS = *Historic Scotland 0131 668 8600*

We have asked attractions with standard or premier entries to supply their own descriptions. We do not include our own opinions or preferences, as we would like the *Days Out Atlas* to provide a comprehensive range of all the relevant attractions. We hope that by doing this you will come to your own conclusions after visiting places listed within the Atlas.

Every entry lists the name, address and telephone number (where available) along with the type of attraction and category into which it has been placed.

Basic Entry

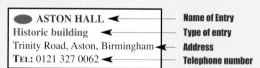

- **ASTON HALL** ◄──── Name of Entry
- Historic building ◄──── Type of entry
- Trinity Road, Aston, Birmingham ◄──── Address
- **TEL:** 0121 327 0062 ◄──── Telephone number

There are two types of enhanced entry; Standard and Premier. Standard entries have a 25-word description, opening times, specialities and facilities.

Standard Entry

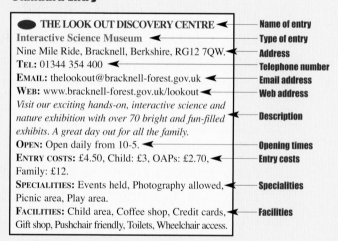

- **THE LOOK OUT DISCOVERY CENTRE** ◄──── Name of entry
- Interactive Science Museum ◄──── Type of entry
- Nine Mile Ride, Bracknell, Berkshire, RG12 7QW. ◄──── Address
- **TEL:** 01344 354 400 ◄──── Telephone number
- **EMAIL:** thelookout@bracknell-forest.gov.uk ◄──── Email address
- **WEB:** www.bracknell-forest.gov.uk/lookout ◄──── Web address
- *Visit our exciting hands-on, interactive science and nature exhibition with over 70 bright and fun-filled exhibits. A great day out for all the family.* ◄──── Description
- **OPEN:** Open daily from 10-5. ◄──── Opening times
- **ENTRY COSTS:** £4.50, Child: £3, OAPs: £2.70, Family: £12. ◄──── Entry costs
- **SPECIALITIES:** Events held, Photography allowed, Picnic area, Play area. ◄──── Specialities
- **FACILITIES:** Child area, Coffee shop, Credit cards, Gift shop, Pushchair friendly, Toilets, Wheelchair access. ◄──── Facilities

Opening Times

Where provided, the company concerned has supplied opening times. Please note that some outlets may be flexible with their dates and hours of opening. It is advisable to contact them before travelling long distances.

Entry Costs

All outlets with enhanced listings have the entry costs included, where supplied. The first cost is for an adult and any concessions are listed afterwards. If in doubt please call before visiting. Group discounts may also apply to some attractions.

Facilities

Outlets with enhanced entries list the facilities they have available. It is advised to call before travelling, to check about particular facilities if you are unsure.

Specialities

Some outlets with enhanced entries list the specialities they have available. It is advisable to call before travelling, to check about particular specialities if you are unsure.

Feedback

If you have any suggestions for places we may have missed or events for our calendar, you can contact us through www.daysoutatlas.co.uk or by phoning us on 01603 633 808. If they meet the criteria, they will be added to the existing details on the website and included within the next edition of the *Days Out Atlas.*

Entry Groups

We have six different types of day out. Each one is explained opposite and identified by its own coloured lozenge.

A Premier entry has a 25-word description, opening times, specialities, facilities and a photograph or logo.

Premier Entry

NEWQUAY ZOO	Name of entry
Zoo	Type of entry
Trenance Leisure Park, Newquay, Cornwall, TR7 2LZ.	Address
TEL: 01637 873 342	Telephone number
EMAIL: info@newquayzoo.co.uk	Email address
WEB: www.newquayzoo.co.uk	Web address
(photograph)	Photograph
Fun for all the family. Set in lush sub-tropical gardens, home to many of the world's endangered species. Regular keeper talks and animal encounters.	Description
OPEN: Apr-Oct: 9.30-6. Nov-Mar: 10-5.	Opening times
ENTRY COSTS: £5.95, Child: £3.95, OAPs: £4.50, Family: £18.50.	Entry costs
SPECIALITIES: Events held, Guided tours available, Photography allowed, Picnic area, Play area.	Specialities
FACILITIES: Child area, Gift shop, Pushchair friendly, Restaurant, Toilets, Wheelchair access.	Facilities

Before travelling long distances, we suggest you call and confirm the opening times and entry costs, as these may vary during different times of the year.

Mention the *Days Out Atlas* if you visit an attraction that has been featured within the Atlas.

Happy Days Out!

The *Days Out Atlas* also has its very own website, www.daysoutatlas.co.uk. Here you can find an online version of the *Days Out Atlas*, so you can search for that perfect day out at anytime! It also has an up-to-date events calendar.

Why not send us a picture from a place you have visited? It may be selected for the Picture of the Week section. We will also keep the pictures on file to use within the next edition of the Atlas.

If you have any feedback about the Atlas or the website you can complete the feedback form on www.daysoutatlas.co.uk or email

www.daysatlas.co.uk

www.daysoutatlas.co.uk

ANIMAL ATTRACTIONS
This group represents all the animal attractions, including zoos, aquariums, bird & aviary centres, farms, safari parks and wildlife parks.

OUTDOOR ACTIVITIES
This group represents all the Outdoor activities including, boat hire & trips, climbing centres and adventure & activity centres.

OUTDOOR ATTRACTIONS
This group represents all the outdoor attractions, including theme parks and gardens.

WATER ACTIVITIES
This group represents all the water activities, including outdoor pursuit centres, swimming and water sports centres.

INDOOR ACTIVITIES
This group represents all the indoor activites, including bowling, ice skating, karting and adventure & activity centres.

HERITAGE & CULTURE
This group represents all the heritage and culture outlets, including museums, galleries, castles, historic houses, abbeys, cathedrals and craft centres.

CALENDAR

The Days Out Atlas Calendar of Events is crammed full of events being held in England, Scotland and Wales. Each event has been placed into one of the following categories; Regional events, Regional festivals, National events, National festivals, Exhibitions, Garden shows, Seasonal events or Sporting events.

Where supplied, we have listed a contact telephone number so if you would like more details about a particular event, the details are only a phone call away!

For up-to-date information and tickets for each event listed, please use the details listed to contact the venue or booking line direct.
If you contact a venue listed on the following pages, please remember to say that you found out about the event from the Days Out Atlas.

DATE	EVENT	VENUE	CONTACT
1 May	Garden Show	A Celebration of Cornish Gardens	01752 894731
1 May	Regional Festival	King's Lynn May Garland Procession	01553 768 930
1-3 May	National Event	Ladies British Open Amateur Foursomes Championship	01334 475 811
1-6 May	National Festival	Cheltenham International Jazz Festival	01242 227 979
1-11 May	Regional Festival	Swindon Festival of Literature	01793 771 080
1-12 May	Regional Festival	Norfolk & Norwich Festival	01603 766 400
1 May - 31 Aug	Regional Festival	Glydenbourne Festival Opera	01273 812 321
2-5 May	Sports Event	Mitsubishi Motors Badminton Horse Trials	01454 218 272
2-6 May	Garden Show	Tulip Festival	01580 200 888
3-5 May	Sports Event	Sagitta Guineas Festival	01638 675 500
3-6 May	Regional Festival	Hastings Traditional Jack in the Green Morris Dance & Folk Festival	01424 781 122
3-6 May	Regional Festival	Spirit of Speyside: Scotland's Whisky Festival	01343 542 666
4-6 May	Exhibition	Spalding Flower Parade	01775 724 843
4-6 May	Garden Show	Spring Gardeners' Weekend	01799 522 842
4-6 May	Seasonal Event	Bath Annual Spring Flower Show	01225 482 624
4-6 May	Garden Show	North London Cactus and Succulents Show	020 8366 4442
4-6 May	Garden Show	Southend Garden Show	
4 May	Sports Event	FA Cup Final	020 7402 7151
4-6 May	Regional Event	Bexhill 100 Festival of Motoring	01424 730 564
4-6 May	Regional Festival	Sweeps Festival	01634 843 666
4-26 May	National Festival	Brighton International Festival	01273 700 747
5-7 May	Garden Show	Tonbridge Gardening Show	01732 770 929
5-6 May	National Event	Weymouth International Beach Kite Festival	01305 785 747
5-6 May	Regional Event	Dover Pageant	01304 242 990
6 May	Regional Event	The East Midlands Festival of Transport	01484 660 622
6 May	Regional Event	North Somerset Show	01275 375 559
8 May	Regional Festival	Helston Flora Day	01326 572 082
9 May	Regional Event	Beating the Bounds	020 7488 5662
9-12 May	Regional Event	Great Northern Needlecraft Fair	01775 722 900
9-12 May	National Event	National Dog Show	01536 791 399
10-12 May	Garden Show	Malvern Spring Gardening Show	01684 584 924
10-12 May	Exhibition	Chelsea Preview	01626 352 233
10-12 May	Garden Show	East of England Garden Show	01702 549 623
10-12 May	Regional Festival	Lancashire Clog-Dancing Festival & Competition	01254 872 595
10-12 May	Regional Festival	Holmfirth Folk Festival	01484 605 059
10-12 May	National Event	London Dolls House Festival	020 8948 1893
10-18 May	Regional Event	Buxton Antiques Fair	01483 422 562
10-26 May	Regional Festival	Bury St Edmunds Festival	01284 757 630
11-12 May	Seasonal Event	Bluebell Days	01565 777 353
11-31 May	Seasonal Event	Rhododendron and Azalea Tme	01444 450 326
11 May	Sports Event	Barbon Hill Climb	01539 740 777
11 May	Plant Fair	Spring Orchid Show	01697 724 76
11-12 May	Regional Event	Windermere Steamboat Centre Model Boat Rally	01539 445 565
11-12 May	National Event	NEC Sports Car Show	01217 672 772
11-12 May	Regional Event	Newark and Nottinghamshire County Show	01636 702 627
11-12 May	Regional Event	Festival of English Food and Wine	01622 765 400
11-25 May	Regional Festival	International Newbury Spring Festival	01635 324 21
11 May - 2 June	Regional Event	Artspace 2002	01491 577 786
12 May	Regional Event	South Suffolk Show	01638 750 879
12 May	Plant Fair	Spring Plant Fair	01372 467 806
14 May	Seasonal Event	Flower Arranging Day	01483 797 332
15-19 May	Sports Event	Royal Windsor Horse Show	01753 860 633
16-18 May	Regional Event	All the Queen's Horses	01753 860 633
17-19 May	Seasonal Event	Spring Garden & Craft Weekend	01727 850 461
17-19 May	Garden Show	Norfolk Garden Show	01702 549 623
17 May - 2 June	Regional Festival	Bath International Music Festival	01225 463 362
18-19 May	Seasonal Event	Bluebell Days	01565 777 353
18 May	Regional Event	Otley Show	01943 462 541
18 May	Regional Event	Hadleigh Farmers Agricultural Association May Show	01473 827 920
18-19 May	Sports Event	Chatsworth Angling Fair	01263 711 736

OF EVENTS

DATE	EVENT	VENUE	CONTACT
18-19 May	Regional Event	BMF Bike Show	01162 548 818
19 May	Seasonal Event	Spring Plant Fair	01938 551 920
19 May	Exhibition	National Garden Scheme Open Day	01483 797 332
19 May	Regional Event	Derbyshire County Show	01332 793 068
20-24 May	Garden Show	Chelsea Flower Show	0870 906 3781
24 May - 9 June	Regional Festival	Swaledale Festival	01969 622 217
24 May - 9 June	Regional Festival	Bath Fringe Festival	01225 480 079
25-26 May	National Event	Air Fete	01638 543 341
25-26 May	Regional Event	Hertforshire County Show	01582 792 626
25-26 May	Regional Event	Medieval Re-enactments	01646 681 510
25-28 May	National Event	Harrogate International Antiques and Fine Art Fair	01277 213 139
25 May - 15 June	Regional Event	Leicester Early Music Festival	01162 709 984
25 May	Regional Event	Claremont in the Evening Walk & Late Night Opening	01372 467 806
26-30 May	Garden Show	Athelhampton Flower Festival	01305 854 363
26 May	Regional Event	Barleylands Woolly Weekend	01268 290 229
26-30 May	Garden Show	Athelhampton Flower Festival	01305 848 363
26 May - 2 June	Regional Event	Mind Body Spirit Festival	020 7371 9191
26 May	Regional Event	RSPB Day	01372 467 806
29-30 May	Garden Show	Woburn Garden Show	01525 290 666
29-30 May	Exhibition	Corpus Christie Carpet of Flowers and Floral Festival	01903 882 297
29-30 May	Garden Show	Cambridge Garden Show	01702 549 623
31 May - 2 June	Garden Show	Holker Garden Festival	01539 558 328
31 May - 2 June	Garden Show	Gardening Scotland	0131 333 09649
31 May - 2 June	Regional Festival	Great Garden & Countryside Festival	01539 558 836
31 May - 2 June	Regional Event	Holker Garden Festival	01539 558 328
31 May - 9 June	Regional Festival	Leominster Festival of the Arts	01568 611 418
31 May	Regional Event	Cotswold Olympic Games	01384 274 041
1-6 June	Exhibition	Flower Festival and Exhibition - Queen of Queen's	01363 772 865
1-4 June	Regional Festival	Bryan's Ground Open Day	01544 260 001
1-4 June	Exhibition	Golden Jubilee Holiday Orchid Weekend	01626 352 233
1 June	Sports Event	Northumbrian Water University Boat Race	01914 333 818
1 June	Exhibition	International Football Memorabilia and Programme Fair	01268 732 041
1-2 June	Regional Event	Biggin Hill International Air Fair	01959 578 100
1-3 June	National Festival	Orange WOW	01912 005 164
1-4 June	National Event	Chatham Navy Days	01634 834 800
1-4 June	Regional Event	World War Two Weekend	01787 310 207
1-9 June	Regional Festival	Durrington Festival	01903 600 516
1 June - 31 Aug	Exhibition	Royal Academy Summer Exhibition	020 7300 8000
1 June	Regional Event	Late Night Opening	01372 467 806
2-4 June	Garden Show	Kent Garden Show	01795 474 660
2 June	Exhibition	Borders Vintage Automobile Club Historic Motoring Extravaganza	01896 860 287
2-3 June	Regional Event	Battle Mediaeval Fair	01424 774 447
2 June	Regional Event	National Gardens Scheme Open Day	01372 467 806
3 June	Seasonal Event	Azalea Time	01444 400 589
3 June	Regional Event	Northumberland County Show	01697 747 848
3 June	Regional Festival	Luton International Carnival	01582 546 091
3 June	Regional Event	Stilton Cheese Rolling	01733 241 206
3 June	Sports Event	Weymouth Trawler Race and Water Carnival	01305 785 747
3 June	Regional Event	Surrey County Show	01483 890 810
3-4 June	Regional Event	Jubilee Craft Fayre	01202 601 483
5-6 June	Regional Event	Staffordshire County Show	01785 258 060
5-6 June	Regional Event	Beating Retreat by the Household Divison Massed Bands	020 7414 2271
6-7 June	Regional Event	Suffolk Show	01473 726 847
6-9 June	Regional Festival	Dickens Festival	01634 843 666
6-12 June	Regional Event	Appleby Horse Fair	01768 351 177
7-9 June	Garden Show	The Garden Show	023 9241 2265
7-9 June	Garden Show	The Festival of Gardening	01707 262 823
7-8 June	Regional Festival	Keswick Beer Festival	01768 773 591
7-9 June	Regional Festival	Godiva Festival	0500 777 220
7-9 June	Regional Festival	Newark on Water Festival	01636 655 723
7-9 June	Garden Show	The Festival of Gardening	01707 262 823

DATE	EVENT	VENUE	CONTACT
8-9 June	Garden Show	Ascot Garden Show	01702 549 623
8 June	Sports Event	Derby Horse Race Meeting	01372 470 047
8-9 June	Regional Event	Thaxted Morris Ring Meeting	01245 420 742
8 June	Regional Event	Late Night Opening	01372 467 806
9 June	Garden Show	National Pelargonium & Geranium Show	020 8366 4442
9 June	Regional Event	Golden Jubilee Air Show	01902 376 200
9 June	Regional Festival	Peterborough Kite Festival	01773 269 687
9 June	Regional Event	London Garden Squares Day	020 7973 3434
9-15 June	Exhibition	Canary Wharf International Motor Expo	01225 425 811
10-28 June	Regional Festival	Spitalfields Festival	020 7377 1362
12-18 June	Exhibition	Grosvenor House Art and Antiques Fair	020 7399 8100
13-16 June	Garden Show	Days of English Roses	01444 450 326
13-16 June	Garden Show	Blenheim Palace Flower Show	01993 811 091
14-17 June	Garden Show	Flower and Garden Festival	01202 861 686
14-16 June	Garden Show	Garden Show	01525 290 666
14-17 June	Regional Festival	The Mersey River Festival	0151 233 6351
14-17 June	National Event	International Ceramics Fair and Seminar	020 7734 5491
15-16 June	Exhibition	Pembrokeshire Flower Arrangers' Competition	01834 811 885
15-16 June	Garden Show	Enfield Rose & Horticultural Show	020 8366 4442
15-16 June	Garden Show	South East Essex Garden Show	01702 549 623
15 June	Regional Event	Late Night Opening at Claremont Landscape Garden	01372 467 806
15 June	Regional Event	Todmorden Agricultural Show	01706 815 648
15 June	National Event	Trooping the Colours - The Queen's Birthday Parade	020 7414 2479
15-16 June	Regional Event	Leamington Peace Festival	
15-21 June	National Festival	International Military & Veterans' Festival	01305 785 747
15-23 June	Regional Festival	Broadstairs Dicken Festival	01843 865 265
16 June	Seasonal Event	Summer Craft Fair - Inspired by the Gardens	01938 551 920
16 June	Exhibition	Well Bred Plant Fair	01834 811 885
17 June	National Event	Garter Ceremony	01753 869 898
18 June	Seasonal Event	Simply Summer	01483 797 332
18 June	Exhibition	Cook What You Grow	01483 797 332
18 June	Seasonal Event	Summertime Garden Day	01483 797 332
18-19 June	Regional Event	Cheshire County Show	01829 760 020
18-21 June	National Event	Royal Ascot	
19-23 June	Garden Show	BBC Gardeners' World Live	0121 767 4505
19-20 June	Regional Event	Lincolnshire Show	01522 522 900
20-23 June	Regional Festival	Royal Highland Show	0131 335 6216
20-22 June	National Event	Club Med Cup	020 7862 0054
21-23 June	Regional Event	Beverley & East Riding Folk Festival	01377 217 569
21-23 June	Regional Event	Lichfield Folk Festival	01889 582 908
21-23 June	Regional Event	Loo Festival of the Sea 2002	01503 264 698
22-23 June	Garden Show	Garden Festival	01243 818 210
22-23 June	Garden Show	Rose Festival	01805 624 067
22-23 June	Garden Show	Sussex Garden Show	01444 450 326
22-29 June	Regional Event	Brackley Music Festival	01295 712 949
24 June - 7 July	National Event	Wimbledon Lawn Tennis Championships	020 8946 2244
26-27 June	Regional Event	Royal Norfolk Show	01603 748 931
26 June - 7 July	Regional Festival	Cliveden Shakespere Festival	
28 June - 7 July	Regional Festival	Harwich Festival	020 7405 6065
28 June - 14 July	Regional Festival	Exeter festival	
28 June - 31 July	National Festival	9th International Music & Dance Festival, Maidstone	01622 695 283
28-30 June	National Festival	Glastonbury Festival	01749 890 470
29-30 June	Seasonal Event	Floral Festival	01438 869 668
29-30 June	Garden Show	Arley Garden Festival	01565 777 353
29-30 June	National Event	RAF Waddington International Airshow	01522 726 102
30 June - 7 July	Regional Festival	Manx Heritage Flower Festival	01624 686 801
30 June	Regional Event	Longleat Amateir Radio Rally	0117 985 6253
1-7 July	Garden Show	Hampton Court Palace Flower Show	0870 906 3791
1-7 July	Seasonal Event	Herbaceous Border	01438 869 668
1-4 July	Regional Event	Royal Show	024 766 96969
1-31 July	Regional Event	Glasgow Jazz Festival	0141 287 5511
1 July - 31 Aug	National Festival	Cardiff International Festival	02920 873 936
3-7 July	Regional Festival	Wisbech Rose Festival	01945 461 393
3-7 July	National Event	Henley Royal Regatta	01491 575 509
5-7 July	National Event	FIA Formula 1 British Grand Prix	01327 857 663
5-14 July	National Festival	York Early Music Festival	01904 632 220
5-14 July	Regional Festival	Winchester Festival	01962 877 977
6-7 July	Regional Festival	Bryan's Ground Open Day	01544 260 001
6-7 July	Garden Show	Bonsai Show	020 8366 4442
6-7 July	Garden Show	Essex Garden Show	01702 549 623
6-7 July	Regional Event	Jousting Tournament	0131 668 8800
6 July	Regional Festival	South Yorkshire Festival	0114 288 6343
6-7 July	Regional Festival	Amble Sea Fair Festival	01665 712 929
6-7 July	Regional Festival	Sunderland International Kite Festival	0191 514 1235
6-21 July	National Festival	Cheltenham International Festival of Music and Fringe	01242 227 979
6 July - 18 Aug	Regional Festival	Cookson Country Festival	0191 424 7985
7-13 July	Regional Festival	Jersey Garden Festival	01534 500 723
7 July	Regional Event	Clacton Classic Vehicle Show 2002	01255 253 124
9-11 July	National Event	Great Yorkshire Show	01423 541 000
10-14 July	National Festival	Henley Festival	01491 843 400
11-13 July	Regional Event	Stonehaven Folk Festival	01569 763 519
11-21 July	Regional Festival	Buxton Festival	01298 703 950
12-14 July	National Event	Goodwood Festival of Speed	01243 755 055

DATE	EVENT	VENUE
12 July - 14 July	Regional Event	Lord Mayor's Celebrations 2002
12-22 July	Regional Festival	'Ways with Words' Literature Festival
12-14 July	Regional Festival	Rothbury Traditional Music Festival
13-14 July	Garden Show	The Parham Garden Weekend
13 July	National Event	Annual Mountain Bike Bog Snorkelling World Championships
13-14 July	Regional Festival	Tewkesbury Medieval Festival
13-14 July	National Event	Flying Legends Air Show
18 July	Regional Event	Mull Highland Games
18-21 July	Regional Event	Claremont Fete & Firework Display
18-21 July	National Event	Golf: The Open Championship 2002
19-21 July	Garden Show	The Great Gardening Show
19-21 July	Regional Festival	Reading Real Ale & Jazz Festival
19 July - 14 Sept	National Event	BBC Henry Wood Promenade Concert (The Proms)
20 July	Regional Event	Cumberland County Show
20-21 July	National Event	Royal International Air Tattoo
21 July	National Event	The Great Eastern Classic Car Rally
22-25 July	National Event	Royal Welsh Show
22-28 July	National Event	Farnborough International Airshow
25 July - 3 Aug	Regional Festival	King's Lynn Festival
25 July - 4 Aug	National Event	Manchester 2002 - The 17th Commonwealth Games
26-28 July	Garden Show	Gateshead Summer Flower Show
26-28 July	Regional Event	Royal Lancashire Show
26-28 July	Regional Festival	North Wiltshire Festival 2002
27-28 July	Garden Show	Summer Gardening & Fuchsia Show
27-28 July	National Event	Sunderland International Air Show
27-28 July	National Event	The National Show for Minature Roses
29 July - 5 Aug	National Event	Jazz on the Waterfront - Hull Jazz Festival
29 July - 9 Aug	Exhibition	Savill Garden Sculpture Exhibition
30 July - 1 Aug	Regional Event	New Forset & Hampshire County Show
31 July	Regional Event	Nantwich & South Cheshire Show
1 Aug	Regional Event	Ambleside Traditional Lakeland Sports
2-9 Aug	National Festival	Sidmouth International Festival
2-24 Aug	National Event	Edinburgh Military Tattoo
3 Aug	Exhibition	Annual Fuchsia Show
3-4 Aug	Regional Event	Traquair Fair
3-10 Aug	National Event	Skandia Life Cowes Week 2002
4-26 Aug	National Event	Edinburgh Festival Fringe
6 Aug	Regional Event	Gosport Vehicle Rally
8 Aug	National Event	Jersey Battle of Flowers
9-11 Aug	Garden Show	Ayr Flower Show
9-11 Aug	National Festival	Saltburn International, Festival
9-11 Aug	National Festival	Brecon Jazz Festival
10 Aug	Regional Event	Abernethy Highland Games

CONTACT
03 212 126
01591 610 236
01223 835 000
01372 467 806
01334 472 112
01483 797 332
0118 699 049
020 7589 8212
01228 560 364
01285 713 300
01277 227 708
01982 553 683
020 7227 1043
01553 767 557
0161 228 2002
0191 433 3000
01254 813 769
01249 706 536
020 8366 4442
0191 553 2002
01727 850 461
01482 615 673
01753 847 518
023 8022 3909
01270 780 306
01539 434 087
01296 393 293
0131 225 1188
01580 880 467
01896 830 323
01983 293 303
0131 226 5257
01534 639 000
01292 618 395
01947 840 928
01874 625 557
01479 821 091

DATE	EVENT	VENUE	CONTACT
11 Aug	Regional Event	Perth Highland Games	01738 627 782
11-31 Aug	National Event	Edinburgh International Festival	0131 473 2000
13-31 Aug	Regional Event	Anglesey County Show	01407 720 880
15-18 Aug	National Event	Cutty Sark Tall Ships' Race	023 9282 6722
16-17 Aug	Garden Show	Shrewsbury Flower Show	01743 234 050
16-18 Aug	Regional Event	Northampton Hot-Air Balloon Festival	01604 238 971
16-26 Aug	National Festival	Ross on Wye International Festival	01594 544 446
17-18 Aug	Garden Show	British Gladiolus Show	020 8366 4442
17 Aug	Garden Show	Warkworth Flower Show	
17-18 Aug	National Festival	Isle of Wight Garlic Festival	01983 853 411
17-23 Aug	Regional Event	Whitby Folk Week	01757 708 424
17-25 Aug	Regional Festival	Llandrindod Wells Victorian Festival	01597 823 441
17 Aug	National Festival	Glastonbury Classical Extravaganza	01749 890 470
18 Aug	Seasonal Event	Gentian Time	01444 400 589
18 Aug	Regional Festival	Great Jubilee Picnic Festival	01444 235 475
18 Aug	Regional Event	Crieff Highland Gathering	01738 627 782
19-27 Aug	National Festival	Glastonbury Festival of Dance	01458 835 717
22-27 Aug	National Festival	International Beatles Festival	0151 236 9091
22-27 Aug	Regional Festival	Presteigne Festival of Music & Arts	01544 267 800
24-26 Aug	Garden Show	Autumn Gardeners' Weekend	01799 522 842
24-26 Aug	Garden Show	Kempton Park Garden Show	01702 549 623
24-25 Aug	Regional Event	Knights of Longshanks Combat Displays	01248 714 795
24-26 Aug	National Event	Plymouth Navy Days 2002	01752 555 914
24-31 Aug	Regional Festival	Bude Jazz Festival	01288 356 360
25 Aug	National Event	Teddies 2002:British Teddy Bear Festival	01273 697 974
25-26 Aug	National Event	Nottinghill Carnival	020 8964 0544
26 Aug	Garden Show	Bude Horticultural Show	01288 352 114
28Aug	Regional Event	Vale of Glamorgan Agricultural Show	01446 710 099
28-31 Aug	National Event	Picture Postcard Show	0151 339 5422
28 Aug - 1 Sept	Regional Event	Great Dorest Steam Fair	01258 860 361
29-31 Aug	National Event	Port of Dartmouth Royal Regatta	01803 832 432
29 Aug	Regional Event	Buckinghamshire County Show	01296 398 515
31 Aug - 1 Sept	Garden Show	Suffolk Autumn Garden Show	01702 549 623
30 Aug - 1 Sept	Regional Festival	Flyde Folk Festival	01253 872 317
30 Aug - 11 Nov	National Event	Blackpool Illuminations	01253 478 222
1 Sept	Regional Event	Egremont Crab Fair & Sports	01946 821 554
5 Sept	Plant Fair	Arley Plant-Hunters' Fair	01565 777 353
6-8 Sept	Flower Show	Dundee Flower Show & Food Festival	01382 434 940
7-8 Sept	Garden Show	Sussex Garden Show	01444 450 326
7-8 Sept	Seasonal Event	Autumn Flowers	
7-8 Sept	Garden Show	Enfield Chrysanthemum Show	020 8366 4442
7 Sept	Regional Event	Braemar Gathering	01339 755 377
7-8 Sept	Regional Event	Berwick Military Tattoo	01289 307 426
7-8 Sept	Regional Event	Medieval Extravaganza	01291 420 241
13-15 Sept	Garden Show	Harrogate Great Autumn Flower Show	0870 758 3333
13-22 Sept	National Event	Southampton International Boat Show	01784 223 600
14-15 Sept	Garden Show	Bonsai Show	020 8366 4442
15 Sept	Exhibition	National Garden Scheme Open Day	01483 797 332
15 Sept	Regional Event	National Gardens Scheme Open Day	01372 467 806
17-18 Sept	Garden Show	The Great Autumn Show	0870 906 3721
21 Sept	Regional Festival	City Farm and Gardens Festival	020 8366 4442
21-22 Sept	Regional Event	Newbury & Royal County of Berkshire Show	01635 247 111
21-22 Sept	Regional Event	Miniature Steam & Model Weekend	01798 831 370
21-22 Sept	Regional Event	Autumn Vintage Vehicle Show	01798 831 370
27 Sept	National Event	The Ryder Cup	01675 470 256
28-29 Sept	Plant Fair	Malvern Autumn Garden and Country Show	01684 584 924
28-29 Sept	Regional Festival	Enfield Chrysanthemum Show	020 8366 4442
29 Sept	Seasonal Event	Fungus Foray	01661 881 636
1 Oct	Exhibition	Cook What You Grow	01483 797 332
1-6 Oct	National Event	Horse of the Year Show	020 8900 9282
1-3 Oct	Regional Event	Captain Cook Festival	
4-10 Oct	National Event	Bristol Poetry Festival 2002	0117 942 6976
5-20 Oct	Regional Festival	Swansea Festival of Music & the Arts	01792 411 570
9-13 Oct	Seasonal Event	Autumn Gold Flower Festival	01622 765 400
11-18 Oct	National Event	Royal National Mod - Stornaway	01463 615 625
12-13 Oct	Garden Show	Enfield Chrysanthemum Show	020 8366 4442
14 Oct - 3 Nov	Regional Event	Cardiff International Festival of Music Theatre	029 2090 1111
20-31 Oct	National Festival	Festival of Animated Theatre, Brighton	01273 643 010
27-29 Oct	Garden Show	Edmonton Chrysanthemum Show	020 8366 4442
27-29 Oct	Garden Show	National Gardens Scheme Open Day	020 8366 4442
1-30 Nov	National Festival	Newcastle Comedy Festival	0191 230 4406
1 Nov - 25 Dec	Regional Event	St Nicholas Fayre - York	01904 554 433
2-3 Nov	Seasonal Event	Autumn Colour	01438 869 668
5 Nov	Regional Event	Inverness Grand Bonfire & Fireworks Party	01463 724 224
9 Nov	Regional Event	Claremont at Dawn	01372 467 806
9 Nov	Regional Event	Lord Mayor's Fireworks Display - London	020 7606 3030
9 Nov	Regional Event	Lord Mayor's Show - London	01483 577 123
10 Nov	Regional Event	Autumn Colour at Claremont	01372 467 806
15-24 Nov	National Festival	Mid Wales Beer Festival	01591 610 666
20 Nov - 1 Dec	Regional Festival	Huddersfield Contemporary Music Festival	01484 425 082
31 Dec	National Event	Hogmanay Paty, Edinburgh	
31 Dec - 1 Jan '03	Regional Festival	Stonehaven Fireballing Festival	01224 582 272

www.daysoutsatlas.co.uk

DAYS OUT ATLAS

MAPS

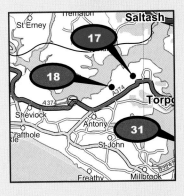

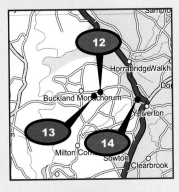

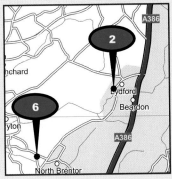

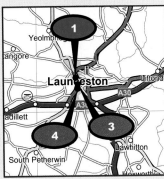

🟢 ANIMAL ATTRACTIONS
🔴 HERITAGE & CULTURE
⚫ INDOOR ACTIVITIES
🔴 OUTDOOR ATTRACTIONS
🟢 OUTDOOR ACTIVITIES
🔴 WATER ACTIVITIES

CORNWALL

● ANIMAL ATTRACTIONS
● HERITAGE & CULTURE
○ INDOOR ACTIVITIES
● OUTDOOR ATTRACTIONS
● OUTDOOR ACTIVITIES
● WATER ACTIVITIES

1 **ADVENTURELINE**
Farm
North Trefula Farm, Redruth
TEL: 01209 820 847

2 **CORNISH ENGINES**
Museum
Pool, Redruth
TEL: 01209 315 027

3 **GEOLOGICAL MUSEUM & ART GALLERY**
Museum
Camborne School of Mines, University of Exeter
Pool, Redruth
TEL: 01209 714 866

4 **TATE GALLERY**
Gallery
Porthmeor Beach, St Ives
TEL: 01736 796 226

5 **BARBARA HEPWORTH MUSEUM & SCULPTURE GARDEN**
Garden
Barnoon Hill, St Ives
TEL: 01736 796 226

6 **TREWYN GARDEN**
Garden
St Ives
TEL: 01736 794 937

7 **ST MAWES CASTLE**
Castle
St Mawes, Truro
TEL: 01326 270 526

8 **NATIONAL LIGHTHOUSE CENTRE**
Museum
Former Buoy Store, Wharf Road, Penzance
TEL: 01736 360 077

9 **FUN FACTORY**
Adventure & activity centre
1 St Georges Road, Newquay
TEL: 01637 877 555

10 **PARADISE PARK**
Garden
Hayle, St Ives
TEL: 01736 757 407

11 **CHYSAUSTER ANCIENT VILLAGE**
Archaeological site
Penzance
TEL: 08317 979 34

12 **CARN EUNY ANCIENT VILLAGE**
Ancient Monuments
Sancreed, Penzance, Plymouth
TEL: Not available

13 **GODOLPHIN ESTATE**
Country park
Godolphin Cross, Helston
TEL: 01326 561 407

14 **TRENGWAINTON GARDEN NT**
Garden
Madron, Penzance
TEL: 01736 362 297

15 **POLDARK MINE & HERITAGE COMPLEX**
Heritage centre
Trenear, Helston
TEL: 01326 563 166

16 **ST MICHAEL'S MOUNT**
Castle
West End, Marazion
TEL: 01736 710 507/710265

---

17 **TREVARNO ESTATE GARDENS & THE NATIONAL MUSEUM OF GARDENING**
Trevarno Manor, Sithney, Helston, Cornwall, TR13 0RU.
TEL: 01326 574 274
EMAIL: enquiry@trevarno.fsnet.co.uk

Unforgettable gardening experience, beautiful Victorian and Georgian gardens with the splendid fountain garden conservatory, unique range of crafts and the amazing National Museum of Gardening.
OPEN: Open all year. Closed Chrismas & Boxing Day.
ENTRY COSTS: £4.50, Child: £1.50 Under 5 free, OAPs: £3.95, Disabled £2.50.
SPECIALITIES: Comprehensive range of Trevarno crafts.
FACILITIES: Wheelchair access, Toilets, Coffee shop, Dogs allowed, Sell plants.

---

18 **MARITIME MUSEUM**
Museum
Chapel Street, Penzance
TEL: 01736 368 890

19 **TREREIFE GARDEN**
Garden
Penzance
TEL: 01736 362 750

20 **NATIONAL SEAL SANCTUARY**
Nature centre
Gweek, Helston
TEL: 01326 221 874

21 **FLAMBARDS VICTORIAN VILLAGE GARDEN**
Theme park
Helston
TEL: 01326 573 404

22 **LAND'S END VISITOR CENTRE AND CONSERVATION SITE**
Visitor centre
Sennen, Penzance
TEL: 01736 871 220

23 **LIZARD COUNTRYSIDE CENTRE**
Heritage centre
Trelowarren Mawgan, Helston
TEL: 01326 221 661

24 **HALLIGGYE FOGOU**
Tunnel Trips
Helston, Lizard
TEL: 01179 750 700

25 **GOONHILLY EARTH STATION VISITOR CENTRE**
Visitor centre
Goonhilly Downs
TEL: 0800 679 593

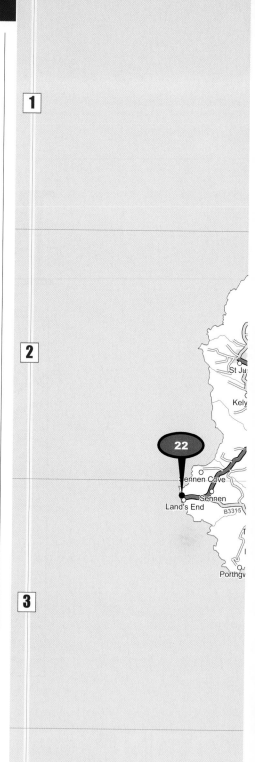

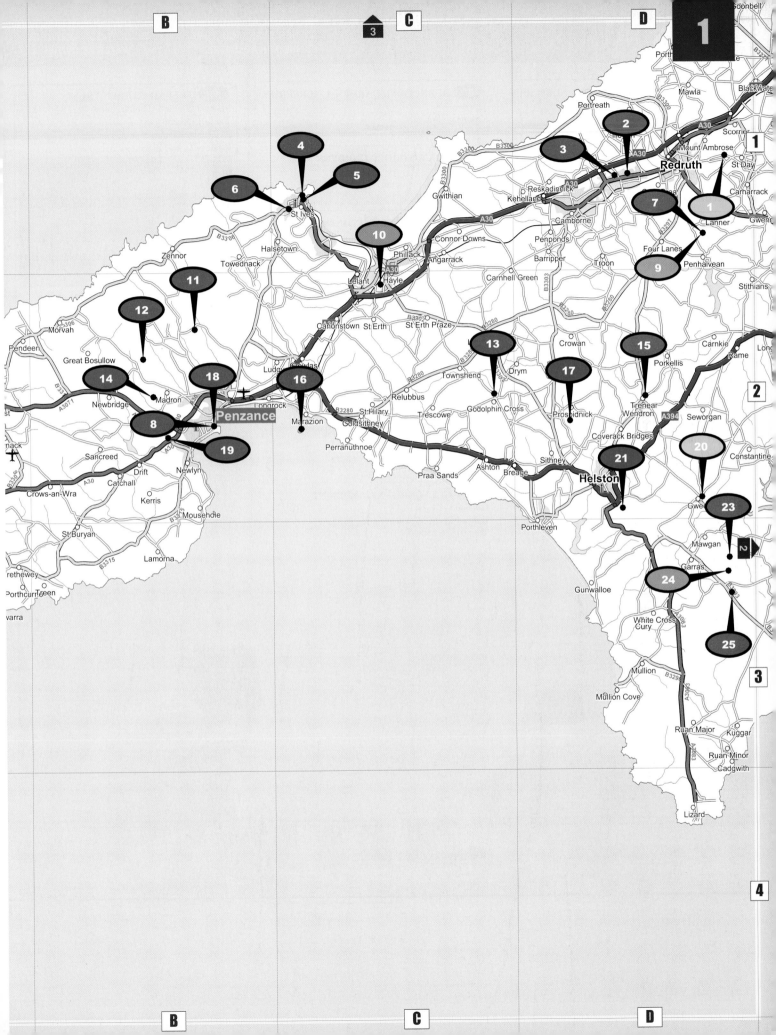

● ANIMAL ATTRACTIONS ● OUTDOOR ATTRACTIONS
● HERITAGE & CULTURE ● OUTDOOR ACTIVITIES
○ INDOOR ACTIVITIES ● WATER ACTIVITIES

1 TREWITHEN GARDENS & NURSERIES
Garden
Grampound Road, Truro
TEL: 01726 883 647

2 CREED HOUSE
Historic building
Creed, Grampound
TEL: 01872 530 372

3 LOST GARDENS OF HELIGAN
Garden
Pentewan, St Austell
TEL: 01726 845 100

4 NATIONAL LOBSTER HATCHERY
Farm
Padstow
TEL: 01841 533 877

5 ROYAL CORNWALL MUSEUM
Museum
River Street, Truro
TEL: 01872 272 205

6 WORLD OF MODEL RAILWAYS
Model village
Meadow Street, Mevagissey
TEL: 01726 842 457

7 TRELISSICK GARDEN NT
Garden
Feock, Truro
TEL: 01872 862 090

8 BURNCOOSE GARDEN & NURSERIES
Garden
Gwennap, Redruth
TEL: 01209 860 316

9 FOX ROSEHILL GARDENS
Garden
Melville Road, Falmouth
TEL: 01326 319 377

10 NATIONAL MARITIME MUSEUM CORNWALL
Museum
Discovery Quay, Falmouth
TEL: 01326 313 388

11 PENDENNIS CASTLE EH
Castle
Castle Drive, Falmouth
TEL: 0117 975 0700

12 CARWINION GARDENS
Garden
Mawnam Smith, Falmouth
TEL: 01326 250 258

13 MEUDON HOTEL & GARDENS
Garden
Mawnam Smith, Falmouth
TEL: 01326 250 541

15 GLENDURGAN GARDEN NT
Garden
Helford River, Mawnam Smith, Fairford
TEL: 01326 250 906

14 TREBAH GARDEN TRUST
Mawnan Smith, Falmouth, Cornwall, TR11 5JZ.
TEL: 01326 250 448
EMAIL: mail@trebah-garden.co.uk
WEB: www.trebah-garden.co.uk

*Stunningly beautiful subtropical ravine garden
running down to a private beach on Helford river.
A riot of colour and scent throughout the year.*
OPEN: Open daily 10.30-5 (last admission).
ENTRY COSTS: £4.50, Child: £2.50 Under 5's free,
OAPs: £4, Disabled: £2.50, RHS members: Free.
FACILITIES: Toilets, Credit cards, Wheelchair access,
Restaurant, Dogs allowed, Child area, Coffee shop,
Sell plants, Gift shop, HTA gift tokens.

Building sandcastles

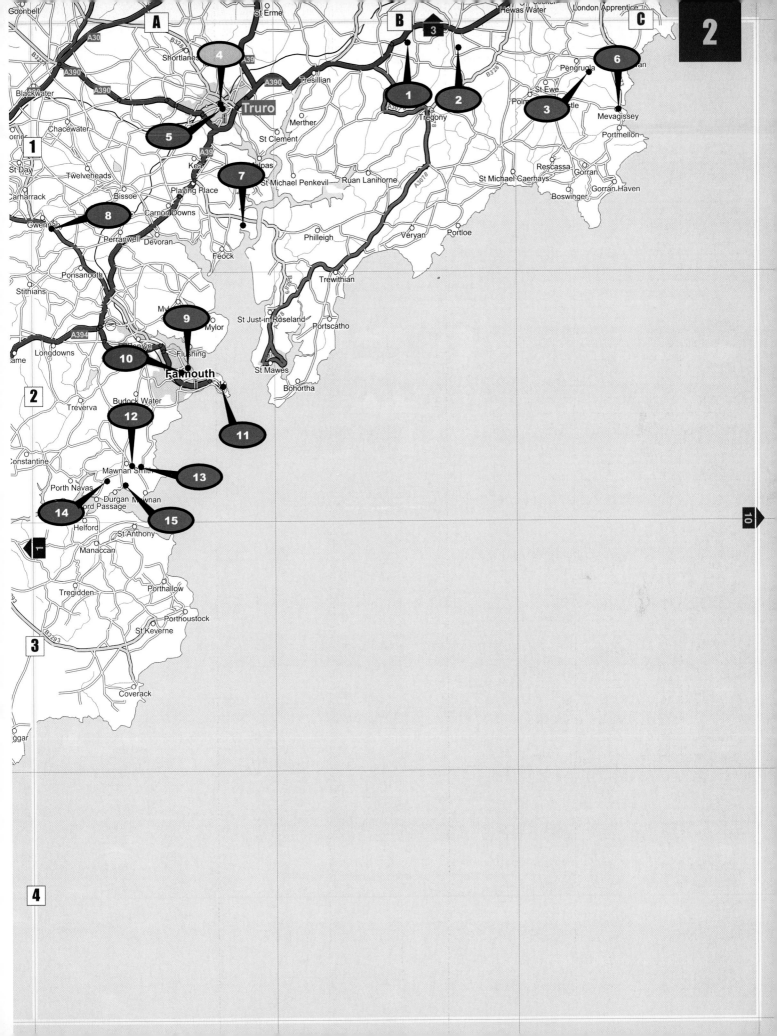

CORNWALL

● ANIMAL ATTRACTIONS   ● OUTDOOR ATTRACTIONS
● HERITAGE & CULTURE   ● OUTDOOR ACTIVITIES
○ INDOOR ACTIVITIES   ● WATER ACTIVITIES

1 TINTAGEL CASTLE
Castle
Tintagel   TEL: 01840 770 328

2 KING ARTHUR'S GREAT HALLS
Historic building
Fore Street, Tintagel   TEL: 01840 770 526

3 OLD POST OFFICE
Historic building
Fore Street, Tintagel   TEL: 01804 770 024

4 BRITISH CYCLING MUSEUM
Museum
The Old Station, Camelford   TEL: 01840 212 811

5 NORTH CORNWALL MUSEUM & GALLERY
Museum
The Clease, Camelford   TEL: 01840 212 954

6 LONG CROSS VICTORIAN GARDENS
Garden
Trelights, Port Isaac   TEL: 01208 880 243

7 POTTERS MUSEUM OF CURIOSITY
Museum
Courtyard Bolventor, Bodmin Moor, Bolventor   TEL: 01566 868 38

8 SMUGGLERS AT JAMAICA INN
Museum
Bolventor, Launceston   TEL: 01566 860 25

9 PRIDEAUX PLACE
Historic building
Padstow   TEL: 01841 532 411

10 DONKEY SANCTUARY
Wildlife park
Lower Maidenland, St Kew, Bodmin   TEL: 01208 841 710

11 COLLIFORD LAKE PARK COMPLEX
Farm
Bolventor   TEL: 01208 821 469

12 PENCARROW
Garden
Washaway, Bodmin   TEL: 01208 841 369

13 SHIRES FAMILY ADVENTURE PARK
Theme park
Trelow Farm St Issey, Wadebridge   TEL: 01841 540 276

14 BODMIN JAIL
Historic building
Berycombe Road, Bodmin   TEL: 01208 762 92

15 JAPANESE GARDEN & BONSAI NURSERY
Garden
St Mawgan Village, Newquay   TEL: 01637 860 116

16 MILITARY MUSEUM BODMIN
Museum
The Keep, Bodmin   TEL: 01208 728 10

17 SPIRIT OF THE WESTERN AMERICAN
Museum
Winnards Perch   TEL: 01637 881 160

18 LANHYDROCK NT
Garden
Lanhydrock, Bodmin   TEL: 01208 733 20

19 NEWQUAY SEA LIFE CENTRE
Sea life centre
Towan Promenade, Newquay   TEL: 01637 872 822

20 TUNNELS THROUGH TIME
Wax work
St Michaels Road, Newquay   TEL: 01637 873 379

21 NEWQUAY ZOO
Zoo
Trenance Leisure Park, Newquay, Cornwall, TR7 2LZ.
TEL: 01637 873 342
EMAIL: info@newquayzoo.co.uk
WEB: www.newquayzoo.co.uk

Fun for all the family. Set in lush sub-tropical gardens, home to many of the world's endangered species. Regular keeper talks and animal encounters.
OPEN: Apr-Oct: 9.30-6. Nov-Mar: 10-5.
ENTRY COSTS: £5.95, Child: £3.95, OAPs: £4.50, Family: £18.50.
SPECIALITIES: Events held, Guided tours available, Photography allowed, Picnic area, Play area.
FACILITIES: Child area, Gift shop, Pushchair friendly, Restaurant, Toilets, Wheelchair access.

22 SPRINGFIELDS FUN PARK & PONY CENTRE
Farm
Springfields Farm, St Columb Major, Newquay   TEL: 01637 881 224

23 RESTORMEL CASTLE
Castle
Restormel Road, Lostwithiel   TEL: 01208 872 687

24 NEWQUAY PEARL
Unusual
Quintrell Downs, Newquay   TEL: 01637 872 991

25 PORFELL ANIMAL LAND
Wildlife park
Trecangate, Lanreath, Liskeard   TEL: 01503 220 211

26 DAIRY LAND FARM WORLD
Farm
Summercourt, Newquay   TEL: 01872 510 246

27 TRERICE NT
Garden
Kestle Mill, Newquay   TEL: 01637 875 404

28 TRENANCE HERITAGE COTTAGES
Historic building
Newquay   TEL: 01637 873 922

29 LAPPA VALLEY STEAM RAILWAY & LEISURE PARK
Railway
Newlyn East, Newquay   TEL: 01872 510 317

30 WHEAL MARTYN CHINA CLAY HERITAGE CENTRE
Heritage centre
Carthew, St Austell   TEL: 01726 850 362

31 EDEN PROJECT
Garden
Bodelva, St Austell   TEL: 01726 222 900

32 WORLD IN MINIATURE
Theme park
Halt Road, Goonhaven, Truro   TEL: 01872 572 828

33 PINE LODGE GARDEN & NURSERY
Garden
Cuddra, Holmbush, St Austell   TEL: 01726 735 00

34 CHARLESTOWN SHIPWRECK AND HERITAGE CENTRE
Heritage centre
Quay Rd, Charlestown, St. Austell   TEL: 01726 698 97

35 ST CATHERINE'S CASTLE
Castle
Fowey   TEL: 01179 750 700

36 CALLESTOCK CIDER FARM
Museum
Penhallow, Truro   TEL: 01872 573 356

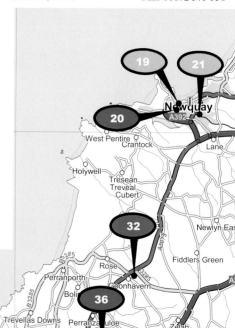

1   A   B

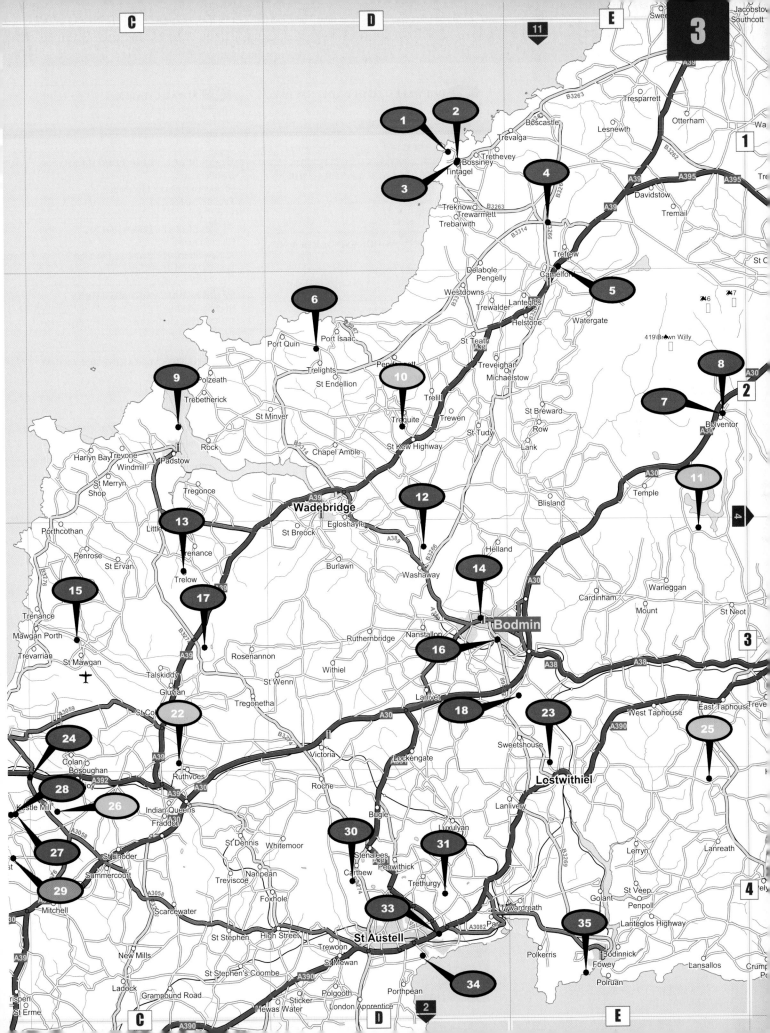

- ANIMAL ATTRACTIONS
- HERITAGE & CULTURE
- INDOOR ACTIVITIES
- OUTDOOR ATTRACTIONS
- OUTDOOR ACTIVITIES
- WATER ACTIVITIES

1 LAUNCESTON STEAM RAILWAY
Railway
St Thomas Road, Launceston
TEL: 01566 775 665

2 LYDFORD CASTLE
Unusual
Lydford, Okehampton
TEL: 01822 820 441

3 LAWRENCE HOUSE
Museum
9 Castle Street, Launceston
TEL: 01566 773 277

4 LAUNCESTON CASTLE
Castle
Launceston
TEL: 01566 772 365

5 HIDDEN VALLEY ADVENTURE & CONSERVATION PARK
Nature centre
Tredidon, St Thomas, Launceston
TEL: 01566 864 63

6 ROWDEN GARDENS
Garden
Rowden, Tavistock
TEL: 01822 810 275

7 ENDSLEIGH HOUSE & GARDENS
Garden
Milton Abbot
TEL: 01822 870 248

8 HURLERS STONE CIRCLES
Unusual
Minions
TEL: 01179 750 700

9 MORWELLHAM QUAY
Museum
Morwellham, Tavistock
TEL: 01822 832 766

10 KING DONIERT'S STONE
Ancient monument
St Cleer
TEL: 01179 750 700

11 COTEHELE NT
Garden
St Dominick, Saltash
TEL: 01579 351 346

12 BUCKLAND ABBEY NT
Historic building
Yelverton
TEL: 01822 853 607

13 GARDEN HOUSE
Garden
Buckland Monachorum, Yelverton
TEL: 01822 854 769

14 PAPERWEIGHT CENTRE
Museum
4 Buckland Terrace, Yelverton
TEL: 01822 854 250

15 DOBWALLS FAMILY ADVENTURE PARK
Adventure & activity centre
Dobwalls, Liskeard
TEL: 01579 320 325

16 CATCHFRENCH MANOR GARDENS
Garden
St Germans, Saltash
TEL: 01503 240 759

17 ANTONY WOODLAND GARDEN NT
Garden
Near Antony House, Torpoint
TEL: 01752 812 364

18 ANTONY HOUSE
Historic house
Antony Estate, Torpoint
TEL: 01752 812 191

19 SALTRAM NT
Garden
Plymton, Plymouth
TEL: 01752 336 546

20 MONKEY SANCTUARY
Animal Sanctuary
St Martin, Murrayton, Looe
TEL: 01503 262 532

21 ELIZABETHAN GARDENS
Garden
New Street, The Barbican, Dartmouth
TEL: 01803 301 010

22 PRYSTEN HOUSE
Historic house
Catherine Street, Plymouth
TEL: 01752 661 414

23 MERCHANT'S HOUSE MUSEUM
Museum
33 St Andrew Street, Plymouth
TEL: 01752 264 878

24 ROYAL CITADEL
Ancient monument
The Hoe, Plymouth
TEL: 01752 775 841

25 BLACK FRIARS DISTILLERY
Distillery
60 Southside Street, Plymouth
TEL: 01752 665 292

26 ELIZABETHAN HOUSE
Historic house
32 New Street, The Barbican, Plymouth
TEL: 01752 253 871

27 BARBICAN GLASSWORKS
Heritage centre
The Old Fish Market, The Barbican, Plymouth
TEL: 01752 224 777

28 NATIONAL MARINE AQUARIUM
Aquarium
Rope Walk, Coxside, Plymouth
TEL: 01752 600 301

29 SMEATON'S TOWER
Historic building
The Hoe, Hoe Road, Plymouth
TEL: 01752 603 300

30 PLYMOUTH DOME
Museum
The Hoe, Plymouth
TEL: 01752 603 300

31 MOUNT EDGCUMBE HOUSE & GARDENS
Historic house
Cremyll, Torpoint
TEL: 01752 822 236

32 LAND OF LEGEND & MODEL VILLAGE
Model village
The Old Forge, Mill Hill, Polperro
TEL: 01503 272 378

Fun at a science museum

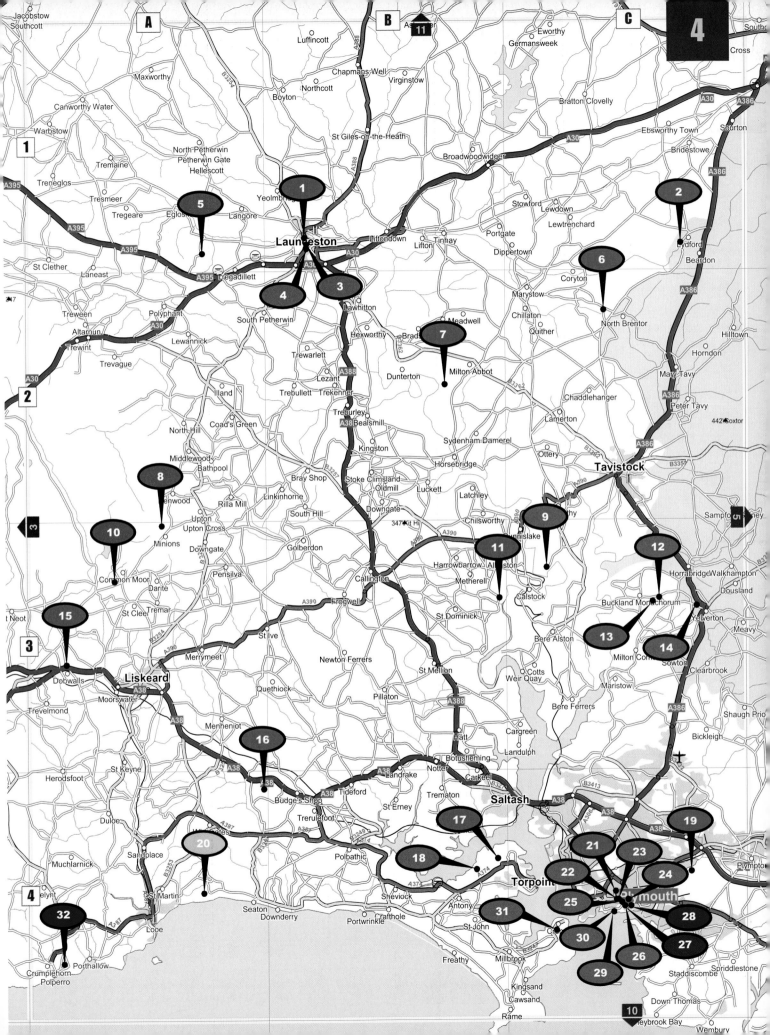

- ● ANIMAL ATTRACTIONS
- ● HERITAGE & CULTURE
- ○ INDOOR ACTIVITIES
- ● OUTDOOR ATTRACTIONS
- ● OUTDOOR ACTIVITIES
- ● WATER ACTIVITIES

1 CLEAVE HOUSE
Garden
Sticklepath, Okehampton
TEL: 01837 840 481

2 CASTLE DROGO NT
Castle
Drewsteignton, Exeter
TEL: 01647 433 306

3 MYTHIC GARDEN
Garden
Stone Farm, Chagford, Newton Abbot
TEL: 01647 231 311

4 MINIATURE PONY CENTRE
Riding
Wormhill Farm, North Bovey
TEL: 01647 432 400

5 CANONTEIGN FALLS & LAKELAND
Country park
Lower Ashton, Exeter
TEL: 01647 252 434

6 BECKY FALLS WOODLAND ESTATE
Country park
Manaton, Bovey Tracey
TEL: 01647 221 259

7 DEVON GUILD OF CRAFTSMEN
Gallery
The Riverside Mill, Bovey Tracey
TEL: 01626 832 223

8 UGBROOKE HOUSE
Historic house
Ugbrooke, Chudleigh, Newton Abbot
TEL: 01626 852 179

9 HOUSE OF MARBLES AND TEIGN VALLEY GLASS
Factory tour
The Old Pottery Pottery Road, Bovey Tracey
TEL: 01626 835 358

10 CHURCH HOUSE
Historic building
Widecombe in the Moor, Newton Abbot
TEL: 01364 621 321

11 GORSE BLOSSOM MINIATURE RAILWAY & WOODLAND PARK
Railway
Bickington, Newton Abbot
TEL: 01626 821 361

12 HIGH MOORLAND VISITOR CENTRE
Visitor centre
The Old Duchy Hotel, Tavistock Road, Princetown
TEL: 01822 890 414

13 NEWTON ABBOT RACECOURSE
Racecourse
Newton Road, Kingsteignton, Newton Abbot
TEL: 01626 353 235

14 BRADLEY MANOR
Historic house
Newton Abbot
TEL: 01626 545 13

15 HEDGEHOG HOSPITAL AT PRICKLY BALL FARM
Farm
Denbury Road, East Ogwell, Newton Abbot
TEL: 01626 362 319

16 BUCKFAST ABBEY
Abbey
Buckfastleigh
TEL: 01364 645 500

17 BUCKFAST BUTTERFLY FARM & DARTMOOR OTTER SANCTUARY
Farm
Buckfastleigh
TEL: 01364 642 916

18 SOUTH DEVON RAILWAY
Railway
The Railway Station, Buckfast Leigh
TEL: 01364 642 338

19 COMPTON CASTLE
Castle
Compton Marldon, Paignton
TEL: 01803 872 112

20 PENNYWELL DEVON'S FARM & WILDLIFE CENTRE
Farm
Lower Dean, Buckfastleigh
TEL: 01364 642 023

21 DEEP EXHIBITION
Aquarium
The Quay, Brixham
TEL: 01803 858 444

22 DARTINGTON HALL
Historic building
Dartington, Totnes
TEL: 01803 862 367

23 HIGH CROSS HOUSE
Historic house
Dartington Hall, Totnes
TEL: 01803 864 114

24 BERRY POMEROY CASTLE
Castle
Berry Pomeroy, Totnes
TEL: 01803 866 618

25 TOTNES CASTLE
Castle
Totnes
TEL: 01803 864 406

26 TOTNES MUSEUM
Museum
70 Fore Street, Totnes
TEL: 01803 863 821

27 GUILDHALL
Historic building
5 Ramparts Walk Totnes
TEL: 01803 862 147

28 PAIGNTON ZOO & BOTANICAL GARDENS
Zoo
Totnes Road, Paignton Devon, TQ4 7EU.
TEL: 01803 697 500
EMAIL: info@paigntonzoo.org.uk
WEB: www.paigntonzoo.org.uk
You can cover thousands of miles in just a few hours on foot, at the worldwide nature trail at Paignton Zoo.
OPEN: Apr-Oct: 10-6. Nov-Mar: 10-5. Closed Christmas Day.
ENTRY COSTS: £8, Child: £5.75, OAPs: £6.50, Family: £24.70.
SPECIALITIES: Events held, Photography allowed, Picnic area, Play area.
FACILITIES: Child area, Coffee shop, Credit cards, Gift shop, Pushchair friendly, Restaurant, Toilets, Wheelchair access.

29 BOWDEN HOUSE GHOSTLY TALES
Historic house
Totnes
TEL: 01803 863 664

30 AVENUE COTTAGE GARDENS
Garden
Ashprington, Otley
TEL: 01803 732 769

31 HEMERDON HOUSE
Historic house
Plympton, Plymouth
TEL: 01752 841 410

32 GREENWAY HOUSE & GARDENS NT
Historic house
Churston Ferrers, Brixham
TEL: 01803 842 382

33 WOODLANDS LEISURE PARK
Country park
Blackawton, Totnes
TEL: 01803 712 598

34 NEWCOMEN MEMORIAL ENGINE
Factory tour
The Engine House, Mayors Avenue, Dartmouth
TEL: 01803 834 224

35 NATIONAL SHIRE HORSE ADVENTURE PARK
Adventure & activity centre
Yealmpton, Plymouth
TEL: 01752 880 268

36 FLETE
Historic house
Ermington, Ivybridge
TEL: 01752 830 308

37 DARTMOUTH CASTLE
Castle
Castle Road, Dartmouth
TEL: 01803 833 588

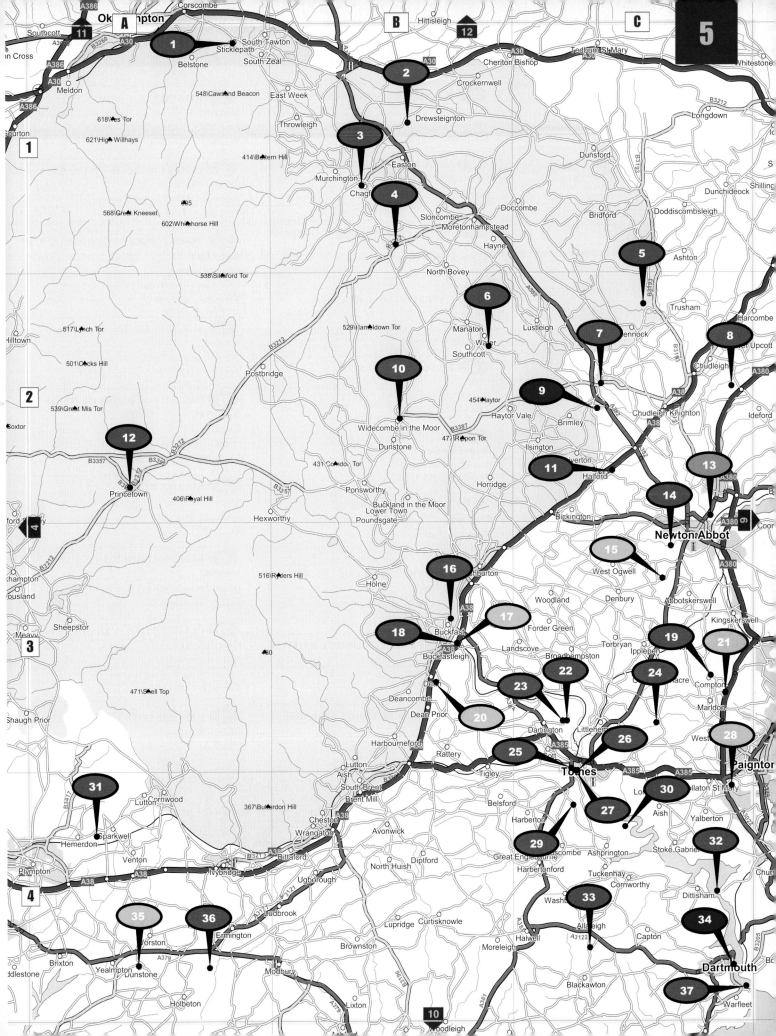

● ANIMAL ATTRACTIONS   ● OUTDOOR ATTRACTIONS
● HERITAGE & CULTURE   ● OUTDOOR ACTIVITIES
○ INDOOR ACTIVITIES   ● WATER ACTIVITIES

1 **EXETER UNIVERSITY GARDENS**
Garden
Streatham Farm, Prince of Wales Road, Exeter
TEL: 01392 263 059

2 **SAND**
Historic house
Sidbury, Sidmouth
TEL: 01395 597 230

3 **UNDERGROUND PASSAGES**
Tour
Romangate Passage, High Street, Exeter
TEL: 01392 265 858

4 **ROYAL ALBERT MEMORIAL MUSEUM**
Museum
Queen Street, Exeter
TEL: 01392 265 858

5 **EXETER CATHEDRAL**
Cathedral
Exeter
TEL: 01392 214 219

6 **ST NICHOLAS PRIORY**
Priory
Mint Lan, Exeter
TEL: 01392 265 858

7 **CREALY PARK**
Adventure & activity centre
Sidmouth Road, Clyst St Mary, Exeter
TEL: 01395 233 200

8 **RSPB NATURE RESERVE AYLESBEARE COMMON**
RSPB
Hawkerland Brake Barn, Aylesbeare, Exeter
TEL: 01404 813 964

9 **PECO GARDENS**
Garden
Beer, Seaton
TEL: 01297 215 42

10 **DONKEY SANCTUARY**
Donkey Sanctuary
Sidmouth, Devon, EX10 0NU.
TEL: 01395 578 222
EMAIL: thedonkeysanctuary@compuserve.com
WEB: www.thedonkeysanctuary.org.uk

The Donkey Sanctuary is a beautiful and relaxing place to visit. Home to over 480 donkeys, many of whom have been rescued from lives of neglect or cruelty.

OPEN: Open daily from 9-dusk.
ENTRY COSTS: Free.
SPECIALITIES: Photography allowed, Picnic area.
FACILITIES: Credit cards, Dogs allowed, Gift shop, Pushchair friendly, Restaurant, Toilets, Wheelchair access.

11 **BRANSCOMBE MANOR MILL**
Museum
The Old Bakery & Forge, Branscombe, Seaton
TEL: 01297 881 691

12 **NORMAN LOCKYER OBSERVATORY**
Observatory
Solcombe Hill, Sidmouth
TEL: 01395 579 941

13 **BICTON PARK BOTANICAL GARDENS**
Garden
East Budleigh, Budleigh Salterton
TEL: 01395 568 465

14 **OTTERTON MILL CENTRE**
Museum
Otterton, Budleigh Salterton
TEL: 01395 568 521

15 **POWDERHAM CASTLE**
Castle
Powderham, Kenton, Exeter
TEL: 01626 890 243

16 **A LA RONDE**
Historic house
Summer Lane, Exmouth
TEL: 01395 265 514

17 **EXETER RACECOURSE**
Racecourse
Kennford, Exeter
TEL: 01392 832 599

18 **FAIRLYNCH MUSEUM**
Museum
27 Fore Street, Budleigh, Salterton
TEL: 01395 442 666

19 **GREAT EXMOUTH MODEL RAILWAY**
Railway
Sea Front, Exmouth
TEL: 01395 278 383

20 **BABBACOMBE MODEL VILLAGE**
Model village
Hampton Avenue, Torquay
TEL: 01803 328 669

21 **BYGONES**
Museum
Fore Street, St Marychurch, Torquay
TEL: 01803 326 108

22 **KENTS CAVERN SHOWCAVES**
Archaeological site
Ilsham Road, Wellswood, Torquay
TEL: 01803 215 136

23 **TORRE ABBEY HISTORIC HOUSE & GALLERY**
Historic house
The Kings Drive, Torquay
TEL: 01803 293 593

24 **TORQUAY MUSEUM**
Museum
529 Babbacombe Road, Torquay
TEL: 01803 293 975

25 **PAIGNTON & DARTMOUTH STEAM RAILWAY**
Railway
Queens Park Station, Torbay Road, Paignton
TEL: 01803 555 872

26 **GOLDEN HINDE**
Ships
The Quay, Brixham
TEL: 01803 856 223

27 **BRIXHAM MUSEUM**
Museum
Bolton Cross, New Road, Brixham
TEL: 01803 856 267

28 **COLETON FISHACRE HOUSE & GARDEN NT**
Historic house
Coleton, Kingswear, Dartmouth
TEL: 01803 752 466

29 **BAYARDS COVE FORT**
Historic building
Dartmouth
TEL: 01803 732 769

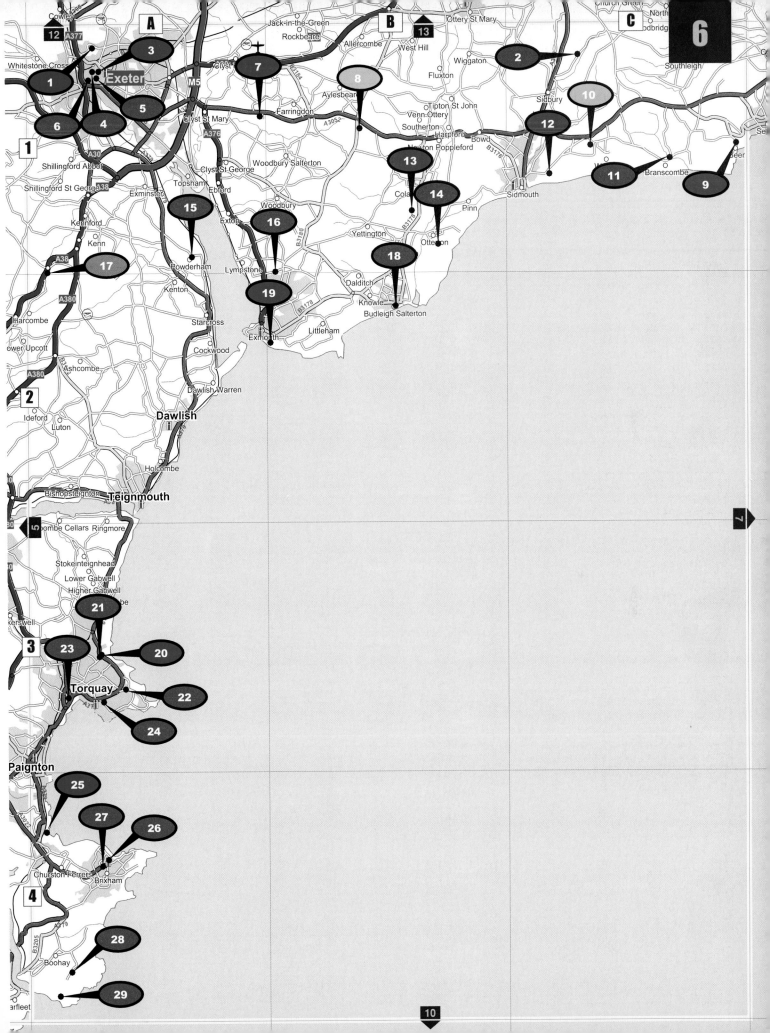

DORSET

- ● ANIMAL ATTRACTIONS
- ● HERITAGE & CULTURE
- ○ INDOOR ACTIVITIES
- ● OUTDOOR ATTRACTIONS
- ● OUTDOOR ACTIVITIES
- ● WATER ACTIVITIES

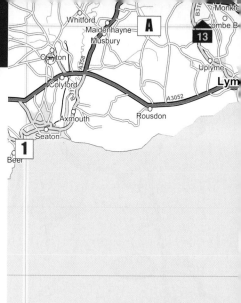

1 LYME REGIS UNDERCLIFF

Walks

Tourist Information Centre, Church Street,
Lyme Regis
TEL: 01297 442 138

2 DINOSAURLAND

Museum

Coombe Street, Lyme Regis
TEL: 01297 443 541

3 NEW BARN FIELD CENTRE

Heritage centre

Bradford Peverell
TEL: 01305 268 865

4 DORSET COUNTY MUSEUM

Museum

High West Street, Dorchester
TEL: 01305 262 735

5 DORSET TEDDY BEAR MUSEUM

Museum

25 High West Street, Dorchester, Dorset, DT1 1UW.
TEL: 01305 269 741
EMAIL: info@teddybearhouse.co.uk
WEB: www.teddybearhouse.co.uk
*A visit to Teddy Bear House is in fact a visit to the
home of Mr Edward Bear and his large family of
human-sized teddy bears!*
OPEN: Open daily 10-5.
ENTRY COSTS: £2.95, Child: £1.50, Family: £7.95

6 KEEP MILITARY MUSEUM

Museum

Bridport Road, Dorchester
TEL: 01305 264 066

7 TUTANKHAMUN EXHIBITION

Museum

High West Street, Dorchester, Dorset, DT1 1UW.
TEL: 01305 269 741
EMAIL: info@tutankhamun-exhibition.co.uk
*Come and visit the ancient world of Egypt and
learn more about Tutankhamun's tomb.*
OPEN: Open daily 10-5.
ENTRY COSTS: £4.75, Child: £2.95, OAPs: £3.75,
Family: £13.75.
FACILITIES: Gift shop.

8 TEDDY BEAR HOUSE

Museum

Antelope Walk, Dorchester, Dorset, DT1 1BE.
TEL: 01305 263 200
*A museum and collectors shop specialising in limited
editions, one-of-a-kind bears, shop exclusives by
top artists.*
OPEN: Open daily 9.30-8.
ENTRY COSTS: Free.

9 DINOSAUR MUSEUM

Museum

Icen Way, Dorchester, Dorset, DT1 1EW.
TEL: 01305 269 880
EMAIL: info@dinosaur-museum.org.uk
WEB: www.dinosaur-museum.org.uk
*Learn all you want to know about Dinosaurs! Fun
for people of all ages!*
OPEN: Open daily 9.30-5.30
ENTRY COSTS: £2.95, Child: £1.50, Family: £7.95.
FACILITIES: Gift shop.

10 ST CATHERINES CHAPEL

Historic building

Abbotsbury
TEL: 0117 975 0700

**11 ABBOTSBURY SUB-TROPICAL
GARDENS**

Garden

Bullersway, Abbotsbury
TEL: 01305 871 387

12 SMUGGLERS BARN

Farm

Abbotsbury, Weymouth
TEL: 01305 871 130

13 ABBOTSBURY SWANNERY

Swannery

New Barn Road, Abbotsbury
TEL: 01305 871 858

14 SEA LIFE PARK

Sea life centre

Lodmoor Country Park, Greenhill, Weymouth
TEL: 01305 788 255

15 MODEL WORLD

Model village

Lodmoor Country Park, Preston Road, Weymouth
TEL: 01305 781 797

16 BENNETTS WATER GARDEN

Garden

Putton Lane, Chickerall, Weymouth
TEL: 01305 785 150

17 RSPB NATURE RESERVE RADIPOLE

Nature centre

Weymouth
TEL: 01305 778 313

18 PAVILION COMPLEX

Entertainment centre

The Esplanade, Weymouth
TEL: 01305 785 747

**19 DEEP SEA ADVENTURE & SHARKY'S
PLAY ZONE**

Museum

9 Custom House, Quay Old Harbour, Weymouth
TEL: 01305 760 690

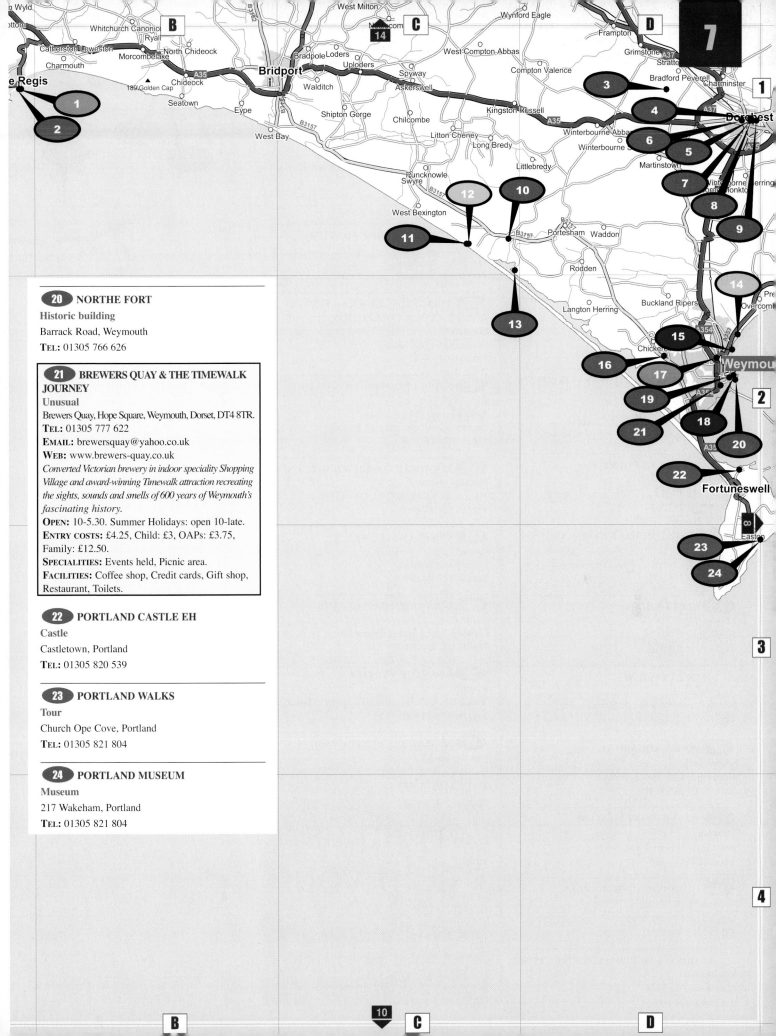

20 NORTHE FORT
Historic building
Barrack Road, Weymouth
TEL: 01305 766 626

21 BREWERS QUAY & THE TIMEWALK JOURNEY
Unusual
Brewers Quay, Hope Square, Weymouth, Dorset, DT4 8TR.
TEL: 01305 777 622
EMAIL: brewersquay@yahoo.co.uk
WEB: www.brewers-quay.co.uk
Converted Victorian brewery in indoor speciality Shopping Village and award-winning Timewalk attraction recreating the sights, sounds and smells of 600 years of Weymouth's fascinating history.
OPEN: 10-5.30. Summer Holidays: open 10-late.
ENTRY COSTS: £4.25, Child: £3, OAPs: £3.75, Family: £12.50.
SPECIALITIES: Events held, Picnic area.
FACILITIES: Coffee shop, Credit cards, Gift shop, Restaurant, Toilets.

22 PORTLAND CASTLE EH
Castle
Castletown, Portland
TEL: 01305 820 539

23 PORTLAND WALKS
Tour
Church Ope Cove, Portland
TEL: 01305 821 804

24 PORTLAND MUSEUM
Museum
217 Wakeham, Portland
TEL: 01305 821 804

DORSET

ANIMAL ATTRACTIONS
HERITAGE & CULTURE
INDOOR ACTIVITIES
OUTDOOR ATTRACTIONS
OUTDOOR ACTIVITIES
WATER ACTIVITIES

1 TOLPUDDLE MARTYRS MUSEUM
Museum
Tolpuddle, Dorchester
TEL: 01305 848 237

2 ATHELHAMPTON HOUSE & GARDENS
Historic house
Athelhampton, Dorchester
TEL: 01305 848 363

3 UPTON COUNTRY PARK
Country park
Upton Road, Poole
TEL: 01202 672 625

4 HARDY'S COTTAGE
Historic building
Higher Bockhampton, Dorchester
TEL: 01305 262 366

5 BOURNEMOUTH BEARS - DORSET'S TEDDY BEAR MUSEUM
Museum
Old Christchurch Lane, Bournemouth
TEL: 01202 293 544

6 SCAPLEN'S COURT
Museum
High Street, Poole
TEL: 01202 683 138

7 KINGSTON MAURWARD GARDENS
Country park
Kingston Maurward College, Dorchester
TEL: 01305 215 000

8 CLOUDS HILL
Mill
Wareham
TEL: 01929 405 616

9 OCEANARIUM
Aquarium
Pier Approach, West Beach, Bournemouth
TEL: 01202 311 993

10 POOLE AQUARIUM
Theme park
Hennings Wharf, The Quay, Poole
TEL: 01202 686 712

11 WATERFRONT MUSEUM
Museum
Poole Quay, 4 High Street, Poole
TEL: 01202 683 138

12 COMPTON ACRES GARDEN
Garden
Canford Cliffs Road, Poole
TEL: 01202 700 778

13 MONKEY WORLD APE RESCUE CENTRE
Wildlife park
Longthorns, Wareham
TEL: 0800 456 600

14 TANK MUSEUM
Museum
Bovington Camp, Wareham
TEL: 01929 405 096

15 RSPB NATURE RESERVE ARNE
Nature centre
Fyldata, Arne
TEL: 01929 553 360

16 WAREHAM TOWN MUSEUM
Museum
East Street, Wareham
TEL: 01929 553 448

17 MILL HOUSE CIDER MUSEUM & DORSET CLOCK COLLECTION
Museum
Owermoigne, Dorchester
TEL: 01305 852 220

18 STUDLAND BEACH & NATURE RESERVE
Nature centre
Countryside Office, Studland, Swanage
TEL: 01929 450 259

19 LULWORTH COVE HERITAGE CENTRE
Heritage centre
Main Road, Lulworth Cove, West Lulworth
TEL: 01929 400 587

20 CORFE CASTLE NT
Castle
Castle View, Wareham
TEL: 01929 481 294

21 LULWORTH CASTLE PARK
Castle
Lulworth Park, Lulworth, Wareham
TEL: 01929 400 510

22 SWANAGE RAILWAY
Railway
Station House Railway Station Approach, Swanage
TEL: 01929 425 800

23 DURLSTON COUNTRY PARK
Country park
Lighthouse Road, Swanage
TEL: 01929 427 965

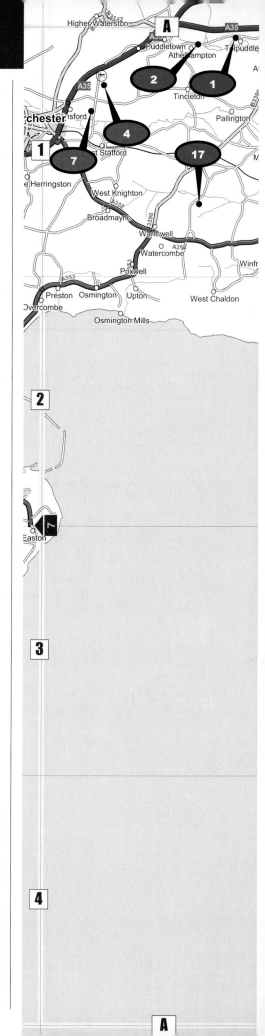

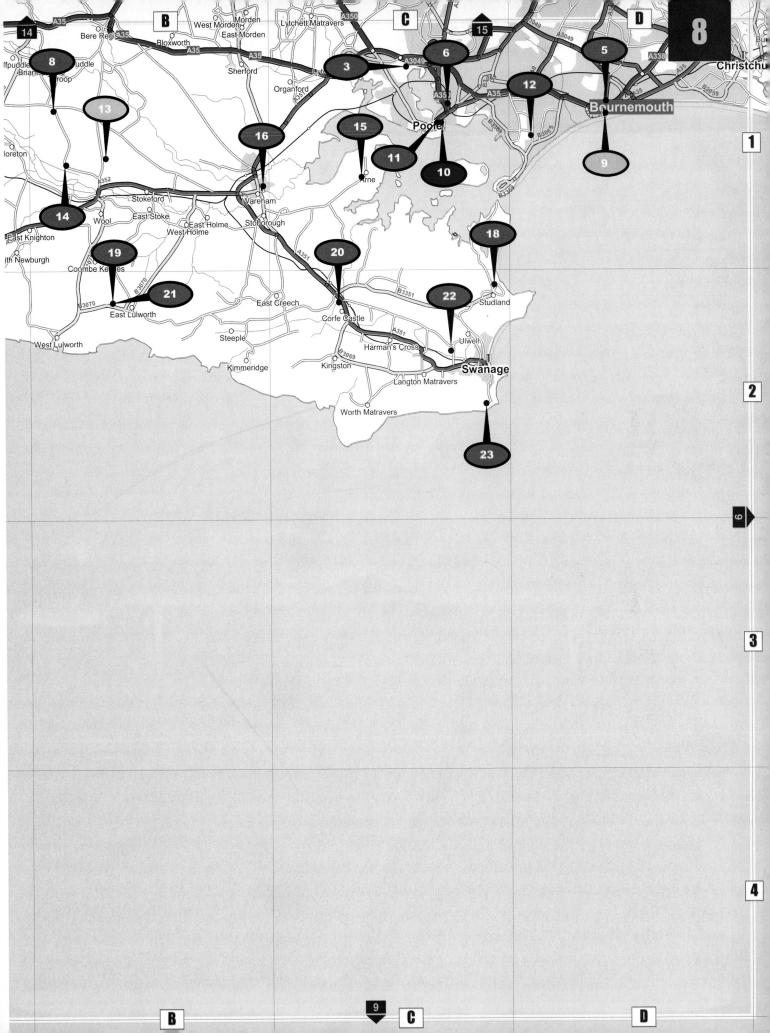

● ANIMAL ATTRACTIONS   ● OUTDOOR ATTRACTIONS
● HERITAGE & CULTURE   ● OUTDOOR ACTIVITIES
○ INDOOR ACTIVITIES   ● WATER ACTIVITIES

1 HIGHCLIFFE CASTLE
Castle
Rothsay Drive, Highcliffe-on-Sea, Christchurch
TEL: 01425 278 807

2 CHRISTCHURCH CASTLE & NORMAN HOUSE
Castle
Christchurch
TEL: 01179 750 700

3 RED HOUSE MUSEUM & GARDENS
Museum
Quay Road, Christchurch
TEL: 01202 482 860

4 HURST CASTLE
Castle
Pebble Spit, Keyhaven
TEL: 01590 642 344

5 YARMOUTH CASTLE
Castle
Quay Street, Yarmouth
TEL: 01983 760 678

6 ROMAN VILLA
Roman site
Cypress Road, Newport
TEL: 01983 529 720

7 CARISBROOKE CASTLE
Castle
Newport
TEL: 01983 522 107

8 CALBOURNE WATERMILL & RURAL MUSEUM
Museum
Calbourne, Newport
TEL: 01983 531 227

9 DIMBOLA LODGE
Historic building
Terrance Lane, Freshwater Bay
TEL: 01983 756 814

10 CHESSELL POTTERY
Factory shop
Calbourne
TEL: 01983 531 248

11 NEEDLES PLEASURE PARK
Theme park
Alum Bay, Totland Bay
TEL: 01983 752 401

12 NEEDLES OLD BATTERY
Historic building
West Highdown, Totland
TEL: 01983 754 772

13 BRIGHSTONE SHOP & MUSEUM
Historic building
North Street, Brighstone
TEL: Not available

14 OLD TOWN HALL NEWTOWN
Historic house
Upper Lane, Brighstone, Newport
TEL: 01983 741 052

15 YAFFORD WATER MILL FARM PARK
Museum
Yafford Shorwell, Newport
TEL: 01983 740 610

16 ST CATHERINE'S ORATORY
Historic building
Niton
TEL: Not available

17 BLACKGANG CHINE FANTASY PARK
Theme park
Blackgang, Ventnor
TEL: 01983 730 330

Bicton Park, Devon, Map 6-13

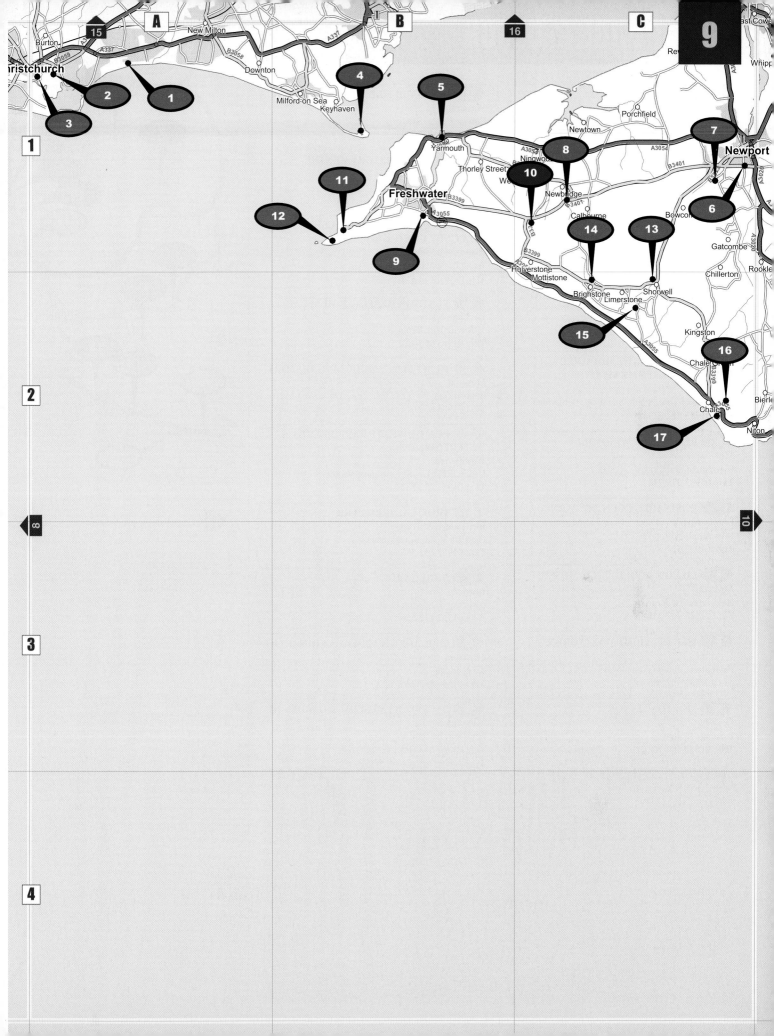

1 OSBORNE HOUSE EH
Historic house
York Avenue, East Cowes
TEL: 01983 200 022

2 BRICKFIELDS HORSE COUNTRY
Riding
Binstead
TEL: 01983 566 801

3 WALTZING WATERS
Unusual
Brading Road, Ryde
TEL: 01983 811 333

4 ISLE OF WIGHT STEAM RAILWAY
Railway
Station Road, Havenstreet Village, Ryde
TEL: 01983 882 204

5 ISLE OF WIGHT SHIPWRECK CENTRE & MARITIME MUSEUM
Museum
Providence House, Sherborne Street, Bembridge
TEL: 01983 872 223

6 BEMBRIDGE WINDMILL
Mill
High Street, Bembridge
TEL: 01983 873 945

7 ROBIN HILL COUNTRY PARK
Country park
Down End, Newport
TEL: 01983 527 352

8 LILLIPUT DOLL & TOY MUSEUM
Museum
High Street, Sandown
TEL: 01983 407 231

9 ISLE OF WIGHT WAX WORKS
Unusual
High Street, Brading, Sandown
TEL: 01983 407 286

10 MORTON MANOR
Garden
Brading, Sandown
TEL: 01983 406 168

11 DINOSAUR ISLE
Museum
Culver Parade, Sandown
TEL: 01983 404 344

12 NATURAL HISTORY CENTRE
Museum
Godshill
TEL: 01983 840 333

13 APPULDURCOMBE HOUSE & FALCONRY CENTRE EH
Historic building
Wroxall, Ventnor
TEL: 01983 852 484

14 VENTNOR HERITAGE MUSEUM
Heritage centre
11 Spring Hill, Ventnor
TEL: 01983 855 407

15 MUSEUM OF SMUGGLING HISTORY
Museum
Botanic Gardens, The Undercliffe Drive, Ventnor
TEL: 01983 853 677

16 ISLE OF WIGHT RARE BREEDS & WATERFOWL PARK
Wildlife park
Undercliff Drive, St Lawrence, Ventnor
TEL: 01983 852 582

17 TROPICAL BIRD PARK
Bird centre & aviary
Old Park Road, St Lawrence
TEL: 01983 852 583

18 HIGH GARDEN
Garden
Courtwood, Newton Ferrers
TEL: 01752 872 528

19 COOKWORTHY MUSEUM OF RURAL LIFE
Museum
Kingsbridge
TEL: 01548 853 235

20 OVERBECKS MUSEUM & GARDEN NT
Museum
Sharpitor, Salcombe
TEL: 01548 842 893

Help us help you

mention the
Days Out Atlas
when visiting
anywhere on this page.

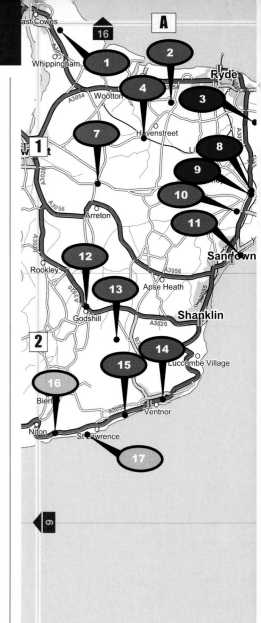

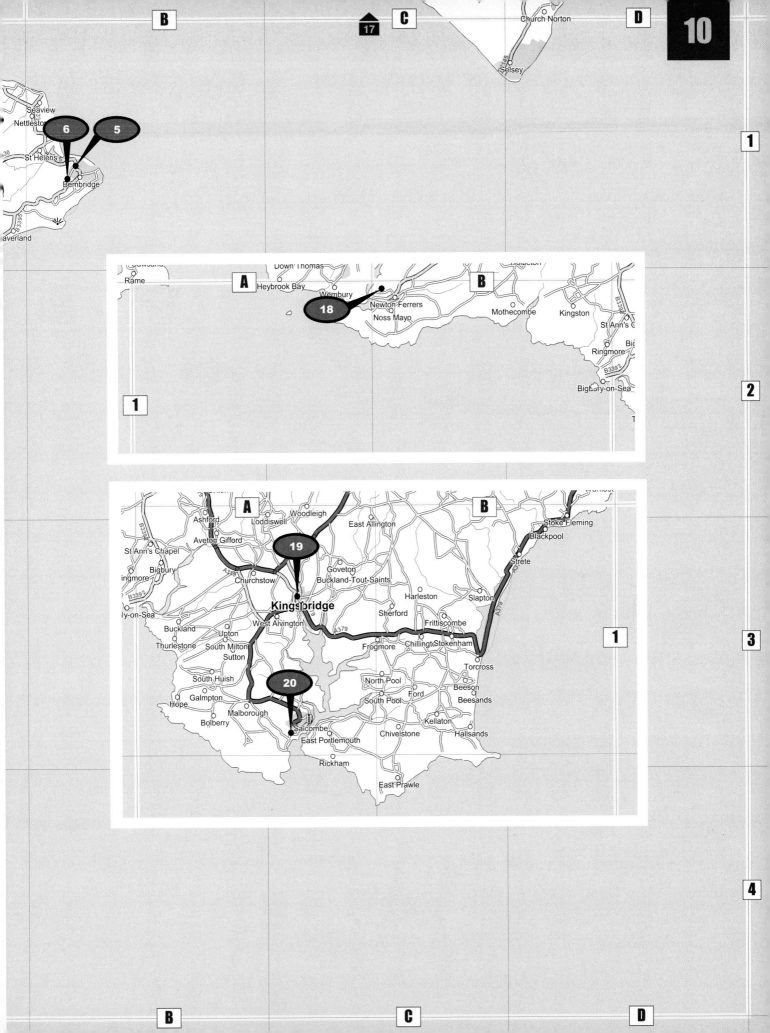

- ● ANIMAL ATTRACTIONS
- ● HERITAGE & CULTURE
- ○ INDOOR ACTIVITIES
- ● OUTDOOR ATTRACTIONS
- ● OUTDOOR ACTIVITIES
- ● WATER ACTIVITIES

1 EXMOOR ZOOLOGICAL PARK
Wildlife park
South Stowford, Bratton Flemming, Barnstaple
Tel: 01598 763 352

2 CROYDE GEM ROCK & SHELL MUSEUM
Museum
10 Hobbs Hill, Croyde   Tel: 01271 890 407

3 EXMOOR STEAM RAILWAY
Railway
Bratton Fleming, Barnstaple   Tel: 01598 710 711

4 MARWOOD HILL GARDENS
Garden
Marwood Hill, Barnstaple   Tel: 01271 342 528

5 BRANNAM'S POT FACTORY
Factory tour
Roundswell Industrial Estate, Barnstaple
Tel: 01271 343 035

6 NORTH DEVON MARITIME MUSEUM
Museum
Odun House, Odun Road, Appledore
Tel: 01237 474 852

7 TAPELEY PARK
Garden
Tapeley House, Instow   Tel: 01271 342 558

8 SECRET GARDEN
Garden
2a Cross St, Northam, Bideford Tel: 01237 474 403

9 BIG SHEEP
Farm
Abbotsham, Bideford   Tel: 01237 477 916

10 COBBATON COMBAT COLLECTION
Museum
Cobbaton, Chittlehampton, Umberleigh
Tel: 01769 540 740

11 QUINCE HONEY FARM
Farm
North Road, South Molton   Tel: 01769 572 401

12 SOUTH MOLTON MUSEUM
Museum
Town Hall, Broad St, South Molton Tel: 01769 572 951

13 HARTLAND ABBEY & GARDENS
Historic building
Cuckoo Wood Cottage, Hartland, Bideford
Tel: 01237 441 264

14 DOCTON MILL
Historic building
Lymebridge, Hartland, Bideford Tel: 01237 441 369

15 MILKY WAY ADVENTURE PARK
Adventure & activity centre
Clovelly, Bideford   Tel: 01237 431 255

16 TORRINGTON 1646
Heritage centre
Castle Hill, South Street, Torrington
Tel: 01805 626 146

17 ROSEMOOR GARDEN RHS
Garden
Great Torrington   Tel: 01805 624 067

18 GNOME RESERVE & WILDFLOWER GARDEN
Garden
West Putford, Bradworthy   Tel: 0870 845 9012

19 BUDE-STRATTON TOWN MUSEUM
Museum
The Lower Wharf, Bude   Tel: 01225 477 785

20 PENHALLAM
Roman site
Week St Mary   Tel: 01179 750 700

21 FINCH FOUNDRY
Historic building
Sticklepath, Oakhampton   Tel: 01837 840 046

22 OKEHAMPTON CASTLE
Roman site
Okehampton   Tel: 01837 528 44

23 MUSEUM OF DARTMOOR LIFE
Museum
West Street, Okehampton   Tel: 01837 522 95

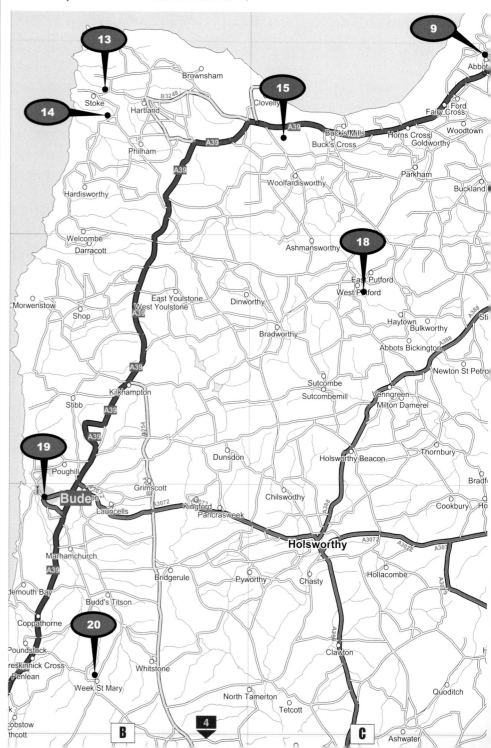

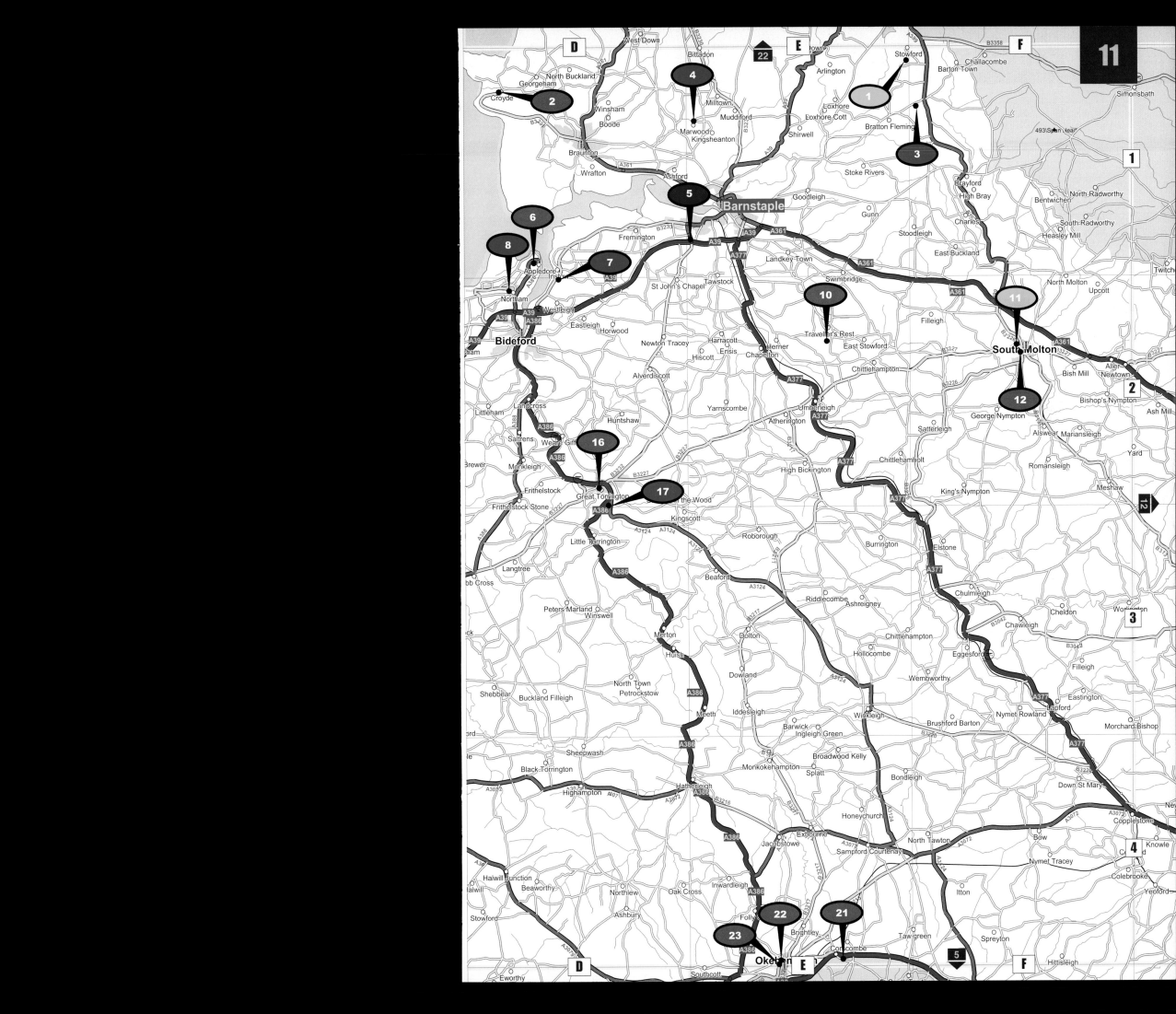

1 **BAKELITE MUSEUM**
Museum
Orchard Mill, Bridge Street, Williton
TEL: 01984 632 133

2 **CLEEVE ABBEY**
Abbey
Washford, Watchet
TEL: 01984 640 377

3 **TROPIQUARIA**
Zoo
Washford Cross, Watchet
TEL: 01984 640 688

4 **COLERIDGE COTTAGE**
Historic house
35 Lime Street, Nether Stowey, Bridgwater
TEL: 01278 732 662

5 **ORCHARD WYNDHAM**
Historic house
Williton, Taunton
TEL: 01984 632 309

6 **BRIDGEWATER CAMEL COMPANY**
Unusual
Orchard Farm, Plainsfield Over Stowey, Bridgewater
TEL: 01278 733 186

7 **COMBE SYDENHAM COUNTRY PARK**
Country park
Monksilver, Taunton
TEL: 01984 656 284

8 **BEE WORLD & ANIMAL CENTRE**
Farm
Lower Stream Farm Station Stogumber, Taunton
TEL: 01984 656 545

9 **BARFORD PARK**
Historic house
Spaxton, Bridgewater
TEL: 01278 671 269

10 **GAULDEN MANOR**
Historic house
Tolland Lydeard, St Lawrence, Taunton
TEL: 01984 667 213

11 **SOMERSET COUNTY MUSEUM**
Museum
Taunton Castle, Taunton
TEL: 01823 355 504

12 **SHEPPY'S CIDER FARM CENTRE**
Craft centre
Three Bridges, Bradford on Tone, Taunton
TEL: 01823 461 233

13 **COTHAY MANOR**
Historic building
Greenham, Wellington
TEL: 01823 672 283

14 **KNIGHTSHAYES COURT NT**
Garden
Bolham, Tiverton
TEL: 01884 254 665

15 **TIVERTON CASTLE**
Castle
Park Hill, Tiverton
TEL: 01884 253 200

16 **GRAND WESTERN HORSEBOAT COMPANY**
Boat hire
Canal Hill, Tiverton
TEL: 01884 253 345

17 **COLD HARBOUR MILL WORKING WOOL MUSEUM**
Museum
Uffculme, Cullompton
TEL: 01884 840 960

18 **TIVERTON MUSEUM**
Museum
St Andrew Street, Tiverton
TEL: 01884 256 295

19 **BICKLEIGH CASTLE**
Castle
Bickleigh, Tiverton
TEL: 01884 855 363

20 **FURSDON**
Historic house
Cadbury, Thorverton, Exeter
TEL: 01392 860 860

21 **ALLHALLOWS MUSEUM OF LACE & ANTIQUITIES**
Museum
High Street, Honiton
TEL: 01404 449 66

22 **KILLERTON HOUSE NT**
Historic house
Broadclyst, Exeter
TEL: 01392 881 345

23 **ESCOT COUNTRY PARK & GARDENS**
Country park
Escott Ottery, St Mary
TEL: 01404 822 188

24 **MARKER'S COTTAGE**
Historic house
Broad Clyst, Exeter
TEL: 01392 461 546

25 **FARWAY COUNTRYSIDE PARK**
Country park
Farway, Colyton
TEL: 01404 871 224

26 **CADHAY**
Historic house
Ottery St Mary
TEL: 01404 812 432

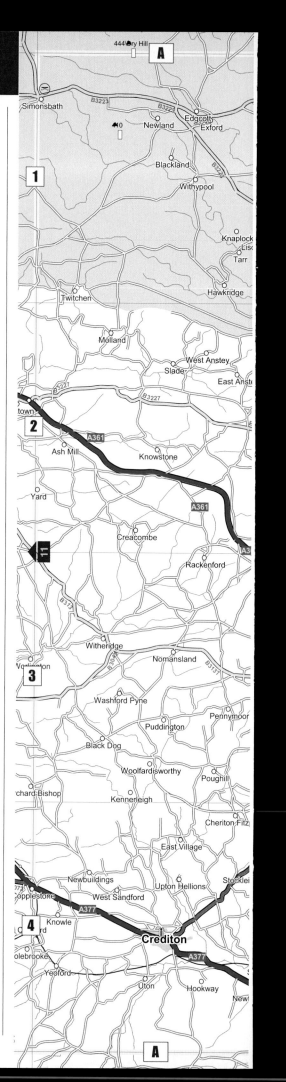

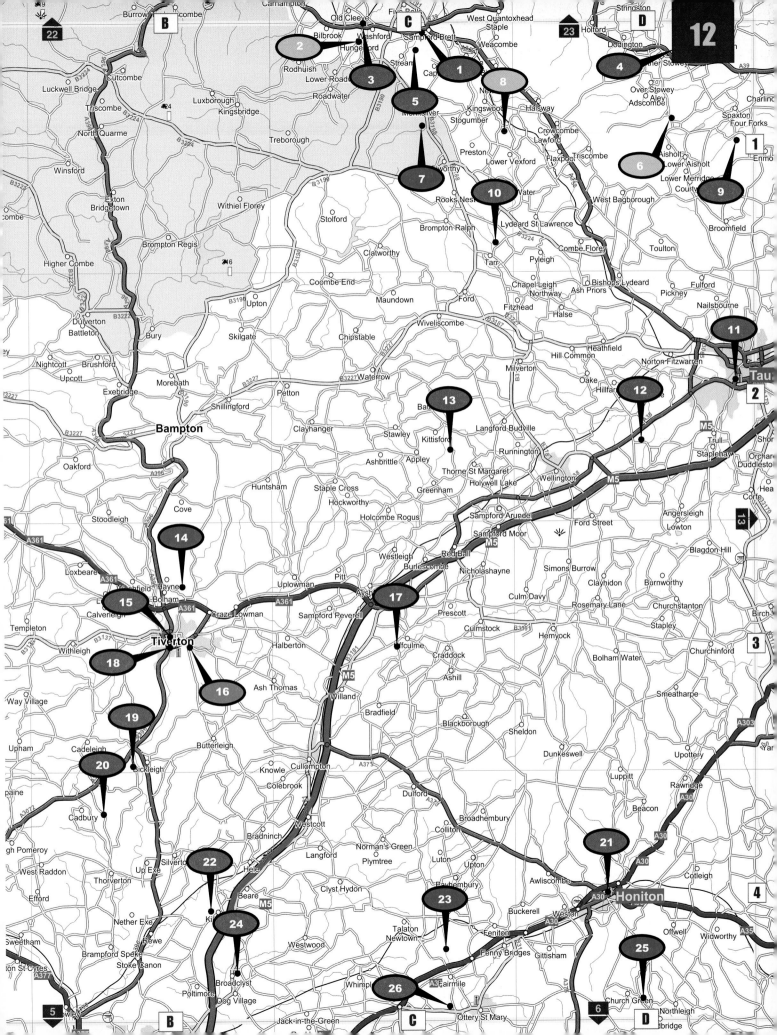

DEVON · SOMERSET · DORSET

1 **CANNINGTON COLLEGE HERITAGE GARDENS**
Garden
Cannington, Bridgwater
TEL: 01278 655 200

2 **GLASTONBURY TRIBUNAL**
Historic building
Glastonbury
TEL: 0117 975 0700

3 **GLASTONBURY LAKE VILLAGE MUSEUM**
Museum
9 High Street, Glastonbury
TEL: 01458 832 954

4 **GLASTONBURY ABBEY**
Abbey
Abbey Gatehouse, Magdalene Street, Glastonbury
TEL: 01458 832 267

5 **SOMERSET RURAL LIFE MUSEUM**
Museum
Abbey Farm, Chilkwell Street, Glastonbury
TEL: 01458 831 197

6 **WEST PENNARD COURT BARN**
Historic building
Newtown, West Pennard, Glastonbury
TEL: 01985 843 600

7 **ADMIRAL BLAKE MUSEUM**
Museum
Blake Street, Bridgewater
TEL: 01278 456 127

8 **SHOE MUSEUM**
Museum
40 High Street, Street
TEL: 01458 443 131

9 **WESTONZOYLAND PUMPING STATION**
Museum
Hoopers Lane, Westonzoyland, Bridgwater
TEL: 01823 412 713

10 **STEMBRIDGE TOWER MILL**
Mill
Mill Road High Ham, Langport
TEL: 01985 843 600

11 **HESTERCOMBE GARDENS**
Garden
Cheddon Fitzpaine, Taunton
TEL: 01823 413 923

12 **WILLOWS & WETLANDS VISITOR CENTRE**
Visitor centre
Mere Green Court, Mere Green, Stoke St Gregory
TEL: 01823 490 249

13 **STOKE-SUB-HAMDON PRIORY**
Priory
North Street, Stoke-Sub-Hamdon
TEL: 01985 843 600

14 **LYTES CARY MANOR**
Historic house
Kingsdon, Charlton Mackrell, Somerton
TEL: 01985 843 600

15 **MUCHELNEY ABBEY**
Abbey
Muchelney, Langport
TEL: 01458 250 664

16 **PRIEST'S HOUSE**
Historic house
Muchelney, Langport
TEL: 01458 252 621

17 **FLEET AIR ARM MUSEUM**
Museum
Royal Naval Air Station, Yeovilton, Yeovil
TEL: 01935 841 524

18 **TAUNTON RACECOURSE**
Racecourse
Orchard Portman, Taunton
TEL: 01823 337 172

19 **HATCH COURT**
Garden
Hatch Beauchamp, Taunton
TEL: 01823 480 120

20 **LOWER SEVERALLS GARDEN & NURSERY**
Garden
Crewkerne
TEL: 01460 732 34

21 **TREASURER'S HOUSE**
Historic house
Church Street, Martock
TEL: 01985 843 600

22 **EAST LAMBROOK MANOR GARDENS**
Garden
East Lambrook, South Petherton
TEL: 01460 240 328

23 **BARRINGTON COURT & GARDEN NT**
Historic building
Barrington, Ilminster
TEL: 01460 241 938

24 **MONTACUTE HOUSE NT**
Historic building
Montacute, Yeovil
TEL: 01935 823 289

25 **MUSEUM OF SOUTH SOMERSET**
Museum
Hendford, Yeovil
TEL: 01935 424 774

26 **PERRY BROS CIDER MILLS**
Factory shop
Orchardland, Dowlish Wake
TEL: 01460 526 81

27 **TINTINHULL HOUSE GARDEN NT**
Garden
Farm Street, Tintinhull, Yeovil
TEL: 01935 822 545

28 **CRICKET ST THOMAS WILDLIFE PARK**
Wildlife park
Chard
TEL: 01460 301 11

29 **CHARD & DISTRICT MUSEUM**
Museum
High Street, Chard
TEL: 01460 650 91

30 **WILDLIFE PARK AT CRICKET ST THOMAS**
Wildlife park
Crickest St Thomas, Chard
TEL: 01460 301 11

31 **FORDE ABBEY**
Historic building
Chard
TEL: 01460 221 290

33 **BURROW FARM GARDENS**
Garden
Dalwood, Axminster
TEL: 01404 831 285

34 **PARNHAM HOUSE**
Garden
Beaminster
TEL: 01308 862 204

35 **MAPPERTON GARDENS**
Garden
Beaminster
TEL: 01308 862 645

36 **SHUTE BARTON**
Historic house
Shute, Axminster
TEL: 01297 346 92

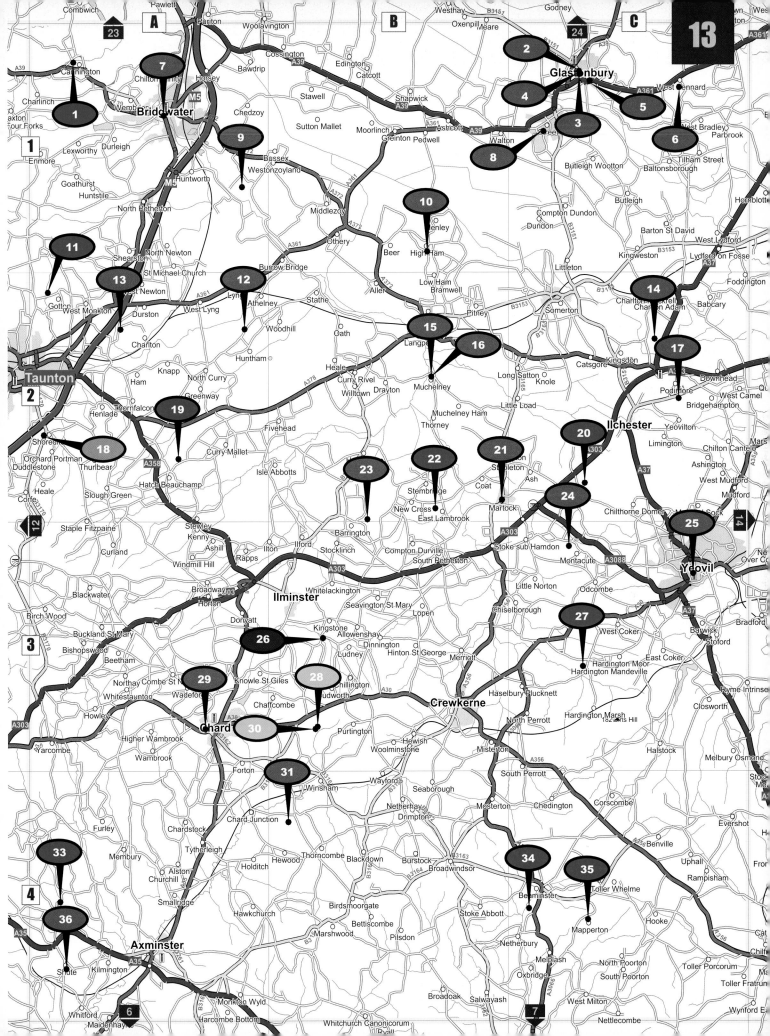

DORSET · SOMERSET · WILTSHIRE

1 STOURTON NT
Historic house
Stourton, Warminster
TEL: 01747 841 152

2 STOURHEAD HOUSE
Historic house
Stourton, Warminster
TEL: 01747 840 417

3 FARMER GILES FARMSTEAD
Country park
Teffont, Salisbury, Wiltshire, SP3 5QY.
TEL: 01722 716 338
WEB: www.farmergiles.co.uk

The farmstead is a wonderful day out for the family. Feed, see and learn about farm animals, cuddle the rabbits. Restaurant, Bar and Museum. Full wheelchair access.
OPEN: Mar 21-Nov 3: daily 10-6. Nov-Mar: Sat-Sun
ENTRY COSTS: £3.95, Child: £2.85, OAPs: £3.50, Family: £13.
SPECIALITIES: Guided tours available, Picnic area, Indoor & Outdoor play areas, Rides.
FACILITIES: Child area, Credit cards, Dogs allowed, Gift shop, Pushchair friendly, Toilets.

4 PHILIPPS HOUSE & DINTON PARK NT
Historic building
Dinton, Salisbury
TEL: 01985 843 600

5 BISON CENTRE & FARM
Farm
West Knoyle
TEL: 01747 830 263

6 LITTLE CLARENDON
Historic building
Dinton, Salisbury
TEL: 01985 843 600

7 HADSPEN GARDEN & NURSERY
Garden
Hadspen House, Castle Cary
TEL: 01749 813 707

8 WINCANTON RACECOURSE
Racecourse
Wincanton
TEL: 01963 323 44

9 OLD WARDOUR CASTLE EH
Castle
Tisbury, Salisbury
TEL: 01747 870 487

10 HAYNES MOTOR MUSEUM
Museum
Sparkford, Yeovil
TEL: 01963 440 804

11 SHAFTESBURY ABBEY RUINS & MUSEUM
Abbey
Park Walk, Shaftesbury
TEL: 01747 852 910

12 LARMER TREE GARDENS
Garden
Tollard Royal, Salisbury
TEL: 01725 516 228

13 WORLDWIDE BUTTERFLY & WILDLIFE
Butterfly farm
Compton House, Over Compton, Sherborne, Dorset, DT9 4QN.
TEL: 01935 474 608
EMAIL: butterflies@wwb.co.uk
WEB: www.worldlife.co.uk
Come and encounter exotic plants, butterflies, giant Stick Insects and other creatures.
OPEN: Apr-Sep; open daily from 10-5.
ENTRY COSTS: £4.95, Child: £2.95, OAPs: £3.95, Family: £14.95.
FACILITIES: Bookshop, Child area, Credit cards, Gift shop, Gift tokens, Pushchair friendly, Restaurant, Toilets, Wheelchair access.

14 SHERBORNE OLD CASTLE
Castle
Castleton, Sherborne
TEL: 01935 812 730

15 SHERBORNE CASTLE
Castle
New Road, Sherborne
TEL: 01935 813 182

16 KNOWLTON CHURCH & EARTHWORKS
Archaeological site
Cranbourne
TEL: 01179 750 700

17 BLANDFORD FORUM ROYAL SIGNALS MUSEUM
Museum
Blandford Camp, Blandford Forum
TEL: 01258 482 258

18 MINTERNE GARDENS
Historic house
Minterne Magna, Dorchester
TEL: 01300 341 370

19 MILTON ABBEY
Abbey
Milton Abbas, Blandford
TEL: 01258 880 489

20 KINGSTON LACY NT
Historic building
Wimborne Minster
TEL: 01202 883 402

21 PRIEST'S HOUSE MUSEUM & GARDEN
Museum
23-27 High Street, Wimborne
TEL: 01202 882 533

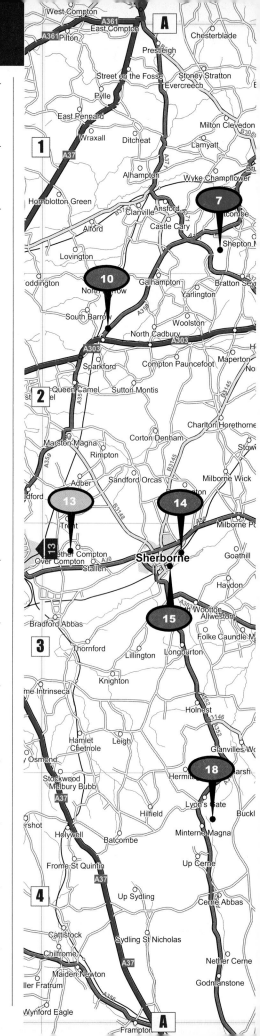

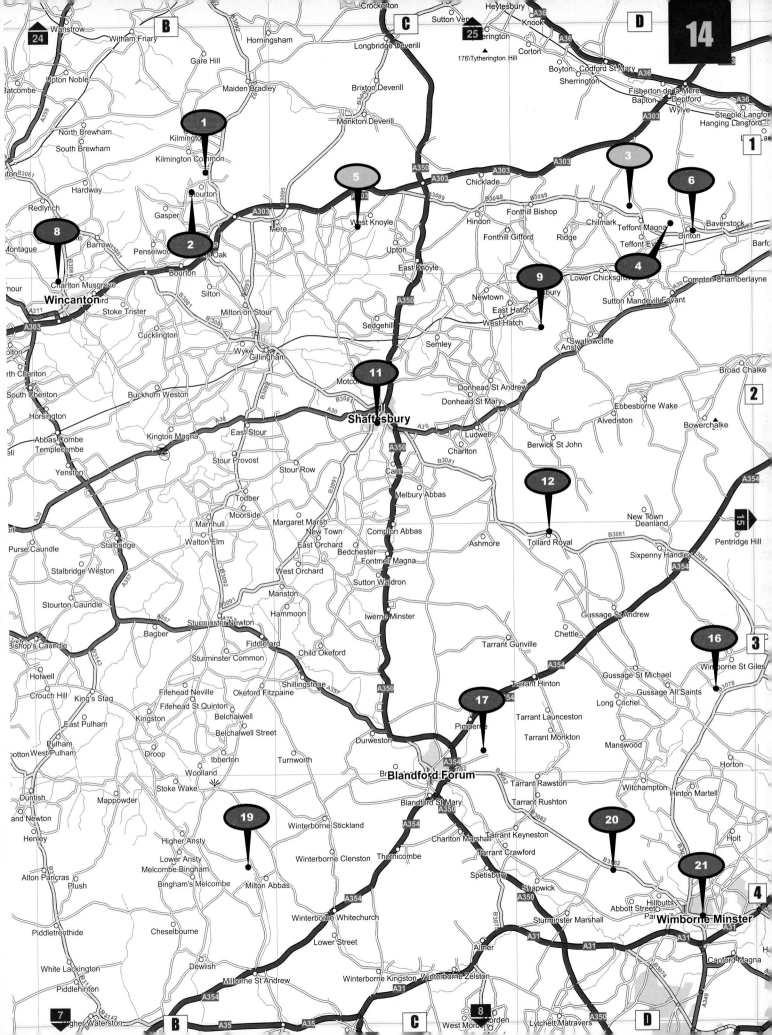

WILTS · HANTS · DORSET

- ANIMAL ATTRACTIONS
- HERITAGE & CULTURE
- INDOOR ACTIVITIES
- OUTDOOR ATTRACTIONS
- OUTDOOR ACTIVITIES
- WATER ACTIVITIES

1 MUSEUM OF ARMY FLYING
Museum
Middle Wallop, Stockbridge   Tel: 01980 674 421

2 HEALE GARDENS & PLANT CENTRE
Garden
Heale House, Middle Woodford, Salisbury
Tel: 01722 782 504

3 HOUGHTON LODGE GARDENS
Garden
Hampshire Hydroponicum, Houghton, Stockbridge
Tel: 01264 810 912

4 OLD SARUM CASTLE EH
Castle
Castle Road, Salisbury   Tel: 01722 335 398

5 SHAFTSBURY TOWN MUSEUM
Museum
Gold Hill, Shaftesbury   Tel: 01747 852 157

6 WILTON HOUSE
Historic house
Wilton, Salisbury   Tel: 01722 746 720

7 MEDIEVAL HALL
Historic building
Sarum St Michael, Cathedral Close, Salisbury
Tel: 01722 412 472

8 ROYAL GLOUCESTERSHIRE BERKSHIRE & WILTSHIRE REGIMENT MUSEUM
Museum
The Wardrobe, 58 The Close, Salisbury
Tel: 01722 414 536

9 MALMESBURY HOUSE
Historic building
The Close, Salisbury   Tel: 01722 327 027

10 MOMPESSON HOUSE
Historic building
The Close, Salisbury   Tel: 01722 335 659

12 SALISBURY AND SOUTH WILTSHIRE MUSEUM
Museum
The King's House, 65 The Close, Salisbury
Tel: 01722 332 151

13 SALISBURY RACECOURSE
Racecourse
Netherhampton, Salisbury   Tel: 01722 326 461

14 MOTTISFONT ABBEY & GARDEN NT
Abbey
Mottisfont, Romsey   Tel: 01794 340 757

15 SIR HAROLD HILLIER GARDENS & ARBORETUM
Garden
Jermyns Lane, Ampfield, Romsey   Tel: 01794 368 787

16 BROADLANDS
Garden
Broadlands Park, Romsey   Tel: 01794 505 010

11 SALISBURY CATHEDRAL
Cathedral
33 The Close, Salisbury, Wiltshire, SP1 2EJ.
Tel: 01722 555 120
Email: visitors@salcath.co.uk
Web: www.salisburycathedral.org.uk

Britain's finest medieval Cathedral, boasts England's tallest (123m/404ft) spire, best preserved Magna Carta (1215AD), largest Cathedral Close and Europe's oldest working clock (1386AD).
Open: Sep-May & Sun (all year) 7.15am-6.15pm. Jun-Aug (excl Sun) 7.15am-8.15pm.
Entry costs: Requested Voluntary donation £3.50, Child: £2, OAPs: £2.50, Family: £8.
Specialities: Guided tours available.
Facilities: Gift shop, Restaurant, Wheelchair access, Dogs allowed.

17 HAMPTWORTH LODGE
Historic building
Landford, Salisbury   Tel: 01794 390 215

18 BREAMORE HOUSE AND MUSEUM
Historic house
Breamore, Fordingbridge   Tel: 01725 512 468

19 ROCKBOURNE ROMAN VILLA
Museum
The Roman Villas Rockbourne, Fordingbridge
Tel: 01725 518 541

20 PAULTONS PARK
Theme park
Ower, Romsey, Hampshire, SO51 6AL.
Tel: 023 8081 4455
A day out to remember for all the family! Ride the Log Flume, explore Dinosaurland. Plenty for youngsters too - Tiny Tots Town, Kids Kingdom, animated nursery rhymes, children's rides and loads more.
Open: Mar 9-Oct 3: 10-6.30. Nov-Dec: Sat-Sun.
Entry costs: £11, Child: £10, OAPs: £10, Family: £39.
Facilities: Coffee shop, Gift shop, Pushchair friendly, Restaurant, Toilets, Wheelchair access.

21 CRANBORNE MANOR GARDENS
Garden
Cranborne, Wimbourne   Tel: 01725 517 248

22 TOTTON AND ELING HERITAGE CENTRE
Heritage centre
122 Eling Lane, Totton, Southampton
Tel: 023 8066 6339

23 ELING TIDE MILL
Mill
Eling Hill, Totton, Southampton   Tel: 023 8086 9575

24 FURZEY GARDENS
Garden
Minstead, Lyndhurst   Tel: 023 8081 2464

25 DORSET HEAVY HORSE CENTRE
Shire Horse Centre
Edmondsham, Verwood, Wimborne
Tel: 01202 824 040

26 NEW FOREST OTTER & OWL PARK
Wildlife park
Longdown, Ashurst   Tel: 023 8029 2408

27 LONGDOWN DAIRY FARM
Farm
Longdown Ashurst, Southampton   Tel: 023 8029 3326

28 MOORS VALLEY COUNTRY PARK
Country park
Ashley Heath   Tel: 01425 470 721

29 NEW FOREST OWL SANCTUARY
Bird centre & aviary
Crow Lane, Ringwood   Tel: 01425 476 487

30 BEAULIEU
Museum
John Montagu Building, Beaulieu, Brockenhurst
Tel: 01590 612 345

31 NEW FOREST MUSEUM & VISITOR CENTRE
Museum
Main Car Park, High Street, Lyndhurst
Tel: 023 8028 3914

32 MATCHAMS KARTING EXPERIENCE
Karting
Ringwood   Tel: 01425 473 305

33 STAPEHILL ABBEY CRAFTS & GARDENS
Craft centre
276 Wimborne Road West, Stapehill, Ferndown
Tel: 01202 861 686

34 KNOLL GARDENS & NURSERY
Garden
Hampreston, Ferndown, Wimborne
Tel: 01202 873 931

35 ARTSWAY
Gallery
Station Rd, Sway, Lymington   Tel: 01590 682 260

36 SPINNERS GARDEN
Garden
School Lane, Boldre, Lymington   Tel: 01590 673 347

37 ALICE IN WONDERLAND FAMILY PARK
Theme park
Hurn, Bournemouth   Tel: 01202 483 444

38 NEW FOREST WINE
Vineyard
Hollybush Vineyard, Brockenhurst   Tel: 01590 622 246

39 STREETWISE SAFETY CENTRE
Adventure & activity centre
Unit 1 Roundways, Elliot Road, Bournemouth
Tel: 01202 591 330

40 SADLERS GARDENS
Garden
31 Rawley Road, Pennington, Lymington
Tel: 01590 672 728

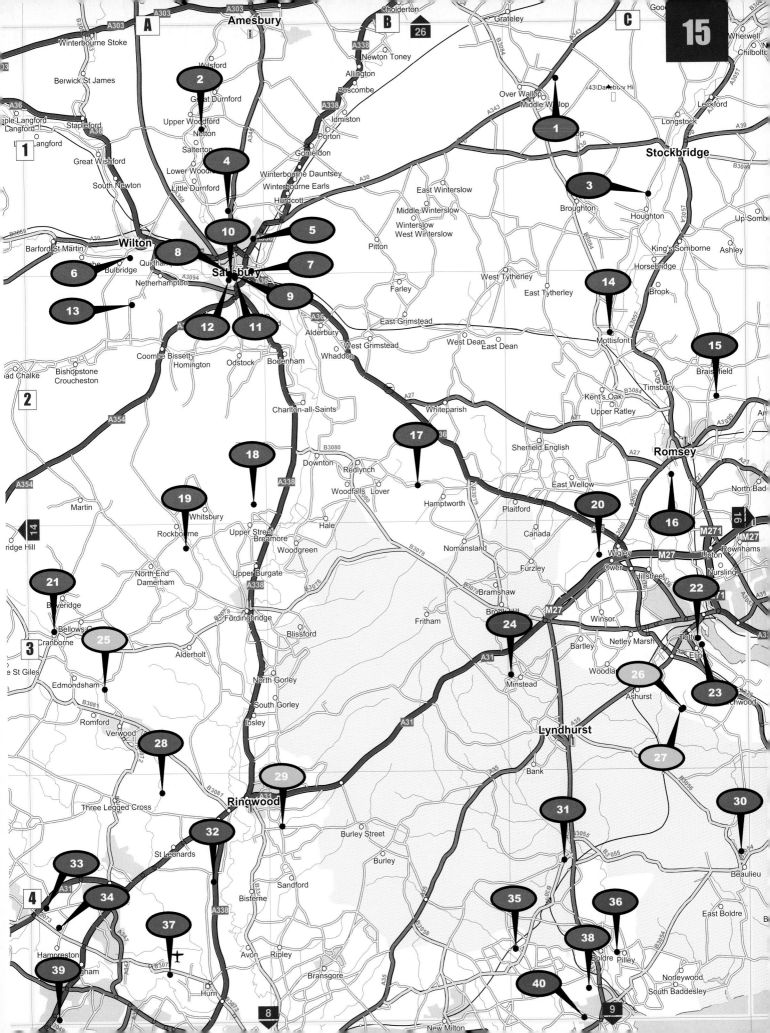

● ANIMAL ATTRACTIONS   ● OUTDOOR ATTRACTIONS
● HERITAGE & CULTURE   ● OUTDOOR ACTIVITIES
○ INDOOR ACTIVITIES   ● WATER ACTIVITIES

1 NORTHINGTON GRANGE
Historic building
Northington
TEL: 020 7320 5588

2 WATERCRESS LINE
Railway
Station Road, Alresford
TEL: 01962 733 810

3 AVINGTON PARK
Historic house
Avington, Winchester
TEL: 01962 779 260

4 GREAT HALL OF WINCHESTER CASTLE
Castle
The Castle, Castle Avenue, Winchester
TEL: 01962 846 476

5 ROYAL GREEN JACKETS
Museum
Peninsula Barracks, Romsey Road, Winchester
TEL: 01962 863 846

6 GURKHA MUSEUM
Museum
Penninsula Barracks, Romsey Road, Winchester
TEL: 01962 842 832

7 KING'S ROYAL HUSSARS MUSEUM IN WINCHESTER
Museum
Peninsula Barracks, Romsey Road, Winchester
TEL: 01962 828 539

8 WINCHESTER CITY MUSEUM & WESTGATE MUSEUM
Museum
The Square, High Street, Winchester
TEL: 01962 848 269

9 WINCHESTER CITY MILL & SHOP
Mill
Bridge Street, Winchester
TEL: 01962 870 057

10 ROYAL HAMPSHIRE REGIMENT MUSEUM & MEMORIAL GARDEN
Museum
Serle's House, Southgate Street, Winchester
TEL: 01962 863 658

11 WOLVESEY CASTLE EH
Castle
College Street, Wolvesey, Winchester
TEL: 01962 854 766

12 WINCHESTER CATHEDRAL
Cathedral
Winchester
TEL: 01962 853 137

13 MARWELL ZOOLOGICAL PARK
Zoo
Colden Common, Winchester
TEL: 01962 777 407

14 BISHOP'S WALTHAM PALACE
Historic house
Bishops Waltham, Southampton
TEL: 01489 892 460

15 HAWTHORN'S URBAN WILDLIFE
Museum
The Common, Southampton
TEL: 023 8067 1921

16 TUDOR HOUSE MUSEUM GARDEN
Garden
Cultural Services, Civic Centre, Southampton
TEL: 023 8063 5904

17 MEDIEVAL MERCHANT'S HOUSE
Historic house
58 French Street, Southampton
TEL: 023 8022 1503

18 SOUTHAMPTON HALL OF AVIATION
Museum
Albert Road South, Southampton
TEL: 023 8063 5830

19 NETLEY ABBEY
Abbey
Netley
TEL: 023 9237 8291

20 TITCHFIELD ABBEY
Abbey
Titchfield
TEL: 023 9252 7667

21 FORT NELSON
Museum
The Royal Armouries Museum of Artillery,
Down End Road, Fareham
TEL: 01329 233 734

Shopping - an alternative day out

22 CALSHOT CASTLE
Castle
Southampton
TEL: 023 8089 2023

23 EXPLOSION!
Museum
Priddy's Hard, Priory Road, Gosport
TEL: 023 9250 5600

24 BUCKLER'S HARD VILLAGE & MARITIME MUSEUM
Museum
Bucklers Hard, Near Beaulieu, Brockenhurst
TEL: 01590 616 203

25 EXBURY GARDENS
Garden
Exbury, Southampton
TEL: 023 8089 8625

26 LEPE COUNTRY PARK
Country park
Lepe, Exbury, Southampton
TEL: 023 8089 9108

27 SIR MAX AITKEN MUSEUM
Museum
High Street, Cowes
TEL: 01983 295 144

28 COWES LIBRARY & MARITIME MUSEUM
Museum
Beckford Road, Cowes
TEL: 01983 293 394

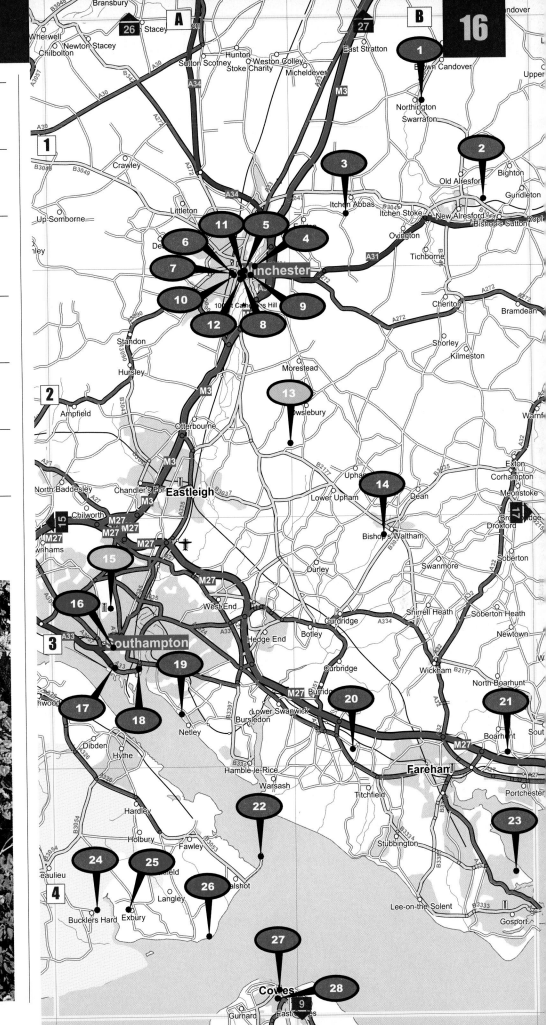

● ANIMAL ATTRACTIONS
● HERITAGE & CULTURE
○ INDOOR ACTIVITIES
● OUTDOOR ATTRACTIONS
● OUTDOOR ACTIVITIES
● WATER ACTIVITIES

1 WITLEY COMMON INFORMATION CENTRE
Visitor centre
Witley Centre, Haslemere Road, Witley
TEL: 01428 683 207

2 JANE AUSTEN'S HOUSE
Historic house
Winchester Rd, Chawton, Alton TEL: 01420 832 62

3 GILBERT WHITE'S HOUSE & GARDEN
Garden
The Wakes, Selborne TEL: 01420 511 275

4 RAMSTER GARDENS
Garden
Ramster, Chiddingfold TEL: 01428 654 167

5 HASLEMERE EDUCATIONAL MUSEUM
Museum
High Street, Haslemere TEL: 01428 642 112

6 BOHUNT MANOR
Garden
Liphook TEL: 01428 722 208

7 HOLLYCOMBE STEAM COLLECTION
Museum
Midhurst Road, Liphook TEL: 01428 724 900

8 PETERSFIELD PHYSIC GARDEN
Garden
16 High Street, Petersfield TEL: 01730 233 371

9 BEAR MUSEUM
Museum
38 Dragon Street, Petersfield TEL: 01730 265 108

10 QUEEN ELIZABETH COUNTRY PARK
Garden
Gravel Hill, Horndean, Waterlooville
TEL: 023 9259 5040

11 UPPARK NT
Garden
South Harting, Petersfield TEL: 01730 825 415

12 BUTSER ANCIENT FARM
Farm
Bascombe Copse, Chalton TEL: 023 9259 8838

13 GEORGE GALE HAMPSHIRE BREWERY
Factory tour
Horndean TEL: 023 9271 4422

14 WEALD & DOWNLAND OPEN AIR MUSEUM
Museum
Singleton, Chichester TEL: 01243 811 363

15 WEST DEAN GARDENS
Garden
West Dean, Chichester TEL: 01243 818 210

16 GOODWOOD RACECOURSE
Racecourse
Goodwood, Chichester TEL: 01243 755 022

17 STANSTED PARK
Country park
Rowland's Castle TEL: 023 9241 3090

18 GARDEN IN MIND
Garden
Stansted Park, Rowland's Castle TEL: 023 9241 3149

19 GOODWOOD HOUSE
Historic house
Goodwood, Chichester TEL: 01243 755 000

20 STAUNTON COUNTRY PARK
Garden
Middle Park Way, Havant TEL: 023 9245 3405

21 GUMBER BOTHY GUMBER FARM
Farm
Slindon Estate, Arundel Warden, Arundel
TEL: 01243 814 554/814 484

22 FONTWELL PARK RACECOURSE
Racecourse
Fontwell Park, Arundel TEL: 01243 543 335

23 DENMANS GARDEN
Garden
Denmans, Fontwell, Arundel TEL: 01243 542 808

24 ROYAL MILITARY POLICE MUSEUM
Museum
Roussillon Barracks Broyle Road, Chichester
TEL: 01243 534 225

25 HAVANT MUSEUM
Museum
East Street, Havant TEL: 023 9245 1155

26 TANGMERE MILITARY AVIATION MUSEUM TRUST
Museum
Tangmere, Chichester TEL: 01243 775 223

27 CHICHESTER DISTRICT MUSEUM
Museum
29 Little London, Chichester TEL: 01243 784 683

28 FISHBOURNE ROMAN PALACE & GARDENS
Roman site
Salthill Road, Fishbourne, Chichester
TEL: 01243 785 859

29 PALLANT HOUSE
Historic house
9 North Pallant, Chichester TEL: 01243 774 557

30 CHICHESTER CATHEDRAL
Cathedral
West Street, Chichester TEL: 01243 782 595

31 PORTCHESTER CASTLE
Castle
Castle St, Portchester, Fareham TEL: 023 9237 8291

32 APULDRAM ROSES
Garden
Apuldram Lane, Dell Quay, Chichester
TEL: 01243 785 769

33 CHARLES DICKENS' BIRTHPLACE
Historic building
393 Old Commercial Road, Portsmouth
TEL: 023 9282 7261

34 GUNWHARF QUAYS
Visitor centre
Portsmouth TEL: 023 9275 5940

35 ROYAL NAVAL MUSEUM
Museum
H M Naval Base, Portsmouth TEL: 023 9272 7562

36 NATURAL SCIENCE MUSEUM AND BUTTERFLY HOUSE
Museum
Cumberland House, Eastern Parade, Portsmouth
TEL: 023 9282 7261

37 MARY ROSE SHIP HALL & EXHIBITION
Museum
College Road, HM Naval Base, Portsmouth
TEL: 023 927 5521

38 HMS VICTORY
Museum
Main Road H M Naval Base, Portsmouth
TEL: 023 9229 5390

39 FLAGSHIP PORTSMOUTH
Museum
College Road, H M Naval Base, Portsmouth
TEL: 023 9286 1512

40 HMS WARRIOR 1860
Museum
Main Road H M Naval Base, Portsmouth
TEL: 023 9229 1379

41 ROYAL NAVY SUBMARINE MUSEUM & HMS ALLIANCE
Museum
Haslar Jetty Road, Gosport TEL: 023 9252 9217

42 CITY MUSEUM & RECORDS OFFICE
Museum
Museum Road, Portsmouth TEL: 023 9282 7261

43 ROYAL MARINES MUSEUM
Museum
Eastney Esplanade, Southsea TEL: 023 9281 9385

44 SOUTHSEA PIER
Entertainment centre
Southsea, Portsmouth TEL: Not available

45 PORTSMOUTH SEA LIFE CENTRE
Aquarium
Clarence Esplanade, Southsea Portsmouth
TEL: 023 9287 5222

46 D-DAY MUSEUM & OVERLORD EMBROIDERY
Museum
Clarence Esplanade, Southsea TEL: 023 9282 7261

47 SOUTHSEA CASTLE & MUSEUM
Castle
Clarence Esplanade, Southsea TEL: 023 9282 7261

48 EARNLEY GARDENS
Garden
Almodington Lane, Earnley TEL: 01243 512 637

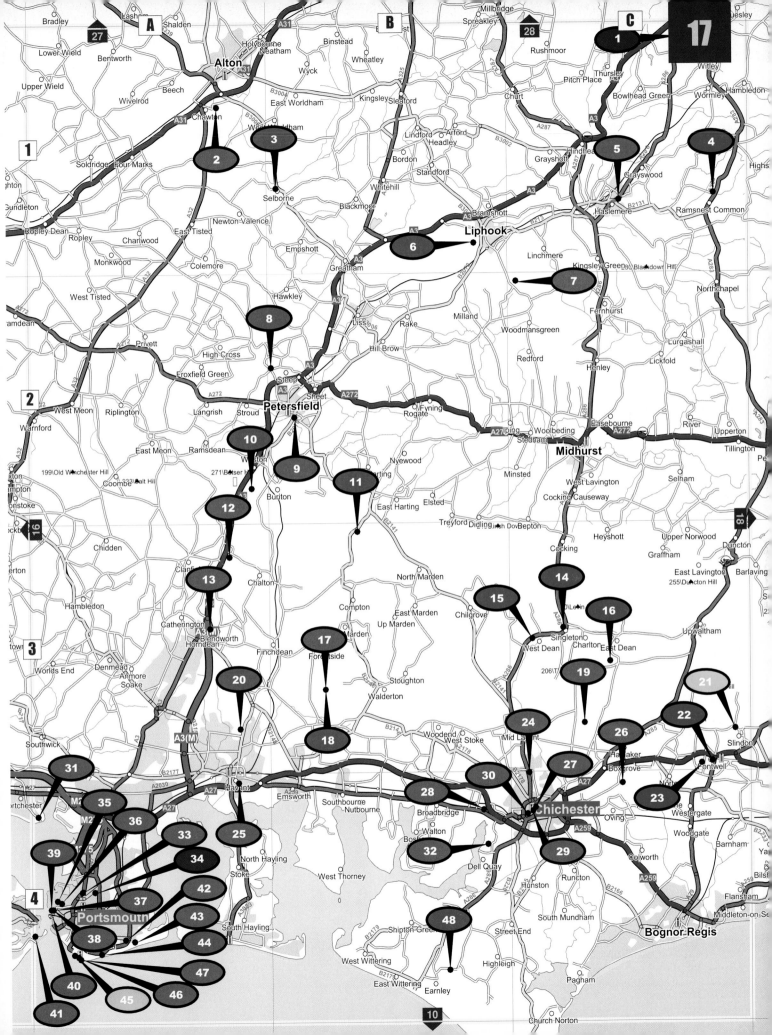

EAST & WEST SUSSEX · SURREY

- ANIMAL ATTRACTIONS
- HERITAGE & CULTURE
- INDOOR ACTIVITIES
- OUTDOOR ATTRACTIONS
- OUTDOOR ACTIVITIES
- WATER ACTIVITIES

1 GATWICK ZOO
Zoo
Russ Hill, Glovers Road, Charlwood
TEL: 01293 862 312

2 WINKWORTH ARBORETUM NT
Garden
Hascombe Road, Godalming
TEL: 01483 208 477

3 BUCHAN COUNTRY PARK
Garden
Horsham Road, Crawley
TEL: 01293 542 088

4 HIGH BEECHES WOODLAND & WATER GARDENS
Garden
High Beeches, Handcross
TEL: 01444 400 589

5 HORSHAM MUSEUM
Museum
9 The Causeway, Horsham
TEL: 01403 254 959

6 NYMANS GARDEN NT
Garden
Handcross, Haywards Heath
TEL: 01444 400 321

7 FISHERS FARM PARK
Farm
Newpound Lane, Wisborough Green, Billingshurst
TEL: 01403 700 063

8 LEONARDSLEE GARDENS
Garden
Lower Beeding, Horsham
TEL: 01403 891 212

9 SOUTHWATER COUNTRY PARK
Country park
Cripplegate Lane, Southwater, Horsham
TEL: 01403 731 218

10 PETWORTH HOUSE & PARK NT
Historic house
Petworth
TEL: 01798 342 207

11 HENFIELD MUSEUM
Museum
Village Hall, High Street, Henfield
TEL: 01273 492 546

12 PARHAM ELIZABETHAN HOUSE & GARDENS
Historic building
Parham Park, Pulborough
TEL: 01903 744 888

13 BIGNOR ROMAN VILLA & MUSEUM
Roman site
Bignor Lane, Bignor, Pulborough
TEL: 01798 869 259

14 WOODS MILL COUNTRYSIDE CENTRE
Country park
Sussex Wildlife Trust, Woods Mill, Henfield
TEL: 01273 492 630

15 AMBERLEY MUSEUM
Museum
Station Road, Amberley, Arundel
TEL: 01798 831 370

16 STEYNING MUSEUM
Museum
Church Street, Steyning
TEL: 01903 813 333

17 BRAMBER CASTLE
Castle
Bramber
TEL: Not available

18 ST MARY'S HOUSE & GARDENS
Historic house
The Street, Bramber, Steyning
TEL: 01903 816 205

19 WWT ARUNDEL
Wildlife park
Mill Road, Arundel
TEL: 01903 883 355

20 ARUNDEL HERITAGE CENTRE
Heritage centre
61 High Street, Arundel
TEL: 01903 882 268

21 ARUNDEL CASTLE
Castle
Arundel
TEL: 01903 882 173

22 FOREDOWN TOWER
Historic building
Foredown Road, Portslade, Brighton
TEL: 01273 292 092

23 ARUNDEL TOY & MILITARY MUSEUM
Museum
23 High Street, Arundel
TEL: 01903 882 908

24 BRITISH ENGINEERIUM MUSEUM OF STEAM & MECHANICAL ANTIQUITIES
Museum
Off Nevill Road, Hove
TEL: 01273 559 583

25 PRESTON MANOR
Historic building
Preston Road, Brighton
TEL: 01273 292 770

26 BOOTH MUSEUM OF NATURAL HISTORY
Museum
194 Dyke Road, Brighton
TEL: 01273 292 777

27 MARLIPINS MUSEUM
Museum
High Street, Shoreham-By-Sea
TEL: 01273 462 994

28 HOVE MUSEUM & ART GALLERY
Museum
19 New Church Road, Hove
TEL: 01273 290 200

30 ROYAL PAVILION
Museum
4-5 Pavilion Buildings, Brighton
TEL: 01273 290 900

31 HIGHDOWN
Garden
Littlehampton Road, Goring-by-sea
TEL: 01903 501 054

32 BRIGHTON PALACE PIER
Funfair
Madeira Drive, Brighton
TEL: 01273 609 361

33 LITTLEHAMPTON MUSEUM
Museum
Manor House, Church Street, Littlehampton
TEL: 01903 715 149

34 HARBOUR PARK
Adventure & activity centre
Seafront, Littlehampton
TEL: 01903 721 200

Playing in the waves

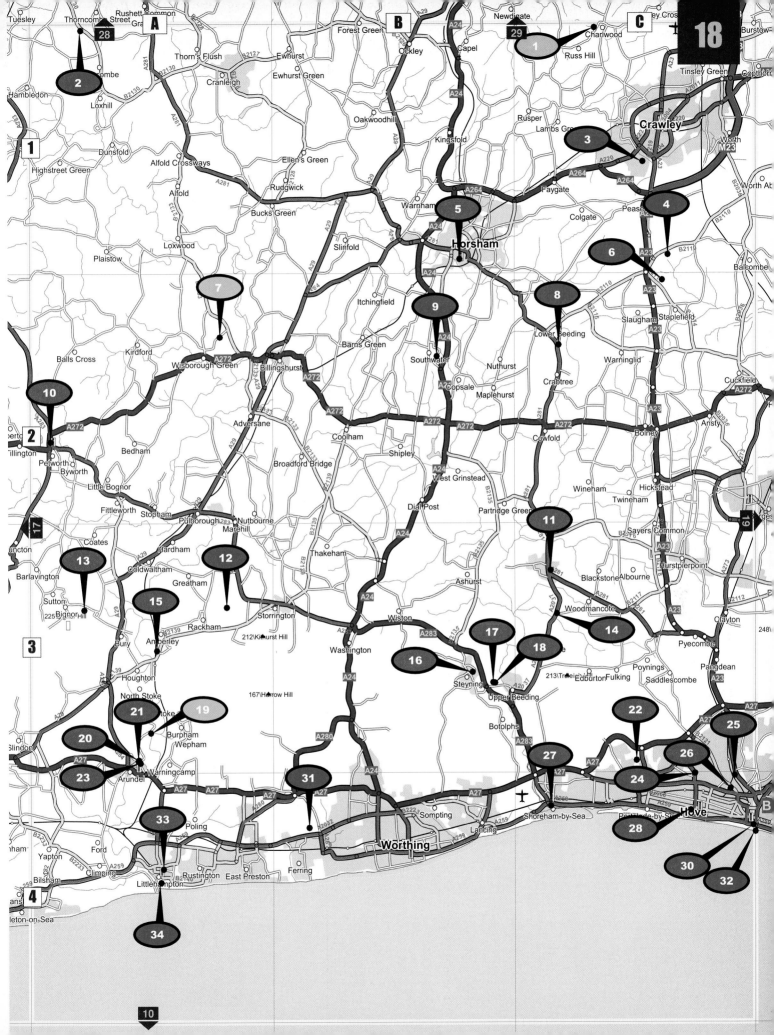

E. & W. SUSSEX · KENT

● ANIMAL ATTRACTIONS ● OUTDOOR ATTRACTIONS
● HERITAGE & CULTURE ● OUTDOOR ACTIVITIES
○ INDOOR ACTIVITIES ● WATER ACTIVITIES

1 TUNBRIDGE WELLS MUSEUM & ART GALLERY
Museum
Civic Centre, Mount Pleasant, Tunbridge Wells
TEL: 01892 526 121

2 A DAY AT THE WELLS
Museum
Corn Exchange, The Pantiles, Tunbridge Wells
TEL: 01892 546 545

3 SACKVILLE COLLEGE
Historic house
Church Lane, East Grinstead
TEL: 01342 321 930

4 GROOMBRIDGE PLACE GARDENS
Garden
Groombridge, Tunbridge Wells
TEL: 01892 863 999

5 SPA VALLEY RAILWAY
Railway
Tunbridge Wells
TEL: 01892 537 715

6 BAYHAM OLD ABBEY
Abbey
Bayham Abbey, Lamberhurst, Tunbridge Wells
TEL: 01892 890 381

7 AMAZING MAIZE MAZE
Maze
Turners Hill Road, Turners Hill
TEL: 01342 718 472

8 STANDEN HILLSIDE GARDEN NT
Garden
East Grinstead
TEL: 01342 323 029

9 PRIEST HOUSE
Museum
North Lane, West Hoathly, East Grinstead
TEL: 01342 810 479

10 WAKEHURST PLACE NT
Garden
Ardingly, Haywards Heath
TEL: 01444 892 701

11 ASHDOWN LLAMA FARM
Farm
Wych Cross
TEL: 01825 712 040

12 BORDE HILL GARDEN
Garden
Balcombe Road, Haywards Heath
TEL: 01444 450 326

13 SHEFFIELD PARK GARDEN NT
Garden
Sheffield Park, Uckfield
TEL: 01825 790 231

14 WILDERNESS WOOD
Garden
Hadlow Down, Uckfield
TEL: 01825 830 509

15 BLUEBELL RAILWAY
Railway
Sheffield Park Station, Uckfield
TEL: 01825 720 800

16 BENTLEY WILDFOWL MOTOR MUSEUM & GARDENS
Historic house
Halland, Lewes
TEL: 01825 840 573

17 DITCHLING MUSEUM
Museum
Church Lane, Ditchling, Hassocks
TEL: 01273 844 744

18 LEWES CASTLE & BARBICAN HOUSE MUSEUM
Castle
169 High Street, Lewes
TEL: 01273 486 290

19 KNOCKHATCH ADVENTURE PARK
Adventure & activity centre
Hempstead Lane, Hailsham
TEL: 01323 442 051

20 ANNE OF CLEVES HOUSE MUSEUM
Historic house
52 Southover, High Street, Lewes
TEL: 01273 474 610

21 FIRLE PLACE
Historic house
Firle, Lewes
TEL: 01273 858 335

22 MONK'S HOUSE
Historic building
Rodmell, Lewes
TEL: 01892 890 651

23 CANDY CASTLE
Adventure & activity centre
Enterprise point, Melbourne Street, Brighton
TEL: 01273 276 060

24 BRIGHTON RACECOURSE
Racecourse
Freshfield Road, Brighton
TEL: 01273 603 580

25 PEVENSEY CASTLE
Castle
Castle Road, Pevensey
TEL: 01323 762 604

26 ENGLISH WINE CENTRE
Vineyard
Alfriston Roundabout, Berwick, Polegate
TEL: 01323 870 164

27 DRUSILLAS PARK
Zoo
Alfriston
TEL: 01323 870 234

28 BRIGHTON SEA LIFE CENTRE
Aquarium
Marine Parade, Brighton
TEL: 01273 604 233

29 PARADISE PARK
Country park
Avis Road, Newhaven
TEL: 01273 616 000

30 EASTBOURNE MINIATURE STEAM RAILWAY FUN PARK
Railway
Lottbridge Drove, Eastbourne
TEL: 01323 520 229

31 REDOUBT FORTRESS
Historic building
Royal Parade, Eastbourne
TEL: 01323 410 300

32 TOWNER ART GALLERY & LOCAL MUSEUM
Museum
High Street, Borough Lane, Eastbourne
TEL: 01323 411 688

33 SEVEN SISTERS SHEEP CENTRE
Farm
The Fridays, East Dean, Eastbourne
TEL: 01323 423 302

34 EASTBOURNE PIER
Pier
Eastbourne
TEL: Not available

35 HOW WE LIVED THEN MUSEUM OF SHOPS & SOCIAL HISTORY
Museum
20 Cornfield Terrace, Eastbourne
TEL: 01323 737 143

36 ROYAL NATIONAL LIFEBOAT INSTITUTION MUSEUM
Museum
King Edwards Parade, Eastbourne
TEL: 01323 730 717

37 WISH TOWER PUPPET MUSEUM
Museum
King Edwards Parade, Eastbourne
TEL: 01323 417 776

38 NEWHAVEN LOCAL & MARITIME MUSEUM
Museum
Paradise Leisure Park, Avis Road, Newhaven
TEL: 01273 514 760

Dover Castle, Kent, Map 32-42

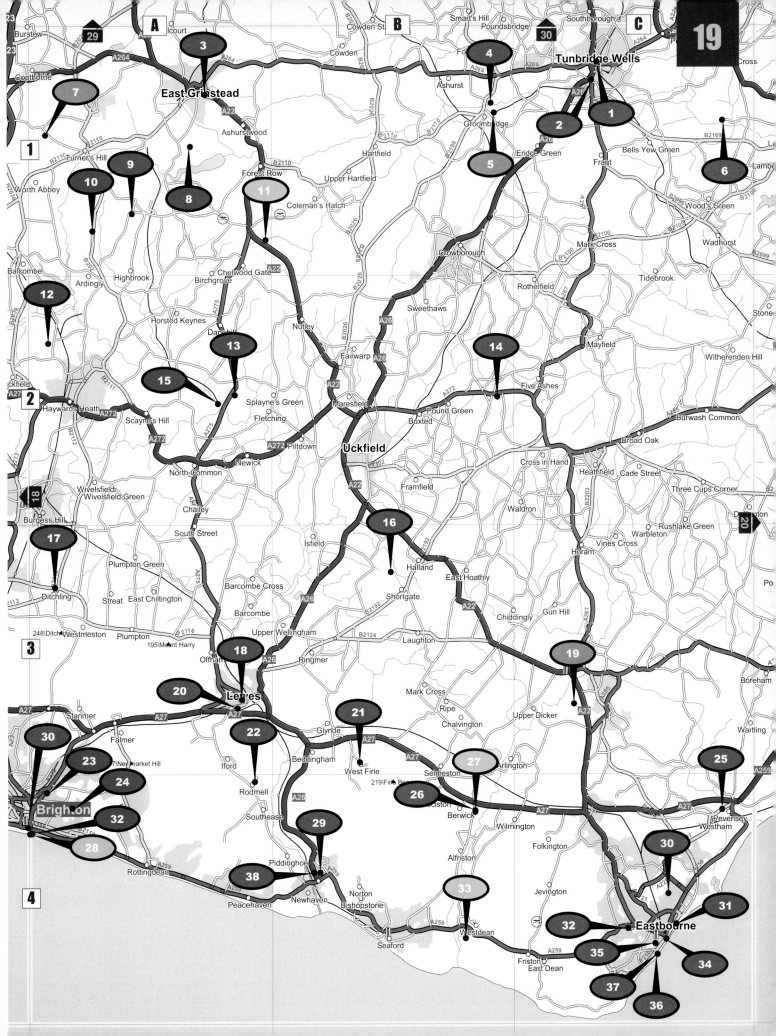

● ANIMAL ATTRACTIONS
● HERITAGE & CULTURE
○ INDOOR ACTIVITIES
● OUTDOOR ATTRACTIONS
● OUTDOOR ACTIVITIES
● WATER ACTIVITIES

1 MARLE PLACE GARDENS
Garden
Brenchley, Tonbridge
TEL: 01892 722 304

2 WILLESBOROUGH WINDMILL
Mill
Ashford
TEL: 01233 625 643

3 LADHAM HOUSE
Historic house
Ladham Road, Goudhurst, Cranbrook
TEL: 01580 211 203

4 SISSINGHURST CASTLE GARDEN NT
Garden
Sissinghurst, Cranbrook
TEL: 01580 710 700

5 OWL HOUSE GARDENS
Garden
Mount Pleasant, Lamberhurst, Tunbridge Wells
TEL: 01892 891 290

6 FINCHCOCKS
Museum
Goudhurst
TEL: 01580 211 702

7 BIDDENDEN VINEYARDS
Vineyard
Little Whatmans, Gribble Bridge Lane, Biddenden
TEL: 01580 291 726

8 SCOTNEY CASTLE GARDEN NT
Garden
Lamberhurst, Tunbridge Wells
TEL: 01892 891 081

9 BEWL WATER
Adventure & activity centre
Lamberhurst
TEL: 01892 890 661

10 BEDGEBURY NATIONAL PINETUM
Garden
Goudhurst, Cranbrook
TEL: 01580 211 044

11 KENT & EAST SUSSEX STEAM RAILWAY
Railway
Tenterden Town Station, Tenterden
TEL: 01580 765 155

12 TENTERDEN & DISTRICT MUSEUM
Museum
Station Road, Tenterden
TEL: 01580 764 310

13 C M BOOTH COLLECTION OF HISTORIC VEHICLES
Museum
63-67 High Street, Rolvenden, Cranbrook
TEL: 01580 241 234

14 GREAT MAYTHAM HALL
Historic building
Rolvenden, Cranbrook
TEL: 01580 241 346

15 PASHLEY MANOR GARDENS
Garden
Ticehurst, Wadhurst
TEL: 01580 200 888

16 KING JOHN'S LODGE
Garden
Sheepstreet Lane, Etchingham
TEL: 01580 819 232

17 BODIAM CASTLE
Historic building
Bodiam, Robertsbridge
TEL: 01580 830 436

Family on the beach

18 **GREAT DIXTER GARDENS**
Garden
Northiam, Rye
TEL: 01797 252 878

19 **BATEMAN'S NT**
Historic house
Burwash, Etchingham
TEL: 01435 882 302

20 **CARR TAYLOR VINEYARD**
Vineyard
Westfield
TEL: 01424 752 501

21 **BUCKLEYS YESTERDAYS' WORLD**
Museum
High Street, Battle
TEL: 01424 775 378

22 **BATTLE ABBEY & BATTLEFIELD**
Battlefield
High Street, Battle
TEL: 01424 773 792

23 **SMUGGLERS ADVENTURE**
Adventure & activity centre
St Clements Caves, Cobourg Place, West Hill
TEL: 01424 422 964

24 **SHIPWRECK HERITAGE CENTRE**
Heritage centre
Rock-a-Nore, Hastings
TEL: 01424 437 452

25 **UNDERWATER WORLD**
Sea life centre
Rock-a-Nore Road, Hastings
TEL: 01424 718 776

26 **OLD TOWN HALL MUSEUM OF LOCAL HISTORY**
Museum
High Street, Hastings
TEL: 01424 781 166

27 **HASTINGS MUSEUM & ART GALLERY**
Museum
Johns Place, Cambridge Road, Hastings
TEL: 01424 781 155

28 **1066 STORY IN HASTINGS CASTLE**
Castle
Castle Hill Road, West Hill, Hastings
TEL: 01424 781 111

29 **CLAMBERS PLAY CENTRE**
Adventure & activity centre
Hastings
TEL: 01424 423 778

30 **HASTINGS EMBROIDERY**
Museum
White Rock Theatre, White Rock, Hastings
TEL: 01424 781 010

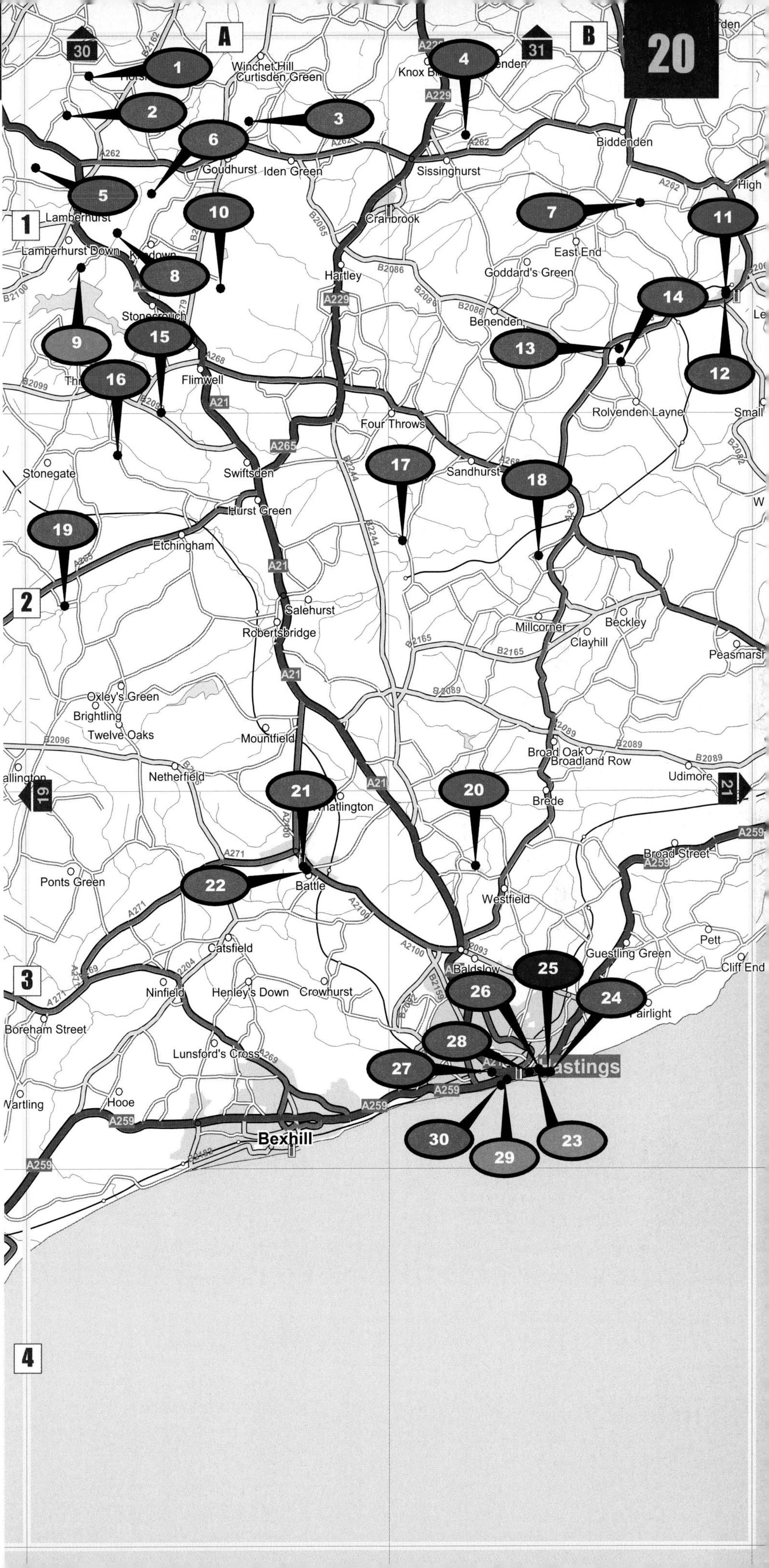

E.SUSSEX · KENT

1 **FOLKESTONE DOWNS**
Country Walks
Folkestone
TEL: 01304 241 806

2 **KENT BATTLE OF BRITAIN MUSEUM**
Museum
Aerodrome Road, Hawkinge, Folkestone
TEL: 01303 893 140

3 **SAMPHIRE HOE**
Country park
Dover
TEL: 01304 241 806

4 **EUROTUNNEL EDUCATION SERVICE**
Visitor centre
Cheriton Parc, Folkestone
TEL: 01303 241 160

5 **EAST CLIFF & WARREN COUNTRY PARK**
Country park
Folkestone
TEL: 01304 241 806

6 **FOLKESTONE MUSEUM & SASSOON GALLERY**
Museum
Folkestone Library, Grace Hill, Folkestone
TEL: 01303 850 123

7 **PORT LYMPNE WILD ANIMAL PARK**
Wildlife park
Lympne, Hythe
TEL: 01303 264 647

8 **LYMPNE CASTLE**
Castle
Castle Close, Lympne, Hythe
TEL: 01303 267 571

9 **SOUTH OF ENGLAND RARE BREEDS CENTRE**
Farm
Woodchurch, Ashford
TEL: 01233 861 493

10 **SMALLHYTHE PLACE**
Museum
Smallhythe Road, Tenterden
TEL: 01580 762 334

11 **DYMCHURCH MARTELLO TOWER**
Historic building
Dymchurch
TEL: 01732 778 000

12 **ROMNEY HYTHE & DYMCHURCH RAILWAY**
Railway
New Romney Station, Littlestone Road, New Romney
TEL: 01797 362 353

13 **LAMB HOUSE**
Historic building
West Street, Rye
TEL: 01892 890 651

14 **STORY OF RYE**
Heritage centre
Rye Heritage Centre, Strand Quay, Rye
TEL: 01797 226 696

15 **CAMBER CASTLE**
Castle
Rye
TEL: 01797 223 862

16 **DUNGENESS VISITOR CENTRE**
Factory tour
Dungeness, Rommey Marsh
TEL: 01797 321 815

17 **OLD LIGHTHOUSE**
Historic building
Dungeness Road, Dungeness, Romney Marsh
TEL: 01797 321 300

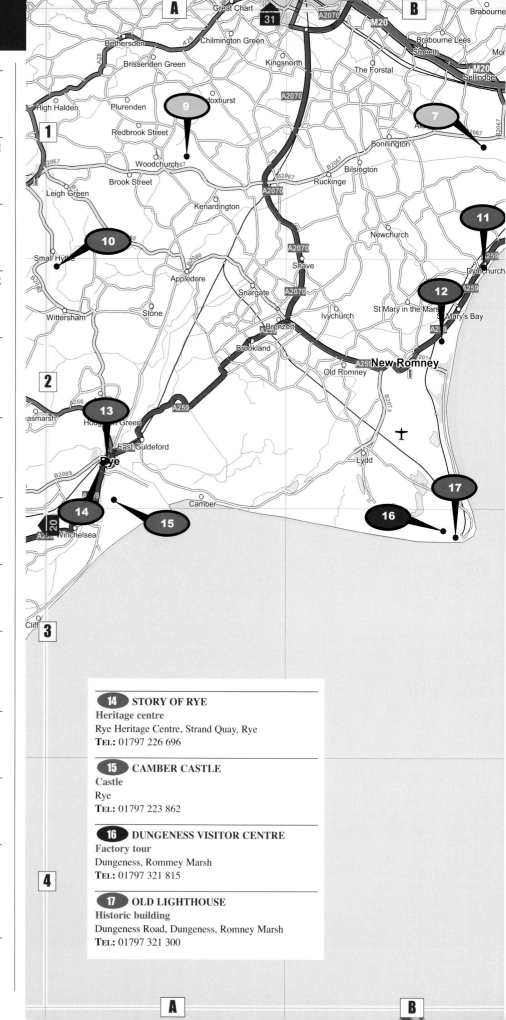

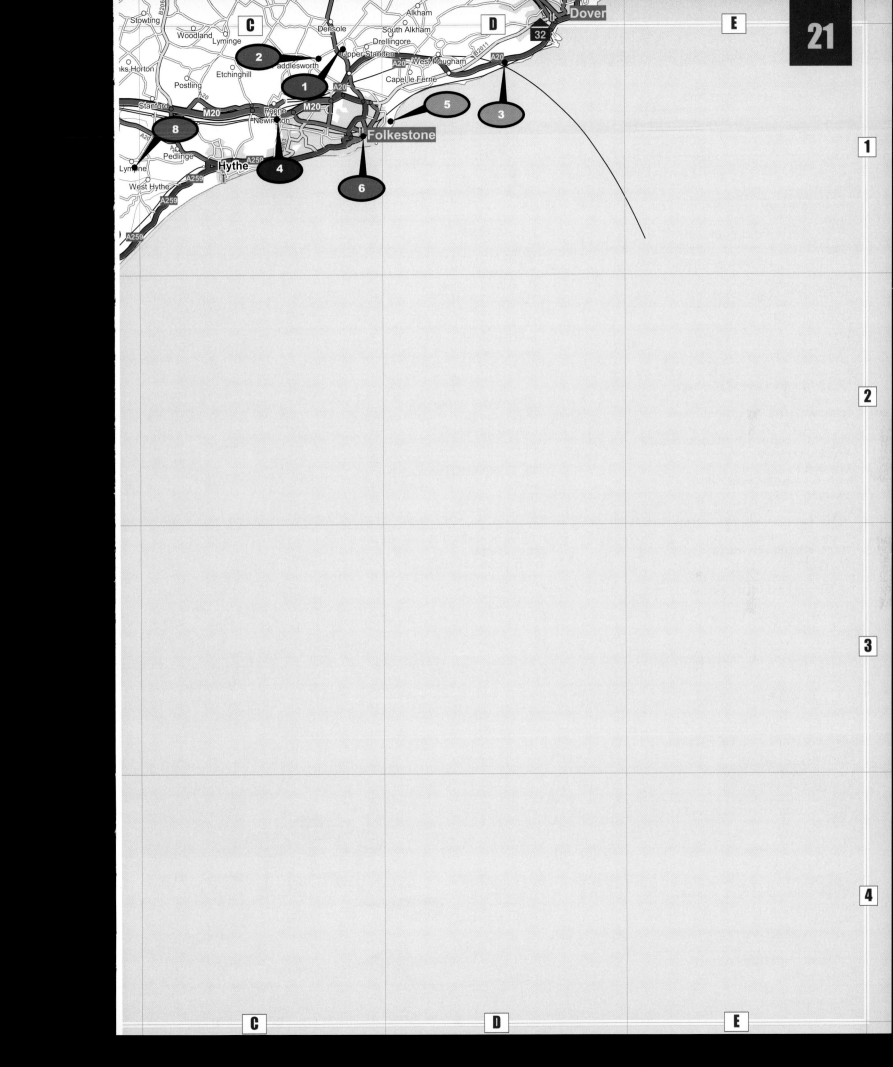

1 **MARGAM COUNTRY PARK**
Country park
Margam, Port Talbot
TEL: 01639 881 635

2 **COITY CASTLE**
Castle
Coity, Bridgend
TEL: 01656 652 021

3 **SOUTH WALES POLICE MUSEUM**
Museum
South Wales Police Headquarters, Cowbridge Road,
Bridgend
TEL: 01656 869 315

4 **OGMORE CASTLE**
Castle
Ogmore
TEL: 01656 653 435

5 **LYN & EXMOOR MUSEUM**
Museum
St Vincent's Cottage, Market Street, Lynton
TEL: 01598 752 317

6 **WATERSMEET HOUSE**
Historic house
Watersmeet Road, Lynmouth
TEL: 01598 753 348

7 **ONCE UPON A TIME THEME PARK**
Theme park
The Old Station, Station Road, Woolacombe
TEL: 01271 867 474

8 **WATERMOUTH CASTLE**
Theme park
Berrynarbor, Ilfracombe
TEL: 01271 867 474

9 **EXMOOR FALCONRY & ANIMAL FARM**
Bird centre & aviary
West Lynch Farm, Allerford, Porlock
TEL: 01643 862 816

10 **OLD CORN MILL & POTTERY**
Watermill
Watermouth Road, Hele, Ilfracombe
TEL: 01271 863 185

11 **COMBE MARTIN MOTORCYCLE COLLECTION**
Museum
Cross Street, Combe Martin, Ilfracombe
TEL: 01271 882 346

12 **CHAMBERCOMBE MANOR**
Historic house
Ilfracombe
TEL: 01271 862 624

13 **HOLNICOTE ESTATE NT**
Historic building
Selworthy, Minehead
TEL: 01643 863 011

14 **WEST SOMERSET RAILWAY**
Railway
The Railway Station, Station Terrace, Minehead
TEL: 01643 704 996

15 **BUTLIN'S SOMERWEST WORLD**
Theme park
The Seafront, Minehead
TEL: 01643 703 331

16 **COMBE MARTIN WILDLIFE & DINOSAUR PARK**
Butterfly farm
Combe Martin, Ilfracombe
TEL: 01271 882 486

17 **YARN MARKET**
Historic building
High Street, Dunster
TEL: 01179 750 700

18 **DUNSTER CASTLE NT**
Castle
Dunster, Minehead
TEL: 01643 821 314

19 **DUNSTER WORKING WATER MILL NT**
Historic building
Mill Lane, Dunster, Minehead
TEL: 01643 821 759

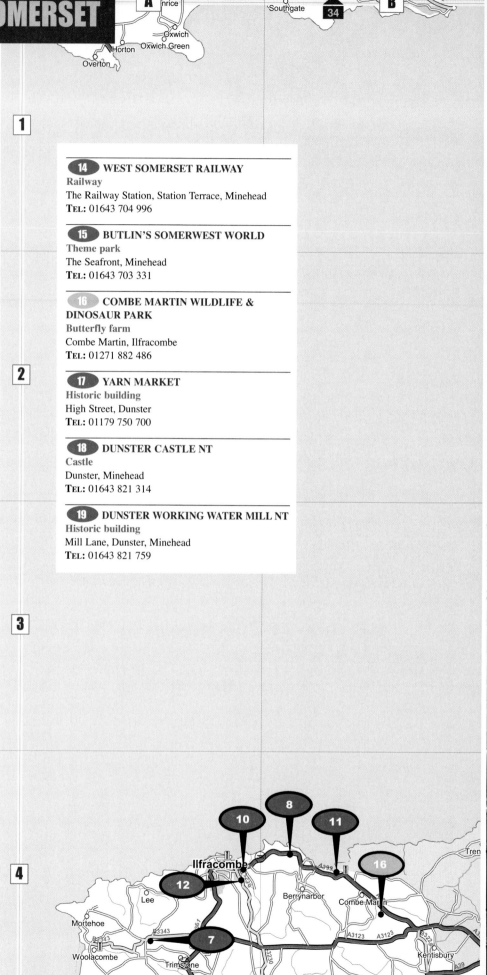

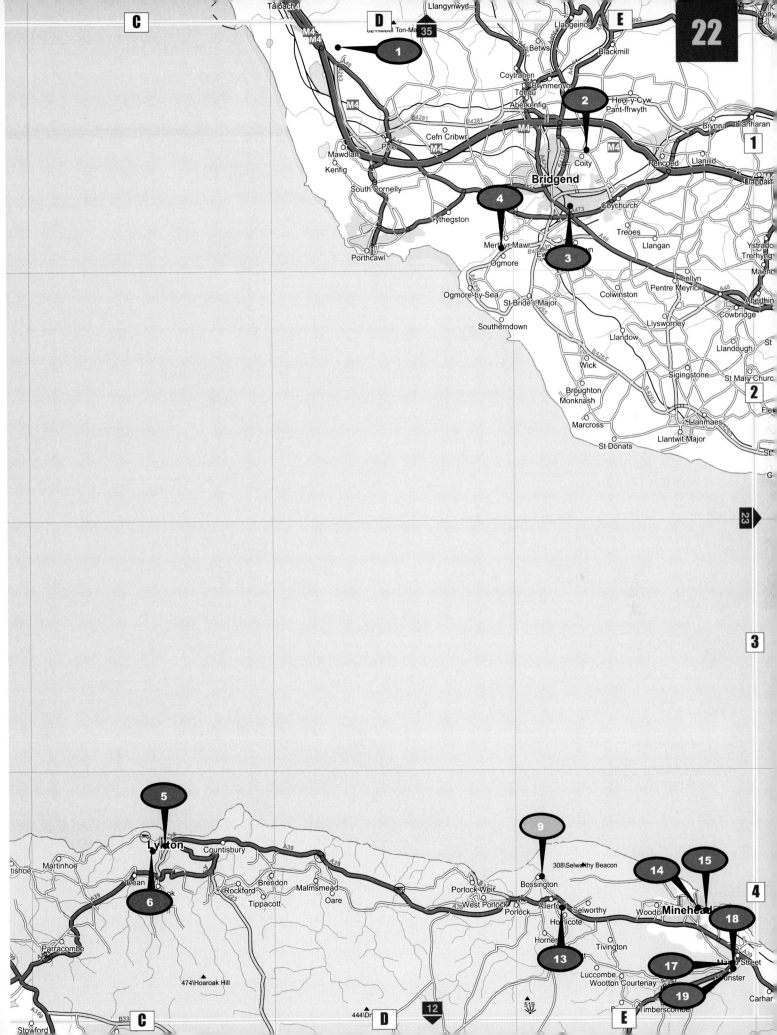

SOMERSET · SOUTH WALES

● ANIMAL ATTRACTIONS   ● OUTDOOR ATTRACTIONS
● HERITAGE & CULTURE   ● OUTDOOR ACTIVITIES
○ INDOOR ACTIVITIES   ● WATER ACTIVITIES

1 NANTGARW CHINA WORKS MUSEUM
Museum
Treforest Industrial Estate, Nantgarw
TEL: 01443 841 703

2 TREDEGAR HOUSE & PARK
Garden
Newport
TEL: 01633 815 880

3 MODEL HOUSE CRAFT & DESIGN CENTRE
Visitor centre
Bull Ring
TEL: 01443 237 758

4 CASTELL COCH
Castle
Forest Farm Industrial Estate, Whitchurch, Cardiff
TEL: 020 2081 0101

5 CAERPHILLY CASTLE
Castle
Caerphilly
TEL: 020 2088 3143

6 RHONDDA HERITAGE PARK
Historic house
Lewis Merthyr, Trehafod
TEL: 01443 682 036

7 LLANDAFF CATHEDRAL
Cathedral
The Cathedral Green, Cardiff
TEL: 029 2056 4554

8 MUSEUM OF WELSH LIFE
Museum
St Fagans, Cardiff
TEL: 029 2057 3500

9 NATIONAL MUSEUM & GALLERY CARDIFF
Museum
Cathays Park, Cardiff
TEL: 029 2039 7951

10 CARDIFF CASTLE
Castle
Castle Street, Cardiff
TEL: 02920 878 100

11 WELSH REGIMENT MUSEUM OF THE ROYAL REGIMENT OF WALES
Museum
Cardiff Castle Grounds, Cardiff
TEL: 029 2022 9367

12 MILLENNIUM STADIUM
Tour
Cardiff
TEL: 0292 023 1495

13 OLD BEAUPRE CASTLE
Castle
Cowbridge
TEL: 01446 773 034

14 DYFFRYN BOTANIC GARDEN
Garden
St Nicholas, Cardiff
TEL: 029 2059 3328

15 ALEXANDRA PARK
Garden
Beach Road, Penarth
TEL: 029 2070 4617

16 WELSH HAWKING CENTRE
Bird centre & aviary
Weycock Road, Barry
TEL: 01446 734 687

17 COSMESTON LAKES MEDIEVAL VILLAGE & COUNTRY PARK
Museum
Lavernock Road, Penarth
TEL: 02920 708 686

18 WESTON-SUPER-MARE HERITAGE CENTRE
Heritage centre
3-6 Wadham Street, Weston-Super-Mare
TEL: 01934 412 144

19 HELICOPTER MUSEUM
Museum
The Heliport Locking, Moor Road, Weston-Super-Mare
TEL: 01934 635 227

20 TIME MACHINE
Museum
Burlington Street, Weston-Super-Mare
TEL: 01934 621 028

21 WESTON-SUPER-MARE SEA LIFE CENTRE
Sea life centre
Marine Parade, Weston-Super-Mare
TEL: 01934 613 361

22 ANIMAL FARM ADVENTURE PARK
Farm
Red Road, Berrow, Burnham-on-sea
TEL: 01278 751 628

23 SECRET WORLD-BADGER & WILDLIFE RESCUE CENTRE
Wildlife park
New Road, East Huntspill, Highbridge
TEL: 01278 783 250

24 MARKET HOUSE MUSEUM
Museum
Market Street, Watchet
TEL: 01984 631 345

25 HOME FARM
Farm
Blue Anchor, Minehead
TEL: 01984 640 817

Dolphins

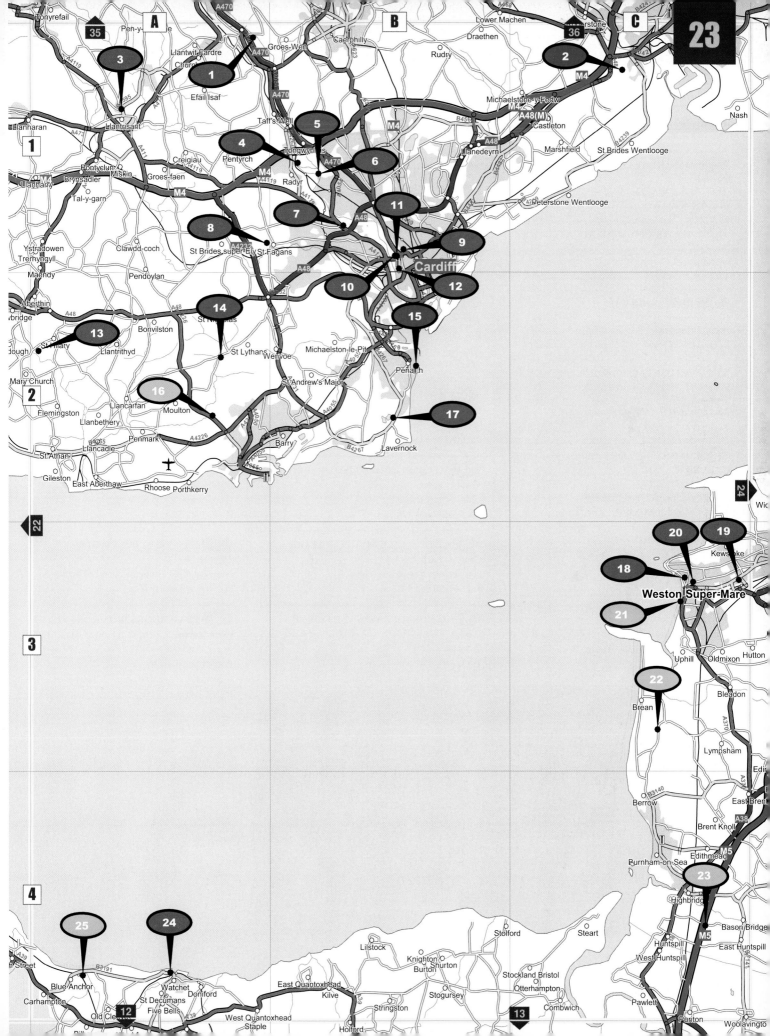

⬤ ANIMAL ATTRACTIONS   ⬤ OUTDOOR ATTRACTIONS
⬤ HERITAGE & CULTURE   ⬤ OUTDOOR ACTIVITIES
◯ INDOOR ACTIVITIES   ⬤ WATER ACTIVITIES

1 BLAISE CASTLE HOUSE
Castle
Henbury, Bristol
TEL: 0117 950 6789

2 WESTBURY COLLEGE GATEHOUSE
Gatehouses
College Road, Westbury-on-Tryn
TEL: 01985 843 600

3 BRISTOL CITY MUSEUM & ART GALLERY
Museum
Queens Road, Clifton
TEL: 01179 223 571

4 RED LODGE
Historic house
Park Row, Bristol
TEL: 01179 211 360

5 BRITISH EMPIRE & COMMONWEALTH MUSEUM
Museum
Bristol
TEL: 0117 925 4980

6 UNIVERSITY OF BRISTOL BOTANIC GARDEN
Garden
North Road, Leigh Woods, Bristol
TEL: 0117 973 3682

7 AT-BRISTOL
Museum
Clifton
TEL: 0845 345 1235

8 EXPLORATORY HANDS-ON SCIENCE CENTRE
Science Centres
Bristol Old Station, Temple Meads, Bristol
TEL: 01179 075 000

9 SS GREAT BRITAIN
Museum
Great Western Dock, Gas Ferry Road, Bristol
TEL: 01179 260 680

10 CLEVEDON COURT
Historic house
Tickenham Road, Clevedon
TEL: 01275 872 257

11 BRISTOL INDUSTRIAL MUSEUM
Museum
Princes Wharf, Wapping Road, Bristol
TEL: 01179 251 470

12 AVON VALLEY RAILWAY
Railway
Bitton Station, Bath Road, Bitton
TEL: 01179 327 296

13 ASHTON COURT ESTATE
Garden
Long Ashton, Bristol
TEL: 01275 375 559

14 ASHTON COURT VISITOR CENTRE
Visitor Centres
Long Ashton, Bristol
TEL: 01179 639 174

15 AVON VALLEY COUNTRY PARK
Country park
Pixash Lane, Keynsham, Bath
TEL: 01179 864 929

16 CHEDDAR CAVES AND GORGE
Cave
Cheddar
TEL: 01934 742 343

17 CHEDDAR GORGE CHEESE COMPANY
Cheese making
The Cliffs Cheddar George, Cheddar
TEL: 01934 742 810

18 KING JOHN'S HUNTING LODGE
Museum
The Square, Axbridge
TEL: 01934 732 012

19 DONNINGTON CASTLE
Castle
Newbury
TEL: Not available

20 WOOKEY HOLE CAVES & PAPERMILL
Cave
Wookey Hole, Wells
TEL: 01749 672 243

21 WELLS CATHEDRAL
Cathedral
Cathedral Green, Wells
TEL: 01749 674 483

22 BISHOP'S PALACE
Historic building
The Henderson Rooms, Wells
TEL: 01749 678 691

23 EAST SOMERSET RAILWAY
Railway
Cranmore Railway Station, Shepton, Mallet
TEL: 01749 880 417

24 PEAT MOORS IRON AGE CENTRE
Visitor centre
Shapwick Road, Westhay
TEL: 01458 860 897

Fun on the beach

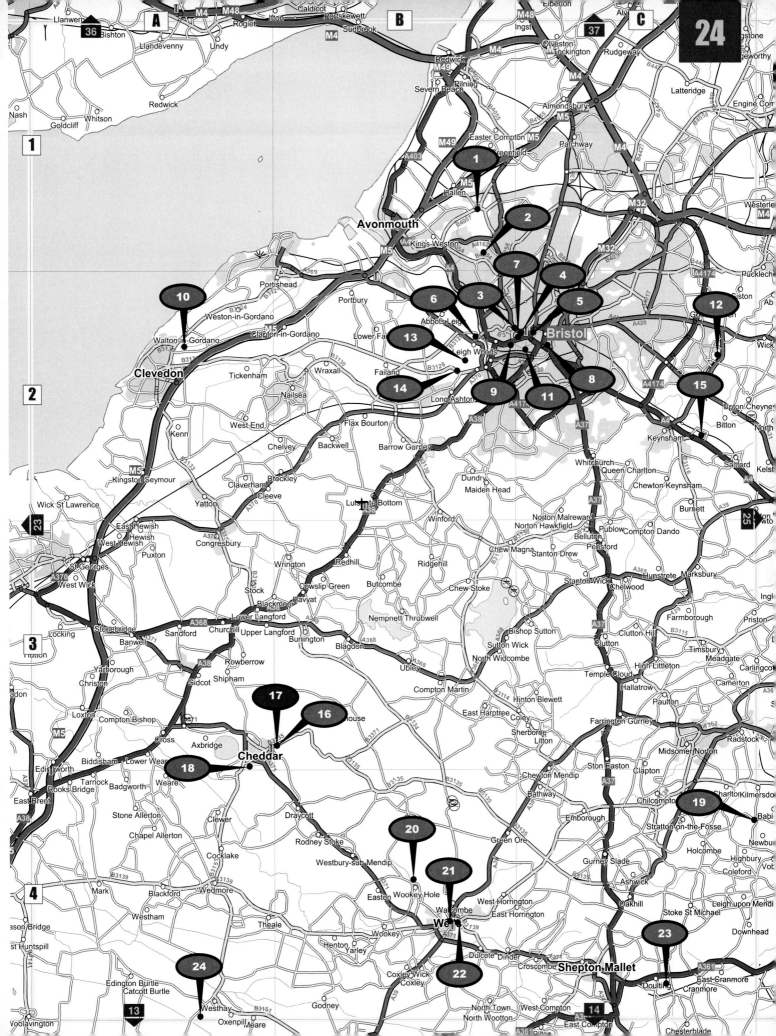

SOMERSET · WILTSHIRE · GLOUCS

● ANIMAL ATTRACTIONS
● OUTDOOR ATTRACTIONS
● HERITAGE & CULTURE
● OUTDOOR ACTIVITIES
○ INDOOR ACTIVITIES
● WATER ACTIVITIES

1 HORTON COURT
Historic house
Horton Chipping, Sodbury
Tel: 01985 843 600

2 CASTLE COMBE
Motor racing circuit
Chippenham
Tel: 01249 782 417

3 DYRHAM PARK NT
Garden
Chippenham
Tel: 0117 937 2501

4 CORSHAM COURT
Garden
Corsham
Tel: 01249 701 610

5 LACOCK ABBEY
Abbey
Lacock, Chippenham
Tel: 01249 730 227

6 FOX TALBOT MUSEUM OF PHOTOGRAPHY
Museum
Lacock, Chippenham
Tel: 01249 730 459

7 BATH BOATING STATION
Boat hire
Forester Road, Bath
Tel: 01225 466 407

8 1 ROYAL CRESCENT
Historic building
Bath
Tel: 01225 428 126

9 BATH ASSEMBLY ROOMS
Historic house
Bennett Street, Bath
Tel: 01225 477 785

10 MUSEUM OF COSTUME
Museum
Bennett Street, Bath
Tel: 01225 477 785

11 MUSEUM OF EAST ASIAN ART
Museum
12 Bennett Street, Bath
Tel: 01225 464 640

12 BUILDING OF BATH MUSEUM
Museum
Countess of Huntingdon's Chapel, The Vineyards, Bath
Tel: 01225 333 895

13 HOLBURNE MUSEUM & CRAFTS STUDY CENTRE
Museum
Great Pulteney Street, Bath
Tel: 01225 466 669

14 GEORGIAN GARDEN
Garden
Gravel Walk, Bath
Tel: 01225 477 752

15 BATH BOTANIC GARDENS
Garden
Royal Victoria Park, Bath
Tel: 01225 482 624

16 ROYAL PHOTOGRAPHIC SOCIETY
Museum
Octagon Galleries, Milsom Street, Bath
Tel: 01225 462 841

17 GUILDHALL
Historic building
High Street, Bath
Tel: 01225 477 724

18 IMPOSSIBLE MICROWORLD MUSEUM
Museum
Monmouth Street, Bath
Tel: 01225 333 003

19 WILLIAM HERSCHEL MUSEUM
Museum
19 New King Street, Bath
Tel: 01225 311 342

20 ROMAN BATHS MUSEUM
Roman site
Pump Room, Stall Street, Bath
Tel: 01225 477 785

21 SALLY LUNN'S REFRESHMENT HOUSE & MUSEUM
Historic house
4 North Parade Passage, Bath
Tel: 01225 461 634

22 BOOK MUSEUM
Museum
Manvers Street, Bath
Tel: 01225 466 000

23 CLAVERTON MANOR
Museum
Claverton, Bath
Tel: 01225 460 503

24 AMERICAN MUSEUM IN BRITAIN
Museum
Claverton Manor, Bath
Tel: 01225 460 503

25 CROWE HALL
Historic house
Widcombe Hill, Bath
Tel: 01225 310 322

26 GREAT CHALFIELD MANOR
Historic building
Great Chalfield, Melksham
Tel: 01225 782 239

27 ENGLISHCOMBE TITHE BARN
Historic building
Rectory Farmhouse, Englishcombe, Bath
Tel: 01225 425 073

28 PRIOR PARK LANDSCAPE GARDEN NT
Garden
Ralph Allen Drive, Bath
Tel: 01225 833 422

29 COURTS GARDEN NT
Garden
Holt, Trowbridge
Tel: 01225 782 340

30 PRISTON MILL
Watermill
Priston, Bath
Tel: 01225 423 894

31 WESTWOOD MANOR
Historic house
Bradford-On-Avon
Tel: 01225 863 374

32 PETO GARDEN
Historic house
Iford Manor, Bradford on Avon
Tel: 01225 863 146

Iford Hill Garden, Map 25

33 TROWBRIDGE MUSEUM
Museum
The Shires, Court Street, Trowbridge
TEL: 01225 751 339

34 FARLEIGH CASTLE EH
Castle
Farleigh Hungerford, Bath
TEL: 01225 754 026

35 NORWOOD FARM
Farm
Bath Road, Norton St Philip, Bath
TEL: 01373 834 356

36 RODE TROPICAL BIRD GARDENS
Garden
Rode, Bath
TEL: 01373 830 326

37 BROKERSWOOD COUNTRY PARK
Country park
Brokerswood, Westbury
TEL: 01373 822 238

38 NUNNEY CASTLE
Castle
Frome
TEL: 01179 750 700

39 LONGLEAT
Safari park
Warminster, Wiltshire, BA12 7NW.
TEL: 01985 844 400
EMAIL: enquiries@longleat.co.uk
WEB: www.longleat.co.uk

Voted 'UK Family Attraction of the Year 2002' by the 'Good Britain Guide' Longleat offers a great day out for all the family. Discover tigers, elephants, lions and giraffe in the Safari Park, get lost in the 'World's Longest Hedge Maze', voyage on the Safari Boats and much much more!
OPEN: All attractions open daily from Mar 16-Nov 3 2002.
ENTRY COSTS: £15, Child: £11, OAPs: £11.
SPECIALITIES: Events held, Guided tours available.
FACILITIES: Child area, Coffee shop, Credit cards, Gift shop, Pushchair friendly, Restaurant, Toilets, Wheelchair access.

40 WALLED GARDEN NURSERY
Garden
Cock Road, Horningsham
TEL: 01985 845 004

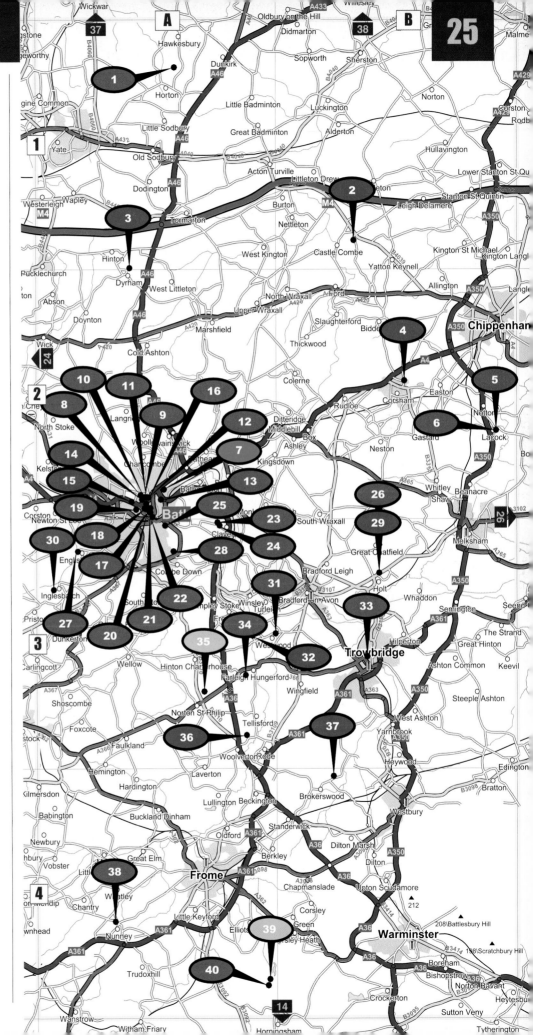

1 UFFINGTON CASTLE
Castle
Uffington
TEL: Not available

2 NATIONAL MONUMENTS RECORD CENTRE
Museum
Kemble Drive, Swindon
TEL: 01793 414 600

3 GREAT WESTERN RAILWAY MUSEUM
Museum
Faringdon Road, Swindon
TEL: 01793 466 555

4 RAILWAY VILLAGE MUSEUM
Museum
34 Faringdon Road, Swindon
TEL: 01793 446 646

5 LYDIARD PARK
Country park
Lydiard Tregoze, Swindon
TEL: 01793 771 419

6 ASHDOWN HOUSE NT
Historic building
Lambourn
TEL: 01488 725 84

7 BOWOOD HOUSE & GARDENS
Historic house
Bowood House, Derry Hill, Calne
TEL: 01249 812 102

8 AVEBURY MANOR & GARDEN NT
Garden
Marlborough
TEL: 01672 539 250

9 ALEXANDER KEILLER MUSEUM
Museum
Avebury
TEL: 01672 539 250

10 ATWELL-WILSON MOTOR MUSEUM
Museum
Downside Stockley Road, Calne
TEL: 01249 813 119

11 BEDWYN STONE MUSEUM
Museum
19 Church Street, Great Bedwyn
TEL: 01672 870 043

12 FLOWER FARMS
Farm
Carvers Hill Farm, Shalbourne, Marlborough
TEL: 01672 870 782

13 CROFTON BEAM ENGINES
Museum
Crofton Pumping Station, Marlborough
TEL: 01672 870 300

14 DEVIZES CANAL WHARF
Museum
Kennet and Avon Canal Trust Museum, Devizes
TEL: 01380 721 279

15 DEVIZES MUSEUM
Museum
41 Long Street, Devizes
TEL: 01380 727 369

16 MARKET LAVINGTON VILLAGE MUSEUM
Museum
Church Street, Market Lavington, Devizes
TEL: 01380 818 736

17 FINKLEY DOWN FARM PARK
Farm
Finkley Down, Andover
TEL: 01264 352 195

18 ANDOVER MUSEUM & MUSEUM OF THE IRON AGE
Museum
6 Church Close, Andover
TEL: 01264 366 283

19 HAWK CONSERVANCY
Falconry
Sarson Lane, Weyhill, Andover, Hampshire, SP11 8DY.
TEL: 01264 773 850
Housing more than 200 birds in its 15 acres of woodland and 7 acres of wildflower meadow it has one the largest collections of birds of prey.
OPEN: Feb 9-Nov 3.
ENTRY COSTS: £6.25, Child: £3.60, OAPs: £5.70, Family: £18.50.
FACILITIES: Coffee shop, Gift shop, Pushchair friendly, Wheelchair access.

20 THRUXTON MOTORING RACING CIRCUIT
Motor racing circuit
Thruxton, Andover
TEL: 01264 772 696

21 WOODHENGE
Ancient monument
Amesbury
TEL: Not available

22 CHOLDERTON RARE BREEDS FARM
Farm
Amesbury Road, Cholderton, Salisbury
TEL: 01980 629 438

23 STONEHENGE
Archaeological site
Salisbury
TEL: 01980 624 715

Help us help you

mention the *Days Out Atlas* when visiting anywhere on this page.

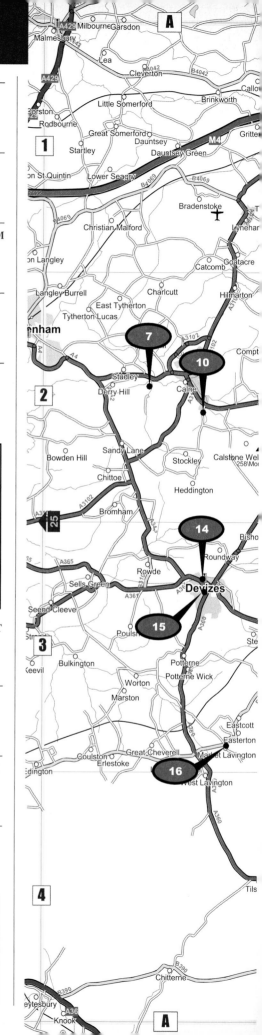

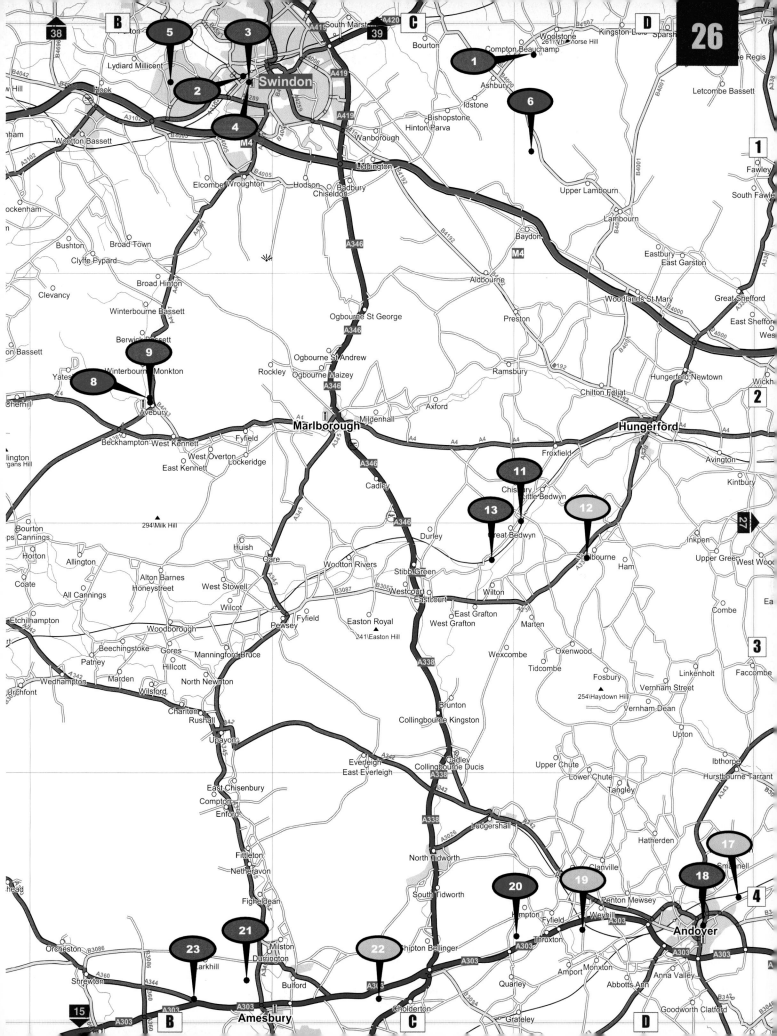

BERKS · HANTS · OXON

● ANIMAL ATTRACTIONS   ● OUTDOOR ATTRACTIONS
● HERITAGE & CULTURE   ● OUTDOOR ACTIVITIES
○ INDOOR ACTIVITIES   ● WATER ACTIVITIES

1 GREYS COURT NT
Garden
Rotherfield Greys, Henley on Thames
TEL: 01491 628 529

2 CANE END VINEYARD
Vineyard
Cane End, Reading
TEL: 01189 722 114

3 BEALE PARK
Wildlife park
Lower Basildon, Reading
TEL: 01734 845 172

4 LIVING RAINFOREST
Garden
Wyld Court Hall, Hampstead Norreys, Newbury
TEL: 01635 202 444

5 MAPLEDURHAM HOUSE & WATERMILL
Historic building
Mapledurham Village, Reading
TEL: 01189 723 350

6 THAMES RIVERCRUISE LTD
Boat trip
Pipers Island, Bridge Street, Caversham, Berkshire, RG4 8AH.
TEL: 0118 948 1088
EMAIL: Booking@thamesrivercruise.co.uk
WEB: www.thamesrivercruise.co.uk
Cruising "The Wind in the Willows" country. Boats available for public & private parties or groups & corporate events.
OPEN: Easter-end Sep. Available rest of year for private parties.
ENTRY COSTS: Depending on trip booked.
FACILITIES: Credit cards, Pushchair friendly, Restaurant, Toilets.

7 MUSEUM OF READING
Museum
The Town Hall, Blagrave Street, Reading
TEL: 01189 399 800

8 BUCKLEBURY FARM PARK
Farm
Bucklebury, Reading
TEL: 01189 714 002

9 WEST BERKSHIRE MUSEUM
Museum
The Wharf, Newbury
TEL: 01635 305 11

10 KENNET AND AVON CANAL VISITOR & INFORMATION CENTRE
Museum
Aldermaston Wharf, Wharf Side Padworth, Reading
TEL: 01189 712 868

11 KENNET HORSE BOAT COMPANY
Boat trip
32 West Mills, Newbury
TEL: 01635 441 54

12 NEWBURY RACECOURSE
Racecourse
Newbury
TEL: 01635 400 15

13 FOXHILL WORLD OF CARRIAGES MUSEUM
Museum
Basingstoke Road, Spencers Wood, Reading
TEL: 01188 833 34

14 SWALLOWFIELD PARK
Historic house
Swallowfield, Reading
TEL: 01189 883 815

15 WELLINGTON COUNTRY PARK & DAIRY MUSEUM
Museum
Odiham Road, Riseley, Reading
TEL: 0118 932 6444

16 SILCHESTER ROMAN CITY WALLS & AMPHITHEATRE
Roman site
Silchester
TEL: Not available

17 SANDHAM MEMORIAL CHAPEL
Historic building
Burghclere
TEL: 01635 278 394

18 VYNE
Garden
Sherborne St John, Basingstoke
TEL: 01256 881 337

19 MILESTONES LIVING HISTORY MUSEUM
Museum
Leisure Park, Basingstoke
TEL: 01256 477 766

20 BASING HOUSE RUINS
Historic building
Redbridge Lane, Old Basing, Basingstoke
TEL: 01256 467 294

21 BASINGSTOKE ICE RINK
Ice skating rink
The Leisure Park, Basingstoke
TEL: 01256 355 266

22 WILLIS MUSEUM
Museum
Market Place, Basingstoke
TEL: 01256 465 902

23 WOOLDINGS VINEYARD
Vineyard
Whitchurch
TEL: 01256 895 200

Rollercoaster

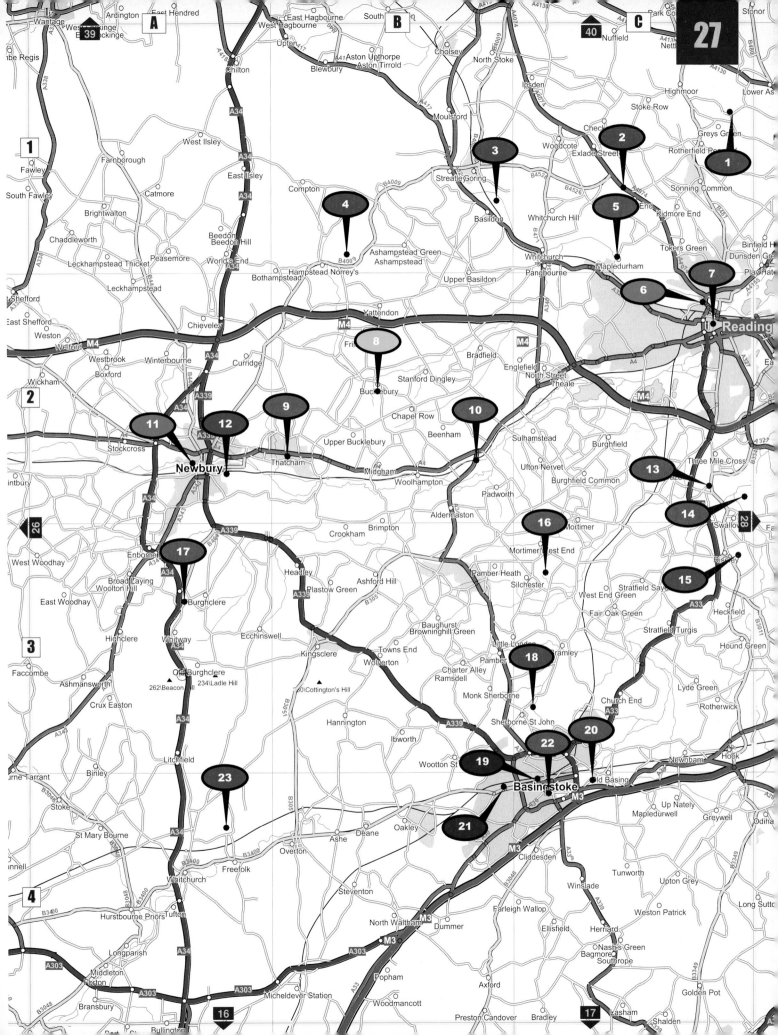

1 CLIVEDEN NT
Garden
Taplow
Tel: 01628 605 069

2 RIVER & ROWING MUSEUM
Museum
Mill Meadows, Henley-on-Thames
Tel: 01491 415 600

3 FROGMORE HOUSE
Historic house
Windsor
Tel: 01753 831 118

4 COURAGE SHIRE HORSE CENTRE
Farm
Cherry Garden Lane, Maidenhead
Tel: 01628 824 848

5 WINDSOR RACECOURSE
Racecourse
Maidenhead Road, Windsor, Berkshire, SL4 5JJ.
Tel: 0870 220 0024
Email: office@windsor-racecourse.co.uk
Web: www.windsor-racecourse.co.uk
Windsor racecourse offers excellent fun and entertainment for all the family, especially on dates when we have our themed events. Call 0870 220 0024 for more information.
Open: Apr 29-Aug 8: Mon evening & some weekends.
Entry costs: £17 Club, £12 Grandstand, £5 Silver Ring.
Specialities: Picnic area, Play area.
Facilities: Credit cards, Gift tokens, Pushchair friendly, Restaurant, Toilets, Wheelchair access.

6 WALTHAM PLACE
Garden
Maidenhead
Tel: 01628 825 517

7 FRENCH BROTHERS
Boat trip
Clewer Boat House, Clewer Court Road, Windsor, Berkshire, SL4 5JH.
Tel: 01753 851 900 or 862 933
Email: info@boat-trips.co.uk
Web: www.boat-trips.co.uk

River Thames passenger boat operators. Commentary on all boat trips. Windsor, Maidenhead and Runnymede. Group discounts available.
Open: Easter-Oct.
Entry costs: From £4.20.
Facilities: Credit cards, Dogs allowed, Pushchair friendly, Toilets, Wheelchair access, Gift shop.

8 CROWN JEWELS OF THE WORLD MUSEUM
Museum
Peascod Street, Windsor
Tel: 01753 833 773

9 HOUSEHOLD CAVALRY MUSEUM
Museum
Combermere Barracks, St Leonards Road, Windsor
Tel: 01753 755 203

10 LEGOLAND WINDSOR
Adventure & activity centre
Windsor, Berkshire.
Tel: 01753 626 200

11 VALLEY GARDENS WINDSOR GREAT PARK
Garden
Access via Wick Road, Englefield Green, Windsor
Tel: 01753 860 222

12 DINTON PASTURES COUNTRY PARK
Country park
Davis Street, Reading
Tel: 0118 934 2016

13 MUSEUM OF ENGLISH RURAL LIFE
Museum
Reading University, Reading
Tel: 01189 318 660

14 JOCKS LANE PARK
Country park
Binfield Road, Bracknell
Tel: 01344 300 380

15 ASCOT RACECOURSE
Racecourse
High Street, Ascot
Tel: 01344 622 211

16 HOLME GRANGE CRAFT VILLAGE
Craft centre
Heathlands Road, Wokingham
Tel: 0118 977 6753

17 CORAL REEF WATER WORLD
Theme park
Nine Mile Ride, Bracknell
Tel: 01344 862 525

19 ROYAL ELECTRICAL MECHANICAL ENGINEERS (REME) MUSEUM OF TECHNOLOGY
Museum
Isaac Newton Road, Arborfield, Reading
Tel: 01189 763 567

Fun on the water flumes

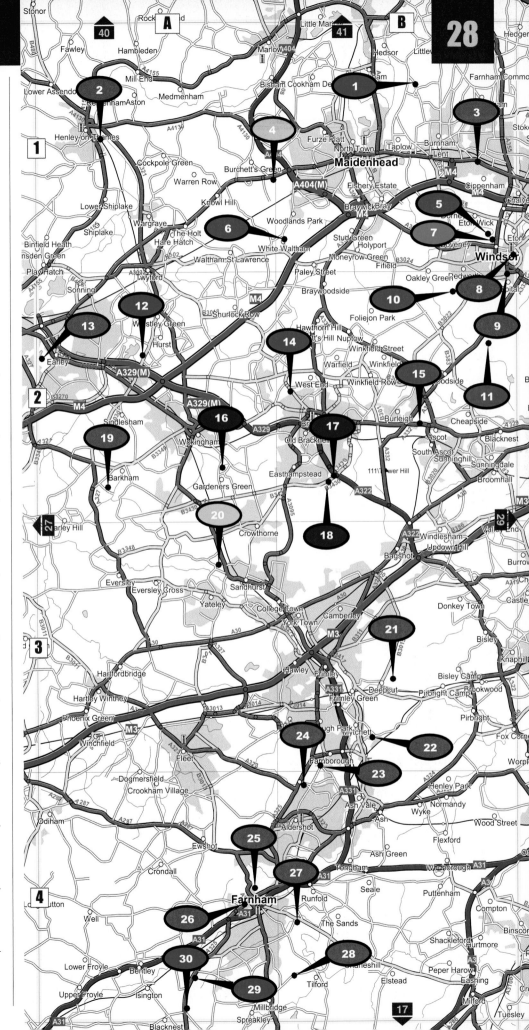

18 THE LOOK OUT DISCOVERY CENTRE

Interactive Science Museum

Nine Mile Ride, Bracknell, Berkshire, RG12 7QW.
TEL: 01344 354 400
EMAIL: thelookout@bracknell-forest.gov.uk
WEB: www.bracknell-forest.gov.uk/lookout
Visit our exciting hands-on, interactive science and nature exhibition with over 70 bright and fun-filled exhibits. A great day out for all the family.
OPEN: Open daily from 10-5.
ENTRY COSTS: £4.50, Child: £3, OAPs: £2.70, Family: £12.
SPECIALITIES: Events held, Photography allowed, Picnic area, Play area.
FACILITIES: Child area, Coffee shop, Credit cards, Gift shop, Pushchair friendly, Toilets, Wheelchair access.

20 TRILAKES ANIMAL PARK & FISHERY

Country park

Yateley Road, Sandhurst
TEL: 01252 873 191

21 ROYAL LOGISTIC CORPS MUSEUM

Museum

Deepcut, Camberley
TEL: 01252 340 871

22 ARMY MEDICAL SERVICES MUSEUM

Museum

Keogh Barracks, Ash Vale, Aldershot
TEL: 01252 340 212

23 ALDERSHOT MILITARY MUSEUM & RUSHMOOR LOCAL HISTORY GALLERY

Museum

Evelyn Woods Road, Queen's Avenue, Aldershot
TEL: 01252 314 598

24 AIRBORNE FORCES MUSEUM

Museum

Browning Barracks, Aldershot
TEL: 01252 349 619

25 FARNHAM CASTLE KEEP

Castle

Castle Hill, Farnham
TEL: 01252 713 393

26 MUSEUM OF FARNHAM

Museum

38 West Street, Farnham
TEL: 01252 715 094

27 WAVERLEY ABBEY

Abbey

Farnham
TEL: Not available

28 RURAL LIFE CENTRE

Museum

Reeds Road, Tilford
TEL: 01252 792 300/795571

29 BIRDWORLD

Garden

Forest Lodge Garden Centre, Holt Pound, Farnham
TEL: 01420 221 40

30 ALICE HOLT WOODLAND PARK

Country park

Bucks Horn, Oak Farnham
TEL: 01420 236 66

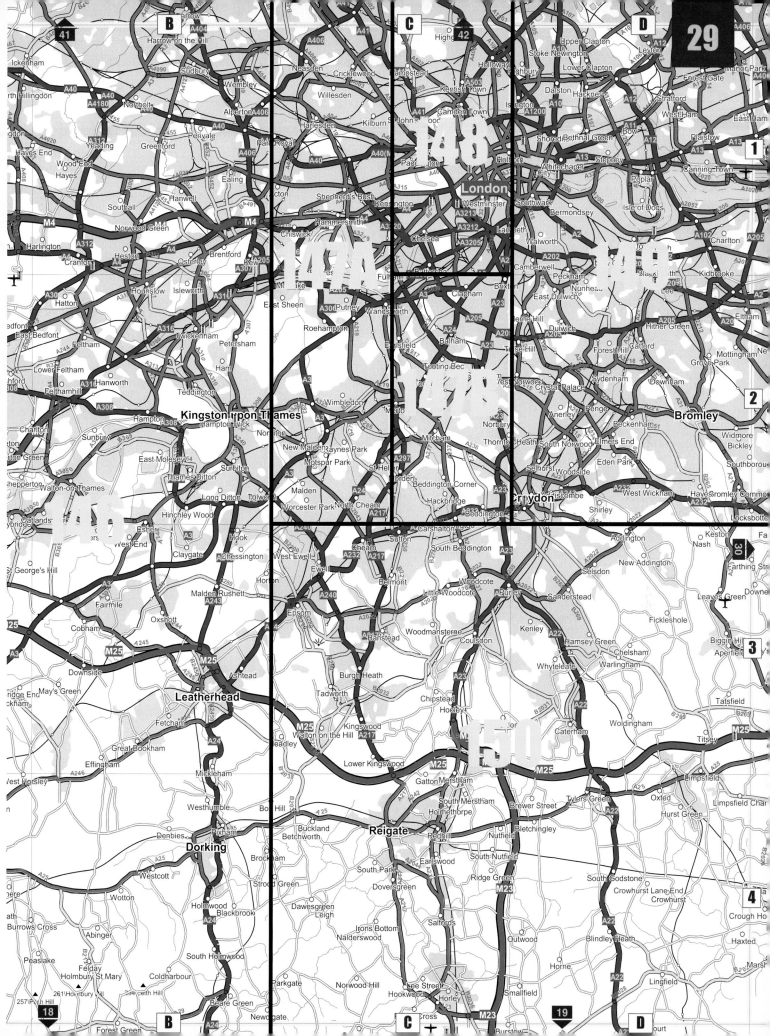

ESSEX · KENT · LONDON

- ANIMAL ATTRACTIONS
- HERITAGE & CULTURE
- INDOOR ACTIVITIES
- OUTDOOR ATTRACTIONS
- OUTDOOR ACTIVITIES
- WATER ACTIVITIES

1 UPMINSTER WINDMILL
Mill
St Mary's Lane, Upminster
TEL: 01708 772 394

2 VALENCE HOUSE MUSEUM & ART GALLERY
Museum
Becontree Avenue, Dagenham
TEL: 020 8595 8404

3 MILLENNIUM CENTRE
Museum
The Chase, Dagenham Road, Romford
TEL: 020 8595 4155

4 HORNCHURCH COUNTRY PARK
Country park
Southend Road, South Hornchurch, Rainham
TEL: 01708 554 451

5 EASTBURY MANOR HOUSE
Historic house
Barking
TEL: 020 8507 0119

6 OUTFALL SAILING CLUB
Sailing
Jenkins Lane, Barking
TEL: 020 8507 4711

7 RAINHAM HALL
Historic house
The Broadway, Rainham
TEL: 01494 528 051

8 NORTH WOOLWICH OLD STATION MUSEUM
Museum
Pier Road, North Woolwich, London
TEL: 020 7474 7244

9 PURFLEET HERITAGE & MILITARY CENTRE
Museum
Purfleet
TEL: 01708 866 764

10 GREENWICH BOROUGH MUSEUM
Museum
232 Plumstead High Street, London
TEL: 020 8855 3240

11 THURROCK MUSEUM
Museum
Thameside Complex, Orsett Road, Grays
TEL: 01375 382 555

12 ERITH MUSEUM
Museum
Erith Library, Walnut Tree Road, Erith
TEL: 01322 526 574

13 MUSEUM OF ARTILLERY IN THE ROTUNDA
Museum
Royal Artillery Institution, Woolwich, London
TEL: 020 8316 5402

14 TILBURY FORT
Garden
Tilbury
TEL: 01375 858 489

15 WORLD OF SILK
Factory shop
Bourne Road, Crayford
TEL: 01322 559 401

16 HALL PLACE
Garden
Bourne Road, Bexley
TEL: 01322 526 574

17 BEXLEY MUSEUM
Museum
Hall Place, Bourne Road, Bexley
TEL: 01322 526 574

18 CHANTRY HERITAGE CENTRE
Heritage centre
Fort Gardens, Commercial Place, Gravesend
TEL: 01474 321 520

19 TROSLEY COUNTRY PARK
Country park
Waterlow Road, Meopham, Gravesend
TEL: 01732 823 570

20 DARTFORD BOROUGH MUSEUM
Museum
Market Street, Dartford
TEL: 01322 343 555

21 CHISLEHURST CAVES
Cave
Old Hill, Chislehurst
TEL: 020 8467 3264

22 TUDOR YEOMAN'S HOUSE
Historic house
Sole Street, Cobham, Gravesend
TEL: 01892 890 651

23 BROMLEY MUSEUM & PRIORY GARDENS
Museum
The Priory Church Hill, Orpington
TEL: 01689 873 826

24 CROFTON ROMAN VILLA
Roman site
Crofton Road, Orpington
TEL: 01689 873 826

25 EYNSFORD CASTLE
Castle
Eynsford
TEL: 01322 862 114

26 LULLINGSTONE CASTLE
Castle
Lullingstone Park, Eynsford
TEL: 01322 862 114

27 LULLINGSTONE ROMAN VILLA
Archaeological site
Lullingstone Lane, Eynsford
TEL: 01732 778 000

Tractor racing

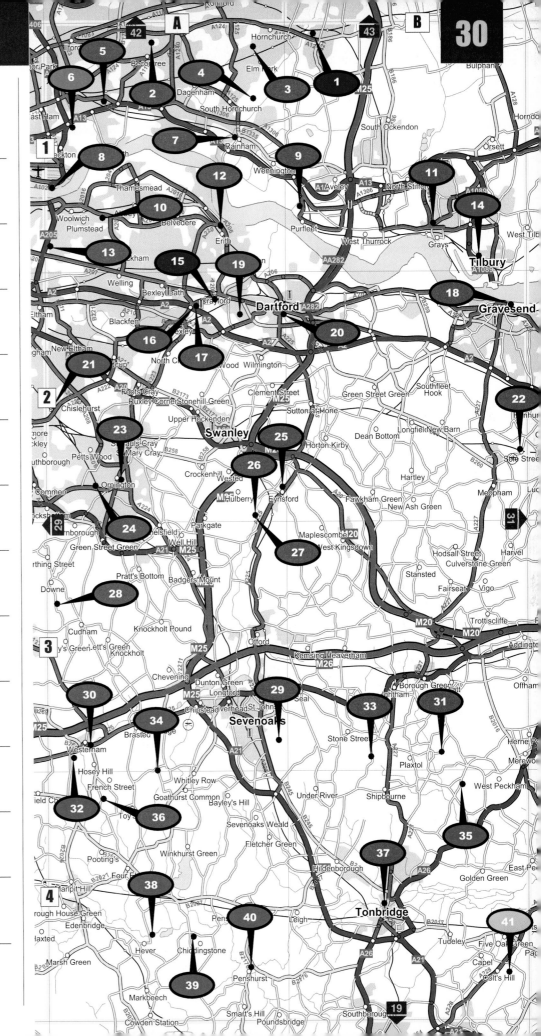

28 DOWN HOUSE HOME OF CHARLES DARWIN
Historic building
Luxted Road, Downe
TEL: 01689 859 119

29 KNOLE NT
Historic house
Sevenoaks
TEL: 01732 462 100

30 QUEBEC HOUSE
Historic house
Quebec Square, Westerham
TEL: 01892 890 651

31 OLD SOAR MANOR
Historic house
Old Soar Road, Plaxtol, Sevenoaks
TEL: 01732 810 378

32 SQUERRYES COURT
Garden
Squerryes, Westerham
TEL: 01959 562 345

33 IGHTHAM MOTE NT
Historic house
Ivy Hatch, Sevenoaks
TEL: 01732 810 378

34 EMMETTS GARDEN NT
Garden
Ide Hill, Sevenoaks
TEL: 01732 750 367

35 OLD WALLED GARDEN
Garden
Oxonhoath, Hadlow
TEL: 01732 810 012

36 CHARTWELL NT
Historic building
Westerham
TEL: 01732 866 368

37 TONBRIDGE CASTLE
Castle
Castle Street, Tonbridge
TEL: 01732 770 929

38 HEVER CASTLE & GARDENS
Garden
Edenbridge
TEL: 01732 865 224

39 CHIDDINGSTONE CASTLE
Garden
Chiddingstone, Edenbridge
TEL: 01892 870 347

40 PENSHURST PLACE & GARDENS
Garden
Penshurst, Tonbridge
TEL: 01892 870 307

41 BADSELL PARK FARM
Farm
Crittenden Road, Matfield, Tonbridge
TEL: 01892 832 223

ESSEX · KENT

● ANIMAL ATTRACTIONS   ● OUTDOOR ATTRACTIONS
● HERITAGE & CULTURE   ● OUTDOOR ACTIVITIES
○ INDOOR ACTIVITIES   ● WATER ACTIVITIES

1 PRITTLEWELL PRIORY MUSEUM
Museum
Priory Park, Victoria Avenue, Southend-on-Sea
TEL: 01702 342 878

2 NATIONAL MOTORBOAT MUSEUM
Museum
Wat Tyler Country Park, Pitsea Hall Lane, Pitsea
TEL: 01268 550 077

3 HADLEIGH CASTLE
Castle
Hadleigh
TEL: 01760 755 161

4 SOUTHEND MUSEUM & PLANETARIUM
Museum
Victoria Avenue, Southend-on-Sea
TEL: 01702 215 131

5 SOUTHCHURCH HALL MUSEUM
Museum
Southchurch Hall Close, Southend-on-Sea
TEL: 01702 467 671

6 PETER PAN'S ADVENTURE ISLAND
Adventure & activity centre
Southend-on-Sea
TEL: 01702 468 023

7 SOUTHEND PIER
Historic building
Southend-on-Sea
TEL: 01702 215 622

8 COALHOUSE FORT
Historic building
Princess Margaret Road, East Tilbury Village, Tilbury
TEL: 01375 844 203

9 MILTON CHANTRY
Historic building
Gravesend
TEL: 01474 321 520

10 GAD'S HILL PLACE
Historic house
Gravesend Road, Higham, Rochester
TEL: 01474 822 366

11 ROCHESTER CASTLE
Castle
The Keep, Rochester
TEL: 01634 402 276

12 UPNOR CASTLE
Castle
High Street, Upper Upnor, Rochester
TEL: 01634 827 980

13 SHORNE WOOD COUNTRY PARK
Country park
Brewers Road, Shorne, Gravesend
TEL: 01474 823 800

14 PADDLE STEAMER KINGSWEAR CASTLE
Boat trip
The Historic Dockyard, Chatham
TEL: 01634 827 648

15 HISTORIC DOCKYARD CHATHAM
Museum
Chatham
TEL: 01634 823 800

16 ROYAL ENGINEERS MUSEUM
Museum
Prince Arthur Road, Gillingham
TEL: 01634 406 397

17 GUILDHALL MUSEUM
Museum
High Street, Rochester
TEL: 01634 848 717

18 OWLETTS
Historic house
The Street, Cobham, Gravesend
TEL: 01892 890 651

19 ROCHESTER CATHEDRAL
Cathedral
High Street, Rochester
TEL: 01634 401 301

20 COBHAM HALL
Historic house
Cobham, Gravesend
TEL: 01474 823 371

21 FORT AMHERST
Historic building
Dock Road, Chatham
TEL: 01634 847 747

22 CHARLES DICKENS CENTRE
Historic house
Eastgate House, High Street, Rochester
TEL: 01634 844 176

23 SITTINGBOURNE & KEMSLEY LIGHT RAILWAY
Railway
Kemsley Down, Station Mill Way, Sittingbourne
TEL: 01634 852 672

24 CAPSTONE FARM COUNTRY PARK
Country park
Capstone Road, Gillingham
TEL: 01634 812 196

25 DOLPHIN SAILING BARGE MUSEUM
Museum
Crown Quay Lane, Sittingbourne
TEL: 01795 423 215

26 MAISON DIEU
Historic house
Ospringe
TEL: 01795 534 542

27 BROGDALE HORTICULTURAL TRUST
Garden
Brogdale Road, Faversham
TEL: 01795 535 286

28 TYLAND BARN KENT'S WILDLIFE & CONSERVATION CENTRE
Wildlife park
Sandling, Maidstone
TEL: 01622 662 012

29 MUSEUM OF KENT LIFE
Museum
Lock Lane, Sandling Maidstone
TEL: 01622 763 936

30 DODDINGTON PLACE GARDENS
Garden
Doddington, Sittingbourne
TEL: 01795 886 101

31 BELMONT PARK
Historic building
Throwley, Faversham
TEL: 01795 890 202

32 MAIDSTONE MUSEUM & ART GALLERY
Museum
St Faiths Street, Maidstone
TEL: 01622 754 497

33 TYRWHITT DRAKE MUSEUM OF CARRIAGES
Museum
Mill Street, Maidstone
TEL: 01622 663 006

34 LEEDS CASTLE
Castle
Maidstone
TEL: 01622 765 400

35 BEECH COURT GARDENS
Garden
Canterbury Road, Challock Ashford
TEL: 01233 740 735

36 BOUGHTON MONCHELSEA PLACE
Garden
Church Hill, Boughton Monchelsea, Maidstone
TEL: 01622 743 120

37 CHURCH HILL COTTAGE GARDENS & NURSERY
Garden
Church Hill, Charing Heath, Ashford
TEL: 01233 712 522

38 YALDING ORGANIC GARDENS
Garden
Benover Road, Yalding, Maidstone
TEL: 01622 814 650

39 HOP FARM COUNTRY PARK
Country park
Maidstone Road, Paddock Wood, Tonbridge
TEL: 01622 872 068

40 INTELLIGENCE CORPS MUSEUM
Museum
Templer, Barracks, Ashford
TEL: 01233 657 208

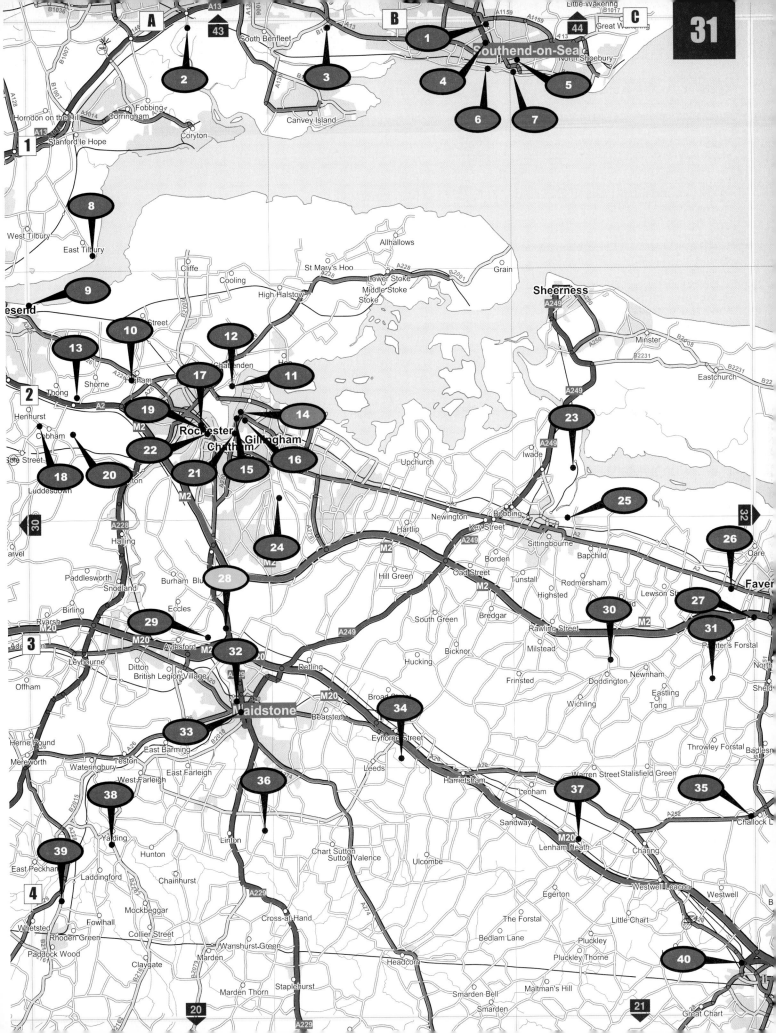

- ANIMAL ATTRACTIONS
- HERITAGE & CULTURE
- INDOOR ACTIVITIES
- OUTDOOR ATTRACTIONS
- OUTDOOR ACTIVITIES
- WATER ACTIVITIES

1 OLD TOWN HALL MUSEUM
Museum
Market Place, Margate   Tel: 01843 231 213

2 DREAMLAND FUN PARK
Theme park
Marine Terrace, Margate   Tel: 01843 227 011

3 RECULVER TOWERS & ROMAN FORT
Historic building
Reculver, Herne Bay   Tel: 01227 740 676

4 HERNE BAY MUSEUM & GALLERY
Museum
William Street, Herne Bay   Tel: 01227 367 368

5 QUEX HOUSE AND GARDENS & POWELL-COTTON MUSEUM
Historic house
Quex Park, Birchington   Tel: 01843 842 168

6 DICKENS HOUSE MUSEUM
Museum
Victoria Parade, Broadstairs   Tel: 01843 862 853

7 CHUFFA TRAINS MUSEUM
Museum
82 High Street, Whitstable   Tel: 01227 277 339

8 WHITSTABLE MUSEUM & GALLERY
Museum
Oxford Street, Whitstable   Tel: 01227 276 998

9 SPITFIRE & HURRICANE MEMORIAL BUILDING
Museum
The Airfield, Manston Rd, Ramsgate   Tel: 01843 821 940

10 RAMSGATE MUSEUM
Museum
Guildford Lawn, Ramsgate   Tel: 01843 593 532

11 MARITIME MUSEUM
Museum
Clock House Pier Yard, Royal Harbour, Ramsgate   Tel: 01843 587 765

12 MINSTER ABBEY
Abbey
Church St Minster, Ramsgate   Tel: 01843 821 254

13 DRUIDSTONE WILDLIFE PARK
Wildlife park
Honey Hill, Blean, Canterbury   Tel: 01227 765 168

14 FLEUR DE LYS HERITAGE CENTRE
Heritage centre
13 Preston Street, Faversham   Tel: 01795 534 542

15 RICHBOROUGH ROMAN FORT
Castle
Richborough, Sandwich   Tel: 01304 612 013

16 FARMING WORLD
Farm
Nash Court, Boughton   Tel: 01227 751 144

17 TOWN HALL
Historic building
King St, Fordwich, Canterbury   Tel: 01227 710 756

18 MOUNT EPHRAIM GARDENS
Garden
Staple St, Hernhill, Faversham   Tel: 01227 751 496

19 WEST GATE MUSEUM
Museum
St Peter's Street, Canterbury   Tel: 01227 452 747

20 ST AUGUSTINE'S ABBEY
Abbey
Longport, Canterbury   Tel: 01227 767 345

21 EASTBRIDGE HOSPITAL OF ST THOMAS
Historic building
High Street, Canterbury   Tel: 01227 471 688

22 CANTERBURY ROMAN MUSEUM
Museum
Butchery Lane, Longmarket, Canterbury   Tel: 01227 785 575

23 CANTERBURY CATHEDRAL
Cathedral
Canterbury   Tel: 01227 762 862

24 CANTERBURY HERITAGE MUSEUM
Heritage centre
Stour Street, Canterbury   Tel: 01227 452 747

25 BUFFS REGIMENTAL MUSEUM
Museum
Royal Museum & Art Gallery, High St, Canterbury   Tel: 01227 452 747

26 CANTERBURY TALES
Visitor centre
St Margaret's St, Canterbury   Tel: 01227 454 888

27 HOWLETTS WILD ANIMAL PARK
Wildlife park
Bekesbourne Lane, Bekesbourne, Canterbury   Tel: 0891 800 605

28 GOODNESTONE PARK GARDENS
Garden
Goodnestone, Canterbury   Tel: 01304 840 107

29 BADGERS HILL FARM
Farm
New Cut Road, Chilham   Tel: 01227 730 573

30 HIGHAM PARK & GARDENS
Garden
Higham Park, Bridge, Canterbury   Tel: 01227 830 830

31 DEAL CASTLE
Castle
Victoria Road, Deal   Tel: 01304 372 762

32 WALMER CASTLE & GARDENS EH
Garden
Kingsdown Rd, Walmer, Deal   Tel: 01304 364 288

33 ELHAM VALLEY VINEYARDS
Vineyard
Elham Valley Road, Barham   Tel: 01227 831 266

34 LYDDEN INTERNATIONAL MOTOR RACING CIRCUIT
Motor racing circuit
Wootton, Canterbury   Tel: 01304 830 557

35 PINES GARDEN
Garden
Beach Road, St Margaret's Bay, Dover   Tel: 01304 852 764

36 BAY MUSEUM & PINES GARDENS
Museum
Beach Road, St. Margarets Bay, Dover   Tel: 01304 852 764

37 KERSNEY ABBEY & RUSSELL GARDENS
Garden
Alkham Valley Road, Temple Ewell, Dover   Tel: 01304 872 434

38 CRABBLE CORN MILL
Museum
Lower Road River, Dover   Tel: 01304 823 292

39 SOUTH FORELAND LIGHTHOUSE NT
Historic building
St Margaret's-at-Cliffe, Dover   Tel: 01304 852 463

40 MACFARLAN'S BUTTERFLY CENTRE
Butterfly farm
Canterbury Rd, Swingfield, Dover   Tel: 01303 844 24

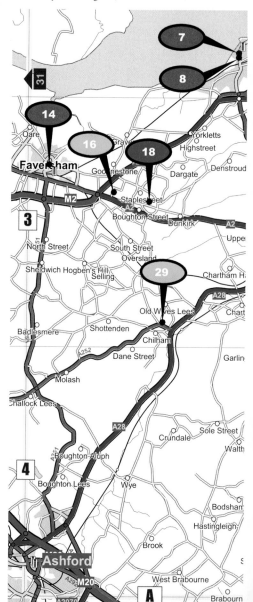

1

2

3

4

41 GATEWAY TO THE WHITE CLIFFS
Country park
Langdon Cliffs, Dover   **TEL:** 01304 202 756

42 DOVER CASTLE & SECOND WORLD WAR TUNNELS
Castle
Dover   **TEL:** 01304 211 067

43 PRINCESS OF WALES'S ROYAL REGIMENT & THE QUEEN'S REGIMENT MUSEUM
Museum
Inner Bailey, Dover Castle, Dover **TEL:** 01304 240 121

44 DOVER OLD TOWN GAOL
Historic building
Dover Town Hall, Biggin Street, Dover
    TEL: 01304 201 200

45 ROMAN PAINTED HOUSE
Historic house
New Street, Dover   **TEL:** 01304 203 279

46 DOVER MUSEUM
Museum
Market Square, Dover   **TEL:** 01304 201 066

47 WESTERN HEIGHTS
Historic building
Dover   **TEL:** 01304 241 806

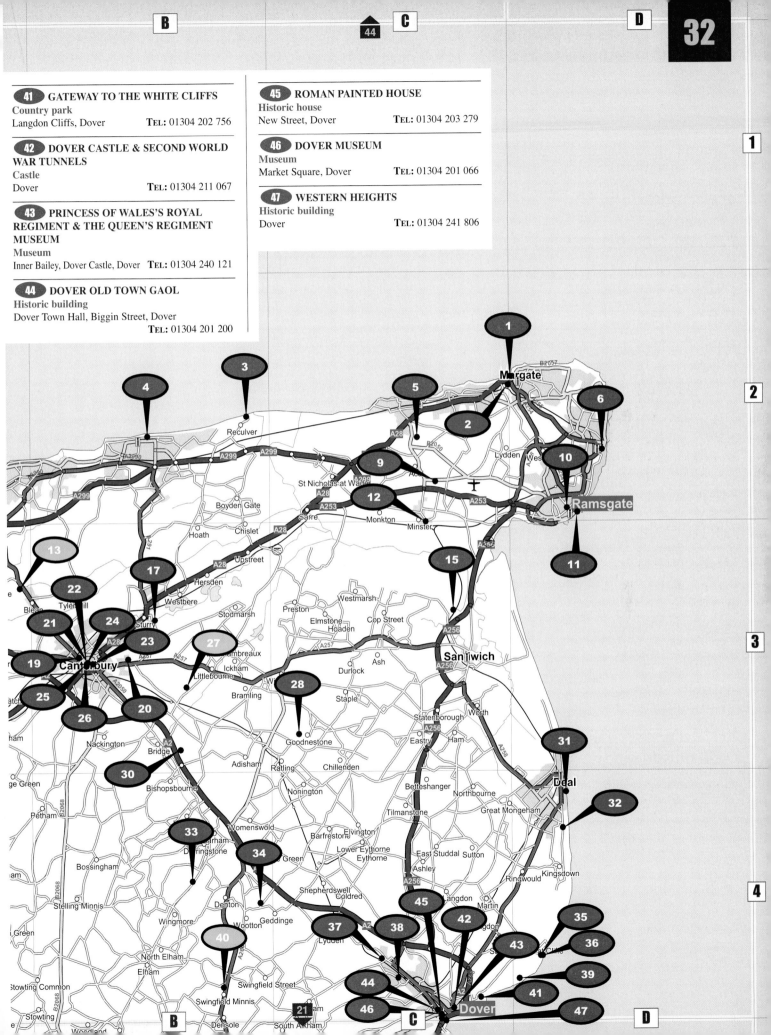

SOUTH WALES

1 PENRHOS COTTAGE
Historic house
Llanycefn, Clunderwen
TEL: 01437 731 328

2 ST DAVIDS BISHOP'S PALACE
Archaeological site
The Close, St Davids, Haverfordwest
TEL: 01437 720 517

3 OCEANARIUM
Aquarium
42 New Street, St Davids
TEL: 01437 720 453

4 ST DAVIDS CATHEDRAL
Cathedral
The Close, St Davids
TEL: 01437 720 199

5 SCOLTON MANOR HOUSE & MUSEUM
Historic house
Spittal, Haverfordwest
TEL: 01437 731 328

6 LLAWHADEN CASTLE
Castle
Llawhaden
TEL: 01437 541 201

7 HAVERFORDWEST CASTLE
Castle
Haverfordwest
TEL: 01437 763 707

8 PICTON CASTLE
Castle
Haverfordwest
TEL: 01437 751 326

9 OAKWOOD PARK
Theme park
Canaston Bridge, Narberth
TEL: 01834 891 373

10 CWM DERI VINEYARD
Vineyard
Martletwy, Narberth
TEL: 01834 891 274

11 COLBY WOODLAND GARDEN NT
Garden
Amroth, Narberth
TEL: 01834 811 885

12 UPTON CASTLE GARDENS
Garden
Cosheton, Pembroke Dock
TEL: 01646 651 782

13 HEATHERTON COUNTRY SPORTS PARK
Adventure & activity centre
St Florence, Tenby
TEL: 01646 651 025

14 CAREW CASTLE
Castle
Carew, Tenby
TEL: 01646 651 657

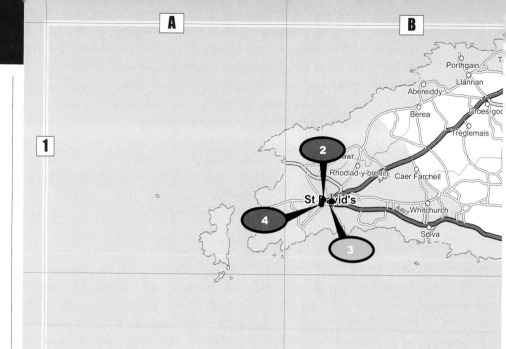

15 MANOR HOUSE WILDLIFE & LEISURE PARK
Wildlife park
St Florence, Tenby
TEL: 01646 651 201

16 MUSEUM OF THE HOME
Museum
Westgate Hill, Pembroke
TEL: 01646 681 200

17 PEMBROKE CASTLE
Castle
Castle Terrace, Pembroke
TEL: 01646 681 510

18 LAMPHEY PALACE
Historic building
Lamphey
TEL: 01646 672 224

19 TENBY MUSEUM & ART GALLERY
Museum
Castle Hill, Tenby
TEL: 01834 842 809

20 TUDOR MERCHANT'S HOUSE
Historic house
Quay Hill, Tenby
TEL: 01834 842 279

21 MANORBIER CASTLE
Castle
Manorbier
TEL: 01834 871 394

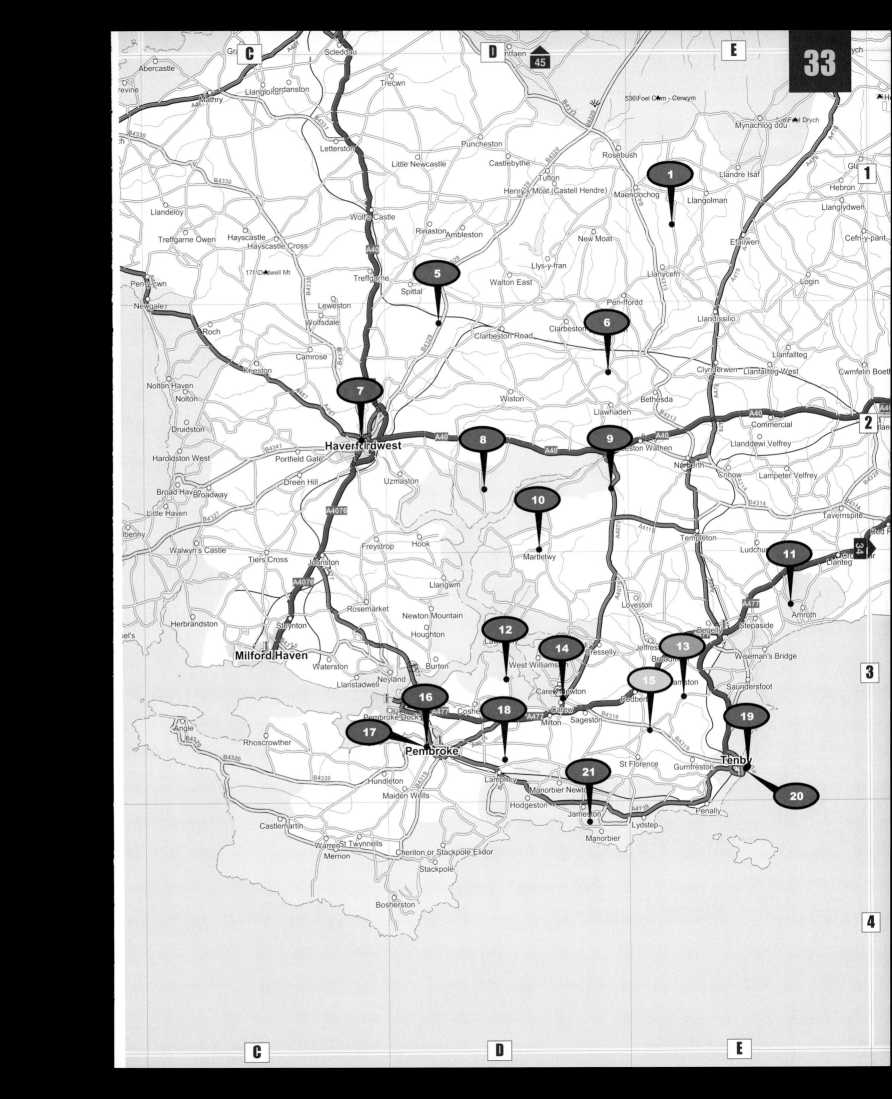

S WALES

● ANIMAL ATTRACTIONS
● HERITAGE & CULTURE
○ INDOOR ACTIVITIES
● OUTDOOR ATTRACTIONS
● OUTDOOR ACTIVITIES
● WATER ACTIVITIES

1 **CWMDU INN SHOP, POST OFFICE & COTTAGES**
Historic building
Cwmdu
TEL: 01558 685 088

2 **DINEFWR PARK NT**
Historic building
Llandeilo
TEL: 01558 823 902

3 **ABERGLASNEY GARDENS**
Llangathen, Carmarthen, Carmarthenshire, SA32 8QH.
TEL: 01558 668 998
EMAIL: info@aberglasney.org.uk
WEB: www.aberglasney.org.uk

Set in the Tywi Valley, the gardens have first class horticultural qualities and a mysterious history, destined to become one of the most fascinating gardens in the UK.
OPEN: Apr-Oct: 10-6 (last admission 5). Nov-Dec: Mon-Fri & 1st Sun of month, 10.30-3.
ENTRY COSTS: £5, Child: £2.50 Under 5s Free, OAPs: £4, Family: £12.
SPECIALITIES: Walled garden, Woodland plants, Exotic plants, Hardy plants, Lilies.
FACILITIES: Toilets, Credit cards, Wheelchair access, Restaurant, Own gift tokens, Pushchair friendly.

4 **CARMARTHENSHIRE COUNTY MUSEUM**
Museum
Abergwili
TEL: 01267 231 691

5 **DRYSLWYN CASTLE**
Castle
Dryslwyn
TEL: 029 2050 0200

6 **GELLI AUR COUNTRY PARK**
Country park
Golden Grove, Carmarthen
TEL: 01558 668 885

7 **GROVELAND ADVENTURE WORLD**
Theme park
The Grove, Llangynin
TEL: 01994 231 181

8 **DYLAN THOMAS' BOAT HOUSE**
Historic house
Dylan's Walk, Laugharne
TEL: 01994 427 420

9 **KIDWELLY CASTLE**
Castle
5 Castle Road, Kidwelly
TEL: 01554 890 104

10 **PEMBREY MOTOR RACING CIRCUIT**
Motor racing circuit
Pembrey
TEL: 01554 891 042

11 **CEFN COED COLLIERY MUSEUM**
Museum
Neath Road, Crynant, Neath
TEL: 01639 750 556

12 **SWANSEA MARITIME & INDUSTRIAL MUSEUM**
Museum
Maritime Square, Maritime Quarter, Swansea
TEL: 01792 650 351

13 **PEMBREY COUNTRY PARK**
Country park
Burry Port
TEL: 01554 833 913

14 **WWT LLANELLI**
Bird centre & aviary
Llwynhendy, Llanelli
TEL: 01554 741 087

15 **GLYNN VIVIAN ART GALLERY & MUSEUM**
Museum
Alexandra Road, Swansea
TEL: 01792 655 006

16 **WEOBLEY CASTLE**
Castle
Llanrhidian, Swansea
TEL: 01792 390 012

17 **SINGLETON BOTANIC GARDENS**
Garden
Singleton Park, Swansea
TEL: 01792 302 420

18 **EGYPT CENTRE**
Museum
University Campus, Oystermouth Road, Swansea
TEL: 01792 295 960

19 **TALIESIN ARTS CENTRE**
Craft centre
University of Wales, Singleton Park, Swansea
TEL: 01792 296 883

20 **RHOSSILI VISITOR CENTRE**
Visitor centre
Coastguard Cottages, Rhossili, Gower
TEL: 01792 390 707

21 **NATIONAL BOTANIC GARDEN OF WALES**
Garden
Middleton Hall, Llanarthne
TEL: 01558 668 768

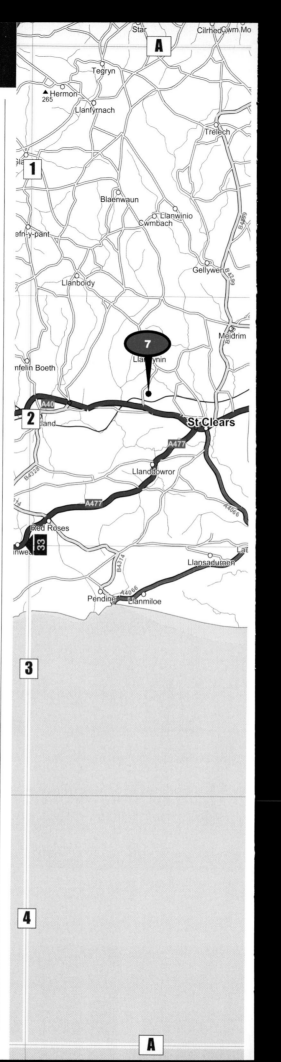

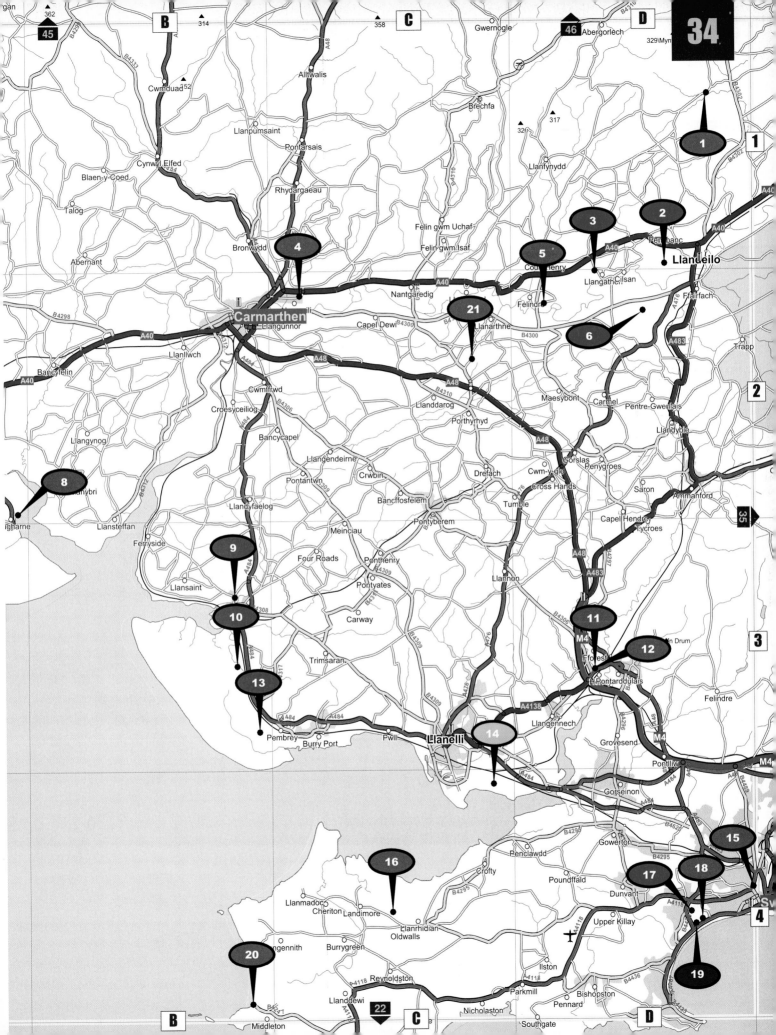

1 BRECKNOCK MUSEUM
Museum
Captain's Walk, Brecon
TEL: 01874 624 121

2 SOUTH WALES BORDERERS MUSEUM
Museum
The Barracks, Brecon
TEL: 01874 613 310

3 CARREG CENNEN CASTLE & FARM
Castle
Trapp, Llandeilo
TEL: 01558 822 291

4 DAN-YR-OGOF SHOWCAVES
Cave
Brecon Road, Penycae, Swansea
TEL: 01639 730 284

5 BRECON BEACONS NATIONAL PARK
Country park
Brecon Road, Penycae, Swansea
TEL: 01639 730 395

6 GARWNANT VISITOR CENTRE
Forest Visitor Centres
Cwm Taf Merthyr Tydfill, Coed Taf Fawr
TEL: 01685 723 060

7 BRECON MOUNTAIN RAILWAY
Railway
Pant Station, Merthyr Tydfil
TEL: 01685 722 988

8 CYFARTHFA CASTLE MUSEUM & ART GALLERY
Museum
Cyfarthfa Park, Merthyr Tydfil
TEL: 01685 723 112

9 JOSEPH PARRY'S COTTAGE
Historic building
Chapel Row, George Town, Merthyr Tydfil
TEL: 01685 721 858

10 MERTHYR TYDFIL HERITAGE TRUST
Heritage centre
Ynysfach Road, Merthyr Tydfil
TEL: 01685 721 858

11 PENSCYNOR WILDLIFE PARK
Wildlife park
Penscynor Cilfrew, Neath
TEL: 01639 642 189

12 ABERDULAIS FALLS
Waterfall
Aberdulais, Neath
TEL: 01639 636 674

13 NEATH ABBEY
Abbey
Monastery Road, Neath
TEL: 01792 812 387

14 LLANCAIACH FAWR MANOR
Historic house
Nelson, Treharris
TEL: 01443 412 248

15 SOUTH WALES MINERS MUSEUM
Museum
Percy Road, Cynonville, Port Talbot
TEL: 01639 850 564

16 AFAN FOREST PARK & COUNTRYSIDE CENTRE
Forest Visitor Centres
Cynonville, Port Talbot
TEL: 01639 850 564

17 PLANTASIA
Garden
Parc Towe, Swansea
TEL: 01792 474 555

18 DYLAN THOMAS CENTRE
Museum
Somerset Place, Swansea
TEL: 01792 463 980

19 SWANSEA MUSEUM
Museum
Victoria Road, Maritime Quarter, Swansea
TEL: 01792 653 763

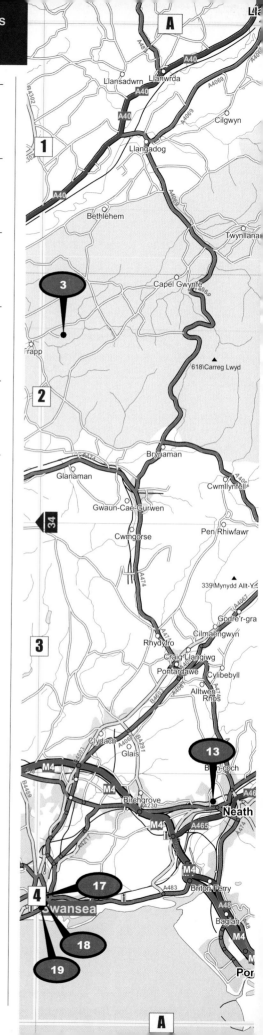

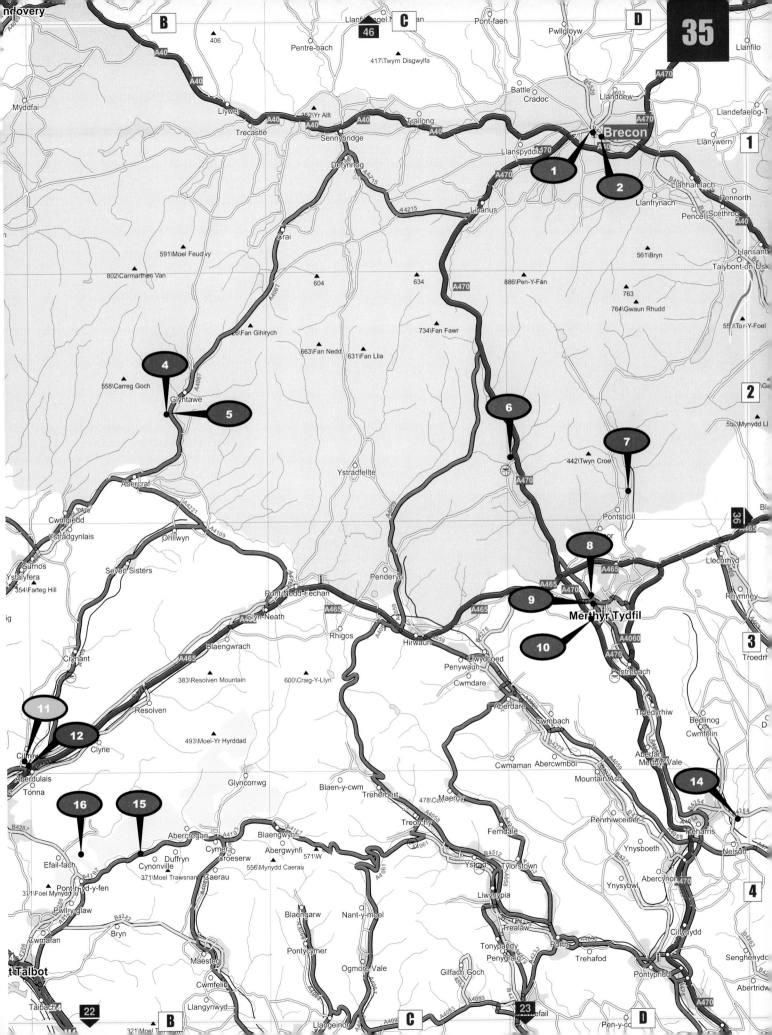

● ANIMAL ATTRACTIONS
● HERITAGE & CULTURE
○ INDOOR ACTIVITIES
● OUTDOOR ATTRACTIONS
● OUTDOOR ACTIVITIES
● WATER ACTIVITIES

1 LONGTOWN CASTLE
Castle
Abbey Dore, Hereford
TEL: 01604 730 320

2 LLANTHONY PRIORY
Priory
Llanthony, Abergavenny
TEL: 02920 826 185

3 GROSMONT CASTLE
Castle
Grosmont, Wales
TEL: 01981 240 301

4 TRETOWER COURT
Garden
Tretower, Crickhowell
TEL: 01874 730 279

5 SKENFRITH CASTLE
Castle
Abergavenny
TEL: 01874 625 515

6 WHITE CASTLE
Castle
Whitecastle, Abergavenny
TEL: 01600 780 380

7 HEN GWRT
Roman site
Abergavenny
TEL: 02920 826 185

8 ABERGAVENNY MUSEUM & CASTLE
Castle
Castle Street, Abergavenny
TEL: 01873 854 282

9 BIG PIT MINING MUSEUM
Museum
Blaenafon
TEL: 01495 790 311

10 RAGLAN CASTLE
Castle
Raglan
TEL: 01291 690 228

11 VALLEY INHERITANCE MUSEUM
Museum
Park Buildings, Park Road, Pontypool
TEL: 01495 752 036

12 GWENT RURAL LIFE MUSEUM
Museum
The Malt Barn, New Market Street, Usk
TEL: 01291 673 777

13 GREENMEADOW COMMUNITY FARM
Farm
Greenforge Way, Cwmbran
TEL: 01633 862 202

14 GELLIGROES MILL
Historic building
Pontllanfraith, Blackwood
TEL: 01495 222 322

15 BOATING LAKE
Boat hire
Llanfrechfa Way, Cwmbran
TEL: 01633 867 642

16 PENHOW CASTLE
Castle
Penhow, Newport
TEL: 01633 400 800

17 ROMAN LEGIONARY MUSEUM
Museum
High Street, Caerleon, Newport
TEL: 01633 423 134

18 CAERLEON FORTRESS BATHS AMPHITHEATRE AND BARRACKS
Roman site
High Street, Caerleon, Newport
TEL: 02920 826 185

Enjoying the sunshine

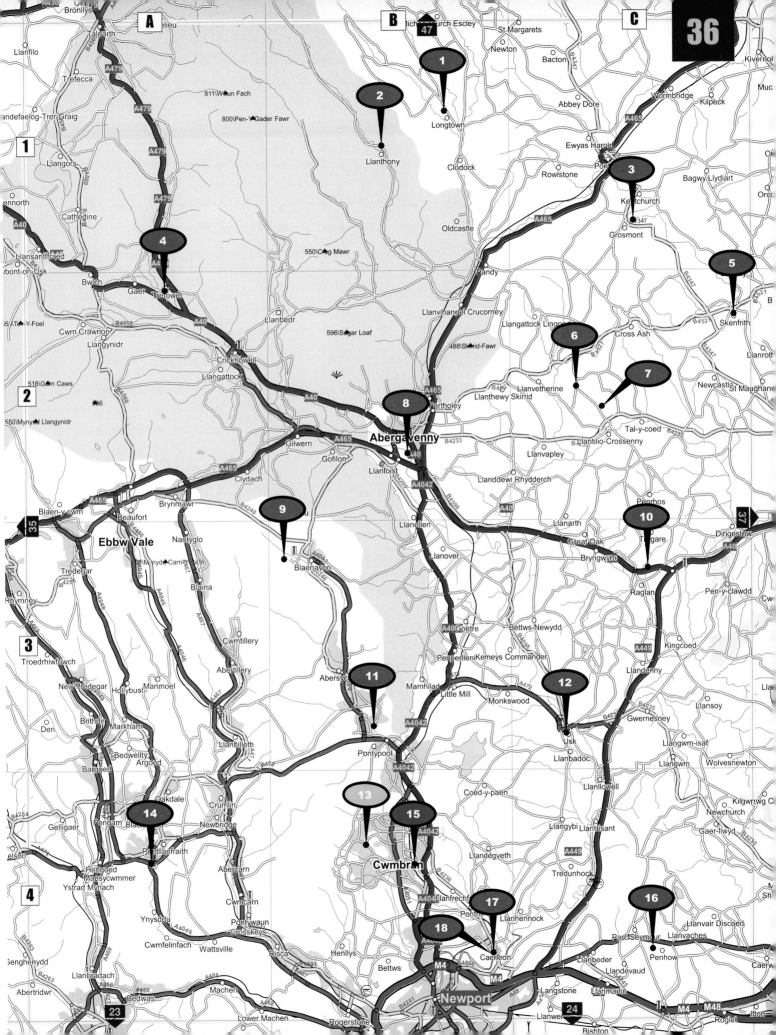

GLOUCS · HEREFORD · S WALES

1 BROCKHAMPTON ESTATE
Country park
Bringsty
TEL: 01885 482 077

2 SHAMBLES
Museum
Church Street, Newent
TEL: 01531 822 144

3 NATIONAL BIRDS OF PREY CENTRE
Bird centre & aviary
Great Boulsdon, Newent
TEL: 01531 820 286

4 MARKET HOUSE HERITAGE CENTRE
Heritage centre
Market Place, Ross-on-Wye
TEL: 01432 260 675

5 GOODRICH CASTLE
Castle
Goodrich, Ross-on-Wye
TEL: 01600 890 538

6 AMAZING HEDGE PUZZLE
Garden
Simonds Yat West, Ross-on-Wye
TEL: 01600 890 360

7 SPLENDOURS OF THE ORIENT
Garden
Jubilee Park, Symonds Yat West
TEL: 01600 890 668

8 WESTBURY COURT GARDEN NT
Garden
Westbury Court, Westbury-on-Severn
TEL: 01452 760 461

9 LITTLE DEAN HALL
Archaeological site
Newnham Road, Littledean, Cinderford
TEL: 01594 824 213

10 NELSON MUSEUM
Museum
Priory Street, Monmouth
TEL: 01600 713 519

11 KYMIN NT
Historic building
Monmouth
TEL: 01874 625 515

12 CASTLE & REGIMENTAL MUSEUM
Museum
The Castle, Monmouth
TEL: 01600 772 175

13 HARDWICKE COURT
Historic house
Bristol Road, Hardwicke, Gloucester
TEL: 01452 720 212

14 ST AUGUSTINES' FARM
Farm
Arlingham, Gloucester
TEL: 01452 740 277

15 DEAN HERITAGE CENTRE
Heritage centre
Camp Mill, Soudley, Cinderford
TEL: 01594 822 170

16 PUZZLE WOOD
Country park
Forest of Dean
TEL: 01594 833 187

17 CLEARWELL CAVES ANCIENT IRON MINES
Factory tour
Royal Forest of Dean, Coleford
TEL: 01594 832 535

18 FRAMPTON MANOR
Historic house
Frampton-on-Severn, Gloucester
TEL: 01452 740 698

19 ST BRIAVELS CASTLE
Castle
St Briavels
TEL: 01604 730 320

20 WWT SLIMBRIDGE
Wildlife park
Slimbridge, Gloucester
TEL: 01453 890 333

21 DEAN FOREST RAILWAY
Railway
Norchard Centre, Forest Road, Lydney
TEL: 01594 843 423

22 WOODCHESTER MANSION
Historic building
Woodchester Park, Nympsfield, Stonehouse
TEL: 01453 750 455

23 TINTERN ABBEY
Abbey
Tintern, Chepstow
TEL: 01291 689 251

24 CATTLE COUNTRY ADVENTURE PARK
Adventure & activity centre
Berkeley Heath
TEL: 01453 810 510

25 JENNER MUSEUM
Museum
Church Lane, High Street, Berkeley
TEL: 01453 810 631

26 BERKELEY CASTLE
Castle
Berkeley
TEL: 01453 810 332

27 OWLPEN MANOR
Historic house
Owlpen, Dursley
TEL: 01453 860 261

28 HUNTS COURT
Garden
North Nibley, Dursley
TEL: 01453 547 440

29 OLDBURY POWER STATION
Factory tour
Oldbury-on-Severn, Bristol
TEL: 01454 893 500

30 CHEPSTOW MUSEUM
Museum
Gwy House, Bridge Street, Chepstow
TEL: 01291 625 981

31 CHEPSTOW CASTLE
Castle
Bridge Street, Chepstow
TEL: 01291 624 065

32 CHEPSTOW RACECOURSE
Racecourse
Chepstow
TEL: 01291 622 260

33 NEWARK PARK
Historic house
Ozleworth, Wotton-under-Edge
TEL: 01453 842 644

34 THORNBURY CASTLE
Castle
Castle Street, Thornbury
TEL: 01454 281 182

35 CAERWENT ROMAN TOWN
Roman site
Caerwent, Newport
TEL: 02920 826 185

36 CALDICOT CASTLE & COUNTRY PARK
Castle
Church Road, Caldicot
TEL: 01291 420 241

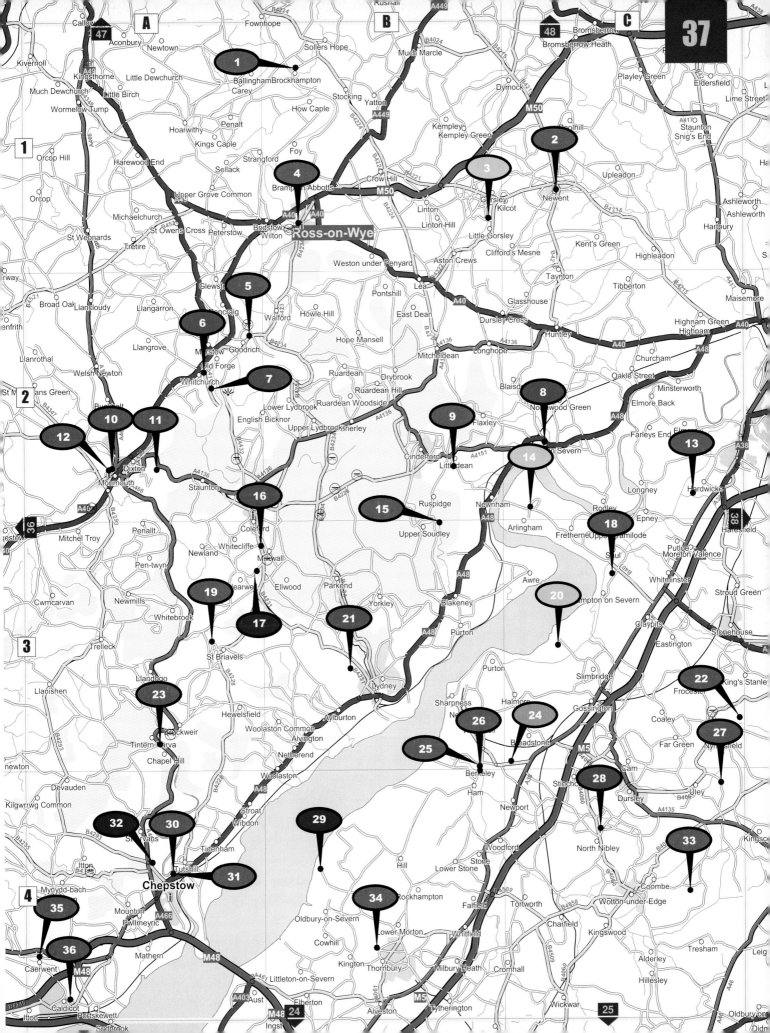

GLOUCESTERSHIRE · WILTSHIRE

● ANIMAL ATTRACTIONS
● HERITAGE & CULTURE
○ INDOOR ACTIVITIES
● OUTDOOR ATTRACTIONS
● OUTDOOR ACTIVITIES
● WATER ACTIVITIES

1 TEWKESBURY ABBEY
Abbey
Church Street, Tewkesbury   Tel: 01684 273 736

2 JOHN MOORE COUNTRYSIDE MUSEUM
Museum
41 Church Street, Tewkesbury   Tel: 01684 297 174

3 GLOUCS WARKS RAILWAY
Railway
The Railway Station, Toddington, Winchcombe
Tel: 01242 621 405

4 HAILES ABBEY
Abbey
Winchcombe, Cheltenham   Tel: 01242 602 398

5 ODDA'S CHAPEL EH
Historic building
Deerhurst   Tel: 0117 975 0700

6 WINCHCOMBE FOLK & POLICE MUSEUM
Museum
Old Town Hall, Winchcombe   Tel: 01242 602 925

7 SUDELEY CASTLE & GARDENS
Castle
Winchcombe, Cheltenham   Tel: 01242 602 308

---

8 COTSWOLD FARM PARK
Farm Park
Guiting Power, Stow on the Wold, Cheltenham,
Gloucestershire, GL54 5UG.
Tel: 01451 850 307
Email: info@cotswoldfarmpark.co.uk
Web: www.cotswoldfarmpark.co.uk

*Home to Britain's most comprehensive collection of
rare breeds of farm animals. Fun activities and
demonstrations for all ages, whatever the weather!*
Open: Mar 23-Sep 15; open daily from 10.30-5.
Then weekends until end of Oct & Autumn half
term; 10.30-4.
Entry costs: £4.75, Child: £3, OAPs: £4.25,
Family: £14.50.
Specialities: Picnic area, Photography allowed,
Play area, Audio tour, Farm safari rides.
Facilities: Child area, Gift shop, Pushchair friendly,
Restaurant, Toilets, Wheelchair access.

---

9 ASHLEWORTH TITHE BARN
Historic building
Ashleworth, Gloucester   Tel: 01684 850 051

10 CHELTENHAM HALL OF FAME
Museum
Cheltenham Racecourse, Prestbury Park, Cheltenham
Tel: 01242 513 014

11 PUMP ROOM MUSEUM
Museum
Pittville Park, East Approach Drive, Cheltenham
Tel: 01242 523 852

12 HOLST BIRTHPLACE MUSEUM
Museum
4 Clarence Road, Pittville, Cheltenham
Tel: 01242 524 846

13 NATURE IN ART
Museum
Wallsworth Hall, Twigworth, Gloucester
Tel: 01452 731 422

14 CHELTENHAM ART GALLERY & MUSEUM
Museum
Clarence Street, Cheltenham   Tel: 01242 237 431

15 FOLLY FARM WATERFOWL
Nature centre
Bourton-on-the-Water, Cheltenham Tel: 01451 820 285

16 GLOUCESTER CATHEDRAL
Cathedral
College Green, Gloucester   Tel: 01452 528 095

17 GLOUCESTER FOLK MUSEUM
Museum
99-103 Westgate Street, Gloucester
Tel: 01452 526 467

18 SOLDIERS OF GLOUCS MUSEUM
Museum
Commercial Road, Gloucester Tel: 01452 522 682

19 BEATRIX POTTERS HOUSE OF GLOUCS
Museum
9 College Court, Gloucester   Tel: 01452 422 856

20 NATIONAL WATERWAYS MUSEUM
Museum
Llanthony Warehouse, Gloucester Docks, Gloucester
Tel: 01452 318 054

21 GLOUCS CITY MUSEUM & ART GALLERY
Museum
City East Gate, Broomswick Road, Gloucester
Tel: 01452 524 131

**22 ROBERT OPIE COLLECTION
MUSEUM OF ADVERTISING & PACKAGING**
Museum
Albert Warehouse, The Docks, Gloucester
Tel: 01452 302 309

23 CRICKLEY HILL COUNTRY PARK
Country park
Crickley Hill Gloucester   Tel: 01452 863 170

**24 COTSWOLD HERITAGE CENTRE-
MUSEUM OF RURAL LIFE**
Museum
Fosseway, Northleach   Tel: 01242 522 878

25 COTSWOLD HERITAGE CENTRE
Heritage centre
Fosseway, Northleach, Cheltenham
Tel: 01451 860 715

26 GREAT WITCOMBE ROMAN VILLA
Roman site
Great Witcombe   Tel: 01179 750 700

**27 KEITH HARDING'S WORLD OF
MECHANICAL MUSIC**
Museum
Oak House, High Street, Northleach
Tel: 01451 860 181

28 PRINKNASH ABBEY
Abbey
Cranham, Gloucester   Tel: 01452 812 066

29 CHEDWORTH ROMAN VILLA
Roman site
Yanworth, Cheltenham   Tel: 01242 890 256

30 WOODCHESTER PARK NT
Country park
Old Ebworth Centre, Ebworth Estate, Stroud
Tel: 01452 814 213

31 PAINSWICK ROCOCO GARDEN
Garden
Painswick House, Painswick Tel: 01452 813 204

32 LITTLE FLEECE BOOKSHOP
Historic house
Bisley St, Painswick, Stroud   Tel: 01452 812 103

33 BARNSLEY HOUSE GARDEN
Garden
Barnsley House, Barnsley, Cirencester
Tel: 01285 740 561

34 CORINIUM MUSEUM
Museum
Park Street, Cirencester   Tel: 01285 655 611

35 CIRENCESTER LOCK-UP
Museum
Trinity Road, Cirencester   Tel: 01285 655 611

36 CIRENCESTER AMPHITHEATRE
Roman site
Cirencester   Tel: Not available

37 RODMARTON MANOR
Historic house
Rodmarton, Cirencester   Tel: 01285 841 253

38 CHAVENAGE
Historic house
Chavenage, Tetbury   Tel: 01666 502 329

**39 WESTONBIRT ARBORETUM &
PLANT CENTRE**
Garden
Westonbirt Arboretum, Westonbirt, Tetbury
Tel: 01666 880 544

40 HODGES BARN GARDENS
Garden
Shipton Moyne, Tetbury   Tel: 01666 880 202

41 ABBEY HOUSE GARDENS
Garden
Market Cross, Malmesbury   Tel: 01666 822 212

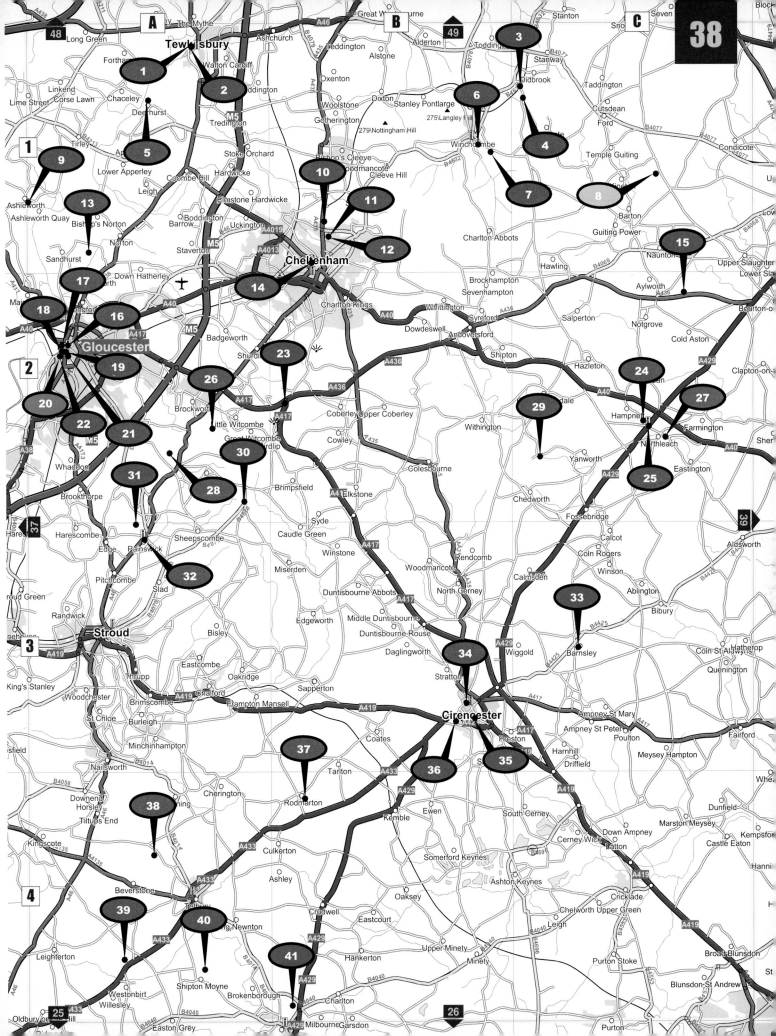

1 WATERFOWL SANCTUARY & CHILDREN'S FARM
Farm
Wiggington Heath, Norton, Banbury
TEL: 01608 730 252

2 COTSWOLD FALCONRY CENTRE
Bird centre & aviary
Batsford Park, Moreton-in-Marsh
TEL: 01386 701 043

3 DEDDINGTON CASTLE
Castle
Deddington
TEL: Not available

4 CHASTLETON HOUSE
Historic house
Chastleton, Moreton-in-Marsh
TEL: 01608 674 355

5 OXFORDSHIRE NARROWBOATS
Boat hire
Canal Wharf, Station Road, Lower Heyford, Bicester
TEL: 01869 340 348

6 ROUSHAM HOUSE
Historic house
Steeple Aston, Bicester
TEL: 01869 347 110

7 COTSWOLDS MOTOR MUSEUM & TOY COLLECTION
Museum
The Old Mill, Bourton-on-the-Water, Gloucestershire, GL54 2BY.
TEL: 01451 821 255

Full of motoring memorabilia including cars, motorcycles, pedal cars, metal motoring signs and a fabulous toy collection. It is also home to Brum, the little yellow car from the hit BBC childrens TV series!

OPEN: Feb-Nov: open daily.
ENTRY COSTS: £2.50, Child: £1.75.
SPECIALITIES: Photography allowed.
FACILITIES: Gift shop, Wheelchair access.

8 MODEL VILLAGE
Unusual
Old New Inn, Bourton-on-the-Water
TEL: 01451 820 467

9 BIRDLAND
Bird centre & aviary
Rissington Road, Bourton on the Water, Cheltenham
TEL: 01451 820 480

10 OXFORDSHIRE MUSEUM
Museum
Fletcher's House, Park Street, Woodstock
TEL: 01993 811 456

11 BLENHEIM PALACE
Historic house
Woodstock, Oxford
TEL: 01993 811 325

12 NORTH LEIGH ROMAN VILLA
Roman site
North Leigh
TEL: Not available

13 COGGESS FARM MUSEUM
Museum
Church Lane, Coggess, Witney
TEL: Not available

14 GO BANANAS
Adventure & activity centre
34-36 Market Square, Witney
TEL: 01993 779 877

15 COTSWOLD WILDLIFE PARK
Wildlife park
Burford, Oxford, Oxfordshire, OX18 4JW.
TEL: 01993 823 006
WEB: www.cotswoldwildlifepark.co.uk
Wide variety of animals, many endangered. Set in 160 acres of landscaped parkland with beautiful gardens, around a listed Victorian manor. Good facilities for the disabled.
OPEN: Open daily from 10am, last admission 4.30 (Mar-Sep) or 3.30 (Oct-Feb). Closed Christmas Day.
ENTRY COSTS: £7, Child: £4.50, OAPs: £4.50.
SPECIALITIES: Photography allowed, Picnic area, Play area, Rides, Mid-late summer plant displays.
FACILITIES: Wheelchair access, Toilets, Gift shop, Restaurant, Coffee shop.

16 STANTON HARCOURT MANOR HOUSE & GARDENS
Historic house
Stanton Harcourt
TEL: 01865 880 117

17 COTSWOLD WOOLEN WEAVERS
Factory tour
Filkins, Lechlade
TEL: 01367 860 491

18 KELMSCOTT MANOR
Historic house
Kelmscott, Lechlade
TEL: 01367 252 486

19 KINGSTON BAGPUIZE HOUSE
Historic house
Kingston Bagpuize, Abingdon
TEL: 01865 820 259

20 BUSCOT PARK
Garden
Faringdon
TEL: 01367 240 786

21 MILLETS FARM CENTRE
Farm
Kingsford Farm, Frilford
TEL: 01865 392 200

22 ABINGDON MUSEUM
Museum
County Hall, Market Place, Abingdon
TEL: 01235 523 703

23 GREAT COXWELL BARN NT
Historic building
Rotherfield Greys, Henley-on-Thames
TEL: 01793 762 209

24 ROVES FARM
Farm
Sevenhampton, Highworth, Swindon
TEL: 01793 763 939

25 ARDINGTON HOUSE
Historic house
Church Street, Ardington, Wantage
TEL: 01235 821 566

26 VALE & DOWNLAND MUSEUM CENTRE
Museum
Church Street, Wantage
TEL: 01235 771 447

Jaguar

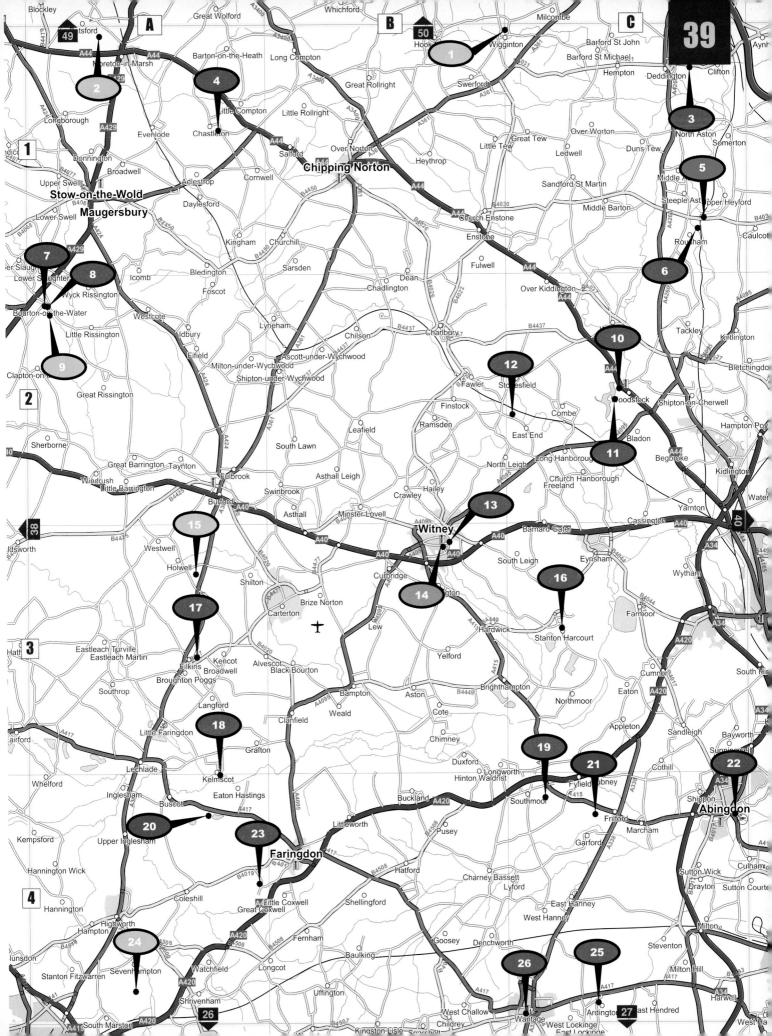

BUCKS · OXFORDSHIRE

- ANIMAL ATTRACTIONS
- HERITAGE & CULTURE
- INDOOR ACTIVITIES
- OUTDOOR ATTRACTIONS
- OUTDOOR ACTIVITIES
- WATER ACTIVITIES

1 AYNHO PARK
Parks
Aynho, Banbury
TEL: 01869 810 636

2 WINSLOW HALL
Historic house
Winslow
TEL: 01296 712 323

3 CLAYDON HOUSE
Historic house
Middle Claydon, Buckingham
TEL: 01296 730 349

4 BUCKINGHAMSHIRE RAILWAY CENTRE
Museum
Quainton Road Station, Quainton, Aylesbury
TEL: 01296 655 450

5 WADDESDON MANOR NT
Garden
Aylesbury
TEL: 01296 651 226

6 BOARSTALL DUCK DECOY
Historic building
Boarstall, Aylesbury
TEL: 01844 237 488

7 OAK FARM RARE BREEDS PARK
Farm
Broughton, Aylesbury
TEL: 01296 415 709

8 BUCKINGHAMSHIRE COUNTY MUSEUM & ROALD DAHL CHILDREN'S GALLERY
Museum
Church Street, Aylesbury
TEL: 01296 331 441

9 NETHER WINCHENDEN HOUSE
Historic house
Aylesbury
TEL: 01844 290 101

10 ST TIGGYWINKLES WILDLIFE CENTRE
Wildlife park
Wildlife Hospital Trust, Aston Road, Haddenham
TEL: 01844 292 640

11 WELLPLACE ZOO
Farm
Ipsden
TEL: 01491 680 473

12 BUCKS GOAT CENTRE
Farm
Layby Farm Stoke, Mandeville
TEL: 01296 612 983

13 PITT RIVERS MUSEUM
Museum
South Parks Road, Oxford
TEL: 01865 270 927

14 OXFORD UNIVERSITY MUSEUM OF NATURAL HISTORY
Museum
Parks Road, Oxford
TEL: 01865 272 950

15 ASHMOLEAN MUSEUM
Museum
Beaumont Street, Oxford
TEL: 01865 278 000

16 MUSEUM OF THE HISTORY OF SCIENCE
Museum
Broad Street, Oxford
TEL: 01865 277 280

17 OXFORD STORY
Museum
6 Broad Street, Oxford
TEL: 01865 790 055

18 WATERPERRY GARDENS
Garden
Wheatley, Oxford
TEL: 01844 339 226

19 TOWN HALL PLATE ROOM
Historic building
St Aldate's, Oxford
TEL: 01865 249 811

20 MUSEUM OF OXFORD
Museum
St Aldate's, Oxford
TEL: 01865 815 559

21 CHRIST CHURCH CATHERDRAL
Cathedral
Oxford
TEL: 01865 276 154

22 OXFORD BOTANIC GARDENS
Garden
Rose Lane, Oxford
TEL: 01865 276 920

23 MUSEUM OF MODERN ART OXFORD
Museum
30 Pembroke Street, Oxford
TEL: 01865 722 733

24 RYCOTE CHAPEL
Historic building
Rycote Park, Milton Common, Thame
TEL: 01844 339 346

25 PRINCES RISBOROUGH MANOR HOUSE
Historic house
Princes Risborough
TEL: 01494 528 051

26 CHINNOR & PRINCES RISBOROUGH RAILWAY
Railway
Chinnor
TEL: 01844 353 535

27 HARCOURT ARBORETUM
Garden
Oxford Lodge, Peacock Gate, Nuneham Courtenay
TEL: 01865 343 501

28 WALLED GARDEN
Garden
2 Castle Road, Shirburn, Watlington
TEL: 01491 612 882

29 WEST WYCOMBE PARK & CAVES NT
Garden
West Wycombe
TEL: 01494 524 411

30 PENDON MUSEUM OF MINIATURE LANDSCAPE & TRANSPORT
Model village
High Street, Long Wittenham, Abingdon
TEL: 01865 407 365

31 DIDCOT RAILWAY CENTRE
Railway
Didcot
TEL: 01235 817 200

32 WALLINGFORD MUSEUM
Museum
Flint House, High Street, Wallingford
TEL: 01491 835 065

33 STONOR PARK
Historic house
Stonor, Henley-on-Thames
TEL: 01491 638 587

34 NUFFIELD PLACE
Historic house
Huntercombe, Henley-on-Thames
TEL: 01491 641 224

Feeding the sheep

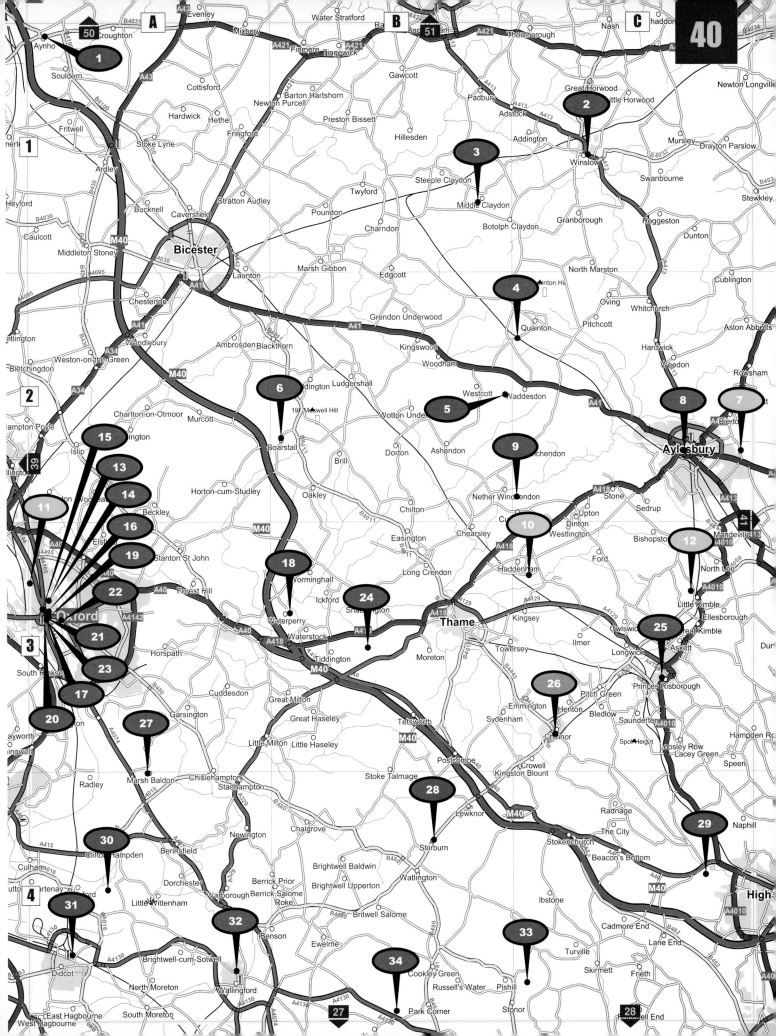

HERTS · BUCKS · MIDDX · BEDS

● ANIMAL ATTRACTIONS   ● OUTDOOR ATTRACTIONS
● HERITAGE & CULTURE   ● OUTDOOR ACTIVITIES
○ INDOOR ACTIVITIES   ● WATER ACTIVITIES

1 WOBURN ABBEY
Abbey
Woburn, Milton Keynes
TEL: 01525 290 666

2 HITCHIN MUSEUM & ART GALLERY
Museum
Paynes Park, Hitchin
TEL: 01462 434 476

3 STOCKGROVE COUNTRY PARK
Country park
Brick Hill Road, Heath and Reach, Leighton Buzzard
TEL: 01525 237 660

4 BEDFORDSHIRE & HERTFORDSHIRE REGIMENT
Museum
Wardown Park, Luton
TEL: 01582 746 722

5 LUTON MUSEUM & ART GALLERY
Museum
Wardown Park, Old Bedford Road, Luton
TEL: 01582 746 739

6 PITSTONE WINDMILL
Mill
Ivinghoe, Tring
TEL: 01582 872 303

7 JOHN DONY FIELD CENTRE
Wildlife park
Hancock Drive, Bushmead, Luton
TEL: 01582 486 983

8 MEAD OPEN FARM
Farm
Stanbridge Road, Billington
TEL: 01525 852 954

9 ASCOTT NT
Historic building
Wing, Leighton Buzzard
TEL: 01296 688 242

10 STOCKWOOD CRAFT MUSEUM & GARDENS
Museum
Stockwood Park, Farley Hill, Luton
TEL: 01582 738 714

11 DUNSTABLE DOWNS
Country park
Dunstable Downs Countryside Centre,
Whipsnade Road, Kensworth
TEL: 01582 608 489

12 WHIPSNADE TREE CATHEDRAL NT
Historic building
Dunstable
TEL: 01582 872 406

13 WHIPSNADE WILDLIFE ANIMAL PARK
Wildlife park
Whipsnade, Dunstable
TEL: 01582 872 171

14 SHAW'S CORNER NT
Historic house
Ayot St Lawrence, Welwyn
TEL: 01438 820 307

15 ASHRIDGE ESTATE NT
Historic house
Ringshall, Berkhamsted
TEL: 01442 851 227

16 WALTER ROTHSCHILD ZOOLOGICAL MUSEUM
Museum
Akeman Street, Tring
TEL: 01422 824 181

17 BERKHAMSTED CASTLE
Castle
Castle Hill, Berkhamsted
TEL: 01442 871 737

18 GORHAMBURY HOUSE
Historic house
Gorhambury, St Albans
TEL: 01727 854 051

19 ROMAN THEATRE OF VERULAMIUM
Roman site
Gorhambury Drive, St Michaels, St Albans
TEL: 01727 835 035

20 MUSEUM OF ST ALBANS
Museum
Hatfield Road, St Albans
TEL: 01727 819 340

21 VERULAMIUM MUSEUM & PARK
Museum
St Michaels Street, St Albans
TEL: 01727 819 339

22 KINGSBURY WATER MILL MUSEUM
Watermill
St Michaels Street, St Albans
TEL: 01727 853 502

23 ST ALBANS CATHEDRAL
Cathedral
Sumpter Yard, Holywell Hill, St Albans
TEL: 01727 860 780

24 ORGAN MUSEUM
Museum
Camp Road, St Albans
TEL: 01727 851 557

25 GARDENS OF THE ROSE
Garden
Royal National Rose Society, Chiswell Green,
St Albans
TEL: 01727 850 461

26 MOSQUITO AIRCRAFT MUSEUM
Museum
Salisbury Hall, London Colney Street, St Albans
TEL: 01727 822 051

27 BOWMANS OPEN FARM
Farm
Coursers Road, St Albans
TEL: 01727 822 106

28 SHENLEY PARK
Country park
Radlett Lane, Radlett
TEL: 01923 852 629

29 CONIFER NURSERY
Garden
Hare Lane Nursery, Little Kingshill, Great Missenden
TEL: 01494 862 086

30 CHESLYN HOUSE
Garden
54 Nascot Wood Road, Watford
TEL: 01923 235 946

31 CHENIES MANOR HOUSE
Historic house
Chenies, Rickmansworth
TEL: 01494 762 888

32 AMERSHAM MUSEUM
Museum
49 High Street, Amersham
TEL: 01494 725 754

33 WATFORD MUSEUM
Museum
194 High Street, Watford
TEL: 01923 232 297

34 ALDENHAM COUNTRY PARK
Country park
Dagger Lane, Elstree, Borehamwood
TEL: 020 8953 9602

35 HUGHENDEN MANOR NT
Garden
High Wycombe
TEL: 01494 755 573

36 BATCHWORTH LOCK CENTRE
Boat trip
99 Church Street, Rickmansworth
TEL: 01923 778 382

37 CHILTERN OPEN AIR MUSEUM
Museum
Newland Park, Gorelands Lane, Chalfont St Giles
TEL: 01494 871 117

38 MILTON'S COTTAGE
Historic house
Deanway, Chalfont St Giles
TEL: 01494 872 213

39 WYCOMBE LOCAL HISTORY & CHAIR MUSEUM
Museum
Castle Hill House, Priory Avenue, High Wycombe
TEL: 01494 421 895

40 BEKONSCOT MODEL VILLAGE
Model village
Warwick Road, Beaconsfield
TEL: 01494 672 919

41 WYCOMBE SUMMIT SKI & SNOWBOARD CENTRE
Ski centre
Abbey Barn Lane, High Wycombe
TEL: 01494 474 711

42 HARROW MUSEUM & HERITAGE CENTRE
Museum
Headstone Manor, Pinner View, Harrow
TEL: 020 8861 2626

43 ODDS FARM PARK RARE BREEDS CENTRE
Farm
Green Common Lane, Wooburn Green High,
Wycombe
TEL: 01628 520 188

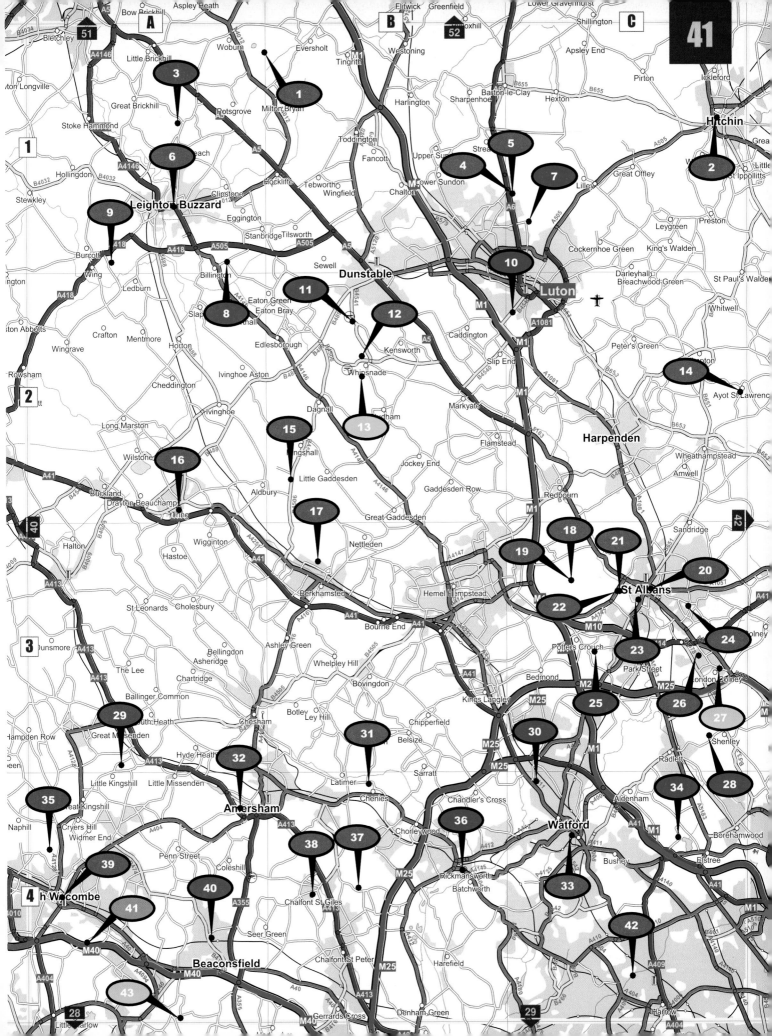

1 FIRST GARDEN CITY HERITAGE MUSEUM
Museum
296 Norton Way, South Letchworth
TEL: 01462 482 710

2 ROSE GARDENS
Garden
Cambridge Road, Hitchin
TEL: 01426 420 402

3 CROMER WINDMILL
Mill
Cromer, Stevenage
TEL: 01279 843 301

4 HOUSE ON THE HILL TOY MUSEUM
Museum
Grove Hill, Stansted
TEL: 01279 813 237

5 MOUNTFITCHET CASTLE & NORMAN VILLAGE
Castle
Grove Hill, Stansted
TEL: 01279 813 237

6 KNEBWORTH HOUSE & COUNTRY PARK
Garden
Knebworth Park, Knebworth
TEL: 01438 813 825

7 RHODES MUSEUM GARDEN
Museum
South Road, Bishop's Stortford
TEL: 01279 651 746

8 FORGE MUSEUM & VICTORIAN COTTAGE GARDEN
Museum
High Street, Much Hadham
TEL: 01279 843 301

9 ADVENTURE ISLAND
Adventure & activity centre
Sawbridgeworth
TEL: 01279 600 907

10 WELWYN ROMAN BATHS
Roman site
Welwyn Village, Welwyn
TEL: 01707 271 362

11 HERTFORD MUSEUM
Museum
19 Bull Plain, Hertford
TEL: 01992 582 686

12 MARK HALL CYCLE MUSEUM & GARDENS
Museum
Muskham Road, Harlow
TEL: 01279 439 680

13 ACTIVITY WORLD
Adventure & activity centre
Hatfield
TEL: 01707 270 789

14 MILL GREEN MUSEUM & MILL
Watermill
Mill Green, Hatfield
TEL: 01707 271 362

15 HATFIELD HOUSE & GARDENS
Historic house
Hatfield House, Hatfield, Hertfordshire, AL9 5NQ.
TEL: 01707 287 010
WEB: www.hatfield-house.co.uk
Celebrated Jacobean house, steeped in Elizabethan and Victorian political history. Standing in its own great park the house is famous for its exquisite furniture, tapestries and paintings.
OPEN: *Mar 30-Sep 30: open daily (house) 12-4. (West garden & park) 11-5.30. (East gardens) Fri only.*
ENTRY COSTS: £7, Child: £3.50. Fridays: all £10.50.
SPECIALITIES: Events held, Guided tours available, Photography allowed, Picnic area, Play area, Rides, Formal organic gardens, Banquets.
FACILITIES: Coffee shop, Credit cards, Dogs allowed, Pushchair friendly, Restaurant, Toilets, Wheelchair access.

16 PARADISE WILDLIFE PARK
Wildlife park
White Stubbs Lane, Broxbourne
TEL: 01992 470 490

17 LEE VALLEY PARK FARMS
Farm
Stubbings Hall Lane, Crooked Mile, Waltham Abbey
TEL: 01992 892 781

18 SQUADRON
Airfield
Hurricane Way, North Weald Airfield, North Weald
TEL: 01992 524 510

19 EPPING FOREST DISTRICT MUSEUM
Museum
39-41 Sun Street, Waltham Abbey
TEL: 01992 716 882

20 CAPEL MANOR
Garden
Bullsmoor Lane, Enfield
TEL: 020 8366 4442

21 LEE VALLEY REGIONAL PARK
Garden
Myddelton House, Bulls Cross, Enfield
TEL: 01992 717 711

22 FORTY HALL MUSEUM
Museum
Forty Hill, Enfield
TEL: 020 8363 8196

23 EPPING FOREST INFORMATION CENTRE
Forest Visitor Centres
Epping Forest Centre, High Beach, Loughton
TEL: 020 8508 0028

24 QUEEN ELIZABETH'S HUNTING LODGE
Historic building
Ranger's Road, Chingford, London
TEL: 020 8529 6681

25 FUN HOUSE
Adventure & activity centre
Edmonton Leisure Centre, Plevna Road, Edmonton
TEL: 020 8807 0712

26 MONKEY BUSINESS
Adventure & activity centre
222 Green Lanes, Palmers Green, London
TEL: 020 8886 7520

27 ARNOS PARK
Garden
Bowes Road, New Southgate, London
TEL: 020 8368 2779

28 HARINGEY MUSEUM & ARCHIVES SERVICE
Museum
Lordship Lane, Tottenham, Haringey
TEL: 020 8808 8772

29 ROYAL AIR FORCE MUSEUM
Museum
Grahame Park Way, Hendon, London
TEL: 020 8205 2266

30 WILLIAM MORRIS GALLERY
Museum
Forest Road, Walthamstow, London
TEL: 020 8527 3782

31 ALEXANDRA PALACE
Historic building
Alexandra Palace Way, Wood Green, London
TEL: 020 8365 2121

32 JEWISH MUSEUM
Museum
80 East End Road, London
TEL: 020 8349 1143

33 COLLEGE FARM
Farm
45 Fitzalan Road, Finchley, London
TEL: 020 8349 0690

34 CHURCH FARMHOUSE MUSEUM
Museum
Greyhound Hill, London
TEL: 020 8203 0130

35 VESTRY HOUSE MUSEUM
Museum
Vestry Road, Walthamstow, London
TEL: 020 8509 1917

36 MARKFIELD BEAM ENGINE & MUSEUM
Museum
Markfield Road, South Tottenham, London
TEL: 020 8800 7061

37 HIGHGATE WOOD
Forest Park
Muswell Hill Road, London
TEL: 020 8444 6129

38 LONDON BUTTERFLY HOUSE
Butterfly farm
Syon Park, Brentford, London
TEL: 020 8560 7272

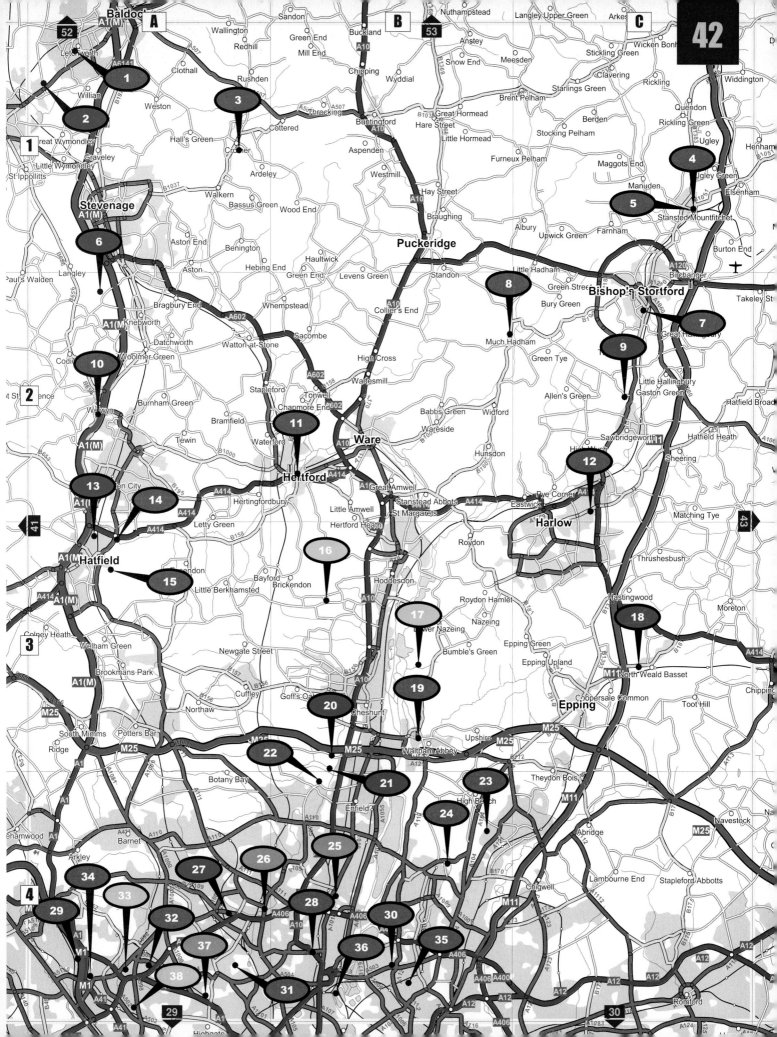

● ANIMAL ATTRACTIONS
● HERITAGE & CULTURE
○ INDOOR ACTIVITIES
● OUTDOOR ATTRACTIONS
● OUTDOOR ACTIVITIES
● WATER ACTIVITIES

1 HILL HALL
Historic house
Epping, Harlow
Tel: 01992 573 810

2 MOLE HALL WILDLIFE PARK
Wildlife park
Mole Hall, Widdington, Saffron Walden
Tel: 01799 540 400

3 GOSFIELD HALL
Historic house
Gosfield, Halstead
Tel: 01787 472 914

4 EASTON LODGE THE FORGOTTEN GARDENS
Garden
Little Easton, Great Dunmow
Tel: 01371 876 979

5 BRAINTREE DISTRICT MUSEUM
Museum
Manor Street, Braintree
Tel: 01376 325 266

6 MARKS HALL ARBORETUM
Garden
Marks Hall, Coggeshall, Colchester
Tel: 01376 563 796

7 WORKING SILK MUSEUM
Museum
New Mills, South Street, Braintree
Tel: 01376 553 393

8 PAYCOCKE'S
Historic house
West Street, Coggeshall, Colchester
Tel: 01376 561 305

9 COGGESHALL GRANGE BARN
Historic house
Grange Hill, Coggeshall, Colchester
Tel: 01376 562 226

10 HATFIELD FOREST NT
Country park
Takeley, Bishop's Stortford
Tel: 01279 870 678

11 MAELDUNE CENTRE
Heritage centre
Plume Building, Market Hill, Maldon
Tel: 01621 851 628

12 MOOT HALL
Historic building
High Street, Maldon
Tel: 01621 857 373

13 CHELMSFORD CATHEDRAL
Cathedral
New Street, Chelmsford
Tel: 01245 294 480

14 CHELMSFORD & ESSEX REGIMENT MUSEUM
Museum
Oaklands Park, Moulsham Street, Chelmsford
Tel: 01245 353 066

15 DANBURY COUNTRY PARK
Country park
Woodhill Road, Chelmsford
Tel: 01245 222 350

16 NEW HALL VINEYARDS
Vineyard
Purleigh
Tel: 01621 828 343

17 HYDE HALL RHS
Garden
Rettendon, Chelmsford
Tel: 01245 400 256

18 ENGLAND'S SECRET NUCLEAR BUNKER
The Unusual
Kelvin Hatch Lane, Brentwood
Tel: 01277 364 883

19 MARSH FARM COUNTRY PARK
Country park
Marsh Farm Road, South Woodhamferrers, Chelmsford
Tel: 01245 321 552

20 VIEW GARDENS
Garden
Chelmsford Road, Rawreth, Wickford
Tel: 01268 761 337

21 OLD MACDONALD'S FARM PARK
Farm
Weald Road, South Weald
Tel: 01277 375 177

22 BARLEYLANDS FARM MUSEUM & VISITORS CENTRE
Museum
Barleylands Road, Billericay
Tel: 01268 290 229

23 UPMINSTER TITHE BARN AGRICULTURAL & FOLK MUSEUM
Museum
Hall Lane, Upminster
Tel: Not available

24 PRIOR'S HALL BARN
Historic building
Widdington
Tel: 01799 522 842

Hatfield Forest, Herts, Map 43-10

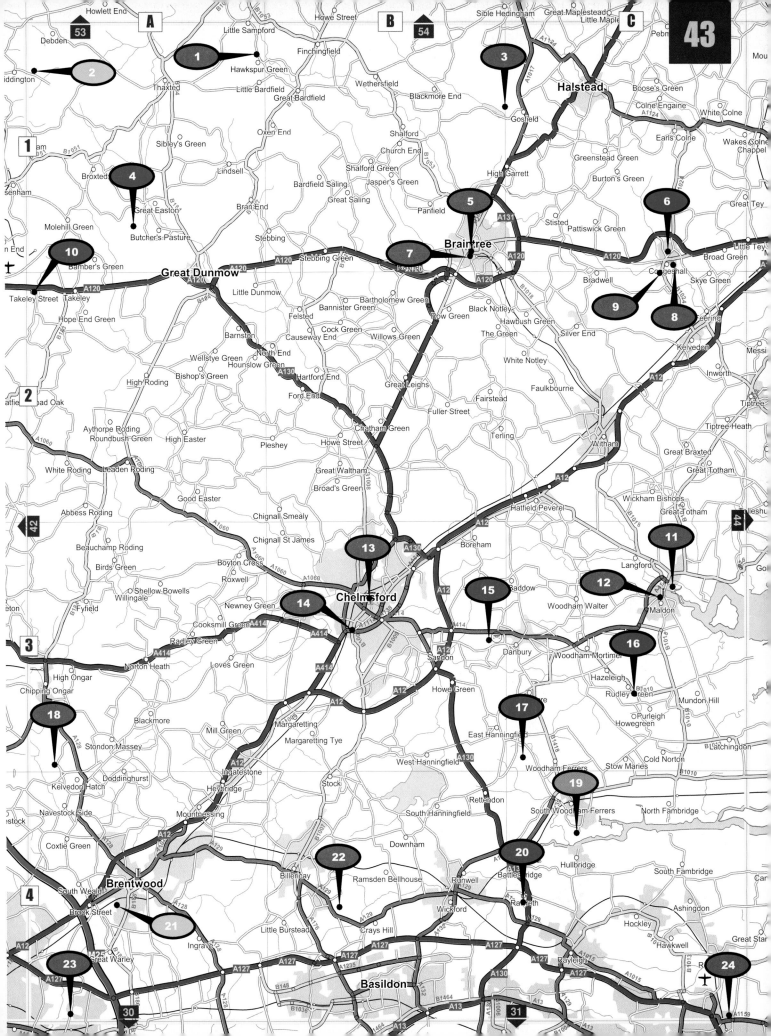

ESSEX

- ● ANIMAL ATTRACTIONS
- ● HERITAGE & CULTURE
- ○ INDOOR ACTIVITIES
- ● OUTDOOR ATTRACTIONS
- ● OUTDOOR ACTIVITIES
- ● WATER ACTIVITIES

1 DEDHAM VALE FAMILY FARM
Farm
Mill Street, Dedham
TEL: 01206 323 111

2 MISTLEY TOWERS
Historic building
Factory Lane, Brantham, Manningtree
TEL: 01206 393 884

3 HARWICH LIFEBOAT MUSEUM
Museum
Wellington Road, Harwich
TEL: 01255 503 429

4 SIR ALFRED MUNNINGS ART MUSEUM
Museum
Castle House, Castle Hill, Dedham
TEL: 01206 322 127

5 HARWICH REDOUBT FORT
Forts
4 Hall Lane, Harwich
TEL: 01255 503 429

6 MISTLEY PLACE PARK ENVIRONMENTAL & ANIMAL RESCUE CENTRE
Wildlife park
New Road, Mistley, Manningtree
TEL: 01206 396 483

7 GNOME MAGIC
Garden
Old Ipswich Road, Colchester
TEL: 01206 231 390

8 HIGH WOODS COUNTRY PARK
Country park
Turner Road, Colchester
TEL: Not available

9 CHILDSPLAY ADVENTURELAND
Adventure & activity centre
Clarendon Way, North Station, Colchester
TEL: 01206 366 566

Seal

10 COLCHESTER CASTLE & MUSEUM
Castle
High Street, Colchester
TEL: 01206 282 931

11 LEXDEN EARTHWORKS & BLUEBOTTLE GROVE
Roman site
Colchester
TEL: 01604 730 320

12 HOLLYTREES MUSEUM
Museum
High Street, Colchester
TEL: 01206 282 937

13 BRIDGE COTTAGE
Historic building
Flatford, East Bergholt, Colchester
TEL: 01206 298 260

14 ROLLERWORLD
Rollerskating
Eastgates, Colchester
TEL: 01206 868 868

15 NATURAL HISTORY MUSEUM
Museum
All Saints Church, High Street, Colchester
TEL: 01206 282 937

16 TYMPERLEYS CLOCK MUSEUM
Museum
Trinity Street, Colchester
TEL: 01206 282 931

17 BETH CHATTO GARDENS
Garden
Clacton Road, Elmstead Market, Colchester
TEL: 01206 822 007

18 BOURNE MILL
Watermill
Bourne Road, Colchester
TEL: 01206 572 422

19 COLCHESTER ZOO
Zoo
Maldon Road, Stanway, Colchester
TEL: 01206 331 292

20 ABBERTON RESERVOIR VISITOR CENTRE
Visitor centre
Church Road, Layer de la Haye
TEL: 01206 738 172

21 LAYER MARNEY TOWER
Historic building
Layer Marney, Colchester
TEL: 01206 330 784

22 CUDMORE GROVE COUNTRY PARK
Country park
Bromans Lane, East Mersea, Colchester
TEL: 01206 383 868

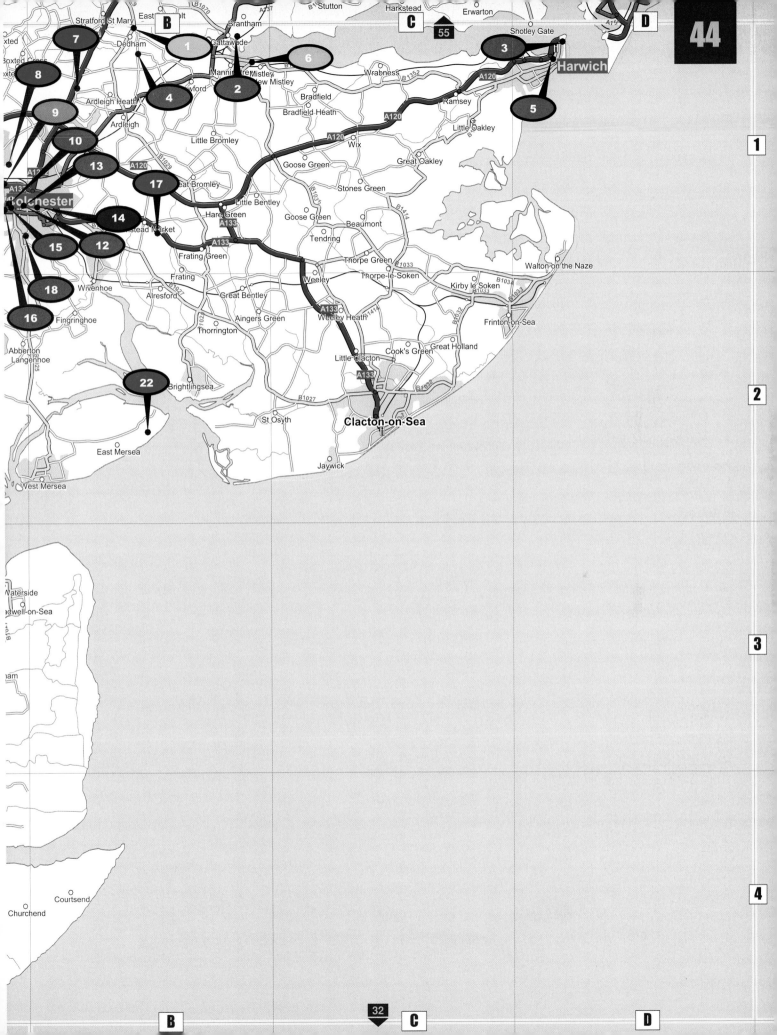

1 ABERAERON CRAFT CENTRE
Craft centre
Aberaeron
TEL: 01545 570 075

 2 ABERAERON WILDLIFE & LEISURE PARK
Wildlife park
Aberarth, Aberaeron
TEL: 01545 570 766

 3 LLANERCHAERON
Historic house
Ciliau Aeron, Lampeter
TEL: 01545 570 200

 4 NEW QUAY HERITAGE CENTRE
Heritage centre
Ty Glyn Basement, Glyn Square, New Quay
TEL: 01545 572 142

 5 WALLED GARDEN AT PIGEONSFORD
Garden
Llangranog, Llandysul
TEL: 01239 654 360

 6 FELINWYNT RAINFOREST & BUTTERFLY CENTRE
Butterfly farm
Felinwynt, Cardigan
TEL: 01239 810 882

 7 CARDIGAN ISLAND COASTAL FARM PARK
Farm
Gwbert-On-Sea, Cardigan
TEL: 01239 612 196

 8 CURLEW WEAVERS WOOLLEN MILL
Factory shop
Troedyraur, Rhydlewis, Newcastle Emlyn
TEL: 01239 851 357

 9 CARDIGAN HERITAGE CENTRE
Heritage centre
Castle Street, Teifi Wharf, Cardigan
TEL: 01239 614 404

10 CILGERRAN CASTLE
Castle
Cilgerran
TEL: 01239 615 007

11 ROCK MILLS WOOLLEN & WATER MILL
Watermill
John Morgan & Son, Capel Dewi, Llandysul
TEL: 01559 362 356

12 NATIONAL CORACLE CENTRE
Visitor centre
Cenarth Falls, Newcastle Emlyn
TEL: 01239 710 507

13 TEIFI VALLEY RAILWAY
Railway
Henllan Station, Yard Henllan, Newcastle Emlyn
TEL: 01559 371 077

14 MUSEUM OF THE WELSH WOOLLEN INDUSTRY
Museum
Dre-Fach Felindre, Llandysul
TEL: 01559 370 929

15 CASTELL HENLLYS IRON AGE FORT
Forts
Pant-Glas Meline, Crymych
TEL: 01239 891 319

16 DYFED SHIRE HORSE FARM & ADVENTURE PLAYLAND
Shire Horse Centres
Carnhuan, Eglwyswrw, Cardigan
TEL: 01834 891 640

17 OCEAN LAB
Aquarium
The Parrog, Goodwick
TEL: 01348 874 737

18 PENTRE IFAN BURIAL CHAMBER
Archaeological site
Brynberian, Newport
TEL: 029 2082 6185

19 MANOROWEN WALLED GARDEN
Garden
Manorowen, Fishguard
TEL: 01348 872 168

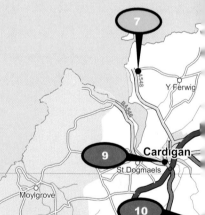

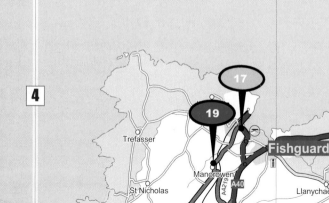

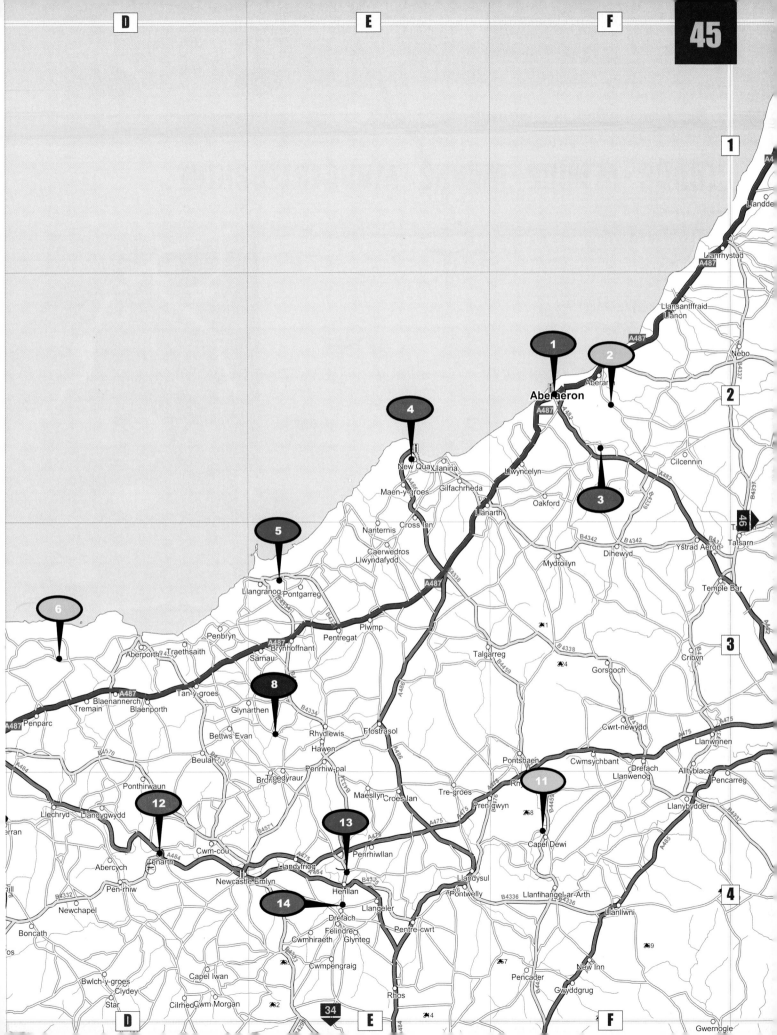

SOUTH WALES

 1 **VALE OF RHEIDOL RAILWAY**
Railway
Park Avenue, Aberystwyth
Tel: 01970 625 819

2 **RHEIDOL HYDRO ELECTRIC POWER STATION AND VISITOR CENTRE**
Factory tour
Cwm Rheidol, Aberystwyth
Tel: 01970 880 667

 3 **FANTASY FARM PARK**
Farm
Hafod Peris, Llanrhystud, Aberystwyth
Tel: 01974 272 285

 4 **STRATA FLORIDA ABBEY**
Abbey
Ffair Rhos, Ystrad Meurig
Tel: 01974 831 261

 5 **ELAN VALLEY VISITOR CENTRE**
Visitor centre
Elan Valley, Rhayader, Elan Valley
Tel: 01597 810 880

6 **ANIMAL RANCH & TROPICAL BUTTERFLY JUNGLE**
Farm
Penuwch, Tregaron
Tel: 01974 821 247

 7 **RADNOSHIRE MUSEUM**
Museum
Temple Street, Llandrindod Wells
Tel: 01597 824 513

 8 **NATIONAL CYCLE EXHIBITION**
Museum
The Automobile Palace, Temple Street, Llandrindod
Tel: 01597 825 531

 9 **WELSH GOLD CENTRE**
Craft centre
Main Square, Tregaron
Tel: 01974 298 415

10 **MODEL AIRCRAFT EXHIBITION**
Museum
Brooklands, Cellan, Lampeter
Tel: 01570 422 604

11 **DOLAUCOTHI GOLD MINES**
Museum
Pumsaint, Llanwrda
Tel: 01558 650 359

Help us help you

mention the
Days Out Atlas
when visiting
anywhere on this page

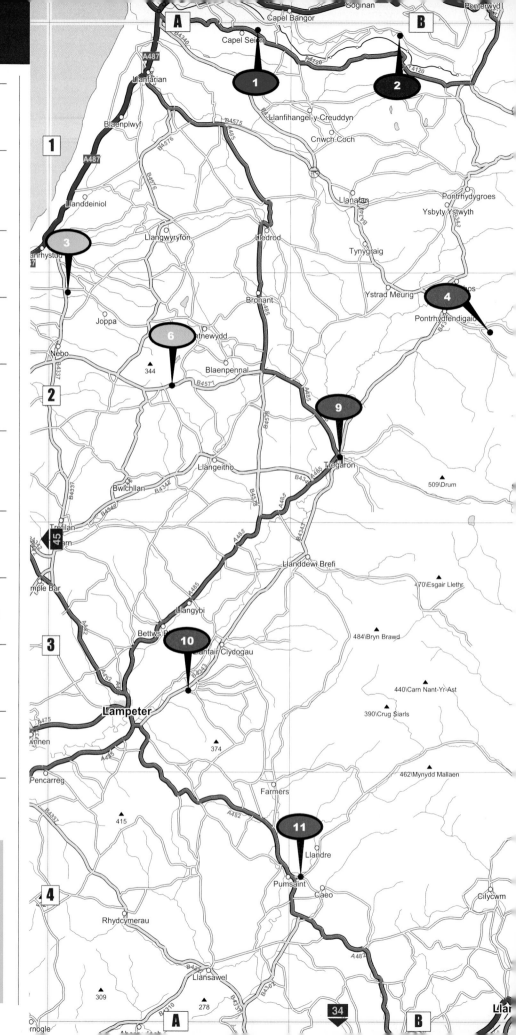

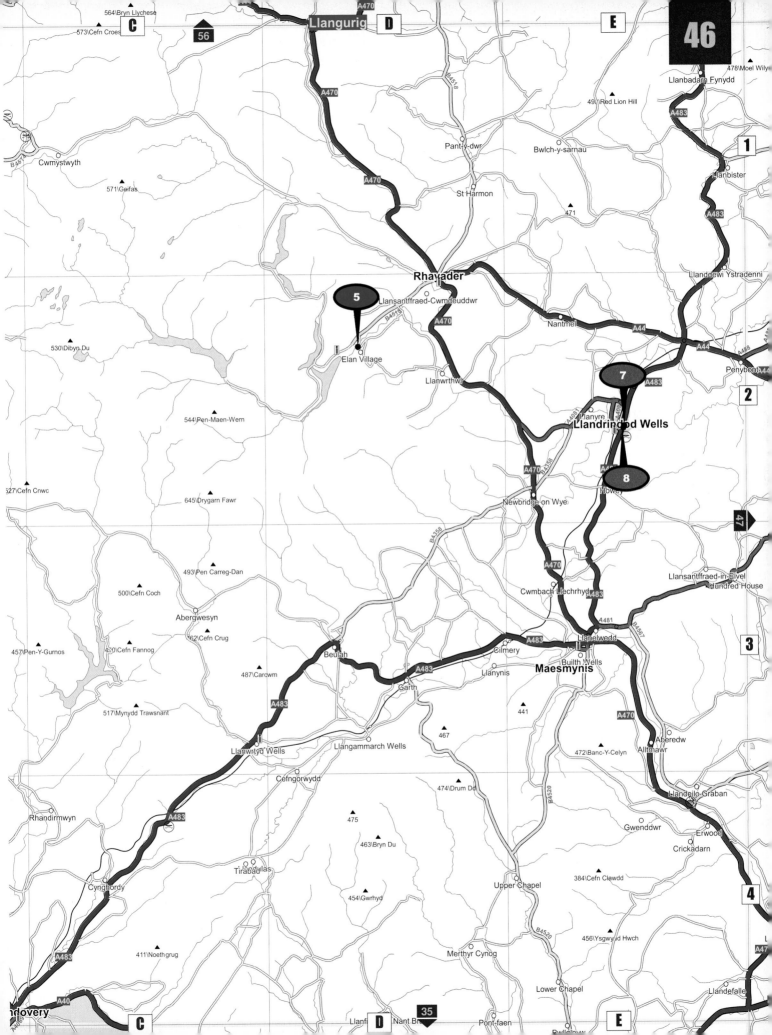

1 LUDLOW MUSEUM
Museum
Castle Street, Ludlow
TEL: 01584 875 384

2 LUDLOW CASTLE
Castle
Castle Square, Ludlow
TEL: 01584 873 355

3 LUDFORD HOUSE
Historic house
Ludford, Ludlow
TEL: 01584 872 542

4 LINGEN NURSERY & GARDENS
Garden
Lingen, Bucknell
TEL: 01544 267 720

5 CROFT CASTLE NT
Historic building
Croft, Leominster
TEL: 01568 780 246

6 STOCKTON BURY GARDENS
Garden
Stockton Bury, Kimbolton, Leominster
TEL: 01568 613 432

7 CWMMAU FARMHOUSE
Historic building
Brilley, Whitney-on-Wye, Hereford
TEL: 01497 831 251

8 QUEEN'S WOOD ARBORETUM
Garden
Dinmore Hill, Leominster
TEL: 01568 798 320

9 DINMORE MANOR
Garden
Dinmore, Hereford
TEL: 01432 830 322

10 ARROW COTTAGE GARDEN
Garden
Weobley
TEL: 01544 318 468

11 KINNERSLEY CASTLE
Castle
Kinnersley
TEL: 01544 327 507

12 MOCCAS COURT
Historic house
Moccas, Hereford
TEL: 01981 500 381

13 WEIR GARDENS
Garden
Swainshill, Hereford
TEL: 01684 850 051

14 CHURCHILL HOUSE MUSEUM & HATTON ART GALLERY
Museum
Venns Lane, Aylestone Hill, Hereford
TEL: 01432 260 693

15 JUNGLE MANIA
Adventure & activity centre
Unit 4, Station Approach, Hereford
TEL: 01432 263 300

16 OLD HOUSE
Museum
High Town, Hereford
TEL: 01432 260 694

17 CIDER MUSEUM & KING OFFA DISTILLERY
Museum
Pomona Place, Whitecross Road, Hereford
TEL: 01432 354 207

18 HEREFORD MUSEUM & ART GALLERY
Museum
Broad Street, Hereford
TEL: 01432 260 692

19 HEREFORD CATHEDRAL
Cathedral
Cathedral Close, Hereford
TEL: 01432 359 880

Horse riding

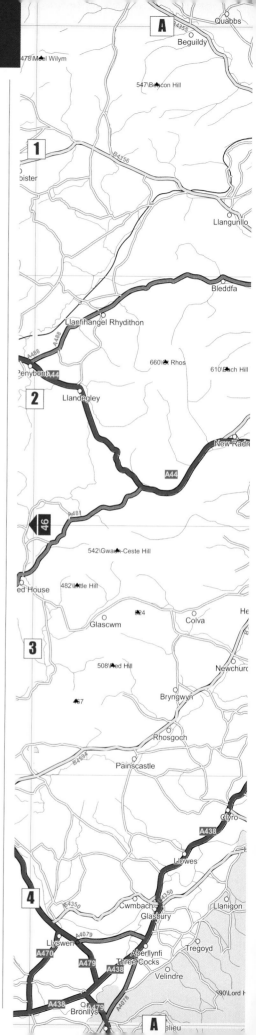

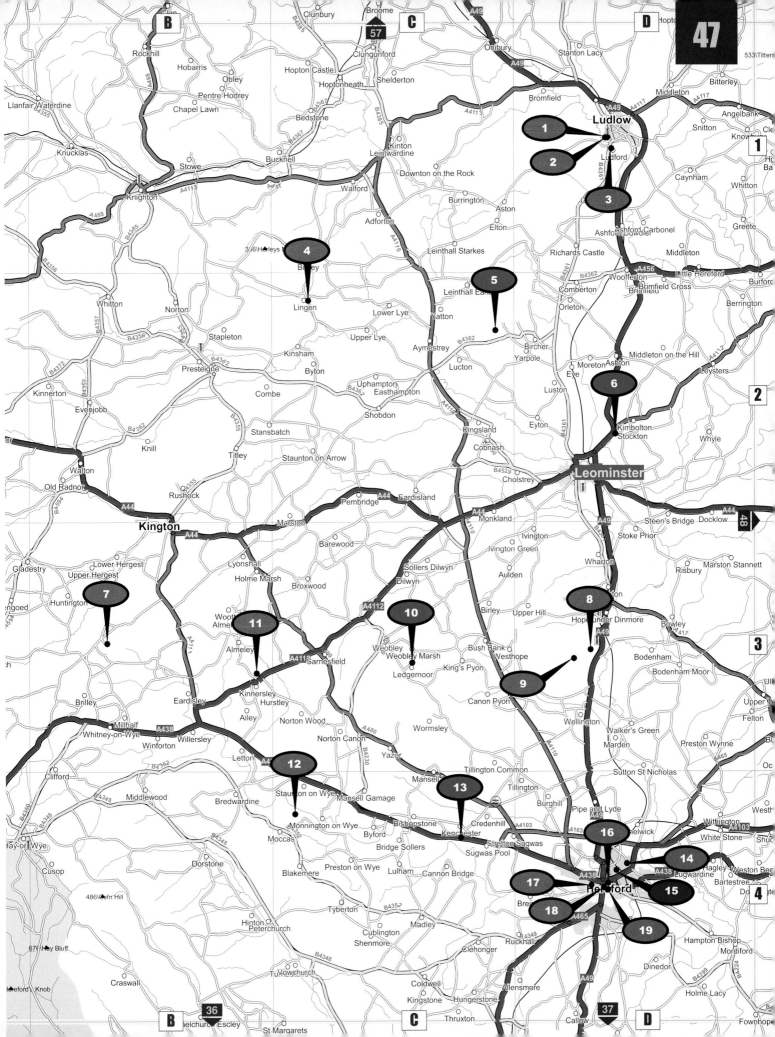

● ANIMAL ATTRACTIONS
● HERITAGE & CULTURE
○ INDOOR ACTIVITIES
● OUTDOOR ATTRACTIONS
● OUTDOOR ACTIVITIES
● WATER ACTIVITIES

1 FALCONRY CENTRE
Bird centre & aviary
Kidderminster Road, South Hagley
TEL: 01562 700 014

2 SEVERN VALLEY RAILWAY
Railway
The Railway Station, Bewdley, Worcestershire, DY12 1BG.
TEL: 01299 403 816
WEB: www.svr.co.uk
A 16-mile journey by steam train along the beautiful Severn Valley. Opportunities for walking and visiting other attractions en-route. A real step back in time.
OPEN: Open daily: Mar 29-Apr 14, May 4-Sep 29, Oct 26-Nov 3 & Dec 26-Jan 1. Sat-Sun: open all year.
ENTRY COSTS: Depends on journey taken.
SPECIALITIES: Events held, Photography allowed, Picnic area, Rides.
FACILITIES: Bookshop, Coffee shop, Credit cards, Dogs allowed, Gift shop, Pushchair friendly, Toilets, Wheelchair access.

3 BEWDLEY MUSEUM
Museum
The Shambles, Load Street, Bewdley
TEL: 01299 403 573

4 STONE HOUSE COTTAGE NURSERIES
Garden
Stone, Kidderminster
TEL: 01562 699 02

5 HARVINGTON HALL
Historic house
Harvington, Kidderminster
TEL: 01562 777 846

6 WYRE FOREST VISITOR CENTRE
Country park
Wyre Forest, Callow Hill, Bewdley
TEL: 01299 266 944

7 HARTLEBURY CASTLE STATE ROOMS
Castle
Stourport Road, Hartlebury, Kidderminster
TEL: 01299 250 410

8 HEREFORD & WORCESTER COUNTY MUSEUM
Museum
Hartlebury Castle, Hartlebury, Kidderminster
TEL: 01299 250 416

9 BURFORD HOUSE GARDENS
Garden
Tenbury Wells, Tenbury Wells
TEL: 01584 810 777

10 LEIGH COURT BARN
Historic building
Witley, Worcester
TEL: 01604 730 320

11 WITLEY COURT EH
Garden
Worcester Road, Great Witley, Worcester
TEL: 01299 896 636

12 EASTGROVE COTTAGE GARDEN NURSERY
Garden
Sankyns Green, Shrawley, Little Witley
TEL: 01299 896 389

13 KYRE PARK GARDENS
Garden
Kyre Park, Tenbury Wells
TEL: 01885 410 247

14 HAWFORD DOVECOTE
Historic building
Hawford
TEL: 01684 850 051

15 WICHENFORD DOVECOTE
Historic building
Wichenford, Worcester
TEL: 01684 850 051

16 LOWER BROCKHAMPTON
Historic house
Brockhampton, Bringsty, Worcester
TEL: 01885 488 099

17 ELGAR'S BIRTHPLACE MUSEUM
Museum
Crown East Lane, Lower Broadheath, Worcester
TEL: 01905 333 224

18 BROMYARD HERITAGE CENTRE
Heritage centre
Rowberry Street, Bromyard
TEL: 01885 482 038

19 MUSEUM OF LOCAL LIFE
Museum
Friar Street, Worcester
TEL: 01905 722 349

20 GREYFRIARS
Historic house
Friar Street, Worcester
TEL: 01905 235 71

21 WORCESTER CATHEDRAL
Cathedral
College Green, Worcester
TEL: 01905 288 54

22 COMMANDERY
Historic building
Sidbury, Worcester
TEL: 01905 355 071

23 ROYAL WORCESTER
Factory tour & shopping
Severn Street, Worcester
TEL: 01905 212 47

24 SPETCHLEY PARK GARDENS
Garden
Spetchley, Worcester
TEL: 01905 345 213

25 BENNETTS FARM PARK
Farm
Lower Wick, Worcester
TEL: 01905 748 102

26 MALVERN MUSEUM
Museum
Abbey Gateway, Abbey Road, Malvern
TEL: 01684 567 811

27 PICTON GARDEN & THE OLD COURT NURSERIES
Garden
Walwyn Road, Colwall, Malvern
TEL: 01684 540 416

28 UPTON HERITAGE CENTRE
Heritage centre
Pepperpot Church Street, Upton-upon-Severn
TEL: 01684 592 679

29 LITTLE MALVERN COURT & GARDENS
Historic house
Little Malvern, Malvern
TEL: 01684 892 988

30 BREDON BARN
Historic building
Bredon, Tewkesbury
TEL: 01684 850 051

31 LEDBURY HERITAGE CENTRE
Heritage centre
The Old Grammar School, Church Lane, Ledbury
TEL: 01531 636 147

32 EASTNOR CASTLE
Castle
Eastnor, Ledbury
TEL: 01531 633 160

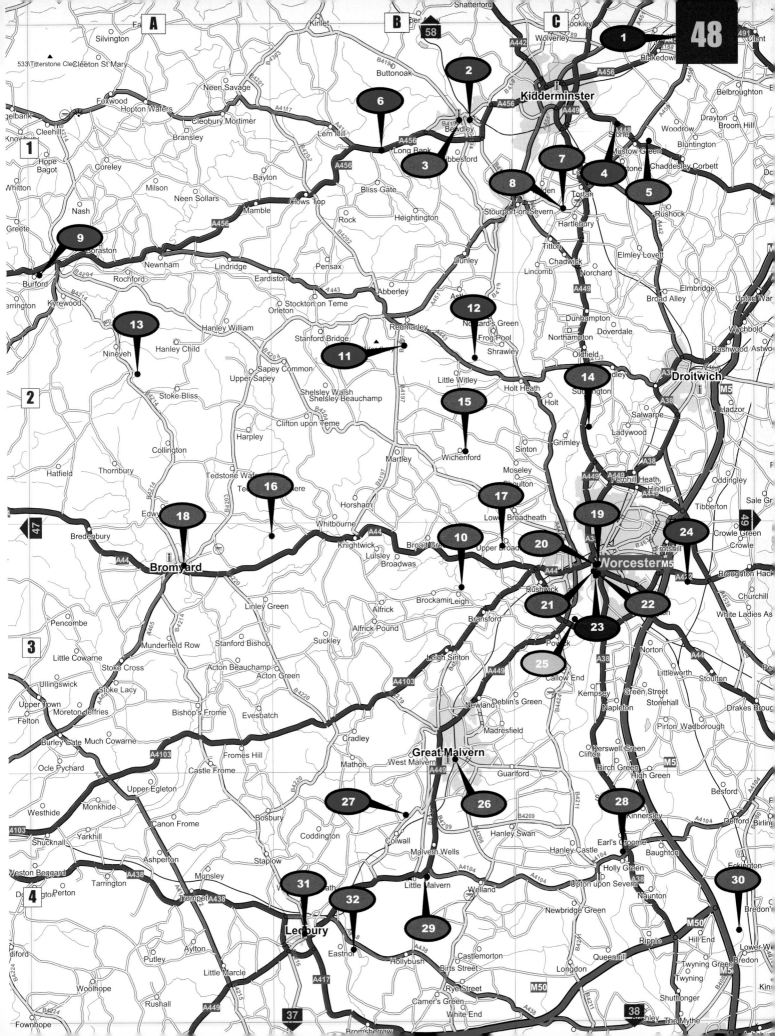

1 WASELEY HILLS COUNTRY PARK
Garden
Gannow Green Lane, Rubery, Rednal
TEL: 01562 710 025

2 PACKWOOD HOUSE NT
Garden
Lapworth, Solihull
TEL: 01564 782 024

3 BADDESLEY CLINTON NT
Garden
Rising Lane, Baddesley Clinton Village, Knowle
TEL: 01564 783 294

4 FORGE MILL NEEDLE MUSEUM & BORDESLEY ABBEY VISITOR CENTRE
Museum
Needle Mill Lane, Riverside, Redditch
TEL: 01527 625 09

5 AVONCROFT MUSEUM OF HISTORIC BUILDINGS
Museum
Redditch Road, Stoke Heath, Bromsgrove
TEL: 01527 831 363

6 HANBURY HALL
Historic house
School Road, Hanbury, Droitwich
TEL: 01527 821 214

7 COUGHTON COURT NT
Garden
Alcester
TEL: 01789 400 777

8 MARY ARDEN'S HOUSE
Garden
Station Road, Wilmcote, Stratford-upon-Avon
TEL: 01789 204 016

9 KINWARTON DOVECOTE
Historic building
Kinwarton, Alcester
TEL: 01684 850 051

10 CHARLECOTE PARK NT
Country park
Charlecote, Wellesbourne, Warwick
TEL: 01789 470 277

11 RAGLEY HALL
Historic house
Alcester
TEL: 01789 762 090

12 SHAKESPEARE BIRTHPLACE
Historic house
Henley Street, Stratford-upon-Avon
TEL: 01789 204 016

13 TEDDY BEAR MUSEUM
Museum
19 Greenhill Street, Stratford-upon-Avon
TEL: 01789 293 160

14 BANCROFT GARDENS
Garden
Waterside, Stratford-upon-Avon
TEL: 01789 260 631

15 ANNE HATHAWAY'S COTTAGE & GARDEN SHOP
Historic building
Cottage Lane, Shottery, Stratford-upon-Avon
TEL: 01789 204 016

16 NASH'S HOUSE & NEW PLACE
Historic building
Chapel Street, Stratford-upon-Avon
TEL: 01789 204 016

17 ROYAL SHAKESPEARE
Theatre
Stratford-upon-Avon
TEL: 01789 296 655

18 STRATFORD-UPON-AVON BUTTERFLY FARM
Butterfly farm
Tramway Walk, Swan's Nest Lane, Stratford-upon-Avon
TEL: 01789 299 288

19 HARVARD HOUSE
Historic house
High Street, Stratford-upon-Avon
TEL: 01789 204 016

20 HALL'S CROFT
Garden
Old Town, Stratford-upon-Avon
TEL: 01789 204 016

21 MIDDLE LITTLETON TITHE BARN
Historic house
Middle Littleton, Evesham
TEL: 01684 850 051

22 VALE WILDLIFE VISITOR CENTRE
Wildlife park
Evesham Country Park, Evesham Road, Evesham
TEL: 01386 443 348

23 FLEECE INN
Historic house
Bretforton, Evesham
TEL: 01386 831 173

24 ALMONRY HERITAGE CENTRE
Museum
Abbey Gate, Evesham
TEL: 01386 446 944

25 HIDCOTE MANOR GARDEN NT
Garden
Hidcote Bartrim, Chipping Camden
TEL: 01386 438 333

26 HONINGTON HALL
Historic house
Honington, Shipston-on-Stour
TEL: 01608 661 434

27 ERNEST WILSON MEMORIAL GARDEN
Garden
High Street, Leas Bourne, Chipping Camden
TEL: 01386 840 884

28 BARN HOUSE
Garden
152 High Street, Broadway
TEL: 01386 858 633

29 BROADWAY TOWER COUNTRY PARK
Country park
Broadway
TEL: 01386 852 390

30 BECKFORD SILK
Factory shop
Beckford, Tewkesbury
TEL: 01386 881 507

31 MILL DENE
Garden
Blockley, Moreton-in-Marsh
TEL: 01386 700 457

32 SNOWSHILL MANOR NT
Historic house
Snowshill, Broadway
TEL: 01386 852 410

33 BATSFORD ARBORETUM
Garden
Batsford Park, Batsford, Moreton-in-Marsh
TEL: 01386 701 441

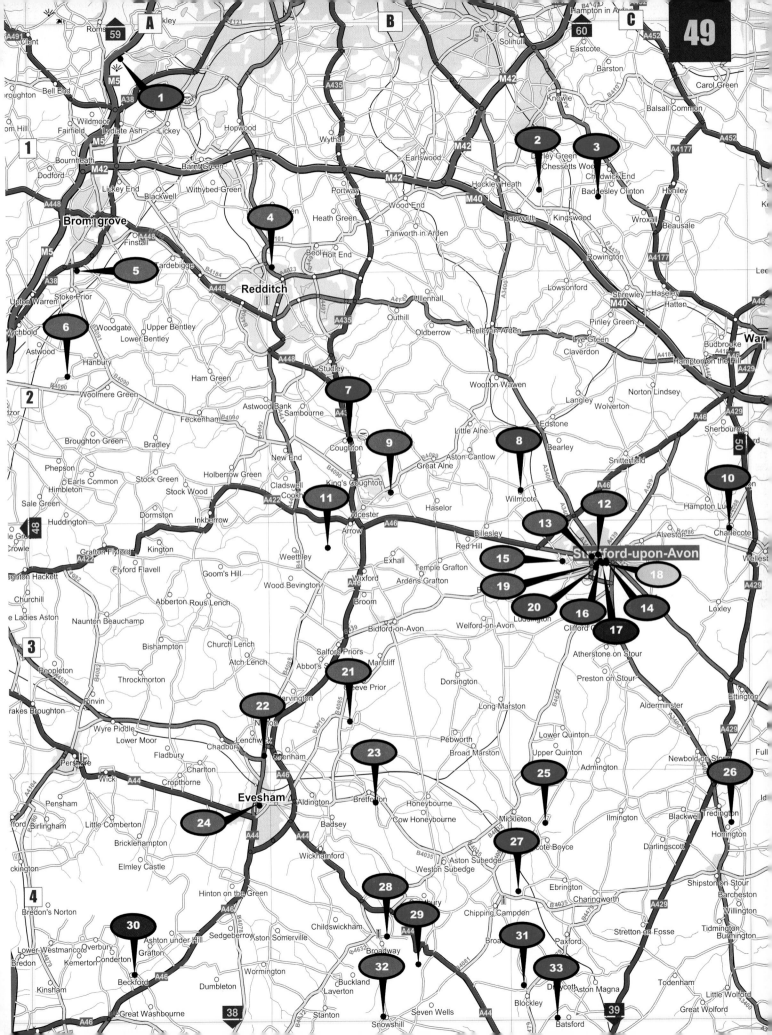

1 STANFORD HALL
Historic house
Lutterworth
TEL: 01788 860 250

2 MUSEUM OF BRITISH ROAD TRANSPORT
Museum
Hales Street, Coventry
TEL: 024 7683 2425

3 COOMBE COUNTRY PARK
Garden
Brinklow Road, Binley, Coventry
TEL: 024 7645 3720

4 COVENTRY CATHEDRAL &
VISITORS CENTRE
Cathedral
7 Priory Row, Coventry
TEL: 024 7622 7597

5 ST MARY'S GUILDHALL
Historic building
Baylby Lane, Coventry
TEL: 024 7683 2381

6 HERBERT ART GALLERY & MUSEUM
Museum
Jordan Well, Coventry
TEL: 024 7683 2381

7 UNIVERSITY OF WARWICK GARDENS
Garden
Gibbet Hill Road, Coventry
TEL: 024 7652 3523

8 LUNT ROMAN FORT
Archaeological site
Coventry Road, Baginton, Coventry
TEL: 024 7683 2565

9 JAMES GILBERT RUGBY FOOTBALL
MUSEUM
Museum
St Matthews Street, Rugby
TEL: 01788 333 888

10 MIDLAND AIR MUSEUM
Museum
Coventry Airport, Coventry
TEL: 024 7630 1033

11 RYTON ORGANIC GARDENS
Garden
Ryton on Dunsmore, Coventry
TEL: 024 7630 3517

12 KENILWORTH CASTLE
Castle
Castle Green, Kenilworth
TEL: 01926 852 078

13 STONELEIGH GARDEN
Garden
Stoneleigh Abbey, Kenilworth
TEL: 01926 858 585

14 DRAYCOTE WATER COUNTRY PARK
Country park
Kites Hardwick, Rugby
TEL: 01827 872 660

15 JEPHSON GARDENS
Garden
Leamington Spa
TEL: 01926 450 000

16 WARWICK CASTLE
Castle
Castle Hill, Warwick
TEL: 01926 406 600

17 WARWICK DOLL MUSEUM
Museum
Oken's House, Castle Street, Warwick
TEL: 01926 495 546

18 WARWICKSHIRE YEOMANRY &
TOWN MUSEUM
Museum
The Court House Vaults, Jury Street, Warwick
TEL: 01926 492 212

19 LORD LEYCESTER HOSPITAL
Historic building
High Street, Warwick
TEL: 01926 491 422

20 MASTER'S GARDEN
Garden
Lord Leycester Hospital, 60 High Street, Warwick
TEL: 01926 491 422

21 WHILTON MILL
Historic building
Whilton Locks, Daventry
TEL: 01327 843 822

22 CHURCH LEYES FARM
Farm
Hollow Way, Napton on the Hill, Southam
TEL: 01926 812 143

23 ASHORNE HALL NICKLELODEON
Museum
Ashorne Hill, Warwick
TEL: 01926 651 444

24 HERITAGE MOTOR CENTRE
Museum
Banbury Road, Gaydon
TEL: 01926 641 188

25 WELLESBOURNE WATERMILL
Watermill
Kineton Road, Wellesbourne, Warwick
TEL: 01789 470 237

26 BURTON DASSETT HILLS COUNTRY PARK
Country park
Northend, Leamington Spa
TEL: 01827 872 660

27 CANONS ASHBY HOUSE NT
Garden
Canons Ashby, Daventry
TEL: 01327 860 044

28 NATIONAL HERB CENTRE
Garden
Banbury Road, Warmington
TEL: 01295 690 999

29 SULGRAVE MANOR
Historic house
Manor Road, Sulgrave, Banbury
TEL: 01295 760 205

30 UPTON HOUSE NT
Garden
Banbury
TEL: 01295 670 266

31 BROOK COTTAGE
Garden
Well Lane, Alkerton, Banbury
TEL: 01295 670 303

32 WROXTON ABBEY
Garden
Wroxton, Banbury
TEL: 01295 730 551

33 BANBURY MUSEUM
Museum
8 Horse Fair, Banbury
TEL: 01295 259 855

34 FUNTASIA
Adventure & activity centre
9-15 Warwick Road, Banbury
TEL: 01295 250 866

35 BROUGHTON CASTLE
Castle
Banbury
TEL: 01295 276 070

Mountain biking

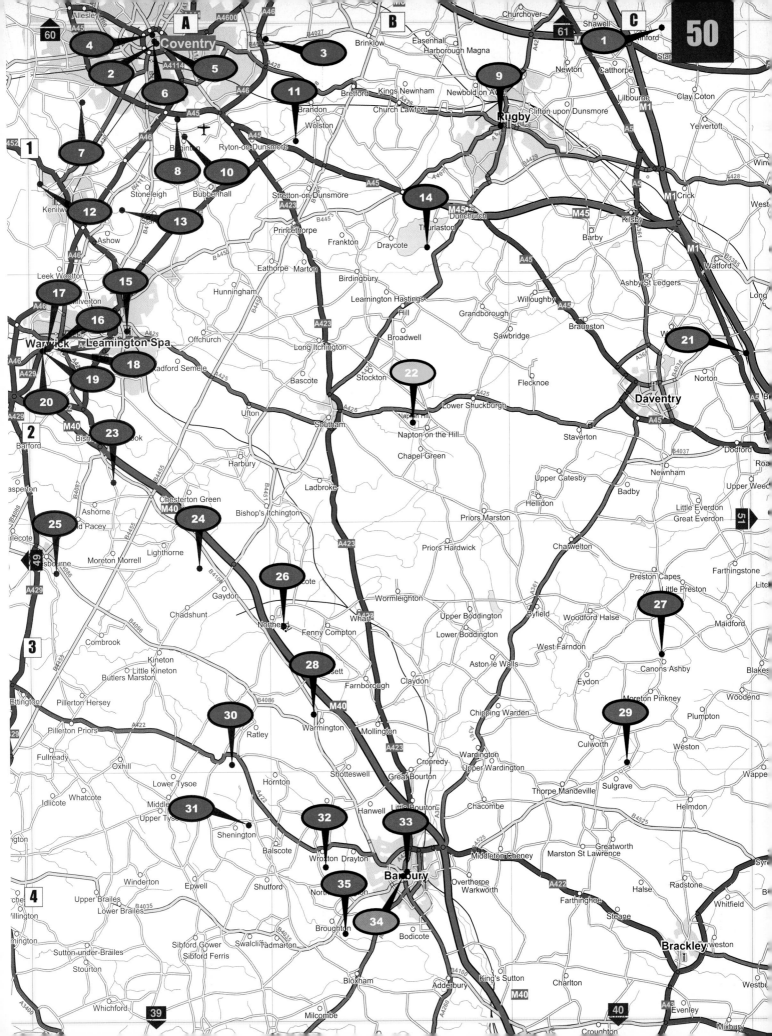

● ANIMAL ATTRACTIONS   ● OUTDOOR ATTRACTIONS
● HERITAGE & CULTURE   ● OUTDOOR ACTIVITIES
○ INDOOR ACTIVITIES   ● WATER ACTIVITIES

1 CARPETBAGGER AVIATION MUSEUM
Museum
Lamport Road, Harrington   TEL: 01604 686 608

2 MANOR HOUSE MUSEUM
Museum
Sheep Street, Kettering   TEL: 01536 534 219

3 KELMARSH HALL
Historic house
Kelmarsh, Northampton   TEL: 01604 686 543

4 WICKSTEED PARK
Theme park
Kettering   TEL: 01536 512 475

5 BRAMPTON VALLEY WAY
Country park
Station House, Railway Terrace, Lamport
TEL: 01604 686 327

6 LAMPORT HALL GARDENS
Garden
Lamport, Northampton   TEL: 01604 686 272

7 COTTESBROOKE HALL & GARDENS
Garden
Cottesbrooke, Northampton   TEL: 01604 505 808

8 MANVELL FARM & ANIMAL SANCTUARY
Farm
Kettering Road, Walgrave   TEL: 01604 781 775

9 COTON MANOR GARDENS
Garden
Guilsborough, Northampton   TEL: 01604 740 219

10 BRIXWORTH COUNTRY PARK
Country park
Northampton Road, Brixworth, Northampton
TEL: 01604 883 920

11 HADDONSTONE SHOW GARDENS
Garden
The Forge House, Church Lane, East Haddon
TEL: 01604 770 711

12 HOLDENBY HOUSE & GARDENS
Garden
Holdenby, Northampton   TEL: 01604 770 074

13 CASTLE THEATRE
Theatre
Castle Way, Wellingborough   TEL: 01933 270 007

14 NORTHAMPTON & LAMPORT RAILWAY
Railway
Pitsford & Brampton Station, Pitsford Rd, Chapel Brampton
TEL: 01604 847 318

15 IRCHESTER COUNTRY PARK
Country park
Gipsy Lane, Little Irchester, Wellingborough
TEL: 01933 276 866

16 ALTHORP HOUSE
Historic house
Althorp, Northampton   TEL: 01604 770 107

17 SYWELL COUNTRY PARK
Country park
Washbrook Lane, Ecton, Northampton
TEL: 01604 810 970

18 BRIGSTOCK COUNTRY PARK
Country park
Lyveden Road, Brigstock, Kettering
TEL: 01536 373 625

19 ABINGTON MUSEUM
Museum
Abington Park, Northampton   TEL: 01604 631 454

20 BILLING AQUADROME
Adventure & activity centre
Crow Lane, Great Billing   TEL: 01604 408 181

21 SANTA POD RACEWAY
Motor racing circuit
Airfield Road, Podington, Wellingborough
TEL: 01234 782 828

22 ROYAL THEATRE
Theatre
Guildhall Road, Northampton   TEL: 01604 632 533

23 DERNGATE
Theatre
19/21 Guildhall Road, Northampton
TEL: 01604 624 811

24 CASTLE ASHBY GARDENS
Garden
Castle Ashby, Northampton   TEL: 01604 696 696

25 DELAPRE ABBEY
Abbey
London Road, Northampton   TEL: 01604 761 074

26 NORTHAMPTON IRONSTONE RAILWAY TRUST
Railway
Hunsbury Hill Country Park, Hunsbury Hill, Northampton
TEL: 0802 420 985

27 HARROLD-ODELL COUNTRY PARK
Country park
Odell Road, Harrold, Bedford   TEL: 01234 720 016

28 OLD DAIRY FARM CENTRE
Farm
Upper Stowe, Weedon, Northampton
TEL: 01327 340 525

29 BLISWORTH TUNNEL BOATS
Boat hire
Gayton Road, Blisworth, Northampton
TEL: 01604 858 868

30 COWPER & NEWTON MUSEUM
Museum
Orchard Side, Market Place, Olney
TEL: 01234 711 516

31 FLAMINGO GARDENS & ZOOLOGICAL PARK
Zoo
Weston Underwood, Olney   TEL: 01234 711 451

32 STOKE BRUERNE CANAL MUSEUM
Museum
Bridge Road, Stoke Bruerne, Towcester
TEL: 01604 862 229

33 INDIAN CHIEF CRUISES
Boat trip
The Boat Inn, Stoke Bruerne   TEL: 01604 862 428

34 STOKE PARK PAVILIONS
Historic building
Stoke Bruerne, Towcester   TEL: 01604 862 172

35 CHICHELEY HALL
Historic house
Chicheley, Newport Pagnell   TEL: 01234 391 252

36 SILVERSTONE CIRCUIT
Motor racing circuit
Towcester   TEL: 01327 320 387

37 LINDA CRUISING COMPANY
Boat trip
Cosgrove Wharf, Lock Lane, Cosgrove
TEL: 01604 862 107

38 MILTON KEYNES MUSEUM OF INDUSTRY & RURAL LIFE
Museum
Stacey Hill Farm, Southern Way, Wolverton
TEL: 01908 316 222

39 GULLIVERS LAND
Theme park
Livingstone Drive, Newlands, Milton Keynes
TEL: 01908 609 001

40 BROMHAM MILL
Watermill
Bridge End, Bromham   TEL: 01234 824 330

41 CECIL HIGGINS ART GALLERY & MUSEUM
Museum
Castle Close, Bedford   TEL: 01234 211 222

42 CITY DISCOVERY CENTRE
Museum
Bradwell Abbey, Milton Keynes   TEL: 01908 227 229

43 STOWE GARDENS NT
Garden
Buckingham   TEL: 01280 822 850

44 BUCKINGHAM CHANTRY CHAPEL
Historic house
Market Hill, Buckingham   TEL: 01494 528 051

45 BLETCHLEY PARK
Historic building
Bletchley, Milton Keynes   TEL: 01908 640 404

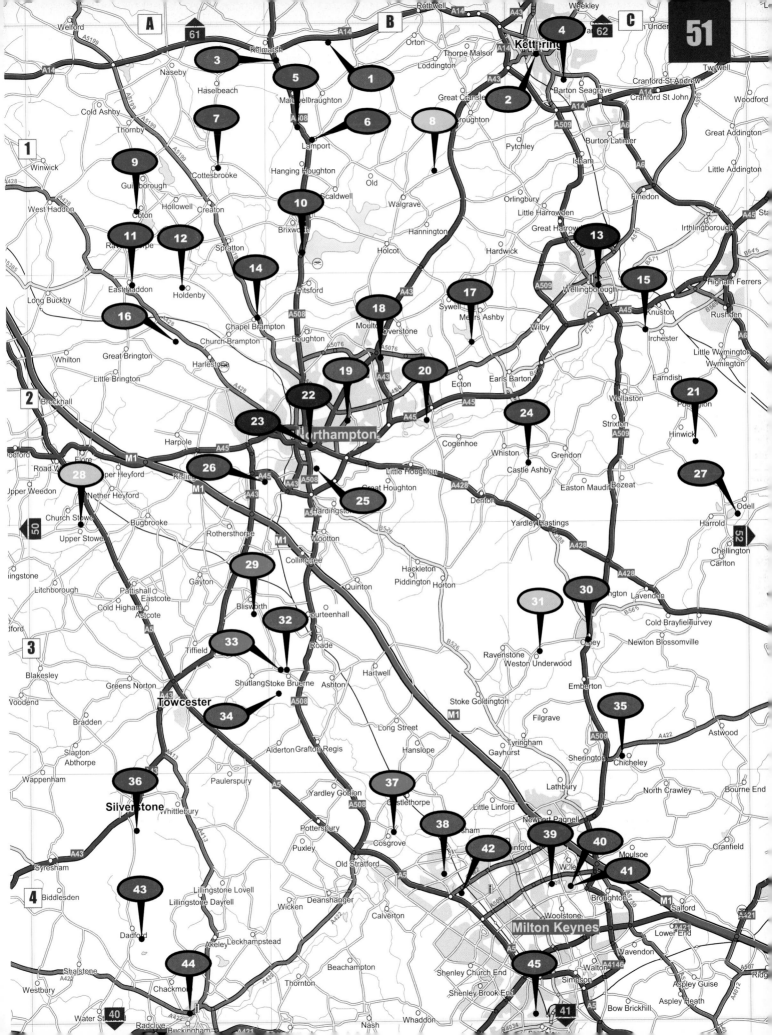

- ● ANIMAL ATTRACTIONS
- ● HERITAGE & CULTURE
- ○ INDOOR ACTIVITIES
- ● OUTDOOR ATTRACTIONS
- ● OUTDOOR ACTIVITIES
- ● WATER ACTIVITIES

1 HOUGHTON MILL
Watermill
Houghton, Huntingdon
TEL: 01480 301 494

2 CROMWELL MUSEUM
Museum
Grammar School Walk, Huntingdon
TEL: 01480 425 830

3 NORRIS MUSEUM
Museum
The Broadway, St Ives, Huntingdon
TEL: 01480 465 101

4 ISLAND HALL
Historic house
Post Street, Godmanchester, Huntingdon
TEL: Not available

5 KIMBOLTON CASTLE
Historic house
Kimbolton School, Kimbolton, Huntingdon
TEL: 01480 860 505

6 ST NEOTS MUSEUM
Museum
The Old Court, 8 New Street, St Neots
TEL: 01480 388 788

7 PRIORY COUNTRY PARK
Country park
Barker Lane, Bedford
TEL: 01234 211 182

8 WILLINGTON DOVECOTE & STABLES
Historic building
21 Chapel Lane, Willington
TEL: 01234 838 278

9 JOHN BUNYAN MUSEUM & LIBRARY
Museum
Bunyan Meeting Free Church, Mill Street, Bedford
TEL: 01234 213 722

10 BEDFORD GUIDED TOURS
Guided Tours
St Pauls Square, Bedford
TEL: 01234 215 226

11 THE LODGE NATURE RESERVE
The RSPB, Potton Road, Sandy, Bedfordshire, SG19 2DL.
TEL: 01767 680 541
EMAIL: thelodge@rspb.org.uk
WEB: www.rspb.org.uk
The organically maintained gardens around the mansion boast large specimen trees, spreading rhododendron, an azalea walk, wisteria, a long herbacous bed and wildlife garden.
OPEN: Mon-Fri 9-9 or dusk if earlier, Sat-Sun 10-9 or dusk if earlier.
ENTRY COSTS: £3, Child: £1, OAPs: £1.50, Family: £6.
SPECIALITIES: Bluebells, Herbaceous plants, Lavender, Trees, Woodland plants.
FACILITIES: Credit cards, Gift shop, Bookshop, Toilets, Wheelchair access.

12 MOOT HALL
Historic house
Elstow Green, Church View, Elstow
TEL: 01234 266 889

13 SHUTTLEWORTH COLLECTION
Museum
Old Warden, Aerodrome, Biggleswade
TEL: 0891 323 310

14 STEWARTBY WATERSPORTS CLUB
Boat hire
Green Lane, Stewartby, Bedford
TEL: 01234 767 751

15 HOUGHTON HOUSE
Historic building
Ampthill, Bedford
TEL: 01223 582 700

16 DE GREY MAUSOLEUM
Historic house
Flitton
TEL: 01525 860 094

17 STONDON MUSEUM
Museum
Station Road, Lower Stondon, Henlow
TEL: 01462 850 339

18 WREST PARK EH
Country park
Silsoe
TEL: 01234 228 337

19 WOBURN SAFARI PARK
Safari park
Woburn, Milton Keynes
TEL: 01525 290 407

Wolterton Hall & Park, Norfolk, 76-24

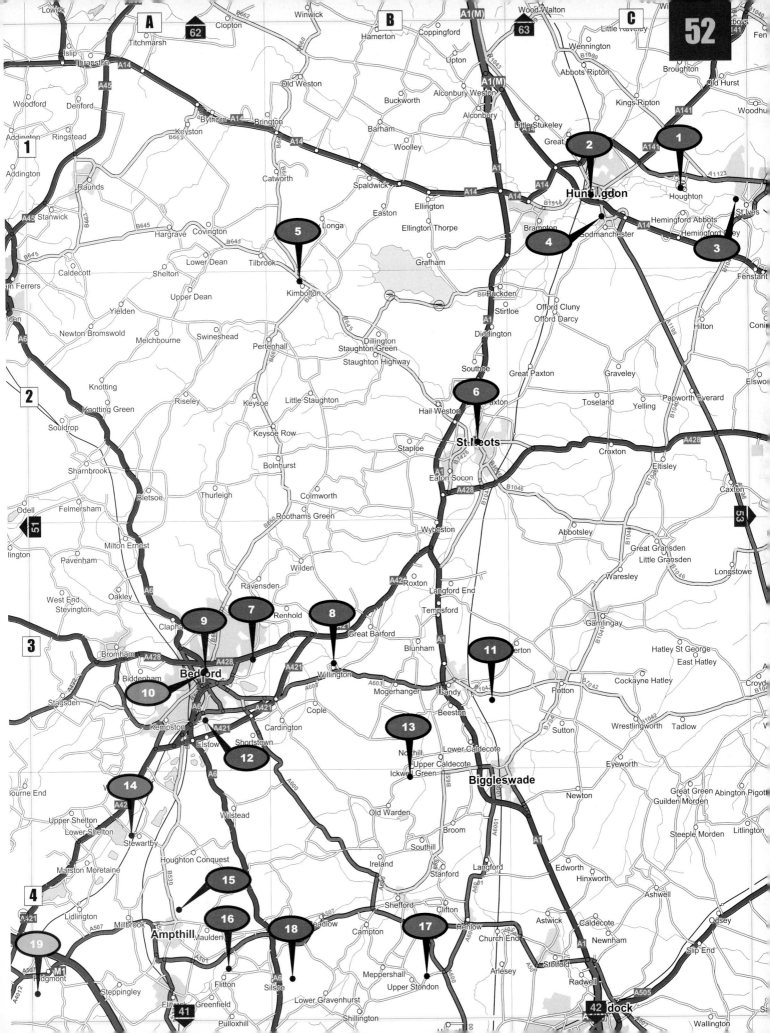

CAMBS · ESSEX · HERTS · SUFFOLK

- ● ANIMAL ATTRACTIONS
- ● HERITAGE & CULTURE
- ○ INDOOR ACTIVITIES
- ● OUTDOOR ATTRACTIONS
- ● OUTDOOR ACTIVITIES
- ● WATER ACTIVITIES

1 **RAPTOR FOUNDATION**
Bird centre & aviary
St Ives Road, Woodhurst, Cambridgeshire, PE28 3BT.
TEL: 01487 741 140
EMAIL: heleowl@aol.com
WEB: www.raptorfoundation.org
*Bird of Prey rescue centre offering a wide variety
of birds to see and photograph. Regular flying
displays with audience participation.*
OPEN: Open daily 10.30-5.
ENTRY COSTS: £2.50, Child: £1.50, OAPs: £1.50.
SPECIALITIES: Guided tours available, Photography
allowed.
FACILITIES: Coffee shop, Gift shop.

2 **WICKEN FEN NT**
Nature centre
Ely
TEL: 01353 720 741

3 **DENNY ABBEY & THE FARMLAND
MUSEUM**
Museum
Ely Road, Chittering, Waterbeach
TEL: 01223 860 489

4 **NATIONAL HORSERACING MUSEUM
& TOURS**
Museum
99 High Street, Newmarket
TEL: 01638 667 333

5 **ANGLESEY ABBEY GARDEN & LODE
MILL NT**
Historic building
Lode, Cambridge
TEL: 01223 811 200

6 **NATIONAL STUD**
Riding
Newmarket
TEL: 01473 584 349

7 **KETTLE'S YARD**
Gallery
Castle Street, Cambridge
TEL: 01223 352 124

8 **CAMBRIDGE & COUNTY FOLK
MUSEUM**
Museum
2-3 Castle Street, Cambridge
TEL: 01223 355 159

9  **ASHBY BOAT COMPANY**
Boat hire
Canal Wharf, Station Road, Stoke Golding
TEL: 01455 212 671

10 **NEWMARKET RACECOURSE**
Racecourse
Westfield House, The Links, Newmarket
TEL: 01638 663 482

11 **VIRTUAL AVIATION**
Airfield
52 Burleigh Street, Cambridge
TEL: 01223 300 300

12 **KING'S COLLEGE**
Historic building
King's Parade, Cambridge
TEL: 01223 331 212

13 **WHIPPLE MUSEUM OF THE
HISTORY OF SCIENCE**
Museum
Free School Lane, Cambridge
TEL: 01223 334 545

14 **SEDGEWICK MUSEUM**
Museum
Department of Earth Sciences, Downing Street,
Cambridge
TEL: 01223 333 456

15 **CAMBRIDGE UNIVERSITY MUSEUM
OF ARCHAEOLOGY & ANTHROPOLOGY**
Museum
Downing Street, Cambridge
TEL: 01223 333 516

16 **SCOTT POLAR RESEARCH
INSTITUTE MUSEUM**
Museum
Lensfield Road, Cambridge
TEL: 01223 336 540

17 **FITZWILLIAM MUSEUM**
Museum
Trumpington Street, Cambridge
TEL: 01223 332 900

18 **CAMBRIDGE UNIVERSITY
BOTANIC GARDEN**
Cory Lodge, Bateman Street, Cambridge, Cambridgeshire,
CB2 1JF.
TEL: 01223 336 265
EMAIL: enquiries@botanic.cam.ac.uk
WEB: www.botanic.cam.ac.uk

*Forty acres of beautifully landscaped gardens and
glasshouses displaying the amazing diversity of the
plant kingdom. Colour and interest all year. Entrance
on Bateman Street. Nine National Collections.*
OPEN: Nov-Jan: 10-4. Feb: 10-5. Mar-Sep: 10-6. Oct: 10-5.
Closed Dec 25-Jan 1.
ENTRY COSTS: £2.50, Child: £2 Under 5s free, OAPs: £2.
SPECIALITIES: Herbaceous plants, Pinetum,
Woodland plants, Alpines.
FACILITIES: Toilets, Coffee shop, Gift shop,
Pushchair friendly, Wheelchair access.

19 **WIMPOLE HALL & HOME FARM NT**
Historic house
Arrington, Royston
TEL: 01223 207 257

20 **CHILFORD HALL VINEYARD**
Vineyard
Balsham Road, Linton, Cambridge
TEL: 01223 892 641

21 **CROSSING HOUSE GARDEN**
Garden
Meldreth Road, Shepreth, Royston
TEL: 01763 261 071

22 **DUXFORD IMPERIAL WAR MUSEUM**
Museum
Duxford, Cambridge
TEL: 01223 835 000

23 **LINTON ZOOLOGICAL GARDENS**
Zoo
Hadstock Road, Linton, Cambridge
TEL: 01223 891 308

24 **ROYSTON & DISTRICT MUSEUM**
Museum
Lower King Street, Royston
TEL: 01763 242 587

25 **AUDLEY END HOUSE EH**
Garden
Audley End, Saffron Walden
TEL: 01799 522 399

26 **AUDLEY END ORGANIC KITCHEN
GARDEN**
Garden
Audley End House, Saffron Walden
TEL: 01799 522 842

Out & About

with

information

from

www.daysoutatlas.co.uk

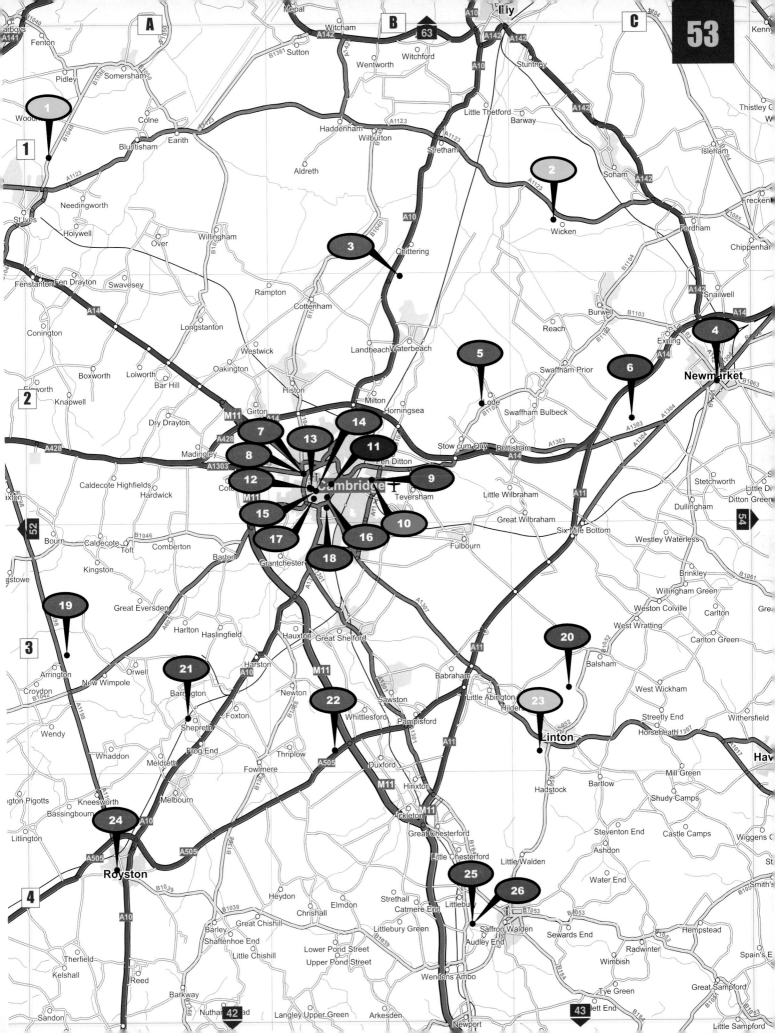

1 REDGRAVE & LOPHAM FEN
Nature centre
Diss
TEL: 01379 688 333

2 EUSTON HALL
Historic building
Euston, Thetford
TEL: 01842 766 366

3 WATSON'S POTTERIES
Factory shop
Wattisfield, Bury St Edmunds
TEL: 01359 251 239

4 WYKEN HALL
Garden
Stanton, Bury St Edmunds
TEL: 01359 250 287

5 THORNHAM ESTATE
Country park
Thornham Magna, Eye
TEL: 01379 783 207

6 WEST STOW COUNTRY PARK & ANGLO-SAXON VILLAGE
Country park
Icklingham Road, West Stow, Bury St Edmunds
TEL: 01284 728 718

7 BURY ST EDMUNDS ABBEY
Abbey
Bury St Edmunds
TEL: 01284 764 667

8 MOYSE'S HALL MUSEUM
Museum
Cornhill, Bury St Edmunds
TEL: 01284 757 488

9 BURY ST EDMUNDS ART GALLERY
Gallery
The Market Cross, Bury St Edmunds
TEL: 01284 762 081

10 ANGEL CORNER
Historic building
8 Angel Hill, Bury St Edmunds
TEL: 01284 763 233

11 ST EDMUNDSBURY CATHEDRAL
Cathedral
Abbey House, Angel Hill, Bury St Edmunds
TEL: 01284 754 933

12 MANOR HOUSE MUSEUM
Museum
Honey Hill, Bury St Edmunds
TEL: 01284 757 076

13 PAKENHAM WATERMILL
Watermill
Mill Road, Pakenham, Bury St Edmunds
TEL: 01359 270 570

14 HAUGHLEY PARK
Historic house
Haughley, Stowmarket
TEL: 01359 240 701

15 ICKWORTH PARK & GARDEN NT
Garden
The Rotunda, Ickworth, Horringer
TEL: 01284 735 270

16 MUSEUM OF EAST ANGLIAN LIFE
Museum
Iliffe Way, Stowmarket
TEL: 01449 612 229

17 REDE HALL FARM PARK
Farm
Rede, Bury St Edmunds
TEL: 01284 850 695

18 BAYLHAM HOUSE RARE BREEDS FARM
Farm
Mill Lane, Baylham
TEL: 01473 830 264

19 LAVENHAM GUILDHALL OF CORPUS CHRISTI NT
Historic building
Market Place, Lavenham, Sudbury
TEL: 01787 247 646

20 LITTLE HALL
Historic house
Lavenham
TEL: 01473 584 349

21 KENTWELL HALL
Historic house
Long Melford, Sudbury
TEL: 01787 310 207

22 CAVENDISH MANOR VINEYARDS & NETHER HALL
Vineyard
Peacocks Road, Cavendish, Sudbury
TEL: 01787 280 221

23 GAINSBOROUGH'S HOUSE
Museum
46 Gainsborough Street, Sudbury
TEL: 01787 372 958

24 COLNE VALLEY RAILWAY & MUSEUM
Railway
Castle Hedingham Station, Yeldman Road, Castle Hedingham
TEL: 01787 461 174

25 HEDINGHAM CASTLE
Castle
Castle Hedingham, Halstead
TEL: 01787 460 261

26 THORINGTON HALL
Historic house
Thorrington Street, Stoke by Nayland, Colchester
TEL: 01263 733 471

27 FLATFORD BRIDGE COTTAGE
Historic building
Flatford, East Bergholt, Colchester
TEL: 01206 298 260

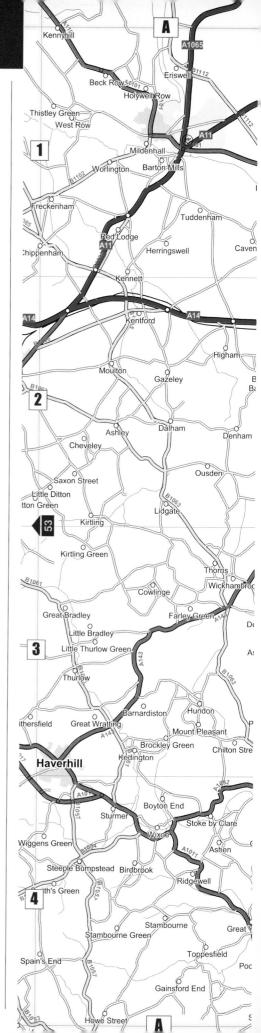

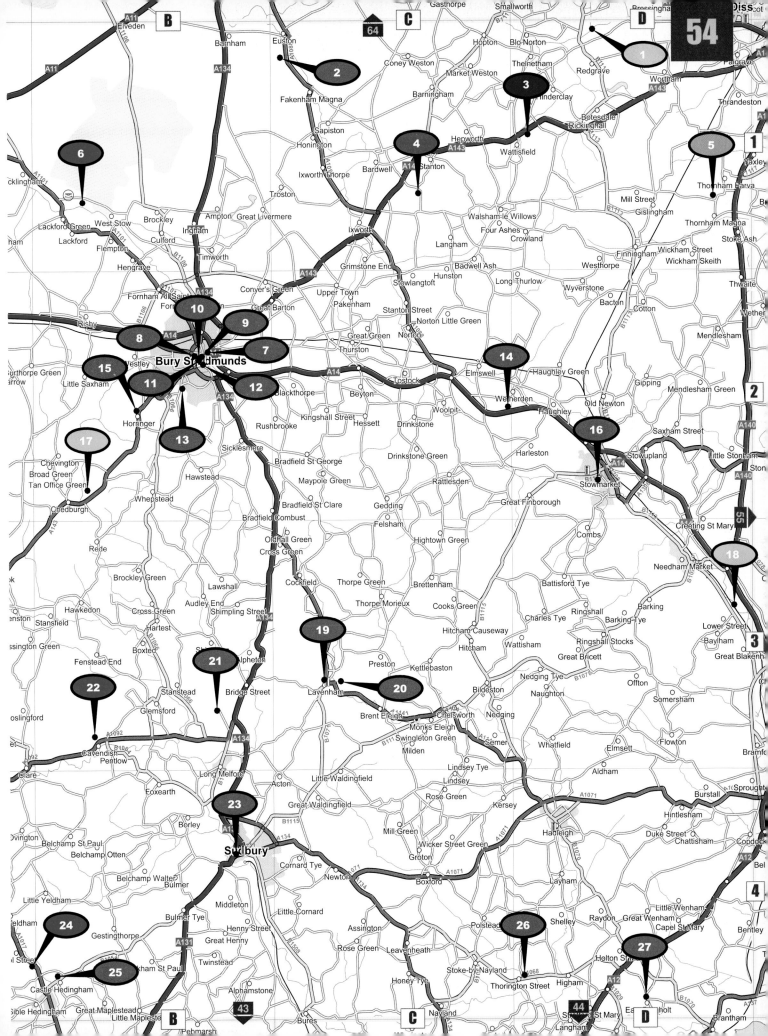

SUFFOLK

- ANIMAL ATTRACTIONS
- HERITAGE & CULTURE
- INDOOR ACTIVITIES
- OUTDOOR ATTRACTIONS
- OUTDOOR ACTIVITIES
- WATER ACTIVITIES

1 WINGFIELD OLD COLLEGE & GARDENS
Historic house
Church Road, Wingfield, Stradbroke
TEL: 01379 384 888

2 AMBER MUSEUM & SHOP
Museum
Market Place, Southwold
TEL: 01502 723 394

3 DUNWICH HEATH & MINSMERE BEACH NT
Nature centre
Dunwich, Saxmundham
TEL: 01728 648 505

4 MINSMERE
Nature centre
Westleton
TEL: 01728 648 281

5 BRUISYARD WINERY VINEYARD & HERB CENTRE
Vineyard
Church Road, Bruisyard, Saxmundham
TEL: 01728 638 281

6 MID SUFFOLK LIGHT RAILWAY MUSEUM
Railway
Brockford Station, Wetheringset-cum-Brockford
TEL: 01473 584 349

7 SAXTEAD GREEN POST MILL
Historic building
Saxtead, Woodbridge
TEL: 01728 685 789

8 SIZEWELL VISITOR CENTRE
Visitor centre
Leiston
TEL: 01728 653 890

9 LONG SHOP MUSEUM
Museum
Main Street, Leiston
TEL: 01728 832 189

10 BRITISH BIRDS OF PREY & NATURE CENTRE
Nature centre
Stonham Barns, Stonham Aspal
TEL: 01449 711 425

11 EASTON FARM PARK
Farm
Pound Corner Easton, Woodbridge
TEL: 01728 746 475

12 MOOT HALL MUSEUM
Museum
Market Cross Place, Aldeburgh
TEL: 01728 452 730

13 SNAPE MALTINGS
Historic building
High Street, Aldeburgh
TEL: 01473 584 349

14 VALLEY FARM CAMARGUE HORSES & WHITE ANIMAL COLLECTION
Stables
Wickham Market, Woodbridge
TEL: 01473 584 349

15 OTLEY HALL
Historic house
Hall Lane, Otley, Ipswich
TEL: 01473 890 264

16 JAMES WHITE CIDER COMPANY
Cider tasting
White's Fruit Farm, Helmingham Road, Ashbocking
TEL: 01473 890 202

17 BUTLEY POTTERY
Factory shop
Butley Barns, Mill Lane, Butley
TEL: 01394 450 785

18 SUTTON HOO NT
Ancient monument
Woodbridge
TEL: 01263 733 471

19 ORFORD CASTLE EH
Castle
Woodbridge
TEL: 01394 450 472

20 SUFFOLK HORSE SOCIETY MUSEUM
Museum
Market Hill, Woodbridge
TEL: 01394 380 643

21 WOODBRIDGE TIDE MILL
Factory tour
Tide Mill Way, Woodbridge
TEL: 01473 626 618

22 CHRISTCHURCH MANSION
Historic house
Soane Street, Ipswich
TEL: 01473 253 246

23 IPSWICH MUSEUM
Museum
High Street, Ipswich
TEL: 01473 213 761

24 390TH BOMB GROUP MEMORIAL AIR MUSEUM
Museum
Parham Airfield, Framlingham
TEL: 01473 584 349

25 LANDGUARD FORT EH
Historic building
Felixstowe
TEL: 01394 277 767

Go exploring
and get more information from
www.daysoutatlas.co.uk

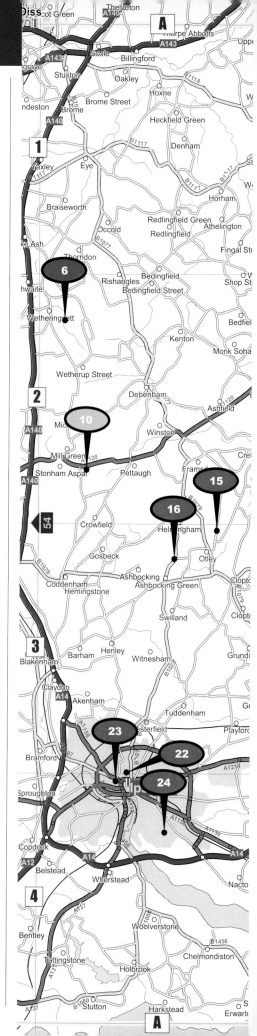

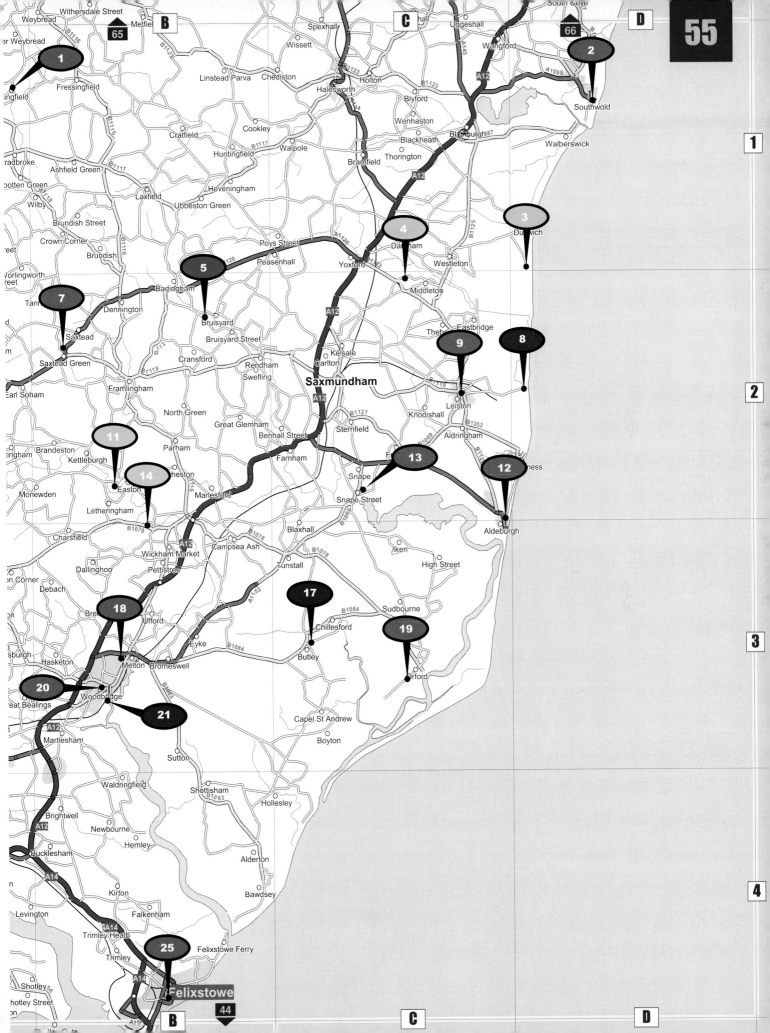

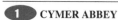

WALES

1 **CYMER ABBEY**
Abbey
Dolgellau   Tel: 01341 422 854

2 **FAIRBOURNE & BARMOUTH STEAM RAILWAY**
Railway
Beach Road, Fairbourne   Tel: 01341 250 362

3 **KING ARTHURS LABYRINTH & CORRIS CRAFT CENTRE**
Cave
Corris   Tel: 01654 761 584

4 **WELSHPOOL & LLANFAIR RAILWAY**
Railway
The Station, Llanfair Caereinion, Welshpool
                             Tel: 01938 810 441

5 **CENTRE FOR ALTERNATIVE TECHNOLOGY**
Education Centre
Pantperthog, Machynlleth   Tel: 01654 702 400

6 **MUSEUM OF MODERN ART WALES**
Museum
Penrallt Street, Machynlleth Tel: 01654 703 355

7 **SENEDD-DY OWAIN GLYNDWR**
Unusual
71 Maen Gwyn Street, Machynlleth
                             Tel: 01654 702 827

8 **TALYLLYN RAILWAY & NARROW GAUGE RAILWAY MUSEUM**
Railway
Wharf Station, Neptune Road, Tywyn
                             Tel: 01654 710 472

9 **BORTH ANIMALARIUM**
Zoo
Borth   Tel: 01970 871 224

10 **WELSH HISTORIC GARDEN TRUST**
Garden
Ty Leri, Talybont   Tel: 01970 832 268

11 **ABERYSTWYTH ELECTRIC CLIFF RAILWAY**
Railway
Constitution Hill, Cliff Terrace, Aberystwyth
                             Tel: 01970 617 642

12 **CEREDIGION ARCHIVES**
Museum
County Offices, Marine Terrace, Aberystwyth
                             Tel: 01970 633 697

13 **NATIONAL LIBRARY OF WALES**
Museum
Penglais Hill, Aberystwyth   Tel: 01970 632 800

14 **LLYWERNOG SILVER LEAD MINE**
Museum
Llywernog, Ponterwyd, Aberystwyth
                             Tel: 01970 890 620

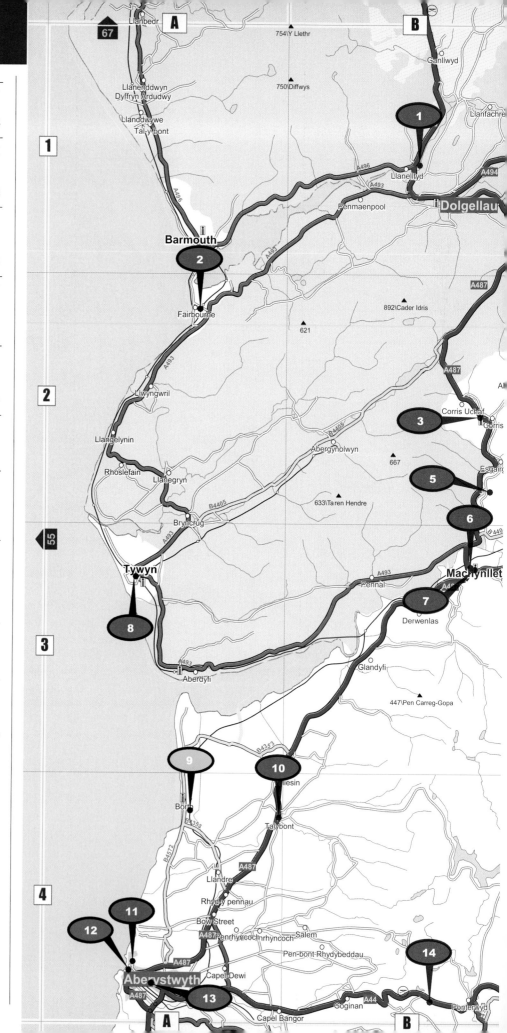

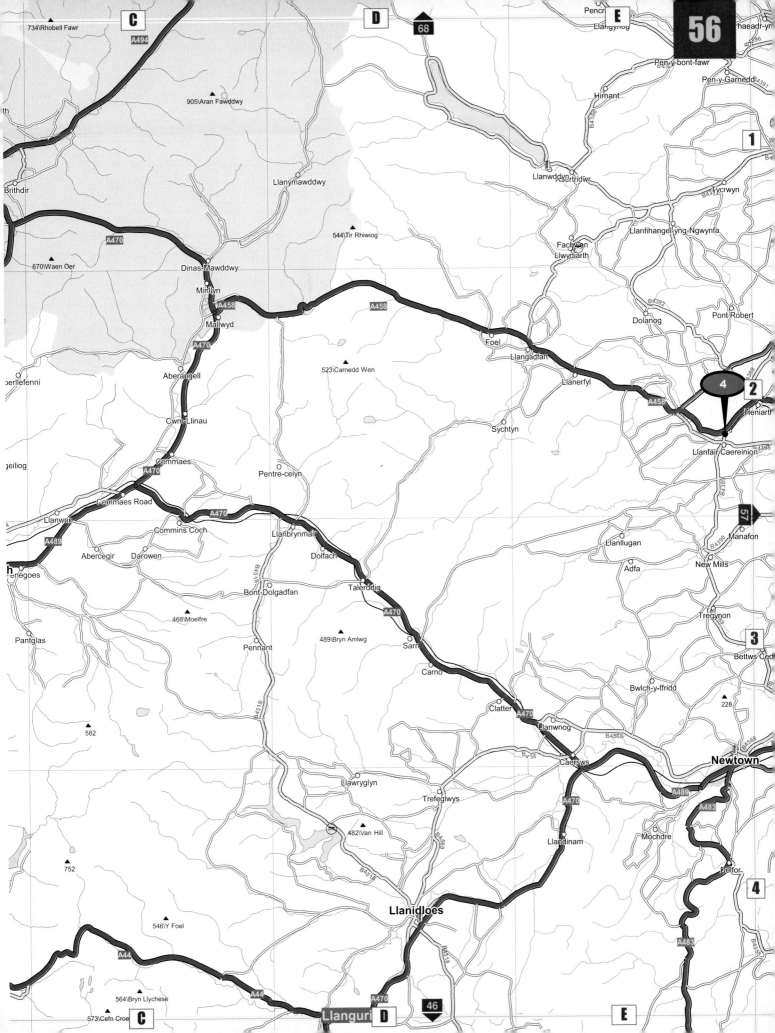

1 MORETON CORBET CASTLE
Castle
Moreton Corbet, Shrewsbury
TEL: 0121 625 6820

2 HAUGHMOND ABBEY
Historic building
Upton Magna, Offington, Shrewsbury
TEL: 01743 709 661

3 SHREWSBURY CASTLE
Castle
Castle Gates, Shrewsbury
TEL: 01743 358 516

4 SHREWSBURY ABBEY
Abbey
Shrewsbury
TEL: 01743 232 723

5 SHREWSBURY MUSEUM & ART GALLERY
Museum
Shrewsbury
TEL: 01743 361 196

6 ROWLEY'S HOUSE MUSEUM
Museum
Barker Street, Shrewsbury
TEL: 01743 361 196

7 CLIVE HOUSE MUSEUM
Museum
College Hill, Shrewsbury
TEL: 01743 354 811

8 SHREWSBURY QUEST
Historic building
193 Abbey Foregate, Shrewsbury
TEL: 01743 243 324

9 RADBROOK CULINARY MUSEUM
Museum
Radbrook College, Radbrook Road, Shrewsbury
TEL: 01743 232 686

10 ATTINGHAM PARK NT
Historic house
Shrewsbury
TEL: 01743 708 123

11 WROXETER ROMAN CITY
Roman site
Wroxeter
TEL: Not available

12 ROMAN SITE EH
Archaeological site
Wroxeter, Shrewsbury
TEL: 01604 735 400

13 POWIS CASTLE GARDENS NT
Garden
Welshpool
TEL: 01938 551 920

14 ACTON BURNELL CASTLE
Castle
Acton Burnell, Shrewsbury
TEL: 01604 730 320

15 ANDREW LOGAN MUSEUM OF SCULPTURE
Gallery
Berriew, Welshpool
TEL: 01686 640 689

16 MOAT HOUSE
Historic house
Longnor, Shrewsbury
TEL: 01743 718 434

17 LANGLEY CHAPEL
Historic building
Acton Burnell, Shrewsbury
TEL: 0121 625 6820

18 CARDING MILL VALLEY & LONG MYND
Moorlands
Chalet Pavilion, Carding Mill Valley, Church Stretton
TEL: 01694 722 631

19 WILDERHOPE MANOR
Historic house
Easthope Longville, Much Wenlock
TEL: 01694 771 363

20 SHIPTON HALL
Historic house
Shipton, Much Wenlock
TEL: 01746 785 225

21 ACTON SCOTT HISTORIC WORKING FARM
Farm
Wenlock Lodge, Acton Scott, Church Stretton
TEL: 01694 781 306

22 WALCOT HALL
Historic house
Bishops Castle, Lydbury North
TEL: Not available

23 STOKESAY CASTLE EH
Castle
Stokesay
TEL: 01588 672 544

Donkeys

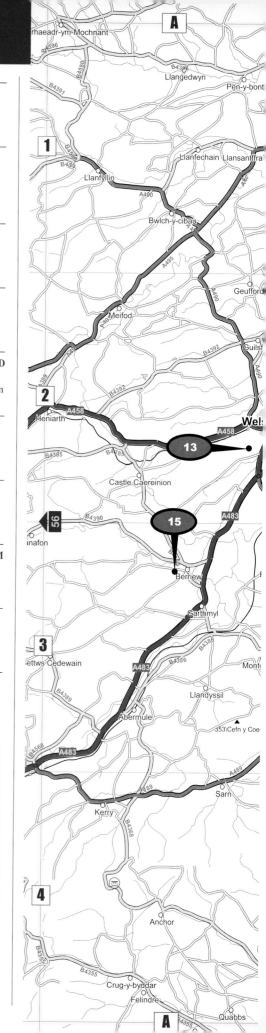

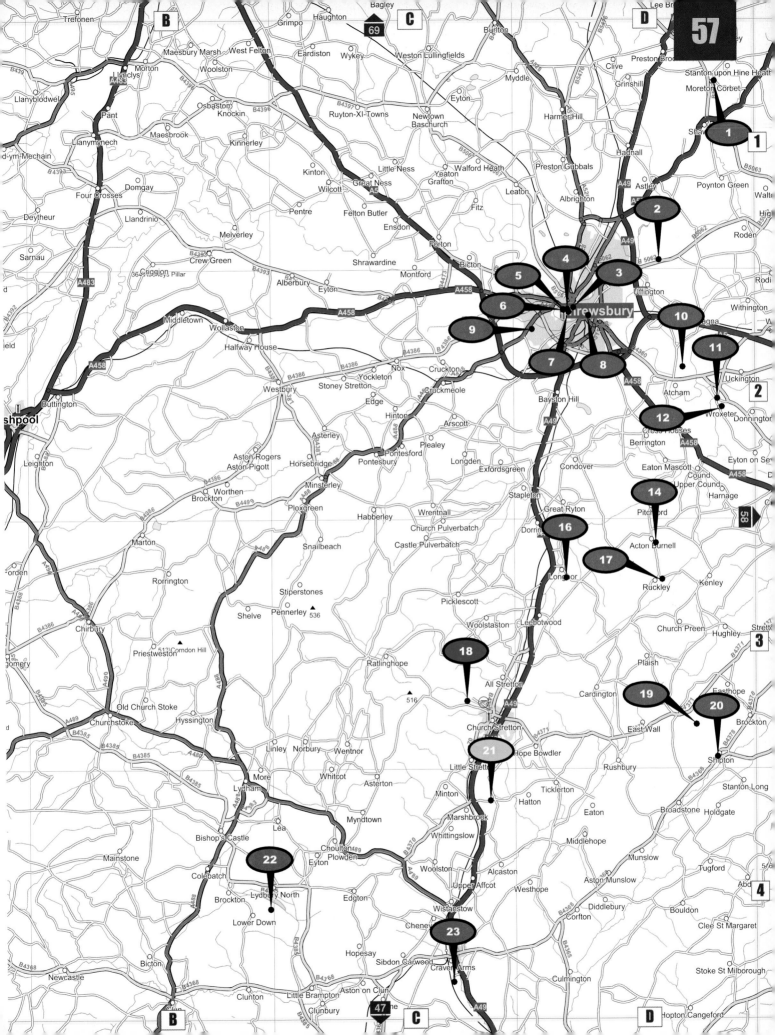

1 ANCIENT HIGH HOUSE
Historic house
Greengate Street, Stafford
TEL: 01785 214 668

2 STAFFORD CASTLE
Castle
Newport Road, Stafford
TEL: 01785 257 698

3 HOO FARM ANIMAL KINGDOM
Farm
Telford
TEL: 01952 677 917

6 WESTON PARK
Historic house
Weston-under-Lizard, Shifnal
TEL: 01952 850 207

7 BOSCOBEL HOUSE EH
Garden
Boscobel Lane, Bishopswood, Stafford
TEL: 01902 850 244

8 TELFORD WONDERLAND
Garden
Telford
TEL: 01952 591 633

9 AEROSPACE MUSEUM
Museum
Cosford
TEL: Not available

10 ROYAL AIR FORCE MUSEUM
Museum
Cosford, Shifnal
TEL: 01902 376 200

11 BLISTS HILL VICTORIAN TOWN
Museum
Legges Way, Madeley, Telford
TEL: 01952 432 166

12 BUILDWAS ABBEY
Abbey
Buildwas
TEL: Not available

13 BROSELEY PIPEWORKS
Museum
King Street, Broseley
TEL: 01952 432 166

14 ROSEHILL HOUSE & DALE HOUSE
Museum
Coalbrookdale
TEL: 01952 433 522

15 IRONBRIDGE GORGE MUSEUMS
Museum
Ironbridge, Telford
TEL: 01952 432 166

16 COALBROOKDALE & MUSEUM OF IRON & FURNACE SITE
Museum
Telford
TEL: 01952 432 166

17 JACKFIELD TILE MUSEUM
Museum
Jackfield, Telford
TEL: 01952 432 166

18 COALPORT CHINA MUSEUM
Museum
Coalport, Telford
TEL: 01952 580 650

19 BENTHALL HALL
Historic house
Benthall, Broseley
TEL: 01952 882 159

20 WENLOCK PRIORY EH
Garden
6 The Bull Ring, Much Wenlock
TEL: 01952 727 466

21 VALLEY PARK NATURE RESERVE
Nature centre
St Peter's Square, Wolverhampton
TEL: Not available

22 WIGHTWICK MANOR
Historic house
Wightwick Bank, Wolverhampton
TEL: 01902 761 108

23 BANTOCK HOUSE MUSEUM IN THE PARK
Museum
Finchfield Road, Wolverhampton
TEL: 01902 552 195

24 PHOENIX ADVENTURE PLAYGROUND
Adventure & activity centre
Cockshutt Lane, Thompson Avenue, Wolverhampton
TEL: 01902 556 324

25 BLACK COUNTRY LIVING MUSEUM
Museum
Tipton Road, Dudley
TEL: 0121 557 9643

26 UPTON CRESSETT HALL
Historic house
Bridgnorth
TEL: 01746 714 307

27 DANIEL'S MILL
Mill
Eardington, Bridgnorth
TEL: 01746 762 753

28 BROADFIELD HOUSE GLASS MUSEUM
Museum
Compton Drive, Kingswinford
TEL: 01384 812 745

29 STUART CRYSTAL
Factory tour & shopping
Wordsley, Stourbridge
TEL: 01384 711 61

30 BUTTER CROSS
Monument
Dunster
TEL: 01179 750 700

31 DUDLEY MUSEUM & ART GALLERY
Museum
St James's Road, Dudley
TEL: 01384 815 571

32 WEST MIDLAND SAFARI & LEISURE PARK
Safari park
Spring Grove, Bewdley
TEL: 01299 402 114

33 KINVER EDGE
Archaeological site
The Warden's Lodge, Compa Kinver, Stourbridge
TEL: 01384 872 418

34 RAYS FARM COUNTRY MATTERS
Farm
Billingsley, Bridgnorth
TEL: 01299 841 255

35 CHARLESTON
Historic house
Stourbridge
TEL: 01323 811 265

Lioness

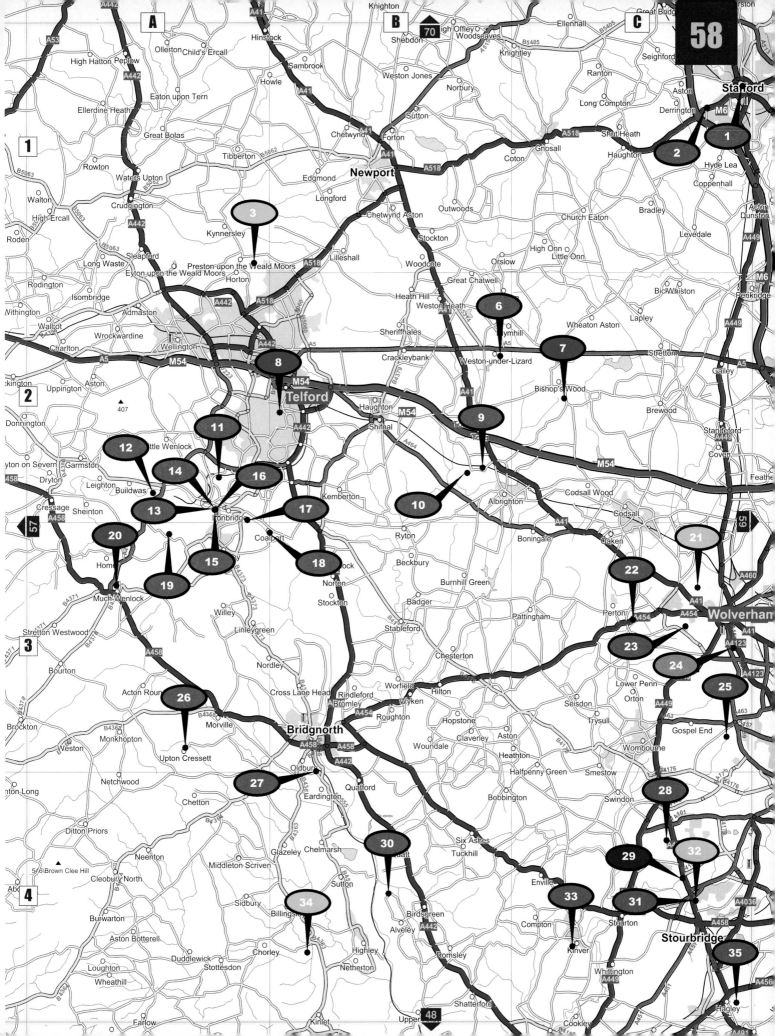

1 SHUGBOROUGH ESTATE NT
Garden
Milford, Stafford
TEL: 01889 881 388

2 MUSEUM OF CANNOCK CHASE
Museum
Valley Heritage Centre, Valley Road, Hednesford
TEL: 01543 877 666

3 LICHFIELD CATHEDRAL
Cathedral
The Close, Lichfield
TEL: 01543 306 240

4 ERASMUS DARWIN CENTRE
Historic house
Darwin House, Beacon Street, Lichfield
TEL: 01543 306 260

5 LICHFIELD HERITAGE CENTRE
Heritage centre
Market Square, Lichfield
TEL: 01543 256 611

6 CHASEWATER COUNTRY PARK
Country park
Pool Road, Walsall
TEL: 01543 452 302

7 STAFFORDSHIRE REGIMENT MUSEUM
Museum
Whittington, Barracks, Lichfield
TEL: 0121 311 3240

8 WALL ROMAN SITE
Roman site
Watling Street Wall, Lichfield
TEL: 01543 480 768

9 MOSELEY OLD HALL NT
Garden
Moseley Old Hall Lane, Fordhouses, Wolverhampton
TEL: 01902 782 808

10 WALSALL LEATHER MUSEUM
Museum
Littleton Street, West Walsall
TEL: 01922 721 153

11 WILLENHALL MUSEUM
Museum
Lichfield Street, Willenhall
TEL: 01922 653 116

12 WALSALL INSIDE OUT
Museum
Lichfield Street, Walsall
TEL: 01922 653 116

13 JEROME K JEROME BIRTHPLACE MUSEUM
Museum
Belsize House, Bradford Place Walsall
TEL: 01922 653 116

14 SUTTON PARK
Country park
Blackroot Hill, Sutton Park, Sutton Coldfield
TEL: 0121 354 1916

15 CORNISH STEAM ENTERPRISE
Museum
14 Bescot Drive, Walsall
TEL: Not available

16 SANDWELL VALLEY COUNTRY PARK
Country park
Salters Lane, West Bromwich
TEL: 0121 553 0220

17 DUDLEY ZOO & CASTLE
Zoo
2 The Broadway, Dudley
TEL: 01384 215 314

18 ASTON HALL
Historic building
Trinity Road, Aston, Birmingham
TEL: 0121 327 0062

19 CASTLE BROMWICH HALL GARDENS
Garden
Chester Road, Castle Bromwich, Birmingham
TEL: 0121 749 4100

20 SOHO HOUSE MUSEUM
Museum
Soho Avenue, Handsworth, Birmingham
TEL: 0121 554 9122

21 DUDLEY CANAL TRUST TRIPS
Boat trip
Pear Tree Lane, Dudley
TEL: 01384 236 275

22 MUSEUM OF THE JEWELLERY QUARTER
Museum
75-79 Vyse Street, Hockley, Birmingham
TEL: 0121 554 3598

23 IMAX THEATRE
Theatre
Millenium Point, Curzon Street, Birmingham
TEL: 0121 202 2222

24 ROCK FACE BIRMINGHAM CLIMBING CENTRE
Adventure & activity centre
Birmingham
TEL: 0121 359 6419

25 BIRMINGHAM CATHEDRAL
Cathedral
Colmore Row, Birmingham
TEL: 0121 236 4333

26 BIRMINGHAM MUSEUM & ART GALLERY
Museum
Chamberlain Square, Birmingham
TEL: 0121 303 2834

27 NATIONAL SEA LIFE CENTRE
Aquarium
The Waters Edge, Brindley Place, Birmingham, West Midlands, B1 2HL.
TEL: 0121 643 6777

The magnificent National Sea-Life Centre overlooks the city's famous canal network and has over 60 displays of different sea and freshwater creatures including the new Otter Sanctuary.
OPEN: Open daily.
FACILITIES: Coffee shop, Credit cards, Gift shop, Toilets.

28 IKON GALLERY
Gallery
1 Oozells Square, Brindley Place, Birmingham
TEL: 0121 248 0708

29 SANDERS PARK
Country park
Kidderminster Road, Bromsgrove
TEL: 01527 832 148

30 BLAKESLEY HALL
Historic building
Blakesley Road, Yardley, Birmingham
TEL: 0121 783 2193

32 SHAKESPEARE EXPRESS
Railway
670 Warwick Road, Tyseley, Birmingham
TEL: 0121 707 4696

31 BIRMINGHAM BOTANICAL GARDENS & GLASSHOUSES
Westbourne Road, Edgebaston, Birmingham, West Midlands, B15 3TR.
TEL: 0121 454 1860
WEB: www.birminghambotanicalgardens.org.uk

Two miles from the city centre. Superb Tropical, Mediterranean and desert glasshouses. Fifteen acres of beautiful landscaped gardens with historic rose, alpine, rock, rhododendron and theme gardens.
OPEN: Mon-Sat 9-dusk, Sun 10-dusk. Closed Christmas Day.
ENTRY COSTS: £5.00, Child: £2.70, OAPs: £2.60, Family: £13.50.
SPECIALITIES: Alpines, Bonsai, Exotic plants, Themed gardens, Citrus.
FACILITIES: Toilets, Credit cards, Wheelchair access, Restaurant, Bookshop, Child area, Coffee shop, Gift shop, Own gift tokens, Sell plants.

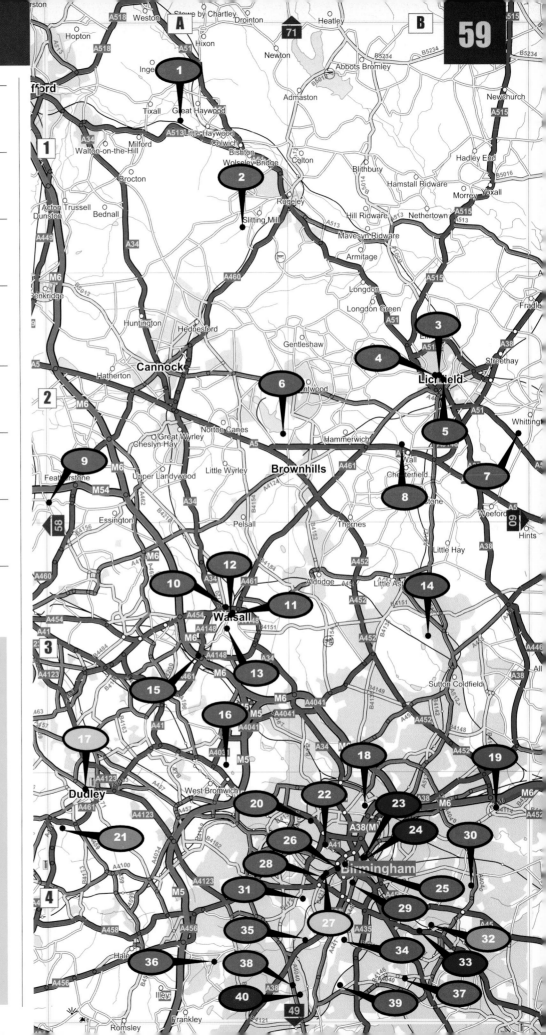

33 BIRMINGHAM RAILWAY MUSEUM
Museum
670 Warwick Road, Tyseley, Birmingham
TEL: 0121 707 4696

34 CANNON HILL PARK
Garden
Moseley, Birmingham
TEL: 0121 442 4226

35 BARBER INSTITUTE OF FINE ARTS
Gallery
University of Birmingham, Edgbaston, Birmingham
TEL: 0121 414 7333

36 WOODGATE VALLEY COUNTRY PARK
Country park
Clapgate Lane, Birmingham
TEL: 0121 421 7575

37 SAREHOLE MILL
Museum
Cole Bank Road, Moseley, Birmingham
TEL: 0121 777 6612

38 SELLY MANOR MUSEUM
Museum
Maple Road, Bournville, Birmingham
TEL: 0121 472 0199

39 KINGS HEATH PARK
Country park
Vicarage Road, Kings Heath, Birmingham
TEL: 0121 444 2848

40 CADBURY WORLD
Factory tour
Linden Road, Bournville, Birmingham
TEL: 0121 451 4180

Help us help you

mention the
Days Out Atlas
when visiting
anywhere on
this page.

1 **DONINGTON GRAND PRIX COLLECTION**
Museum
Donington Park, Castle Donington, Derby
TEL: 01332 811 027

2 **STAUNTON HAROLD CHURCH NT**
Historic building
Staunton Harold
TEL: 01332 863 822

3 **FERRERS CENTRE FOR ARTS & CRAFTS**
Craft centre
Staunton Harold, Ashby-de-la-Zouch
TEL: 01332 865 408

4 **ROSLISTON FORESTRY CENTRE**
Visitor centre
Swadlincote
TEL: 01283 535 039

5 **ASHBY-DE-LA-ZOUCH MUSEUM**
Museum
North Street, Ashby-de-la-Zouch
TEL: 01530 560 090

6 **ASHBY-DE-LA-ZOUCH CASTLE EH**
Castle
South Street, Ashby-de-la-Zouch
TEL: 01530 413 343

7 **MOIRA FURNACE & CRAFT WORKSHOPS**
Museum
Furnace Lane, Moira, Swadlincote
TEL: 01283 224 667

8 **SNIBSTON DISCOVERY PARK**
Museum
Ashby Road, Coalville
TEL: 01530 510 851

9 **DONINGTON-LE-HEALTH MANOR HOUSE**
Historic house
Manor Road, Donington-le-Health, Coalville
TEL: 01530 831 259

10 **MEASHAM MUSEUM**
Museum
56 High Street, Measham
TEL: 01530 273 956

11 **TWYCROSS ZOO PARK**
Zoo
Atherstone, Warwickshire, CV9 3PX.
TEL: 01827 880 250
WEB: www.twycrosszoo.com
Over 1000 animals, including many endangered species-ranging from the tiny Pygmy Marmosets to the impressive silverback Western Lowland Gorillas are all here waiting to see you.
OPEN: Summer: 10-6. Winter: 10-dusk.
ENTRY COSTS: £6.50, Child: £4.50, OAPs: £5.
FACILITIES: Gift shop, Pushchair friendly, Restaurant, Toilets, Wheelchair access.

12 **BATTLEFIELD LINE RAILWAY**
Railway
Market Bosworth
TEL: 01827 880 754

13 **TAMWORTH CASTLE**
Castle
The Holloway, Lady Bank, Tamworth
TEL: 01827 709 626

14 **TROPICAL BIRDLAND**
Bird centre & aviary
Lindridge Lane, Desford
TEL: 01455 824 603

15 **SNOWDOME**
Ski centre
Castle Grounds, River Drive, Tamworth
TEL: 01827 679 05

16 **BOSWORTH WATER TRUST LEISURE & WATER PARK**
Water Parks
Far Caten Lane, Wellsborough, Nuneaton
TEL: 01455 291 876

17 **DRAYTON MANOR PARK**
Theme park
Drayton Manor, Tamworth
TEL: 01827 287 979

18 **MALLORY PARK**
Motor racing circuit
Church Road, Kirkby Mallory
TEL: 01455 842 931

19 **BOSWORTH BATTLEFIELD VISITOR CENTRE & COUNTRY PARK**
Battlefield
Ambion Hill, Sutton Cheney, Nuneaton
TEL: 01455 290 429

20 **WHITEMOOR ANTIQUES & CRAFTS CENTRE**
Craft centre
Main Street, Shenton, Market Bosworth
TEL: 01455 212 250

21 **MIDDLETON HALL**
Historic house
Middleton, Tamworth
TEL: 01827 283 095

22 **ASH END HOUSE CHILDREN'S FARM**
Farm
Middleton Lane, Middleton, Tamworth
TEL: 0121 329 3240

23 **KINGSBURY WATER PARK**
Country park
Bodymoor Heath Lane, Bodymoor Heath, Sutton Coldfield
TEL: 01827 872 660

24 **BROOMEY CROFT CHILDREN'S FARM**
Farm
Bodymoor Heath Lane, Bodymoor Heath, Sutton Coldfield
TEL: 01827 872 660

25 **HINCKLEY & DISTRICT MUSEUM**
Museum
Framework Knitters Cottages, Lower Bond Street, Hinckley
TEL: 01455 251 218

26 **NUNEATON MUSEUM & ART GALLERY**
Museum
Coton Road, Riversley Park, Nuneaton
TEL: 024 7635 0720

27 **ARBURY HALL**
Historic house
Arbury, Nuneaton
TEL: 024 7638 2804

28 **NATIONAL MOTORCYCLE MUSEUM**
Museum
Coventry Road, Bickenhill, Solihull
TEL: 01675 443 311

Having a relaxing drink

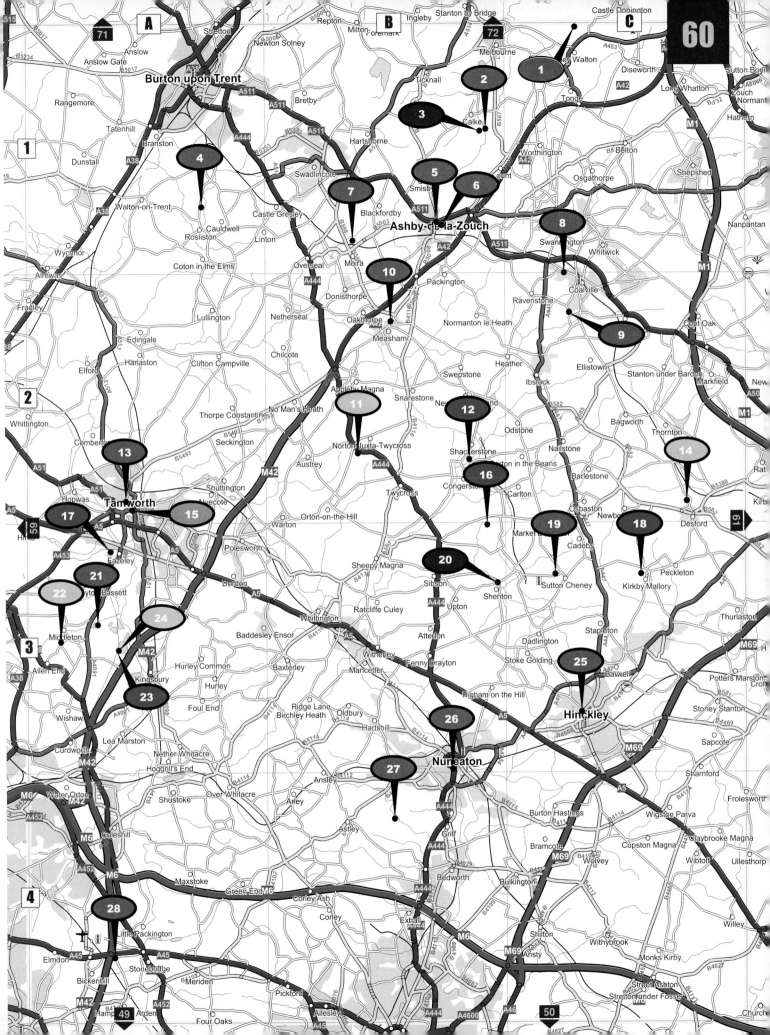

- ● ANIMAL ATTRACTIONS
- ● HERITAGE & CULTURE
- ○ INDOOR ACTIVITIES
- ● OUTDOOR ATTRACTIONS
- ● OUTDOOR ACTIVITIES
- ● WATER ACTIVITIES

1 MANOR FARM ANIMAL CENTRE & DONKEY SANCTUARY
Farm
Castle Hill, East Leake, Loughborough
TEL: 01509 852 525

2 TUMBLEDOWN FARM
Farm
Melton Spinney Road, Thorpe Arnold, Melton Mowbray
TEL: 01664 481 811

3 GREAT CENTRAL RAILWAY
Railway
Great Central Road, Loughborough
TEL: 01509 230 726

4 MELTON CARNEGIE MUSEUM
Museum
Thorpe End, Melton Mowbray
TEL: 01664 569 946

5 BEACON HILL COUNTRY PARK
Country park
Beacon Road, Woodhouse Eaves, Loughborough
TEL: 01509 890 048

6 BRADGATE COUNTRY PARK VISITOR CENTRE
Visitor centre
Bradgate Park, Newtown, Linford
TEL: 01162 362 713

7 BELGRAVE HALL
Historic house
Church Road, Belgrave, Leicester
TEL: 01162 666 590

8 ABBEY PUMPING STATION
Museum
Corporation Road, Leicester
TEL: 01162 995 111

9 GORSE HILL CITY FARM
Farm
Anstey Lane, Leicester
TEL: 01162 537 582

10 HALSTEAD HOUSE FARM & NATURE TRAIL
Farm
Oakham Road, Tilton-on-the-Hill
TEL: 01162 597 239

11 KIRBY MUXLOE CASTLE
Castle
Oakcroft Avenue, Kirby Muxloe
TEL: 01162 386 886

12 NATIONAL SPACE CENTRE
Theme park
Mansion House 41 Guildhall Lane Leicester
TEL: 01162 530 811

13 JEWRY WALL MUSEUM & SITE
Museum
St Nicholas Circle, Leicester
TEL: 01162 473 021

14 GURU NANAK SIKH MUSEUM
Museum
9 Holy Bones, Leicester
TEL: 01162 628 606

15 GUILDHALL
Historic building
Guildhall Lane, Leicester
TEL: 01162 532 569

16 WYGSTON'S HOUSE MUSEUM OF COSTUME
Museum
12 Applegate, Leicester
TEL: 01162 473 056

17 JAIN CENTRE
Historic building
32 Oxford Street, Leicester
TEL: 01162 543 091

18 NEWARKE HOUSES MUSEUM
Museum
The Newarke, Leicester
TEL: 01162 473 222

19 NEW WALK MUSEUM & ART GALLERY
Museum
New Walk, Leicester
TEL: 01162 554 100

20 LEICESTER GAS MUSEUM
Museum
195 Aylestone Road, Leicester
TEL: 01162 503 190

21 FARMWORLD
Farm
Stoughton Farm Park, Gartree Road, Oadby
TEL: 01162 710 355

22 UNIVERSITY OF LEICESTER BOTANIC GARDEN
Garden
Beaumont Hall, Stoughton Drive, Oadby
TEL: 01162 717 725

23 LEICESTERSHIRE RECORD OFFICE
Museum
Long Street, Wigston, Magna
TEL: 01162 571 080

24 WIGSTON FRAMEWORK KNITTERS MUSEUM
Museum
42-44 Bushloe End, Wigston, Magna
TEL: 01162 883 396

25 FOXTON LOCKS COUNTRY PARK
Country park
Gumley Road, Foxton, Market Harborough
TEL: 01162 656 913

26 FOXTON LOCKS CANAL MUSEUM
Museum
Bottom Lock Foxton, Market Harborough
TEL: 01162 792 285

27 HARBOROUGH MUSEUM
Museum
Adam & Eve Street, Market Harborough
TEL: 01858 821 085

28 LUTTERWORTH MUSEUM
Museum
6 McCauley Road, Lutterworth
TEL: 01455 557 635

29 WEST LODGE RURAL CENTRE
Visitor centre
Back Lane, Desborough, Kettering
TEL: 01536 763 762

30 NORTH KILWORTH NARROWBOATS
Boat hire
Kilworth Marina, Kilworth
TEL: 01858 880 484

31 RUSHTON TRIANGULAR LODGE
Historic house
Rushton, Kettering
TEL: 01536 710 761

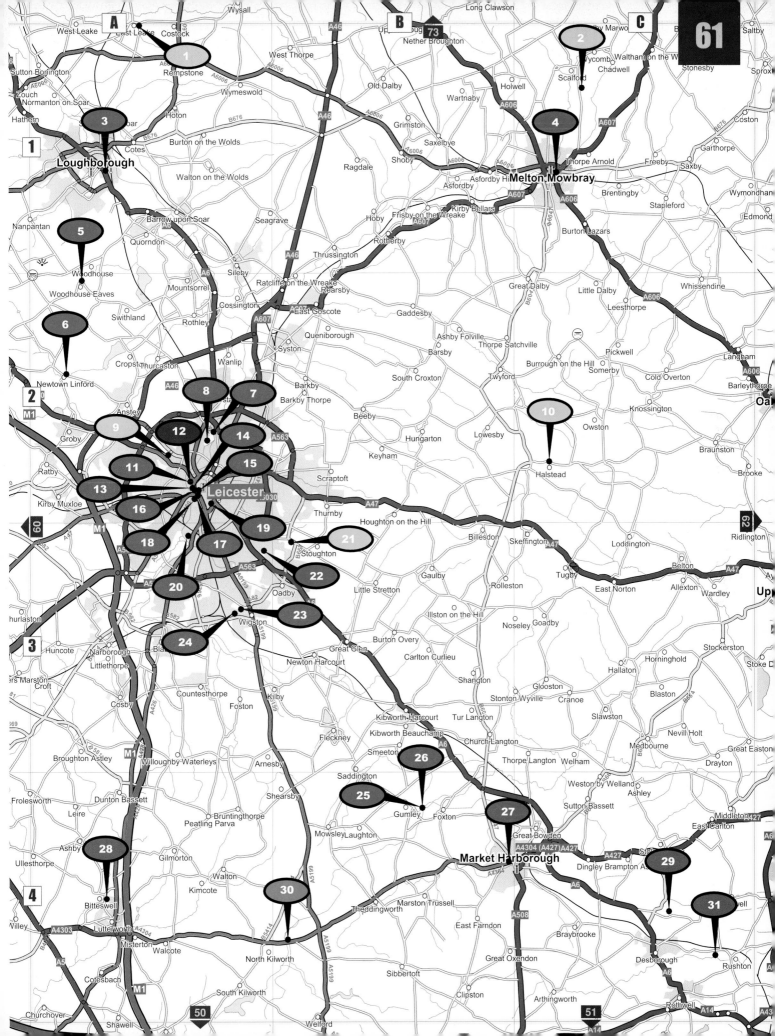

1 WOOLSTHORPE MANOR
Historic house
23 Newton Way, Woolsthorpe-by-Colsterworth, Grantham
TEL: 01476 860 338

2 GRIMSTHORPE CASTLE PARK & GARDENS
Garden
Grimsthorpe, Bourne
TEL: 01778 591 205

3 RUTLAND RAILWAY MUSEUM
Railway
Cottesmore Iron Ore Mines Sidings, Ashwell Road, Cottesmore
TEL: 01572 813 203

4 BARNSDALE GARDENS
Garden
Exton Avenue, Oakham
TEL: 01572 813 200

5 SHAKESPEARE AT TOLETHORPE
Entertainment centre
Rutland Open Air Theatre, Tolethorpe Hall, Stamford
TEL: 01780 754 381

6 TALLINGTON LAKES
Boat hire
Barholm Road, Tallington, Stamford
TEL: 01778 347 000

7 BUTTERFLY & AQUATIC CENTRE
Butterfly farm
Rutland Water
TEL: 01780 460 515

8 RUTLAND COUNTY MUSEUM
Museum
Catmos Street, Oakham
TEL: 01572 723 654

9 OAKHAM CASTLE
Castle
Market Place, Oakham
TEL: 01572 723 654

10 RUTLAND WATER
Water Park
Sykes Lane, Empingham, Oakham
TEL: 01780 460 321

11 ABBEY HOUSE
Historic house
West End Road, Maxey, Stamford
TEL: 01778 344 642

12 PRIEST'S HOUSE
Historic building
Easton on the Hill, Stamford
TEL: 01780 762 619

13 STAMFORD MUSEUM
Museum
Broad Street, Stamford
TEL: 01780 766 317

14 WATERFOWL WORLD
Bird centre & aviary
Peakirk
TEL: 01733 252 271

15 BURGHLEY HOUSE
Historic house
Stamford
TEL: 01780 752 451

16 SACREWELL FARM & COUNTRY STORE
Farm
Thornhaugh, Peterborough
TEL: 01780 782 254

17 ABBEY GATEHOUSE NT
Heritage centre
Abbey School, Ramsey, Peterborough
TEL: 01263 733 471

18 PETERBOROUGH CATHEDRAL
Cathedral
Minster Precincts, Peterborough
TEL: 01733 343 342

19 LONGTHORPE TOWER
Historic building
Peterborough
TEL: 01733 268 482

20 PETERBOROUGH MUSEUM & ART GALLERY
Museum
Priestgate, Peterborough
TEL: 01733 343 329

21 RAILWORLD EXHIBITION CENTRE & MUSEUM
Museum
Oundle Road, Peterborough
TEL: 01733 344 240

22 NENE VALLEY RAILWAY
Railway
Wansford Station, Stibbington, Peterborough
TEL: 01780 784 444

23 BEDE HOUSE
Historic building
Bluecoat Lane, Lyddington, Uppingham
TEL: 01572 822 438

24 BIG SKY ADVENTURE PLAY CENTRE
Adventure & activity centre
24 Wainman Road, Shrewsbury Avenue, Peterborough
TEL: 01733 390 810

25 PREBENDAL MANOR HOUSE
Historic house
Church Street, Nassington, Peterborough
TEL: 01780 782 575

26 ELTON HALL
Historic house
Peterborough
TEL: 01832 280 468

27 DEENE PARK
Garden
Deene, Corby
TEL: 01780 450 278

28 KIRBY HALL EH
Garden
Deene, Corby
TEL: 01536 203 230

29 SOUTHWICK HALL
Historic house
Southwick, Peterborough
TEL: 01832 274 064

30 ROCKINGHAM CASTLE
Castle
Rockingham, Market Harborough
TEL: 01536 770 240

31 NATIONAL DRAGONFLY MUSEUM
Museum
Ashton Mill, Ashton, Oundle
TEL: 01832 272 427

32 LYVEDEN NEW BIELD
Historic house
Oundle
TEL: 01832 205 358

33 BARNWELL COUNTRY PARK
Country park
Barnwell Street, Oundle
TEL: 01832 273 435

34 BOUGHTON HOUSE
Historic house
Kettering
TEL: 01536 515 731

35 HAMERTON WILDLIFE PARK
Wildlife park
Hamerton, Huntingdon
TEL: 01832 293 362

Anglesey Abbey, Cambs, Map53-5

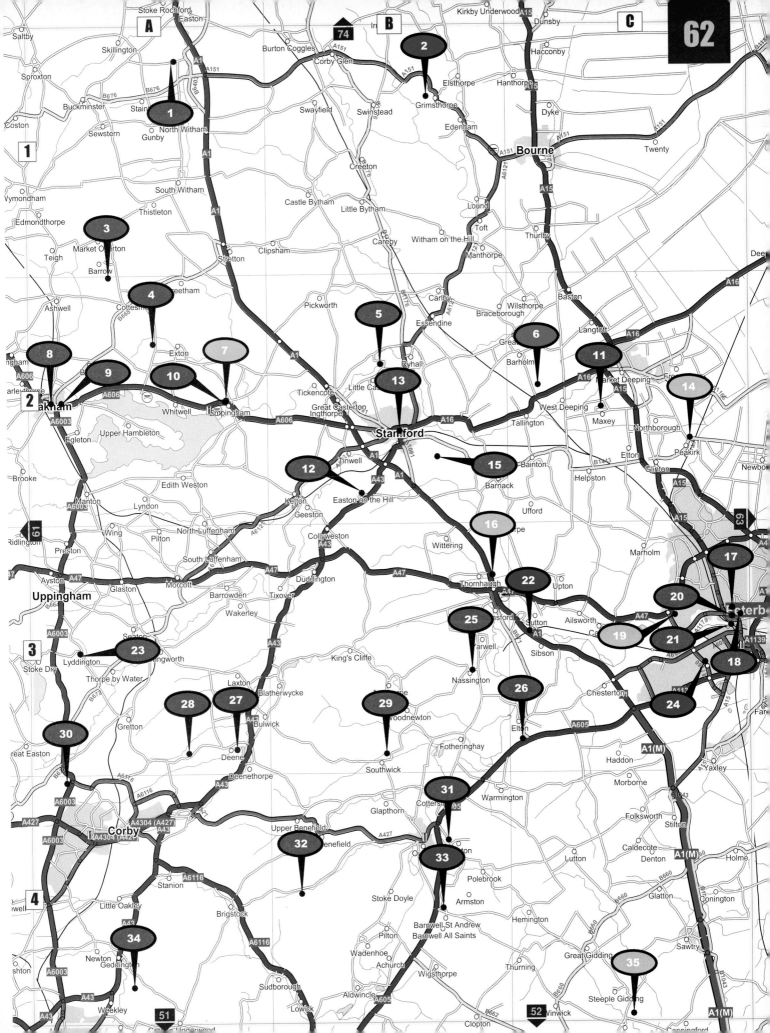

CAMBS · LINCS · NORFOLK

1 SPALDING TROPICAL FOREST
Garden
Glenside North, Pinchbeck, Spalding
TEL: 01775 710 882

2 CASTLE RISING CASTLE
Castle
Castle Rising, King's Lynn
TEL: 01553 631 330

3 BAYTREE OWL CENTRE
Bird centre & aviary
Weston
TEL: 01406 371 907

4 SPRINGFIELDS SHOW GARDENS
Garden
Camelgate, Spalding
TEL: 01775 724 843

5 BUTTERFLY & WILDLIFE PARK
Wildlife park
Long Sutton, Spalding
TEL: 01406 363 833

6 AYSCOUGHFEE HALL MUSEUM & GARDENS
Museum
Churchgate, Spalding
TEL: 01775 725 468

7 GORDON BOSWELL ROMANY MUSEUM
Museum
Clay Lake, Spalding
TEL: 01775 710 599

8 TRUE'S YARD FISHING MUSEUM
Museum
North Street, King's Lynn
TEL: 01553 770 479

9 KING'S LYNN ARTS CENTRE
Art centre
27 King's Street, King's Lynn
TEL: 01553 765 565

10 ST GEORGE'S GUILDHALL NT
Historic building
King Street, King's Lynn
TEL: 01553 765 565

11 CUSTOM HOUSE
Museum
King's Lynn
TEL: 01553 763 044

12 TOWN HOUSE MUSEUM OF LYNN LIFE
Museum
Queen Street, King's Lynn
TEL: 01553 773 450

13 AFRICAN VIOLET CENTRE
Garden
71 Station Road, Terrington St Clement, King's Lynn
TEL: 01553 828 374

14 CAITHNESS GLASS FACTORY & VISITOR CENTRE
Factory tour & shopping
Paxman Road, Hardwick Industrial Estate, King's Lynn
TEL: 01553 765 111

15 PECKOVER HOUSE & GARDEN NT
Historic building
North Brink, Wisbech
TEL: 01945 583 463

16 WISBECH & FENLAND MUSEUM
Museum
Museum Square, Wisbech
TEL: 01945 583 817

17 ELGOOD'S BREWERY
Brewery
North Brink, Wisbech
TEL: 01945 583 160

18 LYNN MUSEUM
Museum
Market Street, King's Lynn
TEL: 01553 775 001

19 FERRY MEADOWS COUNTRY PARK
Country park
Waterville, Peterborough
TEL: 01733 234 443

20 HERMITAGE HALL
Museum
Bridge Farm, Downham Market
TEL: 01366 383 185

21 COLLECTORS WORLD
Museum
Hermitage Hall, Bridge Farm, Downham Market
TEL: 01366 383 185

22 FLAG FEN BRONZE AGE EXCAVATION
Archaeological site
Fourth Drove, Fengate, Peterborough
TEL: 01733 313 414

23 MARCH & DISTRICT MUSEUM
Museum
High Street, March
TEL: 01354 655 300

24 RAMSEY ABBEY GATEHOUSE
Historic building
Abbey School, Ramsey, Huntingdon
TEL: 01263 733 471

25 DRAINAGE ENGINE MUSEUM
Museum
Main Street, Prickwillow, Ely
TEL: 01353 688 360

26 ELY MUSEUM
Museum
The Old Goal Market Street, Ely
TEL: 01353 666 655

27 STAINED GLASS MUSEUM
Museum
Ely Cathedral, Ely
TEL: 01353 660 347

28 ELY CATHEDRAL
Cathedral
Chapter House, Ely
TEL: 01353 667 735

29 OLIVER CROMWELL'S HOUSE
Lived Here
29 St Mary's Street, Ely
TEL: 01353 662 062

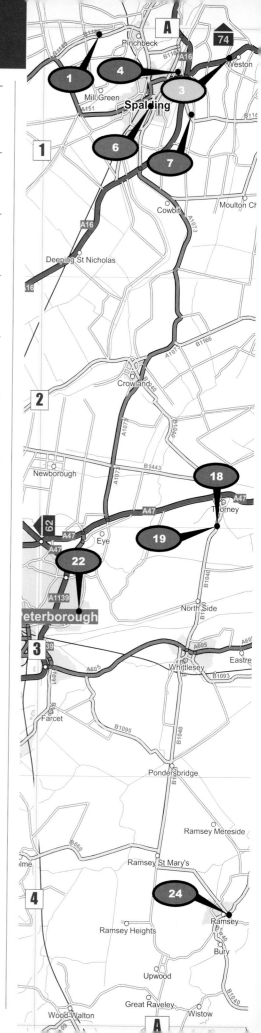

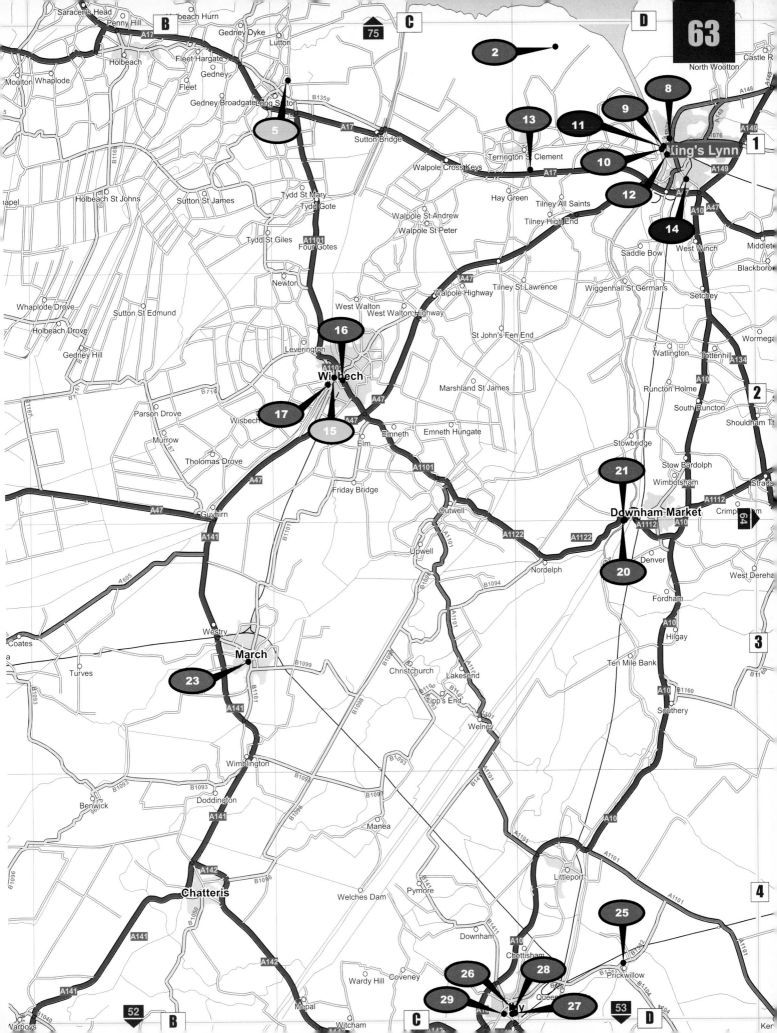

1 FOXLEY WOOD
Nature centre
Dereham
Tel: 01603 625 540

2 NORFOLK WILDLIFE CENTRE & COUNTRY PARK
Wildlife park
Fakenham Road, Lenwade, Norwich
Tel: 01603 872 274

3 DINOSAUR ADVENTURE PARK
Theme park
Weston Park, Lenwade
Tel: 01603 870 245

4 NORFOLK RURAL LIFE MUSEUM & UNION FARM
Museum
Beech House, Gressenhall, Dereham
Tel: 01362 860 563

5 CASTLE ACRE BAILEY GATE
Historic building
Swaffham
Tel: 01604 730 325

6 CASTLE ACRE PRIORY EH
Castle
Back Lane, Stocks Green, Castle Acre
Tel: 01760 755 394

7 ECOTECH DISCOVERY CENTRE & ECOTRICITY WIND TURBINE
Museum
Castle Acre Road, Swaffham
Tel: 01760 726 100

8 SWAFFHAM MUSEUM
Museum
London Street, Swaffham
Tel: 01760 721 230

9 ANGLIAN KARTING CENTRE
Karting
North Pickenham, Swaffham
Tel: 01760 441 777

10 COCKLEY CLEY ICENI VILLAGE & MUSEUMS
Museum
Cockley Cley, Swaffham
Tel: 01760 721 339

11 WYMONDHAM HERITAGE MUSEUM
Museum
10 The Bridewell, Norwich Road, Wymondham
Tel: 01953 600 205

12 TROPICAL BUTTERFLY WORLD
Wildlife park
Great Ellingham, Attleborough
Tel: 01953 453 175

13 HALL FARM
Visitor centre
International League for the Protection of Horses, Snetterton
Tel: 01953 497 219

14 GRIMES GRAVES
Archaeological site
The Lodge, Grimes Grave, Thetford
Tel: 01842 810 656

15 SNETTERTON CIRCUIT
Motor racing circuit
Harling Road, Snetterton, Norwich
Tel: 01953 887 303

16 WEETING CASTLE
Castle
Castle Close, Weeting, Brandon
Tel: 01604 730 320

17 HIGH LODGE FOREST CENTRE
Forest Visitor Centres
Thetford Forest Park, Santon Downham, Brandon
Tel: 01842 810 271

18 BANHAM ZOO & APPLEYARD CRAFT COURT
Zoo
The Grove, Banham
Tel: 01953 887 771

19 BRANDON HERITAGE CENTRE
Heritage centre
George Street, Brandon
Tel: 01842 813 707

20 CHURCH OF HOLY SEPHULCHRE NT
Historic building
Thetford
Tel: 01263 733 471

21 ANCIENT HOUSE MUSEUM
Museum
White Hart Street, Thetford
Tel: 01842 752 599

22 BRESSINGHAM STEAM MUSEUM & GARDENS
Museum
Thetford Road, Diss
Tel: 01379 687 386

23 DISS MUSEUM
Museum
11 Market Hill, Diss
Tel: 01379 650 618

Melford Hall, Suffolk, Map 54

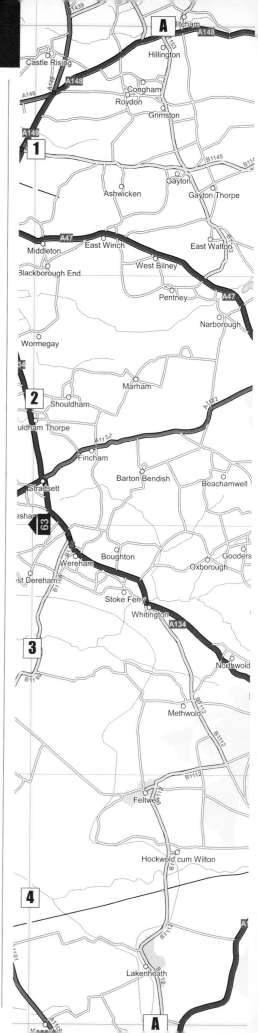

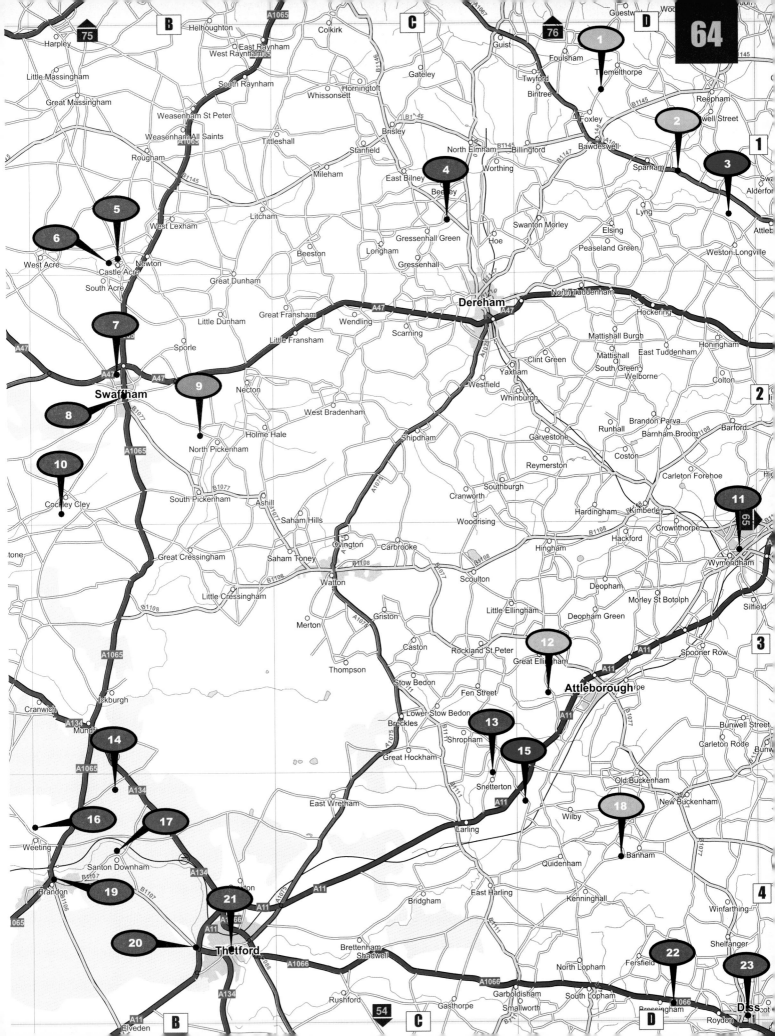

NORFOLK · SUFFOLK

- ANIMAL ATTRACTIONS
- HERITAGE & CULTURE
- INDOOR ACTIVITIES
- OUTDOOR ATTRACTIONS
- OUTDOOR ACTIVITIES
- WATER ACTIVITIES

1 WROXHAM BARNS
Craft centre
Tunstead Road, Hoveton
TEL: 01603 783 762

2 REDWINGS HORSE SANCTUARY
Farm
Hall Lane, Frettenham, Norwich
TEL: 01603 737 432

3 HOVETON HALL GARDENS
Garden
Wroxham, Norwich
TEL: 01603 782 798

4 BROADLAND CYCLE HIRE
Cycle hire
The Rond, Hoveton
TEL: 01603 783 096

5 NORWICH AVIATION MUSEUM
Museum
Old Norwich Road, Horsham St Faith, Norwich
TEL: 01603 893 080

6 NORWICH INDOOR KART CENTRE
Karting
Vulcan Road North, Norwich
TEL: 01603 486 655

7 WATERLOO PARK
Country park
Angel Road, Norwich
TEL: 01603 789 880

8 SLOUGHBOTTOM PARK
Country park
Hellesdon Hall Road, Norwich
TEL: 01603 622 233

9 NUMBER 10
Bowling centre
Barnard Road, Bowthorpe Road, Norwich
TEL: 01603 740 730

11 FUNKY MONKEYS
Adventure & activity centre
Spar Road, Norwich
TEL: 01603 403 220

12 HOLLYWOOD BOWL
Bowling centre
Riverside, Norwich
TEL: 01603 631 311

13 INSPIRE SCIENCE CENTRE
Museum
St Michael's Church, Coslany Street, Norwich
TEL: 01603 612 612

14 NORWICH CATHEDRAL
Cathedral
62 The Close, Norwich
TEL: 01603 764 385/767 617

15 ST PETER HUNGATE CHURCH MUSEUM
Museum
Princes Street, Norwich
TEL: 01603 667 231

16 COW TOWER NT
Historic building
Norwich
TEL: Not available

Harewood House, Yorkshire. Map 88·10

17 PLANTATION GARDEN
Garden
4 Earlham Road, Norwich
TEL: 01603 621 868

18 BRIDEWELL MUSEUM
Museum
Bridewell Alley, Norwich
TEL: 01603 667 228

19 PLANET JAR CADET INDOOR PAINTBALL CENTRE
Paintball centre
Mountergate, Norwich
TEL: 01603 661 040

20 GUILDHALL
Historic building
Gaol Hill, Norwich
TEL: 01603 622 233

21 NORWICH CASTLE MUSEUM
Castle
Castle Meadow, Norwich
TEL: 01603 493 654

22 ROYAL NORFOLK REGIMENTAL MUSEUM
Museum
Market Avenue, Norwich
TEL: 01603 493 649

23 DRAGON HALL
Historic building
115-123 King Street, Norwich
TEL: 01603 663 922

24 NORWICH CITY FOOTBALL CLUB
Football ground
Carrow Road, Norwich
TEL: 01603 760 760

25 LAKENHAM RECREATION GROUND
Country park
City Road, Norwich
TEL: 01603 627 434

26 KARTING COMPANY
Karting
Norwich Common, Wymondham
TEL: 01953 604 705

27 FORNCETT INDUSTRIAL STEAM MUSEUM
Museum
Forncett St Mary
TEL: 01508 488 277

28 OTTER TRUST
Wildlife park
Earsham, Bungay
TEL: 01986 893 470

29 NORFOLK & SUFFOLK AVIATION MUSEUM
Museum
Buckeroo Way, The Street, Flixton
TEL: 01986 896 644

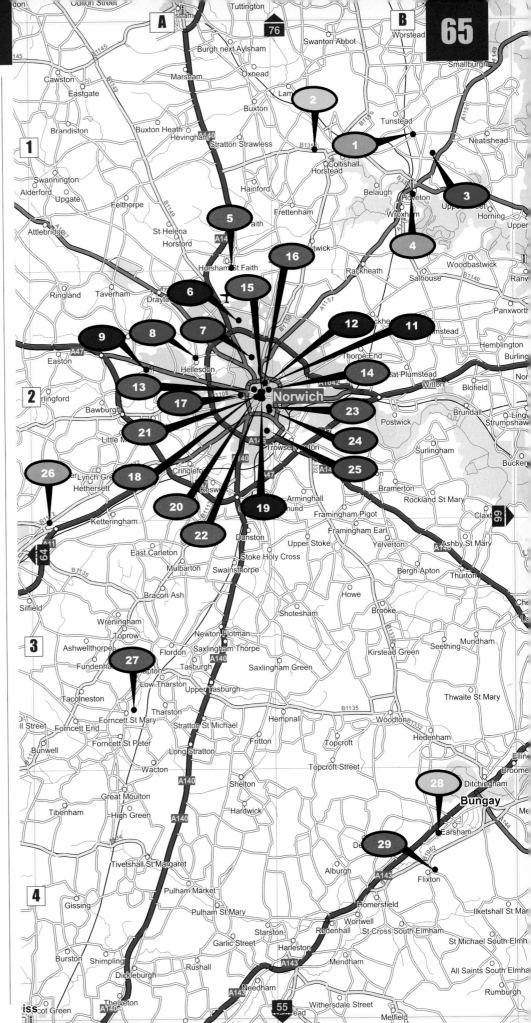

● ANIMAL ATTRACTIONS   ● OUTDOOR ATTRACTIONS
● HERITAGE & CULTURE   ● OUTDOOR ACTIVITIES
○ INDOOR ACTIVITIES   ● WATER ACTIVITIES

1 HORSEY WINDPUMP
Mill
Horsey, Great Yarmouth
TEL: 01493 393 904

2 VILLAGE EXPERIENCE
Unusual
Fleggburgh
TEL: 01493 369 770

3 FAIRHAVEN GARDEN TRUST
Garden
2 Wymers Lane, South Walsham, Norwich
TEL: 01603 270 449

4 CAISTER ROMAN SITE
Roman site
Caister-on-Sea
TEL: Not available

5 CANDLEMAKER & MODEL CENTRE
Craft centre
Stokesby, Great Yarmouth
TEL: 01493 750 242

6 GREAT YARMOUTH RACECOURSE
Racecourse
Jellicoe Road, Great Yarmouth
TEL: 01493 842 527

7 JOYLAND
Theme park
Marine Parade, Great Yarmouth
TEL: 01493 844 094

8 HOLLYWOOD SCREEN ENTERTAINMENTS
Museum
Marine Parade, Great Yarmouth
TEL: 01493 843 504

9 ELIZABETHAN HOUSE MUSEUM
Museum
4 South Quay, Great Yarmouth
TEL: 01493 855 746

10 MARITIME MUSEUM FOR EAST ANGLIA
Museum
25 Marine Parade Great, Yarmouth
TEL: 01493 842 267

11 TOLHOUSE MUSEUM & BRASS RUBBING CENTRE
Museum
Tolhouse Street, Great Yarmouth
TEL: 01493 858 900

12 NELSON'S MONUMENT
Monuments
South Beach Parade, Great Yarmouth
TEL: 01493 858 900

13 AMAZONIA WORLD OF REPTILES
Reptile house
Marine Parade, Great Yarmouth
TEL: 01493 842 202

14 SEA LIFE GREAT YARMOUTH
Sea life centre
Marine Parade, Great Yarmouth
TEL: 01493 330 631

15 MERRIVALE MODEL VILLAGE
Model village
Wellington Pier Gardens, Marine Parade,
Great Yarmouth
TEL: 01493 842 097

16 ROW 111 HOUSE OLD MERCHANTS HOUSE EH
Historic building
South Quay, Great Yarmouth
TEL: 01493 857 900

17 PLEASURE BEACH
Theme park
South Beach Parade, Great Yarmouth
TEL: 01493 844 585

18 KARTING 2000
Karting
Fenner Road, Great Yarmouth
TEL: 01493 854 041

19 BERNEY ARMS WINDMILL
Mill
Great Yarmouth
TEL: 01493 700 605

20 BURGH CASTLE
Castle
Great Yarmouth
TEL: 01493 701 605

21 PETTITTS ANIMAL ADVENTURE PARK
Adventure & activity centre
Camphill, Reedham
TEL: 01493 701 403

22 FRITTON LAKE COUNTRYWORLD
Country park
Fritton, Great Yarmouth
TEL: 01493 488 208

23 ST OLAVE'S PRIORY
Priory
St Olaves
TEL: Not available

24 SOMERLEYTON HALL & GARDENS
Historic building
Somerleyton, Lowestoft
TEL: 01502 730 224

25 RAVENINGHAM HALL GARDENS
Garden
Raveningham, Norwich
TEL: 01508 548 222

Mannington Hall, Norfolk, Map 76-23

26 PLEASUREWOOD HILLS THEME PARK
Theme park
Leisure Way, Corton, Lowestoft
Tel: 01502 586 000

27 MARITIME MUSEUM
Museum
Sparrow Nest Gardens, Whapload Road, Lowestoft
Tel: 01502 561 963

28 LOWESTOFT MUSEUM
Museum
Broad House, Nicholas Everitt Park, Lowestoft
Tel: 01502 511 457

29 EAST POINT PAVILLION VISITOR CENTRE
Visitor centre
Lowestoft
Tel: 01502 533 600

30 PETS CORNER
Farm
Nicholas Everitt Park, Oulton Broad, Lowestoft
Tel: 01502 563 533

31 DISCOVERING
Adventure & activity centre
East Point Pavilion, Royal Plain, Lowestoft
Tel: 01502 533 600

32 ELLOUGH PARK RACEWAY
Karting
Beccles
Tel: 01502 717 718

33 EAST ANGLIA TRANSPORT MUSEUM
Museum
Chapel Road, Carlton Colville, Lowestoft
Tel: 01502 518 459

34 SUFFOLK WILDLIFE PARK
Wildlife park
Whites Lane, Lowestoft
Tel: 01502 740 291

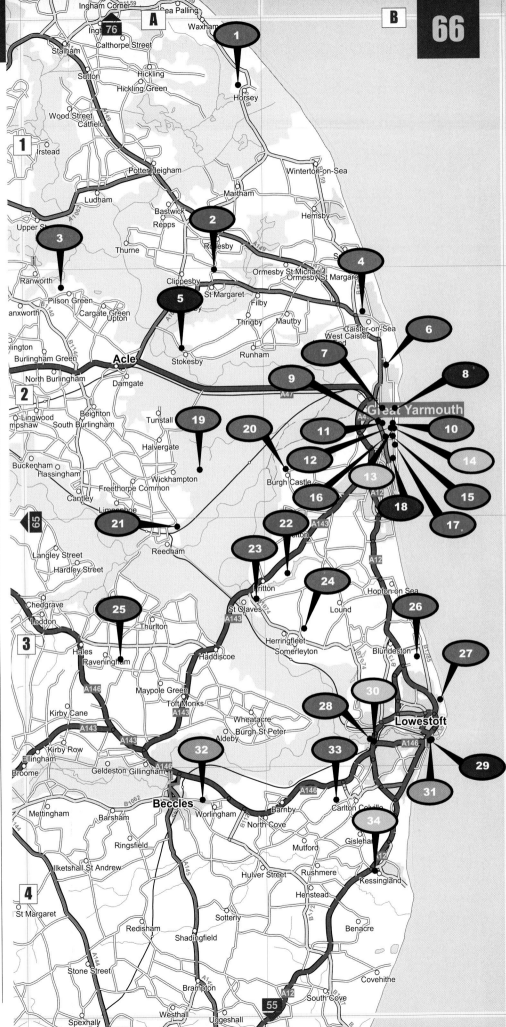

1 PLAS NEWYDD NT
Garden
Llanfairpwyll, Anglesey
Tel: 01248 714 795

2 GREENWOOD CENTRE
Heritage centre
Y Felinheli
Tel: 01248 671 493

3 FOEL FARM PARK
Farm
Foel Farm, Brynsiencyn, Llanfairpwllgwyngyll
Tel: 01248 430 646

4 ANGLESEY SEA ZOO
Aquarium
Brynsiencyn, Llanfairpwllgwyngyll
Tel: 01248 430 411

5 CAERNARFON CASTLE
Castle
Castle Ditch, Caernarfon
Tel: 01286 677 617

6 SEGONTIUM ROMAN FORT & MUSEUM
Roman site
Llanbeblig Road, Caernarfon
Tel: 01286 675 625

7 WELSH SLATE MUSEUM
Museum
Padarn Country Park, Llanberis
Tel: 01286 870 630

8 LLANBERIS LAKE RAILWAY
Railway
Padarn Country Park, Gilfach, Caernarfon
Tel: 01286 870 549

9 SNOWDON MOUNTAIN RAILWAY
Railway
Llanberis, Caernarfon
Tel: 01286 870 223

10 ELECTRIC MOUNTAIN
Factory tour
Llanberis, Caernarfon
Tel: 01286 870 636

11 DOLBADARN CASTLE
Castle
Llanberis, Caernarfon
Tel: 029 2082 9185

12 AIR WORLD
Museum
Caernarfon Air Park, Dinas Dinlle, Caernarfon
Tel: 01286 830 800

13 GLYNLLIFION
Garden
Clynnog Road, Llandwrog, Caernarfon
Tel: 01286 830 222

14 SYGUN COPPER MINE
Museum
Beddgelert
Tel: 01766 510 100

15 PLAS BRONDANW GARDENS
Garden
Llanfrothen, Panrhyndeudreath
Tel: 01766 770 484

16 LLOYD GEORGE MUSEUM & HIGHGATE VICTORIAN COTTAGE
Museum
Llanystumdwy, Criccieth
Tel: 01766 522 071

17 FFESTINIOG RAILWAY
Railway
Harbour Station, Porthmadog
Tel: 01766 512 340

18 CRICCIETH CASTLE
Castle
Castle Street, Criccieth
Tel: 01766 522 227

19 PENARTH FAWR
Historic building
Penarth Fawr
Tel: 01766 810 880

20 PORTMEIRION
Unusual
Penrhyndeudraeth
Tel: 01766 770 228

21 CYFEILION ELLIS WYNNE
Historic house
Lasynys Fawr, Harlech
Tel: 01766 780 846

22 HARLECH CASTLE
Castle
Castle Square, Harlech
Tel: 01766 780 552

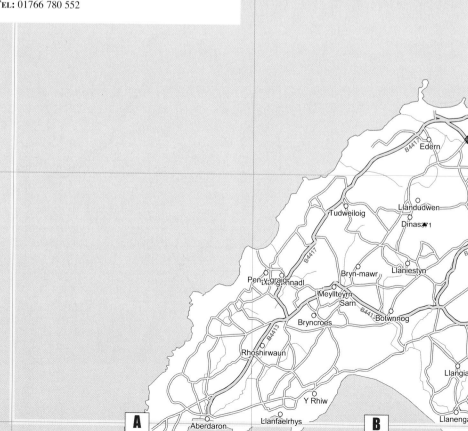

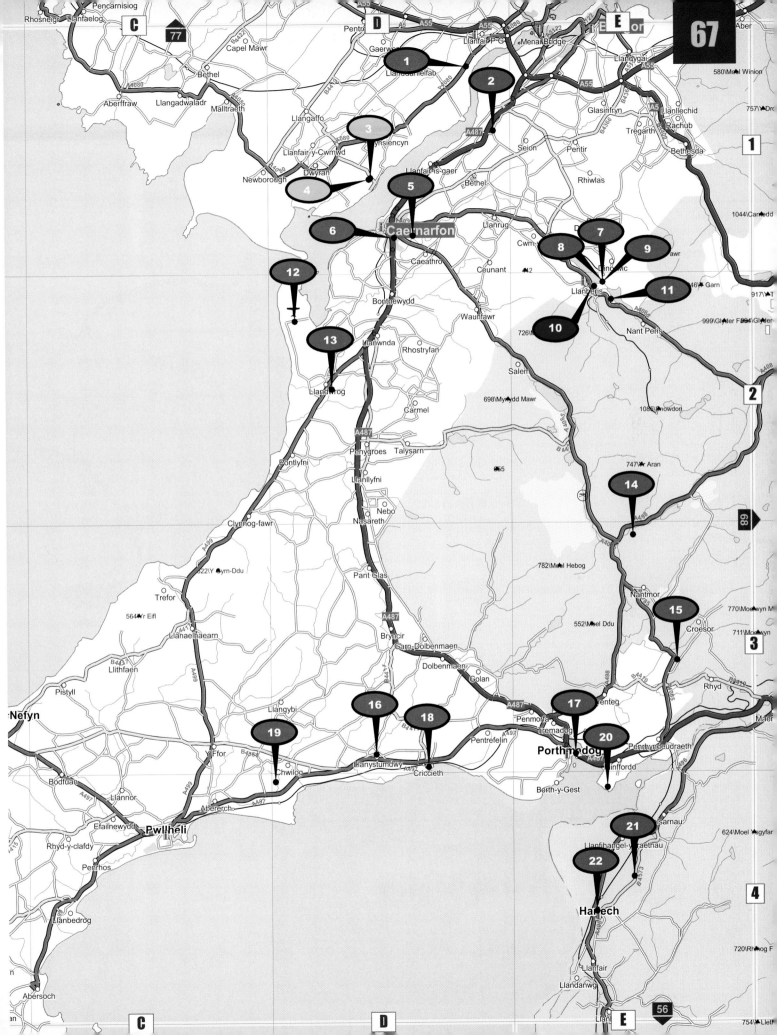

NORTH WALES

1 **DENBIGH CASTLE**
Castle
Castle Hill, Denbigh
TEL: 01745 813 385

2 **ABERGWYNANT FARM TREKKING CENTRE**
Farm
Penmaenpool
TEL: 01341 422 377

3 **MOTOR MUSEUM & CANAL EXHIBITION**
Museum
Llangollen
TEL: 01978 860 324

4 **CONWY RSPB NATURE RESERVE**
Nature reserve
Llandudno Junction, Conwy
TEL: 01492 584 091

5 **TREFRIW WOOLLEN MILLS**
Museum
Trefriw
TEL: 01492 640 462

6 **GWYDIR CASTLE**
Garden
Llanrwst
TEL: 01492 641 687

7 **GWYDYR UCHAF CHAPEL**
Historic building
Gwydyr, Llanrwst
TEL: 01492 640 578

8 **CONWY VALLEY RAILWAY MUSEUM**
Museum
Ffordd Hen Eglwys, Betws-Y-Coed
TEL: 01690 710 568

9 **Y STABLAU VISITOR CENTRE**
Visitor centre
Snowdonia National Park, Betws-Y-Coed
TEL: 01690 710 426

10 **LLYN BRENIG VISITOR CENTRE**
Visitor centre
Cerrigydrudion, Corwen
TEL: 01490 420 463

11 **PENMACHNO WOOLLEN MILL**
Museum
Penmachno, Betws-Y-Coed
TEL: 01690 710 545

12 **TY MAWR**
Historic house
Penmachno, Betws-y-coed, Dolwyddelan
TEL: 01690 760 213

13 **DOLWYDDELAN CASTLE**
Castle
Dolwyddelan
TEL: 01690 750 366

14 **TY'N-Y-COED UCHAF**
Farm
Penmachno, Betws-Y-Coed
TEL: 01690 760 229

15 **GLODDFA GANOL SLATE MINE**
Museum
Blaenau Ffestiniog
TEL: 01766 830 664

16 **LLECHWEDD SLATE CAVERNS**
Cave
Snowdonia, Blaenau Ffestiniog
TEL: 01766 830 306

17 **FFESTINIOG PUMPED STORAGE SCHEME**
Factory tour
Tan-y-Grisiau, Blaenau Ffestiniog
TEL: 01766 830 310

18 **PLAS TAN-Y-BWLCH**
Garden
Maentwrog
TEL: 01766 590 324

19 **BALA LAKE RAILWAY**
Railway
Llanuwchllyn, Bala
TEL: 01678 540 666

20 **COED Y BRENIN VISITOR CENTRE**
Visitor Centres
Ganllwyd, Dolgellau
TEL: 01341 422 289

Portmeirion, Gwynedd, Map 67-20

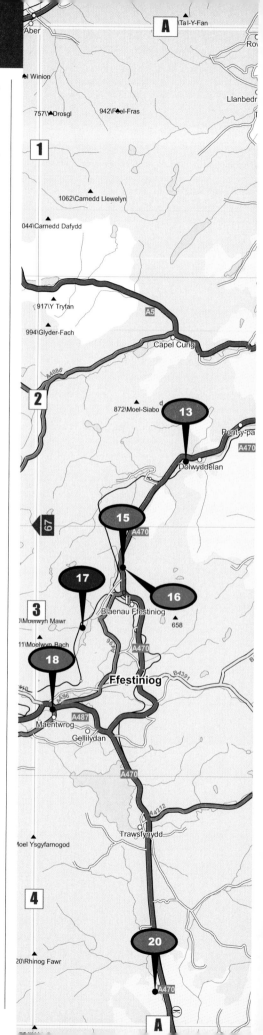

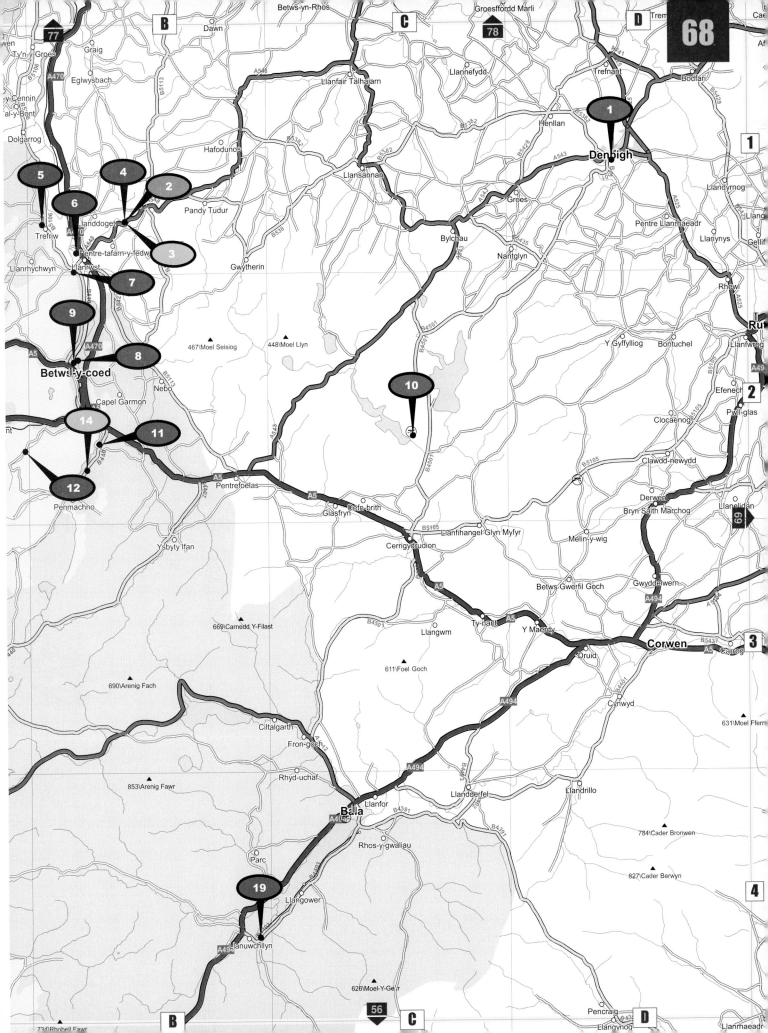

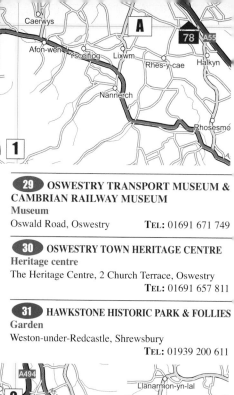

1 MOULDSWORTH MOTOR MUSEUM
Museum
Smithy Lane, Mouldsworth, Chester
Tel: 01928 731 781

2 CHESTER ZOO
Zoo
Upton-by-Chester, Chester, Cheshire, CH2 1LH.
Tel: 01244 380 280
Email: marketing@chesterzoo.co.uk
Web: www.chesterzoo.org

It takes a full day to see the UK's top Zoo. 7000+ animals, with over 500 different species. Natural enclosures and glorious gardens. Free parking.
Open: Open daily from 10am. Last entry varies during season.
Entry costs: £10.50, Child: £8.50, OAPs: £8.50, Family: £35.50.
Specialities: Photography allowed, Picnic area, Play area, Mono-rail.
Facilities: Bookshop, Credit cards, Gift shop, Gift tokens, Pushchair friendly, Restaurant, Toilets, Wheelchair access.

3 CHESHIRE CHEESE EXPERIENCE
Factory tour
Mollington
Tel: 01244 851 982

4 WEPRE COUNTRY PARK
Country park
Wepre Drive, Connah's Quay
Tel: 01244 814 931

5 CHESTER CATHEDRAL
Cathedral
St Werburgh Street, Chester
Tel: 01244 324 756

6 CHESTER HERITAGE CENTRE
Heritage centre
St Michael's Church, Bridge Street Row, Chester
Tel: 01244 402 008

7 CHESTER VISITOR CENTRE
Visitor centre
Vicars Lane, Chester
Tel: 01244 351 609

8 CHESTER RACECOURSE
Racecourse
Chester
Tel: 01244 323 170

9 ON THE AIR THE BROADCASTING MUSEUM
Museum
42 Bridge Street, Row, Chester
Tel: 01244 348 468

10 DEWA ROMAN EXPERIENCE
Roman site
Pierpoint Lane, Chester
Tel: 01244 343 407

11 GROSVENOR MUSEUM
Museum
27 Grosvenor Street, Chester
Tel: 01244 402 008

12 CHESHIRE MILITARY MUSEUM
Museum
The Castle, Chester
Tel: 01244 327 617

13 WATER TOWER
Historic building
City Walls, Chester
Tel: 01244 402 008

14 CHESHIRE FARM ICE CREAM
Farm
Tattenhall
Tel: 01829 770 995

15 BEESTON CASTLE EH
Castle
Beeston, Tarporley
Tel: 01829 260 464

16 PECKFORTON CASTLE
Castle
Stone House Lane, Peckforton, Tarporley
Tel: 01829 260 930

17 CHOLMONDELEY CASTLE GARDEN
Garden
Cholmondeley, Malpas
Tel: 01829 720 383

18 MINERA LEAD MINES
Unusual
Wern Road, Minera, Wrexham
Tel: 01978 751 320

19 BERSHAM INDUSTRIAL HERITAGE CENTRE
Factory tour
Wrexham
Tel: 01978 261 529

20 CLYWEDOG VALLEY
Heritage centre
Bersham Heritage Centre, Bersham, Wrexham
Tel: 01978 261 529

21 ERDDIG NT
Historic house
Wrexham
Tel: 01978 355 314

22 FARMWORLD
Farm
Erddig, Wrexham
Tel: 01978 840 697

23 BANGOR-ON-DEE RACES
Racecourse
Bangor-on-Dee
Tel: 01978 780 323

24 LLANGOLLEN STATION
Railway
The Station, Abbey Road, Llangollen
Tel: 01978 860 951

25 HORSE DRAWN BOATS & CANAL EXHIBITION CENTRE
Museum
The Wharf, Wharf Hill, Llangollen
Tel: 01978 860 702

26 DR WHO EXPERIENCE & INTERNATIONAL MODEL RAILWAY WORLD
Museum
Mill Street, Llangollen
Tel: 01978 860 584

27 CHWAREL WYNN MINE & MUSEUM
Museum
Wynne Quarry, Glyn Ceiriog, Wrexham
Tel: 01691 718 343

28 MERE'S VISITOR CENTRE
Visitor centre
Mereside, Ellesmere
Tel: 01961 622 981

29 OSWESTRY TRANSPORT MUSEUM & CAMBRIAN RAILWAY MUSEUM
Museum
Oswald Road, Oswestry
Tel: 01691 671 749

30 OSWESTRY TOWN HERITAGE CENTRE
Heritage centre
The Heritage Centre, 2 Church Terrace, Oswestry
Tel: 01691 657 811

31 HAWKSTONE HISTORIC PARK & FOLLIES
Garden
Weston-under-Redcastle, Shrewsbury
Tel: 01939 200 611

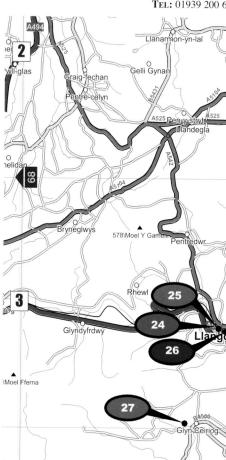

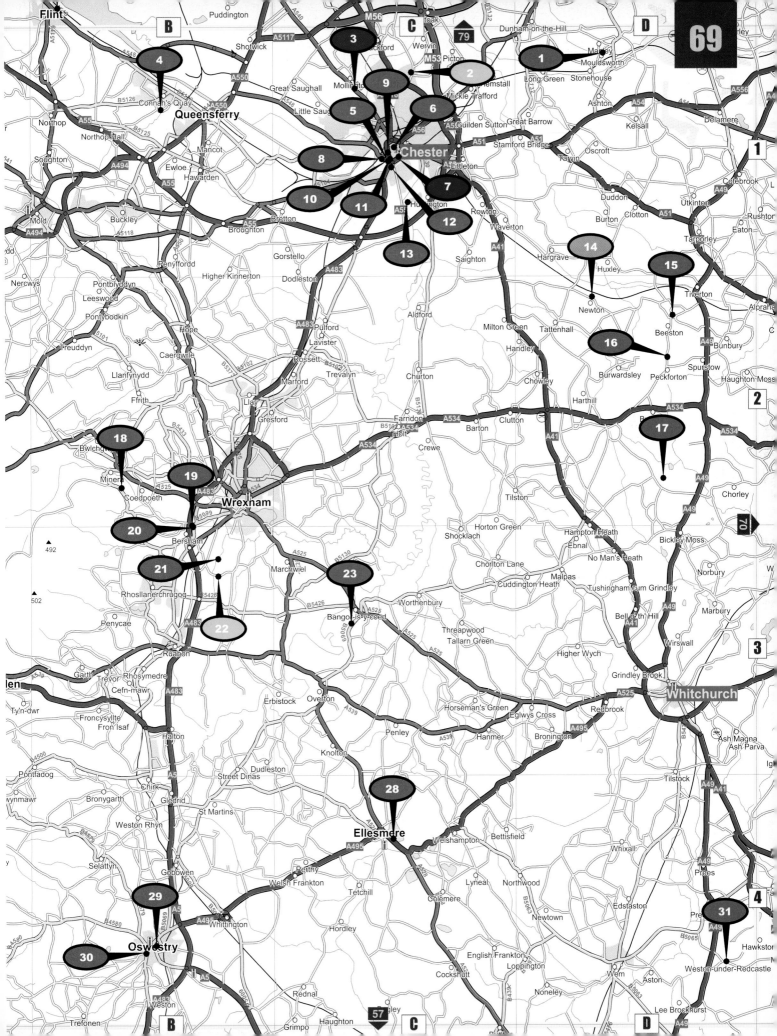

CHESHIRE · SHROPS · STAFFS

● ANIMAL ATTRACTIONS   ● OUTDOOR ATTRACTIONS
● HERITAGE & CULTURE   ● OUTDOOR ACTIVITIES
○ INDOOR ACTIVITIES   ● WATER ACTIVITIES

1 JODRELL BANK ARBORETUM
Arboretum
Lower Withington
TEL: 01477 571 339

2 BLAKEMERE CRAFT CENTRE
Craft centre
Chester Road, Northwich
TEL: 01606 883 261

3 GAWSWORTH HALL
Historic building
Macclesfield
TEL: 01260 223 456

4 MIDDLEWICH NARROWBOATS
Boat hire
74 Canal Terrace, Middlewich
TEL: 01606 832 460

5 OULTON PARK
Motor racing circuit
Tarporley
TEL: 01829 760 301

6 BIDDULPH GRANGE GARDEN NT
Garden
Biddulph Grange, Biddulph, Stoke-on-Trent
TEL: 01782 517 999

7 LITTLE MORETON HALL NT
Garden
Newcastle Road, Congleton
TEL: 01260 272 018

8 LAKEMORE COUNTRY PARK
Country park
Lane Ends Farm, Clay Lane, Haslington
TEL: 01270 253 556

9 RODE HALL
Garden
Church Lane, Scholar Green, Congleton
TEL: 01270 873 273

10 RAILWAY AGE
Railway
Vernon Way, Crewe
TEL: 01270 212 130

11 DORFOLD HALL
Historic house
Chester Road, Acton, Nantwich
TEL: 01270 625 245

12 NANTWICH MUSEUM
Museum
Pillory Street, Nantwich
TEL: 01270 627 104

13 FORD GREEN HALL
Historic building
Ford Green Road, Smallthorne, Stoke-on-Trent
TEL: 01782 233 195

14 HACK GREEN SECRET NUCLEAR BUNKER
Historic building
Baddington, Nantwich
TEL: 01270 629 219

15 WATERWORLD
Boat hire
Festival Park, Stoke-on-Trent
TEL: 01782 205 747

16 POTTERIES MUSEUM & ART GALLERY
Museum
Bethesda Street, Hanley, Stoke-on-Trent
TEL: 01782 232 323

17 ETRURIA INDUSTRIAL MUSEUM
Museum
Lower Bedford Street, Etruria, Stoke-on-Trent
TEL: 01782 233 114

18 PARK HALL COUNTRYSIDE EXPERIENCE
Farm
Park Hall Farm, Burma Road, Oswestry
TEL: 01691 671 749

19 SPODE VISITOR CENTRE
Visitor centre
Church Street, Stoke-on-Trent
TEL: 01782 744 011

20 ROYAL DOULTON VISITOR CENTRE
Visitor centre
Nile Street, Burslem, Stoke-on-Trent
TEL: 01782 292 434

21 AYNSLEY CHINA FACTORY SHOP
Factory tour & shopping
Sutherland Road, Longton, Stoke-on-Trent
TEL: 01782 593 536

22 GLADSTONE WORKING POTTERY MUSEUM
Museum
Uttoxeter Road, Longton, Stoke-on-Trent
TEL: 01782 319 232

23 TRENTHAM PARK GARDENS
Garden
Stone Road, Stoke-on-Trent
TEL: 01782 657 341

24 WHITMORE HALL
Historic house
Whitmore Road, Whitmore, Newcastle
TEL: 01782 680 235

25 DOROTHY CLIVE GARDEN
Willoughbridge, Market Drayton, Shropshire, TF9 4EU.
Garden
TEL: 01630 647 237
WEB: www.dorothyclivegarden.co.uk
This romantic garden is home to choice and unusual plants in informal settings. An alpine scree, water features and a spectacular woodland garden are just some of the delights.
OPEN: Mar 28-Oct 31: 10-5.30.
ENTRY COSTS:
£3.20, Child: £1
Under 11's free, OAPs: £2.70.
SPECIALITIES: Rhododendrons and azaleas, Herbaceous plants, Perennials, Water features, Shrubs.
FACILITIES: Toilets, Wheelchair access, Coffee shop.

26 WEDGWOOD STORY VISITOR CENTRE
Visitor centre
Barlaston, Stoke-on-Trent, Staffordshire, ST12 9ES.
TEL: 01782 204 218
WEB: www.thewedgwoodstory.com
One man, and the company he founded in 1759, changed forever the pottery industry throughout the world. The Wedgwood Story is a celebration of that man and his legacy.
OPEN: Mon-Fri 9-5, Sat-Sun 10-5. Closed Christmas week.
ENTRY COSTS: £6.95, Child: £4.95, OAPs: £4.95, Family: £22.95.
SPECIALITIES: Events held, Photography allowed, Tours available.
FACILITIES: Bookshop, Coffee shop, Credit card, Gift shop, Pushchair friendly, Restaurant, Toilets, Wheelchair access.

27 IZAAK WALTON'S COTTAGE
Lived
Worston Lane, Shallowford, Stafford
TEL: 01785 760 278

River Hodder, Lancs, Map 86

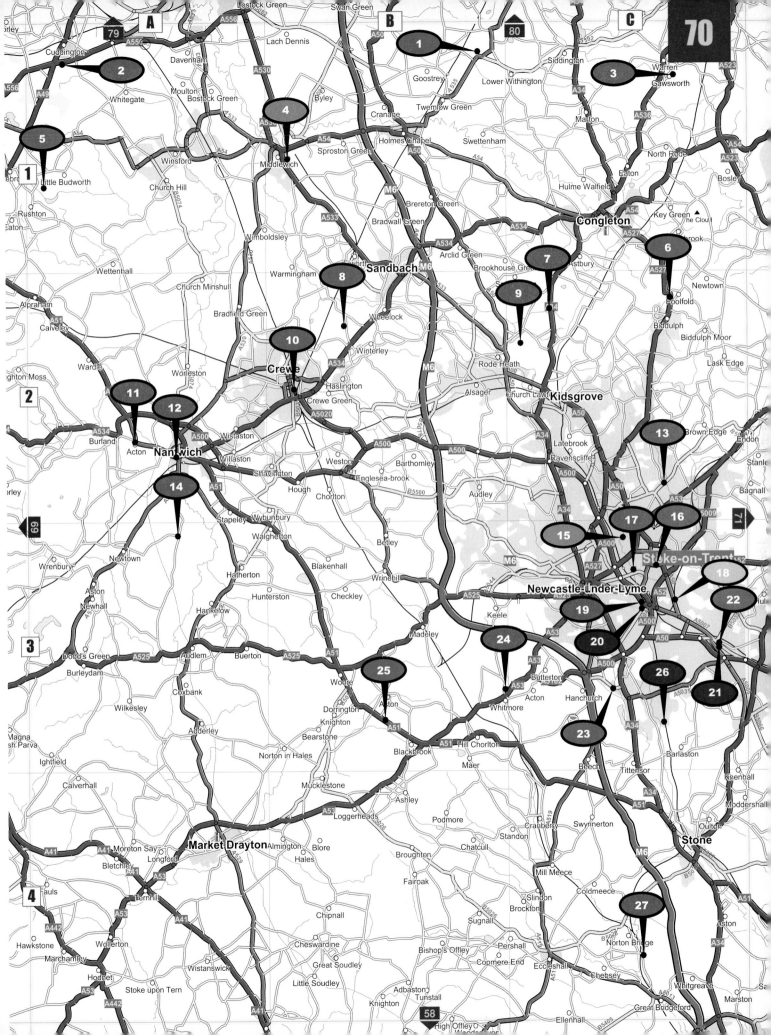

DERBYSHIRE · STAFFORDSHIRE

● ANIMAL ATTRACTIONS ● OUTDOOR ATTRACTIONS
● HERITAGE & CULTURE ● OUTDOOR ACTIVITIES
○ INDOOR ACTIVITIES ● WATER ACTIVITIES

1 CHATSWORTH HOUSE FARMYARD & ADVENTURE PLAYGROUND
Historic house
Edensor, Bakewell
TEL: 01246 582 204

2 OLD HOUSE MUSEUM
Museum
Cunningham Place, Bakewell
TEL: 01629 813 165

3 HADDON HALL
Historic building
Bakewell
TEL: 01629 812 855

4 CAUDWELL'S MILL & CRAFT CENTRE
Museum
Bakewell Road, Rowsley, Matlock
TEL: 01629 734 374

5 TITTESWORTH RESERVOIR VISITOR CENTRE
Visitor centre
Buxton Road, Meerbrook, Leek
TEL: 01538 300 400

6 CHURNET VALLEY RAILWAY
Railway
Cheddleton Station, Station Road, Cheddleton
TEL: 01538 360 522

7 TISSINGTON HALL
Historic house
Ashbourne
TEL: Not available

8 DERWENT CRYSTAL CENTRE
Craft centre
Shawcroft, Ashbourne
TEL: 01335 345 219

9 FOXFIELD STEAM RAILWAY
Railway
Blythe Bridge, Stoke-on-Trent
TEL: 01782 396 210

10 ALTON TOWERS
Theme park
Alton, Stoke-on-Trent
TEL: 0990 204 060

11 CHEADLE RECREATION GROUND
Country park
Tean Road, Stoke-on-Trent
TEL: 01538 754 288

12 BENTLEY FIELDS OPEN FARM
Farm
Bentley Fields, Alkmonton, Cubley Ashbourne
TEL: 01335 330 240

13 UTTOXETER HERITAGE CENTRE
Heritage centre
34-36 Carter Street, Uttoxeter
TEL: 01889 567 176

14 SUDBURY HALL & THE MUSEUM OF CHILDHOOD NT
Historic building
Sudbury, Ashbourne
TEL: 01283 585 305

15 TUTBURY CASTLE
Castle
Tutbury
TEL: 01283 812 129

16 TUTBURY CRYSTAL GLASS
Factory tour & shopping
Burton Street, Tutbury, Burton-upon-Trent
TEL: 01283 813 281

17 AMERTON FARM
Farm
Stow by Chartley, Amerton, Stafford
TEL: 01889 271 998

Rollercoaster

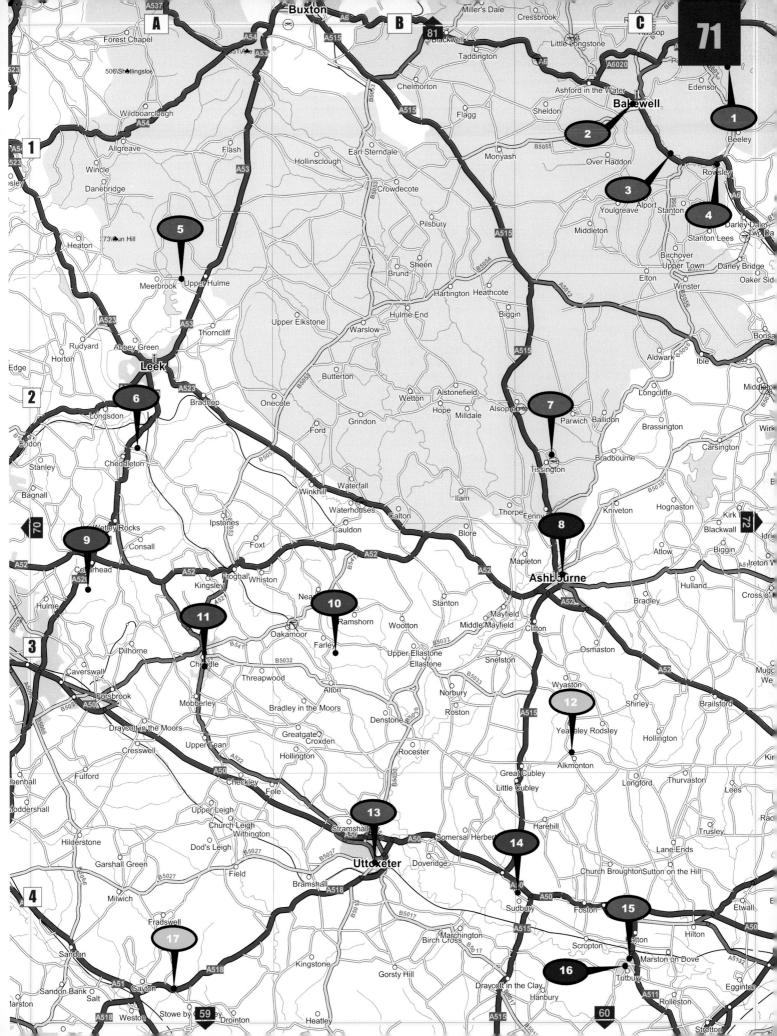

DERBYS · NOTTS · SOMERSET

- ● ANIMAL ATTRACTIONS
- ● HERITAGE & CULTURE
- ○ INDOOR ACTIVITIES
- ● OUTDOOR ATTRACTIONS
- ● OUTDOOR ACTIVITIES
- ● WATER ACTIVITIES

1 SUTTON SCARSDALE HALL
Historic building
Chesterfield
TEL: 01604 735 400

2 STAINSBY MILL
Mill
Hardwick Estate, Doe Lea, Chesterfield
TEL: 01246 850 430

3 HARDSTOFT HERB GARDEN
Garden
Hall View Cottage, Hardstoft, Chesterfield
TEL: 01246 854 268

4 TEVERSAL TRAILS VISITOR CENTRE
Visitor centre
Teversal
TEL: 01623 442 021

5 RIBER CASTLE WILDLIFE PARK
Wildlife park
Riber, Matlock
TEL: 01629 582 073

6 WHISTLESTOP COUNTRYSIDE CENTRE
Visitor centre
Old Railway Station, Bath
TEL: 01629 580 958

7 HEIGHTS OF ABRAHAM-CABLE CARS COUNTRY PARK & CAVERNS
Cave
Matlock Bath, Matlock
TEL: 01629 582 365

8 GULLIVERS KINGDOM THEME PARK
Theme park
Temple Walk, Matlock
TEL: 01629 571 000

9 TEMPLE MINE
Mine
The Pavilion, Matlock Bath, Matlock
TEL: 01629 583 834

10 PEAK DISTRICT MINING MUSEUM
Museum
The Pavilion, Matlock Bath, Matlock
TEL: 01629 583 834

11 ARKWRIGHT'S CROMFORD MILL
Museum
Mill Road, Cromford, Matlock
TEL: 01629 823 256

12 WINGFIELD MANOR
Historic house
Garner Lane, South Wingfield
TEL: 01773 832 060

13 NATIONAL STONE CENTRE
Museum
Porter Lane, Wirksworth, Matlock
TEL: 01629 824 833

14 MIDDLETON TOP ENGINE HOUSE
Heritage centre
Middleton by Wirksworth, Matlock
TEL: 01629 823 204

15 HIGH PEAK JUNCTION WORKSHOP
Railway
High Peak Junction, Cromford
TEL: 01629 822 831

16 CRICH TRAMWAY VILLAGE
Museum
Matlock Road, Crich, Matlock
TEL: 01773 852 565

17 WIRKSWORTH HERITAGE CENTRE
Heritage centre
Crown Yard, Market Place, Wirksworth
TEL: 01629 825 225

18 MIDLAND RAILWAYS CENTRE
Railway
Butterly Station, Ripley
TEL: 01773 747 674

Feeding the sheep

19 DURBAN HOUSE HERITAGE CENTRE
Heritage centre
Durban House, Mansfield Road, Eastwood
TEL: 01773 717 353

20 DENBY POTTERY VISITOR CENTRE
Factory tour & shopping
Denby, Ripley
TEL: 01773 740 799

21 D H LAWRENCE BIRTHPLACE MUSEUM
Museum
8 Victoria Street, Eastwood, Worksop
TEL: 01773 717 353

22 SHIPLEY COUNTRY PARK
Country park
Slack Lane, Heanor
TEL: 01773 719 961

23 EREWASH MUSEUM
Museum
High Street, Illkeston
TEL: 01159 440 440

24 AMERICAN ADVENTURE WORLD
Theme park
Ilkeston
TEL: 01773 531 521

25 KEDLESTON HALL NT
Garden
Derby
TEL: 01332 842 191

26 DERBY INDUSTRIAL MUSEUM
Museum
The Silk Mill, Silk Mill Lane, Derby
TEL: 01332 255 308

27 PICKFORD'S HOUSE SOCIAL HISTORY MUSEUM
Historic house
41 Friargate, Derby
TEL: 01332 255 363

28 DERBY MUSEUM & ART GALLERY
Museum
The Strand, Derby
TEL: 01332 716 659

29 BASS MUSEUM
Museum
Horninglow Street, Burton-upon-Trent
TEL: 01283 511 000

30 ROYAL CROWN DERBY MUSEUM
Museum
194 Osmaston Road, Derby
TEL: 01332 712 800

31 ELVASTON CASTLE COUNTRY PARK
Country park
Elvaston, Thulston, Derby
TEL: 01332 571 342

32 KEGWORTH MUSEUM
Museum
52 High Street, Kegworth
TEL: 01509 672 886

33 CHESTERFIELD MUSEUM & ART GALLERY
Museum
St Mary's Gate, Chesterfield
TEL: 01246 345 727

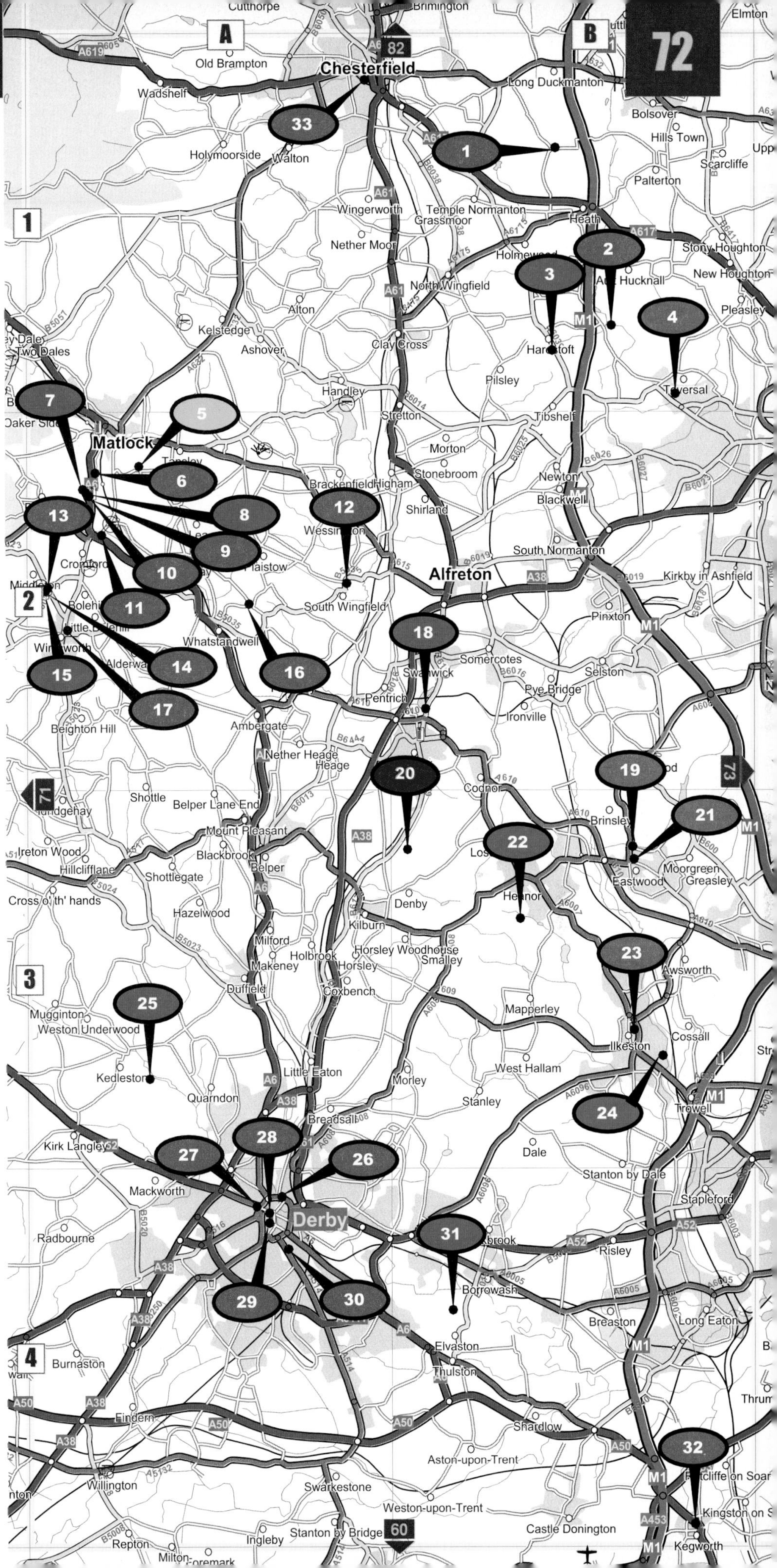

1 WALKS OF LIFE HERITAGE CENTRE
Heritage centre
Tuxford
TEL: 01777 870 427

2 WHALEY THORNS HERITAGE & ENVIRONMENT CENTRE
Heritage centre
Portland Terrace, Langwith
TEL: 01623 742 525

3 SHERWOOD FOREST FUN PARK
Adventure & activity centre
Edwinstowe, Mansfield
TEL: 01623 823 536

4 SHERWOOD FOREST COUNTRY PARK
Country park
Edwinstowe, Mansfield
TEL: 01623 823 202

5 RUFFORD ABBEY & COUNTRY PARK
Country park
Rufford, Ollerton, Newark
TEL: 01623 824 153

6 SHERWOOD FOREST FARM PARK
Farm
Lamb Pens Farm, Edwinstowe, Mansfield
TEL: 01623 823 558

7 RUFFORD CRAFT CENTRE
Craft centre
Rufford Abbey, Rufford, Newark
TEL: 01623 822 944

8 VINA COOKE MUSEUM OF DOLLS & BYGONE CHILDHOOD
Museum
The Old Rectory, Great North Road, Cromwell
TEL: 01636 821 364

9 MANSFIELD MUSEUM & ART GALLERY
Museum
Leeming Street, Mansfield
TEL: 01623 463 088

10 WONDERLAND PLEASURE PARK
Adventure & activity centre
White Post A614, Farnsfield, Mansfield
TEL: 01623 882 773

11 WHITE POST MODERN FARM CENTRE
Farm
Mansfield Road, Farnsfield, Newark
TEL: 01623 882 977

12 NEWARK AIR MUSEUM
Museum
Winthorpe Showground, Lincoln Road, Newark
TEL: 01636 707 170

13 NEWSTEAD ABBEY PARK
Garden
Newstead Abbey, Ravenshead
TEL: 01623 455 900

14 NEWARK CASTLE
Castle
Castle Gate, Newark
TEL: 01636 611 908

15 SOUTHWELL MINSTER
Historic building
Southwell
TEL: 01636 812 649

16 MILLGATE MUSEUM
Museum
48 Mill Gate, Newark
TEL: 01636 679 403

17 LONGDALE CRAFT CENTRE
Craft centre
Longdale Lane, Ravenshead
TEL: 01623 794 858

18 PAPPLEWICK HALL
Historic house
Main Street, Papplewick, Nottingham
TEL: 01159 633 491

19 TIME TRAVEL
Tour
Grantham
TEL: 01476 406 162

20 GREEN'S MILL WINDMILL & SCIENCE MUSEUM
Museum
Windmill Lane, Sneinton, Nottingham
TEL: 01159 156 878

21 TALES OF ROBIN HOOD
Theme park
32-38 Maid Marion Way, Nottingham
TEL: 01159 483 284

22 GALLERIES OF JUSTICE
Museum
Shire Hall, High Pavement, Nottingham
TEL: 01159 520 555

23 LACE CENTRE
Museum
Severns Building, Castle Road, Nottingham
TEL: 01159 413 539

24 MUSEUM OF COSTUME & TEXTILES
Museum
43-51 Castle Gate, Nottingham
TEL: 01159 153 500

25 BREWHOUSE YARD MUSEUM
Museum
Castle Boulevard, Nottingham
TEL: 01159 153 600

26 CAVES OF NOTTINGHAM
Cave
Drury Walk, Broad Marsh Centre Nottingham
TEL: 01159 241 424

27 NOTTINGHAM CASTLE MUSEUM & ART GALLERY
Castle
Nottingham
TEL: 01159 153 700

28 SHERWOOD FORESTERS MUSEUM
Museum
Castle Place, Nottingham
TEL: 01159 465 415

29 WOLLATON PARK
Garden
Wollaton Road, Wollaton, Nottingham
TEL: 01159 153 900

30 NOTTINGHAM INDUSTRIAL MUSEUM
Museum
Courtyard Buildings, Wollaton Park, Nottingham
TEL: 01159 153 910

31 NATIONAL WATER SPORTS CENTRE
Outdoor Centre
Adbolton Lane, Holme Pierrepont, Nottingham
TEL: 01159 821 212

32 CLIFTON PLAYING FIELDS
Country park
Farnborough Road, Nottingham
TEL: 01159 213 125

33 NATURESCAPE WILDFLOWER FARM
Farm
Coachgap Lane, Langar, Nottingham
TEL: 01949 851 045

34 BELVOIR CASTLE
Castle
Belvoir, Grantham
TEL: 01476 870 262

35 RUDDINGTON FRAMEWORK KNITTERS' MUSEUM
Museum
Chapel Street, Ruddington, Nottingham
TEL: 01159 846 914

36 THRUMPTON HALL
Historic house
Main Street, Thrumpton, Nottingham
TEL: 01159 830 333

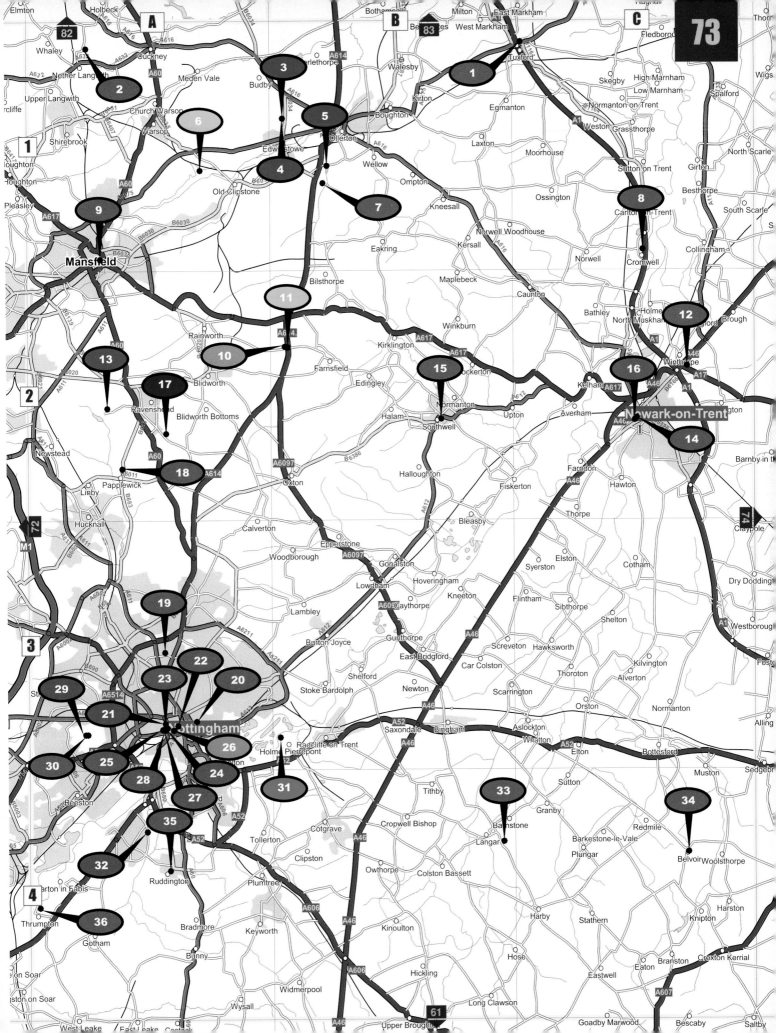

LINCOLNSHIRE

1 **JOHN DAWBER GARDEN**
Garden
The Lawn, Union Road, Lincoln
TEL: 01522 873 622

2 **SIR JOSEPH BANKS CONSERVATORY**
Garden
The Lawn, Union Road, Lincoln
TEL: 01522 873 622

3 **WALTHAM WINDMILL**
Mill
Brigsley Road, Waltham, Grimsby
TEL: 01472 752 122

4 **LAWN VISITORS CENTRE**
Visitor centre
Union Road, Lincoln
TEL: 01522 560 306

5 **LINCOLN CASTLE**
Castle
Castle Hill, Lincoln
TEL: 01522 511 068

6 **LINCOLN CATHEDRAL**
Historic building
Castle Hill, Lincoln
TEL: 01522 544 544

7 **MEDIEVAL BISHOP'S PALACE**
Historic house
Lincoln
TEL: 01522 527 468

8 **LINCOLN GUILDHALL**
Historic building
The Stonebow, Saltergate, Lincoln
TEL: 01522 526 454

9 **HOLMDALE HOUSE GARDEN**
Garden
55 High Street, Martin, Lincoln
TEL: 01526 378 838

10 **TATTERSHALL COLLEGE**
Historic building
Market Place, Tattershall
TEL: 01529 461 499

11 **MRS SMITH'S COTTAGE**
Historic building
Navenby
TEL: 01529 414 155

12 **TATTERSHALL CASTLE**
Castle
Tattershall, Lincoln
TEL: 01526 342 543

13 **BATTLE OF BRITAIN MEMORIAL FLIGHT VISITOR CENTRE**
Museum
Coningsby
TEL: 01526 344 041

14 **CONINGSBY FISH CENTRE**
Farm
New York Road, Gogdyke, Lincoln
TEL: 01526 342 738

15 **FULBECK HALL**
Historic house
Lincoln Road, Fulbeck, Grantham
TEL: 01400 272 205

16 **BELTON HOUSE NT**
Historic house
Grantham
TEL: 01476 566 116

17 **GRANTHAM HOUSE**
Historic house
Castlegate, Grantham
TEL: 01909 486 411

18 **GRANTHAM MUSEUM**
Museum
St Peter's Hill, Grantham
TEL: 01476 568 783

19 **BULB MUSEUM**
Museum
Birchgrove Garden Centre, Surfleet Road, Pinchbeck
TEL: 01775 680 490

Scotch Broom

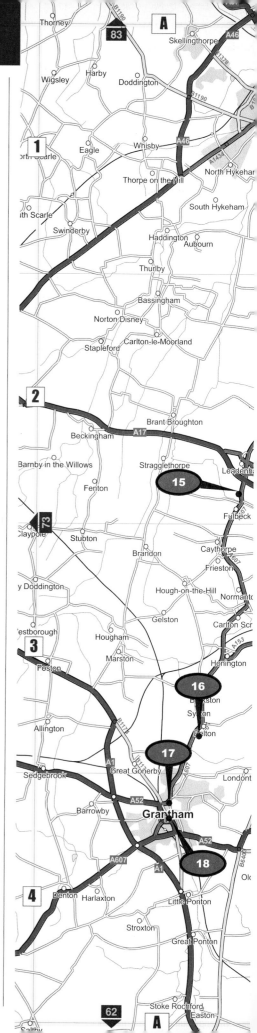

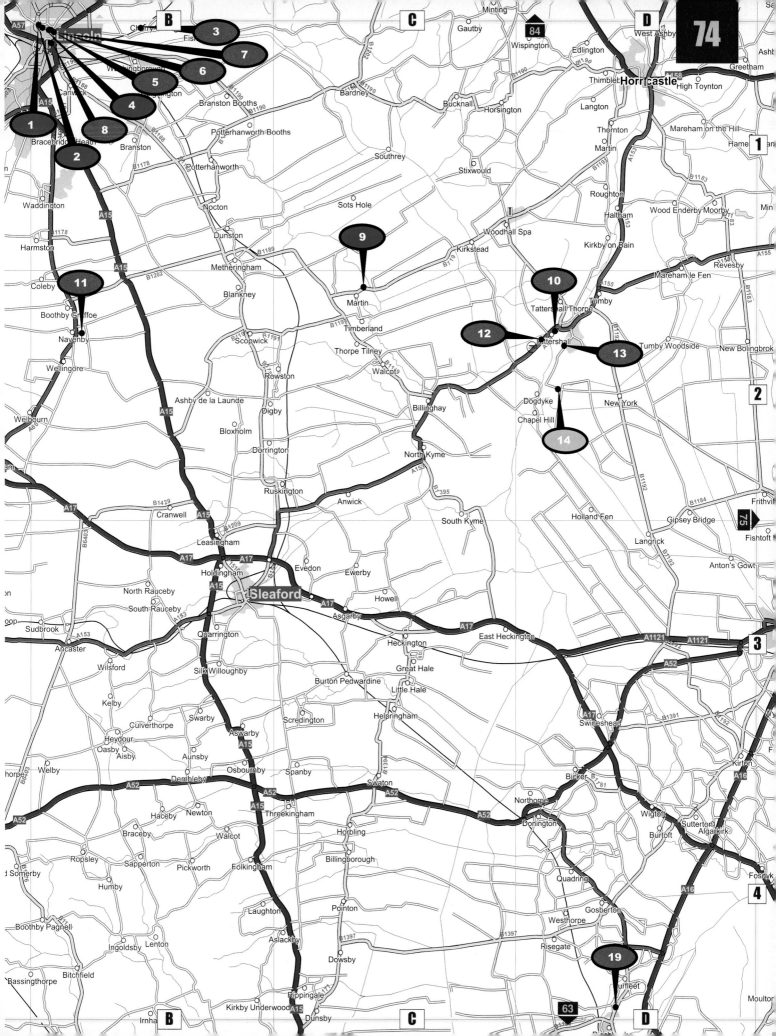

LINCS · NORFOLK

1 MAGICAL WORLD OF FANTASY
Activity Centre
Sea Lane, Ingoldmells, Skegness
TEL: 01754 872 030

2 FUNCOAST WORLD THEME PARK
Theme park
Butlins, Skegness
TEL: 01754 762 311

3 BOLINGBROKE CASTLE
Castle
Old Bolingbroke, Spilsby, Boston
TEL: 01529 461 499

4 SKEGNESS NATURELAND SEAL SANCTUARY
Nature centre
North Parade, Skegness
TEL: 01754 764 345

5 CHURCH FARM MUSEUM
Museum
Church Road, South Skegness
TEL: 01754 766 658

6 LINCOLNSHIRE AVIATION HERITAGE CENTRE
Museum
The Airfield, East Kirkby, Spilsby
TEL: 01790 763 207

7 GIBRALTAR POINT NATURE RESERVE
Nature centre
Gibraltar Road, Skegness
TEL: 01754 762 677

8 SIBSEY TRADER WINDMILL
Museum
Frithville Road, Sibsey, Boston
TEL: 01205 820 065

9 BOSTON GUILDHALL MUSEUM
Museum
South Street, Boston
TEL: 01205 365 954

10 HOLME BIRD OBSERVATORY
Nature centre
Broadwater Road, Holme next the Sea
TEL: 01485 525 406

11 TITCHWELL MARSH RSPB
Nature centre
Hunstanton
TEL: 01485 210 779

13 SEA LIFE HUNSTANTON
Sea life centre
Southern Promenade, Hunstanton
TEL: 01485 533 576

14 NORFOLK LAVENDER
Garden
Caley Hill, Heacham, King's Lynn
TEL: 01485 570 384

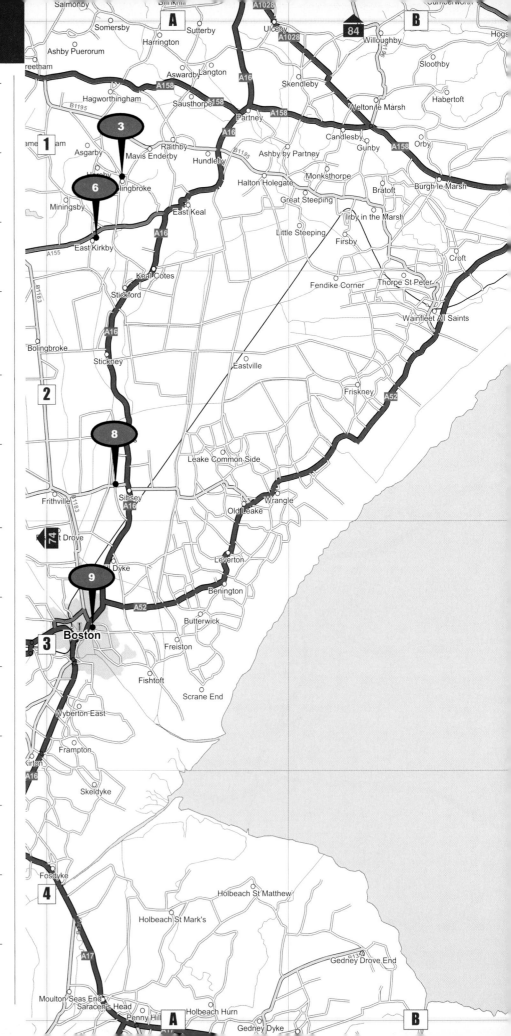

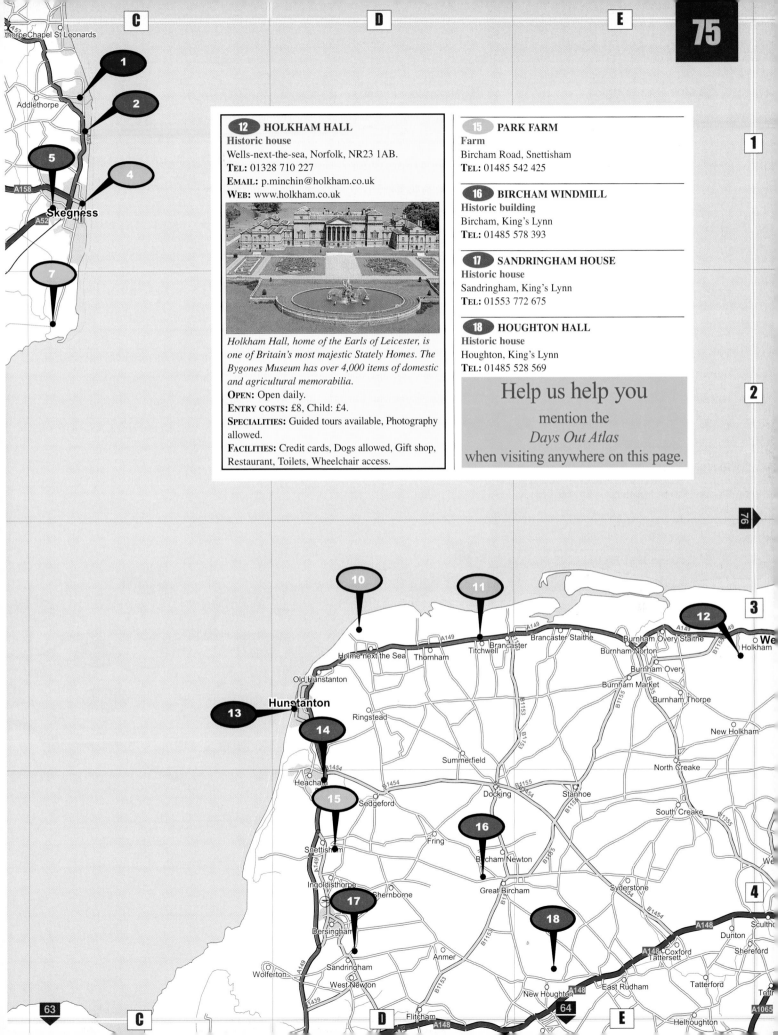

12 HOLKHAM HALL
Historic house
Wells-next-the-sea, Norfolk, NR23 1AB.
TEL: 01328 710 227
EMAIL: p.minchin@holkham.co.uk
WEB: www.holkham.co.uk

Holkham Hall, home of the Earls of Leicester, is one of Britain's most majestic Stately Homes. The Bygones Museum has over 4,000 items of domestic and agricultural memorabilia.
OPEN: Open daily.
ENTRY COSTS: £8, Child: £4.
SPECIALITIES: Guided tours available, Photography allowed.
FACILITIES: Credit cards, Dogs allowed, Gift shop, Restaurant, Toilets, Wheelchair access.

15 PARK FARM
Farm
Bircham Road, Snettisham
TEL: 01485 542 425

16 BIRCHAM WINDMILL
Historic building
Bircham, King's Lynn
TEL: 01485 578 393

17 SANDRINGHAM HOUSE
Historic house
Sandringham, King's Lynn
TEL: 01553 772 675

18 HOUGHTON HALL
Historic house
Houghton, King's Lynn
TEL: 01485 528 569

Help us help you
mention the
Days Out Atlas
when visiting anywhere on this page.

1 BLAKENEY POINT
Walk
Blakeney
TEL: 01263 740 480

2 CLEY MARSHES
Nature centre
Cley
TEL: 01263 740 008

3 WELLS MARITIME MUSEUM
Museum
Old Lifeboat House, West Quay, Wells-next-the-sea
TEL: 01328 711 646

4 BLAKENEY GUILDHALL
Historic building
Blakeney
TEL: 01263 740 898

5 SHERINGHAM MUSEUM
Museum
22-26 Station Road, Sheringham
TEL: 01263 821 871

6 NORTH NORFOLK RAILWAY
Railway
Station Approach, Sheringham
TEL: 01263 822 045

7 PRIORY MAZE & GARDENS
Historic building
Beeston Regis, Sheringham
TEL: 01263 822 986

8 MUCKLEBURGH COLLECTION
Museum
Weybourne Military Camp, Weybourne, Holt
TEL: 01263 588 210

9 NORFOLK SHIRE HORSE CENTRE
Riding
West Runton, Cromer
TEL: 01263 837 339

10 SHERINGHAM PARK NT
Garden
Sheringham
TEL: 01263 823 778

11 CROMER MUSEUM
Museum
Tucker Street, Cromer
TEL: 01263 513 543

12 LITTLE GEMS
Craft centre
Mount Street, Cromer
TEL: 01263 519 519

13 BAYFIELD HALL
Garden
Bayfield, Holt
TEL: 01263 712 219

14 LANGHAM GLASS
Craft centre
North Street, Langham
TEL: 01328 830 511

15 CROMER LIFEBOAT MUSEUM
Museum
Hillside, Cromer
TEL: 01263 512 503

16 BINHAM PRIORY
Historic building
Binham-on-Wells
TEL: 01328 830 434

17 FELBRIGG HALL & GARDEN NT
Historic house
Felbrigg, Roughton
TEL: 01263 837 444

18 LETHERINGSETT WATERMILL
Mill
Letheringsett
TEL: 01263 713 153

19 BACONSTHORPE CASTLE EH
Castle
Baconsthorpe
TEL: 01223 582 700

20 WALSINGHAM ABBEY
Abbey
Walsingham
TEL: 01328 820 510

21 THURSFORD COLLECTION
Museum
Thursford, Fakenham
TEL: 01328 878 477

22 ALBY CRAFTS GARDENS
Garden
Cromer Road, Erpingham, Norwich
TEL: 01263 761 226

25 STRIKERS TEN PIN BOWLING CENTRE
Bowling centre
Tungate Farm, North Walsham
TEL: 01692 407 793

26 NORFOLK MOTOR CYCLE MUSEUM
Museum
Railway Yard, North Walsham
TEL: 01692 406 266

27 PENSTHORPE WATERFOWL PARK
Nature centre
Pensthorpe, Fakenham
TEL: 01328 851 465

28 BLICKLING HALL & GARDEN NT
Historic house
Blickling
TEL: 01263 733 084

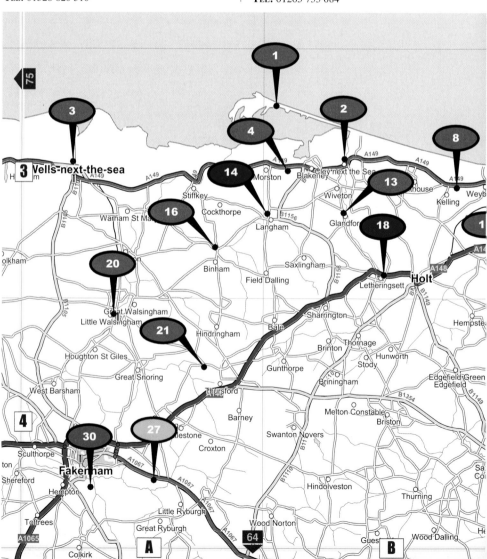

23 MANNINGTON GARDENS
Garden
Saxthorpe, Norwich, Norfolk, NR11 7BB.
TEL: 01263 584 175
WEB: www.manningtongardens.co.uk

Beautiful gardens surround medieval moated manor.
OPEN: Gardens: Jun-Aug: Wed-Fri 11-5, May-Sep:
Sun 12-5. Countryside walks & trails: open daily
from 9am. Car park £1.
ENTRY COSTS: £3, Child: Free, OAPs: £2.50.
SPECIALITIES: Themed garden, Roses, Trees,
Walled garden, Wild flowers.
FACILITIES: Child area, Coffee shop, Gift shop,
Pushchair friendly, Wheelchair access, Toilets.

29 BURE VALLEY RAILWAY
Railway
Aylsham Station, Norwich Road, Aylsham
TEL: 01263 733 858

24 WOLTERTON PARK
Historic house
Erpingham, Aylsham, Norfolk, NR11 7LY.
TEL: 01263 584 175

Historic park around eighteenth-century mansion.
OPEN: Park: Open daily from 9-5 or dusk if earlier.
Car park £2 Hall tours: Fri 2-5 from Apr 26-Oct 26.
ENTRY COSTS: £5.
SPECIALITIES: Events held, Picnic area.

30 FAKENHAM RACECOURSE
Racecourse
Fakenham Racecourse, Fakenham
TEL: 01328 862 388

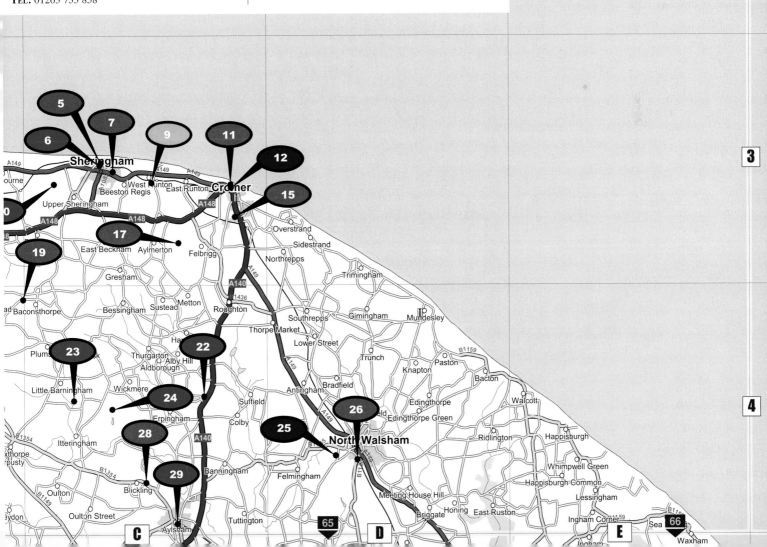

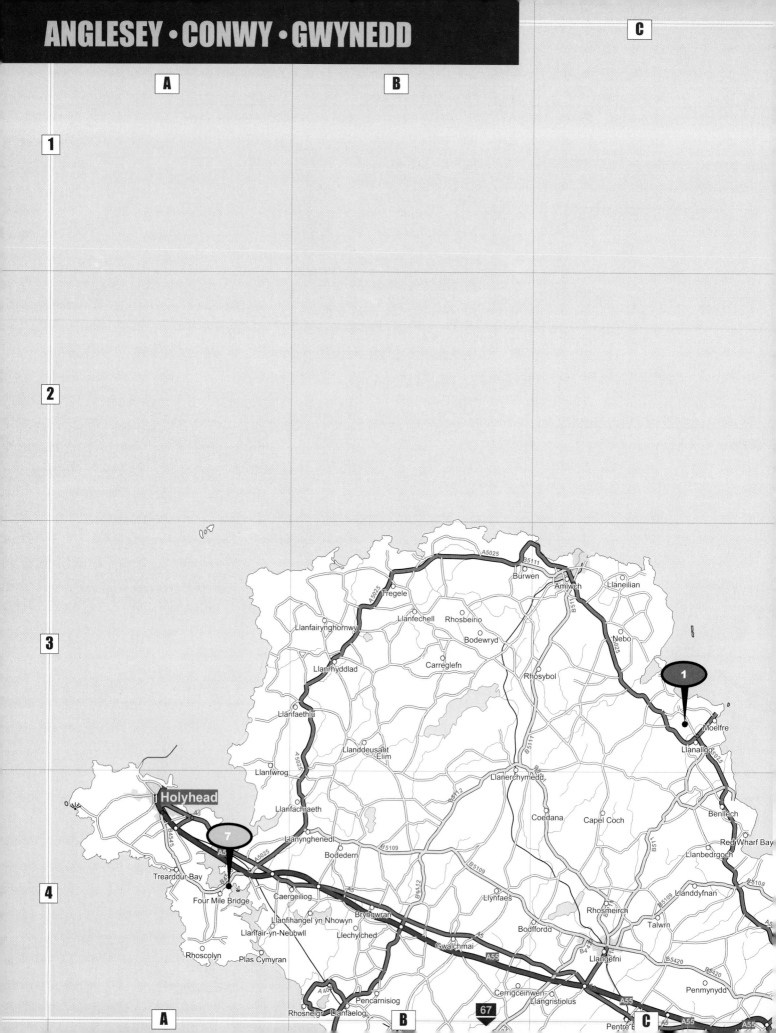

A   B   C

1

2

3

4

Holyhead

Trearddur Bay
Four Mile Bridge
Llanfihangel yn Nhowyn
Llanfair-yn-Neubwll
Rhoscolyn
Plas Cymyran
Caergeiliog
Bryngwran
Llechylched
Gwalchmai
Rhosneigr
Llanfaelog
Pencarnisiog
Bodedern
Llanynghenedl
Llanfachraeth
Llanfaethlu
Llanfwrog
Llanddeusant Elim
Llanrhyddlad
Llanfairynghornwy
Tregele
Llanfechell
Rhosbeirio
Bodewryd
Carreglefn
Rhosybol
Rhosmeirch
Bodffordd
Cerrigceinwen
Llangristiolus
Llangefni
Llanfaes
Coedana
Capel Coch
Llanerchymedd
Nebo
Amlwch
Burwen
Llaneilian
Moelfre
Llanallgo
Benllech
Red Wharf Bay
Llanbedrgoch
Llanddyfnan
Talwrn
Penmynydd
Pentre B

A5025
B5111
B5025
A5
B4545
A5
A5025
B5109
B5112
B5111
B5109
B4
A55
A401
67
A55

7
1

1 DIN LLUGWY ANCIENT VILLAGE
Archaeological site
Llanallgo
Tel: 029 2050 0200

2 LLANDUDNO CABLE CAR
Cable Car
Great Orme, Llandudno
Tel: Not available

3 GREAT ORME MINES
Mines
Pyllau Farm, Pyllau Road, Llandudno
Tel: 01492 870 447

4 LLANDUDNO PIER
Seaside Pier
Llandudno
Tel: 01253 629 600

5 VALLE CRUCIS ABBEY
Abbey
Llangollen
Tel: 01978 860 326

6 WELSH MOUNTAIN ZOO
Zoo
Colwyn Bay
Tel: 01492 532 938

7 RSPB NATURE RESERVE
Nature reserve
Holyhead
Tel: 01407 764 973

8 SMALLEST HOUSE
Historic house
Quay, Conwy
Tel: 01492 593 484

9 CONWY CASTLE
Castle
Castle Street, Conwy
Tel: 01492 592 358

10 ABERCONWY HOUSE
Historic house
Castle Street, Conwy
Tel: 01492 592 246

11 BEAUMARIS GAOL & COURTHOUSE
Museum
Bunkers Hill, Beaumaris
Tel: 01248 810 921

12 BEAUMARIS CASTLE
Castle
Castle Street, Beaumaris
Tel: 01248 810 361

13 MUSEUM OF CHILDHOOD MEMORIES
Museum
1 Castle Street, Beaumaris
Tel: 01248 712 498

14 BUTTERFLY PALACE
Butterfly farm
Penmynydd Road, Menai Bridge
Tel: 01248 712 474

15 PENRHYN CASTLE NT
Castle
Bangor
Tel: 01248 353 084

16 BODNANT GARDENS NT
Garden
Tal y Cafn, Colwyn Bay
Tel: 01492 650 460

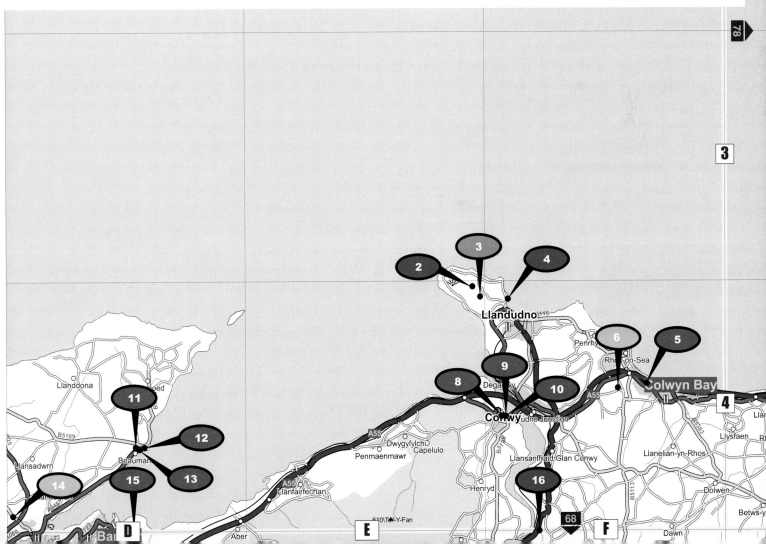

● ANIMAL ATTRACTIONS   ● OUTDOOR ATTRACTIONS
● HERITAGE & CULTURE   ● OUTDOOR ACTIVITIES
○ INDOOR ACTIVITIES   ● WATER ACTIVITIES

1 SILCOCK'S FUNLAND
Theme park
Southport Pier, Southport
TEL: 01704 536 733

2 PLEASURELAND THEME PARK
Theme park
Marine Drive, Southport
TEL: 01704 532 717

3 SOUTHPORT ZOO AND CONSERVATION TRUST
Zoo
Esplanade Princes Park, Southport
TEL: 01704 538 102

4 SOUTHPORT RAILWAY CENTRE
Museum
The Old Engine Shed, Derby Road, Southport
TEL: 01704 530 693

5 BRITISH LAWNMOWER MUSEUM
Museum
106-114 Shakespeare Street, Southport
TEL: 01704 501 336

6 FORMBY SQUIRREL RESERVE
Animal Reserve
Woodland and Beach, Formby
TEL: 01704 878 591

7 CLIMBING HOUSE
Climbing centre
The Clan House Lipton, Close Brasenose Industrial Estate, Bootle
TEL: 0151 922 2999

8 NEW PALACE AMUSEMENT PARK
Theme park
New Brighton
TEL: 0151 639 6041

9 AWESOME WALLS CLIMBING CENTRE
Climbing centre
St Albans Church, Off Great Howard Street, Liverpool
TEL: 0151 298 2422

10 MERSEY FERRIES
Boat trip
Victoria Place, Seacombe, Wallasey
TEL: 0151 630 1030

11 LIVERPOOL MUSEUM
Museum
Liverpool
TEL: 0151 478 4235

12 LIVERPOOL LIBRARIES AND INFORMATION SERVICES
Museum
William Brown Street, Liverpool
TEL: 0151 225 5458

13 ST GEORGE'S HALL
Historic building
William Brown Street, Liverpool
TEL: 0151 707 2391

14 WESTERN APPROACHES
Museum
1-3 Rumford Street, Liverpool
TEL: 0151 227 2008

15 LIVERPOOL TOWN HALL
Historic building
High Street, Liverpool
TEL: 0151 707 2391

16 BEATLES MAGICAL MYSTERY TOUR
Tour
Central Buildings, 41 North John St, Liverpool
TEL: 0151 236 9091

17 HISTORIC WARSHIPS
Museum
East Float Dock Road, Birkenhead
TEL: 0151 650 1573

18 MUSEUM OF LIVERPOOL LIFE
Museum
Mann Island, Liverpool
TEL: 0151 478 4080

19 ALBERT DOCK
Historic building
Edward Pavilion, Liverpool
TEL: 0151 233 6351

20 MERSEYSIDE MARITIME MUSEUM
Museum
Albert Dock, Liverpool
TEL: 0151 478 4499

21 TATE GALLERY LIVERPOOL
Gallery
Albert Dock, Liverpool
TEL: 0151 702 7400

22 BEATLES STORY
Museum
Britannia Vaults, Albert Dock, Liverpool
TEL: 0151 709 1963

23 WOODSIDE VISITOR CENTRE
Visitor centre
Ferry Terminal, Birkenhead
TEL: 0151 647 6780

24 BIRKENHEAD PACKET
Museum
Woodside Ferry Terminal, Woodside
TEL: 0151 647 6780

25 PACIFIC ROAD TRANSPORT MUSEUM
Museum
Tram Shed, Pacific Road, Birkenhead
TEL: 0151 666 2756

26 SHORE ROAD PUMPING STATION
Factory tour
Hamilton Street, Woodside, Birkenhead
TEL: 0151 650 1182

27 BIRKENHEAD PRIORY
Historic building
Priory Street, Birkenhead
TEL: 0151 666 4010

28 WILLIAMSON ART GALLERY & MUSEUM
Museum
Slatey Road, Birkenhead
TEL: 0151 652 4177

29 ARROWE COUNTRY PARK
Country park
Arrowe Park Road, Upton, Wirral
TEL: 0151 678 4200

30 LADY LEVER ART GALLERY
Gallery
Port Sunlight Village, Lower Road, Bebington
TEL: 0151 645 3623

31 DEE ESTUARY WILDLIFE CRUISES
Boat trip
Wirral Country Park, Thurstatson, Wirral
TEL: 0151 648 4371

32 PORT SUNLIGHT HERITAGE CENTRE
Heritage centre
95 Greendale Road, Port Sunlight, Wirral
TEL: 0151 644 6466

33 WIRRAL COUNTRY PARK
Country park
Station Road, Thurstaston, Wirral
TEL: 0151 648 4371

34 VOIRREY EMBROIDERY CENTRE
Museum
Brimstage Hall, Wirral
TEL: 0151 342 3514

35 RHYL SEA LIFE CENTRE
Sea Life Centres
East Parade, Rhyl
TEL: 01745 344 660

36 GYRN CASTLE
Castle
Holywell
TEL: 01745 853 500

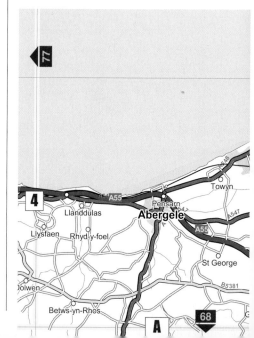

A

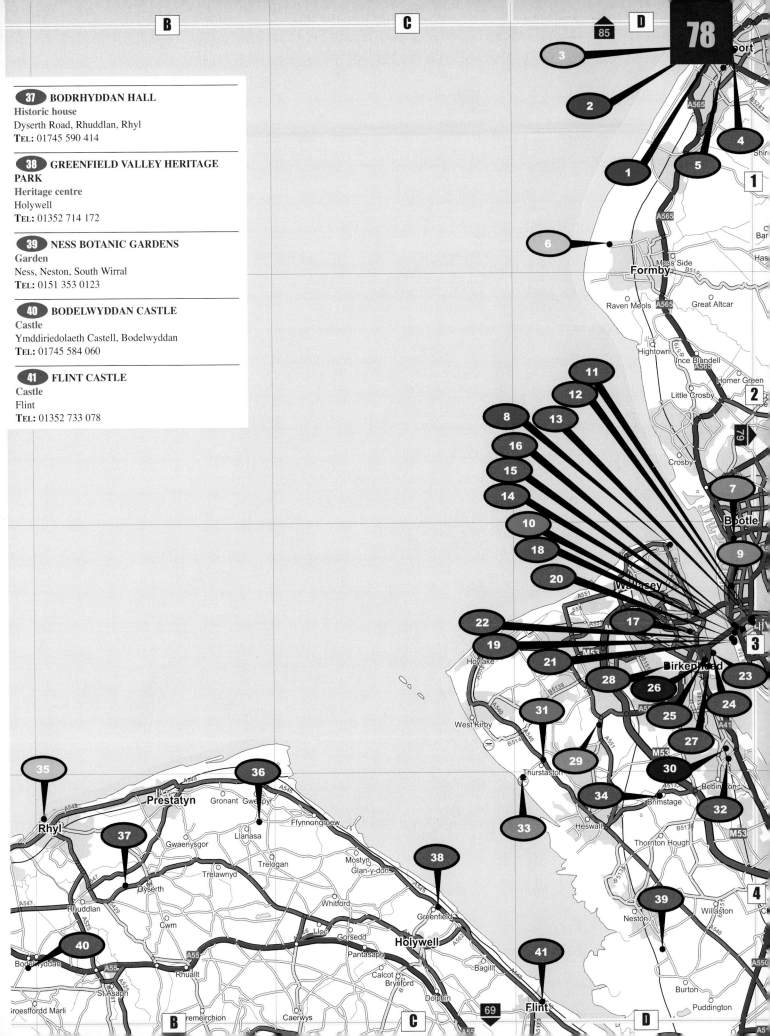

37 **BODRHYDDAN HALL**
Historic house
Dyserth Road, Rhuddlan, Rhyl
TEL: 01745 590 414

38 **GREENFIELD VALLEY HERITAGE PARK**
Heritage centre
Holywell
TEL: 01352 714 172

39 **NESS BOTANIC GARDENS**
Garden
Ness, Neston, South Wirral
TEL: 0151 353 0123

40 **BODELWYDDAN CASTLE**
Castle
Ymddiriedolaeth Castell, Bodelwyddan
TEL: 01745 584 060

41 **FLINT CASTLE**
Castle
Flint
TEL: 01352 733 078

1 ASTLEY HALL
Historic house
Astley Park, Southport Road, Chorley
TEL: 01257 515 555

2 MEOLS HALL
Historic house
Botanic Road, Churchtown, Southport
TEL: 01704 228 326

3 RUFFORD OLD HALL NT
Historic building
Rufford, Ormskirk
TEL: 01704 821 254

4 CAMELOT THEME PARK & RARE BREEDS FARM
Theme park
Park Hall Road, Charnock Richard, Chorley
TEL: 01257 453 044

5 WWT MARTIN MERE
Wildlife park
Fish Lane Burscough, Ormskirk
TEL: 01704 895 181

6 BARROW BRIDGE VILLAGE
Model village
Moss Bank Way, Bolton, Manchester
TEL: 01204 364 333

7 ANIMAL WORLD
Butterfly farm
Moss Bank Park, Moss Bank Way, Bolton
TEL: 01204 846 157

8 HAIGH HALL GARDENS
Garden
Haigh Country Park, Haigh, Wigan
TEL: 01942 832 895

9 ALPHABET ZOO
Zoo
Great George Street, Wigan
TEL: 01942 494 922

10 WIGAN PIER
Historic building
Wallgate, Wigan
TEL: 01942 323 666

11 ORRELL WATER PARK
Boat hire
Lodge Road, Orrell, Wigan
TEL: 01695 625338

12 LILFORD PARK
Wildlife park
Elmridge, The Avenue, Leigh
TEL: 01942 602725

13 HAYDOCK PARK RACECOURSE
Racecourse
Warrington Road, Newton-le-Willows
TEL: 01942 725 963

14 GRAND NATIONAL EXPERIENCE
Racecourse
Ormskirk Road, Aintree, Liverpool
TEL: 0151 522 2921

15 EVERTON FOOTBALL CLUB
Football Club
Goodison Park, Everton
TEL: 0151 330 2266

16 CROXTETH HALL COUNTRY PARK
Garden
Croxteth Hall Lane, Liverpool
TEL: 0151 228 5311

17 KNOWSLEY SAFARI PARK
Safari park
Reading
TEL: 0151 430 9009

18 LIVERPOOL FOOTBALL CLUB & STADIUM TOUR
Football ground
Anfield Road, Liverpool
TEL: 0151 260 6677

19 PRESCOT MUSEUM OF CLOCK & WATCH MAKING
Museum
34 Church Street, Prescot
TEL: 0151 430 7787

20 WALKER ART GALLERY
Gallery
William Brown Street, Liverpool
TEL: 0151 478 4199

21 HOOTON PARK
Museum
North Road, Ellesmere Port
TEL: 0151 350 2598

22 SUDLEY HOUSE
Historic house
Mossley Hill Road, Liverpool
TEL: 0151 724 3245

23 NATIONAL MUSEUMS & GALLERIES ON MERSEYSIDE
Museum
Albert Dock, Liverpool
TEL: 0151 478 4499

24 METROPOLITAN CATHEDRAL OF CHRIST THE KING
Cathedral
Cathedral House, Mount Pleasant, Liverpool
TEL: 0151 709 9222

25 LANDLIFE WILDFLOWERS
Garden
National Wildflower Centre, Court Hey Park, Liverpool
TEL: 0151 737 1819

26 GULLIVER'S WORLD
Theme park
Old Hall, Warrington
TEL: 0151 444 888

27 LIVERPOOL CATHEDRAL
Cathedral
St James Mount, Liverpool
TEL: 0151 709 6271

28 WARRINGTON MUSEUM & ART GALLERY
Museum
Bold Street, Warrington
TEL: 01925 442 392

29 HALEWOOD COUNTRY PARK
Country park
Okell Drive, Halewood
TEL: 0151 488 6151

30 WALTON HALL HERITAGE CENTRE
Heritage centre
Walton Lea Road, Higher Walton, Warrington
TEL: 01925 602 336

31 CATALYST: THE MUSEUM OF THE CHEMICAL INDUSTRY
Museum
Mersey Road, Widnes
TEL: 0151 420 1121

32 SIR PAUL MCCARTNEY'S BIRTHPLACE
Historic building
20 Forthlin Road, Allerton, Liverpool
TEL: 0151 708 8574

33 CALDERSTONE PARK
Garden
Liverpool
TEL: 0151 225 5921

34 REYNOLDS PARK WALLED GARDEN
Garden
Church Road, Woolton, Liverpool
TEL: 0151 724 2371

35 SPEKE HALL NT
Garden
The Walk, Liverpool
TEL: 0151 427 7231

36 EASTHAM COUNTRY PARK
Country park
Ferry Road, Wirral
TEL: 0151 327 1007

37 ARLEY HALL & GARDENS
Historic building
Arley, Great Budworth, Northwich
TEL: 01565 777 479

38 CLAYMOORE NAVIGATION
Boat hire
The Wharf, Preston Brook
TEL: 01928 717 273

39 BOAT MUSEUM
Museum
South Pier Road, Ellesmere Port, South Wirral
TEL: 01513 555 017

40 BLUE PLANET AQUARIUM
Aquarium
Longlooms Road, Little Stanney, Ellesmere Port
TEL: 01930 100 300

41 SALT MUSEUM
Museum
162 London Road, Northwich
TEL: 01606 413 31

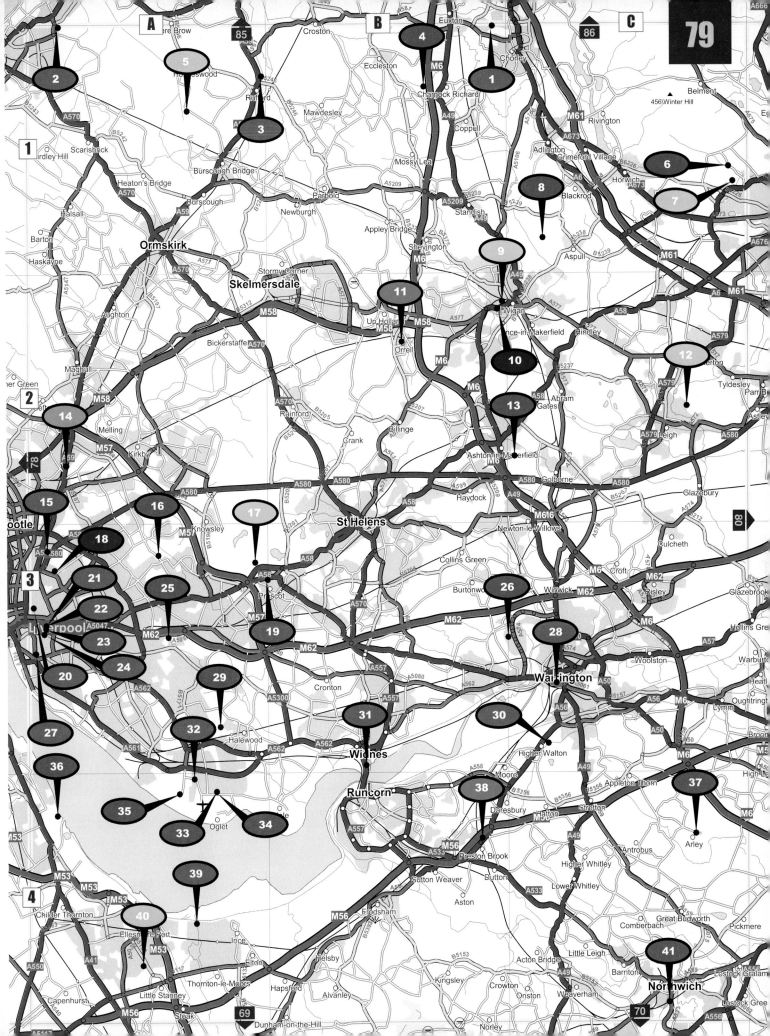

1 TURTON TOWER
Historic house
Tower Drive, Turton, Bolton
TEL: 01204 852 203

2 ROCHDALE PIONEERS MUSEUM
Museum
31 Toad Lane, Rochdale
TEL: 0161 832 4300

3 SMITHILLS COUNTRY PARK
Country park
Smithills Dean Road, Bolton
TEL: 01204 494 612

4 EAST LANCASHIRE RAILWAY & THE BURY TRANSPORT MUSEUM
Railway
Bolton Street Station, Bolton Street, Bury
TEL: 0161 764 7790

5 FUSILIERS' MUSEUM LANCASHIRE
Museum
Wellington Barracks, Bury
TEL: 0161 764 2208

6 WATER PLACE
Theme park
Great Moor Street, Bolton
TEL: 01204 364 616

7 HEATON PARK
Garden
Prestwich, Manchester
TEL: 0161 773 1085

8 CLIFTON COUNTRY PARK & WEST EARTH COLLIERY
Country park
Clifton House Road, Clifton, Salford
TEL: 0161 793 4219

Canal Street, Manchester, Map 80

9 BLACKHEATH COUNTRY PARK
Country park
Hill Top Road, Walkden, Worsley
TEL: 0161 790 7746

10 DAISY NOOK COUNTRY PARK
Country park
Medlock Hall, Daisy Nook, Failsworth
TEL: 0161 308 3909

11 MUSEUM OF TRANSPORT
Museum
Boyle Street, Cheetham, Manchester
TEL: 0161 205 2122

12 MANCHESTER JEWISH MUSEUM
Museum
Cheetham Hill Road, Manchester
TEL: 0161 834 9879

13 LANCASHIRE MINING MUSEUM
Museum
Buile Hill Park, Eccles Old Road, Salford
TEL: 0161 736 1832

14 HISTORY SHOP
Museum
Rodney Street, Wigan, Manchester
TEL: 01942 828 128

15 WORKING CLASS MOVEMENT LIBRARY
Museum
51 The Crescent, Salford
TEL: 0161 736 3601

16 SALFORD LOCAL HISTORY LIBRARY
Museum
Peel Park, The Crescent, Salford
TEL: 0161 736 2649

17 MANCHESTER CRAFT CENTRE
Craft centre
17 Oak Street, Smithfield, Manchester
TEL: 0161 832 4274

18 VIEWPOINT PHOTOGRAPHY GALLERY
Gallery
Old Fire Station, The Crescent, Salford
TEL: 0161 737 1040

19 JOHN RYLANDS UNIVERSITY LIBRARY
Museum
150 Deansgate, Manchester
TEL: 0161 834 5343

20 PUMP HOUSE PEOPLES HISTORY MUSEUM
Museum
Left Bank, Bridge Street, Manchester
TEL: 0161 839 6061

21 GRANADA STUDIOS TOUR
Theme park
Water Street, Manchester
TEL: 0161 832 4999

22 CASTLEFIELD URBAN HERITAGE PARK
Heritage centre
Castlefield, Manchester
TEL: 0161 834 4026

23 MUSEUM OF SCIENCE & INDUSTRY IN MANCHESTER
Museum
Liverpool Road, Castlefield, Manchester
TEL: 0161 832 2244

24 CORNERHOUSE
Theatre
70 Oxford Street, Manchester
TEL: 0161 200 1500

25 LASER QUEST
Unusual
Arch 58, Whitworth Street, Manchester
TEL: 0161 228 2231

26 WATERSPORTS CENTRE
Water sport
5 The Quays, Salford
TEL: 0161 877 7252

27 SALFORD QUAYS HERITAGE CENTRE
Heritage centre
3 The Quays, Salford
TEL: 0161 876 5359

28 ORDSALL HALL MUSEUM
Museum
Taylorson Street, Ordsall, Salford
TEL: 0161 872 0251

29 MANCHESTER MUSEUM
Museum
University of Manchester, Oxford Road, Manchester
TEL: 0161 275 2634

30 MANCHESTER UNITED MUSEUM & TOUR CENTRE
Museum
Sir Matt Busby Way, Manchester
TEL: 0161 877 4002

31 TRAFFORD PARK HERITAGE CENTRE
Heritage centre
386 Third Avenue, Trafford Park, Manchester
TEL: 0161 848 9173

32 GALLERY OF COSTUME
Museum
Platt Hall, Wilmslow Road, Rusholme
TEL: 0161 224 5217

33 SALFORD CITY ARCHIVES CENTRE
Museum
658/662 Liverpool Road, Irlam, Salford
TEL: 0161 775 5643

34 VICARAGE BOTANICAL GARDENS
Garden
Manchester Road, Carrington, Manchester
TEL: 0161 775 2750

35 STOCKPORT AIR RAID SHELTERS
Museum
61 Chestergate, Stockport
TEL: 0161 474 1940

36 **STOCKPORT MUSEUM**
Museum
Vernon Park, Turncroft Lane, Stockport
TEL: 0161 474 4460

37 **BAGULEY HALL**
Historic building
Hall Lane, Manchester
TEL: 0191 261 1585

38 **DUNHAM MASSEY WHITE COTTAGE**
Historic building
Little Bollington, Altrincham
TEL: 0161 928 0075

39 **BRAMALL HALL**
Historic building
Bramall Park, Bramhall
TEL: 0161 485 3708

40 **BROOKSIDE MINIATURE RAILWAY**
Railway
Macclesfield Road, Poynton
TEL: 01625 872 919

41 **QUARRY BANK MILL**
Heritage centre
Styal, Wilmslow
TEL: 01625 527 468

42 **TATTON PARK NT**
Country park
Knutsford
TEL: 01625 534 400

43 **HILLSIDE BIRD OASIS**
Bird centre & aviary
Damson Lane, Mobberley
TEL: 01565 873 282

44 **TABLEY HOUSE COLLECTION TRUST**
Historic building
Tabley Lane, Tabley, Knutsford
TEL: 01565 750 151

45 **NETHER ALDERLEY MILL**
Museum
Congleton Road, Nether Alderley, Macclesfield
TEL: 01625 523 012

46 **WEST PARK MUSEUM**
Museum
Prestbury Road, Macclesfield
TEL: 01625 619 831

47 **MACCLESFIELD SILK MUSEUM & PARADISE MILL**
Museum
Heritage Centre, Roe Street, Macclesfield
TEL: 01625 613 210

48 **PARADISE MILL**
Mill
Park Lane, Macclesfield
TEL: 01625 618 228

49 **CAPESTHORNE HALL**
Historic house
Capesthorne, Siddington, Macclesfield
TEL: 01625 861 221

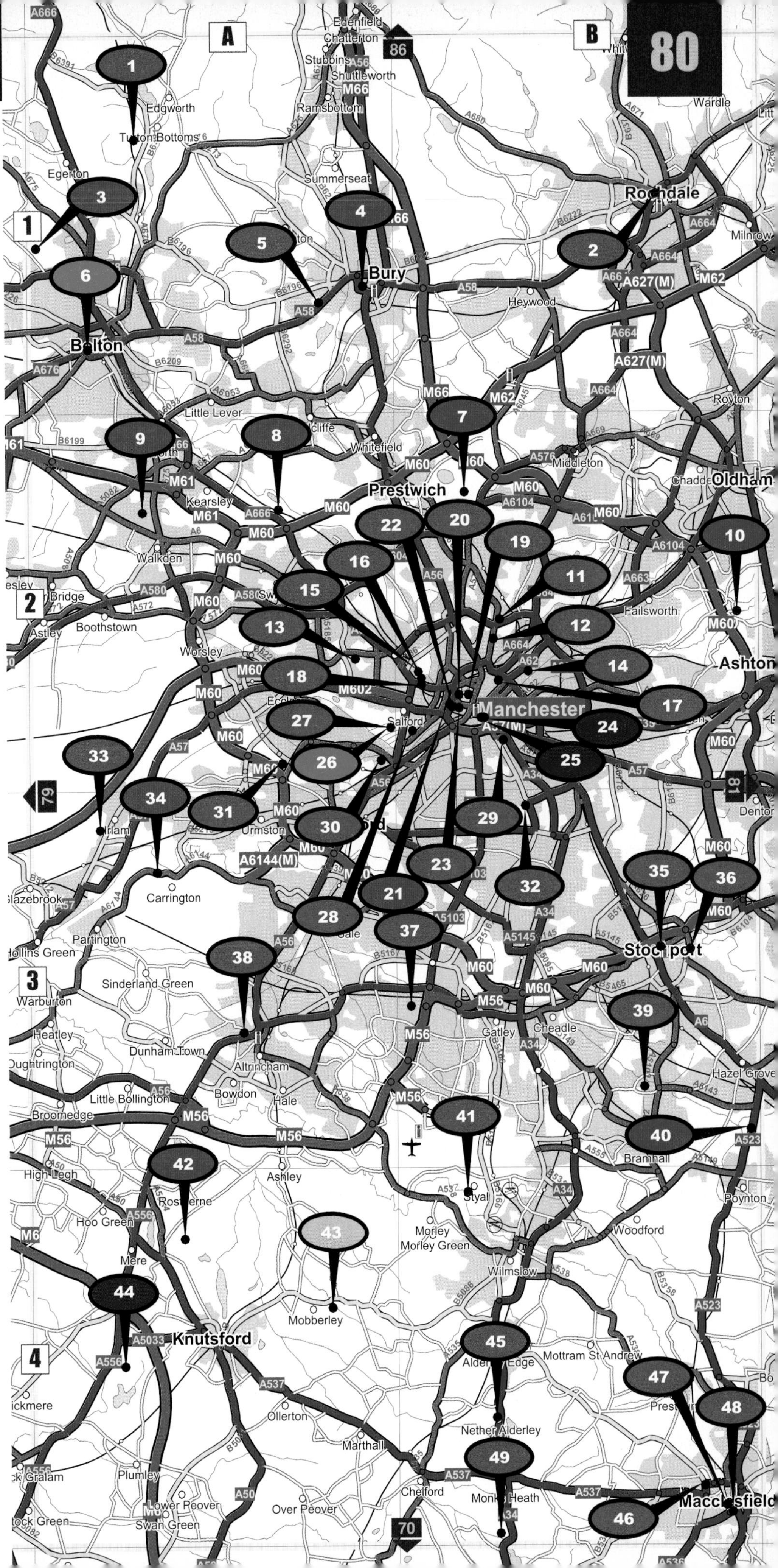

1 OAKWELL HALL COUNTRY PARK
Country park
Nutter Lane, Birstall, Batley
TEL: 01924 326 240

2 AUTOMOBILIA TRANSPORT MUSEUM
Museum
The Heritage Centre, Leeds Road, Huddersfield
TEL: 01422 844 775

3 TOLSON MEMORIAL MUSEUM
Museum
Wakefield Road, Ravensknowle Park, Huddersfield
TEL: 01484 223 830

4 LITTLEBOROUGH COACH HOUSE
Museum
The Heritage Centre, Lodge Street, Littleborough
TEL: 01706 378 481

5 NATIONAL COAL MINING MUSEUM FOR ENGLAND
Museum
Caphouse Colliery New Road, Overton, Wakefield
TEL: 01924 848 806

6 MARSDEN MOOR ESTATE OFFICE
Historic house
Station Road, Marsden, Huddersfield
TEL: 01484 847 016

7 KIRKLEES LIGHT RAILWAY
Railway
Park Mill Way, Clayton West, Huddersfield
TEL: 01484 865 727

8 CANNON HALL COUNTRY PARK
Garden
Cawthorne, Barnsley
TEL: 01226 790 270

9 HOLMFIRTH POSTCARD MUSEUM
Museum
47 Huddersfield Road, Holmfirth, Huddersfield
TEL: 01484 682 231

10 SADDLEWORTH MUSEUM & ART GALLERY
Museum
High Street, Uppermill, Oldham
TEL: 01457 874 093

11 OLDHAM ART GALLERY MUSEUM & LOCAL STUDIES LIBRARY
Museum
Union Street, Oldham
TEL: 01619 114 653

12 PARK BRIDGE HERITAGE CENTRE
Heritage centre
The Stables, Park Bridge, Ashton-under-Lyne
TEL: 0161 330 9613

13 MUSEUM OF THE MANCHESTERS
Museum
Ashton Town Hall, Market Square, Ashton-under-Lyne
TEL: 0161 342 3078

14 PORTLAND BASIN MUSEUM
Museum
Portland Place, Ashton-under-Lyne
TEL: 0161 343 2878

15 GLOSSOP HERITAGE CENTRE
Heritage centre
Bank House, Henry Street, Glossop
TEL: 01457 869 176

16 NEW MILLS HERITAGE & INFORMATION CENTRE
Heritage centre
Rock Mill Lane, New Mills, High Peak
TEL: 01663 746 904

17 SPEEDWELL CAVERN
Cave
Castleton, Hope Valley
TEL: 01433 620 512

18 TREAK CLIFF CAVERN
Cave
Buxton Road, Castleton, Hope Valley
TEL: 01433 620 571

19 BLUE JOHN CAVERN & MINE
Cave
Buxton Road, Sheffield
TEL: 01433 620 638

20 PEAK CAVERN
Cave
Peak Cavern Road, Castleton, Hope Valley
TEL: 01433 620 285

21 LYME PARK NT
Garden
Disley, Stockport
TEL: 01663 762 023

22 OTTER OWL & WILDLIFE PARK CHESTNUT CENTRE
Wildlife park
Castleton Road, Chapel-on-le-Frith
TEL: 01298 814 099

23 PEVERIL CASTLE EH
Castle
Market Place, Castleton, Hope Valley
TEL: 01433 620 613

24 EYAM MUSEUM
Museum
Hawkhill Road, Eyam Hope Valley
TEL: 01433 631 371

25 EYAM HALL
Historic house
Eyam, Hope Valley
TEL: 01433 631 976

26 BUXTON OPERA HOUSE
Theatre
Water Street, Buxton
TEL: 01298 721 90

27 BUXTON MUSEUM & ART GALLERY
Museum
Terrace Road, Buxton
TEL: 01298 246 58

28 POOLE'S CAVERN & BUXTON COUNTRY PARK
Country park
Green Lane, Buxton
TEL: 01298 269 78

Steamboat, Cumbria

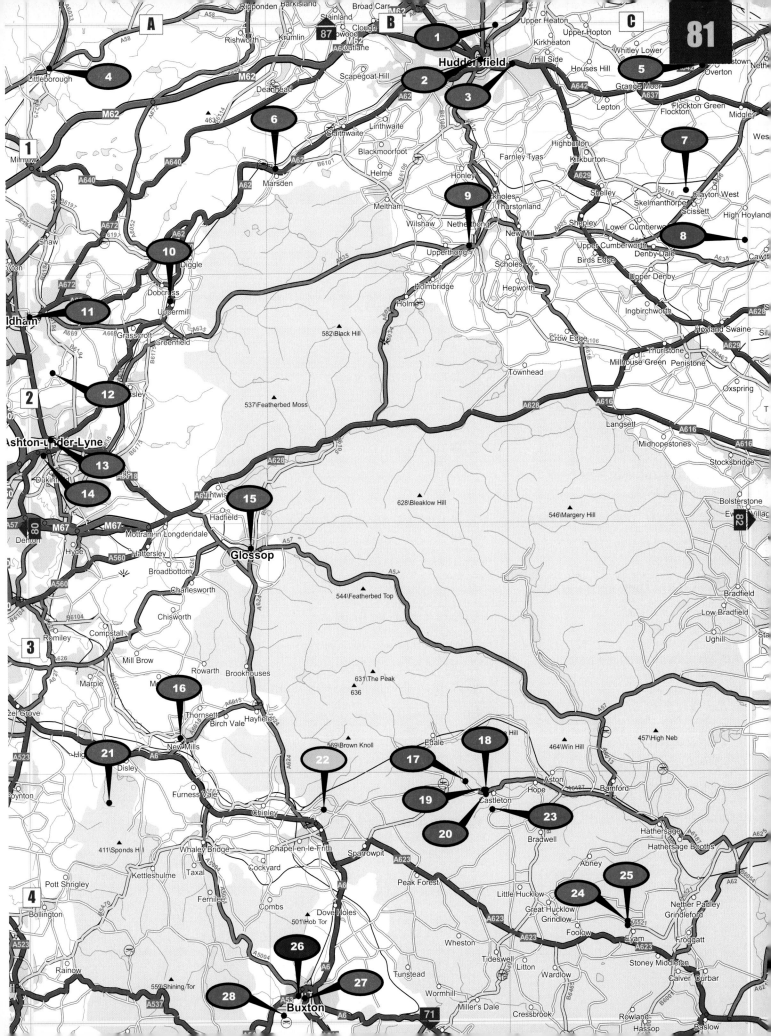

1 NOSTELL PRIORY NT
Historic building
Doncaster Road, Wakefield
TEL: 01924 863 892

2 PUGNEYS COUNTRY PARK
Country park
Asdale Road, Wakefield
TEL: 01924 302 360

3 ANGLERS COUNTRY PARK
Country park
Hawpark Lane, Wintersett, Wakefield
TEL: 01924 830 550

4 YORKSHIRE SCULPTURE PARK
Garden
Bretton Hall, West Breton, Wakefield
TEL: 01924 830 302

5 CAMPSALL COUNTRY PARK
Country park
Churchfield Road, Campsall, Doncaster
TEL: 01302 737 411

6 BRETTON COUNTRY PARK
Country park
Huddersfield Road, Haigh, Barnsley
TEL: 01924 830 550

7 HOWELL WOOD COUNTRY PARK
Country park
South Kirkby, Doncaster
TEL: 01302 737 411

8 HIGHFIELDS COUNTRY PARK
Country park
Doncaster
TEL: 01302 737 411

9 BRODSWORTH HALL EH
Garden
Brodsworth, Doncaster
TEL: 01302 722 598

10 CUSWORTH COUNTRY PARK & CUSWORTH HALL
Country park
Cusworth, Doncaster
TEL: 01302 737 411

11 MUSEUM OF SOUTH YORKSHIRE LIFE
Museum
Cusworth Hall, Cusworth, Doncaster
TEL: 01302 782 342

12 DONCASTER RACECOURSE
Racecourse
Grandstand Ledger Way, Doncaster
TEL: 01302 320 066

13 DONCASTER MUSEUM & ART GALLERY
Museum
Chequer Road, Doncaster
TEL: 01302 734 293

14 BIRDWELL LODGE CRAFT CENTRE
Heritage centre
Birdwell
TEL: 01226 743 489

15 ELSECAR HERITAGE CENTRE
Heritage centre
Wath Road, Elsecar, Barnsley
TEL: 01226 740 203

16 EARTH CENTRE
Adventure & activity centre
Denaby Main, Doncaster
TEL: 01709 322 085

17 WORTLEY HALL
Historic building
Wortley, Sheffield
TEL: 0114 288 2100

18 CONISBROUGH CASTLE
Castle
Castle Hill, Doncaster
TEL: 01709 863 329

19 THRYBERGH COUNTRY PARK
Country park
Doncaster Road, Thrybergh, Rotherham
TEL: 01709 850 353

20 YORK & LANCASTER REGIMENTAL MUSEUM
Museum
Central Library & Arts Centre, Walker Place, Rotherham
TEL: 01709 823 635

21 CLIFTON PARK MUSEUM
Museum
Clifton Park, Clifton Lane, Rotherham
TEL: 01709 823 635

22 HILLSBOROUGH WALLED GARDEN
Garden
Middlewood Road, Sheffield
TEL: 0114 281 2167

23 ROCHE ABBEY
Abbey
Maltby, Rotherham
TEL: 01709 812 739

24 SHEFFIELD ARENA
Entertainment centre
Broughton Lane, Sheffield
TEL: 0114 256 5656

25 KELHAM ISLAND MUSEUM
Museum
Kelham Island, Alma Street, Sheffield
TEL: 0114 272 2106

26 ULLEY COUNTRY PARK
Country park
Pleasey Road, Sheffield
TEL: 01709 365 332

28 CITY MUSEUM
Museum
Weston Park, Sheffield
TEL: 0114 276 8588

29 MILLENNIUM GALLERIES
Gallery
Arundel Gate, Sheffield, Yorkshire, S1 2PP.
TEL: 0114 278 2600
EMAIL: info@sheffieldgalleries.org.uk
WEB: www.sheffieldgalleries.org.uk
Enjoy top quality blockbuster exhibitions and beautiful craft & design; be dazzled by Sheffield's amazing metalwork collections and discover the treasures inside the Ruskin Gallery.
OPEN: Mon-Sat 10-5, Sun 11-5. Please call for Christmas & New Year opening times.
ENTRY COSTS: Free. Entry to special exhibitions is: Adult £4, Child: £2 (5-16), OAPs: £3, Family: £9 (2+2).
FACILITIES: Credit cards, Gift shop, Pushchair friendly, Restaurant, Toilets, Wheelchair access.

30 NATIONAL CENTRE FOR POPULAR MUSIC
Museum
15 Paternoster Row, Sheffield
TEL: 0114 296 2626

31 BOTANICAL GARDENS
Garden
Clarkehouse Road, Sheffield
TEL: 0114 273 4599

32 BISHOPS HOUSE
Historic house
Meersbrook Park, Norton Lees Lane, Sheffield
TEL: 0114 255 7701

33 MR STRAW'S HOUSE
Historic house
7 Blyth Grove, Worksop
TEL: 01909 482 380

34 RENISHAW HALL GARDENS
Historic house
Renishaw Hall, Sheffield
TEL: 01246 432 310

35 CRESWELL CRAGS
Archaeological site
Crags Road, Welbeck, Worksop
TEL: 01909 720 378

36 REVOLUTION HOUSE
Historic house
High Street, Old Whittington, Chesterfield
TEL: 01246 453 554

37 HARLEY GALLERY
Museum
Welbeck, Worksop
TEL: 01909 501 700

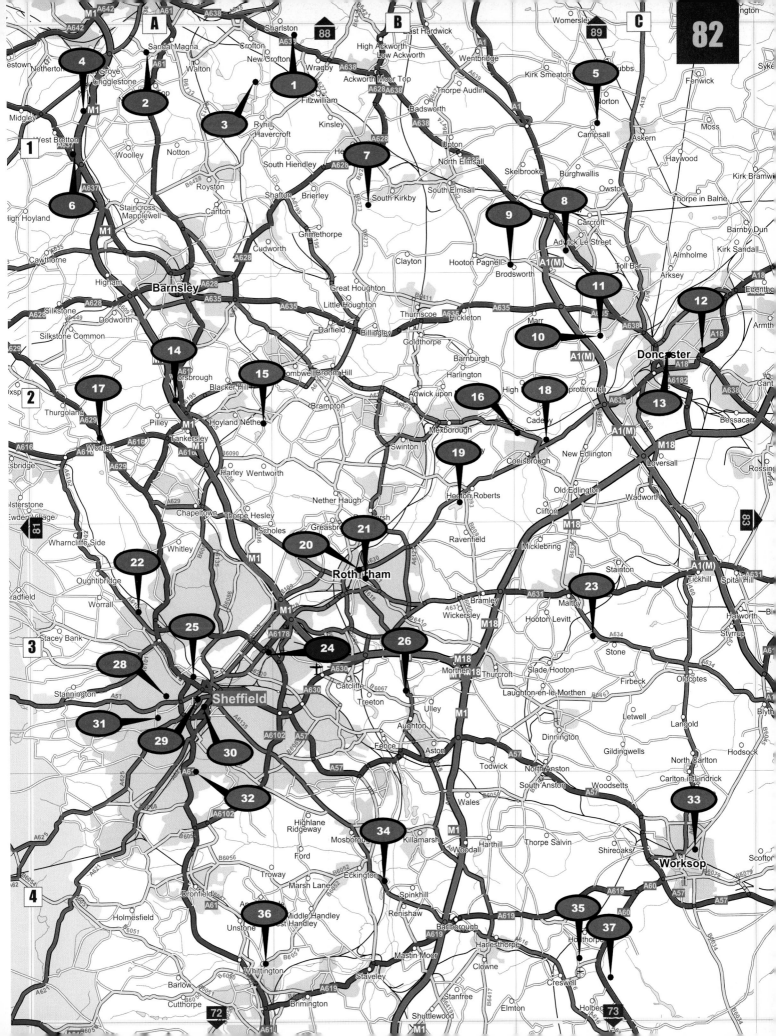

NOTTS · S. YORKS · LINCS

1 NORMANBY HALL VICTORIAN WALLED GARDENS
Country park
Normanby Park, Normanby, Scunthorpe
TEL: 01724 720 588

2 ELSHAM HALL COUNTRY & WILDLIFE PARK
Wildlife park
Elsham, Brigg
TEL: 01652 688 698

3 HATFIELD WATER PARK
Water Parks
Old Thorne Road, Hatfield, Doncaster
TEL: 01302 841 572

4 SANDTOFT TRANSPORT MUSEUM
Museum
Belton Road, Sandtoft, Doncaster
TEL: 01724 711 391

5 BASSETLAW MUSEUM
Museum
Amcott House, Grove Street, Retford
TEL: 01777 713 749

6 EPWORTH OLD RECTORY
Historic house
1 Rectory Street, Epworth, Doncaster
TEL: 01427 872 268

7 BRANDY WHARF CIDER CENTRE
Museum
Brandy Wharf, Waddingham, Gainsborough
TEL: 01652 678 364

8 GAINSBOROUGH HOME AND GARDEN
Garden
Lea Road, Gainsborough
TEL: 01427 612 004

9 WETLANDS WATERFOWL RESERVE & EXOTIC BIRD PARK
Wildlife park
Sutton Retford
TEL: 01777 818 099

10 SUNDOWN KIDDIES ADVENTURELAND
Theme park
Treswell Road, Rampton
TEL: 01777 248 274

11 CLUMBER PARK NT
Historic building
Worksop
TEL: Not available

Water ride

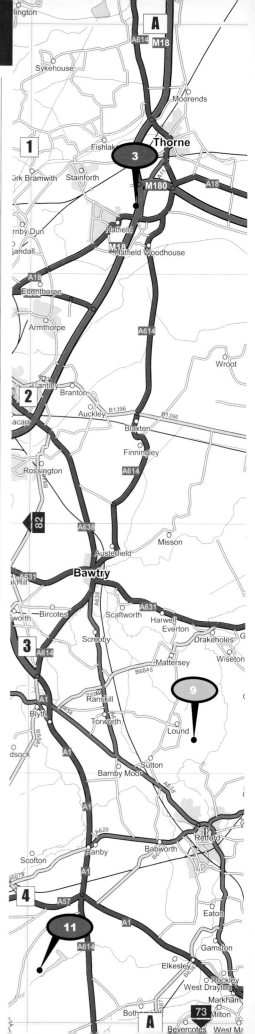

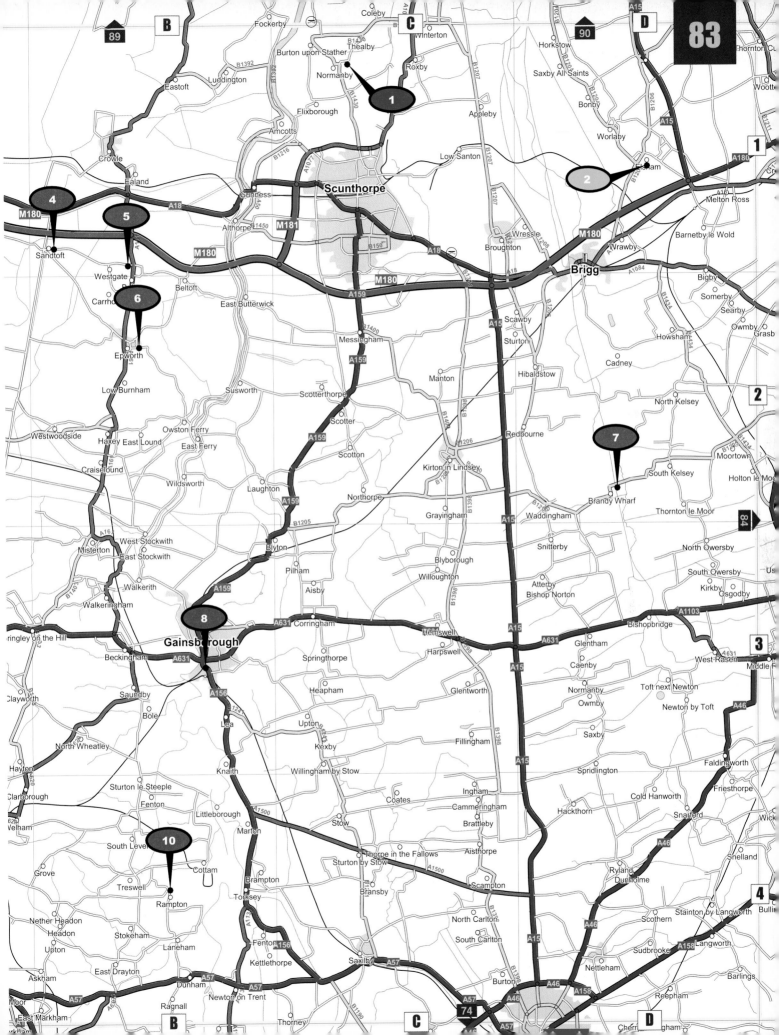

LINCOLNSHIRE

1 NATIONAL FISHING HERITAGE CENTRE
Museum
Alexandra Dock, Grimsby
TEL: 01472 323 345

2 DEEP SEA EXPERIENCE
Aquarium
Central Promenade, Cleethorpes
TEL: 01472 290 220

3 PEOPLE'S PARK
Garden
Welholme Road, Grimsby
TEL: 01472 323 000

4 CLEETHORPES COAST LIGHT RAILWAY
Railway
Lakeside Station, Kings Road, Cleethorpes
TEL: 01472 604 657

5 CLEETHORPES HUMBER ESTUARY DISCOVERY CENTRE
Exhibition Centres
Lakeside, Kings Road, Cleethorpes
TEL: 01472 323 232

6 PLEASURE ISLAND THEME PARK
Theme park
Kings Road, Cleethorpes
TEL: 01472 211 511

7 ALVINGHAM WATERMILL
Watermill
Church Lane, Alvingham, Louth
TEL: 01507 327 544

8 RUSHMOOR HERBS
Country park
Rushmoor County Park, Louth Road, Louth
TEL: 01507 327 184

9 MARKET RASEN RACECOURSE
Racecourse
Legsby Road, Market Rasen
TEL: 01673 843 434

10 ANIMAL GARDENS & SEAL TRUST
Nature centre
North End, Mablethorpe
TEL: 01507 473 346

11 CADWELL PARK CIRCUIT
Motor racing circuit
Old Manor House, Cadwell, Louth
TEL: 01507 343 248

12 RAND FARM PARK
Farm
Rand, Lincoln
TEL: 01673 858 904

13 WRAGBY MAZE & CONIFER CENTRE
Garden
Bardney Road, Wragby
TEL: 01673 857 372

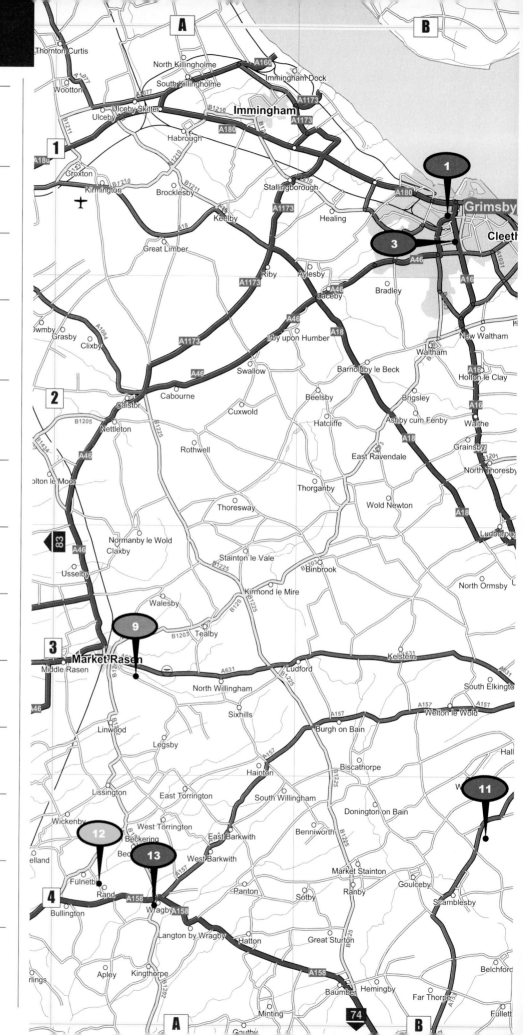

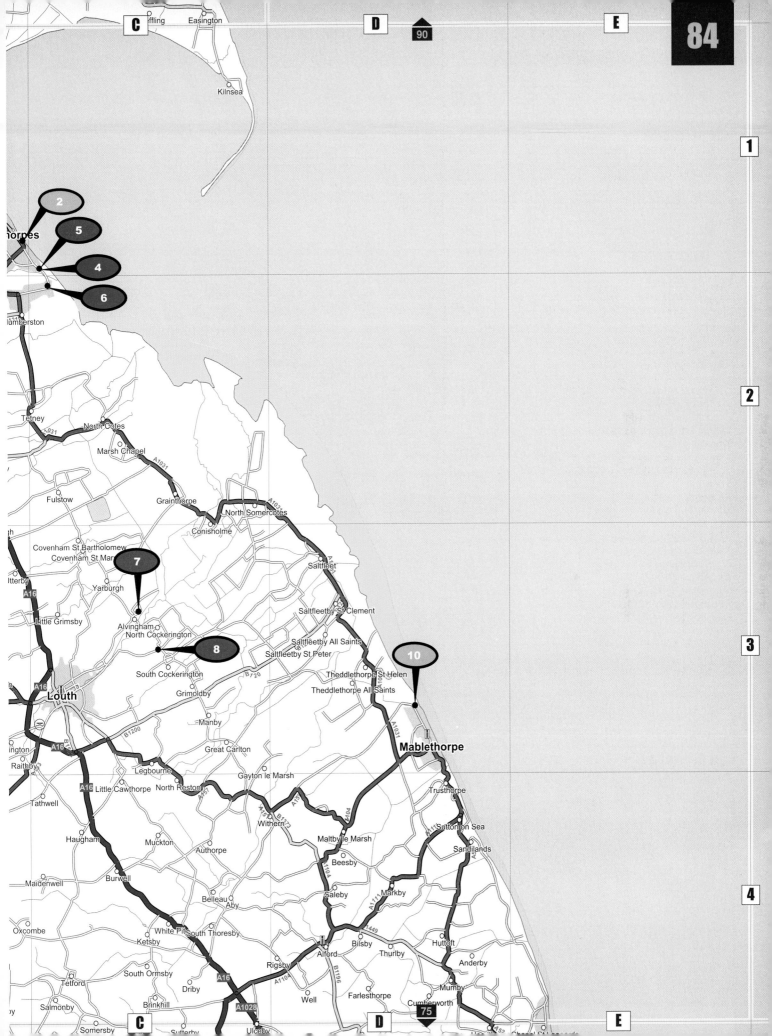

C   ffling   Easington   D   ▲90   E

1

Kilnsea

2
5
4
6

horpes

umberston

2

Tetney
North Cotes
A1031
Marsh Chapel
A1031
Fulstow
Grainthorpe
North Somercotes
Conisholme
Covenham St Bartholomew
Covenham St Mary
7
Yarburgh
Saltfleet
Little Grimsby
Alvingham
North Cockerington
8
Saltfleetby St Clement
Saltfleetby All Saints
Saltfleetby St Peter
South Cockerington
B720
Theddlethorpe St Helen
10
Grimoldby
Theddlethorpe All Saints
Louth
Manby
A16
B1200
ington
A16
Great Carlton
Mablethorpe
Raithby
Legbourne
Gayton le Marsh
A1031
Little Cawthorpe
North Reston
A157
Trusthorpe
Tathwell
A153
B1373
A157
Withern
A104
Sutton on Sea
Haugham
Maltby le Marsh
Sandilands
Muckton
Authorpe
B1104
Beesby
Maidenwell
Burwell
Saleby
A1111
Markby
Belleau
Aby
A16
Oxcombe
White Pit South Thoresby
Ketsby
A1104
Bilsby
Huttoft
Tetford
Rigsby
Thurlby
B1196
Anderby
Driby
Alford
Farlesthorpe
Mumby
Salmonby
Brinkhill
A1028
Well
Cumberworth
y   Somersby   C   Sutterby   D   ▼75   E   A52   Chapel St Leonards

3

4

1

LANCASHIRE · MERSEYSIDE

● ANIMAL ATTRACTIONS   ● OUTDOOR ATTRACTIONS
● HERITAGE & CULTURE   ● OUTDOOR ACTIVITIES
○ INDOOR ACTIVITIES   ● WATER ACTIVITIES

1 FRONTIERLAND
Theme park
Promenade, Morecambe Bay
TEL: 01524 410 024

2 MEGAZONE
Adventure & activity centre
94-96 Marine Road, West Morecambe
TEL: 01524 410 224

3 LANCASTER MARITIME MUSEUM
Museum
St Georges Quay, Lancaster
TEL: 01524 646 37

4 JUDGES' LODGINGS
Museum
Church Street, Lancaster
TEL: 01524 328 08

5 LANCASTER CASTLE
Castle
Shire Hall, Castle Parade, Lancaster
TEL: 01524 649 98

6 LANCASTER CITY MUSEUM
Museum
Market Square, Lancaster
TEL: 01524 646 37

7 KING'S OWN ROYAL REGIMENT MUSEUM
Museum
Lancaster City Museum, Market Square, Lancaster
TEL: 01524 646 37

8 ASHTON MEMORIAL
Garden
Williamson Park, 6 St Marks Place East, Ashton
TEL: 01772 884 444

9 FLEETWOOD MUSEUM
Museum
Queens Terrace, Fleetwood
TEL: 01253 876 621

10 FARMER PARR'S ANIMAL WORLD
Farm
Wyrefield Farm, Rossall Lane, Fleetwood
TEL: 01253 874 389

11 MARSH MILL-IN-WYRE
Mill
Marsh Mill Village, Thornton, Cleveleys
TEL: 01253 860 765

12 BLACKPOOL SOUTH PIER
Pier
Blackpool
TEL: Not available

13 BLACKPOOL NORTH PIER
Pier
Blackpool
TEL: Not available

14 BLACKPOOL TOWER CIRCUS
Unusual
Blackpool
TEL: 01253 292 029

15 BLACKPOOL ZOO PARK
Zoo
East Park Drive, Blackpool
TEL: 01253 765 027

16 BLACKPOOL TOWER
Theme park
Central Promenade, Blackpool
TEL: 01253 222 42

17 TUSSAUDS WAXWORKS
Unusual
87/89 Central Promenade, Blackpool
TEL: 01253 259 53

18 BLACKPOOL SEA LIFE CENTRE
Aquarium
Golden Mile Centre, Promenade, Blackpool
TEL: 01253 622 445

19 BLACKPOOL CENTRAL PIER
Pier
Blackpool
TEL: Not available

20 WORLD OF CORONATION STREET
Museum
Promenade, Blackpool
TEL: 01253 795 774

21 BLACKPOOL PLEASURE BEACH
Theme park
525 Promenade, Ocean Boulevard, Blackpool
TEL: 01253 341 033

22 BLACKPOOL HELICOPTER RIDES
Helicopter flights
Blackpool Airport, Blackpool
TEL: 01253 299 699

23 BLACKPOOL PLEASURE FLIGHTS
Helicopter flights
Blackpool Airport, Blackpool
TEL: 01253 341 567

24 NATIONAL FOOTBALL MUSEUM
Museum
Sir Tom Finney Way, Preston
TEL: 01772 711 600

25 MUSEUM OF LANCASHIRE
Museum
Stanley Street, Preston
TEL: 01772 264 075

26 TOY & TEDDY BEAR MUSEUM
Museum
Clifton Drive, North Lytham, St Annes
TEL: 01253 713 705

27 LYTHAM LIFEBOAT MUSEUM
Museum
East Beach Lytham, St Annes-on-Sea
TEL: 01253 730 155

28 BRITISH COMMERCIAL VEHICLE MUSEUM
Museum
King Street, Leyland, Preston
TEL: 01772 451 011

29 SOUTH RIBBLE MUSEUM & EXHIBITION CENTRE
Museum
The Old Grammar School, Church Road, Leyland
TEL: 01772 422 041

30 BOTANIC GARDENS MUSEUM
Museum
Botanic Road, Churchtown, Southport
TEL: 01704 275 47

Central Pier, Blackpool

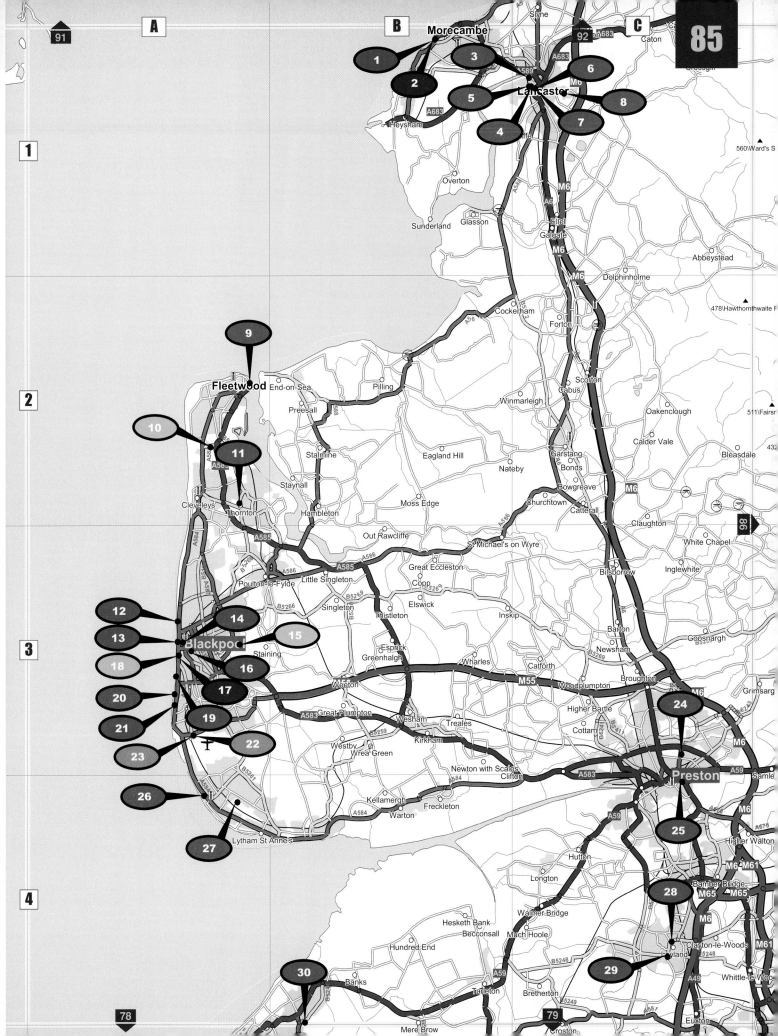

LANCS · YORKSHIRE

● ANIMAL ATTRACTIONS   ● OUTDOOR ATTRACTIONS
● HERITAGE & CULTURE   ● OUTDOOR ACTIVITIES
○ INDOOR ACTIVITIES   ● WATER ACTIVITIES

1 WATERSHED MILL VISITOR CENTRE
Visitor centre
Lancliffe Road, Settle
TEL: 01729 825 539

2 BROWSHOLME HALL
Historic house
Clitheroe Road, Cow Ark, Clitheroe
TEL: 01254 826 719

3 CLITHEROE CASTLE MUSEUM
Museum
Castle Hill, Clitheroe
TEL: 01200 424 635

4 BRITISH IN INDIA MUSEUM
Museum
Newtown Street, Colne
TEL: 01282 613 129

5 STONYHURST COLLEGE
Historic house
Stonyhurst, Clitheroe
TEL: 01254 826 345

6 WHALLEY ABBEY
Abbey
Whalley, Clitheroe
TEL: 01254 822 268

7 WEAVER'S TRIANGLE VISITOR CENTRE
Museum
85 Manchester Road, Burnley
TEL: 01282 452 403

8 SAMLESBURY HALL
Historic building
Crofton New Road, Samlesbury
TEL: 01254 812 010

9 TOWNELEY HALL ART GALLERY & MUSEUMS
Museum
Towneley Park, Burnley
TEL: 01282 424 213

10 BLACKBURN MUSEUM ART GALLERY & LEWIS TEXTILE MUSEUM
Museum
Museum Street, Blackburn
TEL: 01254 667 130

11 BLACKBURN CATHEDRAL
Cathedral
Blackburn
TEL: 01254 514 91

12 WITTON COUNTRY PARK
Garden
Preston Old Road, Blackburn
TEL: 01254 554 23

13 HOGHTON TOWER
Historic house
Hoghton, Preston
TEL: 01254 852 986

14 WHITTAKER PARK & ROSSENDALE MUSEUM
Historic house
Whittaker Park, Haslingden Road, Rossendale
TEL: 01706 217 777

15 HELMSHORE TEXTILE MUSEUMS
Museum
Holcombe Road, Helmshore, Rossendale
TEL: 01706 226 459

Science museum

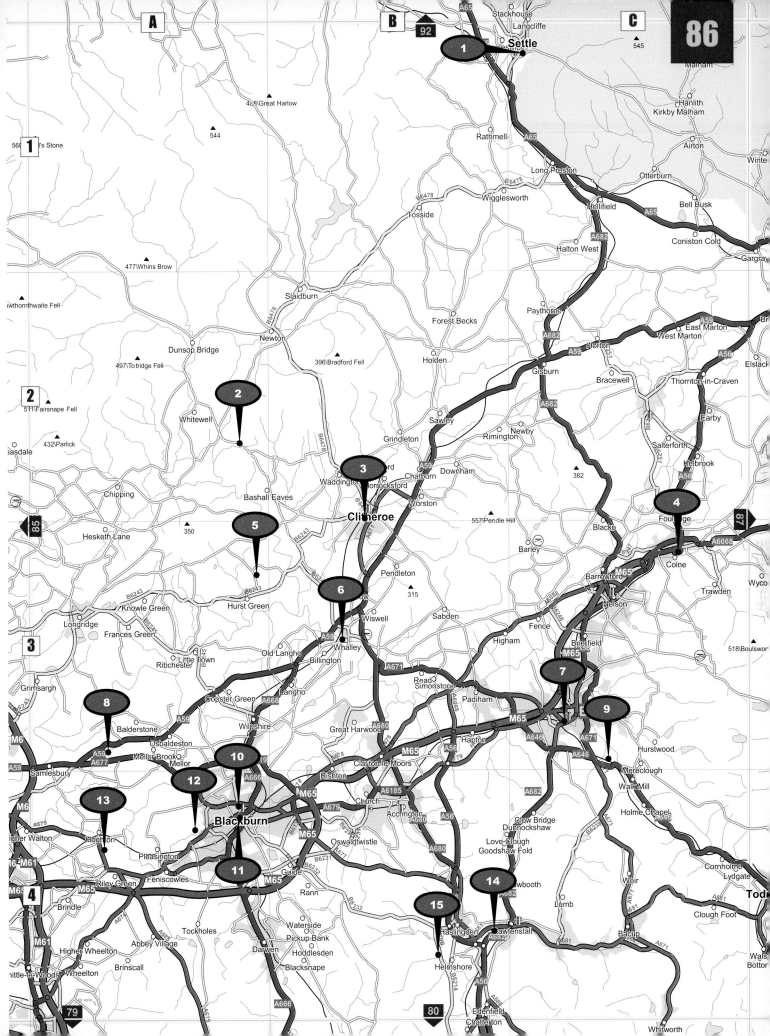

● ANIMAL ATTRACTIONS
● HERITAGE & CULTURE
○ INDOOR ACTIVITIES
● OUTDOOR ATTRACTIONS
● OUTDOOR ACTIVITIES
● WATER ACTIVITIES

1 STUMP CROSS CAVERNS
Cave
Greenhow Hill, Pateley Bridge, Harrogate
TEL: 01756 752 780

2 BRIMHAM ROCKS NT
Walks
Summerbridge, Harrogate
TEL: 01423 780 688

3 PERCEVALL HALL GARDENS
Garden
Skyreholme, Skipton
TEL: 01756 720 311

4 EMBSAY & BOLTON ABBEY STEAM RAILWAY
Railway
Embsay Station, Skipton
TEL: 01756 794 727

5 DARLEY MILL CENTRE
Museum
Darley, Harrogate
TEL: 01423 780 857

6 BOLTON ABBEY
Abbey
Skipton
TEL: 01756 710 533

7 SKIPTON CASTLE
Castle
Skipton
TEL: 01756 792 442

8 CRAVEN MUSEUM
Museum
Town Hall High Street, Skipton
TEL: 01756 706 407

9 PENNINE BOAT TRIPS OF SKIPTON
Boat trip
Wharf Office, Coach Street, Skipton
TEL: 01756 790 829

10 MANOR HOUSE GALLERY & MUSEUM
Museum
Castle Yard, Church Street, Ilkley
TEL: 01943 600 066

11 OTLEY MUSEUM
Museum
Civic Street, Otley
TEL: 01943 461 052

12 EAST RIDDLESDEN HALL NT
Historic house
Bradford Road, Keighley
TEL: 01535 607 075

13 CLIFFE CASTLE MUSEUM & GALLERY
Museum
Spring Gardens Lane, Keighley
TEL: 01535 618 230

14 ST LEONARD'S FARM PARK
Farm
Chapel Lane, Esholt, Bradford
TEL: 01274 598 795

15 VINTAGE RAILWAY CARRIAGE MUSEUM
Museum
Ingrow Railway Centre, Keighley
TEL: 01535 680 425

16 KEIGHLEY & WORTH VALLEY RAILWAY
Railway
Station Road, Haworth, Keighley
TEL: 01535 645 214

17 KIRKSTALL ABBEY
Abbey
Abbey Walk, Abbey Road, Kirkstall
TEL: 0113 263 7861

18 ABBEY HOUSE MUSEUM
Museum
Kirkstall Road, Leeds
TEL: 0113 247 7421

19 BRONTE PARSONAGE MUSEUM
Museum
Church Street, Haworth, Keighley
TEL: 01535 642 323

20 CARTWRIGHT HALL ART GALLERY
Gallery
Lister Park, Keighley Road, Bradford
TEL: 01274 751 535

21 BRADFORD INDUSTRIAL MUSEUM & HORSES AT WORK
Museum
Moorside Road, Eccleshill, Bradford
TEL: 01274 631 756

22 COLOUR MUSEUM
Museum
1 Providence Street, Bradford
TEL: 01274 390 955

23 PUDSEY PARK
Garden
Church Lane, Pudsey
TEL: 0113 255 1334

24 BRADFORD CATHEDRAL
Cathedral
Church Bank, Bradford
TEL: 01274 777 720

25 NATIONAL MUSEUM OF PHOTOGRAPHY
Museum
Bradford
TEL: 01274 202 030

26 BOLLING HALL
Historic house
Bolling Hall Road, Bradford
TEL: 01274 723 057

27 RED HOUSE MUSEUM
Museum
Oxford Road, Gomersal, Cleckheaton
TEL: 01274 335 100

28 BANKFIELD MUSEUM
Museum
Boothtown Road, Akroyd Park, Halifax
TEL: 01422 354 823

29 DUKE OF WELLINGTON'S REGIMENT MUSEUM
Museum
Bankfield Museum, Akroyd Park, Halifax
TEL: 01422 354 823

30 SHIBDEN HALL
Historic house
Lister's Road, Halifax
TEL: 01422 352 246

31 BAGSHAW MUSEUM
Museum
Wilton Park, Batley
TEL: 01924 326 156

32 PIECE HALL
Historic building
Halifax
TEL: 01422 368 725

33 CALDERDALE INDUSTRIAL MUSEUM
Museum
Central Works, Square Road, Halifax
TEL: 01422 358 087

34 CALDERDALE MUSEUMS
Museum
Piece Hall, Halifax
TEL: 01422 358 087

35 EUREKA! THE MUSEUM FOR CHILDREN
Museum
Discovery Road, Halifax
TEL: 01426 983 191

36 NORTH DEAN WOODS
Country park
Greetland
TEL: 01422 393 233

Horse Racing

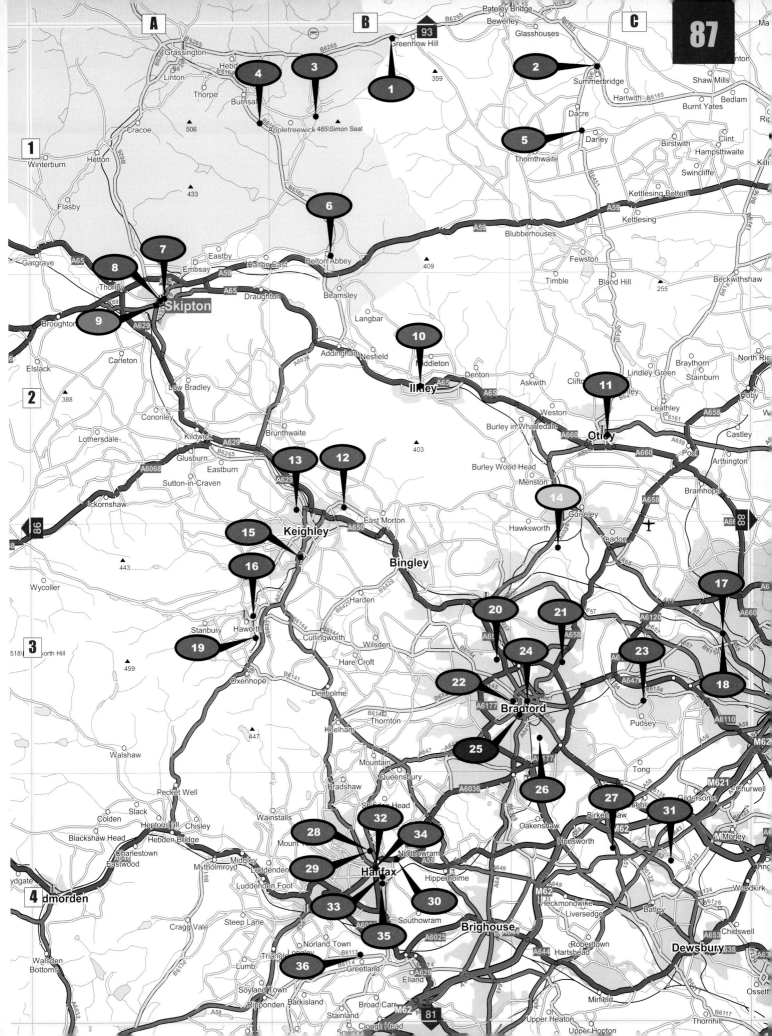

YORKSHIRE

1 RIPLEY CASTLE
Castle
Ripley, Harrogate
TEL: 01423 770 152

2 ALLERTON PARK
Historic house
Knaresborough
TEL: 01423 330 927

3 KNARESBOROUGH CASTLE
Castle
Castle Court, Knaresborough
TEL: 01423 503 340

4 MOTHER SHIPTON'S CAVE & THE PETRIFYING WELL
Cave
High Bridge, Knaresborough
TEL: 01423 864 600

5 MAJOR BRIDGE PARK
Farm
Selby Road, Holme-on-Spalding-Moor
TEL: 01430 860 992

6 ROYAL PUMP ROOM MUSEUM
Museum
Crown Place, Harrogate
TEL: 01423 556 188

7 STOCKELD PARK
Historic house
Wetherby
TEL: 01937 586 101

8 WETHERBY RACECOURSE
Racecourse
York Road, Wetherby
TEL: 01937 582 035

9 BRITISH LIBRARY
Library
Boston Spa, Wetherby
TEL: 020 7412 7332

11 ARK
Historic building
33 Kirkgate, Tadcaster
TEL: 01937 834 113

10 HAREWOOD HOUSE & BIRD GARDEN
Historic house
Leeds, West Yorkshire, LS17 9LQ.
TEL: 0113 2181 010
EMAIL: business@harewood.org
WEB: www.harewood.org.uk

With exquisite House interiors, changing art exhibitions, a premier Bird Garden, thrilling adventure playground, stunning scenery and diverse outdoor activities, there's something for everyone at Harewood.
OPEN: Mar 7-Nov 3. Closed Jul 11.
ENTRY COSTS: Varies. Please contact for more details.
FACILITIES: Child area, Coffee shop, Credit cards, Dogs allowed, Gift shop, Toilets.

12 BRAMHAM PARK
Garden
Wetherby
TEL: 01937 844 265

13 ROUNDHAY PARK
Garden
Roundhay Road, Leeds
TEL: 0113 266 1850

14 HOLLIES PARK
Garden
Westwood Lane, Leeds
TEL: 0113 247 8361

15 MEANWOOD VALLEY URBAN FARM
Farm
Meanwood, Leeds
TEL: 0113 262 9759

16 LOTHERTON HALL
Historic house
Lotherton Lane, Aberford, Leeds
TEL: 0113 281 3259

17 THACKRAY MEDICAL MUSEUM
Museum
Beckett Street, Leeds
TEL: 0113 245 7084

18 ARMLEY MILLS INDUSTRIAL MUSEUM
Museum
Canal Road, Armley, Leeds
TEL: 0113 263 7861

19 GOLDEN ACRE PARK
Garden
Otley Road, Leeds
TEL: 0113 261 0374

20 LEEDS CITY ART GALLERY
Gallery
The Headrow, Leeds
TEL: 0113 247 8248

Jaguar

21 TETLEY'S BREWERY WHARF
Museum
The Waterfront, Leeds
TEL: 0113 242 0666

22 ROYAL ARMOURIES MUSEUM
Museum
Armouries Drive, Leeds
TEL: 09901 066 66

23 TEMPLE NEWSAM HOUSE & PARK
Historic house
Leeds
TEL: 0113 264 7321

24 THWAITE MILLS
Museum
Thwaite Lane, Leeds
TEL: 0113 249 6453

25 MIDDLETON RAILWAY LEEDS
Railway
Moor Road, Hunslet, Leeds
TEL: 0113 271 0320

26 CASTLEFORD MUSEUM
Museum
Carlton Street, Castleford
TEL: 01977 722 085

27 PONTEFRACT CASTLE
Castle
Castle Chain, Pontefract
TEL: 01977 722 740

28 PONTEFRACT RACECOURSE
Racecourse
Park Lane, Pontefract
TEL: 01977 703 224

29 PONTEFRACT MUSEUM
Museum
Salter Row, Pontefract
TEL: 01977 722 740

30 DEWSBURY MUSEUM
Museum
Crow Nest Park, Dewsbury
TEL: 01924 325 100

31 WAKEFIELD MUSEUM
Museum
Wood Street, Wakefield
TEL: 01924 305 351

32 CATHEDRAL CHURCH OF ALL SAINTS
Cathedral
Northgate, Wakefield
TEL: 01924 373 923

33 WAKEFIELD CATHEDRAL
Cathedral
Northgate, Wakefield
TEL: 01924 373 921

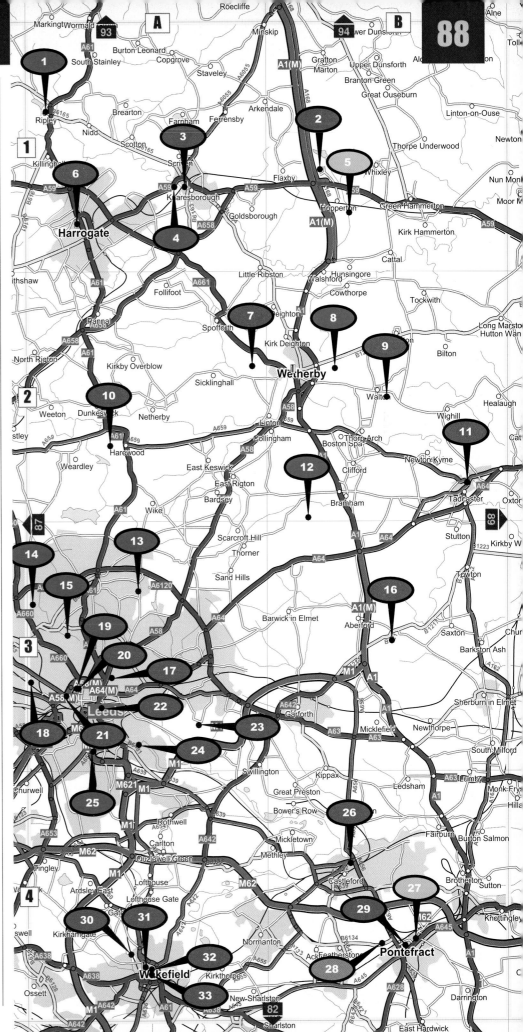

E YORKS · N YORKS · LANCS

● ANIMAL ATTRACTIONS   ● OUTDOOR ATTRACTIONS
● HERITAGE & CULTURE   ● OUTDOOR ACTIVITIES
○ INDOOR ACTIVITIES   ● WATER ACTIVITIES

1 BENINGBROUGH HALL & GARDENS NT
Garden
Beningbrough, York
TEL: 01904 470 666

2 MALTON MUSEUM
Museum
Old Town Hall, Market Place, Malton
TEL: 01653 695 136

3 MURTON PARK
Museum
Murton Lane, Murton, York
TEL: 01904 489 966

4 YORK MINSTER
Cathedral
Deangate, York
TEL: 01904 624 426

5 TREASURER'S HOUSE NT
Historic building
Minster Yard, York
TEL: 01904 624 247

6 YORK CITY ART GALLERY
Gallery
Exhibition Square, York
TEL: 01904 551 861

7 ST WILLIAMS COLLEGE
Historic house
5 College Street, York
TEL: 01904 637 134

8 YORKSHIRE MUSEUM & GARDENS
Museum
Museum Gardens, York
TEL: 01904 629 745

9 YORKSHIRE MUSEUM OF FARMING
Museum
Murton Park, Murton Lane, Murton
TEL: 01904 489 966

10 BARLEY HALL
Historic house
2 Coffee Yard, York
TEL: 01904 610 275

11 NATIONAL RAILWAY MUSEUM
Museum
Leeman Road, York
TEL: 01904 621 261

12 BORTHWICK INSTITUTE OF HISTORICAL RESEARCH
Museum
St Anthony's Hall, Peasholme Green, York
TEL: 01904 642 315

13 YORK BOAT
Boat trip
The Boat Yard, Lendal Bridge, York
TEL: 01904 628 324

14 YORK GUILDHALL
Historic building
Off Coney Street, York
TEL: 01904 613 161

15 ARC
Family Attraction
St Saviorgate, York
TEL: 01904 643 211

16 MERCHANT ADVENTURERS' HALL & GARDEN
Garden
Fossgate, York
TEL: 01904 654 818

17 YORK MODEL RAILWAY
Railway
Tearoom Square, York Station, York
TEL: 01904 630 169

18 VIKING CITY OF JORVIK
Museum
Coppergate, York
TEL: 01904 543 403

19 FAIRFAX HOUSE
Historic house
Castlegate, York
TEL: 01904 655 543

20 MICKLEGATE BAR MUSEUM
Historic building
York
TEL: 01904 634 436

21 ROYAL DRAGOON GUARDS & THE PRINCE OF WALE'S OWN REGIMENT OF YORKSHIRE
Museum
3 Tower Street, York
TEL: 01904 662 790

22 CLIFFORD'S TOWER EH
Castle
Tower Street, York
TEL: 01904 646 940

23 YORK DUNGEON
Museum
12 Clifford Street, York
TEL: 01904 632 599

24 YORK STORY
Heritage centre
Castlegate, York
TEL: 01904 628 632

25 YORK CASTLE MUSEUM
Museum
The Eye of York, York
TEL: 01904 653 611

26 BAR CONVENT
Historic house
17 Blossom Street, York
TEL: 01904 643 238

27 YORK RACECOURSE
Racecourse
York
TEL: 01904 620 911

28 YORKSHIRE AIR MUSEUM & ALLIED AIR FORCES MEMORIAL
Museum
Halifax Way, Elvington
TEL: 01904 608 595

29 BURNBY HALL GARDENS
Garden
The Balk, Pocklington
TEL: 01759 302 068

30 NABURN GRANGE RIDING CENTRE
Riding
Naburn, York
TEL: 01904 728 283

31 MAXWELL HEMMENS PRECISION STEAM MODELS
Museum
Main Street, Thorganby, York
TEL: 01904 448 331

32 SELBY ABBEY
Abbey
Selby
TEL: 01757 703 123

33 HOWDEN ART & CRAFT CENTRE
Craft centre
Howden, Goole
TEL: 01430 430 807

34 HOWDEN MINSTER
Historic building
Howden
TEL: Not available

35 WATERWAYS MUSEUM & ADVENTURE CENTRE
Museum
Dutch River Side, Goole
TEL: 01405 768 730

36 SUNNYHURST WOOD VISITOR CENTRE
Visitor centre
Sunnyhurst Wood, Darwen, Blackburn
TEL: 01254 701 545

37 WOMERSLEY CRAFTS & HERB CENTRE
Craft centre
Womersley Hall, Womersley, Doncaster
TEL: 01977 620 294

Canyoning

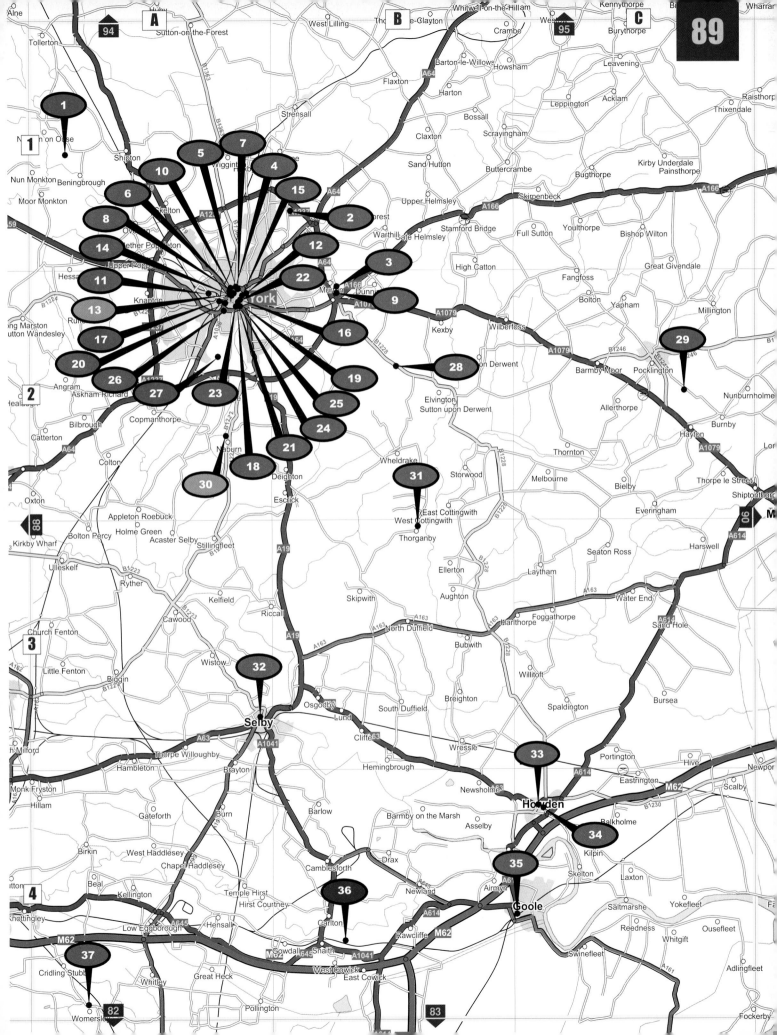

1 **PARK ROSE POTTERY & LEISURE PARK**
Factory shop
Carnaby Covert Lane, Carnaby, Bridlington
TEL: 01262 602 823

2 **JOHN BULL'S WORLD OF ROCK**
Factory shop
Lancaster Road, Carnaby, Bridlington
TEL: 01262 678 525

3 **BURTON AGNES HALL GARDENS**
Burton Agnes, Driffield, East Riding of Yorkshire,
YO25 4NB.
TEL: 01262 490 324
EMAIL: burtonagnes@farmline.com
WEB: www.burton-agnes.com

*Lawns and topiary surround the Elizabethan house
while the walled garden contains a riot of flowers
including a maze and potage.*
OPEN: Apr-Oct: 11-5.
ENTRY COSTS: £2.40, Child: £1, OAPs: £2.15.
SPECIALITIES: Hardy plants, Seeds, Vegetables.
FACILITIES: Toilets, Credit cards, Wheelchair access,
Restaurant, Dogs allowed, Child area, Plant guarantee,
Coffee shop.

4 **CRUCKLEY ANIMAL FARM**
Farm
Foston on the Wolds, Driffield
TEL: 01262 488 337

5 **HORNSEA MUSEUM**
Museum
11 Newbegin, Hornsea
TEL: 01964 533 443

6 **BEVERLEY RECECOURSE**
Racecourse
York Road, Beverley
TEL: 01482 867 488

7 **BEVERLEY GUILDHALL**
Historic building
Register Square, Beverley
TEL: 01482 887 700

8 **MUSEUM OF ARMY TRANSPORT**
Museum
Flemingate, Beverley
TEL: 01482 860 445

9 **SKIDBY MILL & MUSEUM**
Mill
Beverley Road, Skidby, Cottingham
TEL: 01482 848 405

10 **THE DEEP**
Aquarium
Samm's Point, Hull
TEL: 01482 615 789

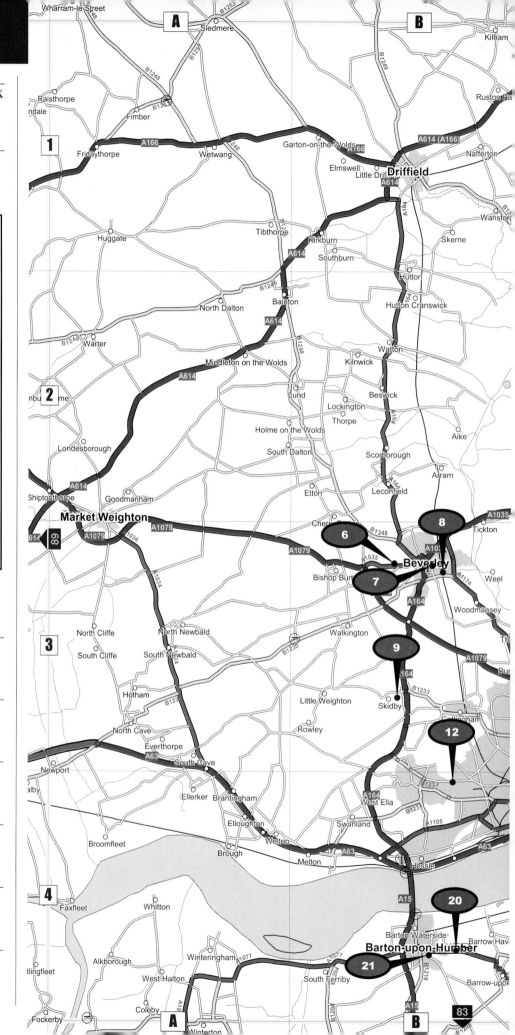

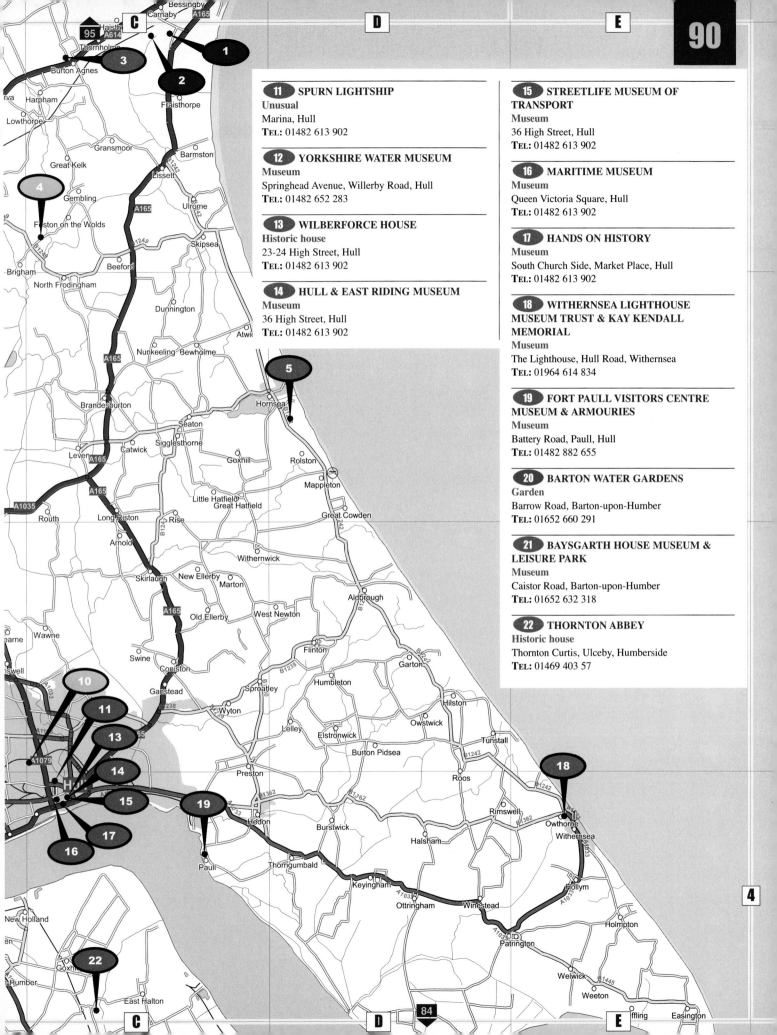

11 **SPURN LIGHTSHIP**
Unusual
Marina, Hull
TEL: 01482 613 902

12 **YORKSHIRE WATER MUSEUM**
Museum
Springhead Avenue, Willerby Road, Hull
TEL: 01482 652 283

13 **WILBERFORCE HOUSE**
Historic house
23-24 High Street, Hull
TEL: 01482 613 902

14 **HULL & EAST RIDING MUSEUM**
Museum
36 High Street, Hull
TEL: 01482 613 902

15 **STREETLIFE MUSEUM OF TRANSPORT**
Museum
36 High Street, Hull
TEL: 01482 613 902

16 **MARITIME MUSEUM**
Museum
Queen Victoria Square, Hull
TEL: 01482 613 902

17 **HANDS ON HISTORY**
Museum
South Church Side, Market Place, Hull
TEL: 01482 613 902

18 **WITHERNSEA LIGHTHOUSE MUSEUM TRUST & KAY KENDALL MEMORIAL**
Museum
The Lighthouse, Hull Road, Withernsea
TEL: 01964 614 834

19 **FORT PAULL VISITORS CENTRE MUSEUM & ARMOURIES**
Museum
Battery Road, Paull, Hull
TEL: 01482 882 655

20 **BARTON WATER GARDENS**
Garden
Barrow Road, Barton-upon-Humber
TEL: 01652 660 291

21 **BAYSGARTH HOUSE MUSEUM & LEISURE PARK**
Museum
Caistor Road, Barton-upon-Humber
TEL: 01652 632 318

22 **THORNTON ABBEY**
Historic house
Thornton Curtis, Ulceby, Humberside
TEL: 01469 403 57

CUMBRIA

1 DOVE COTTAGE & THE WORDSWORTH MUSEUM
Historic house
Dove Cottage, Grasmere, Ambleside
TEL: 01539 435 544

2 RYDAL MOUNT & GARDENS
Garden
Ambleside
TEL: 01539 433 002

3 AMBLESIDE ROMAN FORT EH
Roman site
Ambleside
TEL: 01912 611 585

4 SELLAFIELD VISITORS CENTRE
Tour
Sellafield, Seascale
TEL: 01946 727 027

5 TOWNEND
Historic house
Troutbeck, Windermere
TEL: 01539 432 628

6 HOLEHIRD GARDENS
Garden
Patterdale Road, Windermere   TEL: 01539 446 008

7 ESKDALE WATERMILL
Mill
Boot
TEL: 01946 723 335

8 LAKE DISTRICT VISITOR CENTRE
Visitor centre
At Brockhole, Windermere   TEL: 01539 446 601

9 BROCKHOLE
Garden
Lake District Visitor Centre, Windermere
TEL: 01539 446 601

10 BEATRIX POTTER GALLERY NT
Gallery
Main Street, Hawkshead   TEL: 01539 436 355

11 WINDERMERE STEAMBOAT CENTRE
Boat trip
Rayrigg Road, Windermere   TEL: 01539 445 565

12 RAVENGLASS & ESKDALE RAILWAY
Railway
Ravenglass
TEL: 01229 717 171

13 STEAM YACHT GONDOLA
Boat trip
Pier Cottage, Coniston   TEL: 01539 441 288

14 MUNCASTER WATER MILL
Factory tour
Ravenglass
TEL: 01229 717 232

15 WINDERMERE LAKE CRUISES
Boat trip
Bowness Promenade, Bowness-on-Windermere
TEL: 01539 531 188

16 MUNCASTER CASTLE GARDENS & OWL CENTRE
Garden
Ravenglass
TEL: 01229 717 614

17 BRANTWOOD TRUST
Garden
Brantwood, Coniston   TEL: 01539 441 396

18 HILL TOP NT
Garden
Sawrey, Ambleside
TEL: 01539 436 269

19 GRIZEDALE FOREST PARK VISITOR CENTRE
Visitor centre
Hawkshead, Ambleside   TEL: 01229 860 010

20 STOTT PARK BOBBIN MILL
Factory tour
Finsthwaite, Alveston   TEL: 01539 531 087

21 AQUARIUM OF THE LAKES
Aquarium
Newby Bridge
TEL: 01539 530 153

22 FELL FOOT PARK NT
Garden
Newby Bridge, Ulverston   TEL: 01539 531 273

23 LAKESIDE & HAVERTHWAITE RAILWAY
Railway
Haverthwaite, Ulverston   TEL: 01539 531 594

24 HOLME CRAGG
Garden
Blea Cragg Bridge, Witherslack, Grange-over-Sands
TEL: 01539 552 366

25 MILLOM FOLK MUSEUM
Museum
St Georges Road, Millom   TEL: 01229 772 33

26 CARTMEL RACECOURSE
Racecourse
Cartmel, Grange-over-Sands   TEL: 01539 536 340

27 LAKES GLASS CENTRE
Factory shop
Oubas Hill, Ulverston   TEL: 01229 584 400

28 LAUREL & HARDY MUSEUM
Museum
4c Upper Brook St, Ulverston   TEL: 01229 582 292

29 ULVERSTON HERITAGE CENTRE
Heritage centre
Ulverston
TEL: 01229 580 820

30 HOLKER HALL
Garden
Cark-in-Cartmel, Grange-over-Sands
TEL: 01539 558 328

31 CONISHEAD PRIORY
Historic building
Priory Road, Ulverston   TEL: 01229 584 029

32 SOUTH LAKES WILD ANIMAL PARK
Wildlife park
Crossgates, Dalton-in-Furness   TEL: 01229 466 086

33 FURNESS ABBEY
Abbey
Barrow-in-Furness
TEL: 01229 823 420

34 DOCK MUSEUM
Museum
North Rd, Barrow-in-Furness   TEL: 01229 894 444

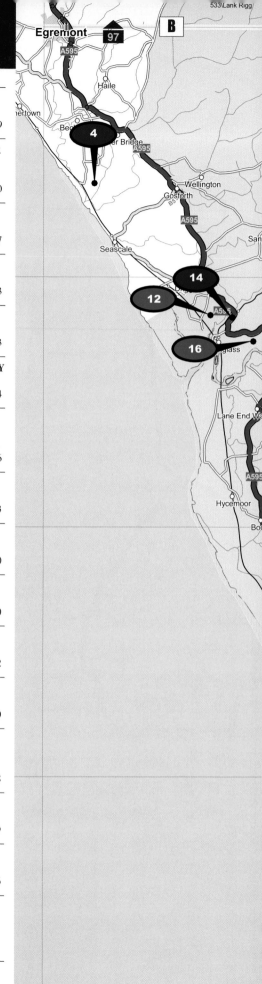

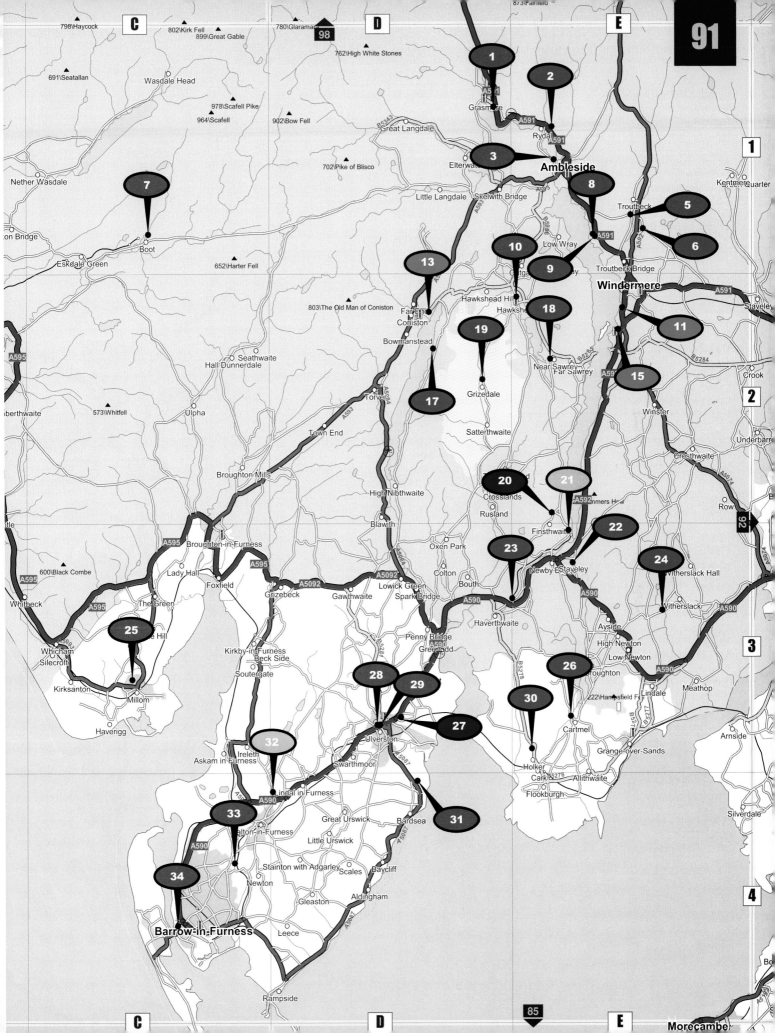

1 KENDAL MUSEUM
Museum
Station Road, Kendal
TEL: 01539 721 374

2 QUAKER TAPESTRY EXHIBITION
Exhibition
Stanoncate, Kendal
TEL: 01539 722 975

3 ABBOT HALL ART GALLERY & MUSEUM
Museum
Kendal
TEL: 01539 722 464

4 SHAP ABBEY
Abbey
Shap
TEL: Not available

5 WENSLEYDALE CREAMERY
Factory shop
Gayle Lane, Hawes
TEL: 01969 667 664

6 LOW SIZERGH BARN
Craft centre
Sizergh
TEL: 01539 560 426

7 SIZERGH CASTLE & GARDEN NT
Castle
Sizergh, Kendal
TEL: 01539 560 070

8 LEVENS HALL
Garden
Kendal
TEL: 01539 560 321

9 HERON CORN MILL & MUSEUM OF PAPERMAKING
Museum
Henry Cooke Waterhouse Mills, Beetham, Milnthorpe
TEL: 01539 565 027

10 LAKELAND WILDLIFE OASIS
Wildlife park
Hale, Milnthorpe
TEL: 01539 563 027

11 LEIGHTON MOSS RSPB NATURE RESERVE
Nature centre
Myers Farm, Storrs Lane, Silverdale
TEL: 01524 701 601

12 LEIGHTON HALL
Historic house
Carnforth
TEL: 01524 734 474

13 WHITE SCAR CAVES
Cave
Ingleton, Carnforth
TEL: 01524 241 244

14 DOCKER PARK
Farm
Arkholme, Carnforth
TEL: 01524 221 331

15 WARTON OLD RECTORY
Historic building
Warton, Carnforth
TEL: 0161 242 1400

16 INGLEBOROUGH SHOW CAVE
Cave
Clapham, Lancaster
TEL: 01524 251 242

17 MALHAM TARN ESTATE NT
Country park
Settle
TEL: 01729 830 416

18 YORKSHIRE DALES FALCONRY & CONSERVATION CENTRE
Bird centre & aviary
Crows Nest, Giggleswick, Settle
TEL: 01729 822 832

The Lakes, Cumbria

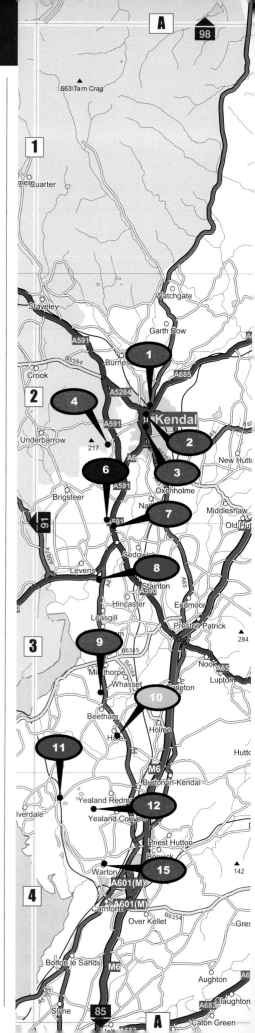

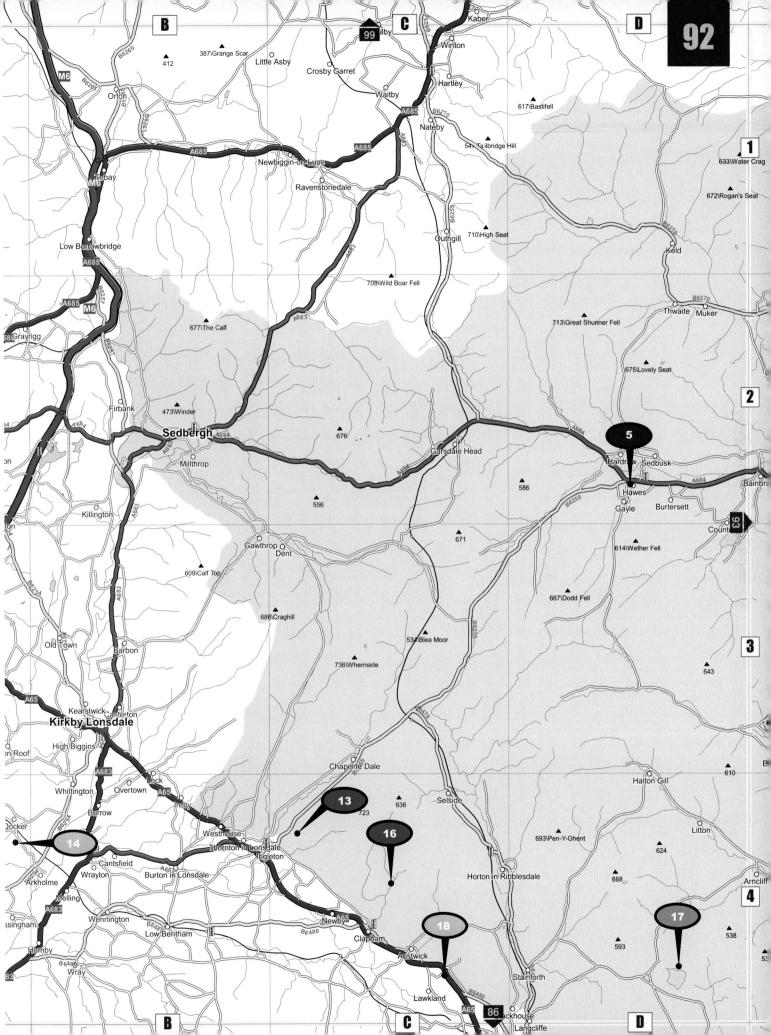

1 CROFT CIRCUIT
Motor racing circuit
Croft-on-Tees, Darlington   **TEL:** 01325 721 815

2 ASKE HALL
Historic house
Aske, Richmond   **TEL:** 01748 850 391

3 RICHMOND CASTLE EH
Castle
Tower Street, Richmond   **TEL:** 01748 822 493

4 RICHMONDSHIRE MUSEUM
Museum
Ryders Wynd, Richmond   **TEL:** 01748 825 611

5 GREEN HOWARDS MUSEUM
Museum
Trinity Church Square, Market Place, Richmond
    TEL: 01748 822 133

6 MILLGATE HOUSE
Garden
Richmond   **TEL:** 01748 823 571

7 SWALEDALE FOLK MUSEUM
Museum
Reeth Green, Reeth, Richmond
    TEL: 01748 884 373

8 CATTERICK BRIDGE RACECOURSE
Racecourse
Catterick Bridge, Richmond   **TEL:** 01748 811 478

9 HAZEL BROW FARM
Farm
Low Row, Richmond   **TEL:** 01748 886 224

10 BOLTON CASTLE
Castle
Leyburn   **TEL:** 01969 623 981

11 BURTON CONSTABLE HALL GARDENS
Garden
Leyburn
TEL: 01677 450 428

12 CRAKEHALL WATER MILL
Mill
Crakehall   **TEL:** 01677 423 240

13 TEAPOTTERY
Factory shop
Leyburn Business Park, Leyburn **TEL:** 01969 623 839

14 YORKSHIRE CARRIAGE MUSEUM
Historic house
Yore Mill, Aysgarth Falls, Leyburn
    TEL: 01969 663 399

15 BIG SHEEP & THE LITTLE COW
Farm
The Old Watermill, Aiskew, Bedale
    TEL: 01677 422 125

16 MIDDLEHAM CASTLE EH
Castle
Middleham, Leyburn   **TEL:** 0191 269 1200

17 FORBIDDEN CORNER
Historic building
Tupgill Park Estate, Coverdale, Leyburn
    TEL: 01969 640 638

18 BRAITHWAITE HALL
Farm
East Witton, Leyburn   **TEL:** 01969 640 287

19 JERVAULX ABBEY
Abbey
Park House, Jervaulx, Ripon   **TEL:** 01677 460 391

20 THORP PERROW ARBORETUM
Garden
The Hall, Thorp Perrow, Bedale   **TEL:** 01677 425 323

21 FALCONRY UK BIRD OF PREY & CONSERVATION CENTRE
Bird centre & aviary
Sion Hill Hall, Kirby Wiske, Thirsk
    TEL: 01845 587 522

22 SION HILL HALL
Historic house
Kirby Wiske, Thirsk   **TEL:** 01845 587 206

23 THEAKSTON BREWERY VISITOR CENTRE
Visitor centre
The Brewery, Masham   **TEL:** 01765 689 057

24 NORTON CONYERS
Historic house
Ripon   **TEL:** 01756 640 333

25 LIGHTWATER VALLEY THEME PARK
Theme park
North Stainley, Ripon   **TEL:** 01765 635 321

26 RIPON WORKHOUSE
Museum
Allhallowgate, Ripon   **TEL:** 01765 690 799

27 RIPON RACES
Racecourse
77 North Street, Ripon   **TEL:** 01765 602 156

28 RIPON PRISON & POLICE MUSEUM
Museum
St Marygate, Ripon   **TEL:** 01765 603 006

29 RIPON CATHEDRAL
Cathedral
Ripon   **TEL:** 01765 604 108

30 FOUNTAINS ABBEY & STUDLEY ROYAL WATER GARDEN NT
Garden
Ripon   **TEL:** 01765 608 888

31 NEWBY HALL & GARDENS
Historic house
Ripon   **TEL:** 01423 322 583

32 KILNSEY PARK & TROUT FARM
Country park
Kilnsey, Skipton   **TEL:** 01756 752 150

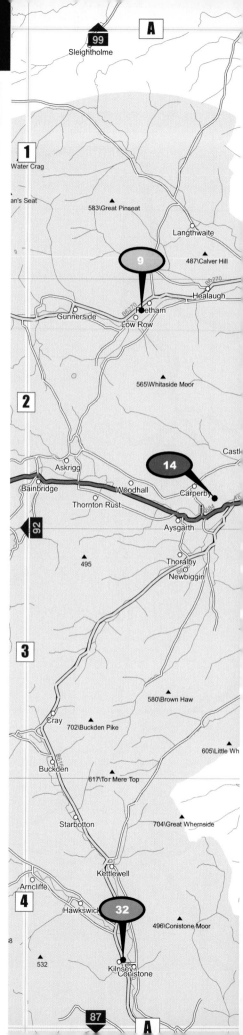

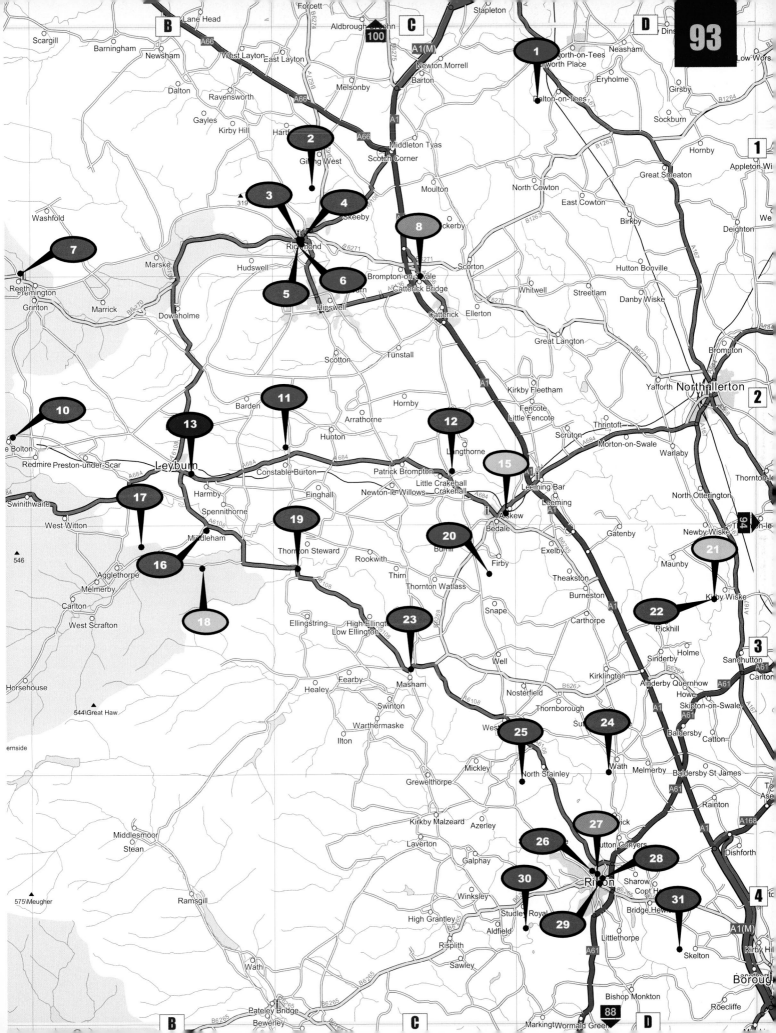

ANIMAL ATTRACTIONS
HERITAGE & CULTURE
INDOOR ACTIVITIES
OUTDOOR ATTRACTIONS
OUTDOOR ACTIVITIES
WATER ACTIVITIES

1 CAPTAIN COOK SCHOOLROOM MUSEUM
Museum
High Street, Great Ayton, Middlesbrough
TEL: 01642 722 030

2 EASBY ABBEY
Abbey
Easby
TEL: 0191 261 1585

3 MOORS CENTRE NORTH YORKSHIRE
Visitor centre
Lodge Lane, Danby, Whitby
TEL: 01287 660 654

4 NORTH YORK MOORS ADVENTURE CENTRE
Adventure & activity centre
Ingleby Cross, , Osmotherley
TEL: 01609 882 571

5 MOUNT GRACE PRIORY EH
Garden
Saddlebridge, Northallerton
TEL: 01609 883 494

6 RYEDALE FOLK MUSEUM
Museum
Hutton-le-Hole, York
TEL: 01751 417 367

7 RIEVAULX TERRACE & TEMPLES NT
Historic building
Helmsley
TEL: 01439 798 340

8 RIEVAULX ABBEY EH
Castle
Rievaulx, York
TEL: 0191 269 1200

9 SUTTON BANK VISITOR CENTRE
Visitor centre
Sutton Bank
TEL: 01845 597 426

10 HELMSLEY CASTLE
Castle
Helmsley
TEL: 01439 770 442

11 HELMSLEY WALLED GARDEN
Garden
Helmsley
TEL: 01439 770 442

12 DUNCOMBE PARK
Garden
Helmsley
TEL: 01439 770 213

13 WORLD OF JAMES HERRIOT
Museum
Skeldale House, 23 Kirkgate, Thirsk
TEL: 01609 779 977

14 THIRSK RACECOURSE
Racecourse
Station Road, Thirsk
TEL: 01845 522 276

15 NUNNINGTON HALL NT
Historic house
Nunnington, Helmsley, York
TEL: 01439 748 283

16 BYLAND ABBEY
Abbey
Coxwold, York
TEL: 01347 868 614

17 SHANDY HALL
Historic building
Coxwold, York
TEL: 01347 868 465

18 NEWBURGH PRIORY
Historic house
Coxwold, York
TEL: 01347 868 435

19 HOVINGHAM HALL
Historic house
Hovingham, York
TEL: 01653 628 206

20 CASTLE HOWARD
Historic house
York
TEL: 01653 648 444

21 ALDBOROUGH ROMAN TOWN & MUSEUM
Museum
High Street, Boroughbridge
TEL: 01423 322 768

22 KIRKHAM PRIORY
Priory
Whitwell-on-the-Hill, Kirkham
TEL: 01653 618 768

23 SUTTON PARK
Historic house
Sutton-on-the-Forest
TEL: 01347 810 249

Tynemouth Castle, Northumberland. Map 106-13

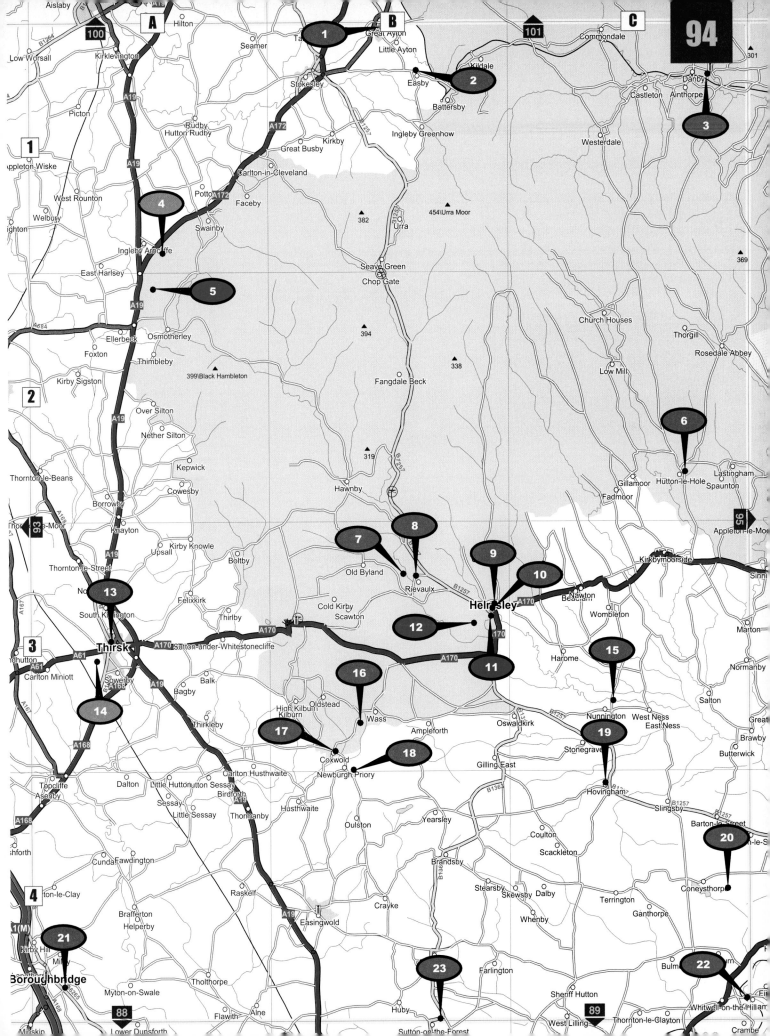

YORKSHIRE

1 MUSIC IN MINIATURE EXHIBITION
Museum
Albion Road, Robin Hood's Bay
TEL: 01947 880 512

2 STAINTONDALE SHIRE HORSE FARM
Farm
Staintondale, Scarborough
TEL: 01723 870 458

3 SCARBOROUGH SEA LIFE & MARINE SANCTUARY
Sea Life Centres
Scalby Mills Road, Scarborough, North Yorkshire, YO12 6RP.
TEL: 01723 376 125

Over 30 displays, a full programme of feeding demonstrations, talks and special presentations, seal rescue hospital, sea turtle convalescence centre and otter sanctuary.
OPEN: Open daily.
ENTRY COSTS: Call to confirm.
FACILITIES: Credit cards, Gift shop, Pushchair friendly, Toilets, Wheelchair access.

4 ATLANTIS
Water Parks
Peasholm Gap, North Bay, Scarborough
TEL: 01723 372 744

5 SCARBOROUGH CASTLE EH
Castle
Castle Road, Scarborough
TEL: 01723 372 451

6 CROPTON BREWERY
Factory tour
Cropton, Pickering
TEL: 01751 417 330

7 TERROR TOWER
Theme park
21 Foreshore Road, Scarborough
TEL: 01723 501 016

8 ROTUNDA MUSEUM
Museum
Vernon Road, Scarborough
TEL: 01723 374 839

9 SCARBOROUGH ART GALLERY
Museum
The Crescent, Scarborough
TEL: 01723 374 753

10 WOOD END MUSEUM
Museum
The Crescent, Scarborough
TEL: 01723 367 326

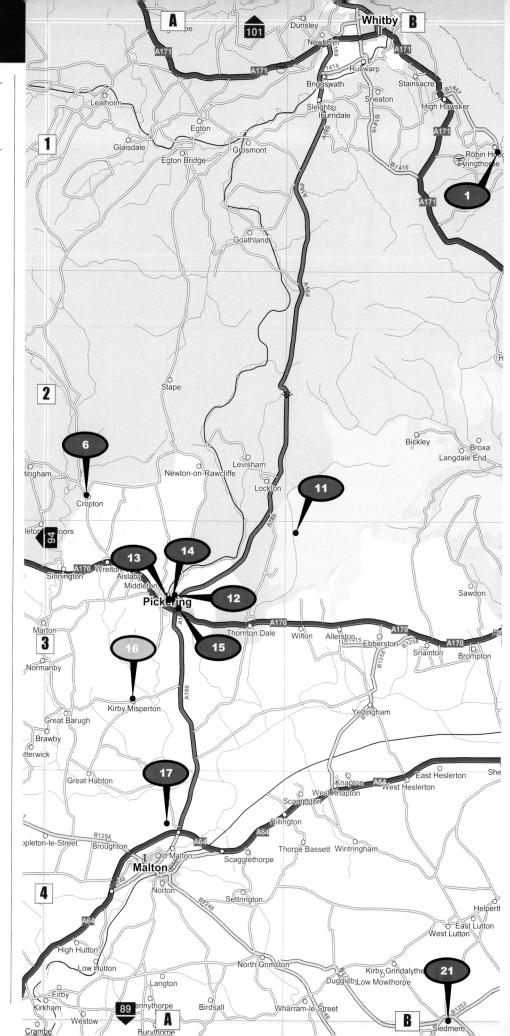

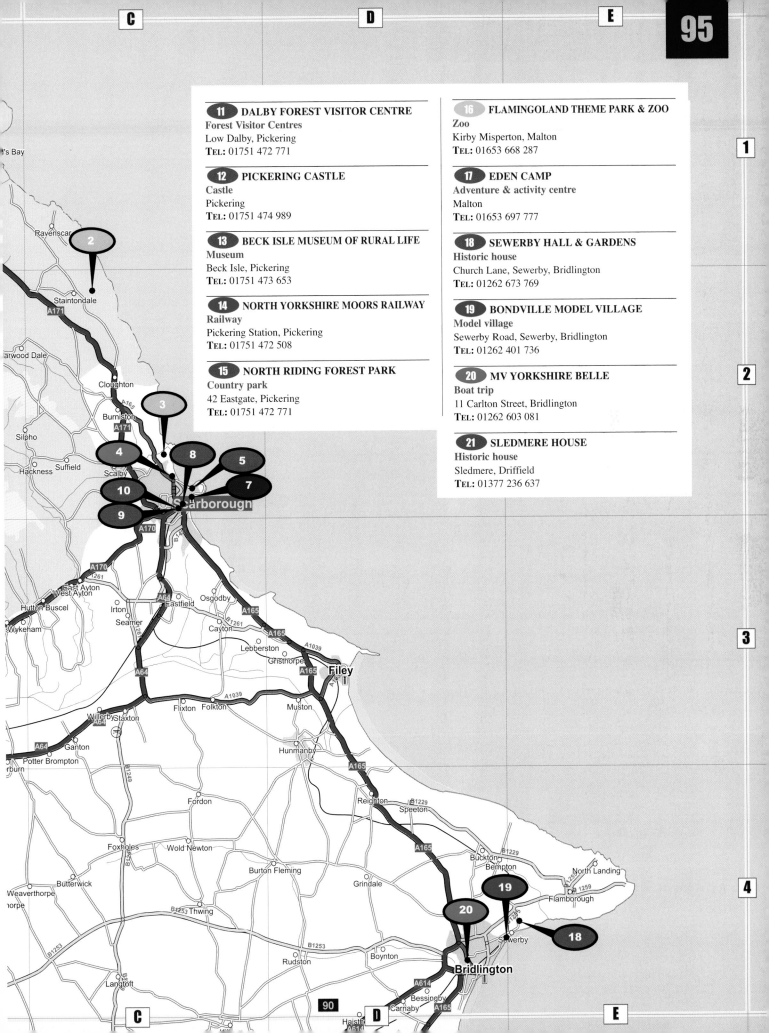

11 DALBY FOREST VISITOR CENTRE
Forest Visitor Centres
Low Dalby, Pickering
TEL: 01751 472 771

12 PICKERING CASTLE
Castle
Pickering
TEL: 01751 474 989

13 BECK ISLE MUSEUM OF RURAL LIFE
Museum
Beck Isle, Pickering
TEL: 01751 473 653

14 NORTH YORKSHIRE MOORS RAILWAY
Railway
Pickering Station, Pickering
TEL: 01751 472 508

15 NORTH RIDING FOREST PARK
Country park
42 Eastgate, Pickering
TEL: 01751 472 771

16 FLAMINGOLAND THEME PARK & ZOO
Zoo
Kirby Misperton, Malton
TEL: 01653 668 287

17 EDEN CAMP
Adventure & activity centre
Malton
TEL: 01653 697 777

18 SEWERBY HALL & GARDENS
Historic house
Church Lane, Sewerby, Bridlington
TEL: 01262 673 769

19 BONDVILLE MODEL VILLAGE
Model village
Sewerby Road, Sewerby, Bridlington
TEL: 01262 401 736

20 MV YORKSHIRE BELLE
Boat trip
11 Carlton Street, Bridlington
TEL: 01262 603 081

21 SLEDMERE HOUSE
Historic house
Sledmere, Driffield
TEL: 01377 236 637

DUMFRIES & GALLOWAY

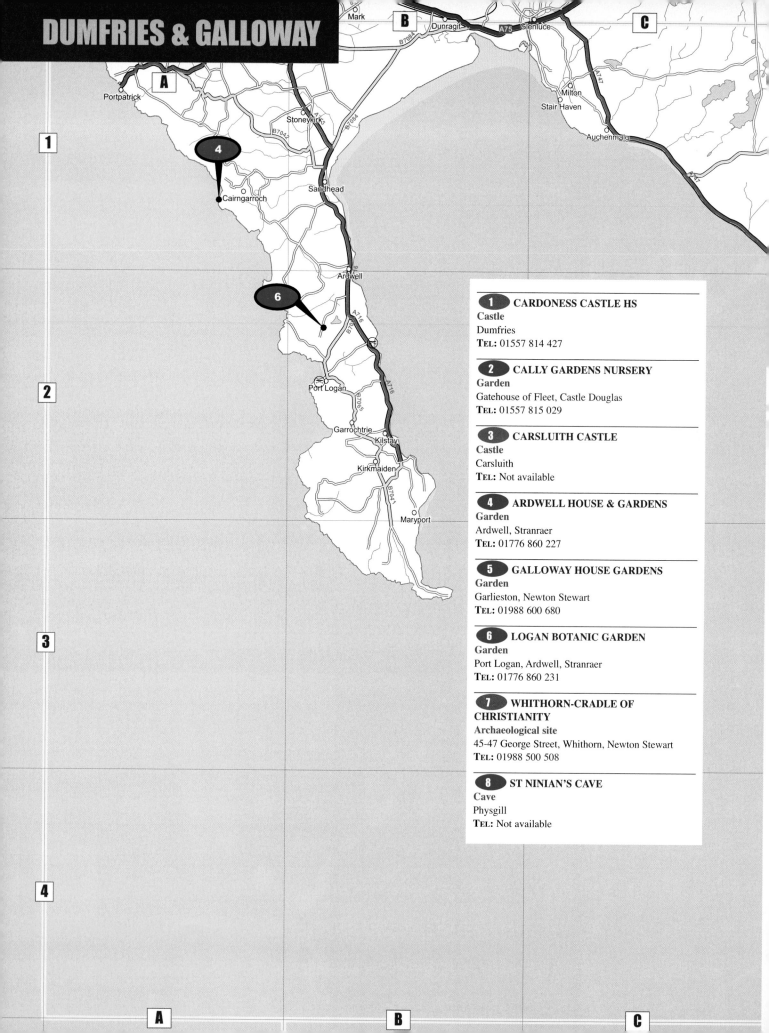

1 CARDONESS CASTLE HS
Castle
Dumfries
TEL: 01557 814 427

2 CALLY GARDENS NURSERY
Garden
Gatehouse of Fleet, Castle Douglas
TEL: 01557 815 029

3 CARSLUITH CASTLE
Castle
Carsluith
TEL: Not available

4 ARDWELL HOUSE & GARDENS
Garden
Ardwell, Stranraer
TEL: 01776 860 227

5 GALLOWAY HOUSE GARDENS
Garden
Garlieston, Newton Stewart
TEL: 01988 600 680

6 LOGAN BOTANIC GARDEN
Garden
Port Logan, Ardwell, Stranraer
TEL: 01776 860 231

7 WHITHORN-CRADLE OF CHRISTIANITY
Archaeological site
45-47 George Street, Whithorn, Newton Stewart
TEL: 01988 500 508

8 ST NINIAN'S CAVE
Cave
Physgill
TEL: Not available

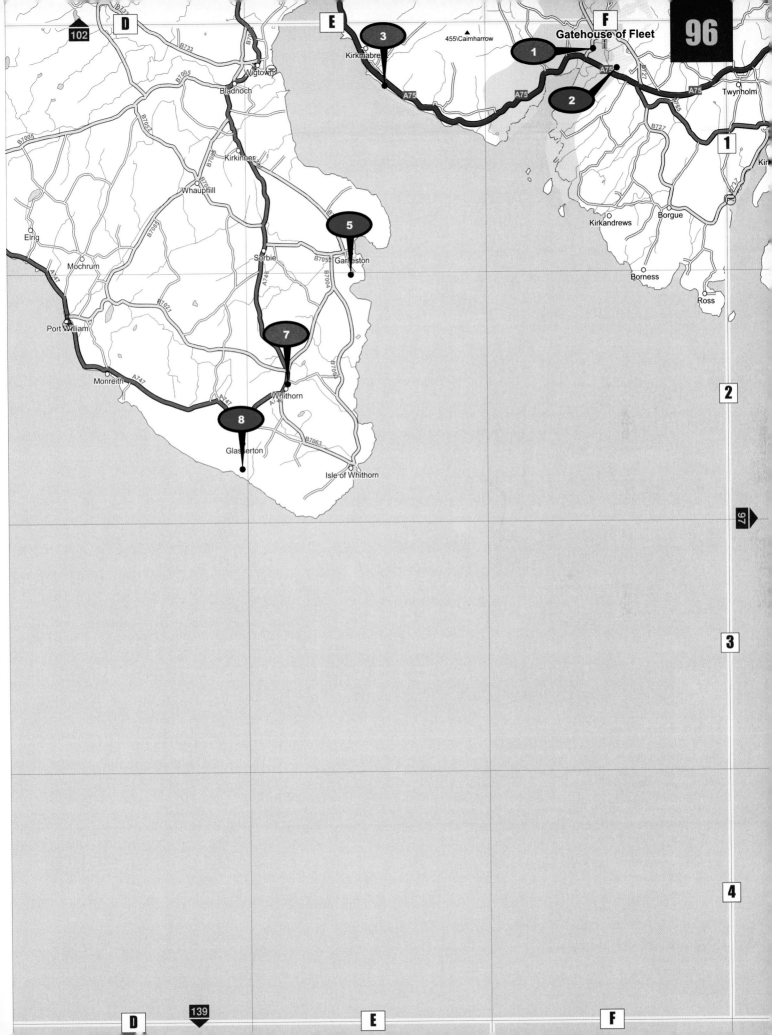

D

E

F

102

B733

B733

Wigtown

Bladnoch

Kirkinner

Whauphill

B703

Elrig

Mochrum

Sorbie

Garlieston

B7052

B7004

Port William

A747

A747

Monreith

Whithorn

Glasserton

B7063

Isle of Whithorn

3

Kirkmabreck

455\Cairnharrow

Gatehouse of Fleet

A75

A75

A75

A75

Twynholm

1

2

B727

Kirkandrews

Borgue

Borness

Ross

5

7

8

139

D

E

F

1

2

97

3

4

1 BROUGHTON HOUSE & GARDEN NTS
Garden
12 High Street, Kirkcudbright
TEL: 01557 330 437

2 STEWARTRY MUSEUM
Museum
St Mary Street, Kirkcudbright
TEL: 01557 331 643

3 MACLELLAN'S CASTLE HS
Castle
Kirkcudbright
TEL: 01557 331 856

4 TOLBOOTH ARTS CENTRE
Gallery
High Street, Kirkcudbright
TEL: 01557 331 556

5 FLYING BUZZARD & VIC 96
Museum
Elizabeth Dock, South Quay, Maryport
TEL: 01900 815 954

6 MARITIME MUSEUM
Museum
1 Senhouse Street, Maryport
TEL: 01900 813 738

7 ISEL HALL
Historic house
Isel, Cockermouth
TEL: Not available

8 TROTTERS WORLD OF ANIMALS
Farm
Coalbeck Farm, Bassenthwaite, Keswick
TEL: 01768 776 239

9 JENNINGS BREWERY TOUR
Unusual
Castle Brewery, Cockermouth
TEL: 01900 823 214

10 PRINTING HOUSE
Museum
Cockermouth
TEL: 01900 824 984

11 CUMBERLAND TOY & MODEL MUSEUM
Museum
Bank's Court Market Place, Cockermouth
TEL: 01900 827 606

12 WORDSWORTH HOUSE NT
Historic house
Main Street, Cockermouth
TEL: 01946 861 235

13 LAKELAND SHEEP & WOOL CENTRE
Farm
Egremont Road, Cockermouth
TEL: 01900 822 673

14 WORKINGTON HALL
Historic building
Ramsey Brow, Workington
TEL: 01900 326 408

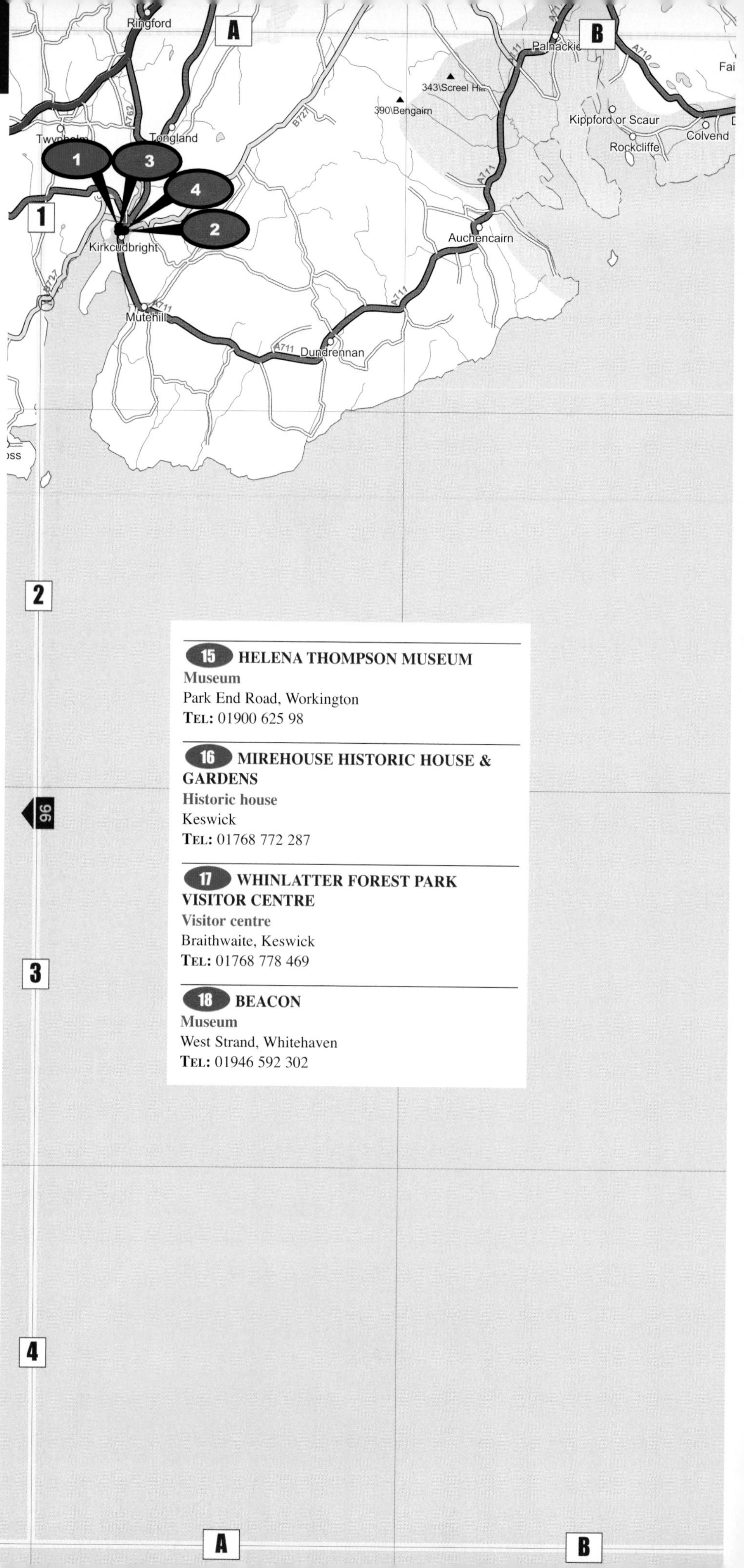

15 HELENA THOMPSON MUSEUM
Museum
Park End Road, Workington
TEL: 01900 625 98

16 MIREHOUSE HISTORIC HOUSE & GARDENS
Historic house
Keswick
TEL: 01768 772 287

17 WHINLATTER FOREST PARK VISITOR CENTRE
Visitor centre
Braithwaite, Keswick
TEL: 01768 778 469

18 BEACON
Museum
West Strand, Whitehaven
TEL: 01946 592 302

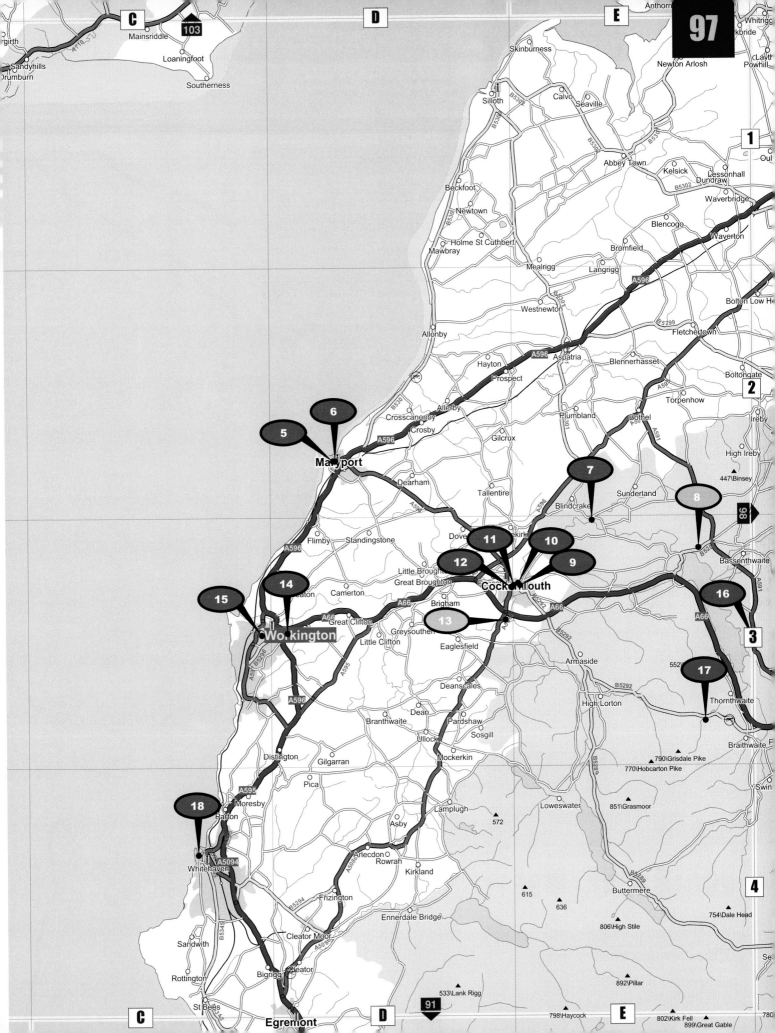

CUMBRIA

● ANIMAL ATTRACTIONS
● HERITAGE & CULTURE
○ INDOOR ACTIVITIES
● OUTDOOR ATTRACTIONS
● OUTDOOR ACTIVITIES
● WATER ACTIVITIES

1 CARLISLE CASTLE
Castle
Carlisle
TEL: 01228 591 922

2 BORDER REGIMENT & KING'S OWN ROYAL BORDER REGIMENT MUSEUM
Museum
Queen Mary's Tower, The Castle, Carlisle
TEL: 01228 532 774

3 TULLIE HOUSE MUSEUM & ART GALLERY
Museum
Castle Street, Carlisle
TEL: 01228 534 664

4 GUILDHALL MUSEUM
Historic building
Green Market, Carlisle
TEL: 01228 819 925

5 CARLISLE CATHEDRAL
Cathedral
7 The Abbey, Castle Street, Carlisle
TEL: 01228 548 151

6 HARDKNOTT CASTLE ROMAN FORT
Castle
Eskdale
TEL: 01229 571 20

7 HAWKSHEAD COURTHOUSE
Historic house
The Square, Hawkshead, Ambleside
TEL: 01539 435 599

8 CARLISLE RACECOURSE
Racecourse
Dirdar Road, Carlisle
TEL: 01228 522 973

9 HUTTON-IN-THE-FOREST
Garden
Penrith
TEL: 01768 484 449

10 EDEN OSTRICH WORLD
Farm
Langwathby Hall Farm, Langwathby, Penrith
TEL: 01768 881 771

11 PENRITH CASTLE EH
Castle
Penrith
TEL: 0191 269 1200

12 PENRITH MUSEUM
Museum
Eden DC Robinson's School, Middlegate, Penrith
TEL: 01768 212 228

13 BROUGHAM CASTLE
Castle
Brougham, Penrith
TEL: 01768 862 488

14 RHEGED DISCOVERY CENTRE
Visitor centre
Redhills, Penrith
TEL: 01768 868 000

15 ACORN BANK GARDEN NT
Garden
Temple Sowerby, Penrith
TEL: 01768 361 893

16 ALPACA CENTRE
Farm
Snuff Mill Lane, Stainton
TEL: 01768 891 440

17 DALEMAIN HISTORIC HOUSE & GARDENS
Garden
Estate Office, Penrith
TEL: 01768 486 450

18 WETHERIGGS COUNTRY POTTERY
Farm
Clifton Dykes, Penrith
TEL: 01768 892 733

19 BROUGH CASTLE
Castle
Brough
TEL: 0191 261 1585

20 LAKELAND BIRD OF PREY CENTRE
Bird centre & aviary
Lowther Castle, Penrith
TEL: 01931 712 746

21 LOWTHER LEISURE & WILDLIFE PARK
Theme park
Hackthorpe, Penrith
TEL: 01931 712 523

22 PENCIL MUSEUM
Museum
Southey Works, Keswick
TEL: 01768 773 626

23 KESWICK MUSEUM & ART GALLERY
Museum
Fitz Park, Station Road, Keswick
TEL: 01768 773 263

24 CARS OF THE STARS MUSEUM
Museum
Standish Street, Keswick
TEL: 01768 737 57

25 APPLEBY CASTLE CONSERVATION CENTRE
Historic building
Boroughgate, Appleby-in-Westmorland
TEL: 01768 351 402

Help us help you

mention the
Days Out Atlas

when visiting anywhere
on this page

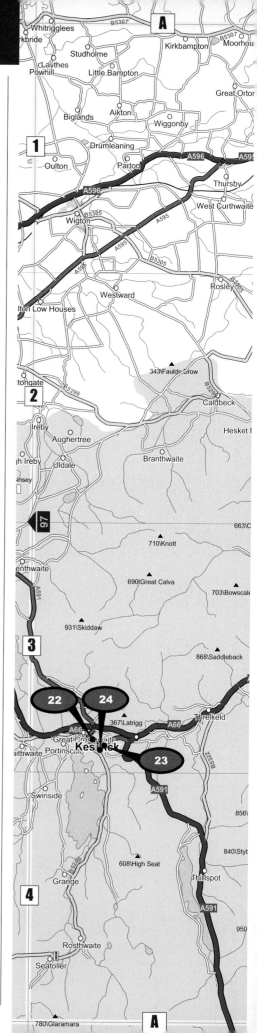

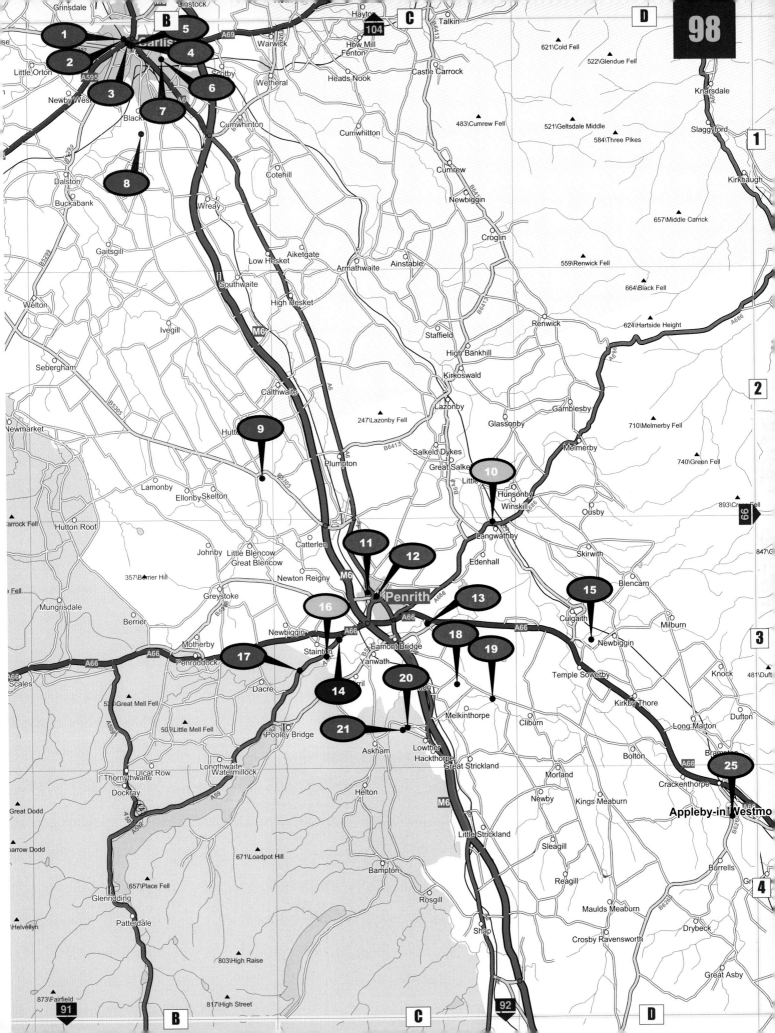

1 SOUTH TYNEDALE RAILWAY
Railway
The Railway Station, Hexham Road, Alston
TEL: 01434 381 696

2 GOSSIPGATE GALLERY
Craft centre
The Butts, Alston
TEL: 01434 381 806

3 ALLENHEADS HERITAGE CENTRE
Heritage centre
Allendale
TEL: 01434 685 326

4 HALL HILL FARM
Farm
Lanchester
TEL: 01388 730 300

5 KILLHOPE LEAD MINING CENTRE
Factory tour
Cowshill, Weardale
TEL: 01388 537 505

6 WEARDALE MUSEUM OF HIGH HOUSE CHAPEL
Museum
Ireshopeburn, Bishop Auckland
TEL: 01388 537 417

7 HAMSTERLEY FOREST VISITOR CENTRE
Visitor centre
Hamsterley Forest, Hamsterley
TEL: 01388 488 312

8 CAULDRON SNOUT
Unusual
Middleton-in-Teesdale
TEL: Not available

9 HIGH FORCE
Unusual
Ettersgill
TEL: 01833 640 209

10 BOWLEES VISITOR CENTRE
Visitor centre
Upper Teesdale, Middleton-in-Teesdale
TEL: 01833 622 292

11 EGGLESTON HALL GARDENS
Garden
Eggleston, Barnard Castle
TEL: 01833 650 115

12 BARNARD CASTLE
Castle
Newgate, Barnard Castle
TEL: 01833 638 212

13 EGGLESTONE ABBEY
Abbey
Marwood, Barnard Castle
TEL: 0191 261 1585

14 ROKEBY PARK
Historic house
Rokeby, Barnard Castle
TEL: 01833 637 334

15 BOWES CASTLE
Castle
Castle Terrace, Bowes, Barnard Castle
TEL: 0191 261 1585

16 OTTER TRUST'S NORTH PENNINES RESERVE
Wildlife park
Vale House Farm, Barnard Castle
TEL: 01833 628 339

Tynemouth Castle, Northumberland Map 106-12

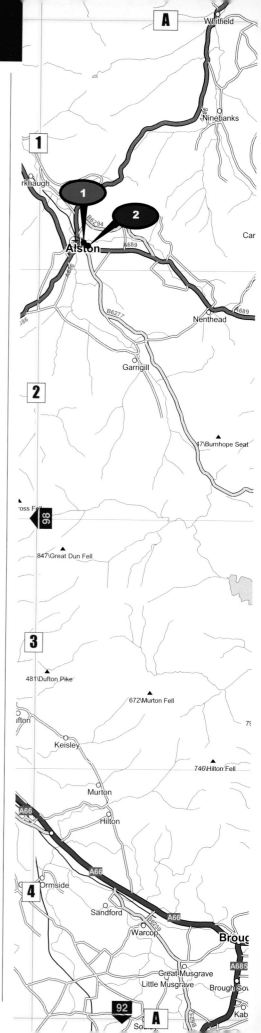

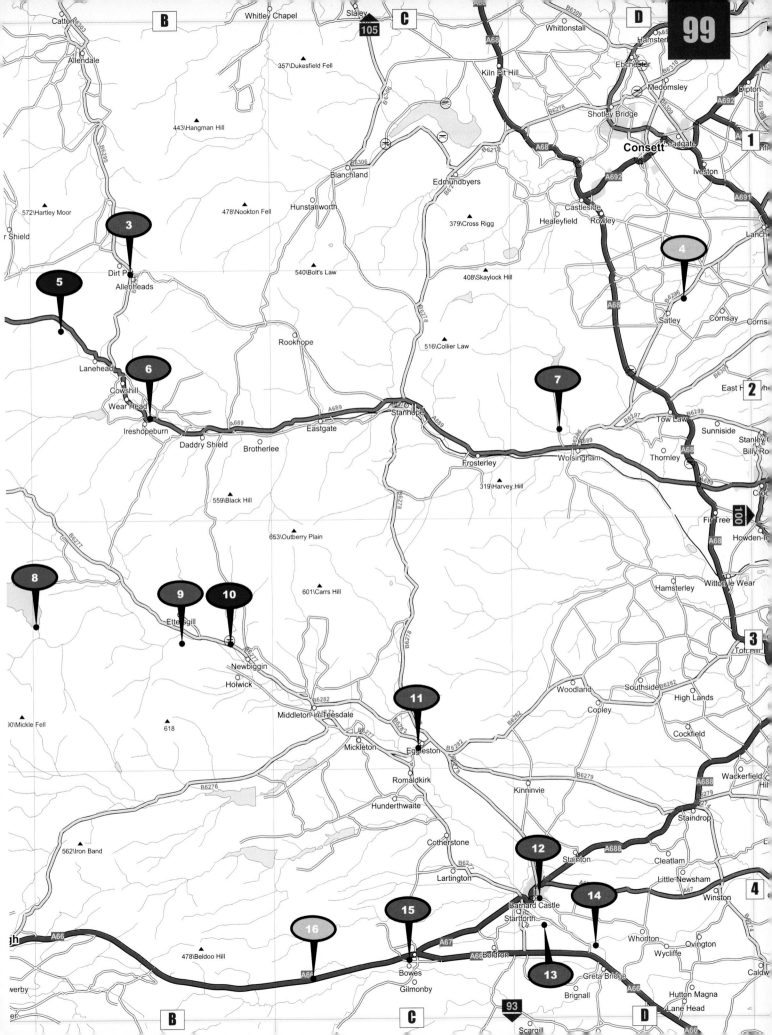

● ANIMAL ATTRACTIONS   ● OUTDOOR ATTRACTIONS
● HERITAGE & CULTURE   ● OUTDOOR ACTIVITIES
○ INDOOR ACTIVITIES   ● WATER ACTIVITIES

1 SUNDERLAND MUSEUM & ART GALLERY
Museum
Borough Road, Sunderland
TEL: 0191 565 0723

2 WASHINGTON OLD HALL
Historic building
The Avenue, District 4, Washington
TEL: 0191 416 6879

3 WILDFOWL & WETLANDS TRUST
Wildlife park
District 15, Washington
TEL: 0191 416 5454

4 NORTH OF ENGLAND OPEN-AIR MUSEUM
Museum
Beamish
TEL: 0191 370 4000

5 RYHOPE ENGINES MUSEUM
Museum
The Waterworks, Sunderland
TEL: 0191 521 0235

6 ANKER'S HOUSE MUSEUM
Museum
Church Chare, Chester-le-Street
TEL: 0191 388 3295

7 FINCHALE PRIORY
Historic building
Brasside Newton Hall, Durham
TEL: 0191 386 3828

8 SEATON HOLME DISCOVERY CENTRE
Museum
Hall Walk Easington, Peterlee
TEL: 0191 527 3333

9 DURHAM LIGHT INFANTRY MUSEUM & DURHAM ART GALLERY
Museum
Aykley Heads, Durham
TEL: 0191 384 2214

10 DURHAM RIVER TRIPS
Boat trip
Elvet Bridge, Durham
TEL: 0191 386 9525

11 DURHAM CASTLE
Castle
Durham
TEL: 0191 374 3800

12 UNIVERSITY OF DURHAM BOTANIC GARDEN
Garden
Green Lane, Old Elvet, Durham
TEL: 0191 374 7971

13 DURHAM HERITAGE CENTRE
Museum
North Bailey, Durham
TEL: 0191 386 8719

14 DURHAM CATHEDRAL
Cathedral
The College, Durham
TEL: 0191 386 4266

15 DURHAM UNIVERSITY MUSEUM OF ARCHAEOLOGY
Museum
The Old Fulling Mill, The Banks, Durham
TEL: 0191 374 3623

16 DURHAM UNIVERSITY ORIENTAL MUSEUM
Museum
Elvet Hill, Durham
TEL: 0191 374 7911

17 LOW BARNS NATURE RESERVE
Nature centre
Witton-le-Wear, Bishop Auckland
TEL: 01388 488 728

18 BINCHESTER ROMAN FORT
Roman site
Vinovia, Bishop Auckland
TEL: 01388 663 089

19 ESCOMB CHURCH
Historic building
Escomb, Bishop Auckland
TEL: 01388 602 861

20 AUCKLAND CASTLE DEER HOUSE & PARK
Garden
Bishop Auckland
TEL: 01388 601 627

21 TIMOTHY HACKWORTH VICTORIAN & RAILWAY MUSEUM
Museum
Hackworth Close, Shildon
TEL: 01388 777 999

22 HMS TRINCOMALEE TRUST
Museum
Jackson Dock, Hartlepool
TEL: 01429 223 193

23 CAPTAIN COOK BIRTHPLACE MUSEUM
Museum
Stewart Park, Marton, Middlesbrough
TEL: 01642 311 211

24 DORMAN MUSEUM
Museum
Linthorpe Road, Middlesbrough
TEL: 01642 813 781

25 GREEN DRAGON MUSEUM
Museum
Theatre Yard, Stockton, Stockton-on-Tees
TEL: 01642 393 936

26 TEESSIDE PRINCESS RIVER CRUISES
Boat trip
Quayside Road, Castlegate Quay, Stockton-on-Tees
TEL: 01642 608 038

27 PIERCEBRIDGE ROMAN FORT
Roman site
Morbium Piercebridge
TEL: 01325 463 795

28 NATURE'S WORLD
Wildlife park
Ladgate Lane, Acklam, Middlesborough
TEL: 01642 594 895

29 DARLINGTON RAILWAY CENTRE & MUSEUM
Museum
North Road Station, Station Road, Darlington
TEL: 01325 460 532

30 PRESTON HALL MUSEUM & PARK
Museum
Yarm Road, Stockton-on-Tees
TEL: 01642 781 184

31 BUTTERFLY WORLD
Wildlife park
Preston Park, Yarm Road, Stockton-on-Tees
TEL: 01642 791 414

32 STANWICK CAMP
Roman site
Aldbrough-St-John, Darlington
TEL: 0117 373 1301

33 TEES COTTAGE PUMPING STATION
Museum
Coniscliffe Road, Darlington
TEL: 01325 487 226

Donkey

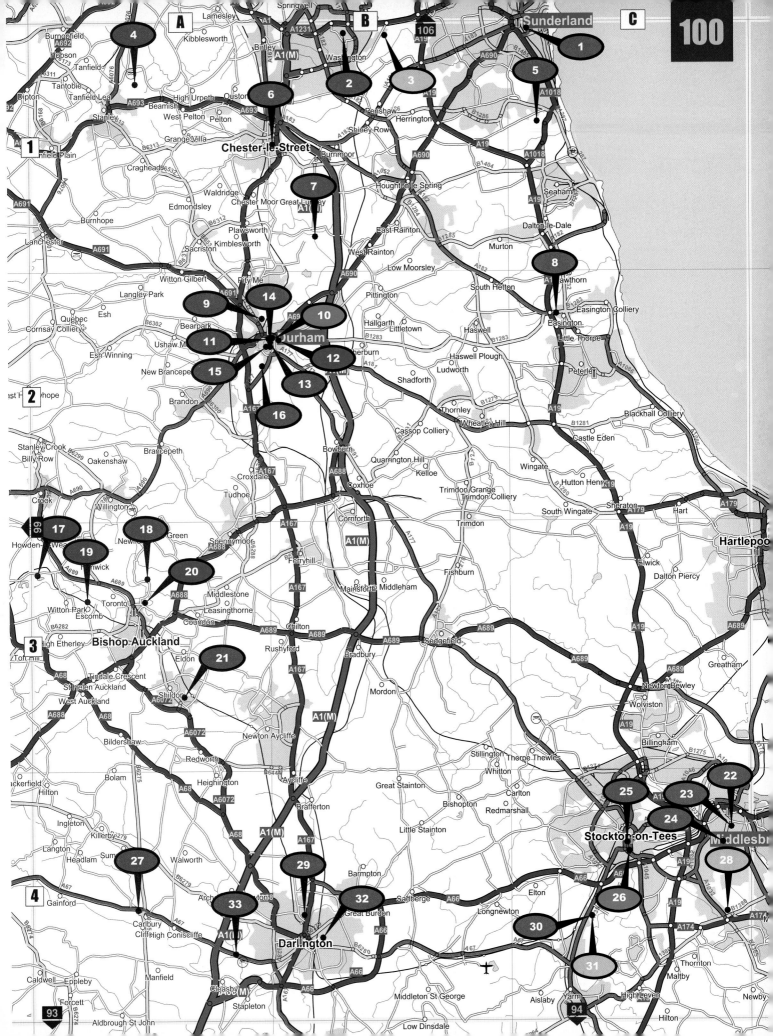

NORTH EAST

● ANIMAL ATTRACTIONS
● HERITAGE & CULTURE
◯ INDOOR ACTIVITIES
● OUTDOOR ATTRACTIONS
● OUTDOOR ACTIVITIES
● WATER ACTIVITIES

1 HARTLEPOOL HISTORIC QUAY
Museum
Museum of Hartlepool, Jackson Dock, Hartlepool
TEL: 01429 222 255

2 HARTLEPOOL POWER STATION
Factory tour
Tees Road, Hartlepool
TEL: 01429 853 888

3 RNLI ZETLAND MUSEUM
Museum
5 King Street, Esplanade, Redcar
TEL: 01642 485 370

4 REDCAR RACECOURSE
Racecourse
Redcar
TEL: 01642 484 068

5 OWL CENTRE
Wildlife park
Kirkleatham, Redcar
TEL: 01642 480 512

6 SALTBURN SMUGGLERS
Museum
Old Saltburn, Saltburn-by-the-Sea
TEL: 01287 625 252

7 TOM LEONARD MINING MUSEUM
Museum
Deepdale, Skinningrove, Loftus
TEL: 01287 642 877

8 CAPTAIN COOK & STAITHES HERITAGE CENTRE
Museum
High Street, Staithes
TEL: 01947 841 454

9 ORMESBY HALL NT
Historic building
Ormesby, Middlesbrough
TEL: 01642 324 188

10 ALBERT PARK
Country park
Marton-in-Cleveland, Middlesbrough
TEL: 01642 246 767

11 STEWART PARK
Country park
Ladgate Lane, Marton-in-Cleveland, Middlesbrough
TEL: 01642 300 202

12 GISBOROUGH PRIORY
Abbey
Church Square, Guisborough
TEL: 01287 633 801

13 MARGROVE SOUTH CLEVELAND HERITAGE CENTRE
Heritage centre
Margrove Park, Boosbeck, Saltburn-by-the-Sea
TEL: 01287 610 368

14 NEWHAM GRANGE LEISURE FARM
Farm
Wykeham, Coulby Newham, Middlesbrough
TEL: 01642 300 202

15 WHITBY ABBEY
Abbey
East Cliff, Whitby
TEL: 01947 603 568

16 CAPTAIN COOK MEMORIAL MUSEUM
Museum
Grape Lane, Whitby
TEL: 01947 601 900

Fun in the waves

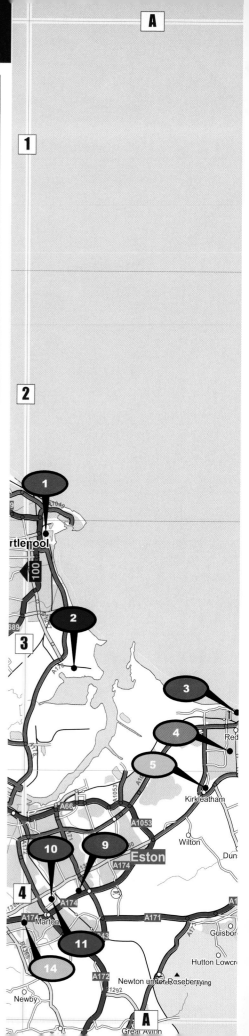

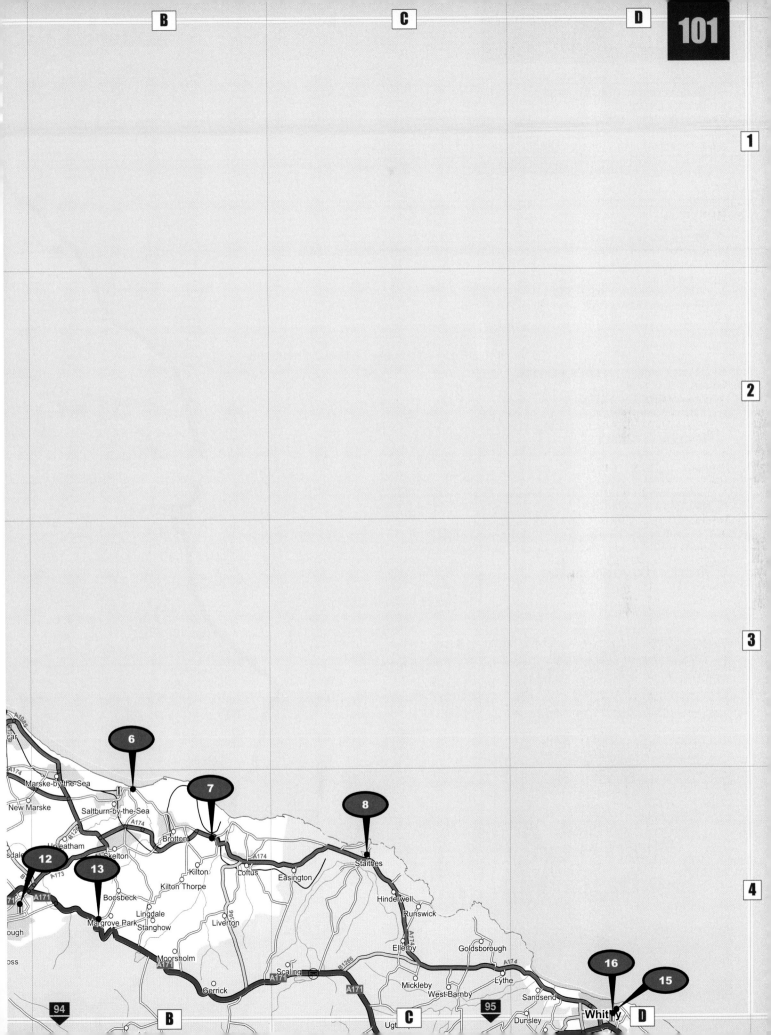

6

7

8

12

13

16

15

A1085

A174

Marske-by-the-Sea

New Marske

Saltburn-by-the-Sea

A174

B1269

Upleatham

Skelton

Brotton

A173

A171

Kilton

Loftus

Easington

Boosbeck

Lingdale

Kilton Thorpe

Stanghow

Liverton

Margrove Park

Moorsholm

A171

Gerrick

Scaling

A171

B1266

Staithes

Hinderwell

Runswick

Ellerby

A174

Goldsborough

A174

Mickleby

West-Barnby

Lythe

Sandsend

Whitby

Dunsley

Ugt

DUMFRIES

1 CLATTERINGSHAWS FOREST WILDLIFE CENTRE
Wildlife park
Clatteringshaws Forest, New Galloway
TEL: 01644 420 285

2 CASTLE KENNEDY GARDENS
Garden
Stair Estates, Rephad, Stranraer
TEL: 01776 702 024

3 STRANRAER MUSEUM
Museum
Old Town Hall, 55 George Street, Stranraer
TEL: 01776 705 088

4 STRANRAER CASTLE
Castle
Stranraer
TEL: 01776 705 888

5 CREETOWN GEM ROCK MUSEUM
Museum
Chain Road, Creetown, Newton Stewart
TEL: 01671 820 357

6 GLENLUCE ABBEY
Abbey
Glenluce
TEL: 01581 300 541

7 GLENWHAN GARDEN
Garden
Dunragit, Stranraer
TEL: 01581 400 222

8 GLENLUCE MOTOR MUSEUM
Museum
Glenluce
TEL: 01581 300 534

Clatteringshaw, Dumfries & Galloway

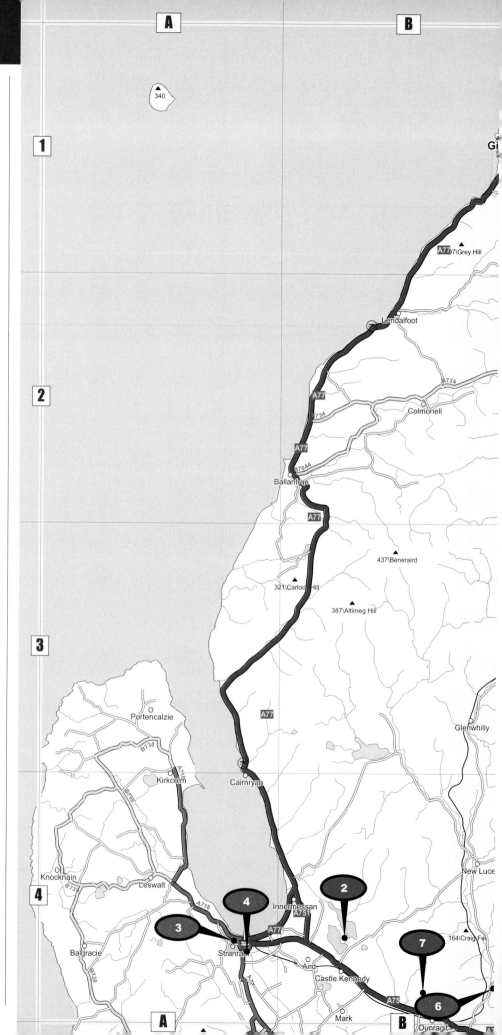

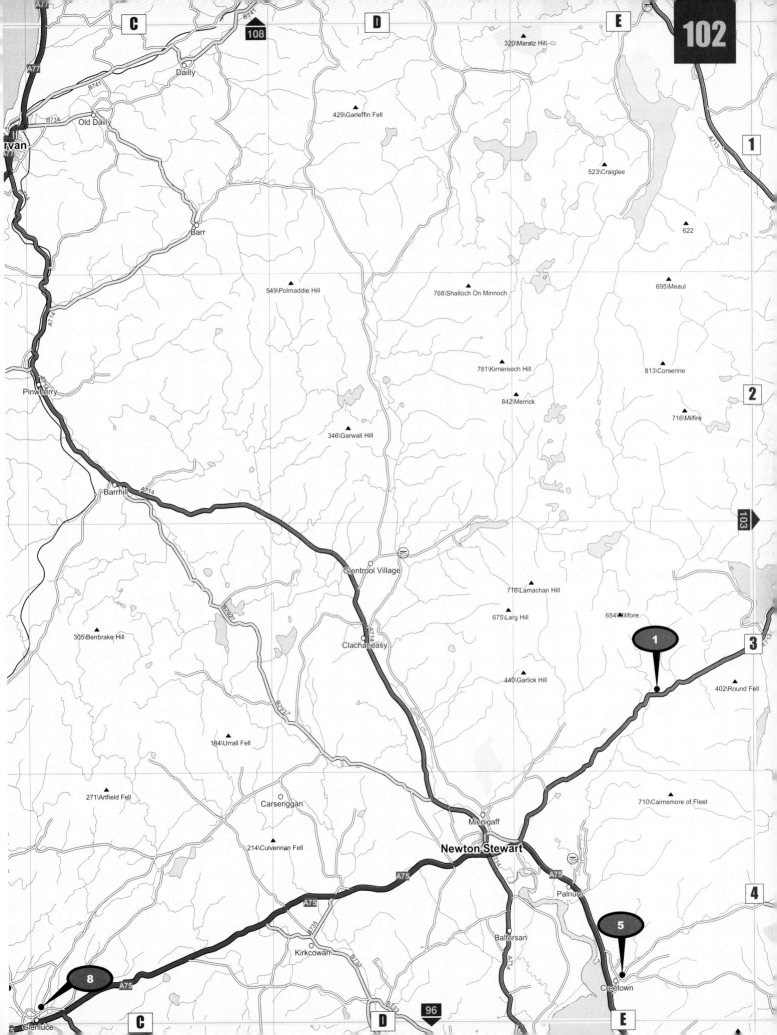

DUMFRIES

1 **DRUMLANRIG CASTLE GARDENS & COUNTRY PARK**
Castle
Thornhill   TEL: 01848 330 248

2 **MAXWELTON HOUSE**
Historic house
Moniaive, Thornhill   TEL: 01848 200 385

3 **ELLISON FARM**
Museum
Hollywood Road, Dumfries   TEL: 01387 740 426

4 **BRUCE'S STONE**
Monument
Moss, Raploch   TEL: 01721 722 502

5 **DUNDRENNAN ABBEY**
Abbey
Kirkcudbright   TEL: 01557 500 262

6 **GRACEFIELD ARTS CENTRE**
Gallery
28 Edinburgh Road, Dumfries   TEL: 01387 262 084

7 **ROBERT BURNS CENTRE**
Museum
Mill Road, Dumfries   TEL: 01387 264 808

8 **OLD BRIDGE HOUSE MUSEUM**
Museum
Mill Road, Dumfries   TEL: 01387 256 904

9 **BURNS HOUSE**
Historic house
Burns Street, Dumfries   TEL: 01387 255 297

10 **DUMFRIES MUSEUM & CAMRA OBSCURA**
Museum
The Observatory, Church Street, Dumfries
     TEL: 01387 253 374

11 **EDINBURGH WOOLLEN MILL**
Visitor centre
Waverley Mills, Langholm   TEL: 01387 380 611

12 **CAERLAVERLOCK CASTLE HS**
Castle
Caerlaverlock, Glencaple, Dumfries
     TEL: 01387 770 244

13 **CAERLAVERLOCK NATIONAL NATURE RESERVE**
Nature centre
Eastpark Farm, Caerlaverlock   TEL: 01387 770 200

14 **GALLOWAY FOREST PARK**
Country park
21 King Street, Castle Douglas, Dumfries
     TEL: 01556 503 626

15 **THREAVE CASTLE & GARDEN NTS**
Garden
Castle Douglas   TEL: 01556 502 575

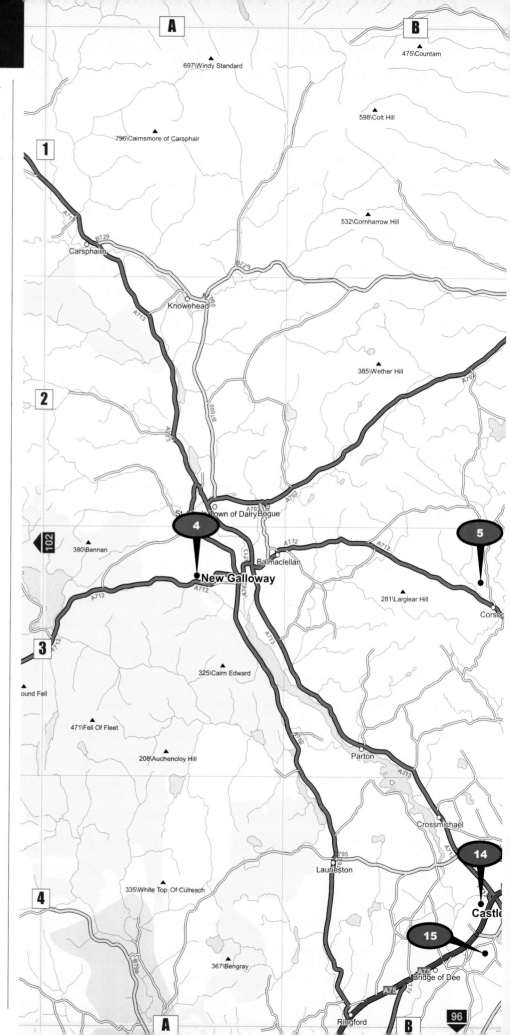

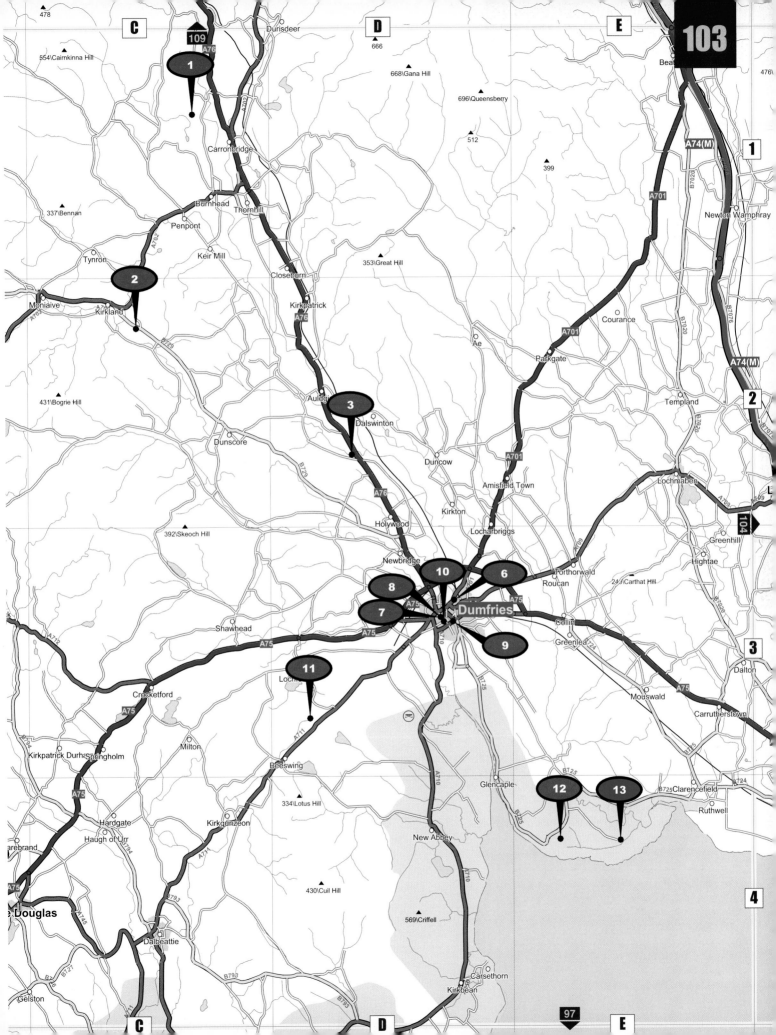

1 HERMITAGE CASTLE
Castle
Liddesdale, Newcastleton
TEL: 01367 376 222

2 LEAPLISH WATERSIDE PARK
Country park
Keilder Water
TEL: 01434 250 312

3 KIELDER CASTLE FOREST PARK CENTRE
Country park
Kielder Castle, Kielder
TEL: 01434 220 643

4 CARLYLE'S BIRTHPLACE
Historic building
The Arched House, High Street, Ecclefechan
TEL: 01576 300 666

5 ROMAN ARMY MUSEUM
Museum
Greenhead, Carlisle
TEL: 01697 747 485

6 POLTROSS BURN MILECASTLE
Archaeological site
Gilsland, Haltwhistle
TEL: Not available

7 WILLOWFORD WALL TURRETS & BRIDGE ABUTMENT
Roman site
Hadrian's Wall, Gilsland
TEL: Not available

8 WALLTOWN CRAGS WALL & TURRET
Roman site
Greenhead
TEL: Not available

9 BIRDOSWALD ROMAN FORT
Roman site
Gisland, Carlisle
TEL: 01697 747 602

10 LANERCOST PRIORY
Historic building
Lanercost, Brampton
TEL: 01697 730 30

11 NAWORTH CASTLE
Castle
Naworth, Brampton
TEL: 01697 732 29

12 CASTLETOWN HOUSE
Historic house
Castletown, Rockcliffe, Carlisle
TEL: 01228 747 92

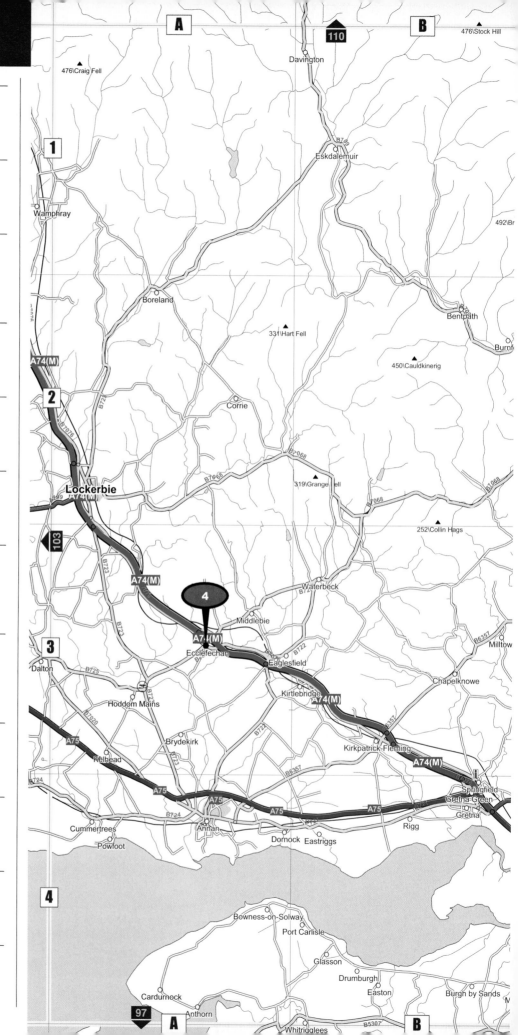

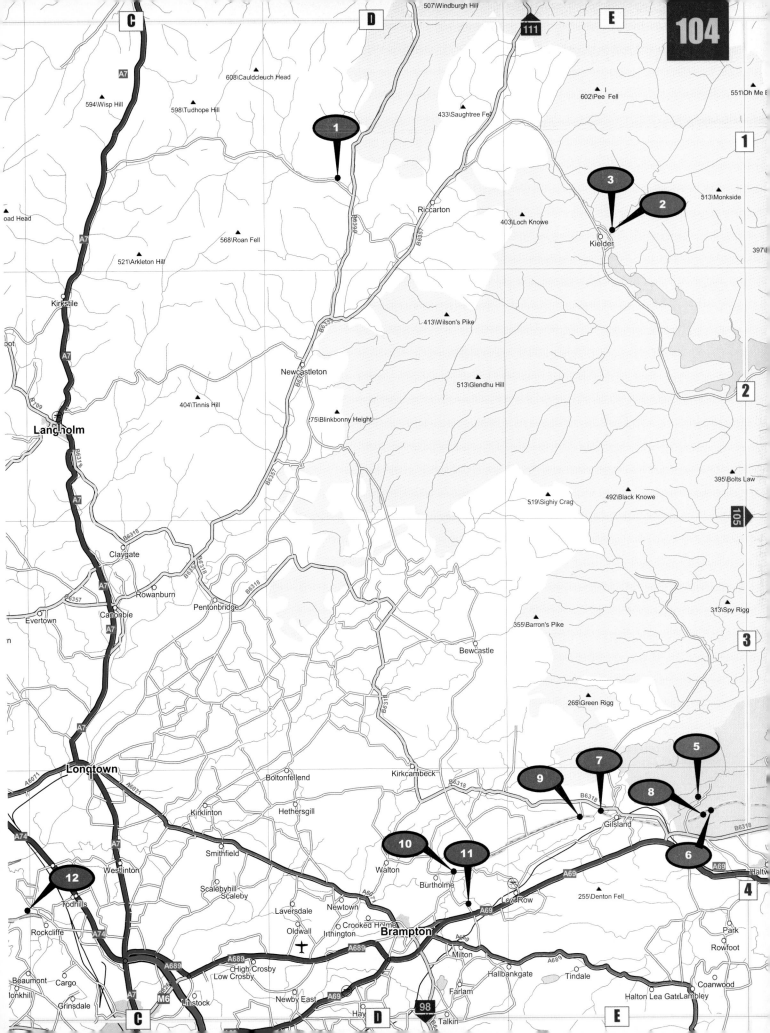

NORTHUMBERLAND

1 CRAGSIDE HOUSE & GARDEN NT
Historic house
Rothbury, Morpeth
TEL: 01669 620 333

2 WALLINGTON HALL NT
Historic house
Cambo, Morpeth
TEL: 01670 774 283

3 BOLAM LAKE COUNTRY PARK
Country park
Belsay, Morpeth
TEL: 01661 881 234

4 BELSAY HALL EH
Garden
Belsay, Newcastle-upon-Tyne
TEL: 01661 881 636

5 KIRKLEY HALL COLLEGE
Historic building
Ponteland
TEL: 01661 860 808

6 CHIPCHASE CASTLE
Castle
Wark, Hexham
TEL: 01434 230 083

7 BLACK CARTS TURRET
Archaeological site
Hadrian's Wall, Chollerford
TEL: Not available

8 BROCOLITIA TEMPLE OF MITHRAS
Archaeological site
Hadrian's Wall, Haydon Bridge, Hexham
TEL: Not available

9 SEWINGSHIELDS WALL TURRETS & MILECASTLE
Archaeological site
Haydon Bridge
TEL: Not available

10 CHESTERS ROMAN FORT & MUSEUM EH
Roman site
Chollerford, Humshaugh, Hexham
TEL: 01434 681 379

11 HOUSESTEADS ROMAN FORT
Roman site
Bardon Mills, Haydon Bridge, Hexham
TEL: 01434 344 363

12 WINSHIELDS ROMAN WALL & MILECASTLE
Roman site
Hadrian's Wall, Corbridge
TEL: Not available

13 AYDON CASTLE
Historic house
Corbridge
TEL: 01434 632 450

14 ROMAN VINDOLANDA
Roman site
Chesterholm Museum, Bardon Mill, Hexham
TEL: 01434 344 277

15 GEORGE STEPHENSON'S BIRTHPLACE
Historic building
Wylam
TEL: 01661 853 457

16 CORBRIDGE ROMAN SITE
Roman site
Corbridge
TEL: 01434 632 349

17 WYLAM RAILWAY MUSEUM
Museum
Falcon Terrace, Wylam
TEL: 01661 852 174

18 BORDER HISTORY MUSEUM
Museum
The Old Gaol, Hallgate, Hexham
TEL: 01434 652 349

19 PRUDHOE CASTLE
Castle
Prudhoe
TEL: 01661 833 459

20 TYNE RIVERSIDE COUNTRY PARK
Country park
Station Road, Prudhoe
TEL: 01661 834 135

21 THOMAS BEWICK'S BIRTHPLACE
Historic building
Station Bank, Mickley, Stocksfield
TEL: 01661 843 276

22 HEXHAM RACECOURSE
Racecourse
High Yarridge, Hexham
TEL: 01434 606 881

Alnwick Castle, Northumberland, Map 112-15

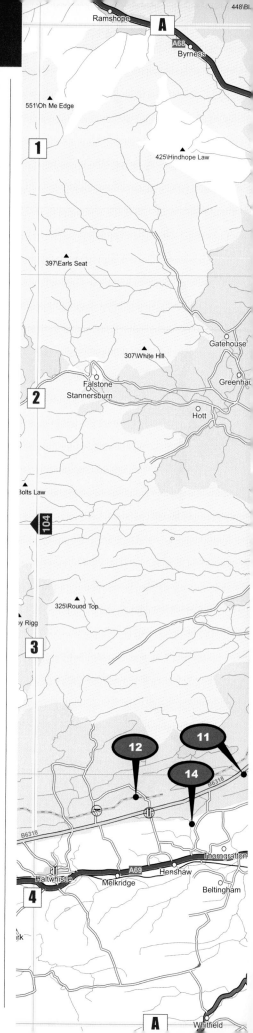

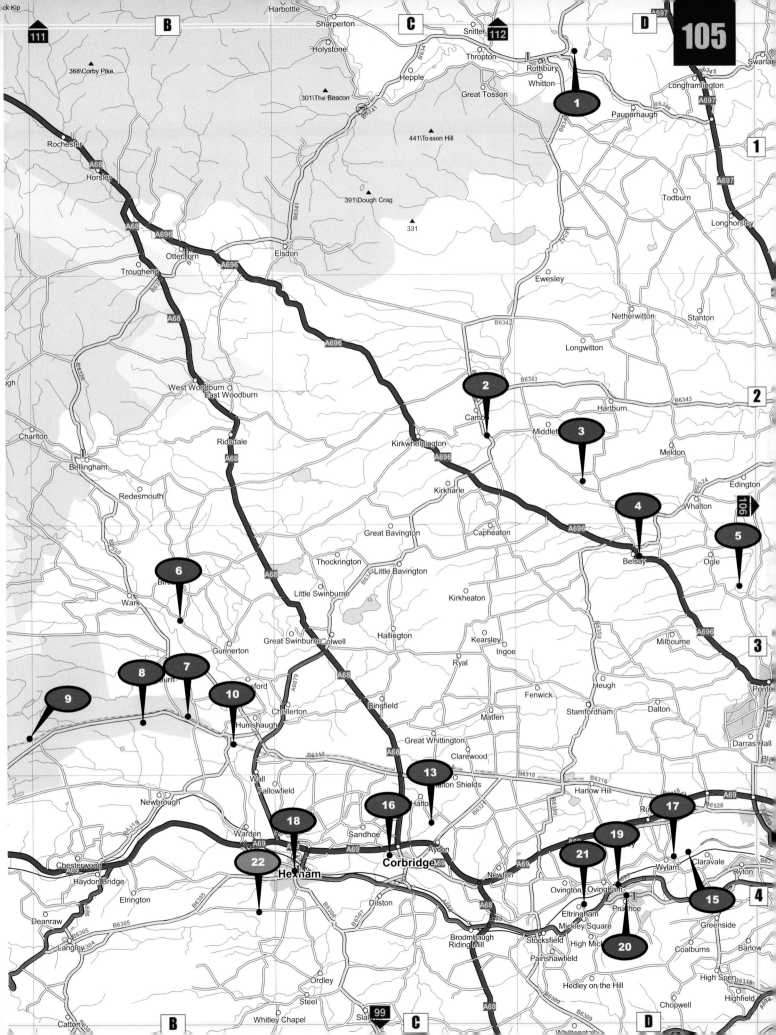

● ANIMAL ATTRACTIONS   ● OUTDOOR ATTRACTIONS
● HERITAGE & CULTURE   ● OUTDOOR ACTIVITIES
○ INDOOR ACTIVITIES   ● WATER ACTIVITIES

1 HAUXLEY NATURE RESERVE & VISITOR CENTRE
Wildlife park
Low Hauxley, Amble-by-the-Sea
TEL: 01665 711 578

2 DRURIDGE BAY COUNTRY PARK
Country park
Red Row, Morpeth
TEL: 01670 760 968

3 MORPETH CHANTRY BAGPIPE MUSEUM
Museum
Chantry Bridge Street, Morpeth
TEL: 01670 519 466

4 BEDLINGTON COUNTRY PARK
Country park
Humford Mill, Church Lane, Bedlington
TEL: 01670 829 550

5 PLESSEY WOODS COUNTRY PARK
Country park
Shields Road, Hartford Bridge, Bedlington
TEL: 01670 824 793

6 SEATON DELAVAL HALL
Historic house
Seaton Sluice, Whitley Bay
TEL: 0191 237 3040

7 ST MARY'S LIGHTHOUSE & VISITOR CENTRE
Historic building
Trinity Cottage, St Mary's Island, Whitley Bay
TEL: 0191 200 8650

8 ST PAUL'S MONASTRY
Historic building
Jarrow
TEL: 0191 489 2106

9 BEDE'S WORLD MUSEUM & HERB GARDEN
Museum
Church Bank, Jarrow
TEL: 0191 489 2106

10 NEWCASTLE RACECOURSE
Racecourse
High Gosforth Park, Newcastle-upon-Tyne
TEL: 0191 236 2020

11 TYNEMOUTH SEA LIFE CENTRE
Aquarium
Grand Parade, Tynemouth
TEL: 0191 258 1031

12 RISING SUN COUNTRY PARK & COUNTRYSIDE CENTRE
Country park
Whitley Road, Benton, Newcastle-upon-Tyne
TEL: 0191 200 7841

13 TYNEMOUTH CASTLE
Castle
East Street, Tynemouth, North Shields
TEL: 0191 257 1090

14 PRESTON TOWERS
Historic house
Preston Road, North Shields
TEL: 0191 259 1828

15 NORTH SHIELDS FISH QUAY
Concert
North Shields
TEL: 0191 200 5423

16 SOUTH SHIELDS MUSEUM & ART GALLERY
Museum
Ocean Road, South Shields
TEL: 0191 456 8740

17 ARBEIA ROMAN FORT & MUSEUM
Museum
Baring Street, South Shields
TEL: 0191 456 1369

18 DIGGERLAND
Adventure & activity centre
Strood
TEL: 01634 291 290

19 WARKWORTH CASTLE & HERMITAGE
Castle
Warkworth
TEL: 01665 711 423

20 BRINKBURN PRIORY
Historic building
Rothbury
TEL: 01665 570 628

21 NEWBURN HALL MOTOR MUSEUM
Museum
35 Townfield Gardens, Newburn
TEL: 0191 264 2977

22 HANCOCK MUSEUM
Museum
Barras Bridge, Newcastle-upon-Tyne
TEL: 0191 222 7418

23 TEMPLE OF MITHRAS EH
Roman site
Carrawburgh, Bardon Mill
TEL: 0191 261 1585

24 MARINE LIFE CENTRE & FISHING MUSEUM
Museum
Seahouses
TEL: 01665 721 257

25 MILITARY VEHICLE MUSEUM
Museum
Exhibition Park Pavilion, Newcastle-upon-Tyne
TEL: 0191 281 7222

26 JESMOND DENE PARK
Garden
Millfield House, Jesmond Dene, Newcastle-upon-Tyne
TEL: 0191 281 0973

27 SEGEDUNUM
Roman site
Buddle Street, Wallsend
TEL: 0191 236 9347

28 MUSEUM OF ANTIQUITIES
Museum
University of Newcastle-upon-Tyne, Newcastle-upon-Tyne
TEL: 0191 222 7849

29 BENWELL ROMAN TEMPLE
Roman site
Newcastle-upon-Tyne
TEL: Not available

30 LAING ART GALLERY
Gallery
New Bridge Street, Newcastle-upon-Tyne
TEL: 0191 232 7734

31 SOUTER LIGHTHOUSE
Historic building
Coast Road, Whitburn, Sunderland
TEL: 0191 529 3161

32 ST NICHOLAS CATHEDRAL
Cathedral
St Nicholas Square, Newcastle-upon-Tyne
TEL: 0191 232 1939

33 CASTLE KEEP
Castle
Castle Garth, Newcastle-upon-Tyne
TEL: 0191 232 7938

34 NEWCASTLE DISCOVERY MUSEUM
Museum
Blandford House, Blandford Square, Newcastle-upon-Tyne
TEL: 0191 232 6789

35 LIFE INTERACTIVE WORLD
Visitor centre
Times Square, Newcastle-upon-Tyne
TEL: 0191 261 6006

36 NEW METROLAND
Theme park
39 Garden Walk, Metrocentre, Gateshead
TEL: 0191 493 2048

37 SWALWELL VISITOR CENTRE
Visitor centre
Derwent Walk Country Park, Swalwell
TEL: 0191 414 2106

38 DERWENT WALK COUNTRY PARK
Country park
Thornley Lane, Rowland's Gill
TEL: 01207 545 212

39 BILL QUAY FARM
Farm
Haining Wood Terrace, Bill Quay, Gateshead
TEL: 0191 438 5340

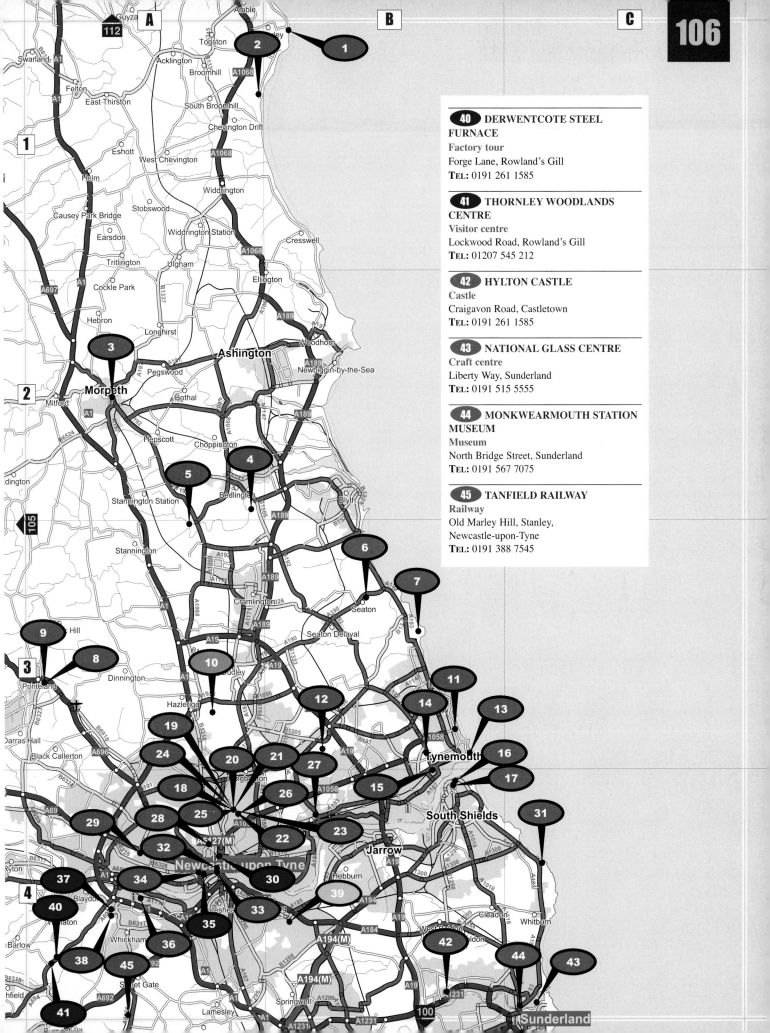

40 **DERWENTCOTE STEEL FURNACE**
Factory tour
Forge Lane, Rowland's Gill
TEL: 0191 261 1585

41 **THORNLEY WOODLANDS CENTRE**
Visitor centre
Lockwood Road, Rowland's Gill
TEL: 01207 545 212

42 **HYLTON CASTLE**
Castle
Craigavon Road, Castletown
TEL: 0191 261 1585

43 **NATIONAL GLASS CENTRE**
Craft centre
Liberty Way, Sunderland
TEL: 0191 515 5555

44 **MONKWEARMOUTH STATION MUSEUM**
Museum
North Bridge Street, Sunderland
TEL: 0191 567 7075

45 **TANFIELD RAILWAY**
Railway
Old Marley Hill, Stanley,
Newcastle-upon-Tyne
TEL: 0191 388 7545

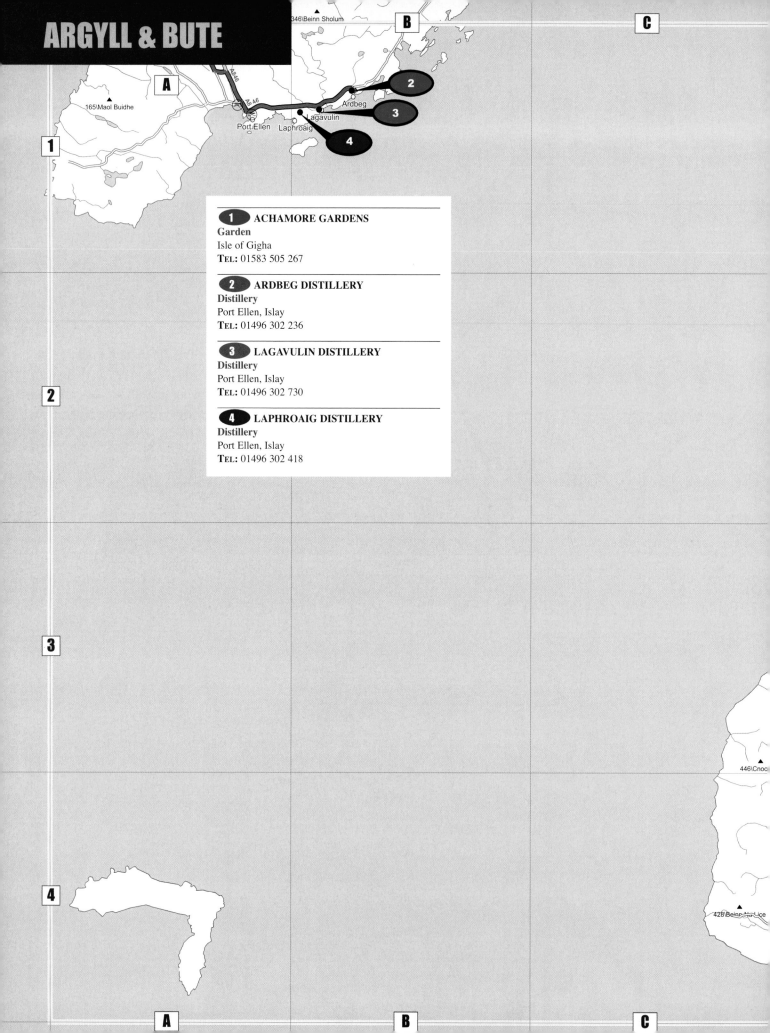

A

B

C

346\Beinn Sholum

165\Maol Buidhe

2

3

A6 A6

Ardbeg

Lagavulin

Port Ellen
Laphroaig

4

1

2

3

1 **ACHAMORE GARDENS**
Garden
Isle of Gigha
TEL: 01583 505 267

2 **ARDBEG DISTILLERY**
Distillery
Port Ellen, Islay
TEL: 01496 302 236

3 **LAGAVULIN DISTILLERY**
Distillery
Port Ellen, Islay
TEL: 01496 302 730

4 **LAPHROAIG DISTILLERY**
Distillery
Port Ellen, Islay
TEL: 01496 302 418

3

446\Cnoc

4

428\Beinn Na Lice

A

B

C

D

247\Cruach Mhic Gougain

E

264\ h T-Samhlaidh

F

Lochranz

1

rminish

1

Tayinloan

A83

Pirnmill

A841

715\Beinn Bharrain

83 eal Abhail

1

792\Beinn Nuis

354\Cruach Nan Gabhar

Muasdale

A83
Glenbarr

454\Beinn An Tuirc

B879

B84

Carradale

512\A'Chruach

B880

2

319

408\Bòrd Mor

503\Beinn Bhreac

A83
Bellochantuy

Saddell

Shiskine

Torbeg

396\Sgreadan Hill

Blackwaterfoot

A84

108

A83

Kilkenzie

A841

3

A83
Kilmichael

B842

Machrihanish

B842

Campbeltown

B842

352\Beinn Ghuilean

385\The State

Moy

4

Southend

D

E

F

SCOTLAND

1 BLACKSHAW FARM PARK
Farm
West Kilbride
TEL: 01294 823 014

2 DALGARVIE MILL MUSEUM
Museum
Dalry Road, Kilwinning
TEL: 01294 552 448

3 EGLINGTON COUNTRY PARK
Country park
Eglington, Irvine
TEL: 01294 316 460

4 NORTH AYRSHIRE MUSEUM
Museum
Manse Street, Kirkgate, Saltcoats
TEL: 01294 464 174

5 DEAN CASTLE COUNTRY PARK
Country park
Dean Road, Kilmarnock
TEL: 01563 574 916

6 GLASGOW VENNEL MUSEUM & ART GALLERY
Museum
10 Glasgow, Vennel, Irvine
TEL: 01294 275 059

7 BIG IDEA
Museum
Irvine
TEL: 08708 403 100

8 SCOTTISH MARITIME MUSEUM
Museum
Laird Forge, Gottries Road, Irvine
TEL: 01294 278 283

9 BRODICK CASTLE NTS
Castle
Isle of Arran
TEL: 01770 302 202

10 DICK INSTITUTE ART GALLERY & MUSEUM
Museum
Elmbank Avenue, Kilmarnock
TEL: 01563 526 401

11 LOUDOUN CASTLE THEME PARK
Theme park
Loudoun Castle, Galston
TEL: 01563 822 296

12 ARRAN BREWERY
Brewery
Isle of Arran
TEL: 01770 302 353

13 CROSSRAGUEL ABBEY
Abbey
Maybole
TEL: 01655 883 113

14 ROYAL DUNDONALD CASTLE
Castle
Dundonald
TEL: 01563 851 489

15 BACHELORS' CLUB
Historic house
Sandgate Street, Tarbloton, Ayr
TEL: 01292 541 940

16 AYR RACECOURSE
Racecourse
2 Whitletts Road, Ayr
TEL: 01292 264 179

17 BURNS NATIONAL HERITAGE PARK
Historic building
Alloway
TEL: 01292 443 700

18 BURN'S COTTAGE
Historic building
Alloway, Ayr
TEL: 01292 441 215

19 TAM O'SHANTER EXPERIENCE
Museum
Alloway, Ayr
TEL: 01292 443 700

20 CULZEAN CASTLE & COUNTRY PARK NTS
Castle
Maybole
TEL: 01655 884 455

21 DUNASKIN OPEN-AIR MUSEUM
Museum
Dalmellington Road, Patna
TEL: 01292 531 144

22 SOUTER JOHNNIE'S COTTAGE
Museum
Main Road, Kirkoswald, Maybole
TEL: 01655 760 603

23 BLAIRQUHAN CASTLE
Castle
Straiton, Maybole
TEL: 01655 770 239

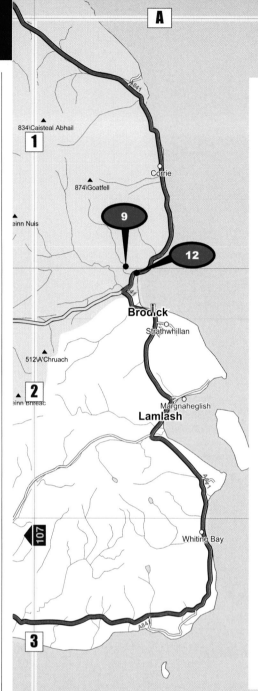

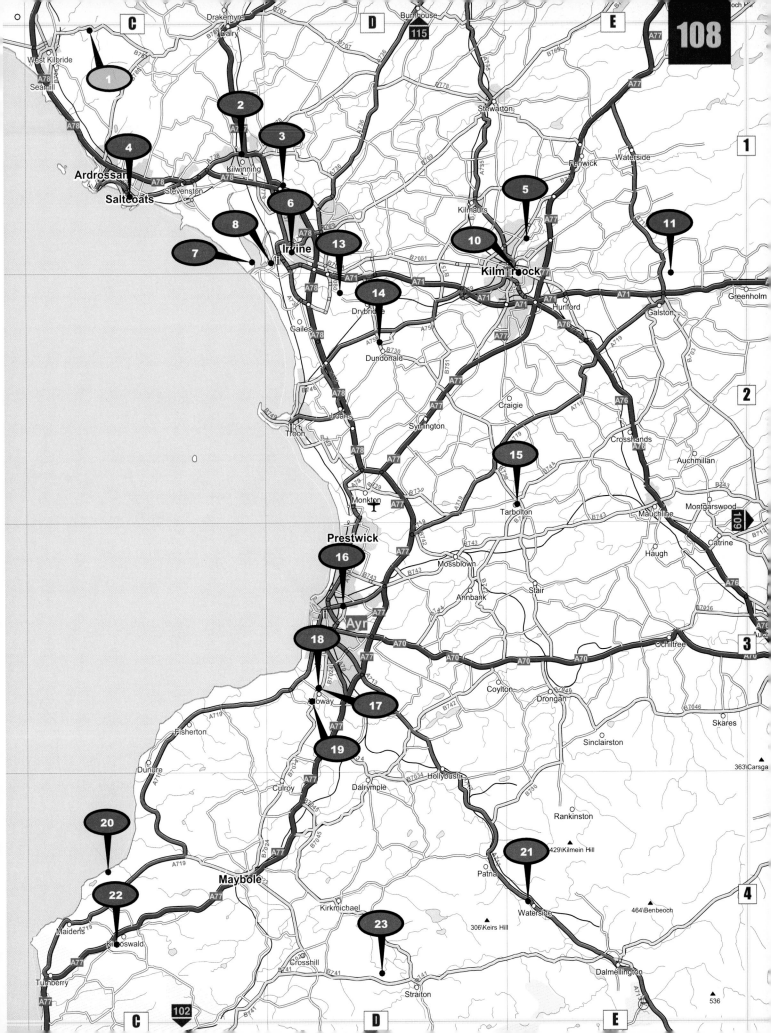

1 CRAIGNETHAN CASTLE

Castle

Lanark

TEL: 01555 860 364

2 JOHN HASTIE MUSEUM

Museum

8 Threestanes Road, Strathaven

TEL: 01355 261 261

3 NEW LANARK WORLD HERITAGE VILLAGE

Heritage centre

New Lanark Mills, Lanark

TEL: 01555 661 345

4 BROUGHTON PLACE

Garden

Broughton, Biggar

TEL: 01899 830 234

5 BIGGAR GASWORKS

Factory tour

Moat Park, Biggar

TEL: 0131 6688 600

6 GREENHILL COVENANTERS HOUSE

Historic House

Kirkstyle, Biggar

TEL: 01899 221 572

7 MOAT PARK HERITAGE CENTRE

Heritage centre

Kirkstyle, Biggar

TEL: 01899 221 050

8 GLADSTONE COURT MUSEUM

Museum

North Back Road, Biggar

TEL: 01899 221 573

9 BAIRD INSTITUTE HISTORY CENTRE & MUSEUM

Museum

Lugar Street, Cumnock

TEL: 01290 421 701

10 MUSEUM OF LEAD MINING

Museum

Biggar

TEL: 01659 743 87

11 SANQUHAR TOLBOOTH MUSEUM

Museum

High Street, Sanquhar

TEL: 01659 251 86

12 GREY MARE'S TAIL

Waterfall

Moffat Valley

TEL: 01556 502 575

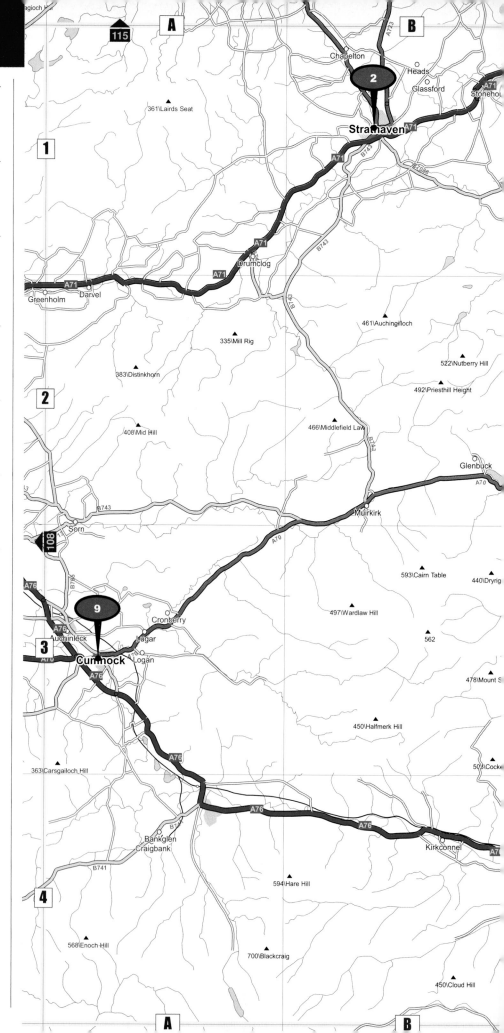

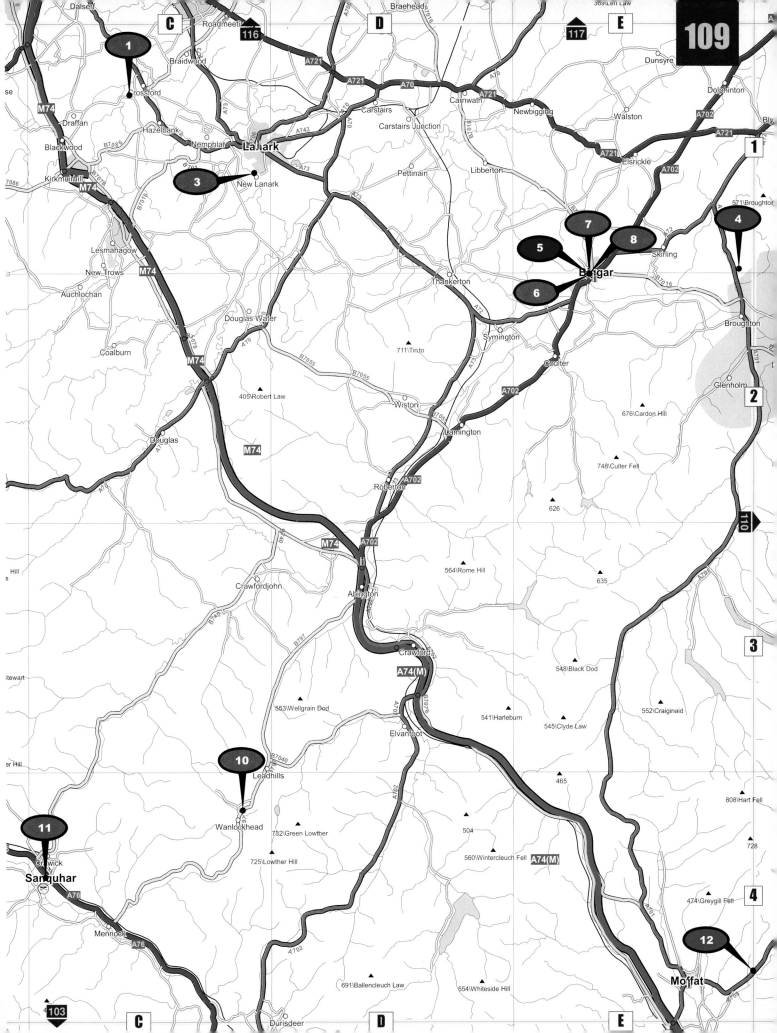

BORDERS

● ANIMAL ATTRACTIONS   ● OUTDOOR ATTRACTIONS
● HERITAGE & CULTURE   ● OUTDOOR ACTIVITIES
○ INDOOR ACTIVITIES   ● WATER ACTIVITIES

1 THIRLESTANE CASTLE
Castle
Lauder
TEL: 01578 722 430

2 TWEEDDALE MUSEUM
Museum
Chambers Institute, High Street, Peebles
TEL: 01721 724 820

3 NEIDPATH CASTLE
Castle
Peebles
TEL: 01721 720 333

4 KAILZIE GARDENS
Garden
Peebles
TEL: 01721 720 007

5 ROBERT SMALL'S PRINTING WORKS
Museum
7/9 High Street, Innerleithen
TEL: 01896 830 206

6 OLD GALA HOUSE
Museum
Scott Crescent, Galashiels
TEL: 01750 200 96

7 LOCHCARRON CASHMERE & WOOL CENTRE
Museum
Huddersfield Street, Galashiels
TEL: 01896 752 091

8 TRAQUAIR HOUSE
Castle
Innerleithen
TEL: 01896 830 323

9 DAWYCK BOTANIC GARDEN
Garden
Peebles
TEL: 01721 760 254

10 HARMONY GARDEN NTS
Garden
Melrose
TEL: 01896 823 464

11 MELROSE MOTOR MUSEUM
Museum
Annay Road, Melrose
TEL: 01896 822 624

12 ABBOTSFORD HOUSE & GARDENS
Garden
Melrose
TEL: 01896 752 043

13 PRIORWOOD GARDEN NTS
Garden
Melrose
TEL: 01896 822 493

14 TEDDY MELROSE TEDDY BEAR MUSEUM
Museum
The Wynd, Melrose
TEL: 01896 823 854

15 TRIMONTIUM EXHIBITION
Museum
The Square, Melrose
TEL: 01896 822 463

16 SIR WALTER SCOTT'S COURTROOM
Museum
Market Place, Selkirk
TEL: 01750 200 96

17 BOWHILL HOUSE & COUNTRY PARK
Historic house
Selkirk
TEL: 01750 222 04

18 HAWICK MUSEUM & SCOTT ART GALLERY
Gallery
Wilton Park Lodge, Hawick
TEL: 01450 373 457

19 DRUMLANRIG'S TOWER
Museum
Tower Knowe, Hawick
TEL: 01450 377 615

20 MELROSE ABBEY HS
Castle
Abbey Street, Melrose
TEL: 0131 668 8800

Sunset on Loch Lomond, Argyll & Bute, Map 115

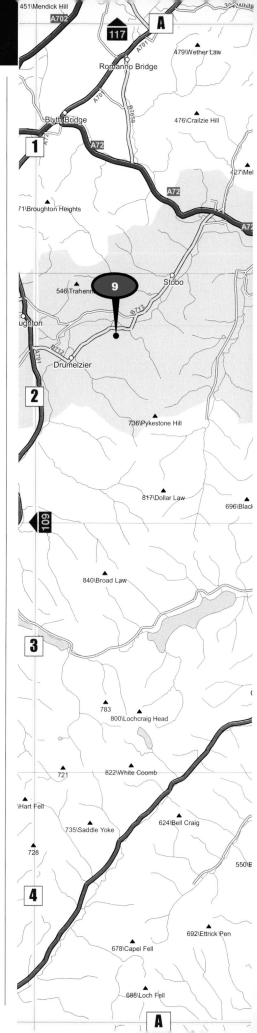

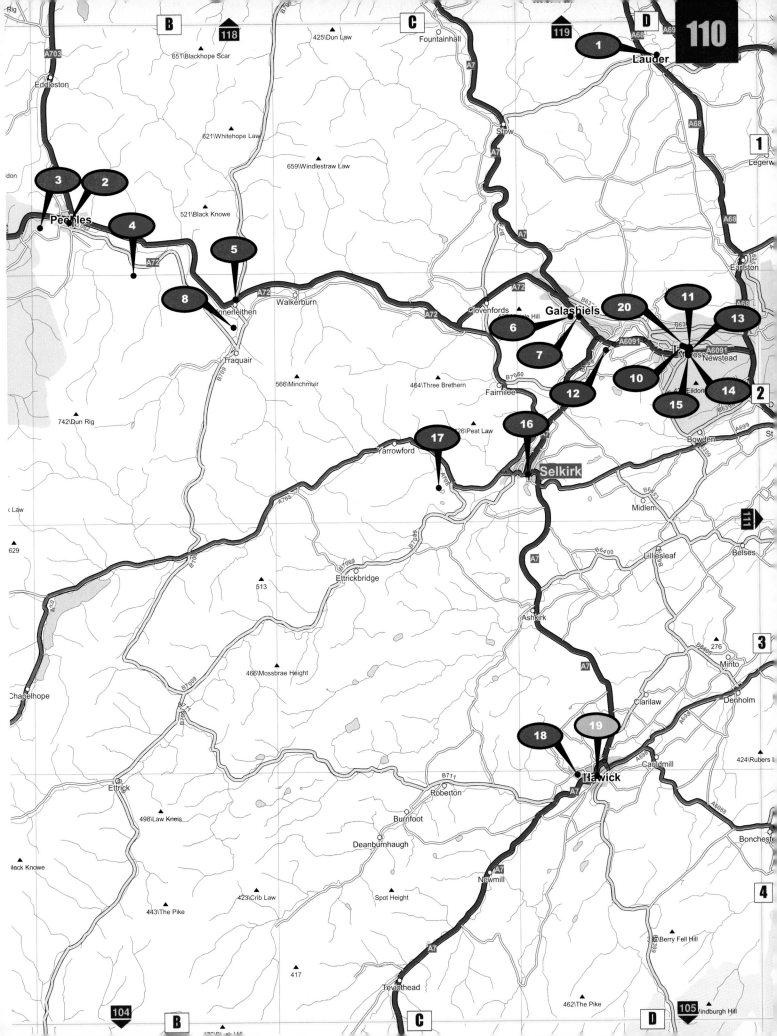

BORDERS · NORTHUMBERLAND

● ANIMAL ATTRACTIONS   ● OUTDOOR ATTRACTIONS
● HERITAGE & CULTURE   ● OUTDOOR ACTIVITIES
○ INDOOR ACTIVITIES   ● WATER ACTIVITIES

1 **NORHAM CASTLE**
Castle
Berwick-upon-Tweed
TEL: 01289 382 329

2 **NORHAM STATION MUSEUM**
Museum
Berwick-upon-Tweed
TEL: 01289 382 217

3 **HIRSEL**
Nature centre
Mansion House, Coldstream
TEL: 01890 882 834

4 **MELLERSTAIN HOUSE**
Historic house
Gordon
TEL: 01573 410 225

5 **SMAILHOLM TOWER**
Museum
Kelso
TEL: 01573 460 365

6 **KELSO RACECOURSE**
Racecourse
Kelso
TEL: 01668 281 611

8 **CHAIN BRIDGE HONEY FARM**
Farm
Horncliffe, Berwick-upon-Tweed
TEL: 01289 386 362

9 **HALLIWELL'S HOUSE MUSEUM**
Museum
Market Square, Selkirk
TEL: 01750 200 96

10 **CRUMSTANE FARM PARK**
Farm
Duns
TEL: 01361 883 268

11 **JEDBURGH CASTLE JAIL & MUSEUM**
Museum
Castlegate, Jedburgh
TEL: 01835 863 254

12 **FLOORS CASTLE**
Castle
Kelso
TEL: 01573 223 333

13 **DRYBURGH ABBEY**
Abbey
Dryburgh, St Boswells
TEL: 01835 822 381

14 **TEVIOT WATER GARDEN**
Garden
Eckford, Kelso
TEL: 01835 850 734

15 **MONTEVIOT HOUSE GARDENS**
Garden
Jedburgh
TEL: 01835 830 380

16 **MARY QUEEN OF SCOTS HOUSE**
Historic house
Queen Marys Buildings, Queen Street, Jedburgh
TEL: 01835 863 331

17 **JEDFOREST DEER & FARM PARK**
Farm
Mervinslaw Estate, Campton, Jedburgh
TEL: 01835 840 364

Jedburgh Abbey, Borders, Map 111

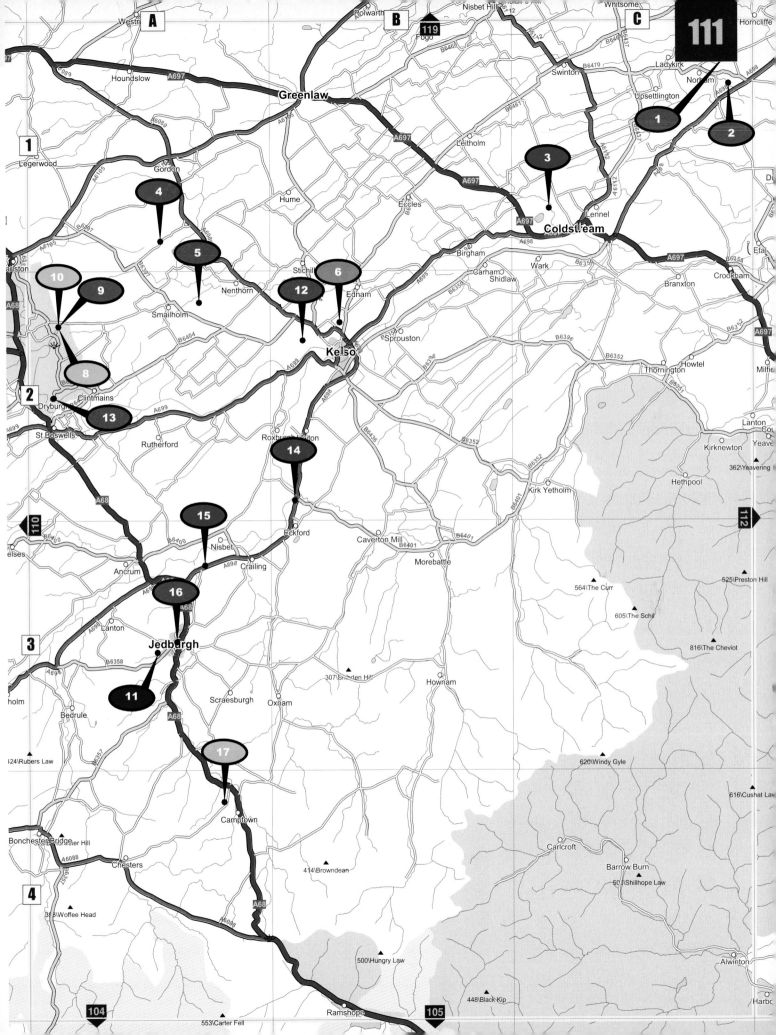

NORTHUMBERLAND

● ANIMAL ATTRACTIONS   ● OUTDOOR ATTRACTIONS
● HERITAGE & CULTURE   ● OUTDOOR ACTIVITIES
○ INDOOR ACTIVITIES   ● WATER ACTIVITIES

1 LINDISFARNE PRIORY
Historic building
Holy Island, Berwick-upon-Tweed
TEL: 01289 389 200

2 LINDISFARNE CASTLE NT
Castle
Holy Island, Berwick-upon-Tweed
TEL: 01289 389 244

3 HEATHERSLAW CORN MILL
Museum
Cornhill-on-Tweed
TEL: 01890 820 338

4 HEATHERSLAW LIGHT RAILWAY COMPANY
Railway
Heatherslaw, Cornhill-on-Tweed
TEL: 01890 820 244

5 LADY WATERFORD HALL
Historic house
Ford, Berwick-upon-Tweed
TEL: 01890 820 224

6 BAMBURGH CASTLE
Castle
Bamburgh
TEL: 01668 214 208

7 GRACE DARLING MUSEUM
Museum
Radcliffe Road, Bamburgh
TEL: 01668 214 465

8 NORSELANDS GALLERY-STUDIO TWO
Craft centre
Old School Warenford, Belford
TEL: 01668 213 465

9 CHILLINGHAM WILD CATTLE PARK
Wildlife park
Chillingham, Alnwick
TEL: 01668 215 250

10 PRESTON TOWER
Historic building
Chathill
TEL: 01665 589 227

11 DUNSTANBURGH CASTLE
Castle
Embleton, Alnwick
TEL: 01665 576 231

12 HOWICK HALL & GARDENS
Historic building
Alnwick
TEL: 01665 577 285

13 NORTHUMBERLAND PARK VISITIOR CENTRE
Visitor centre
Bardon Mill
TEL: 01434 344 396

14 FUSILIERS MUSEUM OF NORTHUMBERLAND
Museum
Alnwick
TEL: 01665 602 152

15 ALNWICK CASTLE
Castle
Alnwick
TEL: 01665 510 777

16 HOUSE OF HARDY MUSEUM & COUNTRYSTORE
Museum
Willowburn, Alnwick
TEL: 01665 510 027

17 EDLINGHAM CASTLE
Castle
Edlingham, Alnwick
TEL: Not available

Hadrian's Wall, Northumberland

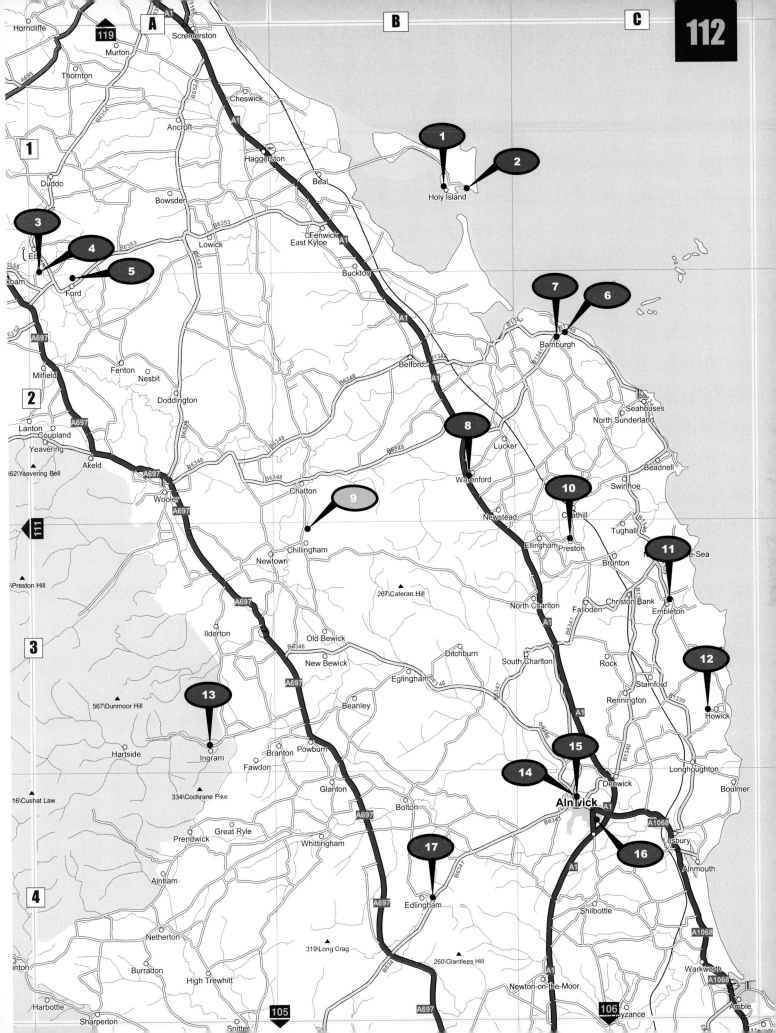

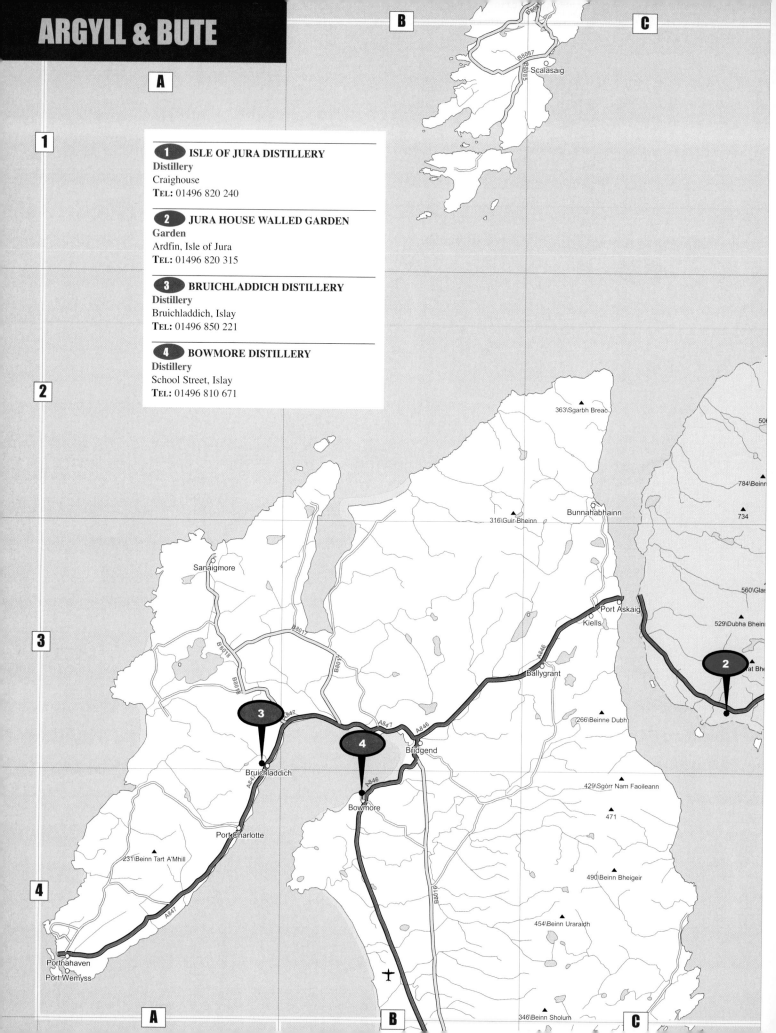

ARGYLL & BUTE

A **B** **C**

1 ISLE OF JURA DISTILLERY
Distillery
Craighouse
Tel: 01496 820 240

2 JURA HOUSE WALLED GARDEN
Garden
Ardfin, Isle of Jura
Tel: 01496 820 315

3 BRUICHLADDICH DISTILLERY
Distillery
Bruichladdich, Islay
Tel: 01496 850 221

4 BOWMORE DISTILLERY
Distillery
School Street, Islay
Tel: 01496 810 671

Scalasaig

363\Sgarbh Breac

Bunnahabhainn

316\Guir-Bheinn

784\Beinn

734

Sanaigmore

Port Askaig

Kiells

560\Glas

529\Dubha Bheinn

Ballygrant

266\Beinne Dubh

at Bhe

Bruichladdich

Bridgend

429\Sgòrr Nam Faoileann

PortCharlotte

Bowmore

471

231\Beinn Tart A'Mhill

490\Beinn Bheigeir

Portnahaven
Port Wemyss

454\Beinn Uraraidh

346\Beinn Sholum

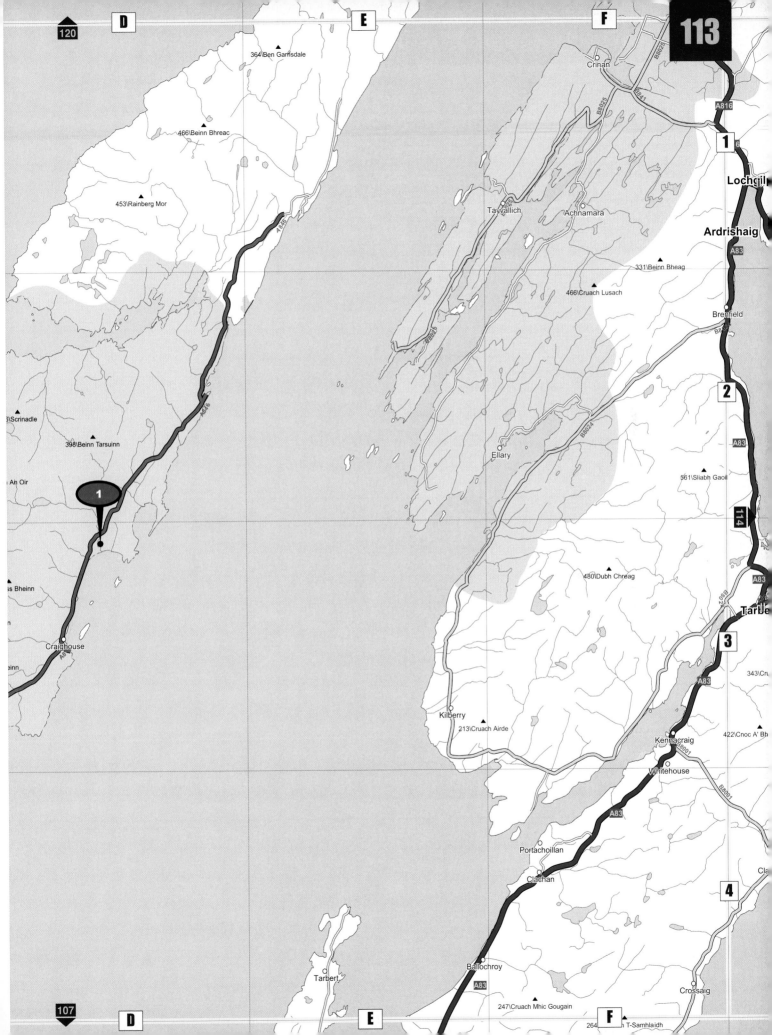

120

364\Ben Garrisdale

466\Beinn Bhreac

453\Rainberg Mor

Crinan

Tayvallich   Achnamara

331\Beinn Bheag

466\Cruach Lusach

Brenfield

\Scrinadle

398\Beinn Tarsuinn

Ah Oir

1

Ellary

561\Sliabh Gaoil

ss Bheinn

480\Dubh Chreag

Craighouse

Tarbe

3

343\Cru

einn

Kilberry   422\Cnoc A' Bh

213\Cruach Airde

Kennacraig

Whitehouse

Portachoillan

Clachan

4

Tarbert

Ballochroy

Crossaig

247\Cruach Mhic Gougain

264\ h T-Samhlaidh

SCOTLAND

● ANIMAL ATTRACTIONS   ● OUTDOOR ATTRACTIONS
● HERITAGE & CULTURE   ● OUTDOOR ACTIVITIES
○ INDOOR ACTIVITIES   ● WATER ACTIVITIES

1 **YOUNGER BOTANIC GARDEN BENMORE**
Garden
Dunoon, Argyll
TEL: 01369 706 261

2 **WEST ARGYLL FOREST DISTRICT**
Country park
Whitegates Road, Lochgilphead, Argyll
TEL: 01546 602 518

3 **GLENARN**
Garden
Rhu, Helensburgh
TEL: 01436 820 493

4 **HILL HOUSE NTS**
Garden
Helensburgh
TEL: 01436 673 900

5 **LINN BOTANIC GARDENS & NURSERY**
Garden
Cove, Helensburgh
TEL: 01436 842 242

6 **MCLEAN MUSEUM & ART GALLERY**
Museum
15 Kelly Street, Greenock
TEL: 01475 715 624

7 **ARDENCRAIG GARDENS**
Garden
High Craigmore, Rothesay
TEL: 01700 504 644

8 **ROTHESAY CASTLE**
Castle
Cattlehill Street, Rothesay
TEL: 01700 502 691

9 **VIKINGAR**
Unusual
Barrfields Greenock Road, Largs
TEL: 01475 689 777

10 **MOUNT STUART GARDENS**
Garden
Isle of Bute
TEL: 01700 503 877

11 **KELBURN CASTLE & COUNTRY CENTRE**
Castle
South Offices Fairlie, Largs
TEL: 01475 568 685

12 **MUSEUM OF THE CUMBRAES**
Museum
Garrison House, Millport
TEL: 01475 530 741

13 **ISLE OF ARRAN DISTILLERY**
Distillery
Lochranza, Isle of Arran
TEL: 01770 830 264

14 **HUNTERSTON POWER STATION**
Factory tour
West Kilbride
TEL: 0800 838 557

Younger Botanic Gardens, Argyll & Bute. Map 114-1

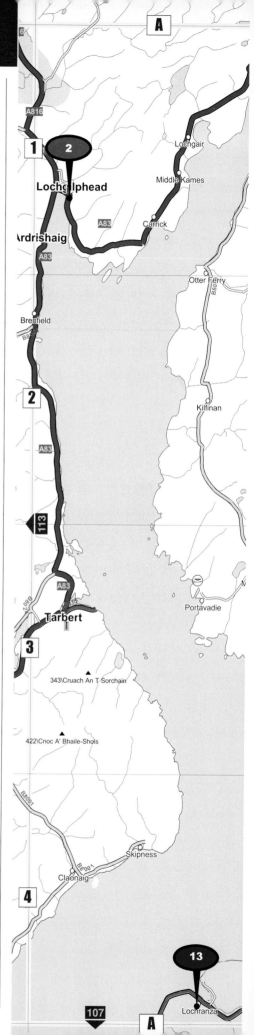

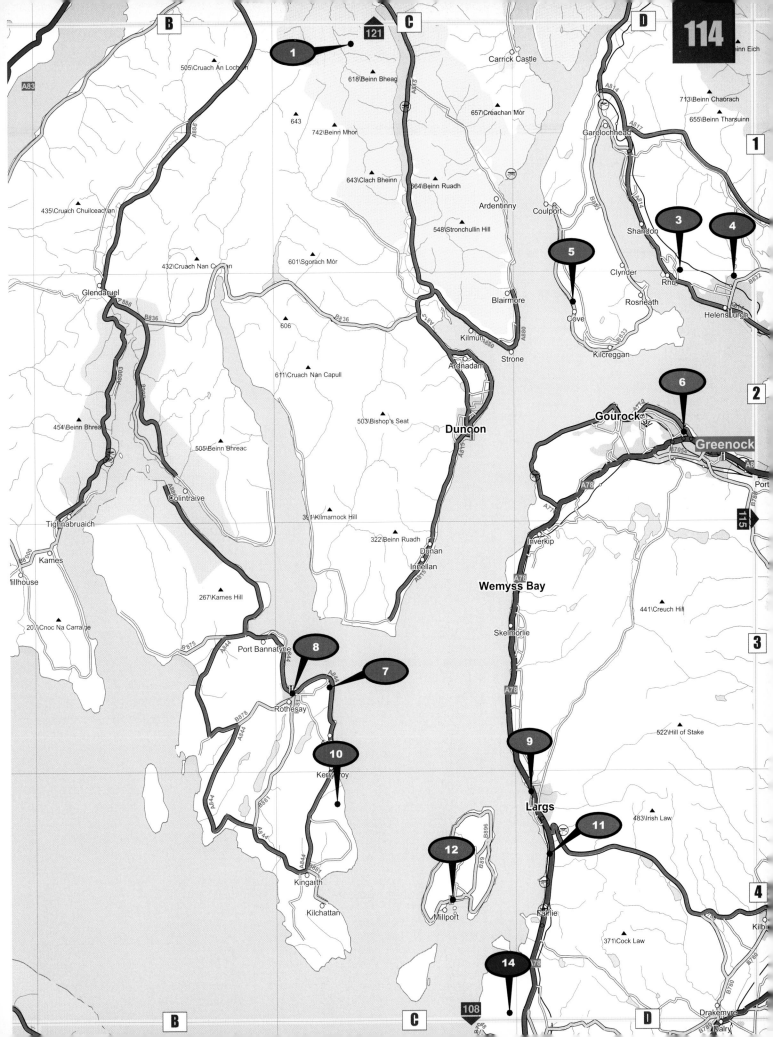

1 BALLOCH CASTLE COUNTRY PARK
Country park
Balloch, Alexandria
TEL: 01389 758 216

2 GLENGOYNE DISTILLERY
Distillery
Dumgoyne
TEL: 01360 550 254

3 LOMOND SHORES
Visitor centre
Old Luss Road, Balloch
TEL: 01389 721 500

4 CLASSIC CAR COLLECTION
Museum
Motor Heritage Centre, Main Street, Alexandria
TEL: 01389 607 862

5 MUGDOCK COUNTRY PARK
Country park
Mugdock Milngavie, Glasgow
TEL: 0141 956 6100

6 DUMBARTON CASTLE
Castle
Castle Road, Dumbarton
TEL: 01389 732 167

7 NEWARK CASTLE
Castle
Castle Road, Port Glasgow
TEL: 01475 741 858

8 AULD KIRK MUSEUM
Museum
Cowgate, Kirkintilloch
TEL: 0141 775 1185

9 FINLAYSTONE
Garden
Langbank
TEL: 01475 540 285

10 GLASGOW BOTANIC GARDENS
Garden
Glasgow
TEL: 0141 334 2422

11 SPRINGBURN MUSEUM
Museum
Atlas Square, Ayr Street, Glasgow
TEL: 0141 557 1405

12 VICTORIA PARK
Country park
North Whiteinch, Glasgow
TEL: 0141 959 2128

13 HUNTERIAN MUSEUM
Museum
University Avenue, Glasgow
TEL: 0141 330 4221

14 MUSEUM OF TRANSPORT
Museum
Kelvin Hall, 1 Bunhouse Road, Glasgow
TEL: 0141 287 2721

15 TENEMENT HOUSE NTS
Historic house
145 Buccleuch Street, Glasgow
TEL: 0141 333 0183

16 ROYAL HIGHLAND FUSILIERS MUSEUM
Museum
518 Sauchiehall Street, Glasgow
TEL: 0141 332 5639

17 PROVAND'S LORDSHIP
Historic house
3 Castle Street, Glasgow
TEL: 0141 552 8819

18 PEOPLE'S PALACE
Museum
Glasgow
TEL: 0141 554 0223

19 GLASGOW CATHEDRAL
Cathedral
Cathedral Square, Glasgow
TEL: 0141 552 6891

20 CLYDEBANK MUSEUM
Museum
Town Hall, Dumbarton Road, Clydebank
TEL: 01389 738 702

21 COLZIUM HOUSE & ESTATE
Historic house
Colzium, Kilsyth
TEL: 01236 823 281

22 GLASGOW SCIENCE CENTRE
Science Museum
Eagle Building, 215 Bothwell Street, Glasgow
TEL: 0141 204 4448

23 ST MUNGO MUSEUM OF RELIGIOUS LIFE & ART
Museum
2 Castle Street, Glasgow
TEL: 0141 553 2557

24 HUTCHESONS' HALL NTS
Historic building
158 Ingram Street, Glasgow
TEL: 0141 552 8391

25 GALLERY OF MODERN ART
Gallery
Queen Street, Glasgow
TEL: 0141 229 1996

26 HOUSE FOR AN ART LOVER
Museum
10 Dunbreck Road, Bellahouston Park, Glasgow
TEL: 0141 353 4770

27 COATS OBSERVATORY
Observatory
49 Oakshaw Street, West Paisley
TEL: 0141 889 2013

28 WEAVER'S COTTAGE
Museum
The Cross, Kilbarchan, Johnstone
TEL: 01505 705 588

29 CROOKSTON CASTLE HS
Castle
170 Brockburn Road, Glasgow
TEL: 0131 668 8800

30 BURRELL COLLECTION
Gallery
2060 Pollokshaws Road, Glasgow
TEL: 0141 287 2550

31 QUEENS PARK
Garden
Glasgow
TEL: 0141 649 0331

32 POLLOCK HOUSE & COUNTRY PARK
Country park
2060 Pollokshaws Road, Glasgow
TEL: 0141 632 9299

33 SCOTLAND STREET SCHOOL MUSEUM
Museum
225 Scotland Street, Glasgow
TEL: 0141 287 0500

34 SCOTTISH NATIONAL MUSEUM OF FOOTBALL
Museum
Hampden Park, Glasgow
TEL: 0141 620 4000

35 GLENIFFER BRAES COUNTRY PARK
Country park
Glen Park, Glenfield Road, Paisley
TEL: Not available

36 HOLMWOOD HOUSE NTS
Garden
61-63 Netherlee Road, Cathcart
TEL: 0141 637 2129

37 LINN PARK
Country park
Glasgow
TEL: 0141 637 1147

38 ROUKEN GLEN PARK
Country park
Rouken Glen Road, Thornliebank, Glasgow
TEL: 0141 553 3095

39 GREENBANK GARDEN NTS
Garden
Clarkson
TEL: 0141 616 2266

40 HUNTER HOUSE
Museum
Maxwellton Road, East Kilbride, Glasgow
TEL: 01355 261 261

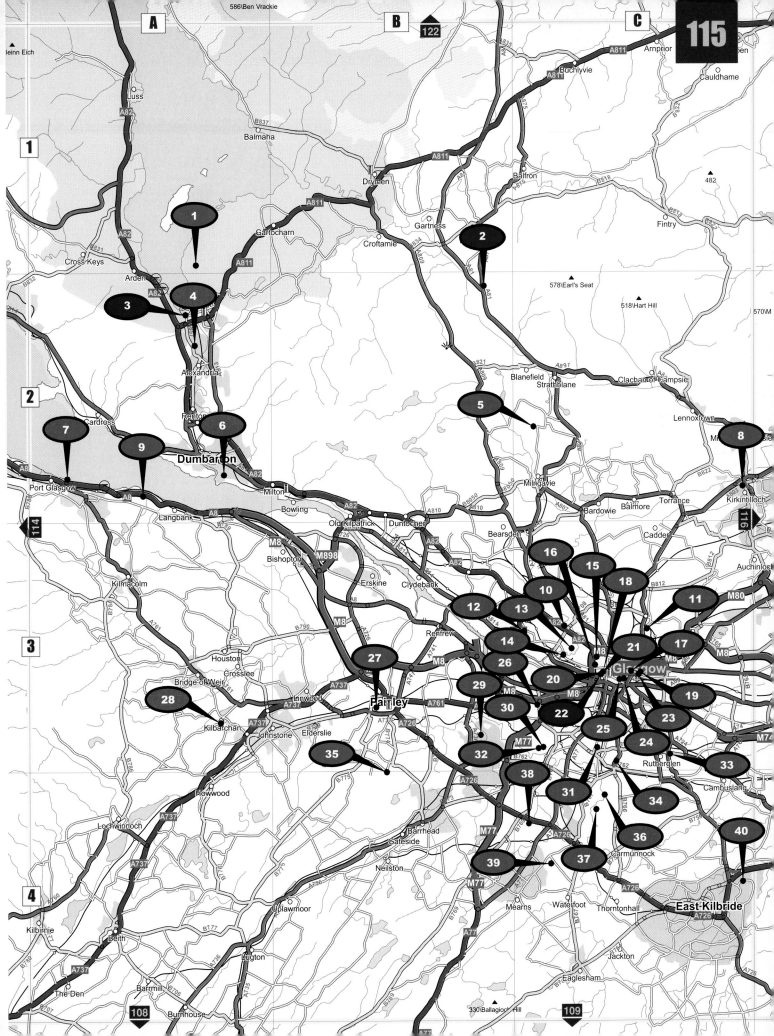

1 BLAIR DRUMMOND SAFARI & ADVENTURE PARK
Safari park
Stirling
TEL: 01786 841 456

2 CAMBUSKENNETH ABBEY HS
Abbey
Stirling
TEL: 0131 668 8800

3 ARGYLLS LODGING HS
Historic building
Stirling
TEL: 0131 668 8800

4 STIRLING CASTLE HS
Castle
Stirling
TEL: 01786 450 000

5 ROYAL BURGH OF STIRLING VISITOR CENTRE
Visitor centre
Castle Wind, Stirling
TEL: 01786 462 517

6 ARGYLL & SUTHERLAND HIGHLANDERS
Museum
Stirling Castle, Stirling
TEL: 01786 475 165

7 STIRLING OLD TOWN JAIL
Historic building
St John Street, Stirling
TEL: 01786 450 050

8 SMITH ART GALLERY & MUSEUM
Museum
Albert Place, Stirling
TEL: 01786 471 917

Stirling Castle, Stirling. Map 116-4

9 ALLOA TOWER NTS
Historic building
Alloa
TEL: 01259 211 701

10 WALLACE MONUMENT
Historic building
St Ninians Road, Stirling
TEL: 01786 472 140

11 BANNOCKBURN HERITAGE CENTRE NTS
Heritage centre
Glasgow Road, Whins of Milton, Stirling
TEL: 01786 812 664

12 DOUNE CASTLE HS
Castle
Castle Road, Doune
TEL: 01786 841 742

13 THE PINEAPPLE
Historic building
Airth
TEL: 01324 831 137

14 CULROSS ABBEY HS
Abbey
Culross
TEL: 0131 668 8800

15 CULROSS PALACE NTS
Garden
Culross
TEL: 01383 880 359

16 GRANGEMOUTH MUSEUM
Museum
Bo'ness Road, Grangemouth
TEL: 01324 504 699

17 BO'NESS & KINNEIL RAILWAY
Railway
Bo'Ness, Falkirk
TEL: 01506 822 298

18 JUPITER URBAN WILDLIFE CENTRE
Wildlife park
Wood Street, Grangemouth
TEL: 01324 494 974

19 KINNEIL MUSEUM & ROMAN FORTLET
Museum
Duchess Anne Cottages, Kinneil Estate, Bo'ness
TEL: 01506 778 530

20 CALLENDAR HOUSE
Historic house
Callendar Park, Falkirk
TEL: 01324 503 770

21 BIRKHILL CLAY MINE
Museum
Birkhill, Dundee
TEL: 01506 825 855

22 CANAL MUSEUM
Museum
Manse Road Basin, Linlithgow
TEL: 01506 671 215

23 PROVAN HALL HOUSE
Historic house
Auchinlea Road, Easterhouse, Glasgow
TEL: 0141 771 4399

24 SUMMERLEE HERITAGE PARK
Heritage centre
Summerlee Heritage Way, Coatbridge
TEL: 01236 431 261

25 DRUMPELLIER COUNTRY PARK
Country park
Townhead Road, Coatbridge
TEL: 01236 422 257

26 INTERPLAY
Country park
Drumpellier Country Park, Townhead Rd, Coatbridge
TEL: 01236 710 556

27 TIME CAPSULE
Unusual
100 Buchanan Street, Coatbridge
TEL: 01236 449 572

28 GLASGOW ZOOPARK
Zoo
Calderpark, Uddingston, Glasgow
TEL: 0141 771 1185

29 BOTHWELL CASTLE
Castle
Bothwell, Uddingston, Glasgow
TEL: 01698 816 894

30 DAVID LIVINGSTONE CENTRE
Museum
Station Road, Blantrye, Glasgow
TEL: 01698 823 140

31 M & D'S SCOTLAND'S THEME PARK
Theme park
Strathclyde Country Park, Motherwell
TEL: 01698 333 999

32 MOTHERWELL HERITAGE CENTRE
Heritage centre
High Road, Motherwell
TEL: 01698 251 000

33 HAMILTON PARK RACECOURSE
Racecourse
Bothwell Road, Hamilton
TEL: 01698 283 806

34 SHOTTS HERITAGE CENTRE
Heritage centre
Shotts
TEL: 01501 821 556

35 HAMILTON LOU PARKS MUSEUM
Museum
129 Muir Street, Hamilton
TEL: 01698 283 981

36 CHATELHERAULT COUNTRY PARK
Country park
Ferniegair, Hamilton
TEL: 01698 426 213

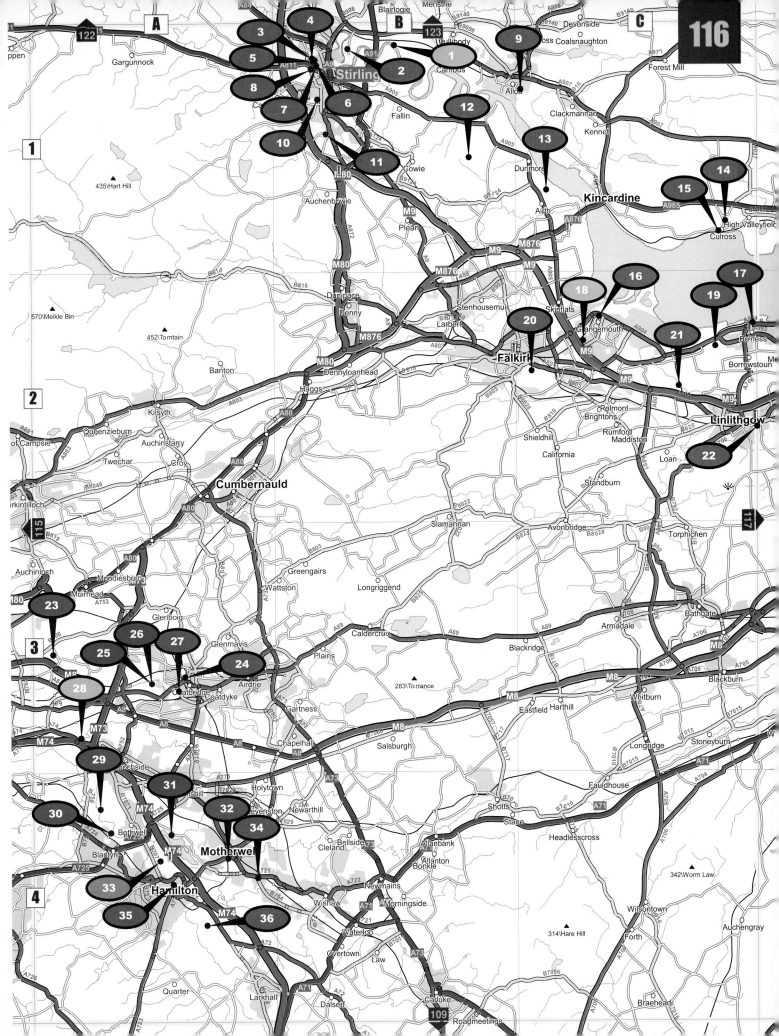

Stirling Castle, Stirling, Map 116-4

1 BUTTERCHURN
Craft centre
Cocklaw Mains Farm, Kelty
TEL: 01383 830 169

2 KNOCKHILL RACING CIRCUIT
Motor racing circuit
Saline, Dunfermline
TEL: 01383 723 337

3 SCOTTISH VINTAGE BUS MUSEUM
Museum
Commerce Park, Crookfur, Dunfermline
TEL: Not available

4 DUNFERMLINE DISTRICT MUSEUM
Museum
Viewfield Terrace, Dunfermline
TEL: 01383 721 814

5 ABBOT HOUSE
Museum
Maygate, Dunfermline
TEL: 01383 733 266

6 DUNFERMLINE HERITAGE TRUST
Heritage Centre
Maygate, Dunfermline
TEL: 01383 733 266

7 DUNFERMLINE ABBEY & PALACE HS
Abbey
Pittencrieff Park, Dunfermline
TEL: 01383 739 026

8 ANDREW CARNEGIE BIRTHPLACE MUSEUM
Museum
Moodie Street, Dunfermline
TEL: 01383 724 302

9 ABERDOUR CASTLE HS
Castle
Aberdour
TEL: 01383 860 519

10 INCHCOLM ABBEY HS
Abbey
Inchcolm Island
TEL: 01383 823 331

11 DEEP SEA WORLD
Aquarium
Forthside Terrace, North Queensferry, Inverkeithing
TEL: 0930 100 300

12 BLACKNESS CASTLE
Castle
Linlithgow
TEL: 01506 834 807

13 HOPETOUN HOUSE
Historic house
South Queensferry
TEL: 0131 331 2451

14 HOUSE OF THE BINNS NTS
Historic house
Linlithgow
TEL: 01506 834 255

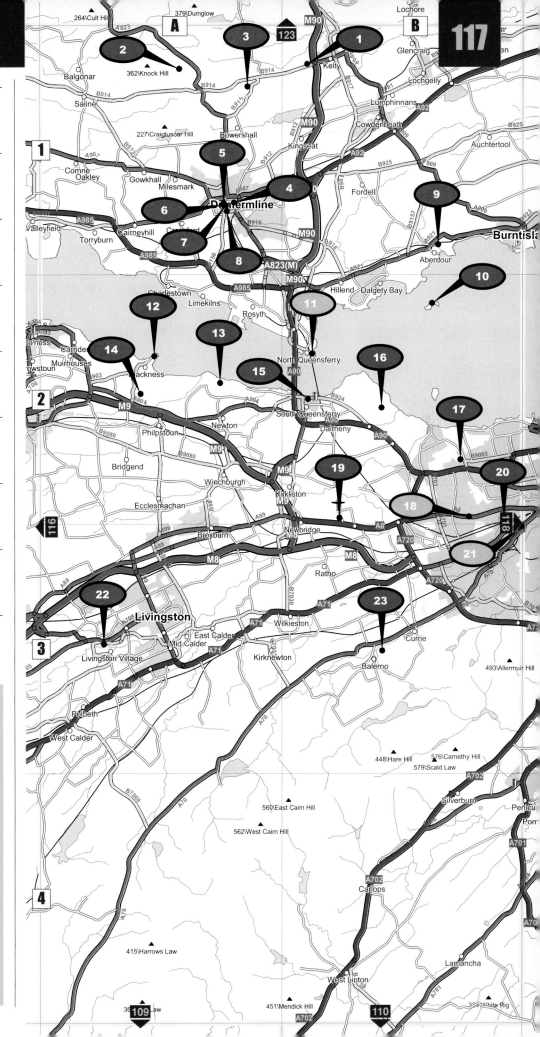

15 QUEENSFERRY MUSEUM
Museum
53 High Street, South Queensferry
TEL: 0131 331 5545

16 DALMENY HOUSE
Historic house
Dalmeny Estate, South Queensferry
TEL: 0131 331 1888

17 LAURISTON CASTLE
Castle
Cramond Road, Edinburgh
TEL: 0131 336 2060

18 EDINBURGH ZOO
Zoo
Murrayfield, Edinburgh
TEL: 0131 334 9171

19 SCOTTISH AGRICULTURAL MUSEUM
Museum
Ingliston, Newbridge
TEL: 0131 333 2674

20 MURRAYFIELD STADIUM
Tour
Edinburgh
TEL: 0131 346 5000

21 GORGIE CITY FARM
Farm
51 Gorgie Road, Edinburgh
TEL: 0131 337 4202

22 ALMOND VALLEY HERITAGE TRUST
Heritage centre
Millfield, Livingston
TEL: 01506 414 957

23 MALLENY GARDEN NTS
Garden
Edinburgh
TEL: 0131 449 2283

Help us help you

mention the
Days Out Atlas
when visiting
anywhere on this page.

1 **RAVENSCRAIG CASTLE HS**
Castle
Kirkcaldy
TEL: 0131 668 8800

2 **BURNTISLAND EDWARDIAN FAIR MUSEUM**
Museum
102 High Street, Burntisland
TEL: 01592 412 860

3 **KIRKCALDY MUSEUM & ART GALLERY**
Museum
War Memorial Gardens, Abbotshall Road, Kirkcaldy
TEL: 01592 412 860

4 **NEWHAVEN HERITAGE MUSEUM**
Museum
24 Pier Place, Edinburgh
TEL: 0131 551 4165

5 **THE ROYAL YACHT BRITANNIA**
Tourist attraction
Ocean Terminal, Leith, Edinburgh, Midlothian, EH6 6JJ.
TEL: 0131 555 5566
EMAIL: enquiries@tryb.co.uk
WEB: www.royalyachtbritannia.co.uk

The experience starts in the visitor centre. Then step aboard for a self-led audio tour around five decks giving an insight into the life on Britannia.
OPEN: Jan-Mar: 10-3.30, close 5pm. Apr-Sep: 9.30-4.30, close 6pm. Oct-Dec: 10-3.30, close 5pm.
ENTRY COSTS: £7.75, Child: £3.75, OAPs: £5.95, Family: £20.
FACILITIES: Credit cards, Gift shop, Gift tokens, Pushchair friendly, Toilets, Wheelchair access.

6 **CLAN TARTAN CENTRE**
Heritage centre
Leith Mills, Bangor Road, Edinburgh
TEL: 0131 553 5161

8 **ROYAL BOTANIC GARDEN EDINBURGH**
Garden
Edinburgh
TEL: 0131 552 7171

9 **PRINCESS STREET GARDENS EAST & WEST**
Garden
Edinburgh
TEL: 0131 529 7913

10 **SCOTTISH NATIONAL PORTRAIT GALLERY**
Gallery
1 Queen Street, Edinburgh
TEL: 0131 624 6200

7 **JAMES PRINGLE WEAVERS AT LEITH MILLS**
Visitor centre
Clan Tartan Centre, 70-74 Bangor Road, Leith, Edinburgh, EH6 5JU.
TEL: 0131 553 5161

Unique shopping experience under one roof. You'll find anything you could possibly want from a Scottish shop and so much more in a relaxed and enjoyable environment.
OPEN: Open daily.
SPECIALITIES: Events held.
FACILITIES: Coffee shop, Credit cards, Gift shop, Pushchair friendly, Toilets, Wheelchair access.

11 **DYNAMIC EARTH**
Museum
William Younger Centre, Holyrood, Edinburgh
TEL: 0131 550 7800

12 **SCOTTISH NATIONAL GALLERY OF MODERN ART**
Gallery
Belford Road, Edinburgh
TEL: 0131 624 6200

13 **PALACE OF HOLYROOD HOUSE**
Historic house
Edinburgh
TEL: 0131 556 7371

14 **GEORGIAN HOUSE**
Historic house
7 Charlotte Square, Edinburgh
TEL: 0131 225 2160

15 **SCOTTISH TARTANS MUSEUM**
Museum
Scotch House, 39/41 Princes Street, Edinburgh
TEL: 0131 556 1252

16 **HUNTLY HOUSE MUSEUM**
Museum
141 Canongate, Edinburgh
TEL: 0131 529 4143

17 **STILLS GALLERY**
Gallery
23 Cockburn Street, Edinburgh
TEL: 0131 622 6200

18 **PEOPLE'S STORY**
Museum
163 Canongate, Edinburgh
TEL: 0131 529 4057

19 **JOHN KNOX HOUSE**
Historic building
45 High Street, Edinburgh
TEL: 0131 556 9579

20 **HOLYROOD ABBEY HS**
Abbey
Canongate, Edinburgh
TEL: 0131 668 8800

21 **NATIONAL GALLERY OF SCOTLAND**
Gallery
The Mound, Edinburgh
TEL: 0131 624 6200

22 **SCOTTISH PARLIAMENT**
Historic building
Mound Place, Edinburgh
TEL: 0131 348 5000

23 **MUSEUM OF CHILDHOOD**
Museum
Royal Mile, Edinburgh
TEL: 0131 529 4142

24 **NATIONAL WAR MUSEUM OF SCOTLAND**
Castle
Edinburgh Castle, Edinburgh
TEL: 0131 225 7534

25 **EDINBURGH CASTLE HS**
Castle
Castlehill, Edinburgh
TEL: 0131 225 9846

26 **SCOTCH WHISKY HERITAGE CENTRE**
Heritage centre
354 Castlehill, Royal Mile, Edinburgh
TEL: 0131 220 0441

27 **PARLIAMENT HOUSE**
Historic building
Parliament Square, Edinburgh
TEL: 0131 225 2595

28 **WRITERS' MUSEUM**
Historic house
Lady Stair's Close, Lawnmarket, Edinburgh
TEL: 0131 529 4901

29 **GLADSTONE'S LAND**
Historic house
477b Lawnmarket, Edinburgh
TEL: 0131 226 5856

30 **CAMERA OBSCURA & OUTLOOK TOWER**
Museum
Castlehill, Royal Mile, Edinburgh
TEL: 0131 226 3709

31 **ROYAL SCOTS DRAGOON GUARDS MUSEUM**
Museum
The Castle, Castlehill, Edinburgh
TEL: 0131 220 4387

32 **SHAMBELLIE HOUSE MUSEUM OF COSTUME**
Museum
New Abbey, Dumfries
TEL: 0131 225 7534

33 **MUSEUM OF SCOTLAND**
Museum
Chambers Street, Edinburgh
TEL: 0131 225 7534

34 **MUSSELBURGH RACECOURSE**
Racecourse
Linkfield Road, Edinburgh
TEL: 0131 665 2859

35 INVERESK LODGE NTS
Garden
Musselburgh
TEL: 0131 665 1855

36 GLENKINCHIE DISTILLERY
Distillery
Pentcaitland, Tranent
TEL: 01875 342 004

37 NEWHAILES ESTATE NTS
Garden
Musselburgh
TEL: 0131 665 0253

38 GOSFORD HOUSE
Historic house
Longniddry
TEL: 01875 870 201

39 SCOTTISH SEA BIRD CENTRE
Bird centre & aviary
North Berwick Harbour, North Berwick
TEL: 01620 893 621

40 LINLITHGOW PALACE HS
Historic building
Kirkgate, Linlithgow
TEL: Not available

41 RUSSELL COLLECTION OF EARLY
KEYBOARD INSTRUMENTS
Museum
St Cecilia's Hall, Niddry Street, Cowgate
TEL: 0131 650 2805

42 ROYAL OBSERVATORY VISITOR CENTRE
Visitor centre
Blackford Hill, Edinburgh
TEL: 0131 668 8405

43 DALKEITH COUNTRY PARK
Country park
High Street, Dalkeith
TEL: 0131 663 5684

44 EDINBURGH BUTTERFLY & INSECT WORLD
Garden
Dobbies Garden World, Lasswade
TEL: 0131 663 4932

45 SCOTTISH MINING MUSEUM
Museum
Newtongrange, Dalkeith
TEL: 0131 663 7519

46 PRESTONGRANGE INDUSTRIAL
HERITAGE MUSEUM
Factory tour
Morison's Heaven, Preston Pans
TEL: 0131 653 2904

47 CRICHTON CASTLE
Castle
Crichton
TEL: 01875 320 017

48 EDINBURGH CRYSTAL VISITOR CENTRE
Factory Tour
Eastfield Industrial Estate, Penicuik
TEL: 01968 675 128

49 ARNISTON HOUSE
Historic house
Gorebridge
TEL: 01875 830 238

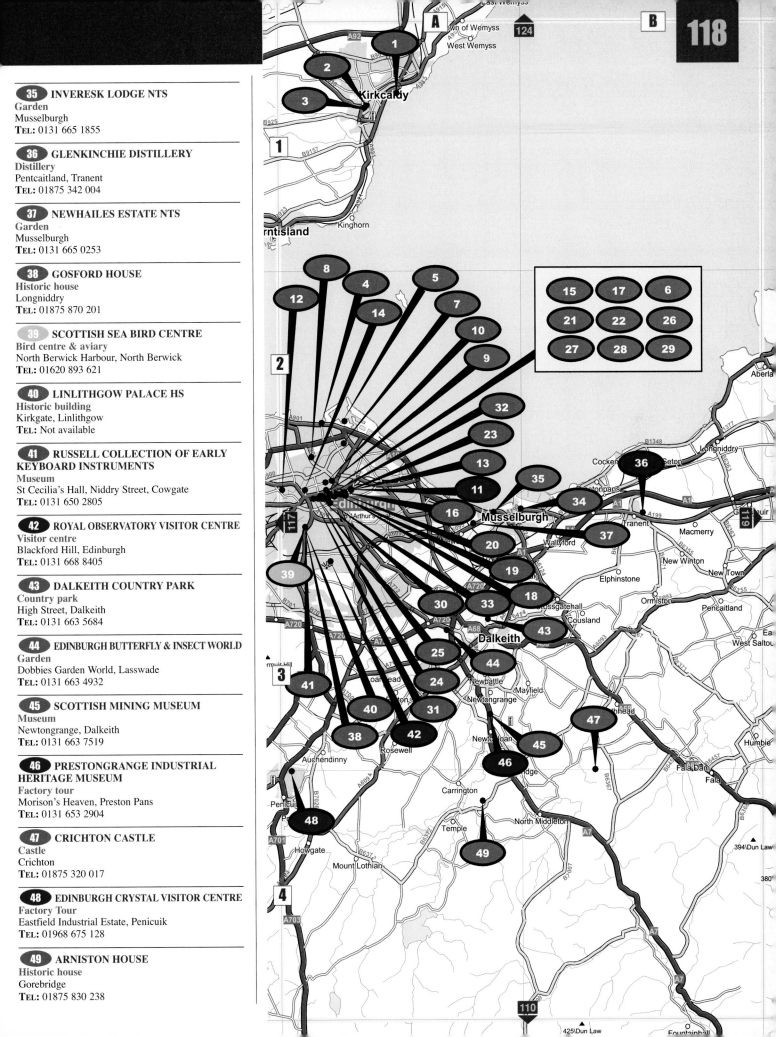

1 NORTH BERWICK MUSEUM
Museum
School Road, North Berwick
TEL: 01620 895 457

2 TANTALLON CASTLE
Castle
North Berwick
TEL: 01620 892 727

3 DIRLETON CASTLE HS
Castle
Dirleton
TEL: 01620 850 330

4 MYRETON MOTOR MUSEUM
Museum
Aberlady, Longniddry
TEL: 01875 870 288

5 MUSEUM OF FLIGHT
Museum
East Fortune Airfield, North Berwick
TEL: 01620 880 308

**6 PRESTON MILL & PHANTASSIE
DOOCOT NTS**
Museum
Preston Road, East Linton
TEL: 01620 860 420

7 SALTIRE HERITAGE CENTRE
Heritage centre
White Cottage, Main Street, Athelstaneford
TEL: 01620 880 243

8 HAILES CASTLE HS
Castle
East Linton
TEL: 0131 668 8800

9 STEVENSON HOUSE
Historic house
Haddington, Edinburgh
TEL: 01620 823 217

10 TORNESS POWER STATION
Factory tour
Dunbar
TEL: 0800 250 255

11 LENNOXLOVE HOUSE & GARDENS
Historic house
Haddington
TEL: 01620 823 720

12 DUNGLASS COLLEGIATE CHURCH
Historic building
Cocksburnpath
TEL: 0131 668 8800

13 EYEMOUTH MUSEUM
Museum
Manse Road, Eyemouth
TEL: 01890 750 678

14 ST ABB'S HEAD NTS
Nature centre
Northfield, St Abb's Eyemouth
TEL: 01890 771 443

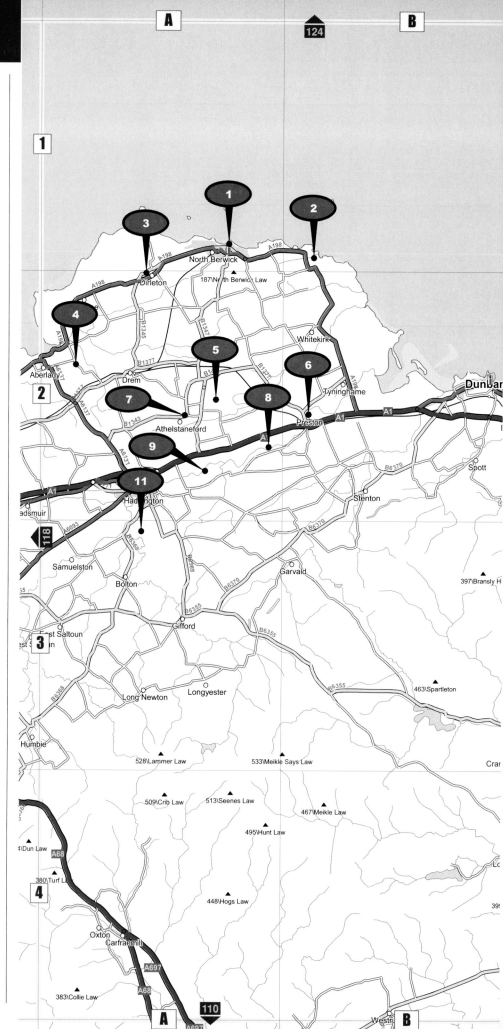

15 **AYTON CASTLE**
Museum
Ayton, Eyemouth
TEL: 01890 781 212

16 **MANDERSTON**
Historic house
Duns
TEL: 01361 883 450

17 **JIM CLARK ROOM**
Museum
44 Newtown Street, Duns
TEL: 01361 883 960

18 **PAXTON HOUSE**
Historic house
Berwick-upon-Tweed
TEL: 01289 386 291

19 **KING'S OWN SCOTTISH BORDERERS MUSEUM**
Museum
The Barracks, Berwick-upon-Tweed
TEL: 01289 307 426

20 **CELL BLOCK MUSEUM**
Museum
Marygate, Berwick-upon-Tweed
TEL: 01289 330 900

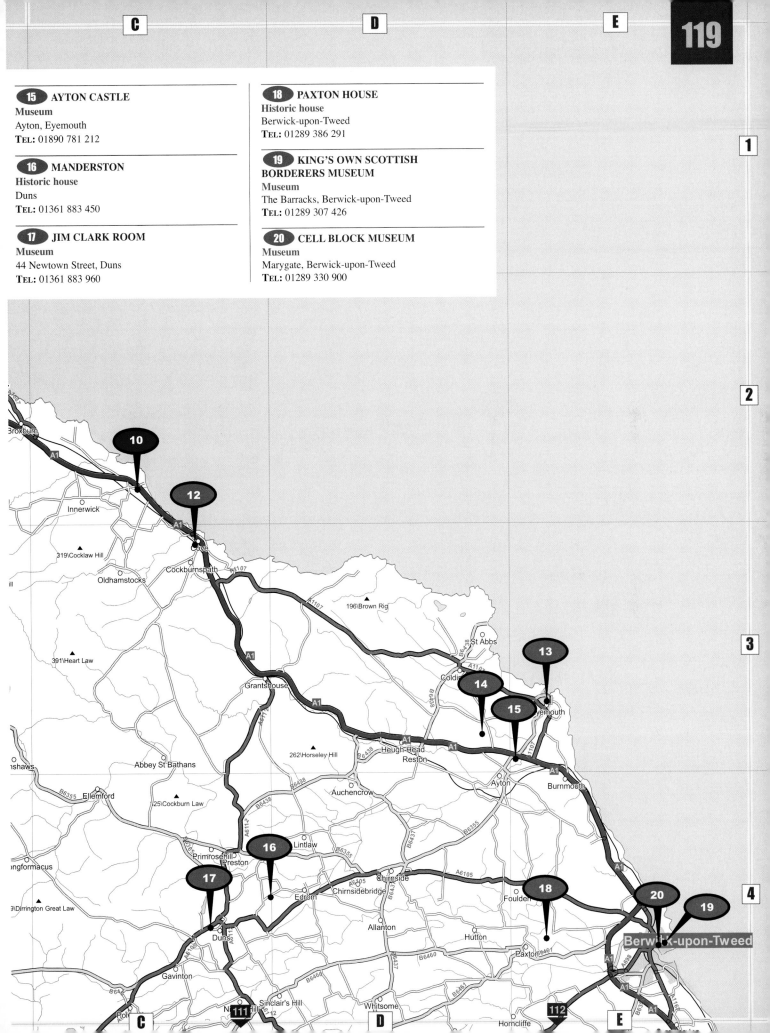

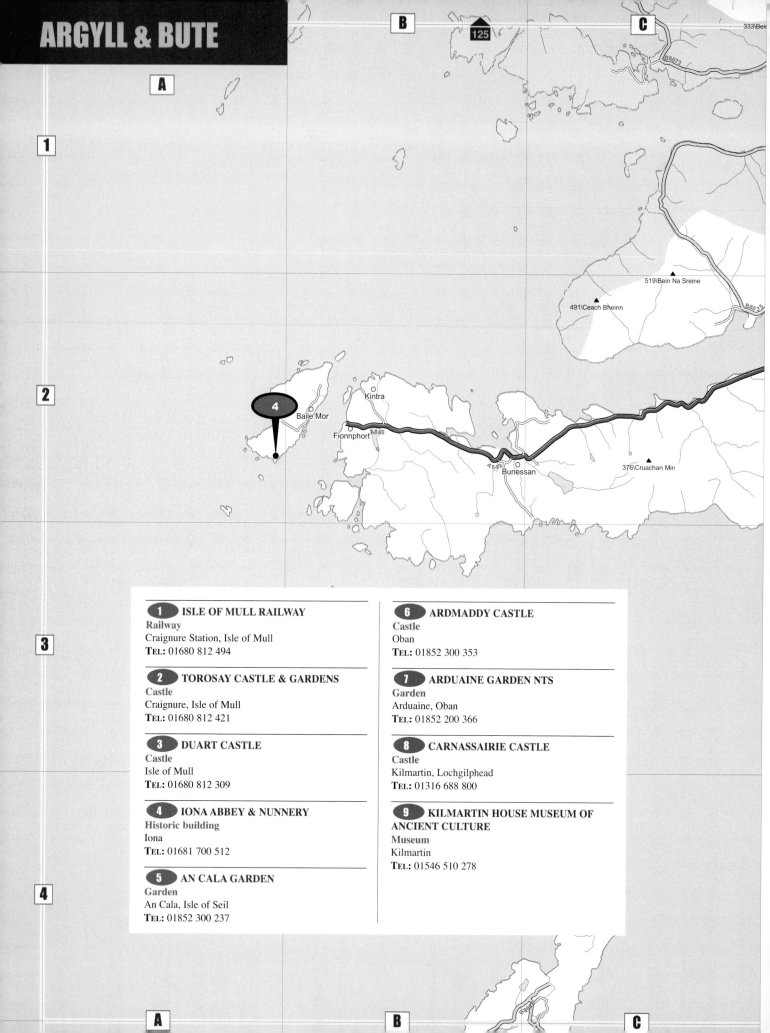

ARGYLL & BUTE

B 125

C 333\Bein

A

1

519\Bein Na Sreine

491\Ceach Bheinn

2

Kintra

4
Baile Mor

Fionnphort A849

A849

Bunessan

376\Cruachan Min

3

1 **ISLE OF MULL RAILWAY**
Railway
Craignure Station, Isle of Mull
TEL: 01680 812 494

2 **TOROSAY CASTLE & GARDENS**
Castle
Craignure, Isle of Mull
TEL: 01680 812 421

3 **DUART CASTLE**
Castle
Isle of Mull
TEL: 01680 812 309

4 **IONA ABBEY & NUNNERY**
Historic building
Iona
TEL: 01681 700 512

5 **AN CALA GARDEN**
Garden
An Cala, Isle of Seil
TEL: 01852 300 237

6 **ARDMADDY CASTLE**
Castle
Oban
TEL: 01852 300 353

7 **ARDUAINE GARDEN NTS**
Garden
Arduaine, Oban
TEL: 01852 200 366

8 **CARNASSAIRIE CASTLE**
Castle
Kilmartin, Lochgilphead
TEL: 01316 688 800

9 **KILMARTIN HOUSE MUSEUM OF ANCIENT CULTURE**
Museum
Kilmartin
TEL: 01546 510 278

4

A **B** **C**

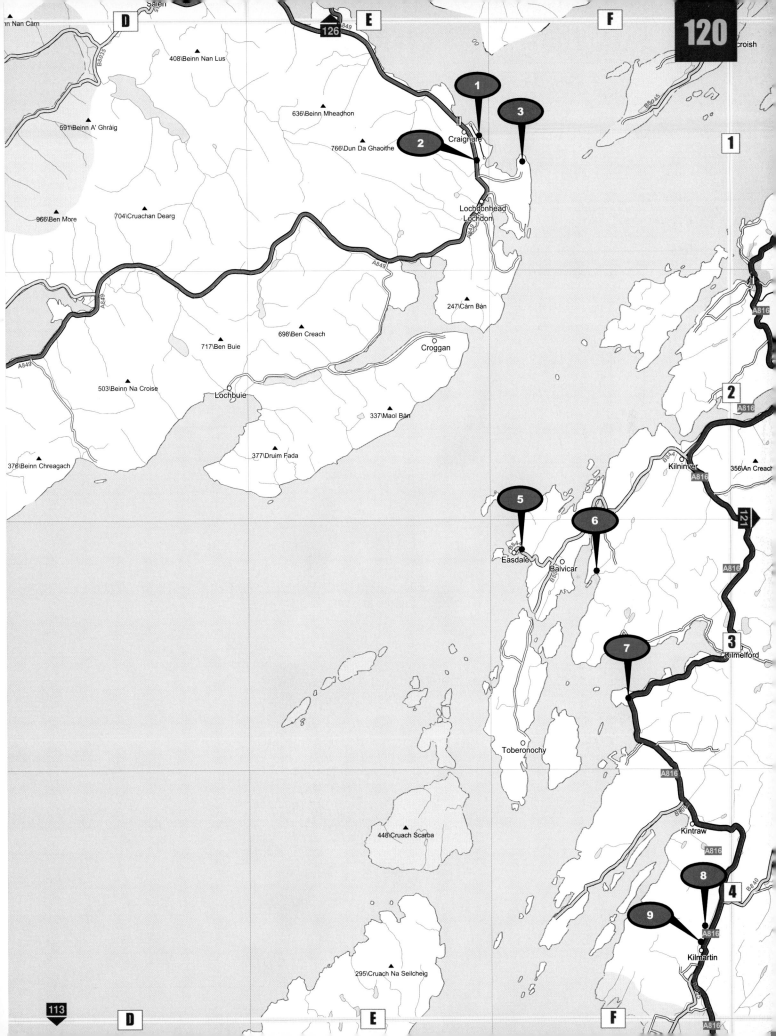

ARGYLL & BUTE

1 OBAN SEA LIFE CENTRE
Aquarium
Barcaldine, Oban
TEL: 01631 720 386

2 ARDCHATTEN PRIORY GARDEN
Garden
Oban
TEL: 01631 750 238

3 ACHNACLOICH
Garden
Connel, Oban
TEL: 01631 710 221

4 DUNSTAFFNAGE CASTLE & CHAPEL
Castle
Dunbeg, Oban
TEL: 01631 562 465

5 BONAWE IRON FURNACE
Factory Tour
Taynuilt
TEL: 01866 822 432

6 BARGUILLEAN ANGUS GARDEN
Garden
Taynuilt
TEL: 01866 822 381

7 OBAN DISTILLERY
Distillery
Stafford Street, Oban
TEL: 01631 572 004

8 OBAN RARE BREEDS FARM
Farm
New Barran Farm, Glencruitten, Oban
TEL: 01631 770 608

9 CRUACHAN POWER STATION
Factory tour
Dalmally
TEL: 01866 822 673

10 ARDANAISEIG HOTEL GARDEN
Garden
Loch Awe, Kilchrenan
TEL: 01866 833 333

11 TREE SHOP
Garden
Ardkinglas Estate Nurseries, Cairndow
TEL: 01499 600 263

12 ARDKINGLAS WOODLAND GARDEN
Garden
Cairndow
TEL: 01499 600 261

13 INVERARAY CASTLE
Castle
Inveraray
TEL: 01499 302 203

14 INVERARAY JAIL
Museum
Church Square, Inveraray
TEL: 01499 302 381

15 AUCHINDRAIN TOWNSHIP-OPEN AIR MUSEUM
Museum
Furnace, Inveraray
TEL: 01499 500 235

16 CRARAE GARDENS NTS
Garden
Minard, Inveraray
TEL: 01546 886 614

17 ARGYLL FOREST PARK
Country park
Argyll
TEL: Not available

Skiing in the highlands - Map 131

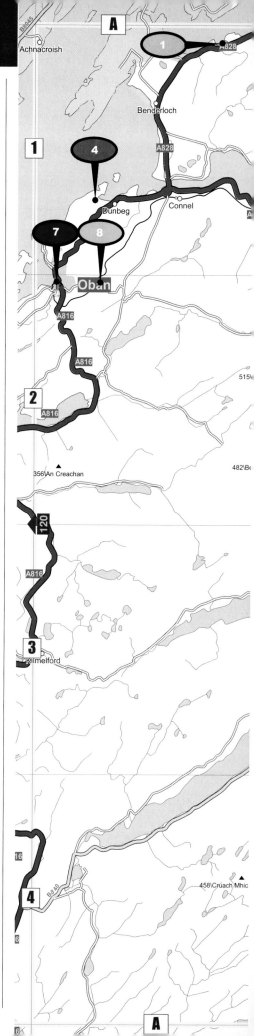

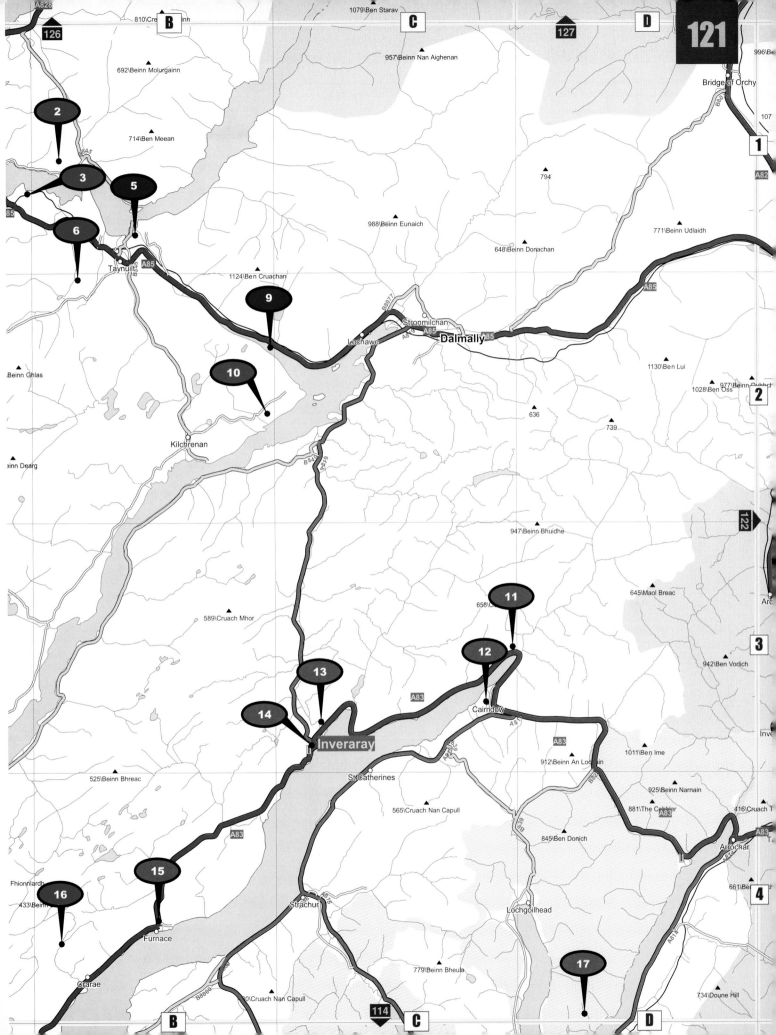

PERTHSHIRE

● ANIMAL ATTRACTIONS
● HERITAGE & CULTURE
○ INDOOR ACTIVITIES
● OUTDOOR ATTRACTIONS
● OUTDOOR ACTIVITIES
● WATER ACTIVITIES

1 BREADALBANE FOLKLORE CENTRE
Museum
Killin
TEL: 01567 820 254

2 AUCHINGARRICH WILDLIFE CENTRE
Wildlife park
Comrie
TEL: 01764 679 469

3 DRUMMOND TROUT FARM & FISHERY
Farm
Comrie, Perth
TEL: 01764 670 500

4 KILMAHOG WOOLEN MILL
Mill
Kilmahog, Callander
TEL: 01877 330 268

5 ROB ROY & TROSSACHS VISITOR CENTRE
Visitor centre
Ancaster Square, Callander
TEL: 01877 330 342

6 DOUNE MOTOR MUSEUM
Museum
Carse of Cambus, Doune
TEL: 01786 841 203

7 INCHMAHOME PRIORY
Historic building
Priory Boathouse, Stirling
TEL: 01877 385 294

8 SCOTTISH WOOL CENTRE
Visitor centre
Aberfoyle, Stirling, FK8 3UQ.
TEL: 01877 382 850

Regular duck & sheepdog Demonstrations, as seen on Ch 4's Big Breakfast. 'The Story of Scottish Wool' is a live show in our main theatre, Spinning demonstrations and quality fashions.
OPEN: Open daily 9.30-6.
SPECIALITIES: Events held.
FACILITIES: Coffee shop, Credit cards, Gift shop, Pushchair friendly, Toilets, Wheelchair access.

9 QUEEN ELIZABETH FOREST PARK VISITOR CENTRE
Visitor centre
Trossachs Road, Aberfoyle, Stirling
TEL: 01877 382 258

Wades Bridge, Aberfeldy. Map 128

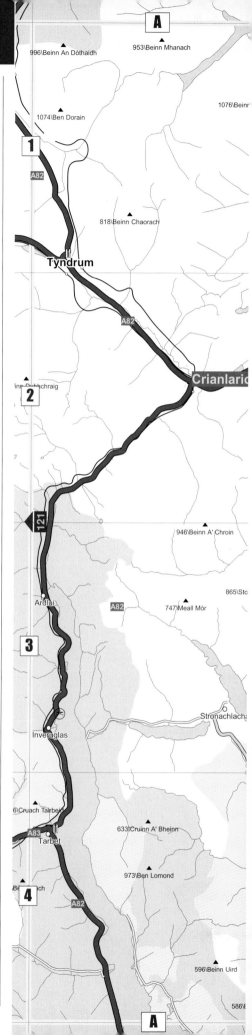

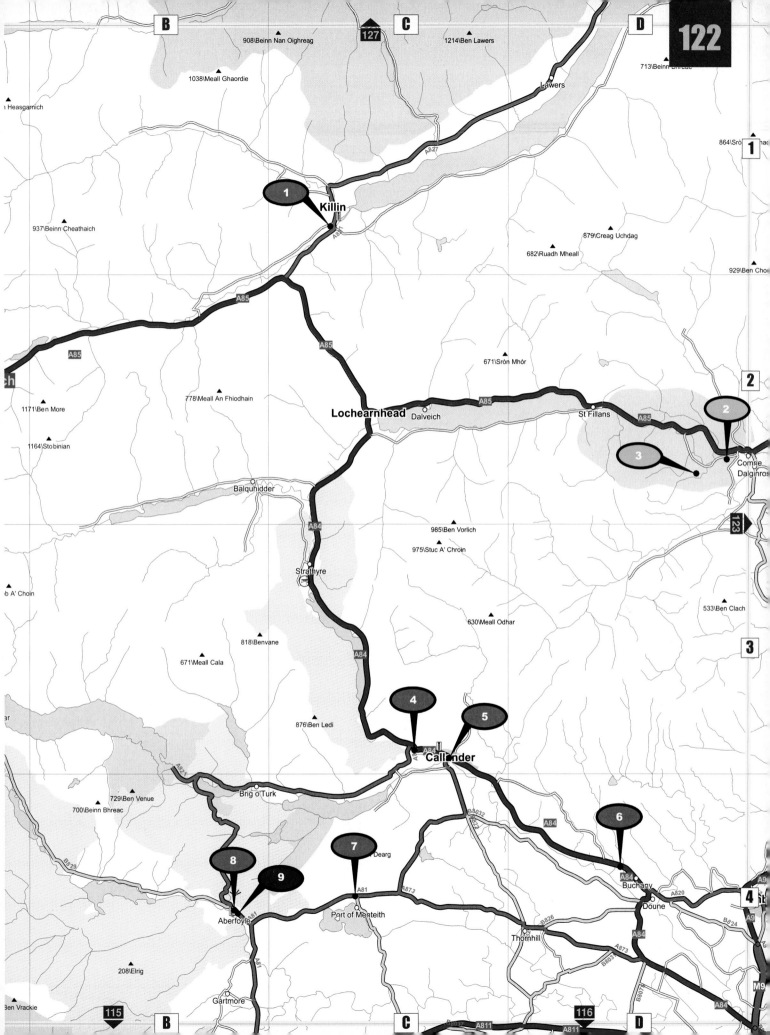

PERTHSHIRE

1 PERTHSHIRE VISITOR CENTRE
Visitor centre
Bankfoot
TEL: 01738 787 696

2 PERTH RACECOURSE
Racecourse
Scone Palace Park, Penhow
TEL: 01738 551 597

3 SCONE PALACE
Garden
Perth
TEL: 01738 552 300

4 NOAH'S ARK
Adventure & activity centre
Old Gallows Road, Western Edge, Perth
TEL: 01738 445 568

5 CAITHNESS GLASS FACTORY & VISITOR CENTRE
Factory shop
Inveralmond, Perth
TEL: 01738 637 373

6 HUNTINGTOWER CASTLE HS
Castle
Huntingtower, Perth
TEL: 01738 627 231

7 GLENTURRET DISTILLERY
Distillery
The Hosh, Crieff
TEL: 01764 656 565

8 BLACK WATCH REGIMENTAL MUSEUM
Museum
Balhousie Castle, Hay Street, Perth
TEL: 01313 108 530

9 PERTH MUSEUM & ART GALLERY
Museum
George Street, Perth
TEL: 01738 632 488

10 WORKING VICTORIAN OATMEAL MILL
Factory tour
Lower City Mills, West Mill Street, Perth
TEL: 01738 627 958

11 BRANKLYN GARDEN NTS
Garden
Perth
TEL: 01738 625 535

12 BELL'S CHERRYBANK GARDENS
Garden
Cherrybank, Perth
TEL: 01738 621 111

13 DRUMMOND CASTLE GARDENS
Castle
Muthill, Crieff
TEL: 01764 681 257

14 LOCHLEVEN CASTLE
Castle
Kinross
TEL: 01316 688 800

15 CASTLE CAMPBELL HS
Castle
Dollar
TEL: 01259 742 408

16 RSPB NATURE RESERVE VANE FARM
Nature centre
Kinross
TEL: 01577 862 355

The Black Watch Museum, Perth

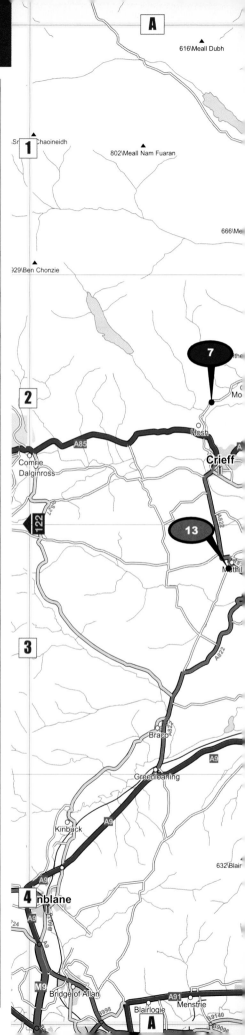

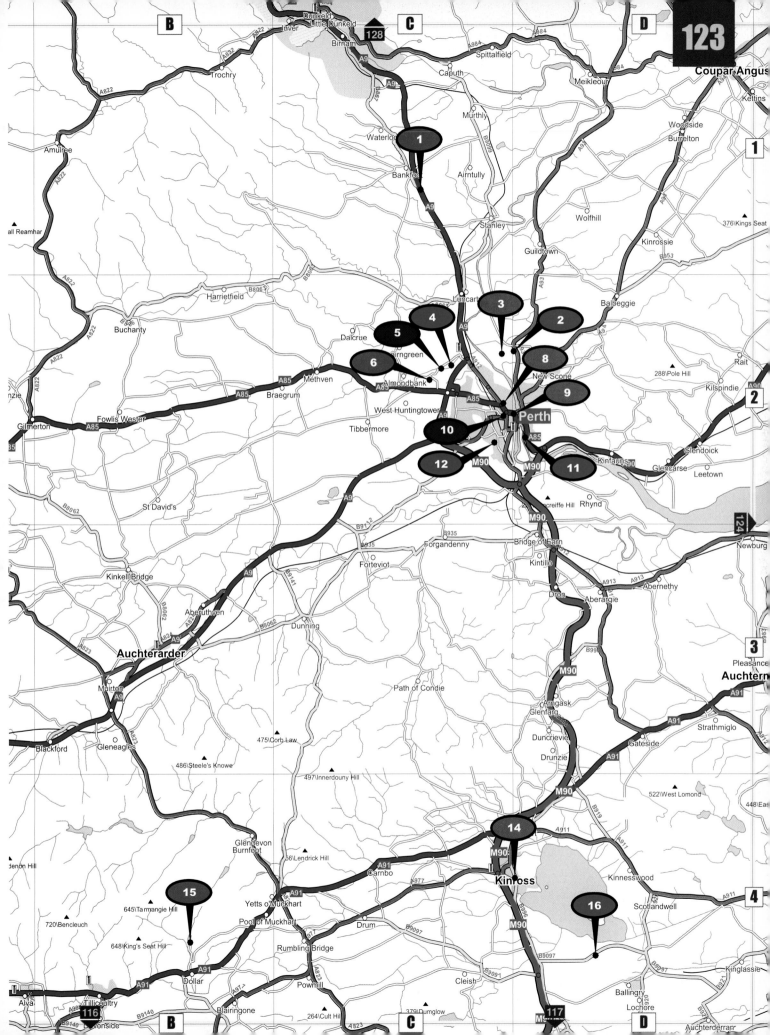

1 ARBROATH ABBEY
Abbey
Arbroath
TEL: 01241 878 756

2 ARBROATH MUSEUM
Museum
Signal Tower, Arbroath
TEL: 01241 875 598

3 BARRY MILL
Historic building
Barry, Carnoustie, Angus
TEL: 01241 856 761

4 CAMPERDOWN COUNTRY PARK
Country park
Coupar Angus Road, Dundee
TEL: 01382 433 815

5 SWEET FACTORY
Factory tour & shopping
Keillers Buildings, 34 Mains Loan, Dundee
TEL: 01382 461 435

6 MILLS OBSERVATORY
Historic building
Balgay Park, Dundee
TEL: 01382 667 138

7 MCMANUS MUSEUM & ART GALLERIES
Museum
Albert Square, Dundee
TEL: 01382 434 000

8 BARRACK STREET MUSEUM
Museum
Barrack Street, Dundee
TEL: 01382 432 067

9 VERDANT WORKS
Museum
West Henderson's Wynd, Dundee
TEL: 01382 225 282

10 HM FRIGATE UNICORN
Museum
Victoria Dock, Dundee
TEL: 01382 200 900

11 DISCOVERY POINT
Heritage centre
Discovery Quay, Dundee
TEL: 01382 201 245

12 UNIVERSITY OF DUNDEE BOTANIC GARDEN
Garden
Dundee
TEL: 01382 566 939

13 LIVE SCIENCE SENSATION DUNDEE
Unusual
Green Market, Dundee
TEL: 01382 228 800

14 MEGGINCH CASTLE
Castle
Errol, Perth
TEL: 01821 642 222

15 BRITISH GOLF MUSEUM
Museum
Bruce Embankment, St Andrews
TEL: 01334 460 046

16 ST ANDREWS SEA LIFE CENTRE
Aquarium
The Scores, St Andrews
TEL: 01334 474 786

17 ST ANDREWS CATHEDRAL & ST RULE'S TOWER HS
Cathedral
St Andrews
TEL: 01334 477 196

18 ST ANDREWS BOTANIC GARDEN
Garden
Canongate, St Andrews
TEL: 01334 476 452

19 SCOTTISH DEER CENTRE
Wildlife park
Rankeilour, Cupar, Fife, KY15 4NQ.
TEL: 01337 810 391

Pop along to the Scottish Deer centre and come face to face with Scottish wildlife. You will find over 140 deer, wolves, and amazing birds of prey.
OPEN: Open daily 10-6.
ENTRY COSTS: £4.50, Child: £3, OAPs: £3.50, Family: £13.50.
SPECIALITIES: Guided tours available, Fitness required.
FACILITIES: Coffee shop, Credit cards, Gift shop, Pushchair friendly, Toilets, Wheelchair access.

20 FIFE ANIMAL PARK
Nature centre
Birniefield, Collessie
TEL: 01337 831 830

21 HILL OF TARVIT MANSION-HOUSE NTS
Historic house
Cupar
TEL: 01334 653 127

22 FIFE FOLK MUSEUM
Museum
The Weigh House, High Street, Ceres
TEL: 01334 828 180

23 CAMBO GARDENS
Garden
Kingsbarns, St Andrews
TEL: 01333 450 054

24 SCOTLAND'S SECRET BUNKER
Historic building
Crown Buildings, St Andrews
TEL: 01333 310 301

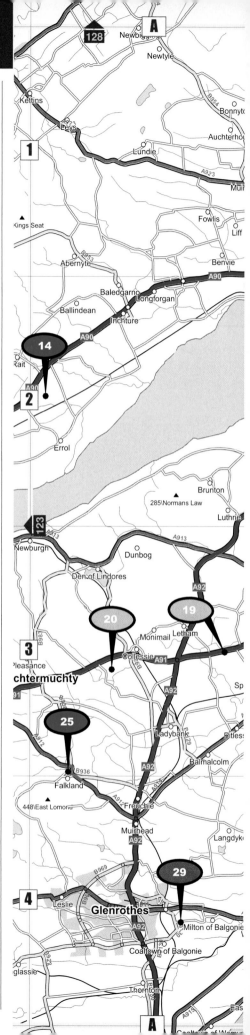

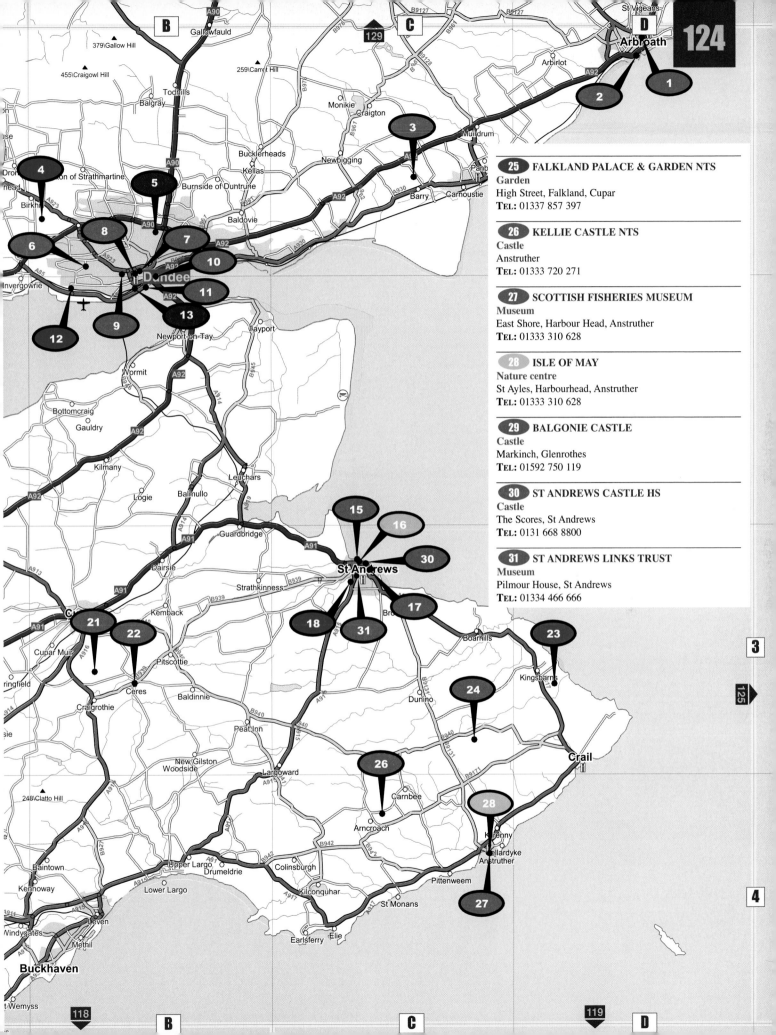

25 FALKLAND PALACE & GARDEN NTS
Garden
High Street, Falkland, Cupar
TEL: 01337 857 397

26 KELLIE CASTLE NTS
Castle
Anstruther
TEL: 01333 720 271

27 SCOTTISH FISHERIES MUSEUM
Museum
East Shore, Harbour Head, Anstruther
TEL: 01333 310 628

28 ISLE OF MAY
Nature centre
St Ayles, Harbourhead, Anstruther
TEL: 01333 310 628

29 BALGONIE CASTLE
Castle
Markinch, Glenrothes
TEL: 01592 750 119

30 ST ANDREWS CASTLE HS
Castle
The Scores, St Andrews
TEL: 0131 668 8800

31 ST ANDREWS LINKS TRUST
Museum
Pilmour House, St Andrews
TEL: 01334 466 666

SCOTLAND

B

C

2

3

Bousd

B8072

B8071

Arnabost

Arinagour

Acha

4

Caoles

B8069

Clachan-Mor

B8068

Ruaig

B8069

Ballevullin

Kilkenneth

B8065

B8069

B8069

Scarinish

Barrapoll

Crossapoll

A

B

C

SCOTLAND

1 GLENFINNAN MONUMENT
Historic building
Glenfinnan
TEL: 01397 722 250

2 NEVIS CABLE CAR
Cable car
Torlundy, Fort William
TEL: 01397 705 825

3 WEST HIGHLAND MUSEUM
Museum
Cameron Square, Fort William
TEL: 01397 702 169

4 BEN NEVIS DISTILLERY
Distillery
Lochy Bridge, Fort William
TEL: 01397 700 200

5 ARDTORNISH GARDEN
Garden
Oban
TEL: 01967 421 288

The Commando Monument, Spean Bridge, Map 131

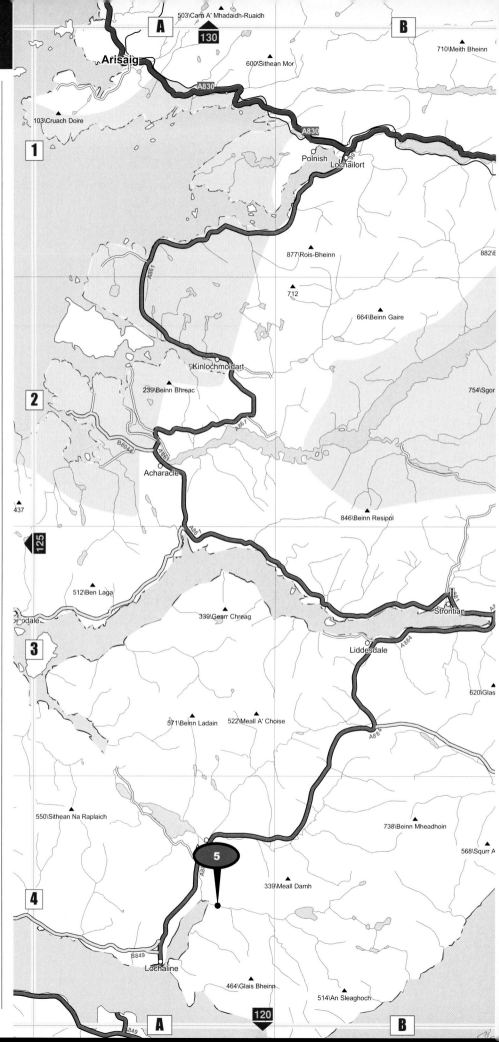

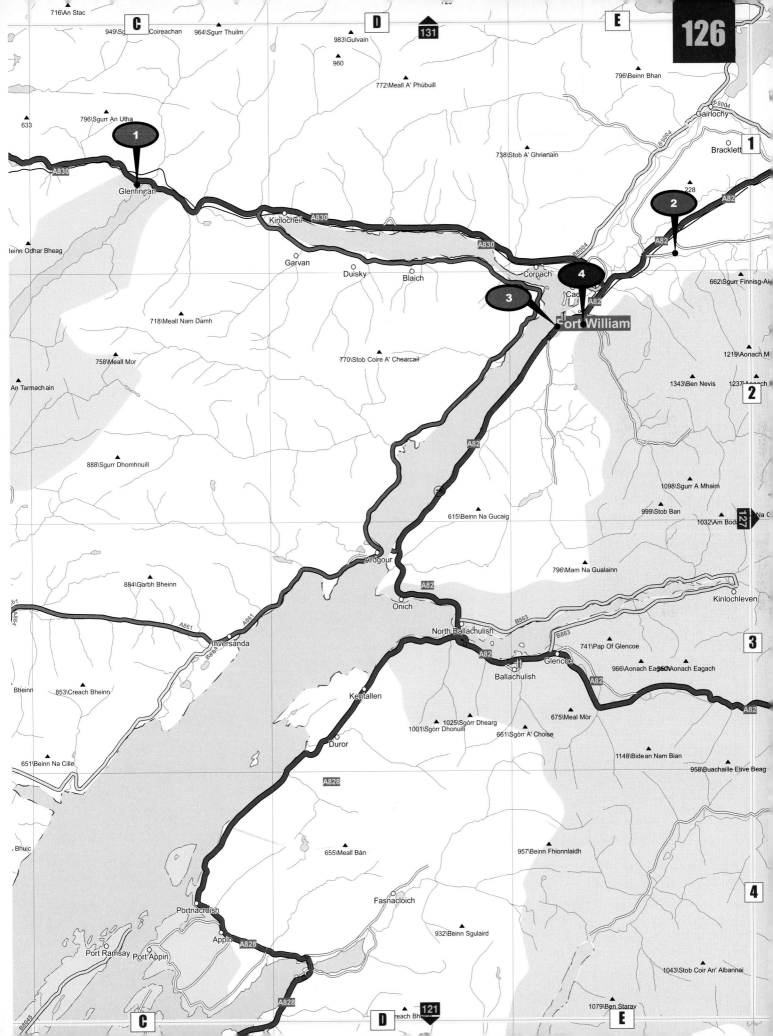

SCOTLAND

Glencoe

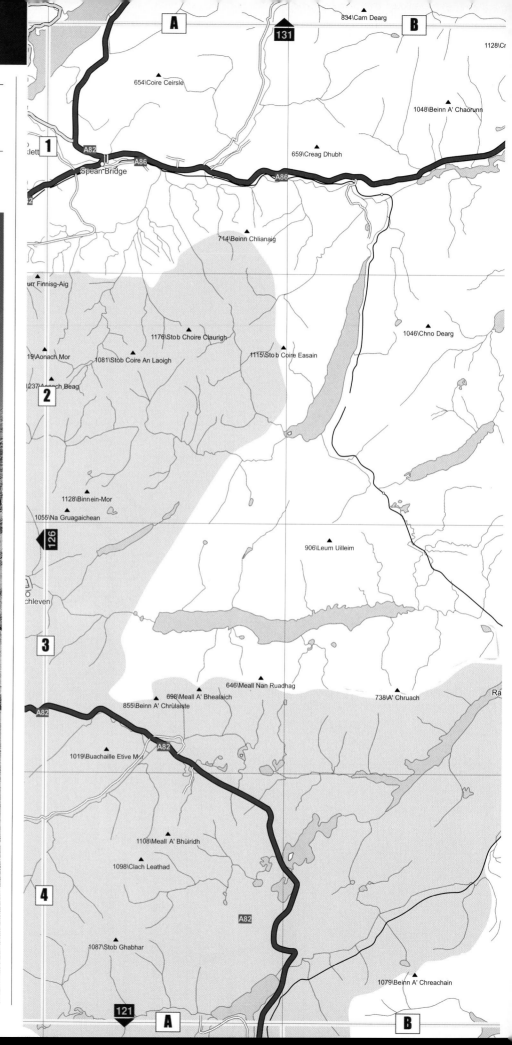

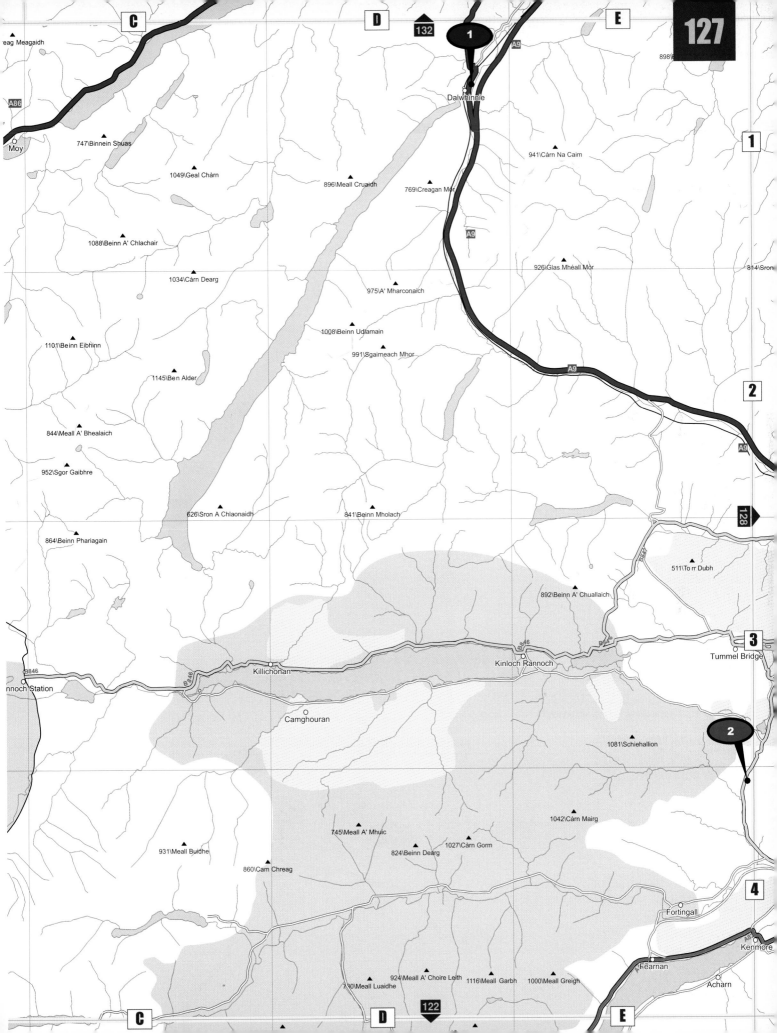

eag Meagaidh

A86

Moy

747\Binnein Shuas

1049\Geal Chàrn

896\Meall Cruaidh

769\Creagan Mòr

941\Càrn Na Caim

926\Glas Mhéall Mòr

814\Sron

1088\Beinn A' Chlachair

1034\Càrn Dearg

975\A' Mharconaich

1008\Beinn Udlamain

991\Sgairneach Mhor

1101\Beinn Eibhinn

1145\Ben Alder

844\Meall A' Bhealaich

952\Sgor Gaibhre

626\Sron A Chlaonaidh

841\Beinn Mholach

864\Beinn Phariagain

892\Beinn A' Chuallaich

511\Torr Dubh

Killichonan

Kinloch Rannoch

Tummel Bridge

nnoch Station

Camghouran

1081\Schiehallion

1042\Càrn Mairg

745\Meall A' Mhuic

931\Meall Buidhe

860\Cam Chreag

824\Beinn Dearg

1027\Càrn Gorm

Fortingall

Kenmore

Fearnan

924\Meall A' Choire Leith

730\Meall Luaidhe

1116\Meall Garbh

1000\Meall Greigh

Acharn

Dalwhinnie

A9

A9

A9

B846

B846

B846

B846

128

PERTHSHIRE

1 **CAIRNWELL MOUNTAIN SPORTS**
Ski centre
Gulabin Lodge, Glenshee
TEL: 01250 885 238

2 **BLAIR CASTLE**
Castle
Blair Atholl, Pitlochry
TEL: 01796 481 207

3 **CLAN DONNACHAIDH MUSEUM**
Museum
Bruar, Pitlochry
TEL: 01796 483 264

4 **KILLIECRANKIE VISITOR CENTRE**
Visitor centre
Killiecrankie, Pitlochry
TEL: 01796 473 233

5 **QUEEN'S VIEW VISITOR CENTRE**
Visitor centre
Tay Forest Park, Strathtummel, Pitlochry
TEL: 01350 727 284

6 **HYDRO-ELECTRIC VISITOR CENTRE
DAM & FISH PASS**
Visitor centre
Pitlochry Power Station, Pitlochry
TEL: 01796 473 152

7 **BLAIR ATHOL DISTILLERY**
Distillery
Pitlochry
TEL: 01796 482 003

8 **EDRADOUR DISTILLERY**
Distillery
Pitlochry
TEL: 01796 472 095

9 **CLUNY HOUSE GARDENS**
Garden
Aberfeldy
TEL: 01887 820 795

10 **CASTLE MENZIES**
Castle
Weem
TEL: 01887 820 982

11 **DEWAR'S WORLD OF WHISKY**
Distillery
Aberfeldy Distillery, Aberfeldy
TEL: 01887 822 011

12 **BOLFRACKS**
Garden
Aberfeldy
TEL: 01887 820 207

13 **THE HERMITAGE NTS**
Historic building
The Cross, Dunkeld
TEL: 01350 728 641

14 **MEIGLE SCULPTURED STONE MUSEUM**
Museum
Dunndee Road, Meigle
TEL: 01828 640 612

15 **DUNKELD NTS**
Historic building
The Cross, Dunkeld
TEL: 01350 727 460

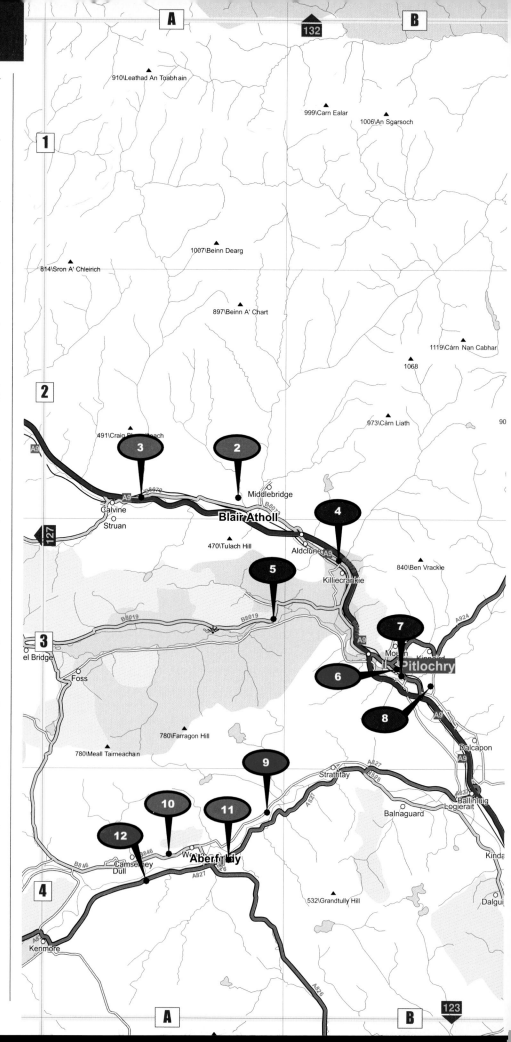

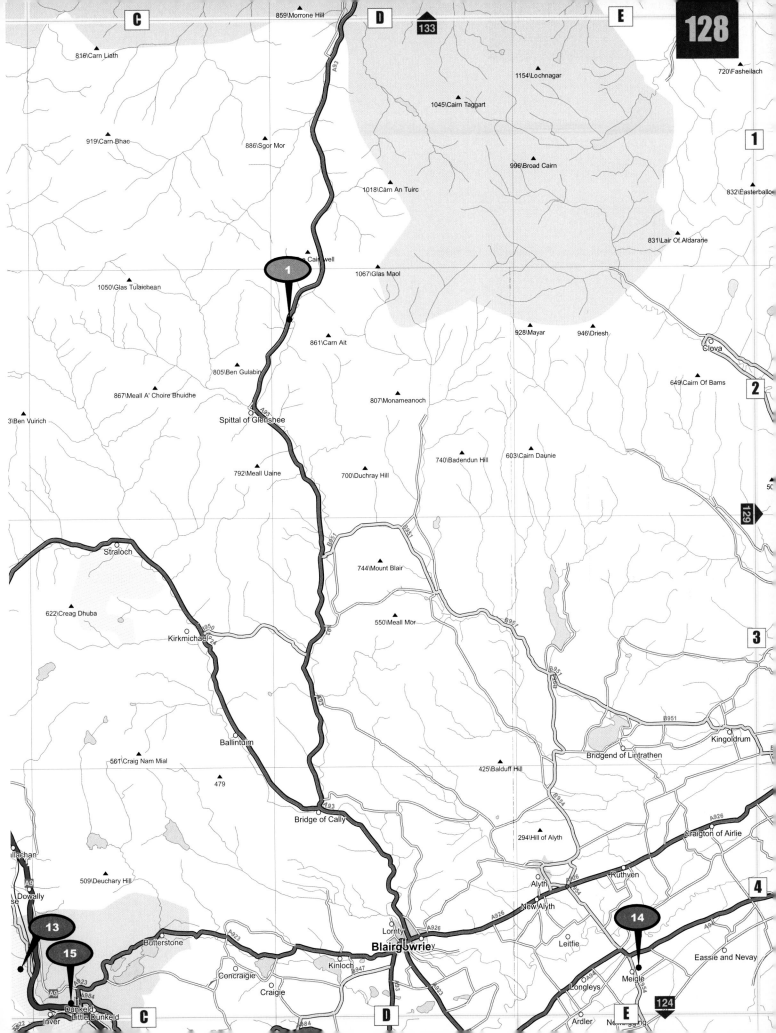

859\Morrone Hill

816\Carn Liath

1154\Lochnagar

720\Fasheilach

1045\Cairn Taggart

919\Carn Bhac

886\Sgor Mor

996\Broad Cairn

832\Easterballo

1018\Carn An Tuirc

831\Lair Of Aldararie

Cairnwell

1050\Glas Tulaichean

1067\Glas Maol

928\Mayar

946\Driesh

Clova

861\Carn Ait

805\Ben Gulabin

807\Monameanoch

649\Cairn Of Bams

867\Meall A' Choire Bhuidhe

3\Ben Vuirich

Spittal of Glenshee

129

740\Badendun Hill

603\Cairn Daunie

792\Meall Uaine

700\Duchray Hill

50

Straloch

744\Mount Blair

622\Creag Dhuba

Kirkmichael

B951

550\Meall Mor

Kingoldrum

Ballintuim

Bridgend of Lintrathen

561\Craig Nam Mial

425\Balduff Hill

479

Bridge of Cally

294\Hill of Alyth

Craigton of Airlie

509\Deuchary Hill

Alyth

Ruthven

Dowally
se

illachan

New Alyth

Butterstone

Lornty

Leitfie

Eassie and Nevay

Blairgowrie

Meigle

Kinloch

Longleys

Concraigie

Craigie

Dunkeld
Little Dunkeld

Inver

Ardler

124

SCOTLAND

1 DUNOTTAR CASTLE
Castle
The Lodge, Dunottar, Stonehaven
TEL: 01569 762 173

2 FASQUE
Historic house
Fettercairn, Laurencekirk
TEL: 01561 340 569

3 ARBUTHNOTT HOUSE
Garden
Laurencekirk
TEL: 01561 361 226

4 EDZELL CASTLE HS
Castle
Brechin
TEL: 01356 648 631

5 HOUSE OF DUN NTS
Historic house
Montrose
TEL: 01674 810 264

6 WILLIAM LAMB SCULPTURE STUDIO
Museum
24 Market Street, Montrose
TEL: 01674 673 232

7 MONTROSE BASIN WILDLIFE CENTRE
Nature centre
Montrose
TEL: 01674 676 336

8 J M BARRIE'S BIRTHPLACE HS
Historic building
9 Brechin Road, Kirriemuir
TEL: 01328 228 054

9 HOUSE OF PITMUIES
Historic house
Guthrie, By Forfar, Angus
TEL: 01241 828 245

10 ANGUS FOLK MUSEUM
Museum
Glamis, Forfar
TEL: 01307 840 288

11 GLAMIS CASTLE
Castle
Glamis, Forfar
TEL: 01307 840 393

Help us help you

mention the
Days Out Atlas
when visiting anywhere
on this page.

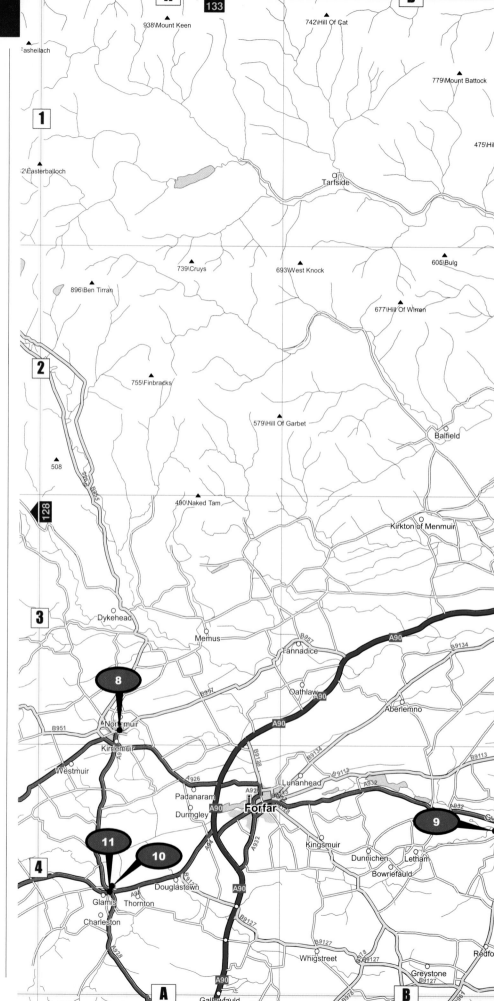

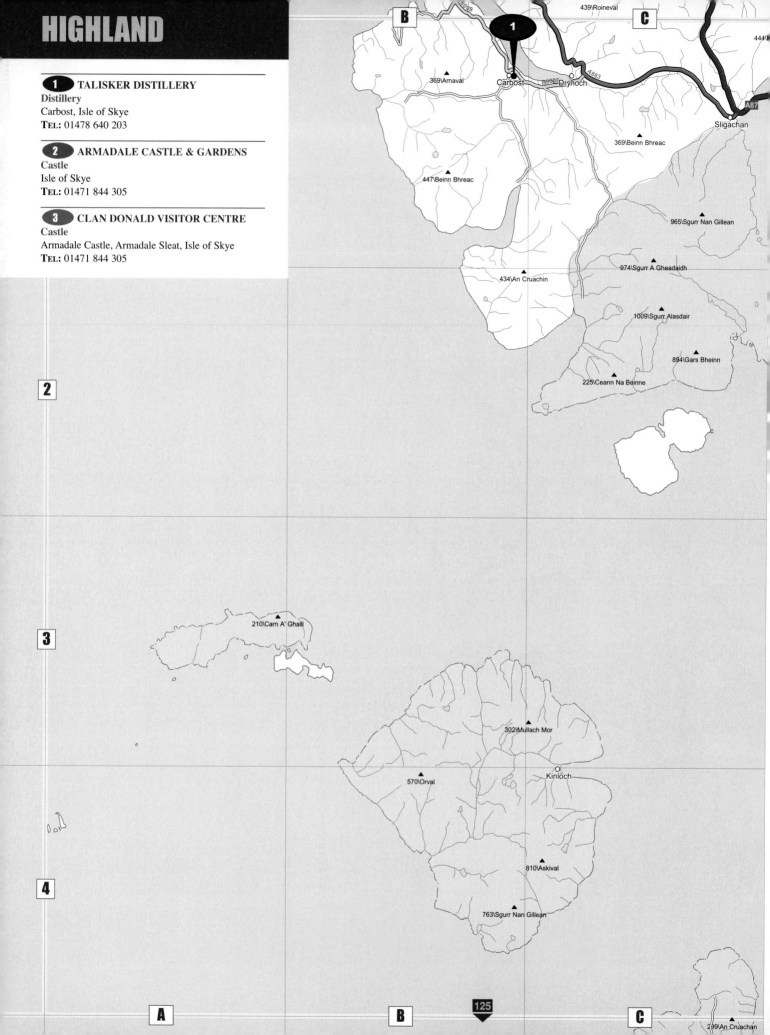

HIGHLAND

1 TALISKER DISTILLERY
Distillery
Carbost, Isle of Skye
TEL: 01478 640 203

2 ARMADALE CASTLE & GARDENS
Castle
Isle of Skye
TEL: 01471 844 305

3 CLAN DONALD VISITOR CENTRE
Castle
Armadale Castle, Armadale Sleat, Isle of Skye
TEL: 01471 844 305

439\Roineval

444\

369\Arnaval

Carbost   Drynoch   A863   Sligachan
A87

369\Beinn Bhreac

447\Beinn Bhreac

965\Sgurr Nan Gillean

974\Sgurr A Gheadaidh

434\An Cruachin

1009\Sgurr Alasdair

894\Gars Bheinn

225\Ceann Na Beinne

210\Carn A' Ghaill

302\Mullach Mor

Kinloch

570\Orval

810\Askival

763\Sgurr Nan Gillean

239\An Cruachan

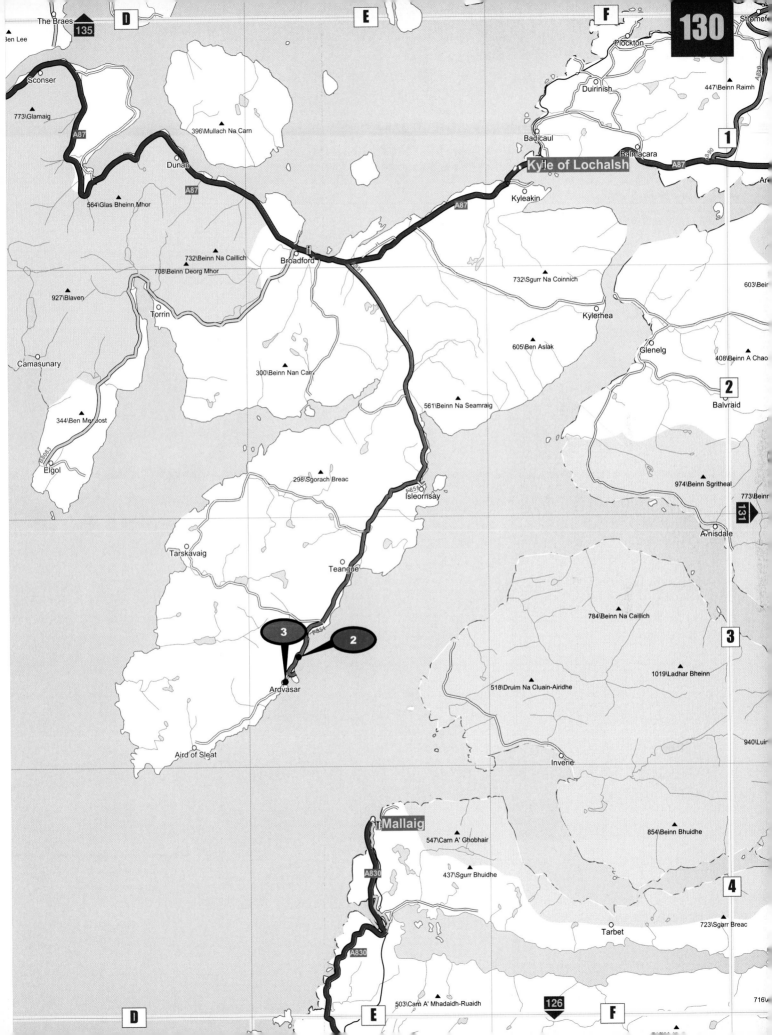

1 EILEAN DONAN CASTLE
Castle
Dornie
Tel: 01599 555 202

2 RARE BREEDS FARM
Farm
Rowanlea, Jenkins Park, Fort Augustus
Tel: 01320 366 433

3 FORT AUGUSTUS ABBEY
Abbey
Fort Augustus
Tel: Not available

4 KYLERHEA OTTER HAVEN
Wildlife park
Strathoich, Fort Augustus
Tel: 01320 366 322

Canyoning

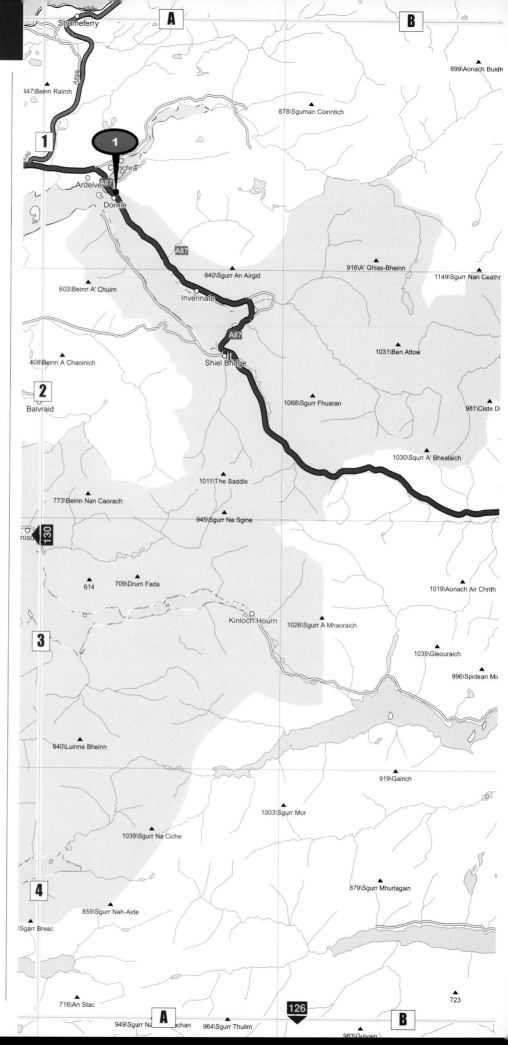

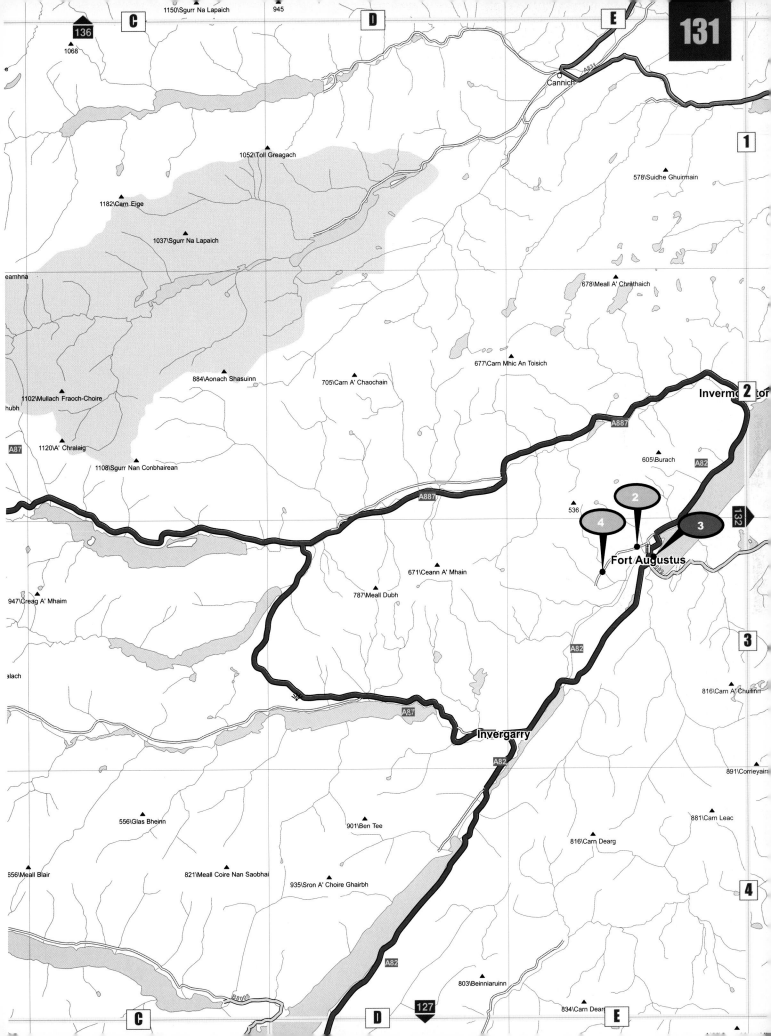

HIGHLAND

1 **ORIGINAL LOCH NESS MONSTER EXHIBITION CENTRE**
Museum
Drumnadrochit
TEL: 01456 450 342

2 **LOCH NESS 2000**
Visitor centre
Drumnadrochit
TEL: 01456 450 573

3 **TOMATIN DISTILLERY**
Distillery
Tomatin
TEL: 01808 511 444

4 **SPEYSIDE HEATHER CENTRE**
Garden
Skye of Curr, Dulnain Bridge, Inverness
TEL: 01479 851 359

5 **LANDMARK HIGHLAND HERITAGE & ADVENTURE PARK**
Heritage centre
Carrbridge
TEL: 08007 313 446

6 **STRATHSPEY STEAM RAILWAY**
Railway
Aviemore Station, Dalfaber Road, Aviemore
TEL: 01479 810 725

7 **CAIRNGORM REINDEER CENTRE**
Farm
Glenmore
TEL: 01479 861 228

8 **GLENMORE VISITOR CENTRE**
Visitor centre
Glenmore Forest Park, Aviemore
TEL: 01479 861 220

9 **HIGHLAND WILDLIFE PARK**
Wildlife park
Kincraig, Kingussie
TEL: 01540 651 270

10 **HIGHLAND FOLK MUSEUM**
Museum
Duke Street, Kingussie
TEL: 01540 661 307

11 **CLAN MACPHERSON HOUSE & MUSEUM**
Historic house
Main Street, Newtonmore
TEL: 01540 673 332

12 **URQUHART CASTLE HS**
Castle
Urquhart
TEL: 01456 450 551

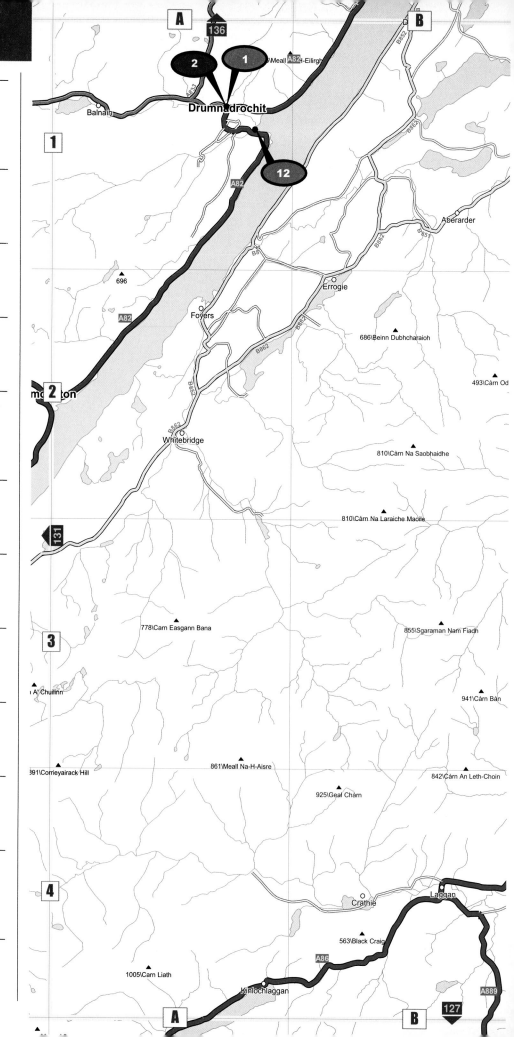

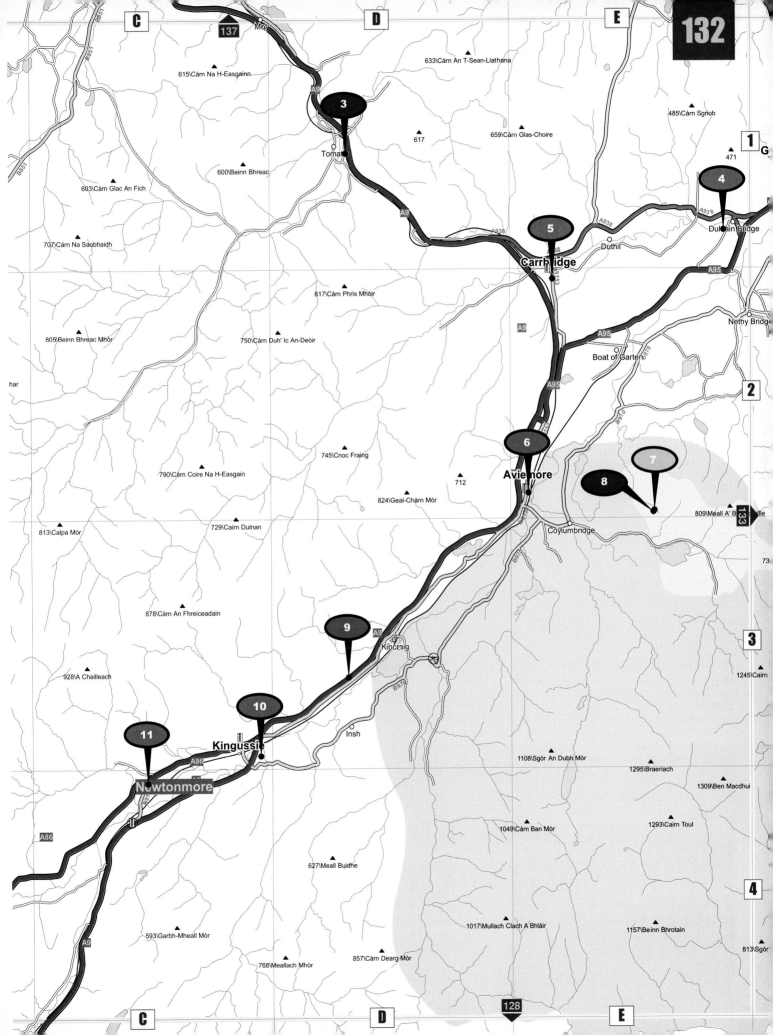

ABERDEENSHIRE

1 **LEITH HALL NTS**
Historic house
Huntly
TEL: 01464 831 216

2 **GLENLIVET DISTILLERY**
Distillery
Ballindalloch
TEL: 01542 783 220

3 **KILDRUMMY CASTLE GARDENS**
Castle
Alford
TEL: 01975 571 203

4 **GRAMPIAN TRANSPORT MUSEUM**
Museum
Main Street, Alford
TEL: 01975 562 292

5 **CRAIGIEVAR CASTLE**
Castle
Alford
TEL: 01339 883 635

6 **CANDACRAIG GARDENS**
Garden
Strathdon
TEL: 01975 651 226

7 **CORGARFF CASTLE HS**
Castle
Corgarff
TEL: 01975 651 460

8 **BALMORAL CASTLE**
Castle
Balmoral, Ballater
TEL: 01339 742 334

9 **ROYAL LOCHNAGAR DISTILLERY**
Distillery
Crathie, Ballater
TEL: 01339 742 700

10 **BRAEMAR CASTLE**
Castle
Braemar, Ballater
TEL: 01339 741 219

11 **BRAEMAR HIGHLAND HERITAGE CENTRE**
Heritage centre
Mar Road, Braemar, Ballater
TEL: 01339 741 944

Balmoral Castle, Aberdeenshire, Map 133-8

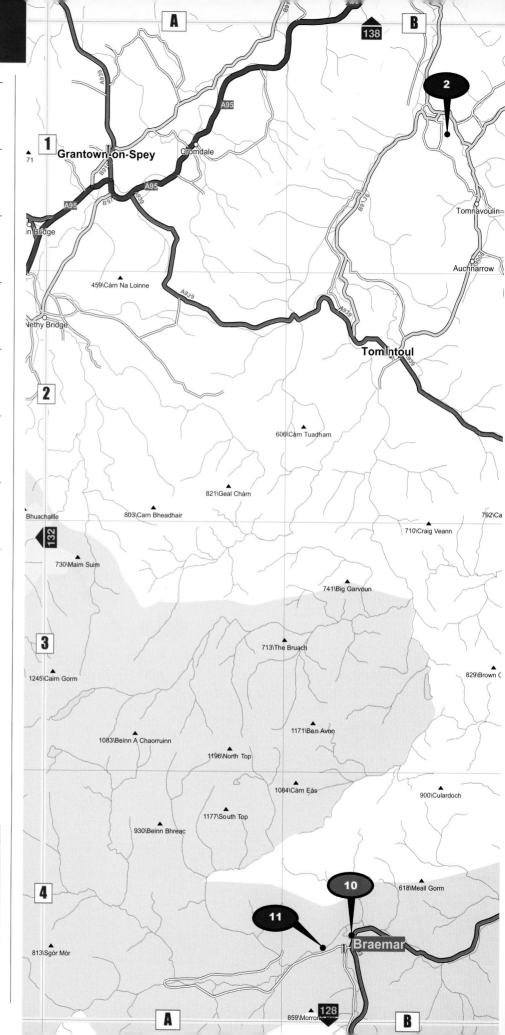

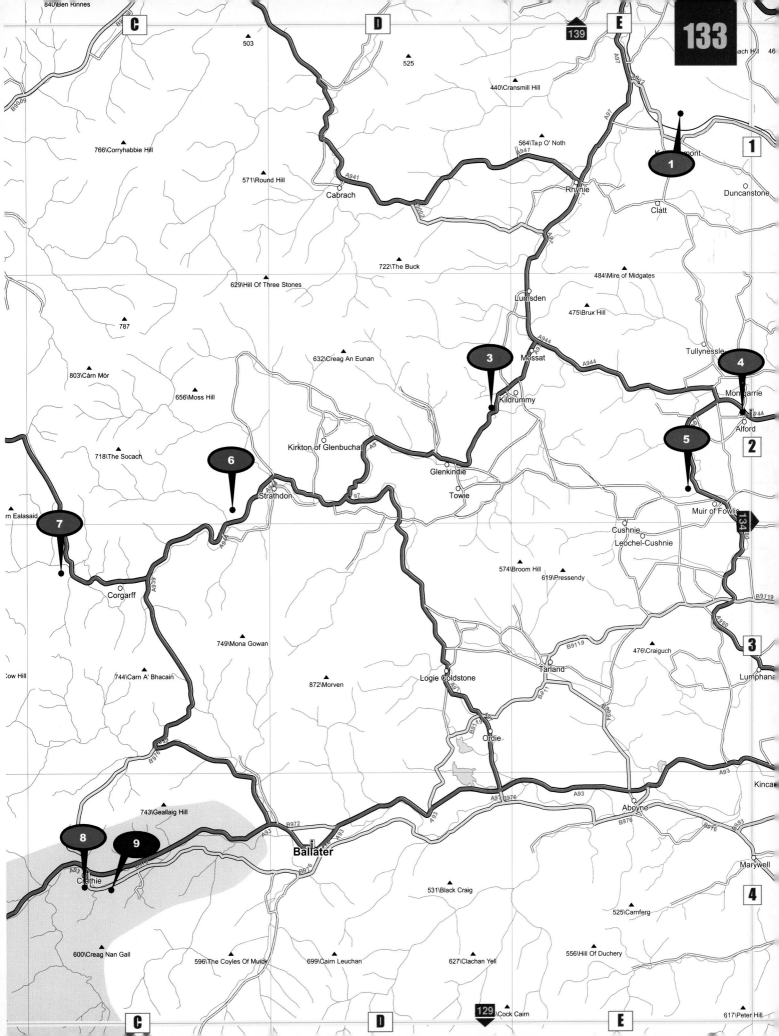

ABERDEENSHIRE

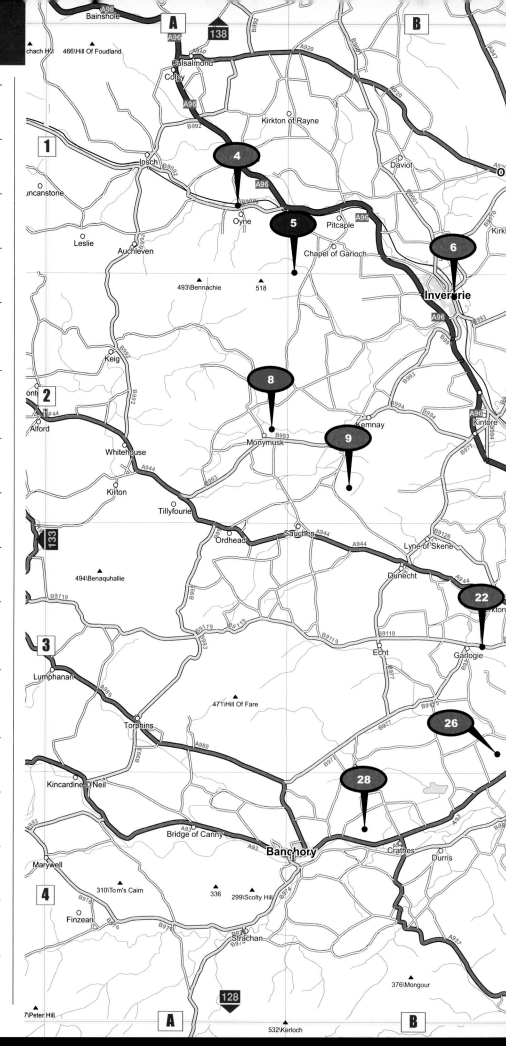

1 HADDO HOUSE NTS
Historic house
Ellon   TEL: 01651 851 440

2 PITMEDDEN GARDEN NTS
Garden
Ellon   TEL: 01651 842 352

3 TOLQUHON CASTLE
Castle
Tolquhon   TEL: 01651 851 286

4 ARCHAEOLINK PREHISTORY PARK
Heritage centre
Oyne, Insch   TEL: 01464 851 500

5 BENNACHIE CENTRE
Visitor centre
Bennachie Forest, Essons, Inverurie
                         TEL: 01467 681 470

6 INVERURIE MUSEUM
Museum
Town House, The Square, Inverurie
                         TEL: 01771 622 906

7 BALMEDIE COUNTRY PARK
Country park
Balmedie   TEL: 01358 742 396

8 MONYMUSK WALLED GARDEN
Garden
Monymusk, Inverurie   TEL: 01467 651 543

9 CASTLE FRASER NTS
Castle
Inverurie   TEL: 01330 833 463

10 SEATON PARK
Garden
Don Street, Old Aberdeen, Aberdeen
                         TEL: 01224 522 734

**11 PETERHEAD MARITIME HERITAGE
CENTRE**
Heritage centre
The Lido, South Rd, Peterhead TEL: 01779 473 000

12 WESTBURN PARK
Garden
Westburn Road, Aberdeen TEL: 01224 522 734

13 LINKS
Garden
Beach Esplanade, Aberdeen TEL: 01224 522 734

14 ABERDEEN FUN BEACH
Funfair
Aberdeen   TEL: 01224 633 339

15 VICTORIA PARK
Garden
Watson Street, Aberdeen TEL: 01224 522 734

16 PROVOST SKENE'S HOUSE
Museum
Guestrow Broad St, Aberdeen TEL: 01224 641 086

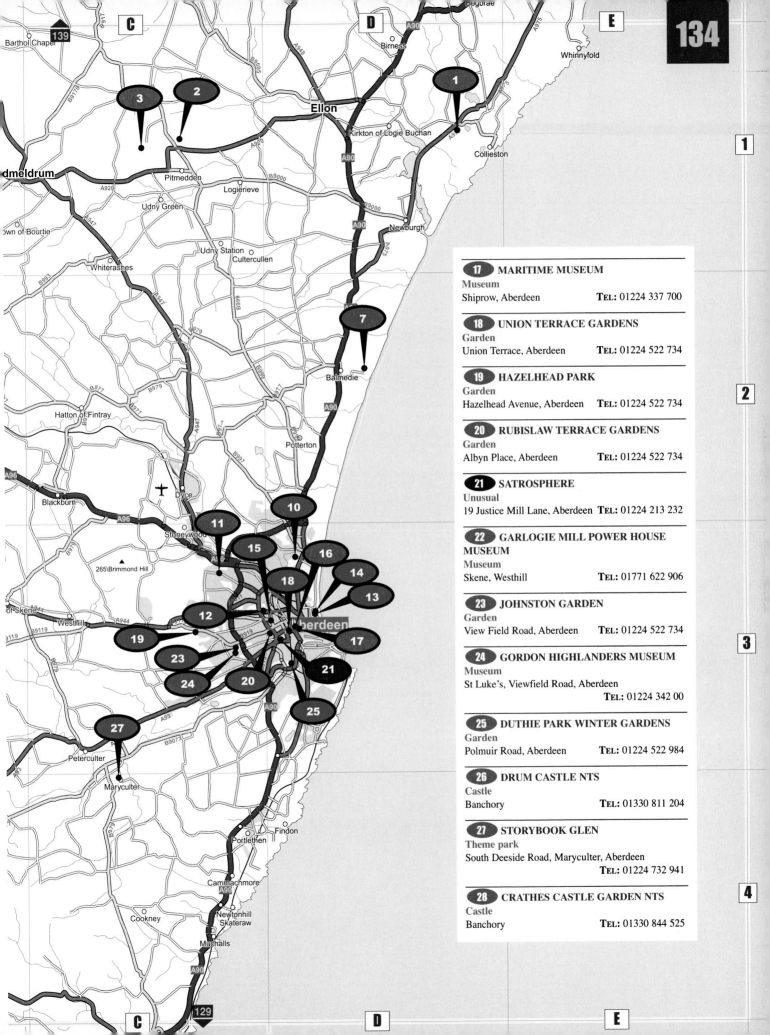

134

17 MARITIME MUSEUM
Museum
Shiprow, Aberdeen — TEL: 01224 337 700

18 UNION TERRACE GARDENS
Garden
Union Terrace, Aberdeen — TEL: 01224 522 734

19 HAZELHEAD PARK
Garden
Hazelhead Avenue, Aberdeen — TEL: 01224 522 734

20 RUBISLAW TERRACE GARDENS
Garden
Albyn Place, Aberdeen — TEL: 01224 522 734

21 SATROSPHERE
Unusual
19 Justice Mill Lane, Aberdeen TEL: 01224 213 232

22 GARLOGIE MILL POWER HOUSE MUSEUM
Museum
Skene, Westhill — TEL: 01771 622 906

23 JOHNSTON GARDEN
Garden
View Field Road, Aberdeen — TEL: 01224 522 734

24 GORDON HIGHLANDERS MUSEUM
Museum
St Luke's, Viewfield Road, Aberdeen
TEL: 01224 342 00

25 DUTHIE PARK WINTER GARDENS
Garden
Polmuir Road, Aberdeen — TEL: 01224 522 984

26 DRUM CASTLE NTS
Castle
Banchory — TEL: 01330 811 204

27 STORYBOOK GLEN
Theme park
South Deeside Road, Maryculter, Aberdeen
TEL: 01224 732 941

28 CRATHES CASTLE GARDEN NTS
Castle
Banchory — TEL: 01330 844 525

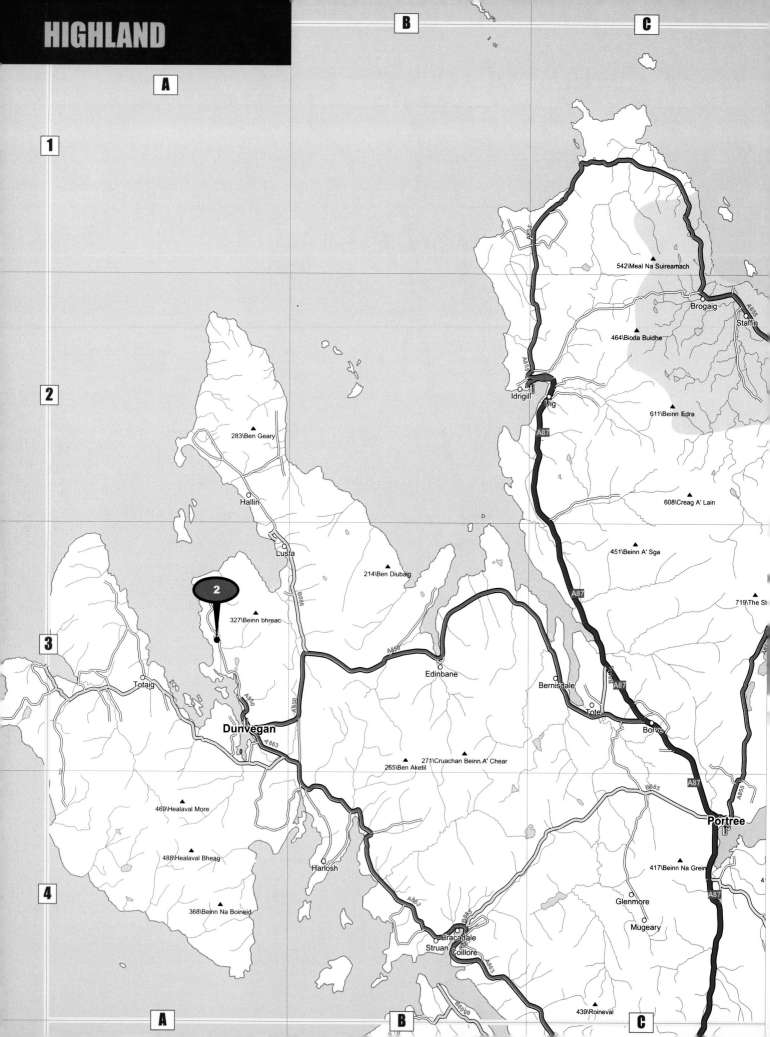

A
B
C

1

2

3

4

A
B
C

542\Meal Na Suireamach

Brogaig
Staffin

464\Bioda Buidhe

Idrigill
Uig

611\Beinn Edra

283\Ben Geary

Hallin

608\Creag A' Lain

451\Beinn A' Sga

Lusta

719\The St

214\Ben Diubaig

327\Beinn bhreac

Totaig

Edinbane

Bernisdale

Tote

Borve

Dunvegan

271\Cruachan Beinn A' Chear
265\Ben Aketil

469\Healaval More

Portree

488\Healaval Bheag

417\Beinn Na Grein

Harlosh

Glenmore

Mugeary

368\Beinn Na Boineid

Bracadale
Struan
Coillore

439\Roineval

1 GAIRLOCH HERITAGE MUSEUM

Museum
Achtercairn, Gairloch
TEL: 01445 712 287

2 DUNVEGAN CASTLE & GARDENS

Castle
Dunvegan, Isle of Skye, Highland, IV55 8WF.
TEL: 01470 521 206
EMAIL: info@dunvegancastle.com
WEB: www.dunvegancastle.com

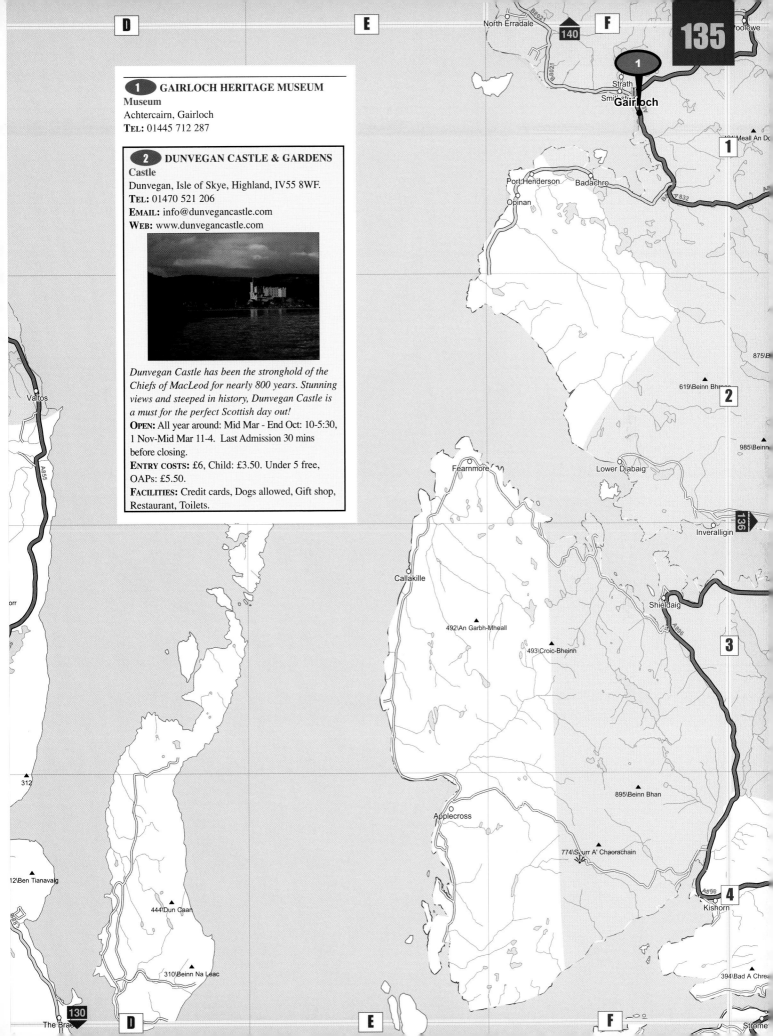

Dunvegan Castle has been the stronghold of the Chiefs of MacLeod for nearly 800 years. Stunning views and steeped in history, Dunvegan Castle is a must for the perfect Scottish day out!
OPEN: All year around: Mid Mar - End Oct: 10-5:30, 1 Nov-Mid Mar 11-4. Last Admission 30 mins before closing.
ENTRY COSTS: £6, Child: £3.50. Under 5 free, OAPs: £5.50.
FACILITIES: Credit cards, Dogs allowed, Gift shop, Restaurant, Toilets.

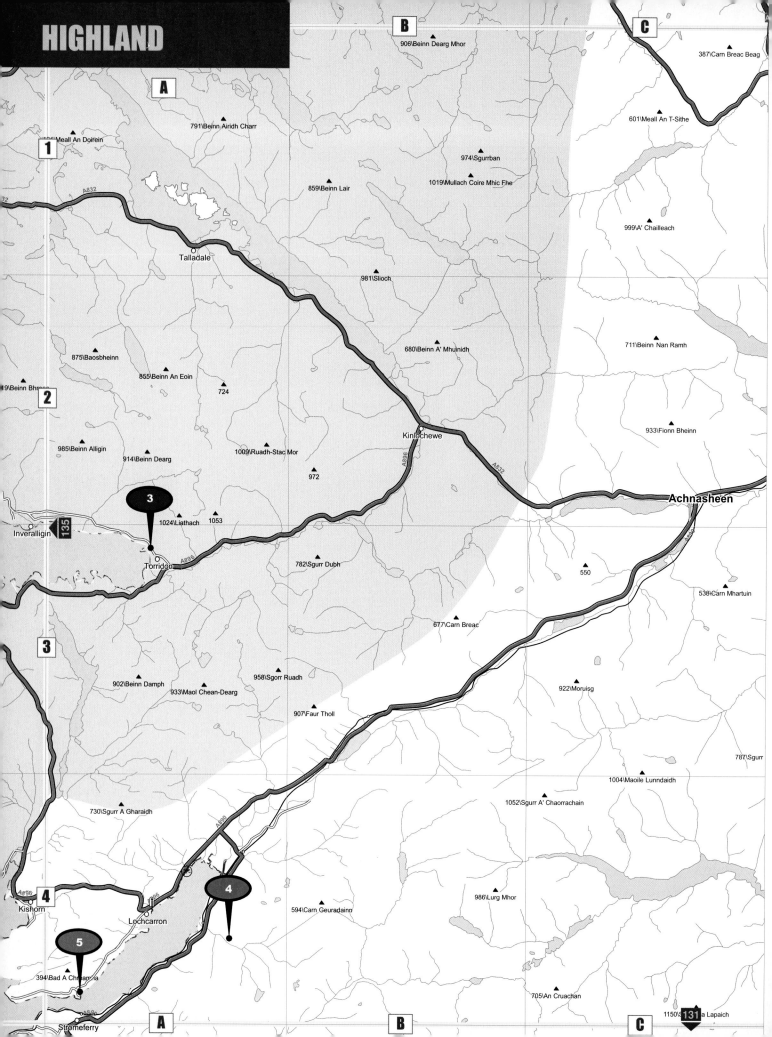

HIGHLAND

A

B

C

906\Beinn Dearg Mhor

387\Carn Breac Beag

601\Meall An T-Sithe

791\Beinn Airidh Charr

1

1041\Meall An Doirein

974\Sgurrban

1019\Mullach Coire Mhic Fhe

859\Beinn Lair

999\A' Chailleach

981\Slioch

A832

Talladale

680\Beinn A' Mhuinidh

711\Beinn Nan Ramh

875\Baosbheinn

855\Beinn An Eoin

933\Fionn Bheinn

724

9\Beinn Bhre...

2

985\Beinn Alligin

914\Beinn Dearg

1009\Ruadh-Stac Mor

Kinlochewe

A896

Achnasheen

A832

972

3

135

550

1024\Liathach 1053

538\Carn Mhartuin

Inveralligin

A896

Torridon

782\Sgurr Dubh

677\Carn Breac

3

902\Beinn Damph

958\Sgorr Ruadh

922\Moruisg

933\Maol Chean-Dearg

907\Faur Tholl

787\Sgurr

1004\Maoile Lunndaidh

730\Sgurr A Gharaidh

1052\Sgurr A' Chaorrachain

A890

4

4

A896

594\Carn Geuradainn

986\Lurg Mhor

Kishorn

A896

Lochcarron

5

705\An Cruachan

394\Bad A Chreamha

1150\S...a Lapaich 131

A896

Stromeferry

A

B

C

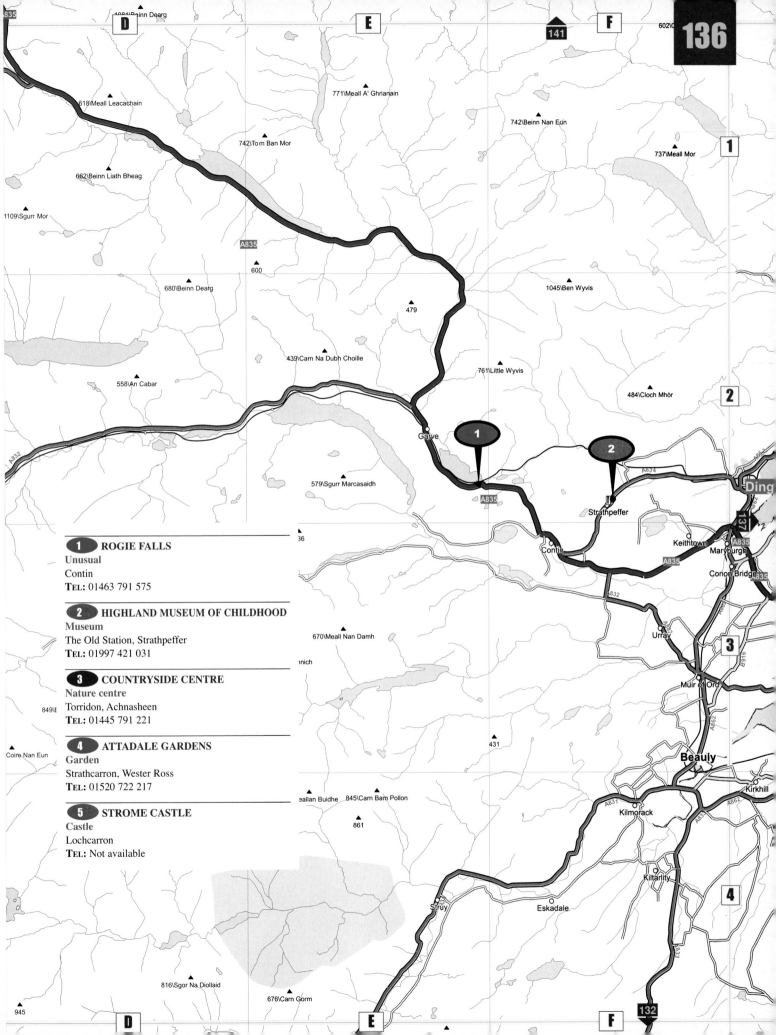

1091\Beinn Dearg
618\Meall Leacachain
771\Meall A' Ghrianain
742\Beinn Nan Eun
737\Meall Mor
742\Tom Ban Mor
662\Beinn Liath Bheag
1109\Sgurr Mor
A835
680\Beinn Dearg
600
1045\Ben Wyvis
479
439\Carn Na Dubh Choille
558\An Cabar
761\Little Wyvis
484\Cloch Mhòr
A832
Garve
1
2
A834
Ding
579\Sgurr Marcasaidh
A835
Strathpeffer
137
Keithtown
Maryburgh
36
Contin
Conon Bridge
A835
A832
670\Meall Nan Damh
Urray
nnich
3
849\E
Muir of Ord
Coire Nan Eun
431
Beauly
Kirkhill
eallan Buidhe
845\Carn Bam Pollon
A831
Kilmorack
861
Kiltarlity
816\Sgor Na Diollaid
Struy
Eskadale
676\Carn Gorm
945

1 ROGIE FALLS
Unusual
Contin
TEL: 01463 791 575

2 HIGHLAND MUSEUM OF CHILDHOOD
Museum
The Old Station, Strathpeffer
TEL: 01997 421 031

3 COUNTRYSIDE CENTRE
Nature centre
Torridon, Achnasheen
TEL: 01445 791 221

4 ATTADALE GARDENS
Garden
Strathcarron, Wester Ross
TEL: 01520 722 217

5 STROME CASTLE
Castle
Lochcarron
TEL: Not available

HIGHLAND

○ ANIMAL ATTRACTIONS   ○ OUTDOOR ATTRACTIONS
○ HERITAGE & CULTURE   ○ OUTDOOR ACTIVITIES
○ INDOOR ACTIVITIES   ○ WATER ACTIVITIES

1 HUGH MILLER'S COTTAGE
Historic building
Church Street, Cromarty
TEL: 01381 600 245

2 CROMARTY COURTHOUSE
Historic Building
Church Street, Cromarty
TEL: 01381 600 418

3 STOREHOUSE OF FOULIS
Visitor centre
Evanton
TEL: 01349 830 000

4 ORDHILL
Country park
Black Isle
TEL: 01463 791 575

5 DINGWALL MUSEUM
Museum
Town House, High Street, Dingwall
TEL: 01349 865 366

7 GROAM HOUSE MUSEUM
Museum
High Street, Rosemarkie, Fortrose
TEL: 01381 621 730

8 FORT GEORGE & QUEEN'S OWN HIGHLANDERS REGIMENTAL MUSEUM HS
Historic building
Inverness
TEL: 01463 224 380

9 ROYAL BRACKLA DISTILLERY
Distillery
Cawdor, Nairn
TEL: 01667 402 002

10 CAWDOR CASTLE & GARDENS
Castle
Nairn
TEL: 01667 404 615

11 CULLODEN BATTLEFIELD NTS
Battlefield
Culloden Moor, Inverness
TEL: 01463 790 607

12 INVERNESS MUSEUM & ART GALLERY
Museum
Castle Wynd, Inverness
TEL: 01463 237 114

13 JACOBITE CRUISES LOCH NESS
Boat trip
Tomnahurich Bridge, Glenurquhart Road, Inverness
TEL: 01463 233 999

14 MONIACK CASTLE & HIGHLAND WINERY
Unusual
Kirkhill, Inverness
TEL: 01463 831 283

15 JAMES PRINGLE WEAVERS OF INVERNESS
Visitor centre
Holm Woollen Mill, Dores Road, Inverness, Highland, IV2 4RB.
TEL: 01463 223 311

JPW of Inverness was established in 1789 making it one of the oldest working weaving mills in Scotland. You can even have a go at weaving yourself (over 16's only). Great shopping facilities.
OPEN: Open daily.
SPECIALITIES: Events held.
FACILITIES: Coffee shop, Credit cards, Gift shop, Pushchair friendly, Toilets, Wheelchair access.

16 DOCHFOUR GARDENS
Garden
Dochfour Estate, Inverness
TEL: 01463 861 218

17 ABRIACHAN GARDENS & NURSERY
Garden
Loch Ness Side, Inverness
TEL: 01463 861 232

Fort George, Highland, Map 137-8

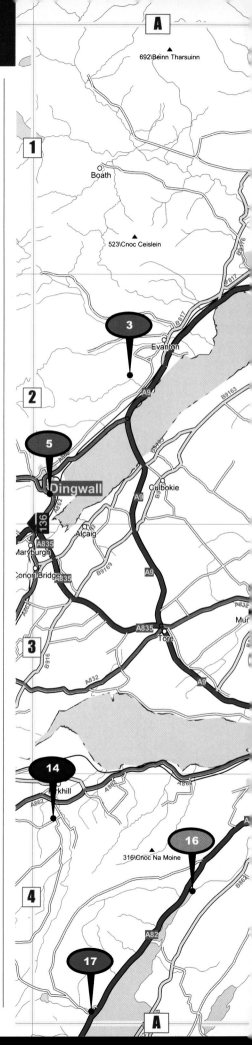

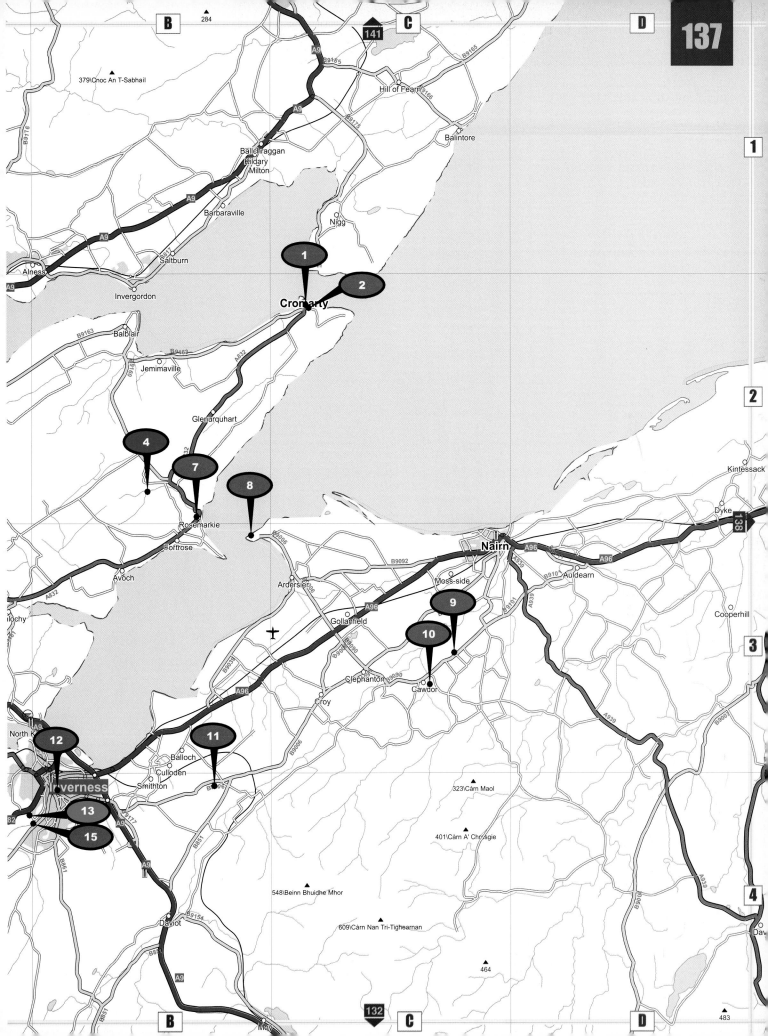

1   SPYNIE PLACE
Historic building
Elgin
TEL: 01343 546 358

2   BUCKIE DRIFTER MARITIME VISITOR CENTRE
Museum
Buckie
TEL: 01542 834 646

3   TUGNET ICE HOUSE
Historic building
Spey Bay, Fochabers
TEL: 01309 673 701

4   MORAY MOTOR MUSEUM
Museum
Bridge Street, Elgin
TEL: 01343 544 933

5   GLEN MORAY DISTILLERY
Distillery
Bruceland Road, Elgin
TEL: 01343 542 577

6   ELGIN MUSEUM
Museum
1 High Street, Elgin
TEL: 01343 543 675

7   ELGIN CATHEDRAL
Cathedral
North College Street, Elgin
TEL: 01343 547 171

8   FALCONER MUSEUM
Museum
Tolbooth Street, Forres
TEL: 01309 673 701

9   NELSON TOWER
Historic building
Grant Park, Forres, Moray
TEL: 01309 673 701

10   FOCHABERS FOLK MUSEUM
Museum
High Street, Fochabers
TEL: 01343 821 204

11   BENROMACH DISTILLERY
Distillery
Invererne Road, Forres
TEL: 01309 675 968

12   PLUSCARDEN ABBEY
Abbey
Pluscarden, Elgin
TEL: 01343 890 257

13   DALLAS DHU DISTILLERY MUSEUM
Distillery
Number 1 Cottage, Mamnachie Road, Forres
TEL: 01309 676 548

14   STRATHISLA DISTILLERY
Distillery
Seafield Avenue, Keith
TEL: 01542 783 042

15   DUFFTOWN MUSEUM
Museum
The Tower, The Square, Dufftown
TEL: 01309 673 701

16   SPEYBURN DISTILLERY
Distillery
Rothes, Aberlour
TEL: 01340 831 213

17   GLEN GRANT DISTILLERY
Distillery
Rothes
TEL: 01542 783 318

18   GLEN GRANT GARDEN
Garden
Rothes, Aberlour
TEL: 01542 783 318

19   MACALLAN DISTILLERY
Distillery
Craigellachie, Aberlour
TEL: 01340 871 471

20   CARDHU DISTILLERY
Distillery
Kockando, Aberlour
TEL: 01340 872 555

21   GLENFIDDICH DISTILLERY
Distillery
Dufftown
TEL: 01340 820 373

22   BALVENIE DISTILLERY
Distillery
Dufftown
TEL: 01340 820 000

23   ABERLOUR DISTILLERY
Distillery
Aberlour
TEL: 01340 871 204

24   BALVENIE CASTLE
Castle
Dufftown, Keith
TEL: 01340 820 121

25   GLENFARCLAS DISTILLERY
Distillery
Marypark, Ballindalloch
TEL: 01807 500 257

26   BALLINDALLOCH CASTLE
Castle
Grantown-on-Spey
TEL: 01807 500 205

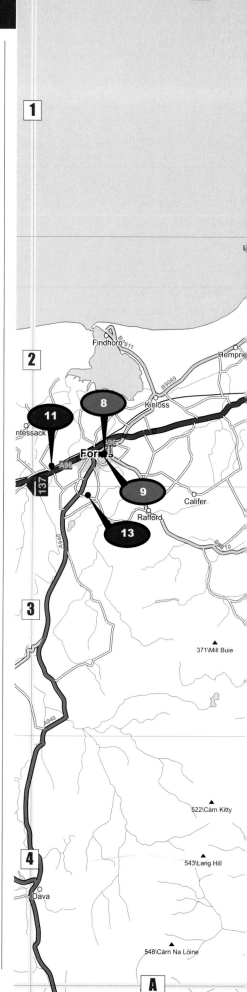

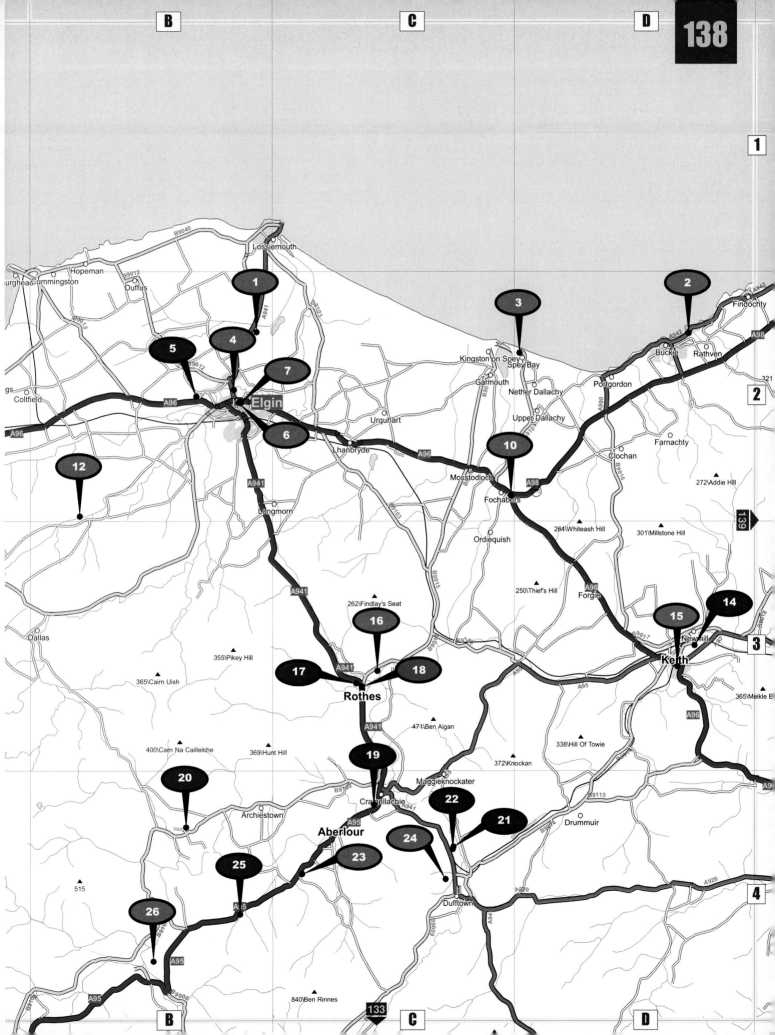

ABERDEENSHIRE

1 MUSEUM OF SCOTTISH LIGHTHOUSES
Museum
Stevenson Road, Fraserburgh   TEL: 01346 511 022

2 BANFF MUSEUM
Museum
High Street, Banff   TEL: 01771 622 906

3 DUFF HOUSE
Historic house
Banff   TEL: 01261 818 181

4 KNOCKDHU DISTILLERY
Distillery
Knock, Huntly
TEL: 01466 771 223

5 DEER ABBEY HS
Abbey
Old Deer   TEL: 0131 668 8800

6 ABERDEENSHIRE FARMING MUSEUM
Museum
Aden Country Park, Peterhead, Mintlaw
  TEL: 01771 622 906

7 DELGATIE CASTLE
Castle
Turriff   TEL: 01888 563 479

8 ARBUTHNOT MUSEUM & ART GALLERY
Museum
St Peter Street, Peterhead   TEL: 01771 622 906

9 NORTH EAST FALCONRY CENTRE
Bird centre & aviary
Carnie, Huntly   TEL: 01466 760 328

10 HUNTLY CASTLE
Castle
Huntly   TEL: 01466 793 191

11 FYVIE CASTLE NTS
Castle
Turriff   TEL: 01651 891 266

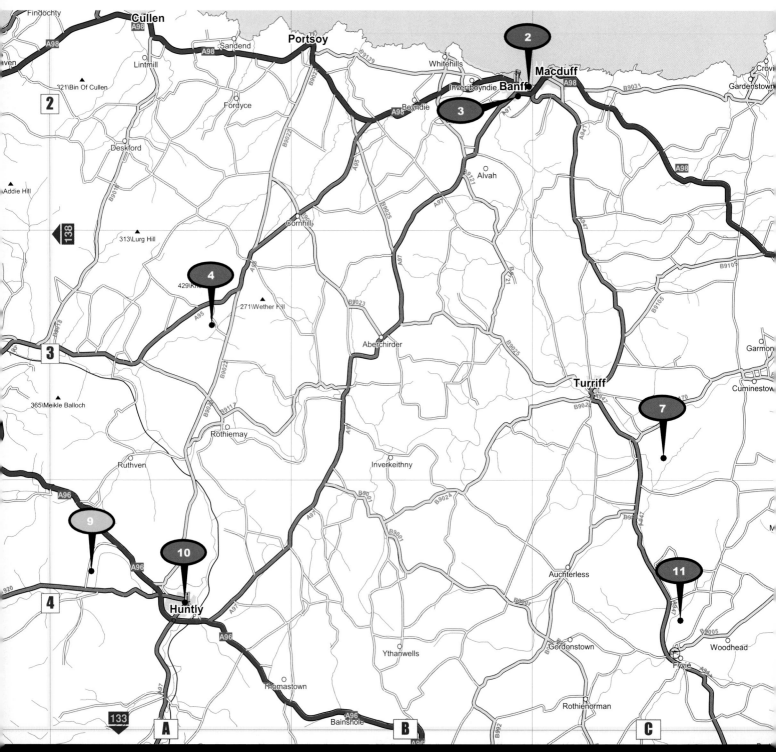

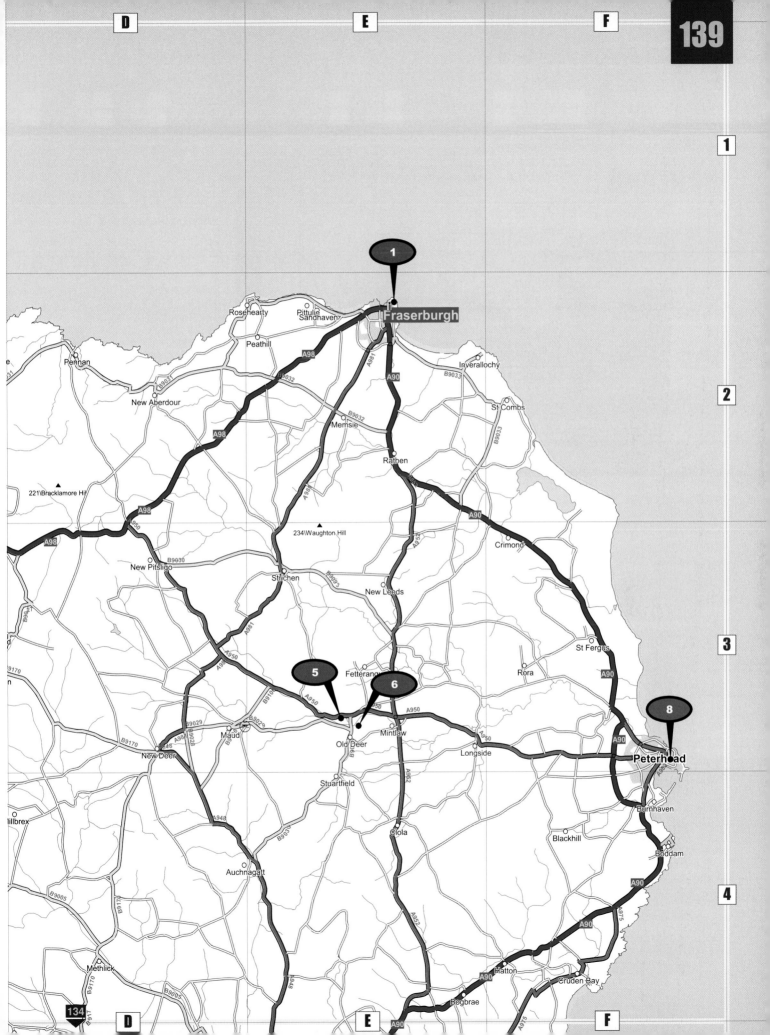

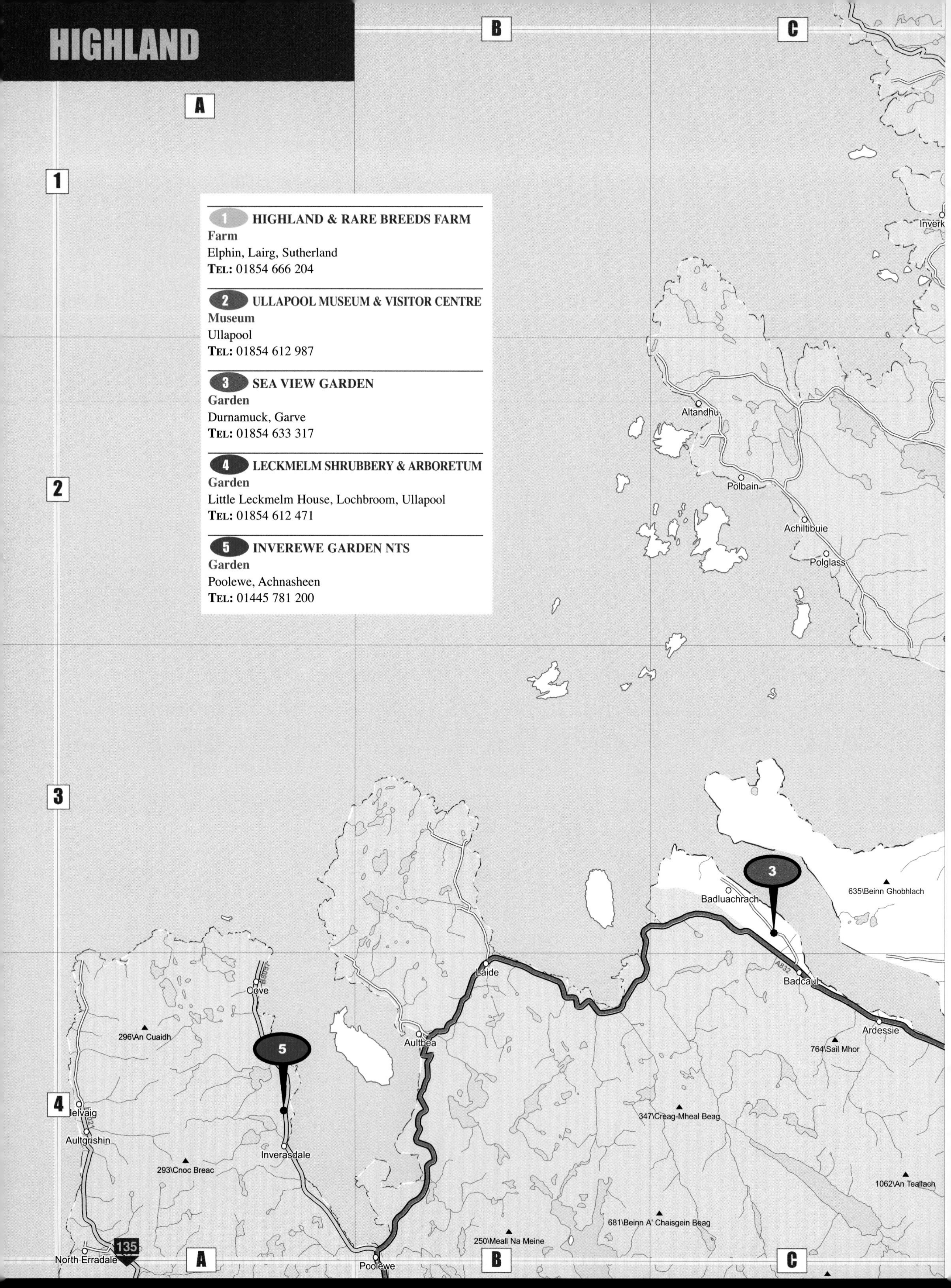

A

B

C

1

2

3

4

1 HIGHLAND & RARE BREEDS FARM
Farm
Elphin, Lairg, Sutherland
TEL: 01854 666 204

2 ULLAPOOL MUSEUM & VISITOR CENTRE
Museum
Ullapool
TEL: 01854 612 987

3 SEA VIEW GARDEN
Garden
Durnamuck, Garve
TEL: 01854 633 317

4 LECKMELM SHRUBBERY & ARBORETUM
Garden
Little Leckmelm House, Lochbroom, Ullapool
TEL: 01854 612 471

5 INVEREWE GARDEN NTS
Garden
Poolewe, Achnasheen
TEL: 01445 781 200

Inverk

Altandhu

Polbain

Achiltibuie

Polglass

635\Beinn Ghobhlach

3

Badluachrach

Badcaul

A832

Laide

Ardessie

Cove

764\Sail Mhor

296\An Cuaidh

Aultbea

5

Melvaig

347\Creag-Mheal Beag

Aultgrishin

Inverasdale

293\Cnoc Breac

1062\An Teallach

681\Beinn A' Chaisgein Beag

250\Meall Na Meine

135

North Erradale

Poolewe

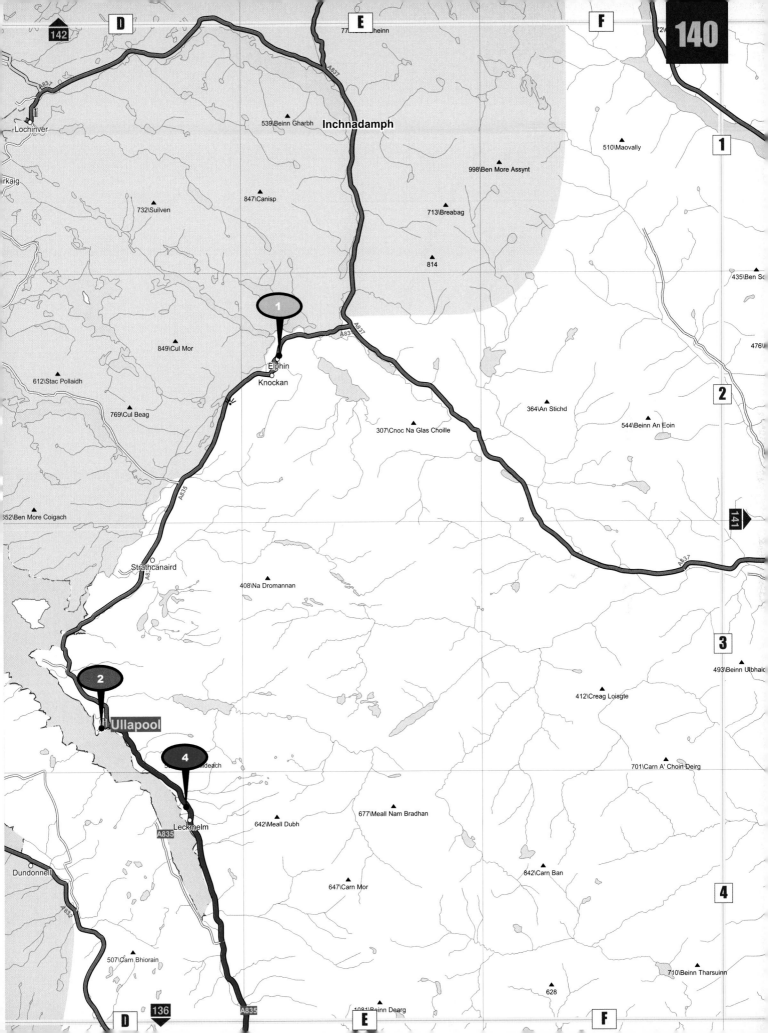

142

Lochinver

rkaig

539\Beinn Gharbh   Inchnadamph

998\Ben More Assynt

510\Maovally

732\Suilven   847\Canisp

713\Breabag

435\Ben Sc

814

476

849\Cul Mor

1

612\Stac Pollaidh

Elphin

Knockan

364\An Stichd

307\Cnoc Na Glas Choille

544\Beinn An Eoin

769\Cul Beag

2

52\Ben More Coigach

141

408\Na Dromannan

Strathcanaird

493\Beinn Ulbhaic

412\Creag Loisgte

3

2

Ullapool

701\Carn A' Choin Deirg

4

ldeach

677\Meall Nam Bradhan

Leckmelm

642\Meall Dubh

A835

842\Carn Ban

Dundonnell

647\Carn Mor

4

507\Carn Bhiorain

710\Beinn Tharsuinn

628

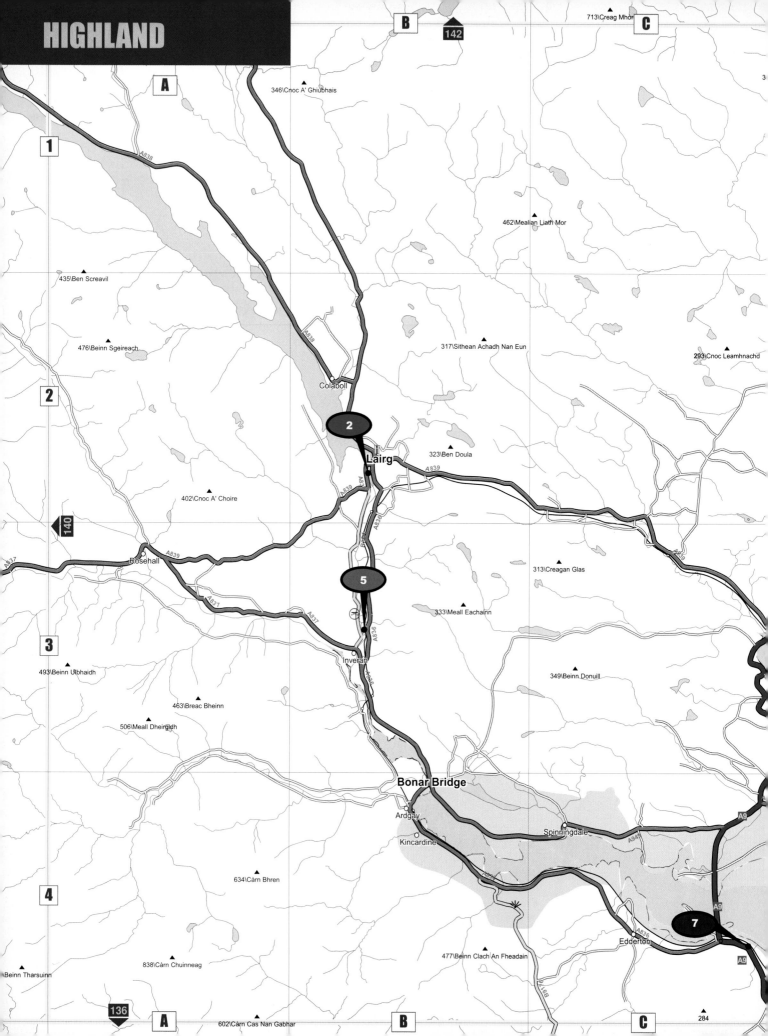

HIGHLAND

346\Cnoc A' Ghiubhais

142

713\Creag Mhor

462\Mealian Liath Mor

435\Ben Screavil

476\Beinn Sgeireach

317\Sithean Achadh Nan Eun

293\Cnoc Leamhnachd

Colaboll

2

Lairg

323\Ben Doula

402\Cnoc A' Choire

140

Rosehall

313\Creagan Glas

5

333\Meall Eachainn

493\Beinn Ulbhaidh

Inveran

349\Beinn Donuill

463\Breac Bheinn

506\Meall Dheirgidh

Bonar Bridge

Ardgay

Spinningdale

Kincardine

634\Càrn Bhren

7

477\Beinn Clach An Fheadain

Edderton

838\Càrn Chuinneag

Beinn Tharsuinn

136

602\Càrn Cas Nan Gabhar

284

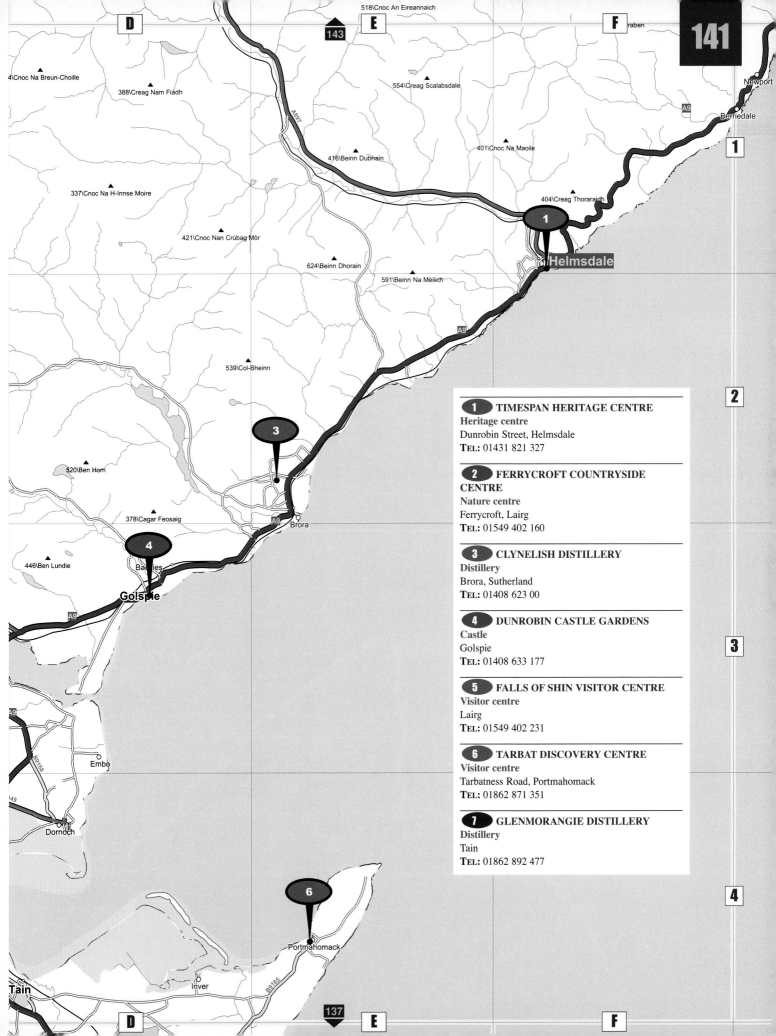

1 TIMESPAN HERITAGE CENTRE
Heritage centre
Dunrobin Street, Helmsdale
TEL: 01431 821 327

2 FERRYCROFT COUNTRYSIDE CENTRE
Nature centre
Ferrycroft, Lairg
TEL: 01549 402 160

3 CLYNELISH DISTILLERY
Distillery
Brora, Sutherland
TEL: 01408 623 00

4 DUNROBIN CASTLE GARDENS
Castle
Golspie
TEL: 01408 633 177

5 FALLS OF SHIN VISITOR CENTRE
Visitor centre
Lairg
TEL: 01549 402 231

6 TARBAT DISCOVERY CENTRE
Visitor centre
Tarbatness Road, Portmahomack
TEL: 01862 871 351

7 GLENMORANGIE DISTILLERY
Distillery
Tain
TEL: 01862 892 477

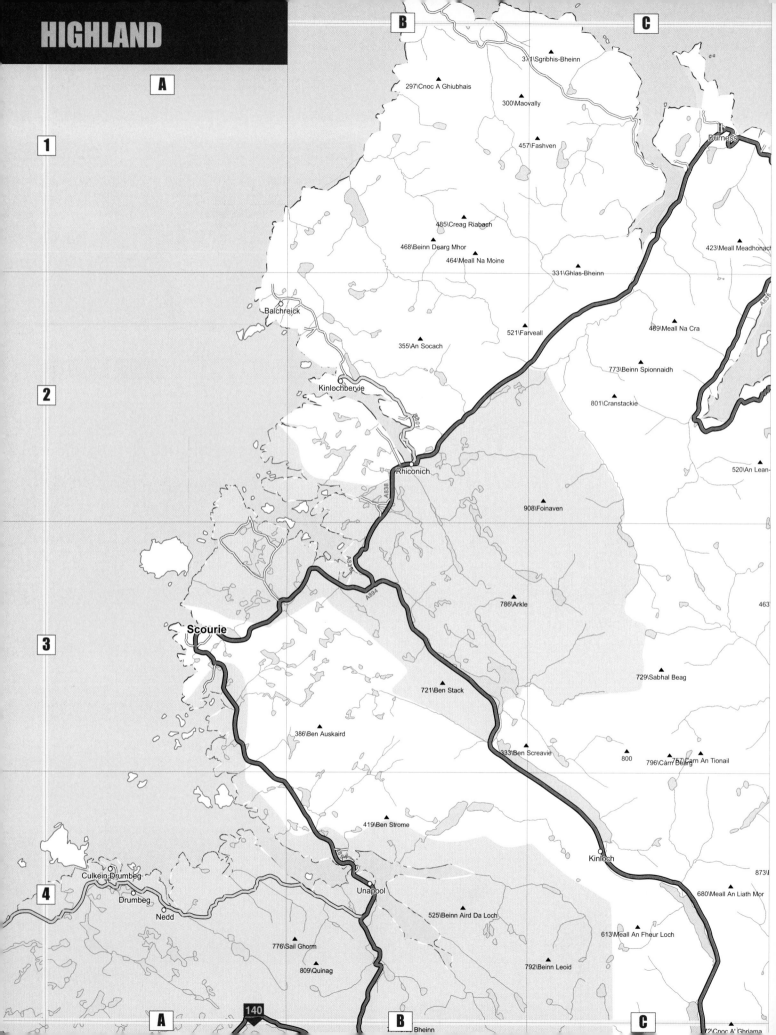

HIGHLAND

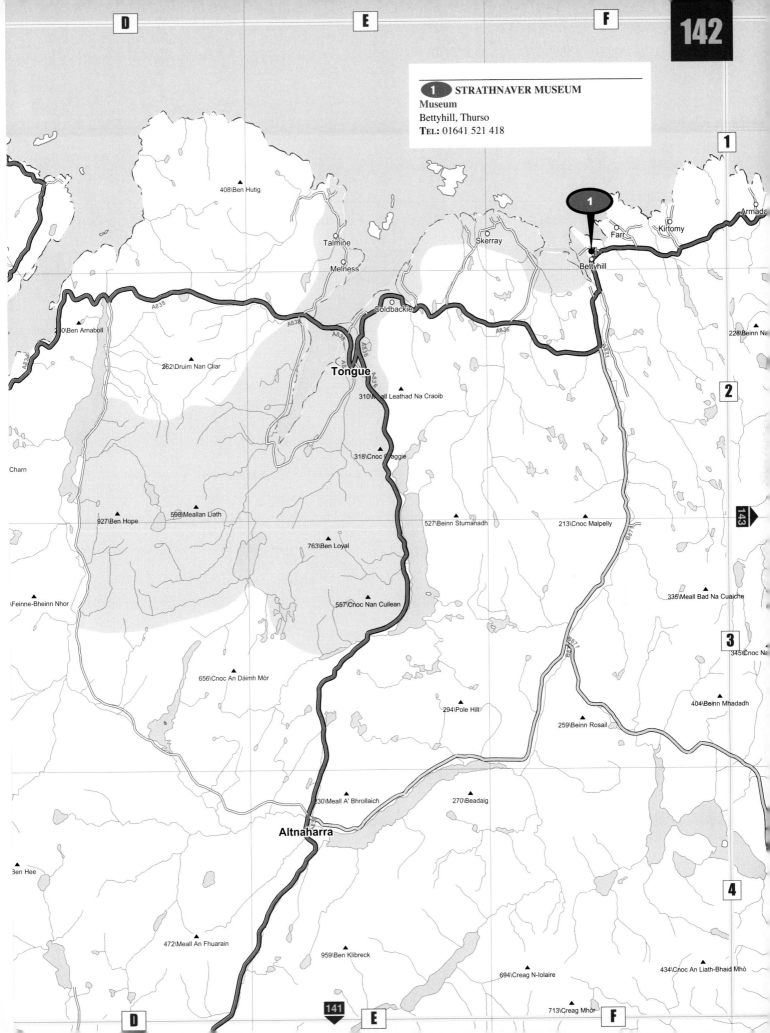

1 **STRATHNAVER MUSEUM**
Museum
Bettyhill, Thurso
TEL: 01641 521 418

1

Armada

Fart

Kirtomy

Bettyhill

228\Beinn Na

408\Ben Hutig

Talmine

Skerray

Melness

Coldbackie

A838

A838

A836

A836

2 0\Ben Arnaboll

262\Druim Nan Cliar

Tongue

A836

310\M all Leathad Na Craoib

2

335\Meall Bad Na Cuaiche

318\Cnoc Maggie

Charn

927\Ben Hope

598\Meallan Liath

527\Beinn Stumanadh

213\Cnoc Malpelly

143

763\Ben Loyal

B871

Feinne-Bheinn Nhor

557\Cnoc Nan Cuilean

3

345\Cnoc Na

656\Cnoc An Dàimh Mòr

294\Pole Hill

404\Beinn Mhadadh

B871

259\Beinn Rosail

230\Meall A' Bhrollaich

270\Beadaig

Altnaharra

Ben Hee

4

472\Meall An Fhuarain

959\Ben Klibreck

434\Cnoc An Liath-Bhaid Mhò

694\Creag N-Iolaire

713\Creag Mhòr

F

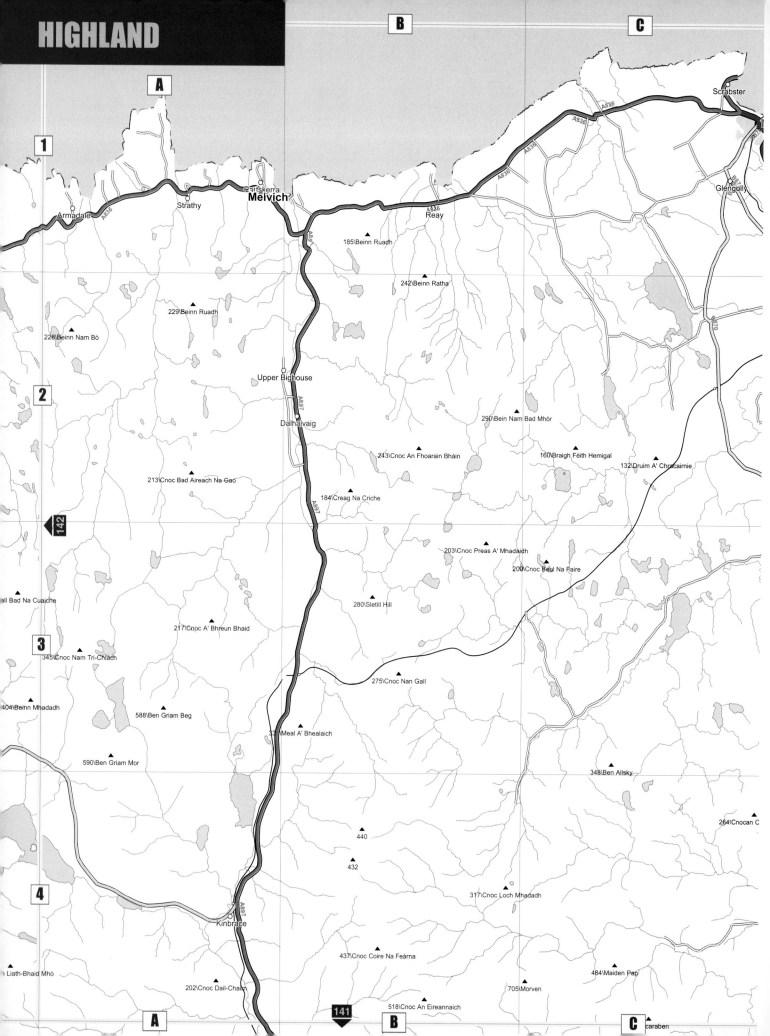

HIGHLAND

A
B
C
1
2
3
4
142
141

Scrabster

Glengolly

Armadale

Strathy

Portskerra

Melvich

Reay

185\Beinn Ruadh

242\Beinn Ratha

229\Beinn Ruadh

228\Beinn Nam Bò

Upper Bighouse

Dalhalvaig

290\Bein Nam Bad Mhòr

243\Cnoc An Fhoarain Bhàin

160\Braigh Féith Hemigal

132\Druim A' Chracairnie

213\Cnoc Bad Aireach Na Gao

184\Creag Na Criche

203\Cnoc Preas A' Mhadaidh

200\Cnoc Beul Na Faire

all Bad Na Cuaiche

280\Sletill Hill

217\Cnoc A' Bhreun Bhaid

345\Cnoc Nam Trì-Chlach

404\Beinn Mhadadh

588\Ben Griam Beg

275\Cnoc Nan Gall

35\Meal A' Bhealaich

590\Ben Griam Mor

348\Ben Alisky

264\Cnocan C

440

432

317\Cnoc Loch Mhadadh

Kinbrace

n Liath-Bhaid Mhò

202\Cnoc Dail-Chairn

437\Cnoc Coire Na Feàrna

484\Maiden Pap

705\Morven

518\Cnoc An Eireannaich

caraben

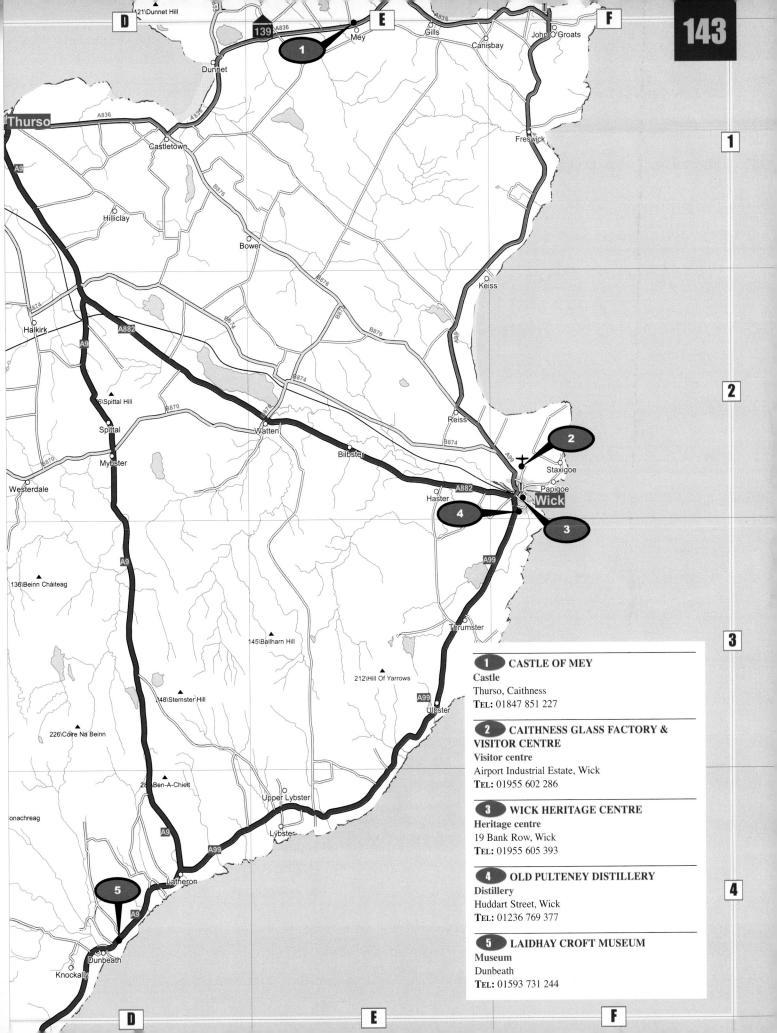

1 **CASTLE OF MEY**
Castle
Thurso, Caithness
TEL: 01847 851 227

2 **CAITHNESS GLASS FACTORY &
VISITOR CENTRE**
Visitor centre
Airport Industrial Estate, Wick
TEL: 01955 602 286

3 **WICK HERITAGE CENTRE**
Heritage centre
19 Bank Row, Wick
TEL: 01955 605 393

4 **OLD PULTENEY DISTILLERY**
Distillery
Huddart Street, Wick
TEL: 01236 769 377

5 **LAIDHAY CROFT MUSEUM**
Museum
Dunbeath
TEL: 01593 731 244

ISLANDS

● ANIMAL ATTRACTIONS
● HERITAGE & CULTURE
○ INDOOR ACTIVITIES
● OUTDOOR ATTRACTIONS
● OUTDOOR ACTIVITIES
● WATER ACTIVITIES

1 KING CHARLES CASTLE
Castle
Tresco
TEL: 01179 750 700

2 CROMWELL'S CASTLE
Castle
Tresco
TEL: 01179 750 700

3 TRESCO ABBEY GARDENS
Garden
Tresco, Isles of Scilly
TEL: 01720 424 105

4 GARRISON WALLS
Castle
St Mary's
TEL: 01179 750 700

5 BLACK HOUSE MUSEUM
Museum
Arnol
TEL: 01851 710 395

6 CALANAIS STANDING STONES & VISITOR CENTRE
Archaeological site
Callanish
TEL: 01851 621 422

7 MUSEUM NAN EILEAN
Museum
Francis Street, Stornoway
TEL: 01851 703 773

8 DUALCHAS BARRA HERITAGE CENTRE
Heritage centre
Castlebay
TEL: 01871 810 413

9 SHETLAND MUSEUM
Museum
Lower Hillhead, Lerwick
TEL: 01595 695 057

10 JARLSHOF PREHISTORIC & NORSE SETTLEMENT HS
Archaeological site
Sumburgh Head
TEL: 01950 460 112

11 MAES HOWE HS
Historic building
Stenness
TEL: 01856 761 606

12 ST MAGNUS CATHEDRAL
Cathedral
Broad Street, Kirkwall
TEL: 01856 874 894

13 HIGHLAND PARK DISTILLERY
Distillery
Holm Road, Kirkwall
TEL: 01856 874 619

14 BISHOP'S & EARL'S PALACES HS
Historic building
Kirkwall
TEL: 01856 875 461

15 TANKERNESS HOUSE MUSEUM
Museum
Broad Street, Kirkwall
TEL: 01856 873 191

16 ORKNEY MARITIME & NATURAL HISTORY MUSEUM
Museum
Alfred Street, Stromness
TEL: 01856 850 025

17 BALFOUR CASTLE
Castle
Shapinsay
TEL: 01856 711 282

18 ORKNEY FARM & FOLK MUSEUM
Museum
Harray
TEL: 01856 771 411

19 SKARA BRAE HS
Historic building
Sandwick, St Margarets Hope
TEL: 0131 668 8800

Stenness Loch, Orkney. Map 144

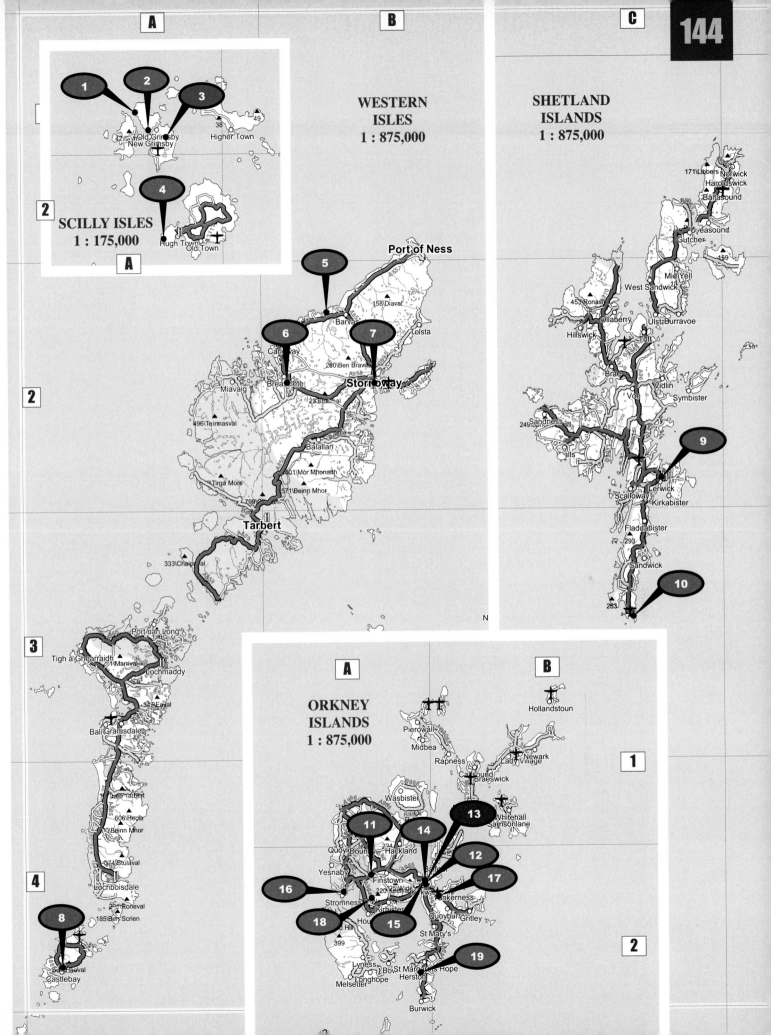

A

B

C

1

2

3

4

WESTERN
ISLES
1 : 875,000

SHETLAND
ISLANDS
1 : 875,000

SCILLY ISLES
1 : 175,000

Old Grimsby
New Grimsby
Higher Town
42
38
49

Hugh Town
Old Town

Port of Ness
158\Diaval
Barvas
Lolsta
Carloway
280\Ben Bravas
Breaclete
Stornoway
233\Eirl al
496\Teinnasval
Miavaig
Balallan
401\Mòr Mhonadh
Tirga More
571\Beinn Mhor
799\Cain
Tarbert
333\Chaipaval

Port nan Long
Marrival
Tigh a Ghearraidh
Lochmaddy
347\Eaval
Bail Gramsdale
Ben Tarbert
606\Hecla
20\Beinn Mhor
374\Stulaval
Lochboisdale
Roneval
185\Ben Scrien
Beoval
Castlebay

171\Libbers Norwick
Haroldswick
Baltasound
Uyeasound
Gutcher
159
Mid Yell
West Sandwick
453\Ronas
Ollaberry
Burravoe
Hillswick
Ulsta
Toft
Brae
Vidlin
Voe
Symbister
249\Sandness Hill
als
Lerwick
Scalloway
Kirkabister
Fladdabister
293
Sandwick
283

ORKNEY
ISLANDS
1 : 875,000

Hollandstoun
Pierowall
Midbea
Rapness
Lady Village
Newark
Calfsound
Braeswick
Whitehall
Samsonlane
Wasbister
Quoyl Doun y
Hackland
224
Yesnaby
Finstown
Bal n
Quoyburr Gritley
Stromness
Kirbister
25\Wid
Kirkwall
Tankerness
Orphir
Kirbister
Houb
Hill
St Mary's
399
Lyness
St Margaret's Hope
Herston
Melsetter
Longhope
Burwick

ISLANDS

1 GIBBS OF THE GROVE
Museum
Andreas Road, Ramsey   TEL: 01624 648 000

2 CURRAGHS WILDLIFE PARK
Wildlife park
Ballaugh   TEL: 01624 897 323

3 GREAT LAXEY WHEEL & MINES TRAIL
Unusual
Laxey   TEL: 01624 648 000

4 PEEL CASTLE TRAIL
Castle
St Patrick's Isle, Peel   TEL: 01624 648 000

5 HOUSE OF MANANNAN
Museum
Peel   TEL: 01624 648 000

6 ODIN'S RAVEN
Museum
Manx Museum, Kingswood Grove, Douglas   TEL: 01624 675 522

7 ISLANDS TREASURE HOUSE MANX MUSEUM
Museum
Douglas   TEL: 01624 648 000

8 ISLE OF MAN RAILWAYS
Railway
Strathallan Crescent, Douglas   TEL: 01624 663 366

9 ISLE OF MAN RAILWAY MUSEUM
Museum
Port Erin Station, Strand Road, Port Erin   TEL: 01624 662 525

10 CASTLE RUSHEN KINGS & LORDS OF MANN
Castle
Castletown   TEL: 01624 648 000

11 PEGGY STORY
Museum
Castletown   TEL: 01624 648 000

12 CREGNEASH VILLAGE FOLK MUSEUM
Museum
Cregneash   TEL: 01624 648 000

13 LE FRIQUET BUTTERFLY CENTRE
Butterfly farm
Le Friquet Castel   TEL: 01481 543 78

14 CANDIE GARDENS
Garden
Candie Road, St Peter Port   TEL: 01481 720 904

15 GUERNSEY MUSEUM & ART GALLERY
Museum
St Peter Port   TEL: 01481 726 518

16 HAUTEVILLE HOUSE-MAISON D'EXIL DE VICTOR HUGO
Historic house
38 Hauteville, St Peter Port   TEL: 01481 721 911

17 CASTLE CORNET
Castle
St Peter Port   TEL: 01481 721 657

18 GERMAN MILITARY UNDERGROUND HOSPITAL AND AMMUNITION STORE
Museum
Rue Des Buttes, St Andrew   TEL: 01481 239 100

19 GUERNSEY BIRD GARDENS
Garden
La Villiaze, St Andrews   TEL: 01481 236 690

20 THE ART PARK
Garden
Sausmarez Manor St Martin   TEL: 01481 235 571

21 GERMAN OCCUPATION MUSEUM
Museum
Les Houards Forest   TEL: 01481 238 205

22 JERSEY ZOOLOGICAL PARK
Zoo
Les Augres Manor, Trinity   TEL: 01534 860 000

23 HAMPTONNE COUNTRY LIFE MUSEUM
Museum
La Rue de la Patente, St Lawrence   TEL: 01534 863 955

24 ERIC YOUNG ORCHID FOUNDATION
Garden
Victoria Village, Trinity   TEL: 01534 861 963

25 GERMAN UNDERGROUND HOSPITAL
Museum
Les Charrieres Malorey, St Lawrence   TEL: 01534 863 442

26 ST PETER'S BUNKER MUSEUM
Museum
La Petite Rue de L'Eglise, St Peter   TEL: 01534 481 048

27 MONT ORGUEIL CASTLE
Castle
La Route de la Cote, St Martin   TEL: 01534 853 292

28 FORT GREY SHIPWRECK MUSEUM
Museum
Rocquaine Bay, St Pierre Du Bois   TEL: 01481 726 518

29 LA HOUGUE BIE MUSEUM
Museum
Princes Tower Road, St Saviour   TEL: 01534 853 823

30 JERSEY MUSEUM
Museum
Weighbridge, St Helier   TEL: 01534 633 300

31 MARITIME MUSEUM
Museum
New North Quay, St Helier   TEL: 01534 811 043

32 ELIZABETH CASTLE
Castle
La Rue de la Patente, St Lawrence   TEL: Not available

33 SAMARES MANOR
Historic house
La Grande Route de St Clement, St Clement   TEL: 01534 870 551

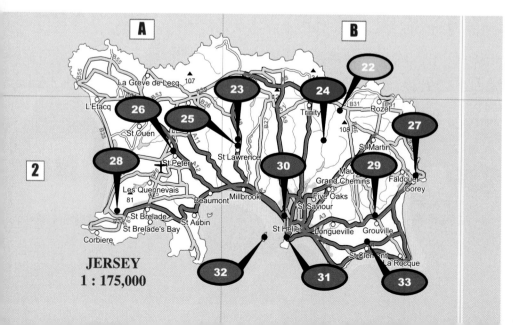

JERSEY
1 : 175,000

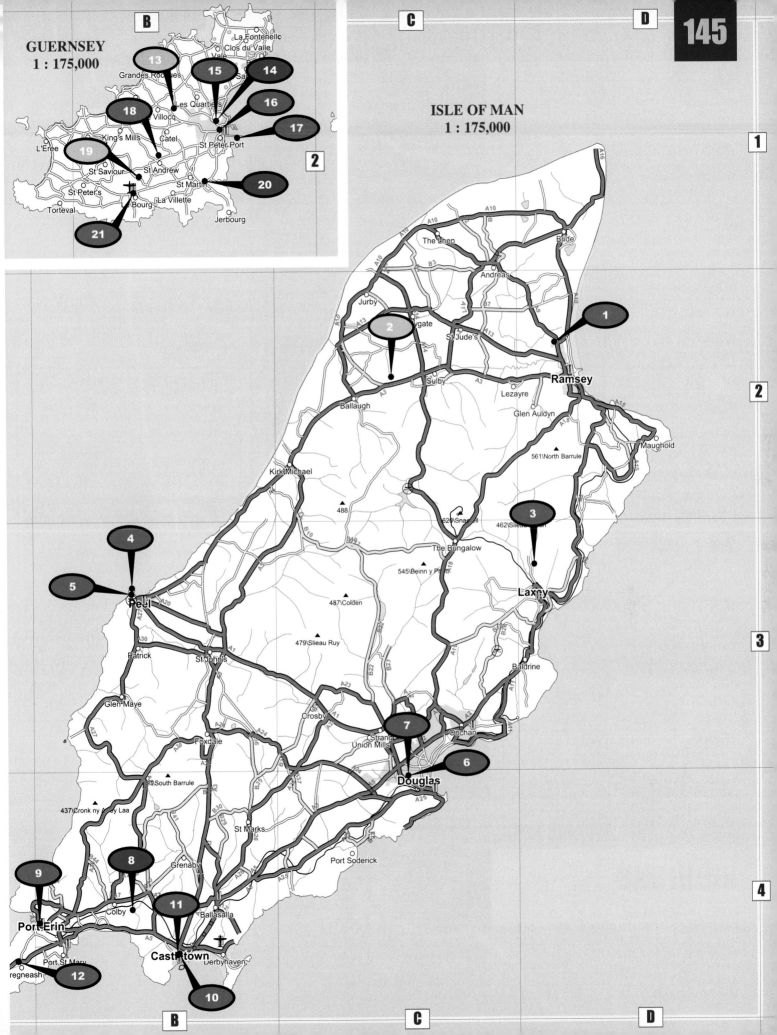

GUERNSEY
1 : 175,000

ISLE OF MAN
1 : 175,000

B C D

1

2

3

4

Guernsey labels: La Fontenello, Clos du Valle, Vale, Grandes Rocques, Les Quartiers, Villocq, King's Mills, Catel, St Peter Port, L'Eree, St Saviour, St Andrew, St Peter's, La Villette, St Martin, Torteval, Le Bourg, Jerbourg

Guernsey numbered markers: 13, 15, 14, 18, 16, 17, 19, 20, 21

Isle of Man labels: The Lhen, Bride, Andreas, Jurby, Ballaugh, Sulby, Lezayre, Glen Auldyn, Ramsey, Maughold, 561\North Barrule, Kirk Michael, 488, 620\Snaefell, 462\Slieau Dhoo, The Bungalow, 545\Beinn y Phott, Laxey, 487\Colden, Peel, Patrick, St John's, 479\Slieau Ruy, Baldrine, Glen Maye, Crosby, Foxdale, Union Mills, Onchan, Douglas, South Barrule, 437\Cronk ny Arrey Laa, St Marks, Port Soderick, Grenaby, Colby, Ballasalla, Port Erin, Port St Mary, Cregneash, Castletown, Derbyhaven

Isle of Man numbered markers: 1, 2, 3, 4, 5, 6, 7, 8, 9, 10, 11, 12

BERKS · LONDON · MIDDX · SURREY

● ANIMAL ATTRACTIONS
● HERITAGE & CULTURE
○ INDOOR ACTIVITIES
● OUTDOOR ATTRACTIONS
● OUTDOOR ACTIVITIES
● WATER ACTIVITIES

1 **FANTASY ISLAND PLAYCENTRE**
Theme park
Vale Farm, Watford Road, Wembley
Tel: 020 8904 9044

2 **WEMBLEY STADIUM TOURS**
Football ground
Empire Way, Wembley
Tel: 020 8902 8833

3 **PITSHANGER MANOR & GALLERY**
Historic house
Mattock Lane, Ealing, London
Tel: 020 8567 1227

4 **BOSTON MANOR HOUSE**
Historic house
1-19 Boston Manor Road, Brentford
Tel: 020 8560 5441

5 **OSTERLEY PARK NT**
Country park
Jersey Road, Isleworth
Tel: 020 8568 7714

6 **MUSICAL MUSEUM**
Museum
368 High Street, Brentford
Tel: 020 8560 8108

7 **ROYAL BOTANIC GARDENS KEW**
Garden
Kew, Richmond
Tel: 020 8940 1171

8 **WINDSOR CASTLE**
Castle
Windsor
Tel: 01753 831 118

9 **SYON HOUSE & PARK**
Historic house
Brentford
Tel: 020 8560 0881

10 **FROGMORE GARDENS**
Garden
Windsor
Tel: 01753 868 286

11 **TWICKENHAM EXPERIENCE & MUSEUM OF RUGBY**
Museum
Rugby Football Union, Rugby Road, Twickenham
Tel: 020 8892 2000

12 **ISABELLA PLANTATION**
Garden
Richmond Park, Richmond
Tel: 020 8948 3209

13 **MARBLE HILL HOUSE EH**
Historic house
Richmond Road, Twickenham
Tel: 020 8892 5115

14 **HAM HOUSE NT**
Garden
Ham, Richmond
Tel: 020 8940 1950

15 **STRAWBERRY HILL HORACE WALPOLE'S GOTHIC VILLA**
Historic house
Waldegrave Road, Twickenham
Tel: 020 8240 4224

16 **RUNNYMEDE**
Country park
Coopers Hill Lane, Egham
Tel: 01784 432 891

17 **SAVILL GARDEN, WINDSOR GREAT PARK** Garden
Access via Wick Lane, Englefield Green, Egham, Surrey.
Tel: 01753 847 518
Email: savillgarden@crownestate.org.uk
Web: www.savillgarden.co.uk
Tranquil 35-acre garden within Windsor Great Park. Spectacular spring displays in the woodland; sweepng summer herbaceous borders and formal rose beds; superb autumn leaf colour.

Open: Mar-Oct: 10-6. Nov-Feb: 10-4. Closed Christmas & Boxing Day.
Entry Costs: £5-£3 Child: £2-£1, OAPs: £4.50-£2.50.
Specialities: Rhododendrons and azaleas, Roses, Camellias, Ferns, Herbaceous plants.
Facilities: Toilets, Credit cards, Wheelchair access, Restaurant, Coffee shop, Gift shop, Own gift tokens, Sell plants, Pushchair friendly.

18 **BUSHY PARK**
Country park
London
Tel: Not available

19 **KEMPTON PARK RACECOURSE**
Racecourse
Kempton, Sunbury-on-Thames
Tel: 01932 782 292

20 **HAMPTON COURT PALACE & GARDENS**
Garden
East Molesey
Tel: 020 8781 9500

21 **CHERTSEY MUSEUM**
Museum
The Cedars, 33 Windsor Street, Chertsey
Tel: 01932 565 764

22 **SANDOWN PARK RACECOURSE**
Racecourse
Portsmouth Road, Esher
Tel: 01372 463 072

23 **BROOKLANDS MUSEUM**
Museum
Brooklands Road, Weybridge
Tel: 01932 857 381

24 **CLAREMONT HOUSE**
Historic house
Claremont Drive, Esher
Tel: 01372 467 841

25 **CLAREMONT LANDSCAPE GARDEN NT**
Garden
Portsmouth Road, Esher
Tel: 01372 467 806

26 **CHESSINGTON WORLD OF ADVENTURE**
Theme park
Chessington
Tel: 01372 729 560

27 **PAINSHILL LANDSCAPE GARDEN**
Garden
Painshill Park Trust, Portsmouth Road, Cobham
Tel: 01932 868 113

28 **WISLEY GARDEN, ROYAL HORTICULTURAL SOCIETY**
Garden
Wisley, Woking, Surrey, GU23 6QB.
Tel: 01483 224 234
Web: www.rhs.org.uk
Whatever the season, RHS Garden Wisley demonstrates British gardening at its best with 240 acres of glorious garden.
Open: Mon-Fri, 10-6 (or sunset), Sat-Sun 9-6 (or sunset), RHS members only on Sun. Closed Christmas Day.
Entry Costs: £6, Child: £2 Under 6s free.
Specialities: Alpines, Fruit & fruit trees, Roses. Herbaceous plants, Rhododendrons and azaleas.
Facilities: Toilets, Credit cards, Wheelchair access, Restaurant, Gift tokens, Bookshop, Gift shop, Pushchair friendly.

29 **POLESDEN LACEY NT**
Historic house
Great Bookham, Dorking
Tel: 01372 452 048

30 **HATCHLANDS PARK NT**
Historic house
East Clandon, Guildford
Tel: 01483 222 482

31 **BOX HILL NT**
Country park
The Old Fort, Box Hill Road, Tadworth
Tel: 01306 742 809

32 **CLANDON PARK NT**
Garden
West Clandon, Guildford
Tel: 01483 222 482

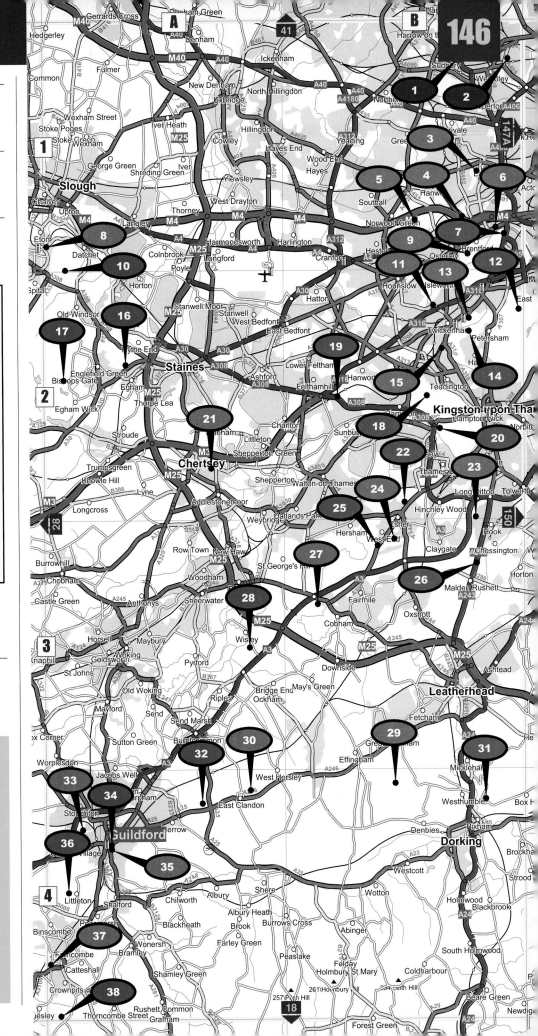

Help us help you

mention the *Days Out Atlas* when visiting anywhere on this page.

● ANIMAL ATTRACTIONS
● HERITAGE & CULTURE
◯ INDOOR ACTIVITIES
● OUTDOOR ATTRACTIONS
● OUTDOOR ACTIVITIES
● WATER ACTIVITIES

1 HOLLAND PARK
Garden
The Stable Yard, Ilchester Place, Kensington
TEL: 020 7602 2226

2 LINLEY SAMBOURNE HOUSE
Historic house
18 Stafford Terrace, Kensington, London
TEL: 020 7937 0663

3 LEIGHTON HOUSE
Historic house
12 Holland Park Road, London
TEL: 020 7602 3316

4 FULLER'S GRIFFIN BREWERY TOURS
Boat trip
Chiswick Lane, London
TEL: 020 8996 2063

5 HOGARTH'S HOUSE
Museum
Hogarth Lane, Great West Road, Chiswick
TEL: 020 8994 6757

6 RAM BREWERY VISITOR CENTRE
Visitor centre
The Brewery Tap, 68 Wandsworth High Street,
London
TEL: 020 8875 7005

7 WIMBLEDON WINDMILL MUSEUM
Mill
Windmill Road, Wimbledon Common, London
TEL: 020 8947 2825

10 WIMBLEDON SOCIETY'S MUSEUM
Museum
22 Ridgway, Wimbledon, London
TEL: 020 8296 9914

11 SOUTHSIDE HOUSE
Historic house
3-4 Woodhayes Road, Wimbledon Common, London
TEL: 020 8946 7643

8 WIMBLEDON LAWN TENNIS TOUR
Tour
Centre Court, All England Club, Church Road,
Wimbledon, SW19 5AE.
TEL: 020 8946 6131
EMAIL: MUSEUM@AELTC.COM
WEB: www.wimbledon.org/museum

Professionally guided tour, includes the Fred Perry Statue, No 1 Court, The Millennium Building, Press Interview Room, Centre Court and finishes in the museum. Pre-booking essential.
OPEN: Mar 29-Jun 4 & Jul 15-Sep 15; open daily.
Sep 22-Oct 27: Sat-Sun.
ENTRY COSTS: £12.75, Child: £10.75, OAPs: £11.75.
SPECIALITIES: Guided tours available.
FACILITIES: Coffee shop, Credit cards, Gift shop, Toilets.

9 WIMBLEDON LAWN TENNIS MUSEUM
Museum
Centre Court, All England Club, Church Road,
Wimbledon, SW19 5AE.
TEL: 020 8946 6131
EMAIL: MUSEUM@AELTC.COM
WEB: www.wimbledon.org/museum

WIMBLEDON
LAWN TENNIS MUSEUM

With views of the Centre Court, the Championship trophies and footage of the great players in action. The museum also includes memorabilia from recent champions, equipment and paintings.
OPEN: Open daily 10.30-5. During Championships museum only open to tournament visitors. Closed Middle Sun of Championships, Mon after the Championships also Dec 24-26 & Jan 1.
ENTRY COSTS: £5.50, Child: £3.50, OAPs: £4.50.
SPECIALITIES: Events held, Guided tours available.
FACILITIES: Coffee shop, Credit cards, Gift shop, Toilets, Wheelchair access.

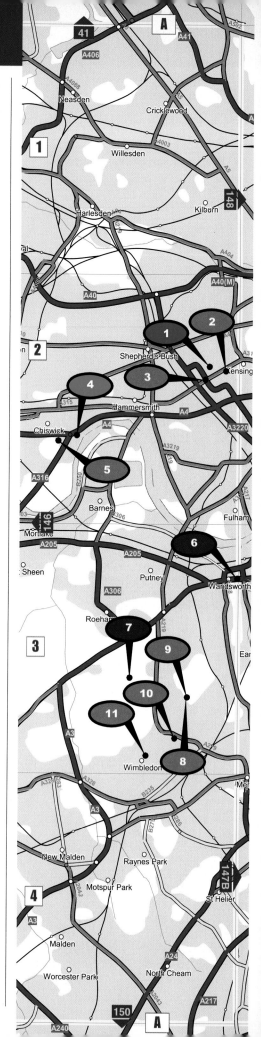

1 **DISCOVERY ZONE**
Adventure & activity centre
St Johns Hill, Clapham, London
TEL: 020 7223 1717

2 **WANDSWORTH MUSEUM**
Museum
11 Garratt Lane, Wandsworth, London
TEL: 020 8871 7074

3 **WANDLE INDUSTRIAL MUSEUM**
Museum
The Vestry Hall Annexe, London Road, Mitcham
TEL: 020 8648 0127

4 **CAREW MANOR & DOVECOTE**
Historic house
Church Road, Wallington
TEL: 020 8770 4781

5 **HONEYWOOD HERITAGE CENTRE**
Museum
Honeywood Walk, Carshalton
TEL: 020 8770 4297

Bank of England Museum, London, Map 149-28

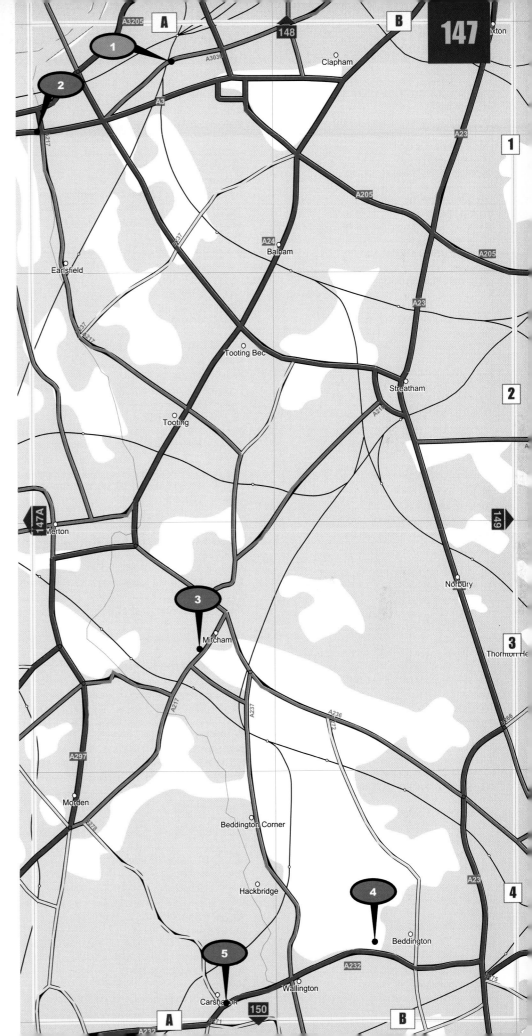

LONDON

- ANIMAL ATTRACTIONS
- HERITAGE & CULTURE
- INDOOR ACTIVITIES
- OUTDOOR ATTRACTIONS
- OUTDOOR ACTIVITIES
- WATER ACTIVITIES

1 HIGHGATE CEMETERY
Historic building
Swains Lane, London TEL: 020 8340 1834

2 BURGH HOUSE
Historic house
New End Square, London TEL: 020 7431 0144

3 KEATS HOUSE
Historic building
Keats Grove, Hampstead, London TEL: 020 7435 2062

4 FREUD MUSEUM
Museum
20 Maresfield Gardens, Hampstead, London
TEL: 020 7435 2002

5 JEWISH MUSEUM
Museum
129-131 Albert Street, Camden, London
TEL: 020 7284 1997

6 LONDON ZOO
Zoo
Regent's Park, London TEL: 020 7722 3333

7 LORD'S TOUR
Cricket ground
Lord's Ground, London TEL: 020 7432 1033

8 REGENT'S PARK & QUEEN MARY`S ROSE GARDEN
Garden
Inner Circle, Regent's Park, London
TEL: 020 7298 2000

9 DICKENS HOUSE MUSEUM
Historic house
48 Doughty Street, London TEL: 020 7405 2127

10 SHERLOCK HOLMES MUSEUM
Historic house
221b Baker Street, London TEL: 020 7935 8866

11 MADAME TUSSAUD'S
Museum
Marylebone Road, London TEL: 020 7487 0200

12 LONDON PLANETARIUM
Museum
Marylebone Road, London TEL: 020 7935 6861

13 POLLOCK'S TOY MUSEUM
Museum
1 Scala Street, London TEL: 020 7636 3452

14 BRITISH MUSEUM
Museum
Great Russell Street, London TEL: 020 7636 1555

15 WALLACE COLLECTION
Gallery
Hertford House, Manchester Square, London
TEL: 020 7935 0627

16 DR JOHNSON'S HOUSE
Historic building
17 Gough Square, London TEL: 020 7353 3745

17 BBC EXPERIENCE
Education Centre
Broadcasting House, Oxford Circus, London
TEL: 0870 603 0304

18 APSLEY HOUSE
Museum
Hyde Park Corner, London TEL: 020 7499 5676

19 LONDON TRANSPORT MUSEUM
Museum
Covent Garden Piazza, Covent Garden, London
TEL: 020 7836 8557

20 LONDON TOY & MODEL MUSEUM
Museum
21-23 Craven Hill, London TEL: 020 7706 8000

21 COURTAULD GALLERY
Gallery
Somerset House, The Strand, London
TEL: 020 7848 2526

22 ROCK CIRCUS
Museum
The London Pavilion, 1 Piccadilly Circus, London
TEL: 020 7734 7203

23 NATIONAL PORTRAIT GALLERY
Gallery
2 St Martin's Place, London TEL: 020 7306 0055

24 FARADAY'S LABORATORY & MUSEUM
Museum
21 Albemarle Street, London TEL: 020 7409 2992

25 NATIONAL GALLERY
Gallery
Trafalgar Square, London TEL: 020 7747 2885

26 ROYAL ACADEMY OF ARTS
Gallery
Burlington House, Piccadilly, London
TEL: 020 7300 8000

27 BATEAUX LONDON
Boat trip
Embankment Pier, Victoria Embankment, London
TEL: 020 7925 2215

28 MUSEUM OF THE MOVING IMAGE
Museum
South Bank, Waterloo, London TEL: 020 7401 2636

29 HORSE GUARDS PARADE
Historic building
Whitehall, London TEL: 020 7414 2271

30 GREEN PARK
Country park
London TEL: Not available

31 SPENCER HOUSE
Historic house
27 St James's Place, London TEL: 020 7499 8620

32 BANQUETING HOUSE
Historic house
London TEL: 020 7839 7569

33 KENSINGTON PALACE & GARDENS
Historic house
Kensington Palace, London TEL: 020 7376 2452

34 FA PREMIER LEAGUE HALL OF FAME
Museum
Riverside Building, Westminster Bridge Rd, London
TEL: 020 7654 7910

35 LONDON EYE
Unusual
Riverside Building, Westminster Bridge Rd, London
TEL: 020 7654 0800

36 DALI UNIVERSE
Gallery
County Hall, Riverside Building, London
TEL: 020 7620 2720

37 ST JAMES'S PARK
Garden
London TEL: 020 7930 1793

38 LONDON AQUARIUM
Aquarium
County Hall, Westminster Bridge Road, London
TEL: 020 7967 8000

39 LONDON BRASS RUBBING CENTRE
Brass rubbing
The Crypt, St Martins in the Field Church, London
TEL: 020 7930 9306

40 BUCKINGHAM PALACE
Historic house
Buckingham Palace Rd, London TEL: 020 7839 1377

41 WESTMINSTER-GREENWICH THAMES BOAT PASSENGER SERVICES
Boat trip
Westminster Pier, Victoria Embankment, London
TEL: 020 7930 4097

42 CABINET WAR ROOMS
Historic building
Clive Steps, King Charles Street, London
TEL: 020 7930 6961

43 ROYAL MINT SOVEREIGN GALLERY
Museum
7 Grosvenor Gardens, London TEL: 020 7592 8601

44 FLORENCE NIGHTINGALE MUSEUM
Museum
Gassiot House, 2 Lambeth Palace Road, London
TEL: 020 7620 0374

45 PALACE OF WESTMINSTER
Historic building
London TEL: 020 7219 4272

46 WESTMINSTER ABBEY
Cathedral
Parliament Square, London TEL: 020 7222 5152

47 SCIENCE MUSEUM
Museum
Exhibition Road, London   TEL: 020 7942 4455

48 VICTORIA & ALBERT MUSEUM
Museum
South Kensington, London   TEL: 020 7942 2000

49 WESTMINSTER CATHEDRAL
Cathedral
Victoria Street, London   TEL: 020 7798 9055

50 NATURAL HISTORY MUSEUM
Museum
Cromwell Road, London   TEL: 020 7942 5000

51 TATE GALLERY
Gallery
Millbank, London   TEL: 020 7887 8008

52 CHELSEA FOOTBALL CLUB
Football tour
Stamford Bridge, Fulham Road, London
    TEL: 020 7915 2222

53 ROYAL HOSPITAL MUSEUM
Museum
Royal Hospital Road, Chelsea, London
    TEL: 020 7730 0161

54 NATIONAL ARMY MUSEUM
Museum
Royal Hospital Road, Chelsea, London
    TEL: 020 7730 0717

55 CARLYLE'S HOUSE NT
Historic building
24 Cheyne Row, Chelsea, London TEL: 020 7352 7087

56 LINDSEY HOUSE
Historic house
99-100 Cheyne Walk, London   TEL: Not available

57 BATTERSEA PARK CHILDREN'S ZOO
Zoo
London   TEL: 020 8871 7540

58 BATTERSEA PARK
Country park
Battersea, London   TEL: 020 8871 7530

Help us help you
mention the
Days Out Atlas
when visiting
anywhere on this page.

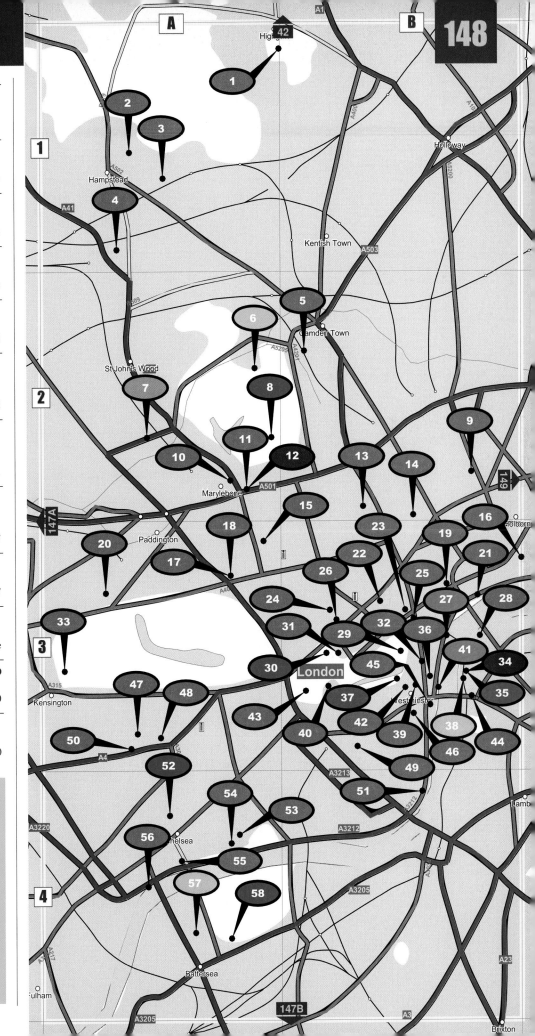

1 FINSBURY PARK
Country park
Seven Sisters Road, London
TEL: Not available

2 SUTTON HOUSE
Historic house
2 & 4 Homerton High Street, Hackney, London
TEL: 020 8986 2264

3 PLASHET PARK ZOO
Zoo
Rutland Road, Forest Gate, London
TEL: 020 8503 5994

4 GEFFRYE MUSEUM HERB GARDEN
Garden
Kingsland Road, London
TEL: 020 7739 9893

5 BETHNAL GREEN MUSEUM OF CHILDHOOD
Museum
Cambridge Heath Road, London
TEL: 020 8983 5200

6 WESLEY'S CHAPEL MUSEUM & HOUSE
Historic building
49 City Road, London
TEL: 020 7253 2262

7 MUSEUM OF THE ORDER OF ST JOHN
Museum
St John's Gate, St John's Lane, London
TEL: 020 7253 6644

8 GUILDHALL
Historic building
Gresham Street, London
TEL: 020 7606 3030

9 RAGGED SCHOOL MUSEUM
Museum
46-50 Copperfield Road, London
TEL: 020 8980 6405

10 BARBICAN CENTRE
Gallery
Silk Street, London
TEL: 020 7638 8891

11 MUSEUM OF LONDON
Museum
150 London Wall, London
TEL: 020 7814 5777

12 NATIONAL POSTAL MUSEUM
Museum
King Edward Building, King Edward Street, London
TEL: 020 7600 8928

13 ST PAULS CATHEDRAL
Cathedral
The Chapter House, St Pauls Churchyard, London
TEL: 020 7246 8346

14 COLLEGE OF ARMS
Historic building
Queen Victoria Street, London
TEL: 020 7248 2762

15 ALL HALLOWS BY THE TOWER
Historic building
Byward Street, London
TEL: 020 7481 2928

16 TOWER OF LONDON
Historic building
Tower Hill, London
TEL: 020 7709 0765

17 SHAKESPEARE'S GLOBE
Historic building
21 New Globe Walk, Bankside, London
TEL: 020 7401 9919

18 TATE MODERN
Museum
Bankside, London
TEL: 020 788 7888

19 GOLDEN HINDE
Museum
St Mary Overie Dock, Cathedral Street, London
TEL: 020 7403 0123

20 THE CLINK
Museum
1 Clink Street, London
TEL: 020 7378 1558

21 SOUTHWARK CATHEDRAL
Cathedral
Montague Close, London
TEL: 020 7407 3708

22 VINOPOLIS
Entertainment centre
1 Bank End, London
TEL: 020 7940 8300

23 HMS BELFAST
Heritage centre
Morgans Lane, Tooley Street London
TEL: 020 7940 6300

24 LONDON DUNGEON
Museum
Tooley Street, London
TEL: 020 7403 7221

25 OLD OPERATING THEATRE MUSEUM & HERB GARRET
Museum
9a St Thomas Street, Southwark, London
TEL: 020 7955 4791

26 SIR WINSTON CHURCHILL'S BRITAIN AT WAR EXPERIENCE
Museum
64-66 Tooley Street, London
TEL: 020 7403 3171

27 DESIGN MUSEUM
Museum
28 Shad, London
TEL: 020 7940 8790

28 TOWER BRIDGE EXPERIENCE
Historic building
Tower Bridge, London
TEL: 020 7407 9222

29 BANK OF ENGLAND MUSEUM
Museum
Bartholomew Lane, London, Greater London, EC2R 8AH.
TEL: 020 7601 5545
WEB: www.bankofengland.co.uk

Come and enjoy an engrossing mix of money, gold, people, forgery, architecture and fun. You can even handle a real gold bar! Free Admisssion.
OPEN: Mon-Fri 10-5. Closed Weekends, Public & Bank Holidays.

30 BRAMAH TEA & COFFEE MUSEUM
Museum
Maguire Street, Butlers Wharf, London
TEL: 020 7378 0222

31 WINCHESTER PALACE
Historic building
Storey Street, London
TEL: 020 7222 1234

32 THAMES BARRIER VISITORS' CENTRE
Visitor centre
Unity Way London
TEL: 020 8305 4188

33 IMPERIAL WAR MUSEUM
Museum
Lambeth Road, London
TEL: 020 7416 5000

34 CUMING MUSEUM
Museum
155-157 Walworth Road, London
TEL: 020 7701 1342

35 CUTTY SARK CLIPPER SHIP
Museum
Greenwich Pier, King William Walk, Greenwich
TEL: 020 8858 3445

36 LIVESEY MUSEUM
Museum
682 Old Kent Road, London
TEL: 020 7639 5604

37 ROYAL OBSERVATORY GREENWICH
Historic building
Greenwich Park, London
TEL: 020 8858 4422

38 NATIONAL MARITIME MUSEUM
Museum
Romney Road, Greenwich, London
TEL: 020 8858 4422

39 FAN MUSEUM
Museum
12 Crooms Hill, London
TEL: 020 8305 1441

40 BRUNEL'S ENGINE HOUSE
Historic building
Railway Avenue, Rotherhithe, London
TEL: 020 8248 3545

41 HORNIMAN MUSEUM & GARDENS
Museum
100 London Road, Forest Hill, London
TEL: 020 8699 1872

42 CRYSTAL PALACE PARK
Garden
Crystal Palace Road, London
TEL: 020 8313 4407

43 PRIORY GARDENS
Garden
High Street, Orpington
TEL: 020 8464 3333

44 OLD PALACE
Historic house
Old Palace Road, Croydon
TEL: 020 8688 2027

45 CROYDON CLOCKTOWER
Historic building
Katharine Street, Croydon
TEL: 020 8253 1030

Help us help you

mention the *Days Out Atlas* when visiting anywhere on this page.

SURREY · KENT

1 CARSHALTON HOUSE
Historic house
St Philomena's School, Pound Street, Carshalton
TEL: 020 8770 4781

2 LITTLE HOLLAND HOUSE
Historic house
40 Beeches Avenue, Carshalton
TEL: 020 8770 4781

3 BOURNE HALL MUSEUM
Museum
Spring Street, Ewell, Epsom
TEL: 020 8394 1734

4 HISTORICAL WALKS OF LONDON TOURS
Guided Tours/Walks
3 Florence Road, South Croydon
TEL: 020 8668 4019

5 BIGGIN HILL AIRFIELD
Airfield
Biggin Hill, Westerham
TEL: Not available

6 EPSOM RACECOURSE
Racecourse
Epsom Downs, Epsom
TEL: 01372 726 311

7 PRIORY MUSEUM
Museum
Bell Street, Reigate
TEL: 01737 245 065

8 REIGATE HILL & GATTON PARK NT
Country park
Reigate
TEL: 01342 843 225

9 LANGSHOTT MANOR
Garden
Langshott, Gatwick
TEL: 01293 786 680

10 LINGFIELD PARK RACECOURSE
Racecourse
Lingfield
TEL: 01342 834 800

Horse riding

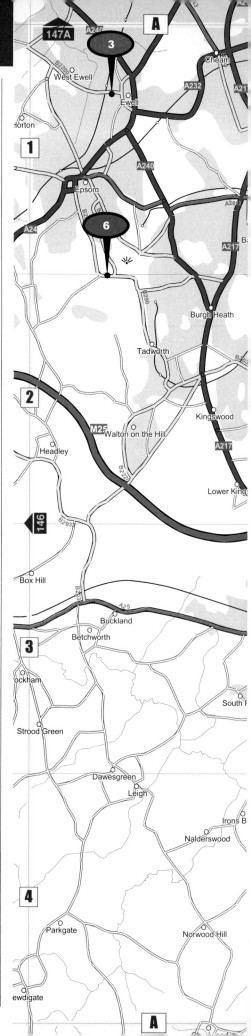

DAYS OUT ATLAS

Sourcing: We originally contacted more than 4,000 companies sourced from the Yellow Pages and Tourist Information Centres. Researchers also visited outlets confirming data for their entry and location. Each outlet contacted was asked to confirm their details and map location. Where companies did not manage to respond in time, we took informed decisions based upon the company name, source information and postcode, and included them where appropriate.

Locations are mapped using GeoConcept software; the post code provides coordinates which gives accuracy to the nearest 100 metres.

Each outlet has been contacted and given the opportunity to be listed in one of three ways; *a basic listing, a standard listing (box and text) or a premier listing (box, text and picture).* The latter two listings are paid entries.

For further information please contact the **Days Out Atlas** on 01603 633 808 or email info@daysoutatlas.co.uk.

HAVE WE MISSED ANYONE?

To ensure the **Days Out Atlas** is as up to date and accurate as possible we would like to hear about anywhere we have missed.

Please complete the form below and send it to:

**Days Out Atlas,
St Faiths House, Mountergate,
Norwich, Norfolk NR1 1PY
Or email: info@daysoutatlas.co.uk
Or fax us on: 01603 632 808
Or visit: www.daysoutatlas.co.uk**

. . . .

NAME OF LOCATION _____

Animal attraction ☐   Heritage & culture ☐   Indoor activity ☐

Outdoor attraction ☐   Outdoor activity ☐   Water activity ☐

Other (please specify) _____

ADDRESS _____

_____

TOWN _____

COUNTY _____ POSTCODE _____

TELEPHONE NUMBER (if known) _____

Please tick this box if you are the manager or owner of the outlet ☐

MR/MRS/MISS NAME _____

ADDRESS _____

_____

TOWN _____

COUNTY _____ POSTCODE _____

EMAIL _____

WEBSITE _____

INDEX
BY OUTLET NAME

GAZETTEER

PLACE	PAGE	GRID
Abbas Combe, Som	14	B2
Abberley, Worcs	48	B2
Abberton, Essex	44	A2
Abberton, Worcs	49	A3
Abbess Roding, Essex	43	A2
Abbey Dore, Heref	36	C1
Abbey Green, Staffs	71	A2
Abbey St Bathans, Border	119	C3
Abbey Town, Cumb	97	E1
Abbey Village, Lancs	86	A4
Abbey Wood, G Lon	30	A1
Abbeystead, Lancs	85	C1
Abbots Bickington, Devon	11	C3
Abbots Bromley, Staffs	59	B1
Abbots Leigh, Som	24	B2
Abbots Ripton, Cambs	52	C1
Abbot's Salford, Warwk	49	B3
Abbotsham, Devon	11	C2
Abbotskerswell, Devon	5	C3
Abbotsley, Cambs	52	C3
Abbott Street, Dorset	14	D4
Abbotts Ann, Hants	26	D4
Abdon, Shrops	57	D4
Aber, Gwyn	77	D4
Aberaeron, Cered	45	F2
Aberangell, Gwyn	56	C2
Aberarder, High	132	B1
Aberargie, Perth	123	D3
Aberarth, Cered	45	F2
Abercarn, Caer	36	A4
Abercastle, Pemb	33	C1
Abercegir, Powys	56	C3
Aberchirder, Aber	139	B3
Abercraf, Powys	35	B2
Abercregan, Neath	35	B4
Abercwmboi, Rhond	35	D3
Abercych, Pemb	45	D4
Abercynon, Rhond	35	D4
Aberdare, Rhond	35	D3
Aberdaron, Gwyn	67	A4
Aberdeen, Aberdeen City	134	D3
Aberdour, Fife	117	B1
Aberdulais, Neath	35	B3
Aberdyfi, Gwyn	56	A3
Aberedw, Powys	46	E3
Abereiddy, Pemb	33	B1
Abererch, Gwyn	67	C4
Aberfan, Merth	35	D3
Aberfeldy, Perth	128	A4
Aberffraw, Angle	67	C1
Aberford, W Yorks	88	B3
Aberfoyle, Stirl	122	B4
Abergavenny, Monm	36	B2
Abergele, Aberc	78	A4
Abergorlech, Carm	34	D1
Abergwesyn, Powys	46	C3
Abergwili, Carm	34	C2
Abergwynfi, Neath	35	C4
Abergynolwyn, Gwyn	56	B2
Aberkenfig, Bridg	22	E1
Aberlady, E Loth	119	A2
Aberlemno, Angus	129	B3
Aberllefenni, Gwyn	56	B2
Aberllynfi, Powys	47	A4
Aberlour, Moray	138	C4
Abermule, Powys	57	A3
Abernant, Carm	34	B1
Abernethy, Perth	123	D3
Abernyte, Perth	124	A1
Aberporth, Cered	45	D3
Abersoch, Gwyn	67	C4
Abersychan, Torf	36	B3
Aberthin, Glam	23	A2
Abertillery, Gwent	36	A3
Abertridwr, Caer	36	A4
Abertridwr, Powys	56	E1
Aberuthven, Perth	123	B3
Aberystwyth, Cered	56	A4
Abingdon, Oxon	39	C4
Abinger, Surrey	146	B4
Abington Pigotts, Cambs	52	C4
Abington, S Lan	109	D3
Ablington, Glouc	38	C3
Abney, Derby	81	C4
Aboyne, Aber	133	E4
Abram, G Man	79	C2
Abridge, Essex	42	C4
Abson, Glouc	25	A2
Abthorpe, Nhants	51	A3
Aby, Lincs	84	C4
Acaster Selby, N York	89	A3
Accrington, Lancs	86	B4
Acha, Argyll	125	C3
Acharacle, High	126	A2
Acharn, High	126	A4
Acharn, Perth	127	E4
Achiltibuie, High	140	C2
Achnacroish, Argyll	121	A1
Achnamara, Argyll	113	F1
Achnasheen, High	136	C2
Achosnich, High	125	E2
Achurch, Nhants	62	B4
Acklam, N York	89	C1
Acklington, Nthumb	106	A1
Ackton, W Yorks	88	B4
Ackworth Moor Top, W Yorks	82	B1
Acle, Norf	66	A2
Acol, Kent	32	C2
Acomb, Nthumb	105	C4
Aconbury, Heref	37	A1
Acton Beauchamp, Heref	48	A3

PLACE	PAGE	GRID
Acton Bridge, Chesh	79	C4
Acton Burnell, Shrops	57	D3
Acton Green, Heref	48	B3
Acton Round, Shrops	58	A3
Acton Trussell, Staffs	59	A1
Acton Turville, Glouc	25	A1
Acton, Chesh	70	A2
Acton, G Lon	147	A2
Acton, Staffs	70	C3
Acton, Suff	54	C4
Adbaston, Staffs	70	B4
Adber, Dorset	14	A2
Adbolton, Notts	73	A3
Adderbury, Oxon	50	B4
Adderley, Shrops	70	A3
Addingham, W Yorks	87	B2
Addington, Bucks	40	C1
Addington, G Lon	150	C1
Addington, Kent	30	B3
Addiscombe, G Lon	149	A4
Addlestonemoor, Surrey	146	A2
Addlethorpe, Lincs	75	C1
Adfa, Powys	56	E3
Adforton, Heref	47	C1
Adisham, Kent	32	B3
Adlestrop, Glouc	39	A1
Adlingfleet, E R of Y	89	C4
Adlington, Lancs	79	C1
Admaston, Shrops	58	A2
Admaston, Staffs	59	B1
Admington, Warwk	49	C3
Adscombe, Som	12	D1
Adstock, Bucks	40	C1
Adversane, W Suss	18	A2
Adwick Le Street, S York	82	C1
Adwick upon Dearne, S York	82	B2
Ae, Dumf	103	D2
Affpuddle, Dorset	8	A1
Afon-wen, Flint	69	A1
Agglethorpe, N York	93	B3
Aike, E R of Y	90	B2
Aiketgate, Cumb	98	C1
Aikton, Cumb	98	A1
Ailey, Heref	47	B3
Ailsworth, Cambs	62	C3
Ainderby Quernhow, N York	93	D3
Aingers Green, Essex	44	B2
Ainstable, Cumb	98	C1
Ainthorpe, N York	94	C1
Aird of Sleat, High	130	D3
Airdrie, N Lan	116	A3
Airmyn, E R of Y	89	B4
Airntully, Perth	123	C1
Airth, Falk	116	C1
Airton, N York	86	C1
Aisby, Lincs	74	B3
Aisby, Lincs	83	C3
Aish, Devon	5	B3
Aish, Devon	5	C4
Aisholt, Som	12	D1
Aiskew, N York	93	C2
Aislaby, Durham	100	C4
Aislaby, N York	95	A3
Aisthorpe, Lincs	83	C4
Akeld, Nthumb	112	A2
Akeley, Bucks	51	A4
Akenham, Suff	55	A3
Albaston, Corn	4	B3
Alberbury, Shrops	57	C2
Albourne, W Suss	18	C3
Albrighton, Shrops	57	D1
Albrighton, Shrops	58	B2
Alburgh, Norf	65	B4
Albury Heath, Surrey	146	A4
Albury, Herts	42	C1
Albury, Surrey	146	A4
Alby Hill, Norf	76	C4
Alcaig, High	137	A2
Alcaston, Shrops	57	C4
Alcester, Warwk	49	B2
Alciston, E Suss	19	B4
Alconbury Weston, Cambs	52	B1
Alconbury, Cambs	52	B1
Aldborough, Norf	76	C4
Aldbourne, Wilts	26	C1
Aldbrough St John, N York	100	A4
Aldbrough, E R of Y	90	D3
Aldbury, Herts	41	A2
Aldcliffe, Lancs	85	C1
Aldclune, Perth	128	B3
Aldeburgh, Suff	55	C2
Aldeby, Norf	66	A3
Aldenham, Herts	41	C4
Alderbury, Wilts	15	B2
Alderford, Norf	65	A1
Alderholt, Dorset	15	A3
Alderley Edge, Chesh	80	B4
Alderley, Glouc	37	C4
Aldermaston, Berks	27	B2
Alderminster, Warwk	49	C3
Aldershot, Hants	28	B4
Alderton, Glouc	38	B1
Alderton, Nhants	51	B3
Alderton, Suff	55	B4
Alderton, Wilts	25	B1
Alderwasley, Derby	72	A2
Aldfield, N York	93	C4
Aldford, Chesh	69	C2
Aldham, Essex	44	A1
Aldham, Suff	54	D3

PLACE	PAGE	GRID
Aldingbourne, W Suss	17	C4
Aldingham, Cumb	91	D4
Aldington, Kent	21	B1
Aldington, Worcs	49	B4
Aldreth, Cambs	53	B1
Aldridge, W Mids	59	B3
Aldringham, Suff	55	C2
Aldsworth, Glouc	38	C3
Aldwark, Derby	71	C2
Aldwark, N York	88	B1
Aldwincle, Nhants	62	B4
Alexandria, Dumb	115	A2
Aley, Som	12	D1
Alfold Crossways, Surrey	18	A1
Alfold, Surrey	18	A1
Alford, Aber	133	E2
Alford, Lincs	84	D4
Alford, Som	14	A1
Alfreton, Derby	72	B2
Alfrick Pound, Worcs	48	B3
Alfrick, Worcs	48	B3
Alfriston, E Suss	19	B4
Algarkirk, Lincs	74	D4
Alhampton, Som	14	A1
Alkborough, Lincs	90	A4
Alkham, Kent	32	C4
Alkmonton, Derby	71	C3
All Cannings, Wilts	26	B3
All Saints South Elmham, Suff	65	B4
All Stretton, Shrops	57	C3
Allaleigh, Devon	5	C4
Allanbank, N Lan	116	B4
Allanton, Border	119	D4
Allanton, N Lan	116	B4
Allen End, Warwk	60	A3
Allendale, Nthumb	99	B1
Allenheads, Nthumb	99	B2
Allen's Green, Herts	42	C2
Allensmore, Heref	47	D4
Aller, Devon	11	F2
Aller, Som	13	B2
Allerby, Cumb	97	D2
Allercombe, Devon	6	B1
Allerford, Som	22	E4
Allerston, N York	95	B3
Allerthorpe, E R of Y	89	C2
Allesley, W Mids	60	B4
Allexton, Leics	61	C3
Allgreave, Chesh	71	A1
Allhallows, Kent	31	B1
Allington, Lincs	74	A3
Allington, Wilts	15	B1
Allington, Wilts	25	B2
Allington, Wilts	26	B3
Allithwaite, Cumb	91	E3
Alloa, Clack	116	B1
Allonby, Cumb	97	D2
Alloway, S Ayrs	108	D3
Allowenshay, Som	13	B3
Alltmawr, Powys	46	E3
Alltwalis, Carm	34	C1
Alltwen, Neath	35	A3
Alltyblaca, Cered	45	F3
Allweston, Dorset	14	A3
Almeley Wooton, Heref	47	B3
Almeley, Heref	47	B3
Almer, Dorset	14	C4
Almholme, S York	82	C1
Almington, Staffs	70	B4
Almondbank, Perth	123	C2
Almondsbury, Glouc	24	C1
Alne, N York	94	A4
Alness, High	137	B1
Alnham, Nthumb	112	A4
Alnmouth, Nthumb	112	C4
Alnwick, Nthumb	112	C4
Alperton, G Lon	146	B1
Alphamstone, Essex	54	B4
Alpheton, Suff	54	B3
Alport, Derby	71	C1
Alpraham, Chesh	70	A2
Alresford, Essex	44	B2
Alrewas, Staffs	60	A1
Alsager, Chesh	70	B2
Alsop en le Dale, Derby	71	C2
Alston, Cumb	99	A1
Alston, Devon	13	A4
Alstone, Glouc	38	B1
Alstonefield, Staffs	71	B2
Alswear, Devon	11	F2
Altandhu, High	140	C2
Altarnun, Corn	4	A2
Althorne, Essex	44	A4
Althorpe, Lincs	83	B1
Altnaharra, High	142	E4
Alton Barnes, Wilts	26	B3
Alton Pancras, Dorset	14	B4
Alton, Derby	72	A1
Alton, Hants	17	A1
Alton, Staffs	71	B3
Altrincham, G Man	80	A3
Alva, Clack	123	A4
Alvah, Aber	139	B2
Alvanley, Chesh	79	B4
Alvecote, Warwk	60	A2
Alvediston, Wilts	14	D2
Alveley, Shrops	58	B4
Alverdiscott, Devon	11	D2
Alverton, Notts	73	C3
Alvescot, Oxon	39	A3

PLACE	PAGE	GRID
Alveston, Glouc	37	B4
Alveston, Warwk	49	C3
Alvingham, Lincs	84	C3
Alvington, Glouc	37	B3
Alwinton, Nthumb	111	C4
Alyth, Perth	128	E4
Ambergate, Derby	72	A2
Amberley, W Suss	18	A3
Amble, Nthumb	112	C4
Ambleside, Cumb	91	E1
Ambleston, Pemb	33	D1
Ambrosden, Oxon	40	A2
Amcotts, Lincs	83	C1
Amersham, Bucks	41	A4
Amesbury, Wilts	26	B4
Amisfield Town, Dumf	103	D2
Amlwch, Angle	77	C3
Ammanford, Carm	34	D2
Ampfield, Hants	16	A2
Ampleforth, N York	94	B3
Ampney St Mary, Glouc	38	C3
Ampney St Peter, Glouc	38	C3
Amport, Hants	26	D4
Ampthill, Beds	52	A4
Ampton, Suff	54	B1
Amroth, Pemb	33	E3
Amulree, Perth	123	B1
Amwell, Herts	41	C2
Ancaster, Lincs	74	B3
Anchor, Shrops	57	A4
Ancroft, Nthumb	112	A1
Ancrum, Border	111	A3
Anderby, Lincs	84	D4
Andover, Hants	26	D4
Andoversford, Glouc	38	B2
Andreas, I of M	145	C1
Anerley, G Lon	149	A4
Angarrack, Corn	1	C1
Angelbank, Shrops	47	D1
Angersleigh, Som	12	D2
Angle, Pemb	33	C3
Angram, N York	89	A2
Anmer, Norf	75	D4
Anmore, Hants	17	A3
Anna Valley, Hants	26	D4
Annan, Dumf	104	A4
Annbank, S Ayrs	108	D3
Annfield Plain, Durham	100	A1
Ansford, Som	14	A1
Ansley, Warwk	60	B3
Anslow Gate, Staffs	60	A1
Anslow, Staffs	60	A1
Anstey, Herts	42	B1
Anstey, Leics	61	A2
Anstruther, Fife	124	C4
Ansty, W Suss	18	C2
Ansty, Warwk	60	C4
Ansty, Wilts	14	D2
Anthonys, Surrey	146	A3
Anthorn, Cumb	104	A4
Antingham, Norf	76	D4
Anton's Gowt, Lincs	74	D3
Antony, Corn	4	B4
Antrobus, Chesh	79	C4
Anwick, Lincs	74	C2
Aperfield, G Lon	150	D1
Apethorpe, Nhants	62	B3
Apley, Lincs	84	A4
Apperknowle, Derby	82	A4
Apperley, Glouc	38	A1
Appin, Argyll	126	C4
Appleby Magna, Leics	60	B2
Appleby, Lincs	83	C1
Appleby-in-Westmorland, Cumb	98	D4
Applecross, High	135	E4
Appledore, Devon	11	D1
Appledore, Kent	21	A2
Appleford, Oxon	40	A4
Appleshaw, Hants	26	D4
Appleton Roebuck, N York	89	A2
Appleton Thorn, Chesh	79	C3
Appleton Wiske, N York	94	A1
Appleton, Oxon	39	C3
Appleton-le-Moors, N York	94	C2
Appleton-le-Street, N York	95	A4
Appletreewick, N York	87	B1
Appley Bridge, Lancs	79	B1
Appley, Som	12	C2
Apse Heath, I of W	10	A2
Apsley End, Beds	41	C1
Arbirlot, Angus	124	D1
Arbroath, Angus	124	D1
Arbuthnott, Aber	129	D2
Archdeacon Newton, Durham	100	A4
Archiestown, Moray	138	B4
Arclid Green, Chesh	70	B1
Ardbeg, Argyll	107	B1
Ardeley, Herts	42	A1
Ardelve, High	131	A1
Arden, Argyll	115	A1
Ardens Grafton, Warwk	49	B3
Ardentinny, Argyll	114	C1
Ardersier, High	137	C3
Ardessie, High	140	C4
Ardgay, High	141	B4
Ardgour, High	126	D3
Ardingly, W Suss	19	A1
Ardington, Oxon	39	C4
Ardleigh Heath, Essex	44	B1

PLACE	PAGE	GRID
Ardleigh, Essex	44	B1
Ardler, Perth	128	E4
Ardley, Oxon	40	A1
Ardlui, Argyll	122	A3
Ardminish, Argyll	107	D1
Ardnadam, Argyll	114	C2
Ardrishaig, Argyll	114	A1
Ardrossan, N Ayrs	108	C1
Ardsley East, W Yorks	88	A4
Ardvasar, High	130	E3
Ardwell, Dumf	96	B1
Arford, Hants	17	B1
Argoed, Caer	36	A3
Arinagour, Argyll	125	C3
Arisaig, High	126	A1
Arkendale, N York	88	B1
Arkesden, Essex	53	B4
Arkholme, Lancs	92	B4
Arkley, G Lon	42	A4
Arksey, S York	82	C1
Arlecdon, Cumb	97	D4
Arlesey, Beds	52	B4
Arley, Chesh	79	C4
Arley, Warwk	60	B4
Arlingham, Glouc	37	C2
Arlington, Devon	11	E1
Arlington, E Suss	19	B3
Armadale, High	143	A1
Armadale, W Loth	116	C3
Armaside, Cumb	97	E3
Armathwaite, Cumb	98	C1
Arminghall, Norf	65	B2
Armitage, Staffs	59	B1
Armston, Nhants	62	B4
Armthorpe, S York	83	A2
Arnabost, Argyll	125	C3
Arncliffe, N York	93	A4
Arncroach, Fife	124	C4
Arne, Dorset	8	C1
Arnesby, Leics	61	A3
Arngask, Perth	123	D3
Arnisdale, High	130	F3
Arnold, E R of Y	90	C3
Arnprior, Stirl	115	C1
Arnside, Cumb	91	E3
Aros, Argyll	125	F4
Arrad Foot, Cumb	91	D3
Arram, E R of Y	90	B2
Arrathorne, N York	93	C2
Arreton, I of W	10	A1
Arrington, Cambs	53	A3
Arrochar, Argyll	121	D4
Arrow, Warwk	49	B2
Arscott, Shrops	57	C2
Arthington, W Yorks	87	C2
Arthingworth, Nhants	61	C4
Arundel, W Suss	18	A3
Asby, Cumb	97	D4
Ascog, Argyll	114	C3
Ascot, Berks	28	B2
Ascott-under-Wychwood, Oxon	39	B2
Asenby, N York	94	A4
Asfordby Hill, Leics	61	B1
Asfordby, Leics	61	B1
Asgarby, Lincs	74	C3
Asgarby, Lincs	75	A1
Ash Green, Surrey	28	B4
Ash Magna, Shrops	69	D3
Ash Mill, Devon	12	A2
Ash Parva, Shrops	69	D3
Ash Priors, Som	12	D2
Ash Thomas, Devon	12	C3
Ash Vale, Surrey	28	B4
Ash, Kent	32	C3
Ash, Som	13	C2
Ash, Surrey	28	B4
Ashampstead Green, Berks	27	B1
Ashampstead, Berks	27	B1
Ashbocking Green, Suff	55	A3
Ashbocking, Suff	55	A3
Ashbourne, Derby	71	C3
Ashbrittle, Som	12	C2
Ashburton, Devon	5	B3
Ashbury, Devon	11	D4
Ashbury, Oxon	26	C1
Ashby by Partney, Lincs	75	B1
Ashby cum Fenby, Lincs	84	B2
Ashby de la Launde, Lincs	74	B2
Ashby Folville, Leics	61	B2
Ashby Parva, Leics	61	A4
Ashby Puerorum, Lincs	75	A1
Ashby St Ledgers, Nhants	50	C2
Ashby St Mary, Norf	65	B3
Ashby-de-la-Zouch, Leics	60	B1
Ashchurch, Glouc	38	B1
Ashcombe, Devon	6	A2
Ashcott, Som	13	B1
Ashdon, Essex	53	C4
Ashe, Hants	27	B4
Asheldham, Essex	44	A3
Ashen, Essex	54	A4
Ashendon, Bucks	40	B2
Asheridge, Bucks	41	A3
Ashfield Green, Suff	55	B1
Ashfield, Suff	55	A2
Ashford Bowdler, Shrops	47	D1
Ashford Carbonel, Shrops	47	D1
Ashford Hill, Hants	27	B3
Ashford in the Water, Derby	71	C1
Ashford, Devon	10	A1

PLACE	PAGE	GRID
Ashford, Devon	11	D1
Ashford, Kent	32	A4
Ashford, Surrey	146	A2
Ashill, Devon	12	C3
Ashill, Norf	64	B2
Ashill, Som	13	A3
Ashingdon, Essex	43	C4
Ashington, Nthumb	106	A2
Ashington, Som	13	C2
Ashkirk, Border	110	D3
Ashleworth Quay, Glouc	38	A1
Ashleworth, Glouc	37	C1
Ashley Green, Bucks	41	B3
Ashley, Cambs	54	A2
Ashley, Chesh	80	A3
Ashley, Glouc	38	B4
Ashley, Hants	15	C1
Ashley, Kent	32	C4
Ashley, Nhants	61	C4
Ashley, Staffs	70	B4
Ashley, Wilts	25	B2
Ashmansworth, Hants	27	A3
Ashmansworthy, Devon	11	C3
Ashmore, Dorset	14	C3
Ashorne, Warwk	50	A2
Ashover, Derby	72	A1
Ashow, Warwk	50	A1
Ashperton, Heref	48	A4
Ashprington, Devon	5	C4
Ashreigney, Devon	11	E3
Ashtead, Surrey	146	B3
Ashton Common, Wilts	25	B3
Ashton Keynes, Wilts	38	C4
Ashton under Hill, Worcs	49	A4
Ashton, Chesh	69	D1
Ashton, Corn	1	C2
Ashton, Devon	5	C1
Ashton, Heref	47	D2
Ashton, Nhants	51	B3
Ashton, Nhants	62	B4
Ashton-in-Makerfield, G Man	79	B2
Ashton-under-Lyne, G Man	81	A2
Ashurst, Hants	15	C3
Ashurst, Kent	19	B1
Ashurst, W Suss	18	B3
Ashurstwood, W Suss	19	A1
Ashwater, Devon	11	C4
Ashwell, Herts	52	C4
Ashwell, Rutland	62	A2
Ashwellthorpe, Norf	65	A3
Ashwick, Som	24	C4
Ashwicken, Norf	64	A1
Askam in Furness, Cumb	91	C3
Askern, S York	82	C1
Askerswell, Dorset	7	C1
Askett, Bucks	40	C3
Askham Bryan, N York	89	A2
Askham Richard, N York	89	A2
Askham, Cumb	98	C3
Askham, Notts	83	B4
Askrigg, N York	93	A2
Askwith, N York	87	C2
Aslackby, Lincs	74	C4
Aslockton, Notts	73	C3
Aspatria, Cumb	97	E2
Aspenden, Herts	42	B1
Aspley Guise, Beds	51	C4
Aspley Heath, Beds	51	C4
Aspull, G Man	79	C1
Asselby, E R of Y	89	B4
Assington Green, Suff	54	A3
Assington, Suff	54	C4
Astbury, Chesh	70	C1
Astcote, Nhants	51	A3
Asterley, Shrops	57	C2
Asterton, Shrops	57	C4
Asthall Leigh, Oxon	39	B2
Asthall, Oxon	39	B2
Astley, G Man	80	A2
Astley, Shrops	57	D1
Astley, Warwk	60	B4
Astley, Worcs	48	B2
Aston Abbotts, Bucks	40	C2
Aston Botterell, Shrops	58	A4
Aston Cantlow, Warwk	49	B2
Aston Crews, Heref	37	B1
Aston End, Herts	42	A1
Aston le Walls, Nhants	50	B3
Aston Magna, Glouc	49	C4
Aston Munslow, Shrops	57	D4
Aston on Clun, Shrops	57	C4
Aston Pigott, Shrops	57	B2
Aston Rogers, Shrops	57	B2
Aston Somerville, Worcs	49	B4
Aston Subedge, Glouc	49	B4
Aston Tirrold, Oxon	27	B1
Aston Upthorpe, Oxon	27	B1
Aston, Berks	28	A1
Aston, Chesh	70	A3
Aston, Chesh	79	B4
Aston, Derby	81	C3
Aston, Heref	47	C1
Aston, Herts	42	A1
Aston, Oxon	39	B3
Aston, S York	82	B3
Aston, Shrops	58	A2
Aston, Shrops	58	B3
Aston, Shrops	69	D4
Aston, Staffs	58	C1
Aston, Staffs	70	B3
Aston, Staffs	70	C4

PLACE	PAGE	GRID
Aston-upon-Trent, Derby	72	B4
Astwick, Beds	52	C4
Astwood Bank, Worcs	49	A2
Astwood, Bucks	51	C3
Astwood, Worcs	49	A2
Aswarby, Lincs	74	B3
Aswardby, Lincs	75	A1
Atch Lench, Worcs	49	A3
Atcham, Shrops	57	D2
Athelhampton, Dorset	8	A1
Athelington, Suff	55	A1
Athelney, Som	13	A2
Athelstaneford, E Loth	119	A2
Atherington, Devon	11	E2
Atherstone on Stour, Warwk	49	C3
Atherton, G Man	79	C2
Atlow, Derby	71	C3
Atterby, Lincs	83	D3
Atterton, Leics	60	B3
Attleborough, Norf	64	D3
Attlebridge, Norf	65	A1
Atwick, E R of Y	90	C2
Atworth, Wilts	25	B2
Aubourn, Lincs	74	A1
Auchenblae, Aber	129	D1
Auchenbowie, Stirl	116	B1
Auchencairn, Dumf	97	B1
Auchencrow, Border	119	D4
Auchendinny, M Loth	118	A3
Auchengray, S Lan	116	C4
Auchenmalg, Dumf	96	C1
Auchinleck, E Ayrs	109	A3
Auchinloch, N Lan	116	A3
Auchinstarry, N Lan	116	A2
Auchleven, Aber	134	A1
Auchlochan, S Lan	109	C2
Auchmillan, E Ayrs	108	E2
Auchmithie, Angus	129	C4
Auchnagatt, Aber	139	D4
Auchnarrow, Moray	133	B1
Auchterarder, Perth	123	B3
Auchterderran, Fife	123	D4
Auchterhouse, Angus	124	A1
Auchterless, Aber	139	C4
Auchtermuchty, Fife	124	A3
Auchtertool, Fife	117	B1
Auckley, S York	83	A2
Audlem, Chesh	70	A3
Audley End, Essex	53	B4
Audley End, Suff	54	B3
Audley, Staffs	70	B2
Aughertree, Cumb	98	A2
Aughton, E R of Y	89	B3
Aughton, Lancs	79	A2
Aughton, Lancs	92	A4
Aughton, S York	82	B3
Auldearn, High	137	D3
Aulden, Heref	47	C3
Auldgirth, Dumf	103	D2
Ault Hucknall, Derby	72	B1
Aultbea, High	140	B4
Aultgrishin, High	140	A4
Aunsby, Lincs	74	B3
Aust, Glouc	37	A4
Austerfield, S York	83	A3
Austrey, Warwk	60	B2
Austwick, N York	92	C4
Authorpe, Lincs	84	C4
Avebury, Wilts	26	B2
Aveley, Essex	30	B1
Avening, Glouc	38	A4
Averham, Notts	73	C2
Aveton Gifford, Devon	10	A1
Aviemore, High	132	E2
Avington, Berks	26	D2
Avoch, High	137	B3
Avon Dassett, Warwk	50	B3
Avon, Hants	15	A4
Avonbridge, Falk	116	C2
Avonmouth, Bristol	24	B1
Avonwick, Devon	5	B4
Awliscombe, Devon	12	D4
Awre, Glouc	37	C3
Awsworth, Notts	72	B3
Axbridge, Som	24	A3
Axford, Hants	27	B4
Axford, Wilts	26	C2
Axminster, Devon	13	A4
Axmouth, Devon	7	A1
Aycliffe, Durham	100	B3
Aydon, Nthumb	105	C4
Aylburton, Glouc	37	B3
Aylesbeare, Devon	6	B1
Aylesbury, Bucks	40	C2
Aylesby, Lincs	84	B1
Aylesford, Kent	31	A3
Aylmerton, Norf	76	C3
Aylsham, Norf	76	C4
Aylton, Heref	48	A4
Aylworth, Glouc	38	C2
Aymestrey, Heref	47	C2
Aynho, Nhants	40	A1
Ayot St Lawrence, Herts	41	C2
Ayr, S Ayrs	108	D3
Aysgarth, N York	93	A2
Ayshford, Devon	12	C3
Ayside, Cumb	91	E3
Ayston, Rutland	62	A3
Aythorpe Roding, Essex	43	A2
Ayton, Border	119	D3
Azerley, N York	93	C4
Babbs Green, Herts	42	B2
Babcary, Som	13	C2
Babington, Som	25	A4
Babraham, Cambs	53	B3
Babworth, Notts	83	A4
Backaland, Orkney	144	B1
Backford, Chesh	69	C1
Backies, High	141	D3
Backwell, Som	24	B2
Baconsthorpe, Norf	76	C4
Bacton, Heref	36	C1
Bacton, Norf	76	D4
Bacton, Suff	54	D2
Bacup, Lancs	86	C4
Badachro, High	135	F1
Badbury, Wilts	26	C1
Badby, Nhants	50	C2
Badcaul, High	140	C2
Baddesley Clinton, Warwk	49	C1
Baddesley Ensor, Warwk	60	A3
Badger, Shrops	58	B3
Badgers Mount, Kent	30	A3
Badgeworth, Glouc	38	A2
Badgworth, Som	24	A4
Badicaul, High	130	F1
Badingham, Suff	55	B2
Badlesmere, Kent	32	A3
Badluachrach, High	140	C3
Badsey, Worcs	49	B4
Badsworth, W Yorks	82	B1
Badwell Ash, Suff	54	C1
Bagber, Dorset	14	B3
Bagby, N York	94	A3
Bagillt, Flint	78	C4
Baginton, Warwk	50	A1
Baglan, Neath	35	A4
Bagley, Shrops	69	C4
Bagmore, Hants	27	C4
Bagnall, Staffs	71	A2
Bagot, Shrops	48	A1
Bagshot, Surrey	28	B3
Bagstone, Glouc	24	C1
Bagworth, Leics	60	C2
Bagwy Llydiart, Heref	36	C1
Baile Mor, Argyll	120	B2
Bainbridge, N York	93	A2
Bainshole, Aber	139	B4
Bainton, Cambs	62	C2
Bainton, E R of Y	90	A2
Baintown, Fife	124	B4
Bakewell, Derby	71	C1
Bala, Gwyn	68	C4
Balallan, W Isle	144	B2
Balbeggie, Perth	123	D2
Balblair, High	137	B2
Balchreick, High	142	A2
Balcombe, W Suss	18	C1
Baldersby St James, N York	93	D3
Baldersby, N York	93	D3
Balderstone, Lancs	86	A3
Baldinnie, Fife	124	B3
Baldock, Herts	52	C4
Baldovie, Dundee City	124	B1
Baldrine, I of M	145	D3
Baldslow, E Suss	20	B3
Bale, Norf	76	B4
Baledgarno, Perth	124	A2
Balerno, Edin	117	B3
Balfield, Angus	129	B2
Balfour, Orkney	144	B2
Balfron, Stirl	115	C1
Balgonar, Fife	117	A1
Balgracie, Dumf	102	A4
Balgray, Angus	124	B1
Balham, G Lon	147	B1
Balintore, High	137	C1
Balivanich, W Isle	144	A3
Balk, N York	94	A3
Balkholme, E R of Y	89	C4
Ballachulish, High	126	E3
Ballantrae, S Ayrs	102	B2
Ballasalla, I of M	145	B4
Ballater, Aber	133	D4
Ballaugh, I of M	145	C2
Ballchraggan, High	137	B1
Ballevullin, Argyll	125	A4
Ballidon, Derby	71	C2
Ballindean, Perth	124	A2
Ballinger Common, Bucks	41	A3
Ballingham, Heref	37	A1
Ballingry, Fife	123	D4
Ballinluig, Perth	128	B4
Ballintuim, Perth	128	C3
Balloch, High	137	B3
Ballochroy, Argyll	113	E4
Balls Cross, W Suss	18	A2
Ballygrant, Argyll	113	C3
Balmacara, High	130	F1
Balmaclellan, Dumf	103	A3
Balmaha, Stirl	115	A1
Balmalcolm, Fife	124	A3
Balmedie, Aber	134	D2
Balmore, E Dun	115	C2
Balmullo, Fife	124	B2
Balnaguard, Perth	128	B4
Balnain, High	132	A1
Balquhidder, Stirl	122	B2
Balsall Common, W Mids	49	C1
Balscote, Oxon	50	B4
Balsham, Cambs	53	C3
Baltasound, Shet	144	B1
Baltersan, Dumf	102	D4
Baltonsborough, Som	13	C1
Balvicar, Argyll	120	F3
Balvraid, High	130	F2
Bamber Bridge, Lancs	85	C4
Bamber's Green, Essex	43	A1
Bamburgh, Nthumb	112	C2
Bamford, Derby	81	C4
Bampton, Cumb	98	C4
Bampton, Devon	12	B2
Bampton, Oxon	39	B3
Banbury, Oxon	50	B4
Bancffosfelem, Carm	34	C2
Banchory, Aber	134	B4
Bancycapel, Carm	34	C2
Bancyfelin, Carm	34	B2
Banff, Aber	139	B2
Bangor, Gwyn	67	E1
Bangor-is-y-coed, Wrex	69	C3
Banham, Norf	64	D4
Bank, Hants	15	C3
Bankend, Dumf	103	E4
Bankfoot, Perth	123	C1
Bankglen, E Ayrs	109	A4
Banks, Lancs	85	B4
Banningham, Norf	76	C4
Bannister Green, Essex	43	B2
Banstead, Surrey	150	A1
Banton, N Lan	116	A2
Banwell, Som	24	A3
Bapchild, Kent	31	C3
Bapton, Wilts	14	D1
Bar Hill, Cambs	53	A2
Barbaraville, High	137	B1
Barbon, Cumb	92	B3
Barbrook, Devon	22	C4
Barby, Nhants	50	C1
Barcheston, Warwk	49	C4
Barcombe Cross, E Suss	19	A3
Barcombe, E Suss	19	A3
Barden, N York	93	B2
Bardfield Saling, Essex	43	B1
Bardney, Lincs	74	C1
Bardon, Leics	60	C2
Bardowie, E Dun	115	C2
Bardsea, Cumb	91	D4
Bardsey, W Yorks	88	A2
Bardwell, Suff	54	C1
Barewood, Heref	47	C3
Barford St John, Oxon	39	C1
Barford St Martin, Wilts	15	A1
Barford St Michael, Oxon	39	C1
Barford, Norf	64	D2
Barford, Warwk	49	C2
Barfrestone, Kent	32	C4
Bargoed, Caer	36	A3
Barham, Cambs	52	B1
Barham, Kent	32	B4
Barham, Suff	55	A3
Barholm, Lincs	62	C2
Barkby Thorpe, Leics	61	B2
Barkby, Leics	61	B2
Barkestone-le-Vale, Leics	73	C4
Barkham, Berks	28	A2
Barking Tye, Suff	54	D3
Barking, Suff	54	D3
Barkisland, W Yorks	87	B4
Barkston Ash, N York	88	B3
Barkston, Lincs	74	A3
Barkway, Herts	53	A4
Barlaston, Staffs	70	C3
Barlavington, W Suss	18	A3
Barlborough, Derby	82	B4
Barlestone, Leics	60	C2
Barley, Herts	53	A4
Barley, Lancs	86	C3
Barleythorpe, Rutland	61	C2
Barling, Essex	44	A4
Barlings, Lincs	83	D4
Barlow, Derby	82	A4
Barlow, N York	89	B4
Barlow, Tyne	105	D4
Barmby Moor, E R of Y	89	C2
Barmby on the Marsh, E R of Y	89	B4
Barmouth, Gwyn	56	A1
Barmpton, Durham	100	B4
Barmston, E R of Y	90	C1
Barnack, Cambs	62	B2
Barnard Castle, Durham	99	D4
Barnard Gate, Oxon	39	C2
Barnardiston, Suff	54	A3
Barnburgh, S York	82	B2
Barnby Dun, S York	82	C1
Barnby in the Willows, Notts	74	A2
Barnby Moor, Notts	83	A3
Barnby, Suff	66	B4
Barnes, G Lon	147	A2
Barnet, G Lon	42	A4
Barnetby le Wold, Lincs	83	D1
Barney, Norf	76	A4
Barnham Broom, Norf	64	D2
Barnham, Suff	54	B1
Barnham, W Suss	17	C4
Barningham, Durham	93	B1
Barningham, Suff	54	C1
Barnoldby le Beck, Lincs	84	B2
Barns Green, W Suss	18	B2
Barnsley, Glouc	38	C3
Barnsley, S York	82	A2
Barnstaple, Devon	11	E1
Barnston, Essex	43	A2
Barnston, Mers	78	D4
Barnstone, Notts	73	B4
Barnt Green, Worcs	49	A1
Barnton, Chesh	79	C4
Barnwell All Saints, Nhants	62	B4
Barnwell St Andrew, Nhants	62	B4
Barr, S Ayrs	102	C1
Barrapoll, Argyll	125	A4
Barrasford, Nthumb	105	B3
Barrhead, East Renf	115	B4
Barrhill, S Ayrs	102	C2
Barrington, Cambs	53	A3
Barrington, Som	13	B2
Barripper, Corn	1	D1
Barrmill, N Ayrs	115	A4
Barrow Burn, Nthumb	111	C4
Barrow Gurney, Som	24	B2
Barrow Haven, Lincs	90	B4
Barrow upon Soar, Leics	61	A1
Barrow, Glouc	38	A1
Barrow, Lancs	86	B3
Barrow, Rutland	62	A1
Barrow, Som	14	B1
Barrow, Suff	54	A2
Barrowby, Lincs	74	A4
Barrowden, Rutland	62	A3
Barrowford, Lancs	86	C3
Barrow-in-Furness, Cumb	91	C4
Barrow-upon-Humber, Lincs	90	B4
Barry, Angus	124	C1
Barry, Glam	23	B2
Barsby, Leics	61	B2
Barsham, Suff	66	A4
Barston, W Mids	49	C1
Bartestree, Heref	47	D4
Barthol Chapel, Aber	134	C1
Bartholomew Green, Essex	43	B2
Barthomley, Chesh	70	B2
Bartley, Hants	15	C3
Bartlow, Essex	53	C4
Barton Bendish, Norf	64	A2
Barton Hartshorn, Bucks	40	B1
Barton in Fabis, Notts	73	A4
Barton in the Beans, Leics	60	C2
Barton Mills, Suff	54	A1
Barton Seagrave, Nhants	51	C1
Barton St David, Som	13	C1
Barton Stacey, Hants	27	A4
Barton Town, Devon	11	F1
Barton Waterside, Lincs	90	B4
Barton, Cambs	53	A3
Barton, Chesh	69	C2
Barton, Glouc	38	C1
Barton, Lancs	79	A1
Barton, Lancs	85	C3
Barton, N York	93	C1
Barton-le-Clay, Beds	41	C1
Barton-le-Street, N York	94	C4
Barton-le-Willows, N York	89	B1
Barton-on-the-Heath, Warwk	39	A1
Barton-upon-Humber, Lincs	90	B4
Barvas, W Isle	144	B2
Barway, Cambs	53	C1
Barwell, Leics	60	C3
Barwick in Elmet, W Yorks	88	B3
Barwick, Devon	11	E3
Barwick, Som	13	C3
Baschurch, Shrops	57	C1
Bascote, Warwk	50	B2
Bashall Eaves, Lancs	86	A2
Basildon, Berks	27	B1
Basildon, Essex	43	B4
Basingstoke, Hants	27	C4
Baslow, Derby	81	C4
Bason Bridge, Som	23	C4
Bassenthwaite, Cumb	97	E3
Bassingbourn, Cambs	53	A4
Bassingham, Lincs	74	A2
Bassingthorpe, Lincs	74	B4
Bassus Green, Herts	42	A1
Baston, Lincs	62	C2
Bastwick, Norf	66	A1
Batchworth, Herts	41	B4
Batcombe, Dorset	14	A4
Batcombe, Som	14	A1
Bath, Som	25	A2
Bathampton, Som	25	A2
Bathealton, Som	12	C2
Batheaston, Som	25	A2
Bathford, Som	25	A2
Bathgate, W Loth	116	C3
Bathley, Notts	73	C2
Bathpool, Corn	4	A2
Bathway, Som	24	C4
Batley, W Yorks	87	C4
Batsford, Glouc	49	C4
Battersby, N York	94	B1
Battersea, G Lon	148	A4
Battisford Tye, Suff	54	D3
Battle, E Suss	20	A3
Battle, Powys	35	D1
Battlesbridge, Essex	43	C4
Battleton, Som	12	B2
Baughton, Worcs	48	C4
Baughurst, Hants	27	B3
Baulking, Oxon	39	B4
Baumber, Lincs	84	B4
Baunton, Glouc	38	B3
Baverstock, Wilts	14	D1
Bawburgh, Norf	65	A2
Bawdeswell, Norf	64	D1
Bawdrip, Som	13	A1
Bawdsey, Suff	55	B4
Bawtry, S York	83	A3
Baxterley, Warwk	60	B3
Baycliff, Cumb	91	D4
Baydon, Wilts	26	D1
Bayford, Herts	42	A3
Bayford, Som	14	B2
Bayley's Hill, Kent	30	A4
Baylham, Suff	54	D3
Bayston Hill, Shrops	57	D2
Bayton, Worcs	48	A1
Bayworth, Oxon	39	C3
Beachampton, Bucks	51	B4
Beachamwell, Norf	64	A2
Beacon, Devon	12	D4
Beacon's Bottom, Bucks	40	C4
Beaconsfield, Bucks	41	A4
Beadlam, N York	94	C3
Beadlow, Beds	52	B4
Beadnell, Nthumb	112	C2
Beaford, Devon	11	E3
Beal, N York	89	A4
Beal, Nthumb	112	B1
Bealsmill, Corn	4	B2
Beaminster, Dorset	13	C4
Beamish, Durham	100	A1
Beamsley, N York	87	B2
Beanacre, Wilts	25	B2
Beanley, Nthumb	112	B3
Beardon, Devon	4	C1
Beare Green, Surrey	146	B4
Beare, Devon	12	B4
Bearley, Warwk	49	C2
Bearpark, Durham	100	A2
Bearsden, Dumb	115	B3
Bearsted, Kent	31	B3
Bearstone, Shrops	70	B3
Beattock, Dumf	103	E1
Beauchamp Roding, Essex	43	A3
Beaufort, Gwent	36	A2
Beaulieu, Hants	15	C4
Beauly, High	136	F3
Beaumaris, Angle	77	D4
Beaumont, Cumb	104	B4
Beaumont, Essex	44	C1
Beaumont, Jersey	145	A2
Beausale, Warwk	49	C1
Beaworthy, Devon	11	D4
Bebington, Mers	78	D4
Beccles, Suff	66	A4
Becconsall, Lancs	85	B4
Beck Row, Suff	54	A1
Beck Side, Cumb	91	D3
Beckbury, Shrops	58	B3
Beckenham, G Lon	149	B4
Beckering, Lincs	84	A4
Beckermet, Cumb	91	B1
Beckfoot, Cumb	97	D1
Beckford, Worcs	49	A4
Beckhampton, Wilts	26	B2
Beckingham, Lincs	74	A2
Beckingham, Notts	83	B3
Beckington, Som	25	A4
Beckley, E Suss	20	B2
Beckley, Oxon	40	A2
Beckton, G Lon	30	A1
Beckwithshaw, N York	87	C1
Becontree, G Lon	30	A1
Bedale, N York	93	C2
Bedchester, Dorset	14	C3
Beddingham, E Suss	19	B3
Beddington Corner, G Lon	147	A4
Beddington, G Lon	147	B4
Bedfield, Suff	55	A2
Bedford, Beds	52	A3
Bedham, W Suss	18	A2
Bedingfield Street, Suff	55	A2
Bedingfield, Suff	55	A1
Bedlam Lane, Kent	31	B4
Bedlam, N York	87	C1
Bedlington, Nthumb	106	A2
Bedlinog, Merth	35	D3
Bedmond, Herts	41	C3
Bednall, Staffs	59	A1
Bedrule, Border	111	A3
Bedstone, Shrops	47	C1
Bedwas, Caer	36	A4
Bedwellty, Caer	36	A3
Bedworth, Warwk	60	B4
Beeby, Leics	61	B2
Beech, Hants	17	A1
Beech, Staffs	70	C3
Beechingstoke, Wilts	26	B3
Beedon Hill, Berks	27	A1
Beedon, Berks	27	A1
Beeford, E R of Y	90	C1
Beeley, Derby	71	C1
Beelsby, Lincs	84	B2
Beenham, Berks	27	B2
Beer, Devon	6	C1
Beer, Som	13	B1
Beesands, Devon	10	B1
Beesby, Lincs	84	D4
Beeson, Devon	10	B1
Beeston Regis, Norf	76	C3
Beeston, Beds	52	B3
Beeston, Chesh	69	D2
Beeston, Norf	64	C1
Beeston, Notts	73	A4
Beeswing, Dumf	103	D3
Beetham, Cumb	92	A3
Beetham, Som	13	A3
Beetley, Norf	64	C1
Begbroke, Oxon	39	C2
Begelly, Pemb	33	E3
Beguildy, Powys	47	A1
Beighton Hill, Derby	72	A2
Beighton, Norf	66	A2
Beith, N Ayrs	115	A4
Belaugh, Norf	65	B1
Belbroughton, Worcs	48	C1
Belchalwell Street, Dorset	14	B3
Belchalwell, Dorset	14	B3
Belchamp Otten, Essex	54	B4
Belchamp St Paul, Essex	54	B4
Belchamp Walter, Essex	54	B4
Belchford, Lincs	84	B4
Belford, Nthumb	112	B2
Bell Busk, N York	86	C1
Bell End, Worcs	49	A1
Bell o' th' Hill, Chesh	69	D3
Belleau, Lincs	84	C4
Bellerby, N York	93	B2
Bellingdon, Bucks	41	A3
Bellingham, Nthumb	105	B2
Bellochantuy, Argyll	107	D2
Bellows Cross, Dorset	15	A3
Bells Yew Green, E Suss	19	C1
Bellshill, N Lan	116	A4
Bellside, N Lan	116	B4
Belluton, Som	24	C3
Belmont, G Lon	150	B1
Belmont, Lancs	79	C1
Belper Lane End, Derby	72	A2
Belper, Derby	72	A3
Belsay, Nthumb	105	D3
Belses, Border	110	D3
Belsford, Devon	5	B4
Belsize, Herts	41	B3
Belstead, Suff	55	A4
Belstone, Devon	5	A1
Beltingham, Nthumb	105	A4
Beltoft, Lincs	83	B2
Belton, Leics	60	C1
Belton, Lincs	74	A3
Belton, Lincs	83	B1
Belton, Norf	66	B3
Belton, Rutland	61	C3
Belvedere, G Lon	30	A1
Belvoir, Leics	73	C4
Bembridge, I of W	10	B1
Bempton, E R of Y	95	D4
Benacre, Suff	66	B4
Benderloch, Argyll	121	A1
Benenden, Kent	20	B1
Benhall Street, Suff	55	C2
Beningbrough, N York	89	A1
Benington, Herts	42	A1
Benington, Lincs	75	A3
Benllech, Angle	77	C4
Benniworth, Lincs	84	B4
Benson, Oxon	40	B4
Bentley, E R of Y	90	B3
Bentley, Hants	28	A4
Bentley, Suff	54	D4
Benton, Devon	11	F1
Bentpath, Dumf	104	B2
Bentwichen, Devon	11	F1
Bentworth, Hants	17	A1
Benvie, Angus	124	A1
Benville, Dorset	13	C4
Benwick, Cambs	63	B4
Beoley, Worcs	49	B1
Bepton, W Suss	17	C2
Berden, Essex	42	C1
Bere Alston, Devon	4	C3
Bere Ferrers, Devon	4	C3
Bere Regis, Dorset	8	B1
Berea, Pemb	33	B1
Bergh Apton, Norf	65	B3
Berinsfield, Oxon	40	A4
Berkeley, Glouc	37	B3
Berkhamsted, Herts	41	B3
Berkley, Som	25	A4
Berkswell, W Mids	49	C1
Bermondsey, G Lon	149	A2
Bernisdale, High	135	C3
Berrick Prior, Oxon	40	B4
Berrick Salome, Oxon	40	B4
Berrier, Cumb	98	B3
Berriew, Powys	57	A3
Berrington, Shrops	57	D2
Berrington, Worcs	47	D2
Berrow, Som	23	C4
Berrynarbor, Devon	22	B4
Berry's Green, G Lon	30	A3
Bersham, Wrex	69	B3
Berwick Bassett, Wilts	26	B2
Berwick Hill, Nthumb	106	A3
Berwick St James, Wilts	15	A1
Berwick St John, Wilts	14	D2
Berwick, E Suss	19	B4
Berwick-upon-Tweed, Nthumb	119	E4
Bescaby, Leics	73	C4
Besford, Worcs	48	C4
Bessacarr, S York	82	C2
Bessingby, E R of Y	95	D4
Bessingham, Norf	76	C4
Besthorpe, Norf	64	D3
Besthorpe, Notts	73	C1
Beswick, E R of Y	90	B2
Betchworth, Surrey	150	A3
Bethel, Angle	67	C1
Bethel, Gwyn	67	D1
Bethersden, Kent	21	A1
Bethesda, Gwyn	67	E1
Bethesda, Pemb	33	E2
Bethlehem, Carm	35	A1
Bethnal Green, G Lon	149	A1
Betley, Staffs	70	B3
Betteshanger, Kent	32	C4
Bettiscombe, Dorset	13	B4
Bettisfield, Wrex	69	C4
Bettws Bledrws, Cered	46	A3
Bettws Cedewain, Powys	57	A3
Bettws Evan, Cered	45	D3
Bettws, Newport	36	B4
Bettws-Newydd, Monm	36	C3
Bettyhill, High	142	F1
Betws Gwerfil Goch, Denb	68	D3
Betws, Bridg	22	E1
Betws-y-coed, Aberc	68	B2
Betws-yn-Rhos, Aberc	78	A4
Beulah, Cered	45	D3
Beulah, Powys	46	D3
Bevercotes, Notts	83	A4
Beverley, E R of Y	90	B3
Beverstone, Glouc	38	A4
Bewcastle, Cumb	104	D3
Bewdley, Worcs	48	B1
Bewerley, N York	93	B4
Bewholme, E R of Y	90	C2
Bexhill, E Suss	20	A3
Bexley, G Lon	30	A2
Bexleyheath, G Lon	30	A2
Beyton, Suff	54	C2
Bibury, Glouc	38	C3
Bicester, Oxon	40	A1
Bickenhill, W Mids	60	A4
Bicker, Lincs	74	D3
Bickerstaffe, Lancs	79	A2
Bickerton, N York	88	B2
Bickford, Staffs	58	C2
Bickington, Devon	5	C2
Bickleigh, Devon	4	C3
Bickleigh, Devon	12	B3
Bickley Moss, Chesh	69	D3
Bickley, G Lon	149	B4
Bickley, N York	95	B2
Bicknacre, Essex	43	C3
Bicknoller, Som	12	C1
Bicknor, Kent	31	B3
Bicton, Shrops	57	C1
Bicton, Shrops	57	B4
Biddenden, Kent	20	B1
Biddenham, Beds	52	A3
Biddestone, Wilts	25	B2
Biddisham, Som	24	A3
Biddlesden, Bucks	51	A4
Biddulph Moor, Staffs	70	C2
Biddulph, Staffs	70	C2
Bideford, Devon	11	D2
Bidford-on-Avon, Warwk	49	B3
Bielby, E R of Y	89	C2
Bierley, I of W	10	A2
Bierton, Bucks	40	C2
Bigbury, Devon	10	A1
Bigbury-on-Sea, Devon	10	B1
Bigby, Lincs	83	D1
Biggar, S Lan	109	E1
Biggin Hill, G Lon	150	D1
Biggin, Derby	71	C3
Biggin, Derby	71	B2
Biggin, N York	89	A3
Biggleswade, Beds	52	B4
Bighton, Hants	16	B1
Biglands, Cumb	98	A1

PLACE	PAGE	GRID
Bignor, W Suss	18	A3
Bigrigg, Cumb	97	C4
Bilbrook, Som	12	C1
Bilbrough, N York	89	A2
Bilbster, High	143	E2
Bildershaw, Durham	100	A3
Bildeston, Suff	54	C3
Billericay, Essex	43	B4
Billesdon, Leics	61	B3
Billesley, Warwk	49	B3
Billingborough, Lincs	74	C4
Billinge, Mers	79	B2
Billingford, Norf	55	A1
Billingford, Norf	64	D1
Billingham, Durham	100	C3
Billinghay, Lincs	74	C2
Billingley, S York	82	B2
Billingshurst, W Suss	18	B2
Billingsley, Shrops	58	B4
Billington, Beds	41	A1
Billington, Lancs	86	B3
Billockby, Norf	66	A2
Billy Row, Durham	100	A2
Bilsborrow, Lancs	85	C3
Bilsby, Lincs	84	D4
Bilsham, W Suss	18	A4
Bilsington, Kent	21	B1
Bilsthorpe, Notts	73	B1
Bilton, N York	88	B2
Binbrook, Lincs	84	B3
Binfield Heath, Oxon	28	A1
Bingfield, Nthumb	105	C3
Bingham, Notts	73	B3
Bingham's Melcombe, Dorset	14	B4
Bingley, W Yorks	87	B3
Binham, Norf	76	A3
Binley, Hants	27	A3
Binscombe, Surrey	146	A4
Binstead, Hants	17	B1
Binton, Warwk	49	B3
Bintree, Norf	64	D1
Birch Cross, Staffs	71	B4
Birch Green, Essex	44	A2
Birch Green, Worcs	48	C3
Birch Vale, Derby	81	A3
Birch Wood, Som	13	A3
Birch, Essex	44	A2
Bircham Newton, Norf	75	D4
Birchanger, Essex	42	C1
Bircher, Heref	47	D2
Birchgrove, E Suss	19	A1
Birchgrove, Swan	35	A4
Birchley Heath, Warwk	60	B3
Birchover, Derby	71	C1
Bircotes, Notts	83	A3
Birdbrook, Essex	54	A4
Birdforth, N York	94	A4
Birdham, W Suss	17	B4
Birdingbury, Warwk	50	B1
Birdlip, Glouc	38	A2
Birds Edge, W Yorks	81	C1
Birds Green, Essex	43	A3
Birdsall, N York	95	A4
Birdsgreen, Shrops	58	B4
Birdsmoorgate, Dorset	13	B4
Birgham, Border	111	B1
Birkby, N York	93	D1
Birkenhead, Mers	78	D3
Birkenshaw, W Yorks	87	C4
Birkhill, Angus	124	B1
Birkin, N York	89	A4
Birley, Heref	47	C3
Birling, Kent	31	A3
Birlingham, Worcs	49	A4
Birmingham, W Mids	59	B4
Birnam, Perth	123	C1
Birness, Aber	134	D1
Birstall, Leics	61	A2
Birstwith, N York	87	C1
Birtley, Heref	47	C1
Birtley, Nthumb	105	B3
Birtley, Tyne	100	A1
Birts Street, Worcs	48	B4
Biscathorpe, Lincs	84	B3
Bish Mill, Devon	11	F2
Bisham, Berks	28	A1
Bishampton, Worcs	49	A3
Bishop Auckland, Durham	100	A3
Bishop Burton, E R of Y	90	B3
Bishop Middleham, Durham	100	B3
Bishop Monkton, N York	93	D4
Bishop Norton, Lincs	83	D3
Bishop Sutton, Som	24	C3
Bishop Thornton, N York	87	C1
Bishop Wilton, E R of Y	89	C1
Bishopbridge, Lincs	83	D3
Bishops Cannings, Wilts	26	A3
Bishop's Castle, Shrops	57	B4
Bishop's Caundle, Dorset	14	B3
Bishop's Cleeve, Glouc	38	B1
Bishop's Frome, Heref	48	A3
Bishops Gate, Surrey	146	A2
Bishop's Green, Essex	43	A2
Bishop's Itchington, Warwk	50	A2
Bishops Lydeard, Som	12	D2
Bishop's Norton, Glouc	38	A1
Bishop's Nympton, Devon	11	F2
Bishop's Offley, Staffs	70	B4
Bishop's Stortford, Herts	42	C2
Bishop's Sutton, Hants	16	B1
Bishop's Tachbrook, Warwk	50	A2
Bishop's Waltham, Hants	16	B3
Bishop's Wood, Staffs	58	C2
Bishopsbourne, Kent	32	B4
Bishopsteignton, Devon	6	A2
Bishopston, Swan	34	D4
Bishopstone, Bucks	40	C3
Bishopstone, E Suss	19	B4
Bishopstone, Heref	47	C4
Bishopstone, Wilts	15	A2
Bishopstone, Wilts	26	C1
Bishopstrow, Wilts	25	B4
Bishopswood, Som	13	A3
Bishopthorpe, N York	89	A2
Bishopton, Durham	100	B4
Bishopton, Renf	115	B3
Bishton, Newport	24	A1
Bishton, Staffs	59	A1
Bisley Camp, Surrey	28	B3
Bisley, Glouc	38	A3
Bisley, Surrey	28	B3
Bissoe, Corn	2	A1
Bisterne, Hants	15	A4
Bitchfield, Lincs	74	B4
Bittadon, Devon	22	B4
Bittaford, Devon	5	B4
Bitterley, Shrops	47	D1
Bitteswell, Leics	61	A4
Bitton, Glouc	24	C2
Blaby, Leics	61	A3
Black Bourton, Oxon	39	B3
Black Callerton, Tyne	106	A3
Black Dog, Devon	12	A3
Black Notley, Essex	43	B2
Black Torrington, Devon	11	D4
Blackawton, Devon	5	C4
Blackborough End, Norf	64	A1
Blackborough, Devon	12	C3
Blackbrook, Derby	72	A3
Blackbrook, Staffs	70	B3
Blackbrook, Surrey	146	B4
Blackburn, Aber	134	C2
Blackburn, Lancs	86	A4
Blackburn, W Loth	116	C3
Blackdown, Dorset	13	B4
Blacker Hill, S York	82	A2
Blackfen, G Lon	30	A2
Blackfield, Hants	16	A4
Blackford, Perth	123	B3
Blackford, Som	24	A4
Blackfordby, Leics	60	B1
Blackhall Colliery, Durham	100	C2
Blackheath, G Lon	149	B2
Blackheath, Suff	55	C1
Blackheath, Surrey	146	A4
Blackhill, Aber	139	F4
Blackland, Som	12	A1
Blackmill, Bridg	22	E1
Blackmoor, Hants	17	B1
Blackmoor, Som	24	B3
Blackmoorfoot, W Yorks	81	B1
Blackmore End, Essex	43	B1
Blackmore, Essex	43	A3
Blackness, Falk	117	A2
Blacknest, Berks	28	B2
Blacknest, Hants	28	A4
Blacko, Lancs	86	C2
Blackpool, Devon	10	B1
Blackpool, Lancs	85	A3
Blackridge, W Loth	116	C3
Blackrod, G Man	79	C1
Blackshaw Head, W Yorks	87	A4
Blacksnape, Lancs	86	B4
Blackstone, W Suss	18	C3
Blackthorn, Oxon	40	B2
Blackthorpe, Suff	54	C2
Blackwall, Derby	71	C2
Blackwater, Corn	2	A1
Blackwater, Som	13	A3
Blackwaterfoot, N Ayrs	107	F2
Blackwell, Cumb	98	B1
Blackwell, Derby	71	B1
Blackwell, Derby	72	B2
Blackwell, Warwk	49	C4
Blackwell, Worcs	49	A1
Blackwood, Caer	36	A4
Blackwood, S Lan	109	C1
Bladnoch, Dumf	96	D1
Bladon, Oxon	39	C2
Blaenannerch, Cered	45	D3
Blaenau Ffestiniog, Gwyn	68	A3
Blaenavon, Torf	36	B3
Blaenffos, Pemb	45	C4
Blaengarw, Bridg	35	C4
Blaengwrach, Neath	35	B3
Blaengwynfi, Neath	35	C4
Blaenpennal, Cered	46	A2
Blaenplwyf, Cered	46	A1
Blaenporth, Cered	45	D3
Blaenwaun, Carm	34	A1
Blaen-y-Coed, Carm	34	B1
Blaen-y-cwm, Gwent	36	A2
Blaen-y-cwm, Rhond	35	C4
Blagdon Hill, Som	12	D3
Blagdon, Som	24	B3
Blaich, High	126	D1
Blaina, Gwent	36	A3
Blair Atholl, Perth	128	A2
Blairgowrie, Perth	128	D4
Blairingone, Perth	123	B4
Blairlogie, Stirl	123	A4
Blairmore, Argyll	114	C2
Blaisdon, Glouc	37	C2
Blakedown, Worcs	48	C1
Blakemere, Heref	47	C4
Blakeney, Glouc	37	B3
Blakeney, Norf	76	B3
Blakenhall, Chesh	70	B3
Blakesley, Nhants	51	A3
Blanchland, Nthumb	99	C1
Bland Hill, N York	87	C1
Blandford Forum, Dorset	14	C4
Blandford St Mary, Dorset	14	C4
Blanefield, Stirl	115	C2
Blankney, Lincs	74	B2
Blantyre, S Lan	116	A4
Blaston, Leics	61	C3
Blatherwycke, Nhants	62	B3
Blawith, Cumb	91	D2
Blaxhall, Suff	55	C2
Blaxton, S York	83	A2
Blaydon, Tyne	106	A4
Bleadon, Som	23	C3
Blean, Kent	32	B3
Bleasby, Notts	73	B2
Bleasdale, Lancs	85	C2
Bleddfa, Powys	47	A1
Bledington, Glouc	39	A1
Bledlow, Bucks	40	C3
Blencarn, Cumb	98	D3
Blencogo, Cumb	97	E1
Blendworth, Hants	17	A3
Blennerhasset, Cumb	97	E2
Bletchingdon, Oxon	40	A2
Bletchingley, Surrey	150	C3
Bletchley, Bucks	41	A1
Bletchley, Shrops	70	A4
Bletherston, Pemb	33	D2
Bletsoe, Beds	52	A2
Blewbury, Oxon	27	B1
Blickling, Norf	76	C4
Blidworth Bottoms, Notts	73	A2
Blidworth, Notts	73	A2
Blindcrake, Cumb	97	E2
Blindley Heath, Surrey	150	C4
Blisland, Corn	3	E2
Bliss Gate, Worcs	48	B1
Blissford, Hants	15	B3
Blisworth, Nhants	51	A3
Blithbury, Staffs	59	B1
Blo Norton, Norf	54	D1
Blockley, Glouc	49	C4
Blofield, Norf	65	B2
Blore, Staffs	70	B4
Blore, Staffs	71	B2
Bloxham, Oxon	50	B4
Bloxholm, Lincs	74	B2
Bloxworth, Dorset	8	B1
Blubberhouses, N York	87	C1
Blue Anchor, Som	23	A4
Blue Bell Hill, Kent	31	A3
Blundeston, Suff	66	B3
Blunham, Beds	52	B3
Blunsdon St Andrew, Wilts	38	C4
Bluntington, Worcs	48	C1
Bluntisham, Cambs	53	A1
Blyborough, Lincs	83	C3
Blyford, Suff	55	C1
Blymhill, Staffs	58	B2
Blyth Bridge, Border	110	A1
Blyth, Notts	83	A3
Blyth, Nthumb	106	B2
Blythburgh, Suff	55	C1
Blyton, Lincs	83	C3
Boarhills, Fife	124	C3
Boarhunt, Hants	16	B3
Boarstall, Bucks	40	B2
Boat of Garten, High	132	E2
Boath, High	137	A1
Bobbing, Kent	31	B2
Bobbington, Staffs	58	B4
Boddam, Aber	139	F4
Boddington, Glouc	38	A1
Bodedern, Angle	77	B4
Bodelwyddan, Denb	78	B4
Bodenham Moor, Heref	47	D3
Bodenham, Heref	47	D3
Bodenham, Wilts	15	B2
Bodewryd, Angle	77	B3
Bodfari, Denb	68	D1
Bodffordd, Angle	77	C4
Bodfuan, Gwyn	67	C3
Bodham, Norf	76	C3
Bodicote, Oxon	50	B4
Bodinnick, Corn	3	E4
Bodmin, Corn	3	D3
Bodsham Green, Kent	32	A4
Bogbrae, Aber	139	E4
Bognor Regis, W Suss	17	C4
Bogue, Dumf	103	A2
Bohortha, Corn	2	B2
Bolam, Durham	100	A3
Bolberry, Devon	10	A1
Boldre, Hants	15	C4
Boldron, Durham	99	C4
Bole, Notts	83	B3
Bolehill, Derby	72	A2
Bolham Water, Devon	12	D3
Bolham, Devon	12	B3
Bolingey, Corn	3	B4
Bollington, Chesh	81	A4
Bolney, W Suss	18	C2
Bolnhurst, Beds	52	B2
Bolsover, Derby	72	B1
Bolsterstone, S York	81	C2
Boltby, N York	94	A3
Bolton Abbey, N York	87	B1
Bolton le Sands, Lancs	92	A4
Bolton Low Houses, Cumb	98	A2
Bolton Percy, N York	89	A2
Bolton, Cumb	98	D3
Bolton, E Loth	119	A3
Bolton, E R of Y	89	C2
Bolton, G Man	80	A1
Bolton, Nthumb	112	B4
Boltonfellend, Cumb	104	D3
Boltongate, Cumb	97	E2
Bolventor, Corn	3	E2
Bonar Bridge, High	141	B4
Bonby, Lincs	83	D1
Boncath, Pemb	45	D4
Bonchester Bridge, Border	111	A4
Bondleigh, Devon	11	E4
Bonds, Lancs	85	C2
Bo'ness, Falk	116	C2
Boningale, Shrops	58	C3
Bonkle, N Lan	116	B4
Bonnington, Kent	21	B1
Bonnyrigg, M Loth	118	A3
Bonnyton, Angus	124	A1
Bonsall, Derby	72	A2
Bont-Dolgadfan, Powys	56	C3
Bontnewydd, Cered	46	A2
Bontnewydd, Gwyn	67	D2
Bontuchel, Denb	68	D2
Bonvilston, Glam	23	A2
Boode, Devon	11	D1
Boohay, Devon	6	A4
Booley, Shrops	57	D1
Boosbeck, N York	101	B4
Boose's Green, Essex	43	C1
Boot, Cumb	91	C1
Booth, E R of Y	89	B4
Boothby Graffoe, Lincs	74	B2
Boothby Pagnell, Lincs	74	B4
Boothstown, G Man	80	A2
Bootle, Cumb	91	B2
Bootle, Mers	78	D2
Boraston, Shrops	48	A1
Bordeaux, Guern	145	B2
Borden, Kent	31	B3
Bordon, Hants	17	B1
Boreham Street, E Suss	20	A3
Boreham, Essex	43	B3
Boreham, Wilts	25	B4
Borehamwood, Herts	41	C4
Boreland, Dumf	104	A2
Borgue, Dumf	96	F1
Borley, Essex	54	B4
Borness, Dumf	96	F1
Borough Green, Kent	30	B3
Boroughbridge, N York	94	A4
Borrowash, Derby	72	B4
Borrowby, N York	94	A2
Borrowstoun, Falk	116	C2
Borth, Cered	56	A4
Borth-y-Gest, Gwyn	67	E4
Borve, High	135	C3
Borwick, Lancs	92	A4
Bosbury, Heref	48	A4
Boscastle, Corn	3	E1
Boscombe, Wilts	15	B1
Bosham, W Suss	17	B4
Bosherston, Pemb	33	D4
Bosley, Chesh	70	C1
Bosoughan, Corn	3	C3
Bossall, N York	89	B1
Bossiney, Corn	3	D1
Bossingham, Kent	32	B4
Bossington, Som	22	E4
Bostock Green, Chesh	70	A1
Boston Spa, W Yorks	88	B2
Boston, Lincs	75	A3
Boswinger, Corn	2	C1
Botany Bay, G Lon	42	A3
Botesdale, Suff	54	D1
Bothal, Nthumb	106	A2
Bothampstead, Berks	27	B1
Bothamsall, Notts	83	A4
Bothel, Cumb	97	E2
Bothwell, S Lan	116	A4
Botley, Bucks	41	B3
Botley, Hants	16	B3
Botolph Claydon, Bucks	40	B1
Botolphs, W Suss	18	B3
Bottesford, Leics	73	C3
Bottisham, Cambs	53	C2
Bottomcraig, Fife	124	B2
Bottoms, W Yorks	87	A4
Botusfleming, Corn	4	B3
Botwnnog, Gwyn	67	B4
Boughton Aluph, Kent	32	A4
Boughton Lees, Kent	32	A4
Boughton Street, Kent	32	A3
Boughton, Nhants	51	B2
Boughton, Norf	64	A3
Boughton, Notts	73	B1
Bouldon, Shrops	57	D4
Boulmer, Nthumb	112	C4
Bourn, Cambs	53	A3
Bourne End, Beds	51	C4
Bourne End, Herts	41	B3
Bourne, Lincs	62	C1
Bournemouth, Dorset	8	D1
Bournheath, Worcs	49	A1
Bourton, Dorset	14	B1
Bourton, Oxon	26	C1
Bourton, Shrops	58	A3
Bourton, Wilts	26	A2
Bourton-on-the-Water, Glouc	39	A2
Bousd, Argyll	125	C3
Bouth, Cumb	91	D3
Boveney, Bucks	28	B1
Boveridge, Dorset	15	A3
Bovingdon, Herts	41	B3
Bow Brickhill, Bucks	51	C4
Bow Street, Cered	56	A4
Bow, Devon	11	F4
Bow, G Lon	149	A1
Bow, Orkney	144	A2
Bowburn, Durham	100	B2
Bowcombe, I of W	9	C1
Bowd, Devon	6	B1
Bowden Hill, Wilts	26	A2
Bowden, Border	110	D2
Bowdon, G Man	80	A3
Bower, High	143	E1
Bowerchalke, Wilts	14	D2
Bower's Row, W Yorks	88	B4
Bowershall, Fife	117	A1
Bowes, Durham	99	C4
Bowgreave, Lancs	85	C2
Bowley, Heref	47	D3
Bowlhead Green, Surrey	17	C1
Bowling, Dumb	115	B2
Bowmanstead, Cumb	91	D2
Bowmore, Argyll	113	B4
Bowness-on-Solway, Cumb	104	A4
Bowriefauld, Angus	129	B4
Bowsden, Nthumb	112	A1
Box Hill, Surrey	150	A3
Box, Wilts	25	B2
Boxford, Berks	27	A2
Boxford, Suff	54	C4
Boxgrove, W Suss	17	C3
Boxted Cross, Essex	44	A1
Boxted Heath, Essex	44	A1
Boxted, Essex	44	A1
Boxted, Suff	54	B3
Boxworth, Cambs	53	A2
Boyden Gate, Kent	32	B2
Boyndie, Aber	139	B2
Boynton, E R of Y	95	D4
Boyton Cross, Essex	43	A3
Boyton End, Suff	54	A4
Boyton, Corn	4	B1
Boyton, Suff	55	C3
Boyton, Wilts	14	D1
Bozeat, Nhants	51	C2
Brabourne Lees, Kent	21	B1
Brabourne, Kent	32	A4
Bracadale, High	135	B4
Braceborough, Lincs	62	B2
Bracebridge Heath, Lincs	74	B1
Braceby, Lincs	74	B4
Bracewell, Lancs	86	C2
Brackenfield, Derby	72	A2
Brackletter, High	126	E1
Brackley, Nhants	50	C4
Bracknell, Berks	28	B2
Braco, Perth	123	A3
Bracon Ash, Norf	65	A3
Bradbourne, Derby	71	C2
Bradbury, Durham	100	B3
Bradden, Nhants	51	A3
Bradenham, Bucks	40	C4
Bradenstoke, Wilts	26	A1
Bradfield Combust, Suff	54	C2
Bradfield Green, Chesh	70	A2
Bradfield Heath, Essex	44	C1
Bradfield St Clare, Suff	54	C2
Bradfield St George, Suff	54	C2
Bradfield, Berks	27	B2
Bradfield, Devon	12	C3
Bradfield, Essex	44	C1
Bradfield, Norf	76	D4
Bradfield, S York	81	C3
Bradford Abbas, Dorset	14	A3
Bradford Leigh, Wilts	25	B3
Bradford Peverell, Dorset	7	D1
Bradford, Devon	11	C3
Bradford, W Yorks	87	C3
Bradford-on-Avon, Wilts	25	B3
Bradley in the Moors, Staffs	71	B3
Bradley, Derby	71	C3
Bradley, Hants	27	C4
Bradley, Lincs	84	B2
Bradley, Staffs	58	C1
Bradley, Worcs	49	A2
Bradmore, Notts	73	A4
Bradninch, Devon	12	B4
Bradnop, Staffs	71	A2
Bradpole, Dorset	7	C1
Bradshaw, W Yorks	87	B4
Bradstone, Devon	4	B2
Bradwall Green, Chesh	70	B1
Bradwell Waterside, Essex	44	A3
Bradwell, Derby	81	C4
Bradwell, Essex	43	C1
Bradwell-on-Sea, Essex	44	A3
Bradworthy, Devon	11	C3
Brae, Shet	144	A2
Braegrum, Perth	123	C2
Braehead, S Lan	116	C4
Braemar, Aber	133	B4
Braeswick, Orkney	144	B1
Brafferton, Durham	100	B4
Brafferton, N York	94	A4
Bragbury End, Herts	42	A2
Braidwood, S Lan	109	C1
Brailsford, Derby	71	C3
Braintree, Essex	43	B1
Braiseworth, Suff	55	A1
Braishfield, Hants	15	C2
Braithwaite, Cumb	97	E3
Bramcote, Warwk	60	C4
Bramdean, Hants	16	B2
Bramerton, Norf	65	B2
Bramfield, Herts	42	A2
Bramfield, Suff	55	C1
Bramford, Suff	55	A3
Bramhall, G Man	80	B3
Bramham, W Yorks	88	B2
Bramhope, W Yorks	87	C2
Bramley, Hants	27	C3
Bramley, S York	82	B3
Bramley, Surrey	146	A4
Bramling, Kent	32	B3
Brampford Speke, Devon	12	B4
Brampton Abbotts, Heref	37	B1
Brampton Ash, Nhants	61	C4
Brampton, Cambs	52	C1
Brampton, Cumb	98	D3
Brampton, Cumb	104	D4
Brampton, Lincs	83	B4
Brampton, S York	82	B2
Brampton, Suff	66	A4
Bramshall, Staffs	71	B4
Bramshaw, Hants	15	B3
Bramshott, Hants	17	B1
Bramwell, Som	13	B2
Bran End, Essex	43	A1
Branault, High	125	F2
Brancaster Staithe, Norf	75	E3
Brancaster, Norf	75	D3
Brancepeth, Durham	100	A2
Brandesburton, E R of Y	90	C2
Brandeston, Suff	55	B2
Brandiston, Norf	65	A1
Brandon Parva, Norf	64	D2
Brandon, Durham	100	A2
Brandon, Lincs	74	A3
Brandon, Suff	64	B4
Brandon, Warwk	50	B1
Brandsby, N York	94	B4
Brandy Wharf, Lincs	83	D2
Bransbury, Hants	27	A4
Bransby, Lincs	83	C4
Branscombe, Devon	6	C1
Bransford, Worcs	48	B3
Bransgore, Hants	15	B4
Bransley, Shrops	48	A1
Branston Booths, Lincs	74	B1
Branston, Leics	73	C4
Branston, Lincs	74	B1
Branston, Staffs	60	A1
Brant Broughton, Lincs	74	A2
Brantham, Suff	54	D4
Branthwaite, Cumb	97	D3
Branthwaite, Cumb	98	A2
Brantingham, E R of Y	90	A4
Branton Green, N York	88	B1
Branton, Nthumb	112	B3
Branton, S York	83	A2
Branxton, Nthumb	111	C2
Brassington, Derby	71	C2
Brasted, Kent	30	A3
Bratoft, Lincs	75	B1
Brattleby, Lincs	83	C4
Bratton Clovelly, Devon	4	C1
Bratton Fleming, Devon	11	E1
Bratton Seymour, Som	14	A1
Bratton, Wilts	25	B4
Braughing, Herts	42	B1
Braunston, Nhants	50	C2
Braunston, Rutland	61	C2
Braunton, Devon	11	D1
Brawby, N York	95	A3
Bray Shop, Corn	4	B2
Bray, Berks	28	B1
Braybrooke, Nhants	61	C4
Brayford, Devon	11	F1
Braythorn, N York	87	C2
Brayton, N York	89	A3
Braywick, Berks	28	B1
Braywoodside, Berks	28	B2
Breachwood Green, Herts	41	C1
Breadsall, Derby	72	A3
Breadstone, Glouc	37	C3
Breage, Corn	1	D2
Breamore, Hants	15	B3
Brean, Som	23	C3
Brearton, N York	88	A1
Breasclete, W Isle	144	B2
Breaston, Derby	72	B4
Brechfa, Carm	34	C1
Brechin, Angus	129	C3
Breckles, Norf	64	C3
Brecon, Powys	35	D1
Brede, E Suss	20	B2
Bredenbury, Heref	48	A3
Bredfield, Suff	55	B3
Bredgar, Kent	31	B3
Bredon, Worcs	48	C4
Bredon's Norton, Worcs	49	A4
Bredwardine, Heref	47	B4
Breighton, E R of Y	89	B3
Breinton, Heref	47	D4
Bremhill, Wilts	26	A2
Brendon, Devon	22	C4
Brenfield, Argyll	114	A2
Brent Eleigh, Suff	54	C3
Brent Knoll, Som	23	C4
Brent Mill, Devon	5	B4
Brent Pelham, Herts	42	C1
Brentford, G Lon	146	B1
Brentingby, Leics	61	C1
Brentwood, Essex	43	A4
Brenzett, Kent	21	A2
Brereton Green, Chesh	70	B1
Bressingham, Norf	64	D4
Bretby, Derby	60	B1
Bretford, Warwk	50	B1
Bretforton, Worcs	49	B4
Bretherton, Lancs	85	C4
Brettenham, Norf	64	C4
Brettenham, Suff	54	C3
Bretton, Flint	69	C1
Brewer Street, Surrey	150	C3
Brewood, Staffs	58	C2
Briantspuddle, Dorset	8	B1
Brickendon, Herts	42	B3
Bricklehampton, Worcs	49	A4
Bride, I of M	145	D1
Bridekirk, Cumb	97	D3
Bridestowe, Devon	4	C1
Bridford, Devon	5	C1
Bridge End, Surrey	146	A3
Bridge Hewick, N York	93	D4
Bridge of Allan, Stirl	123	A4
Bridge of Cally, Perth	128	D4
Bridge of Canny, Aber	134	A4
Bridge of Dee, Dumf	103	B4
Bridge of Earn, Perth	123	D3
Bridge of Orchy, Argyll	121	D1
Bridge of Weir, Renf	115	A3
Bridge Sollers, Heref	47	C4
Bridge Street, Suff	54	B3
Bridge, Corn	1	D1
Bridge, Kent	32	B3
Bridgehampton, Som	13	C2
Bridgend of Lintrathen, Angus	128	E3
Bridgend, Argyll	113	B3
Bridgend, Bridg	22	E1
Bridgend, W Loth	117	A2
Bridgerule, Devon	11	B4
Bridgetown, Som	12	B1
Bridgham, Norf	64	C4
Bridgnorth, Shrops	58	B3
Bridgwater, Som	13	A1
Bridlington, E R of Y	95	D4
Bridport, Dorset	7	C1
Bridstow, Heref	37	B1
Brierfield, Lancs	86	C3
Brierley, Glouc	37	B2
Brierley, S York	82	B1
Brig o'Turk, Stirl	122	B4
Brigg, Lincs	83	D1
Briggate, Norf	76	D4
Briggswath, N York	95	B1
Brigham, Cumb	97	D3
Brigham, E R of Y	90	B1
Brighouse, W Yorks	87	B4
Brighstone, I of W	9	C2
Brighthampton, Oxon	39	B3
Brightley, Devon	11	E4
Brightling, E Suss	20	A2
Brightlingsea, Essex	44	B2
Brighton, E Suss	19	A4
Brightons, Falk	116	C2
Brightwalton, Berks	27	A1
Brightwell Baldwin, Oxon	40	B4
Brightwell Upperton, Oxon	40	B4

PLACE	PAGE	GRID
Brightwell, Suff	55	B4
Brightwell-cum-Sotwell, Oxon	40	A4
Brignall, Durham	99	D4
Brigsley, Lincs	84	B2
Brigsteer, Cumb	92	A2
Brigstock, Nhants	62	A4
Brill, Bucks	40	B2
Brilley, Heref	47	B3
Brimfield Cross, Shrops	47	D2
Brimfield, Shrops	47	D2
Brimington, Derby	82	B4
Brimley, Devon	5	C2
Brimpsfield, Glouc	38	B2
Brimpton, Berks	27	B2
Brimscombe, Glouc	38	A3
Brimstage, Mers	78	D4
Brind, E R of Y	89	C3
Brindle, Lancs	86	A4
Brineton, Staffs	58	B2
Brington, Cambs	52	B1
Briningham, Norf	76	B4
Brinkhill, Lincs	84	C4
Brinkley, Cambs	53	C3
Brinklow, Warwk	50	B1
Brinkworth, Wilts	26	A1
Brinscall, Lancs	86	A4
Brinsley, Notts	72	B3
Brinton, Norf	76	B4
Brinyan, Orkney	144	A1
Brisley, Norf	64	C1
Brissenden Green, Kent	21	A1
Bristol, Bristol	24	C2
Briston, Norf	76	B4
Britford, Wilts	15	B2
Brithdir, Caer	36	A3
Brithdir, Gwyn	56	B1
British Legion Village, Kent	31	A3
Briton Ferry, Neath	35	A4
Britwell Salome, Oxon	40	B4
Brixham, Devon	6	A4
Brixton Deverill, Wilts	14	C1
Brixton, Devon	5	A4
Brixton, G Lon	148	B4
Brixworth, Nhants	51	B1
Brize Norton, Oxon	39	B3
Broad Alley, Worcs	48	C2
Broad Blunsdon, Wilts	38	C4
Broad Campden, Glouc	49	C4
Broad Carr, W Yorks	87	B4
Broad Chalke, Wilts	14	D2
Broad Green, Essex	43	C1
Broad Green, Suff	54	B2
Broad Green, Worcs	48	B3
Broad Haven, Pemb	33	C2
Broad Hinton, Wilts	26	B1
Broad Laying, Hants	27	A3
Broad Marston, Worcs	49	B3
Broad Oak, E Suss	19	C2
Broad Oak, E Suss	20	B2
Broad Oak, Heref	37	A2
Broad Street, E Suss	20	B3
Broad Street, Kent	31	B3
Broad Town, Wilts	26	B1
Broadbottom, G Man	81	A3
Broadbridge, W Suss	17	B4
Broadclyst, Devon	12	B4
Broadford Bridge, W Suss	18	B2
Broadford, High	130	E1
Broadhembury, Devon	12	C4
Broadhempston, Devon	5	C3
Broadland Row, E Suss	20	B2
Broadmayne, Dorset	8	A1
Broadmoor, Pemb	33	E3
Broadoak, Dorset	13	B4
Broad's Green, Essex	43	B2
Broadstone, Shrops	57	D4
Broadwas, Worcs	48	B3
Broadway, Pemb	33	C2
Broadway, Som	13	A3
Broadway, Worcs	49	B4
Broadwell, Glouc	39	A1
Broadwell, Oxon	39	A3
Broadwell, Warwk	50	B2
Broadwindsor, Dorset	13	B4
Broadwood Kelly, Devon	11	E4
Broadwoodwidger, Devon	4	B1
Brockamin, Worcs	48	B3
Brockbridge, Hants	16	B2
Brockhall, Nhants	51	A2
Brockham, Surrey	146	B4
Brockhampton, Glouc	38	B1
Brockhampton, Heref	37	B1
Brockholes, W Yorks	81	B1
Brocklesby, Lincs	84	A1
Brockley Green, Suff	54	A3
Brockley Green, Suff	54	B3
Brockley, Som	24	B2
Brockley, Suff	54	B1
Brockton, Shrops	57	B2
Brockton, Shrops	57	B4
Brockton, Shrops	57	D3
Brockton, Staffs	70	C4
Brockweir, Glouc	37	A3
Brockworth, Glouc	38	A2
Brocton, Staffs	59	A1
Brodick, N Ayrs	108	A2
Brodsworth, S York	82	C1
Brogaig, High	135	C2
Brokenborough, Wilts	38	A4
Brokerswood, Wilts	25	B4
Brome Street, Suff	55	A1
Brome, Suff	55	A1
Bromeswell, Suff	55	B3
Bromfield, Cumb	97	E1
Bromfield, Shrops	47	D1
Bromham, Beds	52	A3
Bromham, Wilts	26	A2
Bromley Common, G Lon	149	B4
Bromley, G Lon	149	B4
Bromley, Shrops	58	B3
Brompton Ralph, Som	12	C1
Brompton Regis, Som	12	B1
Brompton, N York	93	D2
Brompton, N York	95	B3
Brompton-on-Swale, N York	93	C1
Bromsberrow Heath, Glouc	37	C1
Bromsberrow, Glouc	48	B4
Bromsgrove, Worcs	49	A1
Bromyard, Heref	48	A3
Bronant, Cered	46	A2
Brongest, Cered	45	E3
Bronington, Wrex	69	D3
Bronllys, Powys	47	A4
Bronwydd, Carm	34	B1
Bronygarth, Shrops	69	B4
Brook Hill, Hants	15	B3
Brook Street, Essex	43	A4
Brook Street, Kent	21	A1
Brook, Hants	15	B3
Brook, Hants	15	C2
Brook, Kent	32	A4
Brook, Surrey	146	A4
Brooke, Norf	65	B3
Brooke, Rutland	61	C2
Brookhouse Green, Chesh	70	C1
Brookhouses, Derby	81	A3
Brookland, Kent	21	A2
Brookmans Park, Herts	42	A3
Brookthorpe, Glouc	38	A2
Brookwood, Surrey	28	B3
Broom Hill, S York	82	B2
Broom Hill, Worcs	48	C1
Broom, Beds	52	B4
Broom, Warwk	49	B3
Broome, Norf	65	B3
Broome, Shrops	57	C4
Broome, Worcs	48	C1
Broomedge, Chesh	80	A3
Broomfield, Som	12	D1
Broomfleet, E R of Y	90	A4
Broomhall, Surrey	28	B2
Broomhaugh, Nthumb	105	C4
Broomhill, Nthumb	106	A1
Brora, High	141	E2
Broseley, Shrops	58	A3
Brotherlee, Durham	99	B2
Brotherton, N York	88	B4
Brotton, N York	101	B4
Brough Sowerby, Cumb	99	A4
Brough, Cumb	99	A4
Brough, E R of Y	90	A4
Brough, Notts	73	C2
Broughton Astley, Leics	61	A3
Broughton Green, Worcs	49	A2
Broughton Hackett, Worcs	48	C3
Broughton Mills, Cumb	91	C2
Broughton Poggs, Oxon	39	A3
Broughton, Border	109	E2
Broughton, Bucks	51	C4
Broughton, Cambs	52	C1
Broughton, Flint	69	B1
Broughton, Glam	22	E2
Broughton, Hants	15	C1
Broughton, Lancs	85	C3
Broughton, Lincs	83	C1
Broughton, N York	87	A2
Broughton, N York	95	A4
Broughton, Nhants	51	B1
Broughton, Oxon	50	B4
Broughton, Staffs	70	B4
Broughton-in-Furness, Cumb	91	C3
Brown Candover, Hants	16	B1
Brown Edge, Staffs	70	C2
Brownhills, Fife	124	C3
Brownhills, W Mids	59	B2
Browninghill Green, Hants	27	B3
Brownsham, Devon	11	B2
Brownston, Devon	5	B4
Broxa, N York	95	B2
Broxburn, E Loth	119	B2
Broxburn, W Loth	117	A2
Broxted, Essex	43	A1
Broxwood, Heref	47	C3
Bruichladdich, Argyll	113	A3
Bruisyard Street, Suff	55	B2
Bruisyard, Suff	55	B2
Brund, Staffs	71	B1
Brundall, Norf	65	B2
Brundish Street, Suff	55	B1
Brundish, Suff	55	B1
Brunthwaite, W Yorks	87	B2
Bruntingthorpe, Leics	61	A4
Brunton, Fife	124	A2
Brunton, Nthumb	112	C3
Brunton, Wilts	26	C3
Brushford Barton, Devon	11	F3
Brushford, Som	12	B2
Bruton, Som	14	A1
Bryanston, Dorset	14	C3
Brydekirk, Dumf	104	A3
Bryn Gates, G Man	79	C2
Bryn Saith Marchog, Denb	68	D2
Bryn, Neath	35	B4
Brynaman, Carm	35	A2
Brynberian, Pemb	45	C4
Bryncir, Gwyn	67	D3
Bryn-coch, Neath	35	A3
Bryncroes, Gwyn	67	B4
Bryncrug, Gwyn	56	A1
Bryneglwys, Denb	69	A3
Brynford, Flint	78	C4
Bryngwran, Angle	77	B4
Bryngwyn, Monm	36	C3
Bryngwyn, Powys	47	A3
Bryn-Henllan, Pemb	45	B4
Brynhoffnant, Cered	45	E3
Brynmawr, Gwent	36	A2
Bryn-mawr, Gwyn	67	B4
Brynmenyn, Brigd	22	E1
Brynna, Rhond	22	E1
Brynsadler, Rhond	23	A1
Brynsiencyn, Angle	67	D1
Bubbenhall, Warwk	50	A1
Bubwith, E R of Y	89	B3
Buchanty, Perth	123	B2
Buchany, Stirl	122	D4
Buchlyvie, Stirl	115	C1
Buckabank, Cumb	98	B1
Buckden, Cambs	52	B2
Buckden, N York	93	A3
Buckenham, Norf	66	A2
Buckerell, Devon	12	D4
Buckfast, Devon	5	B3
Buckfastleigh, Devon	5	B3
Buckhaven, Fife	124	B4
Buckholt, Monm	37	A2
Buckhorn Weston, Dorset	14	B2
Buckie, Moray	138	D2
Buckingham, Bucks	51	A4
Buckland Brewer, Devon	11	C2
Buckland Dinham, Som	25	A4
Buckland Filleigh, Devon	11	D3
Buckland in the Moor, Devon	5	B2
Buckland Monachorum, Devon	4	C3
Buckland Newton, Dorset	14	A4
Buckland Ripers, Dorset	7	D2
Buckland St Mary, Som	13	A3
Buckland, Bucks	41	A2
Buckland, Devon	10	A1
Buckland, Glouc	49	B4
Buckland, Herts	53	A4
Buckland, Oxon	39	B4
Buckland, Surrey	150	A3
Buckland-Tout-Saints, Devon	10	A1
Bucklebury, Berks	27	B2
Bucklerheads, Angus	124	B1
Bucklers Hard, Hants	16	A4
Bucklesham, Suff	55	B4
Buckley, Flint	69	B1
Buckminster, Leics	62	A1
Bucknall, Lincs	74	C1
Bucknell, Oxon	40	A1
Bucknell, Shrops	47	C1
Buck's Cross, Devon	11	C2
Bucks Green, W Suss	18	B1
Buck's Mills, Devon	11	C2
Buckton, E R of Y	95	D4
Buckton, Nthumb	112	B1
Buckworth, Cambs	52	B1
Budbrooke, Warwk	49	C2
Budby, Notts	73	A1
Budd's Titson, Corn	11	B4
Bude, Corn	11	B4
Budge's Shop, Corn	4	B4
Budleigh Salterton, Devon	6	B2
Budock Water, Corn	2	A2
Buerton, Chesh	70	A3
Bugbrooke, Nhants	51	A2
Bugle, Corn	3	D4
Bugthorpe, E R of Y	89	C1
Buildwas, Shrops	58	A2
Builth Wells, Powys	46	E3
Bulbridge, Wilts	15	A1
Bulford, Wilts	26	C4
Bulkeley, Chesh	69	D2
Bulkington, Warwk	60	C4
Bulkington, Wilts	26	A3
Bulkworthy, Devon	11	C3
Bullington, Hants	27	A4
Bullington, Lincs	84	A4
Bulmer Tye, Essex	54	B4
Bulmer, Essex	54	B4
Bulmer, N York	94	C4
Bulphan, Essex	30	B1
Bulwick, Nhants	62	A3
Bumble's Green, Essex	42	B3
Bunbury, Chesh	69	D2
Bunessan, Argyll	120	B2
Bungay, Suff	65	B4
Bunnahabhainn, Argyll	113	C2
Bunny, Notts	73	A4
Buntingford, Herts	42	B1
Bunwell Street, Norf	64	D3
Bunwell, Norf	65	A3
Burchett's Green, Berks	28	A1
Burcombe, Wilts	15	A1
Burcott, Bucks	41	A1
Bures, Essex	54	C4
Burford, Oxon	39	A2
Burford, Shrops	48	A1
Burgess Hill, W Suss	19	A2
Burgh by Sands, Cumb	104	B4
Burgh Castle, Norf	66	B2
Burgh Heath, Surrey	150	A2
Burgh le Marsh, Lincs	75	B1
Burgh next Aylsham, Norf	65	A1
Burgh on Bain, Lincs	84	B3
Burgh St Margaret, Norf	66	A2
Burgh St Peter, Norf	66	A3
Burghclere, Hants	27	A3
Burghead, Moray	138	A1
Burghfield Common, Berks	27	C2
Burghfield, Berks	27	C2
Burghill, Heref	47	D4
Burghwallis, S York	82	C1
Burham, Kent	31	A3
Buriton, Hants	17	B2
Burland, Chesh	70	A2
Burlawn, Corn	3	D3
Burleigh, Berks	28	B2
Burleigh, Glouc	38	A3
Burlescombe, Devon	12	C3
Burley Gate, Heref	48	A3
Burley in Wharfedale, W Yorks	87	C2
Burley Street, Hants	15	B4
Burley Wood Head, W Yorks	87	B2
Burley, Hants	15	B4
Burley, Rutland	62	A2
Burleydam, Chesh	70	A3
Burlingham Green, Norf	66	A2
Burlton, Shrops	69	C4
Burmarsh, Kent	21	B1
Burmington, Warwk	49	C4
Burn, N York	89	A4
Burnaston, Derby	72	A4
Burnby, E R of Y	89	C2
Burneside, Cumb	92	A2
Burneston, N York	93	D3
Burnett, Som	24	C2
Burnfoot, Border	110	C4
Burnfoot, Dumf	104	B2
Burnfoot, Perth	123	B4
Burnham Green, Herts	42	A2
Burnham Market, Norf	75	E3
Burnham Norton, Norf	75	E3
Burnham Overy Staithe, Norf	75	E3
Burnham Overy, Norf	75	E3
Burnham Thorpe, Norf	75	E3
Burnham, Bucks	28	B1
Burnham-on-Crouch, Essex	44	A4
Burnham-on-Sea, Som	23	C4
Burnhaven, Aber	139	F4
Burnhead, Dumf	103	C1
Burnhill Green, Staffs	58	B3
Burnhope, Durham	100	A1
Burnhouse, N Ayrs	115	A4
Burniston, N York	95	C2
Burnley, Lancs	86	C3
Burnmoor, Durham	100	B1
Burnmouth, Border	119	E4
Burnopfield, Durham	106	A4
Burnsall, N York	87	A1
Burnside of Duntrune, Angus	124	B1
Burnt Yates, N York	87	C1
Burntcommon, Surrey	146	A3
Burntisland, Fife	117	C1
Burntwood, Staffs	59	B2
Burnworthy, Som	12	D3
Burpham, Surrey	146	A4
Burpham, W Suss	18	A3
Burradon, Nthumb	112	A4
Burravoe, Shet	144	A2
Burrells, Cumb	98	D4
Burrelton, Perth	123	D1
Burridge, Hants	16	B3
Burrill, N York	93	C3
Burrington, Devon	11	E3
Burrington, Heref	47	C1
Burrington, Som	24	B3
Burrough on the Hill, Leics	61	C2
Burrow Bridge, Som	13	B1
Burrow, Lancs	92	B4
Burrow, Som	22	E4
Burrowhill, Surrey	146	A3
Burrows Cross, Surrey	146	B4
Burry Port, Carm	34	C3
Burrygreen, Swan	34	C4
Burscough Bridge, Lancs	79	A1
Burscough, Lancs	79	A1
Bursea, E R of Y	89	C3
Bursledon, Hants	16	A3
Burstall, Suff	54	D4
Burstock, Dorset	13	B4
Burston, Norf	65	A4
Burstow, Surrey	150	B4
Burstwick, E R of Y	90	D4
Burtersett, N York	92	D2
Burtholme, Cumb	104	D4
Burthorpe Green, Suff	54	A2
Burtoft, Lincs	74	D4
Burton Agnes, E R of Y	90	C1
Burton Coggles, Lincs	62	B1
Burton End, Essex	42	C1
Burton Fleming, E R of Y	95	D4
Burton Hastings, Warwk	60	C4
Burton in Lonsdale, N York	92	B4
Burton Joyce, Notts	73	B3
Burton Latimer, Nhants	51	C1
Burton Lazars, Leics	61	C1
Burton Leonard, N York	88	A1
Burton on the Wolds, Leics	61	A1
Burton Overy, Leics	61	B3
Burton Pedwardine, Lincs	74	C3
Burton Pidsea, E R of Y	90	D3
Burton Salmon, N York	88	B4
Burton upon Stather, Lincs	83	C1
Burton upon Trent, Staffs	60	A1
Burton, Chesh	69	D1
Burton, Chesh	78	D4
Burton, Dorset	9	A1
Burton, Lincs	83	C4
Burton, Pemb	33	D3
Burton, Som	23	B4
Burton, Wilts	25	B1
Burton-in-Kendal, Cumb	92	A3
Burton's Green, Essex	43	C1
Burtonwood, Chesh	79	B3
Burwardsley, Chesh	69	D2
Burwarton, Shrops	58	A4
Burwash Common, E Suss	19	C2
Burwell, Cambs	53	C2
Burwell, Lincs	84	C4
Burwen, Angle	77	B3
Burwick, Orkney	144	A2
Bury Green, Herts	42	C2
Bury St Edmunds, Suff	54	B2
Bury, Cambs	63	A4
Bury, G Man	80	A1
Bury, Som	12	B2
Bury, W Suss	18	A3
Burythorpe, N York	95	A4
Buscot, Oxon	39	A4
Bush Bank, Heref	47	C3
Bushey, Herts	41	C4
Bushley, Worcs	48	C4
Bushton, Wilts	26	B1
Bussex, Som	13	B1
Butcher's Pasture, Essex	43	A1
Butcombe, Som	24	B3
Butleigh Wootton, Som	13	C1
Butleigh, Som	13	C1
Butlers Marston, Warwk	50	A3
Butley, Suff	55	C3
Buttercrambe, N York	89	B1
Butterleigh, Devon	12	B3
Buttermere, Cumb	97	E4
Butterstone, Perth	128	C4
Butterton, Staffs	70	C3
Butterton, Staffs	71	B2
Butterwick, Lincs	75	A3
Butterwick, N York	94	C3
Butterwick, N York	95	C4
Buttington, Powys	57	B2
Buttonoak, Shrops	48	B1
Buxted, E Suss	19	B2
Buxton Heath, Norf	65	A1
Buxton, Derby	81	B4
Buxton, Norf	65	A1
Bwlch, Powys	36	A1
Bwlchgwyn, Wrex	69	B2
Bwlchllan, Cered	46	A2
Bwlch-y-cibau, Powys	57	A1
Bwlch-y-ffridd, Powys	56	E3
Bwlch-y-groes, Pemb	45	D4
Bwlch-y-sarnau, Powys	46	E1
Byers Green, Durham	100	A3
Byfield, Nhants	50	C3
Byfleet, Surrey	146	A3
Byford, Heref	47	C4
Bylchau, Aberc	68	C1
Byley, Chesh	70	B1
Byrness, Nthumb	105	A1
Bythorn, Cambs	52	A1
Byton, Heref	47	C2
Byworth, W Suss	18	A2
Cabourne, Lincs	84	A2
Cabrach, Moray	133	D1
Cabus, Lancs	85	C2
Cadbury, Devon	12	B4
Cadder, E Dun	115	C3
Caddington, Beds	41	B2
Cade Street, E Suss	19	C2
Cadeby, Leics	60	C3
Cadeby, S York	82	C2
Cadeleigh, Devon	12	B3
Cadgwith, Corn	1	D3
Cadley, Wilts	26	C2
Cadley, Wilts	26	C3
Cadmore End, Bucks	40	C4
Cadney, Lincs	83	D2
Caeathro, Gwyn	67	D1
Caenby, Lincs	83	D3
Caeo, Carm	46	B4
Caer Farchell, Pemb	33	B1
Caerau, Brig	35	B4
Caergeiliog, Angle	77	B4
Caergwrle, Flint	69	B2
Caerleon, Newport	36	B4
Caernarfon, Gwyn	67	D1
Caerphilly, Caer	23	B1
Caersws, Powys	56	E3
Caerwedros, Cered	45	E3
Caerwent, Monm	37	A4
Caerwys, Flint	78	C4
Cairndow, Argyll	121	C3
Cairneyhill, Fife	117	A1
Cairngarroch, Dumf	96	A1
Cairnie, Aber	139	A4
Cairnryan, Dumf	102	A3
Caister-on-Sea, Norf	66	B2
Caistor St Edmund, Norf	65	A2
Caistor, Lincs	84	A2
Calbourne, I of W	9	C1
Calcot, Flint	78	C4
Calcot, Glouc	38	C3
Caldbeck, Cumb	98	A2
Caldecote Highfields, Cambs	53	A2
Caldecote, Cambs	53	A3
Caldecote, Cambs	62	C4
Caldecote, Herts	52	C4
Caldecott, Nhants	52	A1
Caldecott, Rutland	62	A3
Calder Bridge, Cumb	91	B1
Calder Grove, W Yorks	82	A1
Calder Vale, Lancs	85	C2
Caldercruix, N Lan	116	B3
Caldicot, Monm	37	A4
Caldwell, N York	100	A4
Calfsound, Orkney	144	B1
Calgary, Argyll	125	D4
Califer, Moray	138	A3
California, Falk	116	C2
California, Norf	66	B1
Calke, Derby	60	B1
Callakille, High	135	E3
Callander, Stirl	122	C3
Callestick, Corn	3	B4
Callington, Corn	4	B3
Callow End, Worcs	48	C3
Callow Hill, Wilts	26	A1
Callow, Heref	47	D4
Calmsden, Glouc	38	C3
Calne, Wilts	26	A2
Calshot, Hants	16	A4
Calstock, Corn	4	C3
Calstone Wellington, Wilts	26	A2
Calthorpe Street, Norf	66	A1
Calthwaite, Cumb	98	C2
Calton, Staffs	71	B2
Calveley, Chesh	70	A2
Calver, Derby	81	C4
Calverhall, Shrops	70	A4
Calverleigh, Devon	12	B3
Calverton, Bucks	51	B4
Calverton, Notts	73	A2
Calvine, Perth	128	A2
Calvo, Cumb	97	E1
Cam, Glouc	37	C3
Camasunary, High	130	D2
Camber, E Suss	21	A2
Camberley, Surrey	28	B3
Camberwell, G Lon	149	A2
Camblesforth, N York	89	B4
Cambo, Nthumb	105	C2
Camborne, Corn	1	D1
Cambridge, Cambs	53	B2
Cambus, Clack	116	B1
Cambusbarron, Stirl	116	B1
Cambuslang, S Lan	115	C4
Camden Town, G Lon	148	B2
Camelford, Corn	3	E1
Camer's Green, Worcs	48	B4
Camerton, Cumb	97	D3
Camerton, Som	24	C3
Camghouran, Perth	127	D3
Cammachmore, Aber	134	C4
Cammeringham, Lincs	83	C4
Campbeltown, Argyll	107	D3
Campsall, S York	82	C1
Campsea Ash, Suff	55	B3
Campton, Beds	52	B4
Camptown, Border	111	A4
Camrose, Pemb	33	C2
Camserney, Perth	128	A4
Canada, Hants	15	C3
Candlesby, Lincs	75	B1
Cane End, Oxon	27	C1
Canewdon, Essex	44	A4
Canford Magna, Dorset	14	D4
Canisbay, High	143	E1
Cann, Dorset	14	C2
Cannich, High	131	E1
Canning Town, G Lon	149	B2
Cannington, Som	13	A1
Cannock, Staffs	59	A2
Cannon Bridge, Heref	47	C4
Canon Frome, Heref	48	A4
Canon Pyon, Heref	47	C3
Canonbie, Dumf	104	C3
Canons Ashby, Nhants	50	C3
Canonstown, Corn	1	C2
Canterbury, Kent	32	B3
Cantley, Norf	66	A2
Cantley, S York	83	A2
Cantsfield, Lancs	92	B4
Canvey Island, Essex	31	B1
Canwick, Lincs	74	B1
Canworthy Water, Corn	4	A1
Caol, High	126	E2
Caoles, Argyll	125	B4
Capel Bangor, Cered	56	A4
Capel Coch, Angle	77	C4
Capel Curig, Aberc	68	A2
Capel Dewi, Carm	34	C2
Capel Dewi, Cered	45	F4
Capel Garmon, Aberc	68	B2
Capel Gwynfe, Carm	35	A1
Capel Hendre, Carm	34	D2
Capel Iwan, Carm	45	D4
Capel le Ferne, Kent	21	D1
Capel Mawr, Angle	67	C1
Capel Seion, Cered	46	A1
Capel St Andrew, Suff	55	C3
Capel St Mary, Suff	54	D4
Capel, Kent	30	B4
Capel, Surrey	18	B1
Capel-Dewi, Cered	56	A4
Capelulo, Aberc	77	E4
Capenhurst, Chesh	79	A4
Capheaton, Nthumb	105	C2
Capton, Devon	5	C4
Capton, Som	12	C1
Caputh, Perth	123	C1
Car Colston, Notts	73	B3
Carbost, High	130	B1
Carbrooke, Norf	64	C3
Carcroft, S York	82	C1
Card, Card	23	B1
Cardenden, Fife	117	B1
Cardigan, Cered	45	C3
Cardington, Beds	52	B3
Cardington, Shrops	57	D3
Cardinham, Corn	3	E3
Cardross, Argyll	115	A2
Cardurnock, Cumb	104	A4
Careby, Lincs	62	B1
Carew Newton, Pemb	33	D3
Carew, Pemb	33	D3
Carey, Heref	37	A1
Carfraemill, Border	119	A4
Cargate Green, Norf	66	A2
Cargo, Cumb	104	C4
Cargreen, Corn	4	C3
Carham, Nthumb	111	B1
Carhampton, Som	23	A4
Carharrack, Corn	1	D1
Cark, Cumb	91	E3
Carkeel, Corn	4	B3
Carlbury, Durham	100	A4
Carlby, Lincs	62	B2
Carlcroft, Nthumb	111	C4
Carleton Forehoe, Norf	64	D2
Carleton Rode, Norf	64	D3
Carleton, N York	87	A2
Carlingcott, Som	25	A3
Carlisle, Cumb	98	B1
Carlops, Border	117	B4
Carloway, W Isle	144	B2
Carlton Colville, Suff	66	B4
Carlton Curlieu, Leics	61	B3
Carlton Green, Cambs	53	C3
Carlton Husthwaite, N York	94	A3
Carlton in Lindrick, Notts	82	C3
Carlton Miniott, N York	94	A3
Carlton Scroop, Lincs	74	A3
Carlton, Beds	51	C3
Carlton, Cambs	53	C3
Carlton, Durham	100	C4
Carlton, Leics	60	C2
Carlton, N York	89	B4
Carlton, N York	93	B3
Carlton, N York	94	B3
Carlton, S York	82	A1
Carlton, Suff	55	C2
Carlton, W Yorks	88	A4
Carlton-in-Cleveland, N York	94	B1
Carlton-le-Moorland, Lincs	74	A2
Carlton-on-Trent, Notts	73	C1
Carluke, S Lan	116	B4
Carmarthen, Carm	34	B2
Carmel, Carm	34	D2
Carmel, Gwyn	67	D2
Carmunnock, Glas	115	C4
Carn Brea, Corn	1	D1
Carnaby, E R of Y	95	D4
Carnbee, Fife	124	C4
Carnbo, Perth	123	C4
Carnforth, Lancs	92	A4
Carnhell Green, Corn	1	C1
Carnkie, Corn	1	D2

PLACE	PAGE	GRID
Carno, Powys	56	D3
Carnon Downs, Corn	2	A1
Carnoustie, Angus	124	C1
Carnwath, S Lan	109	D1
Carol Green, W Mids	49	C1
Carperby, N York	93	A2
Carr Gate, W Yorks	88	A4
Carr Shield, Nthumb	99	A1
Carradale, Argyll	107	E1
Carrbridge, High	132	E1
Carreglefn, Angle	77	B3
Carrhouse, Lincs	83	B2
Carrick Castle, Argyll	114	D1
Carrick, Argyll	114	A1
Carriden, Falk	117	A2
Carrington, G Man	80	A3
Carrington, M Loth	118	A4
Carrog, Denb	68	D3
Carronbridge, Dumf	103	C1
Carrutherstown, Dumf	103	E3
Carseriggan, Dumf	102	D4
Carsethorn, Dumf	103	D4
Carshalton, G Lon	147	A4
Carsington, Derby	71	C2
Carsphairn, Dumf	103	A1
Carstairs Junction, S Lan	109	D1
Carstairs, S Lan	109	D1
Carterton, Oxon	39	B3
Carthew, Corn	3	D4
Carthorpe, N York	93	D3
Cartmel, Cumb	91	E3
Carway, Carm	34	C3
Cassington, Oxon	39	C2
Cassop Colliery, Durham	100	B2
Casterton, Cumb	92	B3
Castle Acre, Norf	64	B1
Castle Ashby, Nhants	51	C2
Castle Bolton, N York	93	A2
Castle Bytham, Lincs	62	B1
Castle Caereinion, Powys	57	A2
Castle Camps, Cambs	53	C4
Castle Carrock, Cumb	98	C1
Castle Cary, Som	14	A1
Castle Combe, Wilts	25	B1
Castle Donington, Leics	72	B4
Castle Douglas, Dumf	103	B4
Castle Eaton, Wilts	38	C4
Castle Eden, Durham	100	C2
Castle Frome, Heref	48	A3
Castle Green, Surrey	146	A3
Castle Gresley, Derby	60	B1
Castle Hedingham, Essex	54	B4
Castle Kennedy, Dumf	102	B4
Castle Pulverbatch, Shrops	57	C3
Castle Rising, Norf	64	A1
Castlebay, W Isle	144	A4
Castlebythe, Pemb	33	D1
Castleford, W Yorks	88	B4
Castlemartin, Pemb	33	C4
Castlemorton, Worcs	48	B4
Castleside, Durham	99	D1
Castlethorpe, Bucks	51	B4
Castleton, Derby	81	B4
Castleton, N York	94	C1
Castleton, Newport	23	C1
Castletown, High	143	D1
Castletown, I of M	145	B4
Castley, N York	87	C2
Caston, Norf	64	C3
Castor, Cambs	62	C3
Catchall, Corn	1	B2
Catcliffe, S York	82	B3
Catcomb, Wilts	26	A1
Catcott Burtle, Som	24	A4
Catcott, Som	13	B1
Catel, Guern	145	B2
Caterham, Surrey	150	C2
Catfield, Norf	66	A1
Catford, G Lon	149	B3
Catforth, Lancs	85	C3
Cathedine, Powys	36	A1
Catherington, Hants	17	A3
Catherston Leweston, Dorset	7	B1
Catmere End, Essex	53	B4
Catmore, Berks	27	A1
Caton Green, Lancs	92	A4
Caton, Lancs	85	C1
Catrine, E Ayrs	108	E3
Catsfield, E Suss	20	A3
Catsgore, Som	13	C2
Cattal, N York	88	B1
Cattawade, Suff	44	B1
Catterall, Lancs	85	C2
Catterick Bridge, N York	93	C2
Catterick, N York	93	C2
Catterlen, Cumb	98	C3
Catterline, Aber	129	E1
Catterton, N York	89	A2
Catteshall, Surrey	146	A4
Catthorpe, Leics	50	C1
Cattistock, Dorset	14	A4
Catton, N York	93	D3
Catton, Nthumb	105	B4
Catwick, E R of Y	90	C2
Catworth, Cambs	52	B1
Caudle Green, Glouc	38	B3
Caulcott, Oxon	40	A1
Cauldhame, Stirl	115	C1
Cauldmill, Border	110	D3
Cauldon, Staffs	71	B2
Cauldwell, Derby	60	A1
Caundle Marsh, Dorset	14	A3
Caunton, Notts	73	C2
Causeway End, Essex	43	B2
Causey Park Bridge, Nthumb	106	A1
Cavendish, Suff	54	B3
Cavenham, Suff	54	A1
Caversfield, Oxon	40	A1
Caverswall, Staffs	71	A3
Caverton Mill, Border	111	B3
Cawdor, High	137	C3
Cawood, N York	89	A3
Cawsand, Corn	4	C4
Cawston, Norf	65	A1

PLACE	PAGE	GRID
Cawthorne, S York	82	A1
Caxton, Cambs	52	C2
Caynham, Shrops	47	D1
Caythorpe, Lincs	74	A3
Caythorpe, Notts	73	B3
Cayton, N York	95	C3
Cefn Cribwr, Bridg	22	D1
Cefn-brith, Aberc	68	C2
Cefngorwydd, Powys	46	D3
Cefn-mawr, Wrex	69	B3
Cefn-y-pant, Carm	33	E1
Cellardyke, Fife	124	C4
Cellarhead, Staffs	71	A3
Cemmaes Road, Powys	56	C2
Cemmaes, Powys	56	C2
Cenarth, Cered	45	D4
Ceres, Fife	124	B3
Cerne Abbas, Dorset	14	A4
Cerney Wick, Glouc	38	C4
Cerrigceinwen, Angle	77	B4
Cerrigydrudion, Aberc	68	C3
Ceunant, Gwyn	67	D1
Chaceley, Glouc	38	A1
Chacewater, Corn	2	A1
Chackmore, Bucks	51	A4
Chacombe, Nhants	50	B4
Chadbury, Worcs	49	A3
Chadderton, G Man	80	B2
Chaddesley Corbett, Worcs	48	C1
Chaddlehanger, Devon	4	C2
Chaddleworth, Berks	27	A1
Chadlington, Oxon	39	B2
Chadshunt, Warwk	50	A3
Chadwell, Leics	61	C1
Chadwick End, W Mids	49	C1
Chadwick, Worcs	48	C1
Chaffcombe, Som	13	B3
Chagford, Devon	5	B1
Chailey, E Suss	19	A2
Chainhurst, Kent	31	A4
Chaldon, Surrey	150	B2
Chale Green, I of W	9	C2
Chale, I of W	9	C2
Chalfont St Giles, Bucks	41	B4
Chalfont St Peter, Bucks	41	B4
Chalford, Glouc	38	A3
Chalgrove, Oxon	40	B4
Challacombe, Devon	11	F1
Challock Lees, Kent	32	A4
Chalton, Beds	41	B1
Chalton, Hants	17	A3
Chalvey, Berks	146	A1
Chalvington, E Suss	19	B3
Chandler's Cross, Herts	41	B4
Chandler's Ford, Hants	16	A2
Chantry, Som	25	A4
Chapel Allerton, Som	24	A4
Chapel Amble, Corn	3	D2
Chapel Brampton, Nhants	51	A2
Chapel Green, Warwk	50	B2
Chapel Haddlesey, N York	89	A4
Chapel Hill, Lincs	74	D2
Chapel Hill, Monm	37	A3
Chapel Lawn, Shrops	47	B1
Chapel le Dale, N York	92	C3
Chapel Leigh, Som	12	D2
Chapel of Garioch, Aber	134	B1
Chapel Row, Berks	27	B2
Chapel St Leonards, Lincs	75	C1
Chapel-en-le-Frith, Derby	81	B4
Chapelhall, N Lan	116	B3
Chapelhope, Border	110	A3
Chapelknowe, Dumf	104	B3
Chapelton, Angus	129	C4
Chapelton, Devon	11	E2
Chapelton, S Lan	109	B1
Chapeltown, S York	82	A2
Chapmans Well, Devon	4	B1
Chapmanslade, Wilts	25	B4
Chapmore End, Herts	42	B2
Chappel, Essex	44	A1
Chard Junction, Som	13	A4
Chard, Som	13	A3
Chardstock, Devon	13	A4
Charfield, Glouc	37	C4
Charing, Kent	31	C4
Charingworth, Glouc	49	C4
Charlbury, Oxon	39	B2
Charlcombe, Som	25	A2
Charlcutt, Wilts	26	A2
Charlecote, Warwk	49	C3
Charles Tye, Suff	54	D3
Charles, Devon	11	F1
Charleshill, Surrey	28	B4
Charleston, Angus	129	A4
Charlestown, Fife	117	A2
Charlestown, W Yorks	87	A4
Charlesworth, Derby	81	A3
Charlinch, Som	13	A1
Charlton Abbots, Glouc	38	B1
Charlton Adam, Som	13	C2
Charlton Horethorne, Som	14	A2
Charlton Kings, Glouc	38	B2
Charlton Mackrell, Som	13	C2
Charlton Marshall, Dorset	14	C4
Charlton Musgrove, Som	14	B1
Charlton, G Lon	149	B2
Charlton, Nhants	50	C4
Charlton, Nthumb	105	B2
Charlton, Shrops	58	A2
Charlton, Som	13	A2
Charlton, Som	24	C4
Charlton, Surrey	146	B2
Charlton, W Suss	17	C3
Charlton, Wilts	14	C2
Charlton, Wilts	26	B3
Charlton, Wilts	38	B4
Charlton, Worcs	49	A3
Charlton-all-Saints, Wilts	15	B2
Charlton-on-Otmoor, Oxon	40	A2
Charlwood, Hants	17	A1
Charminster, Dorset	7	D1
Charmouth, Dorset	7	B1
Charndon, Bucks	40	B1

PLACE	PAGE	GRID
Charney Bassett, Oxon	39	B4
Charnock Richard, Lancs	79	B1
Charsfield, Suff	55	B3
Chart Sutton, Kent	31	B4
Charter Alley, Hants	27	B3
Charterhouse, Som	24	B3
Chartham Hatch, Kent	32	A3
Chartham, Kent	32	A3
Chartridge, Bucks	41	A3
Charwelton, Nhants	50	C3
Chastleton, Oxon	39	A1
Chasty, Devon	11	C4
Chatburn, Lancs	86	B2
Chatcull, Staffs	70	B4
Chatham Green, Essex	43	B2
Chatham, Kent	31	A2
Chathill, Nthumb	112	C2
Chattenden, Kent	31	A2
Chatteris, Cambs	63	B4
Chatterton, Lancs	86	B4
Chattisham, Suff	54	D4
Chatton, Nthumb	112	B2
Chawleigh, Devon	11	F3
Chawton, Hants	17	A1
Cheadle, G Man	80	B3
Cheadle, Staffs	71	A3
Cheam, G Lon	150	A1
Cheapside, Berks	28	B2
Chearsley, Bucks	40	B2
Chebsey, Staffs	70	C4
Checkendon, Oxon	27	C1
Checkley, Chesh	70	B3
Checkley, Staffs	71	A3
Chedburgh, Suff	54	B2
Cheddar, Som	24	A3
Cheddington, Bucks	41	A2
Cheddleton, Staffs	71	A2
Chedgrave, Norf	66	A3
Chedington, Dorset	13	C4
Chediston, Suff	55	C1
Chedworth, Glouc	38	C2
Chedzoy, Som	13	A1
Cheldon, Devon	11	F3
Chelford, Chesh	80	B4
Chellington, Beds	51	C3
Chelmarsh, Shrops	58	B4
Chelmondiston, Suff	55	A4
Chelmorton, Derby	71	B1
Chelmsford, Essex	43	B3
Chelsea, G Lon	148	A4
Chelsfield, G Lon	30	A2
Chelsham, Surrey	150	D1
Chelsworth, Suff	54	C3
Cheltenham, Glouc	38	B1
Chelvey, Som	24	B2
Chelwood Gate, E Suss	19	A1
Chelwood, Som	24	C3
Chelworth Upper Green, Wilts	38	C4
Cheney Longville, Shrops	57	C4
Chenies, Bucks	41	B4
Chepstow, Monm	37	A4
Cherhill, Wilts	26	A2
Cherington, Glouc	38	A4
Cheriton Bishop, Devon	5	B1
Cheriton Fitzpaine, Devon	12	A4
Cheriton or Stackpole Elidor, Pemb	33	D4
Cheriton, Hants	16	B2
Cheriton, Swan	34	C4
Cherry Burton, E R of Y	90	B2
Cherry Willingham, Lincs	83	D4
Chertsey, Surrey	146	A2
Cheselbourne, Dorset	14	B4
Chesham, Bucks	41	A3
Cheshunt, Herts	42	B3
Cheslyn Hay, Staffs	59	A2
Chessetts Wood, Warwk	49	C1
Chessington, G Lon	146	B3
Chester Moor, Durham	100	A1
Chester, Chesh	69	C1
Chesterfield, Derby	72	A1
Chesterfield, Staffs	59	B2
Chester-le-Street, Durham	100	A1
Chesters, Border	111	A4
Chesterton Green, Warwk	50	A2
Chesterton, Cambs	62	C3
Chesterton, Oxon	40	A2
Chesterton, Shrops	58	B3
Chesterwood, Nthumb	105	B4
Cheston, Devon	5	B4
Cheswardine, Shrops	70	B4
Cheswick, Nthumb	112	A1
Chetnole, Dorset	14	A3
Chettisham, Cambs	63	D4
Chettle, Dorset	14	D3
Chetton, Shrops	58	A4
Chetwynd Aston, Shrops	58	B1
Chetwynd, Shrops	58	B1
Cheveley, Cambs	54	A2
Chevening, Kent	30	A3
Chevington Drift, Nthumb	106	A1
Chevington, Suff	54	B2
Chew Magna, Som	24	B3
Chew Stoke, Som	24	B3
Chewton Keynsham, Som	24	C2
Chewton Mendip, Som	24	C3
Chicheley, Bucks	51	C3
Chichester, W Suss	17	C4
Chickerell, Dorset	7	D2
Chicklade, Wilts	14	C1
Chidden, Hants	17	A3
Chiddingly, E Suss	19	C3
Chiddingstone, Kent	30	A4
Chideock, Dorset	7	B1
Chidswell, W Yorks	87	C4
Chieveley, Berks	27	A2
Chignall Smealy, Essex	43	B2
Chignall St James, Essex	43	B3
Chigwell, Essex	42	C4
Chilbolton, Hants	16	A1
Chilcomb, Hants	16	B2
Chilcombe, Dorset	7	C1
Chilcompton, Som	24	C4

PLACE	PAGE	GRID
Chilcote, Leics	60	B2
Child Okeford, Dorset	14	C3
Childer Thornton, Chesh	79	A4
Childrey, Oxon	39	B4
Child's Ercall, Shrops	58	A1
Childswickham, Worcs	49	B4
Childthrome, Dorset	14	A4
Chilgrove, W Suss	17	B3
Chilham, Kent	32	A3
Chillaton, Devon	4	C2
Chillenden, Kent	32	C3
Chillerton, I of W	9	C1
Chillesford, Suff	55	C3
Chillingham, Nthumb	112	B3
Chillington, Devon	10	B1
Chillington, Som	13	B3
Chilmark, Wilts	14	D1
Chilmington Green, Kent	21	A1
Chilson, Oxon	39	B2
Chilsworthy, Corn	4	B2
Chilsworthy, Devon	11	C4
Chilthorne Domer, Som	13	C2
Chilton Candover, Hants	16	B1
Chilton Cantelo, Som	13	C2
Chilton Foliat, Wilts	26	D2
Chilton Street, Suff	54	A3
Chilton Trinity, Som	13	A1
Chilton, Bucks	40	B2
Chilton, Durham	100	B3
Chilton, Oxon	27	A1
Chilworth, Hants	16	A2
Chilworth, Surrey	146	A4
Chimney, Oxon	39	B3
Chinley, Derby	81	A4
Chinnor, Oxon	40	C3
Chipnall, Shrops	70	B4
Chippenham, Cambs	54	A1
Chippenham, Wilts	25	B2
Chipperfield, Herts	41	B3
Chipping Campden, Glouc	49	B4
Chipping Norton, Oxon	39	B1
Chipping Ongar, Essex	43	A3
Chipping Warden, Nhants	50	B3
Chipping, Herts	42	B1
Chipping, Lancs	86	A2
Chipstable, Som	12	C2
Chipstead, Kent	30	A3
Chipstead, Surrey	150	B2
Chirbury, Shrops	57	B3
Chirk, Wrex	69	B3
Chirnside, Border	119	D4
Chirnsidebridge, Border	119	D4
Chirton, Wilts	26	D2
Chiselborough, Som	13	C3
Chiseldon, Wilts	26	C1
Chislehampton, Oxon	40	A3
Chislehurst, G Lon	30	A2
Chislet, Kent	32	B2
Chisley, W Yorks	87	A4
Chiswick, G Lon	147	A2
Chisworth, Derby	81	A3
Chittering, Cambs	53	B1
Chitterne, Wilts	26	A4
Chittlehamholt, Devon	11	E2
Chittlehampton, Devon	11	E2
Chittlehampton, Devon	11	E3
Chittoe, Wilts	26	A2
Chivelstone, Devon	10	B1
Chobham, Surrey	146	A3
Cholderton, Wilts	26	C4
Cholesbury, Bucks	41	A3
Chollerton, Nthumb	105	C3
Cholsey, Oxon	27	B1
Cholstrey, Heref	47	D2
Chop Gate, N York	94	B1
Choppington, Nthumb	106	A2
Chopwell, Tyne	105	D4
Chorley, Chesh	69	D2
Chorley, Lancs	79	C1
Chorley, Shrops	58	A4
Chorleywood, Herts	41	B4
Chorlton Lane, Chesh	69	C3
Chorlton, Chesh	70	B2
Choulton, Shrops	57	C4
Chowley, Chesh	69	D2
Chrishall, Essex	53	B4
Christchurch, Cambs	63	C3
Christchurch, Dorset	9	A1
Christian Malford, Wilts	26	A1
Christon Bank, Nthumb	112	C3
Christon, Som	24	A3
Christow, Devon	5	C1
Chudleigh Knighton, Devon	5	C2
Chudleigh, Devon	5	C2
Chulmleigh, Devon	11	F3
Church Brampton, Nhants	51	A2
Church Broughton, Derby	71	C4
Church Eaton, Staffs	58	C1
Church End, Beds	52	B4
Church End, Essex	43	B1
Church End, Hants	27	C3
Church Enstone, Oxon	39	B1
Church Fenton, N York	89	A3
Church Green, Devon	12	D4
Church Hanborough, Oxon	39	C2
Church Hill, Chesh	70	A1
Church Houses, N York	94	C2
Church Langton, Leics	61	B3
Church Lawford, Warwk	50	B1
Church Lawton, Chesh	70	C2
Church Leigh, Staffs	71	A4
Church Lench, Worcs	49	A3
Church Minshull, Chesh	70	A2
Church Norton, W Suss	17	C4
Church Preen, Shrops	57	D3
Church Pulverbatch, Shrops	57	C2
Church Stowe, Nhants	51	A2
Church Street, Kent	31	A2
Church Stretton, Shrops	57	C3
Church Village, Rhond	23	A1
Church Warsop, Notts	73	A1
Church, Lancs	86	B4
Churcham, Glouc	37	C2
Churchend, Essex	44	A4

PLACE	PAGE	GRID
Churchill, Devon	13	A4
Churchill, Oxon	39	B1
Churchill, Som	24	A3
Churchill, Worcs	48	C1
Churchill, Worcs	48	C3
Churchinford, Som	12	D3
Churchover, Warwk	61	A4
Churchstanton, Som	12	D3
Churchstoke, Powys	57	B3
Churchstow, Devon	10	A1
Churchtown, Lancs	85	C2
Churston Ferrers, Devon	6	A4
Churt, Surrey	17	C1
Churton, Chesh	69	C2
Churwell, W Yorks	87	C4
Chwilog, Gwyn	67	D3
Cilcain, Flint	69	A1
Cilcennin, Cered	45	F2
Cilfrew, Neath	35	A3
Cilfynydd, Rhond	35	D4
Cilgerran, Pemb	45	D4
Cilgwyn, Carm	35	A1
Cilmaengwyn, Neath	35	A3
Cilmery, Powys	46	E3
Cilrhedyn, Pemb	45	D4
Cilsan, Carm	34	D1
Ciltalgarth, Gwyn	68	C3
Cilycwm, Carm	46	B4
Cinderford, Glouc	37	B2
Cippenham, Berks	28	B1
Cirencester, Glouc	38	B3
City, G Lon	149	A2
Clachan Mor, Argyll	125	A4
Clachan of Campsie, E Dun	115	C2
Clachan, Argyll	113	F4
Clachaneasy, Dumf	102	D3
Clackmannan, Clack	116	C1
Clacton-on-Sea, Essex	44	C2
Cladswell, Worcs	49	B2
Clanfield, Hants	17	A3
Clanfield, Oxon	39	B3
Clanville, Hants	26	D4
Clanville, Som	14	A1
Claonaig, Argyll	114	A4
Clapham, Beds	52	A3
Clapham, G Lon	147	B1
Clapham, N York	92	C4
Clapton, Som	24	C3
Clapton-in-Gordano, Som	24	B2
Clapton-on-the-Hill, Glouc	39	A2
Claravale, Tyne	105	D4
Clarbeston Road, Pemb	33	D2
Clarbeston, Pemb	33	D2
Clarborough, Notts	83	A4
Clare, Suff	54	A3
Clarebrand, Dumf	103	B4
Clarencefield, Dumf	103	E4
Clarewood, Nthumb	105	C3
Clarilaw, Border	110	D3
Clatt, Aber	133	E1
Clatter, Powys	56	D3
Clatworthy, Som	12	C1
Claughton, Lancs	85	C2
Claughton, Lancs	92	A4
Claverdon, Warwk	49	C2
Claverham, Som	24	A2
Clavering, Essex	42	C1
Claverley, Shrops	58	B3
Claverton, Som	25	A3
Clawdd-coch, Glam	23	A1
Clawdd-newydd, Denb	68	D2
Clawton, Devon	11	C4
Claxby, Lincs	84	A3
Claxton, N York	89	B1
Claxton, Norf	65	B2
Clay Coton, Nhants	50	C1
Clay Cross, Derby	72	B1
Claybrooke Magna, Leics	60	C4
Claydon, Oxon	50	B3
Claydon, Suff	55	A3
Claygate, Dumf	104	C3
Claygate, Kent	31	A4
Claygate, Surrey	146	B3
Clayhanger, Devon	12	C2
Clayhidon, Devon	12	D3
Clayhill, E Suss	20	B2
Claypits, Glouc	37	C3
Claypole, Lincs	73	C2
Clayton West, W Yorks	81	C1
Clayton, S York	82	B1
Clayton, W Suss	18	C3
Clayton-le-Moors, Lancs	86	B3
Clayton-le-Woods, Lancs	85	C4
Clayworth, Notts	83	A3
Cleadon, Tyne	106	B4
Clearbrook, Devon	4	C3
Clearwell, Glouc	37	A3
Cleasby, N York	100	A4
Cleatlam, Durham	99	D4
Cleator Moor, Cumb	97	D4
Cleator, Cumb	97	D4
Clee St Margaret, Shrops	57	D4
Cleehill, Shrops	48	A1
Cleethorpes, Lincs	84	B1
Cleeton St Mary, Shrops	48	A1
Cleeve Hill, Glouc	38	B1
Cleeve Prior, Worcs	49	B3
Cleeve, Oxon	27	B1
Cleeve, Som	24	A2
Clehonger, Heref	47	C4
Cleish, Perth	123	C4
Cleland, N Lan	116	B4
Clement Street, Kent	30	A2
Clenchwarton, Norf	63	D1
Clent, Worcs	49	A1
Cleobury Mortimer, Shrops	48	A1
Cleobury North, Shrops	58	A4
Clephanton, High	137	C3
Clevancy, Wilts	26	B2
Clevedon, Som	24	A2
Cleveleys, Lancs	85	A2
Cleverton, Wilts	26	A1
Clewer, Som	24	A4

PLACE	PAGE	GRID
Cley next the Sea, Norf	76	B3
Cliburn, Cumb	98	D3
Cliddesden, Hants	27	C4
Cliff End, E Suss	20	B3
Cliffe, Durham	100	A4
Cliffe, Kent	31	A1
Cliffe, N York	89	B3
Clifford Chambers, Warwk	49	C3
Clifford, Heref	47	B3
Clifford, W Yorks	88	B2
Clifford's Mesne, Glouc	37	C1
Clifton Campville, Staffs	60	A2
Clifton Hampden, Oxon	40	A4
Clifton upon Dunsmore, Warwk	50	C1
Clifton upon Teme, Worcs	48	B2
Clifton, Beds	52	B4
Clifton, Cumb	98	C3
Clifton, Derby	71	C3
Clifton, Lancs	85	B3
Clifton, N York	87	C2
Clifton, Oxon	39	C1
Clifton, S York	82	C2
Clifton, Worcs	48	C3
Climping, W Suss	18	A4
Clint Green, Norf	64	D2
Clint, N York	87	C1
Clintmains, Border	111	A2
Clippesby, Norf	66	A2
Clipsham, Rutland	62	B1
Clipston, Nhants	61	B4
Clipston, Notts	73	B4
Clipstone, Beds	41	A1
Clitheroe, Lancs	86	B2
Clive, Shrops	57	D1
Clixby, Lincs	84	A2
Clocaenog, Denb	68	D2
Clochan, Moray	138	D2
Clodock, Heref	36	B1
Clola, Aber	139	E4
Clophill, Beds	52	B4
Clopton Corner, Suff	55	A3
Clopton, Nhants	62	B4
Clopton, Suff	55	A3
Clos du Valle, Guern	145	B2
Closeburn, Dumf	103	D1
Closworth, Som	13	C3
Clothall, Herts	42	A1
Clotton, Chesh	69	D1
Clough Foot, W Yorks	86	C4
Clough Head, W Yorks	87	B4
Cloughton, N York	95	C2
Clova, Angus	128	E2
Clovelly, Devon	11	C2
Clovenfords, Border	110	C2
Clow Bridge, Lancs	86	C4
Clowne, Derby	82	B4
Clows Top, Worcs	48	B1
Clun, Shrops	57	B4
Clunbury, Shrops	57	C4
Clungunford, Shrops	47	C1
Clunton, Shrops	57	B4
Clutton Hill, Som	24	C3
Clutton, Chesh	69	C2
Clutton, Som	24	C3
Clydach, Monm	36	A2
Clydach, Swan	35	A3
Clydebank, Dumb	115	B3
Clydey, Pemb	45	D4
Clyffe Pypard, Wilts	26	B1
Clynder, Argyll	114	D1
Clynderwen, Carm	33	E2
Clyne, Neath	35	B3
Clynnog-fawr, Gwyn	67	C2
Clyro, Powys	47	A4
Clyst Honiton, Devon	6	A1
Clyst Hydon, Devon	12	C4
Clyst St George, Devon	6	A1
Clyst St Mary, Devon	6	A1
Cnwch Coch, Cered	46	B1
Coad's Green, Corn	4	A2
Coalburn, S Lan	109	C2
Coalburns, Tyne	105	D4
Coaley, Glouc	37	C3
Coalport, Shrops	58	A3
Coalsnaughton, Clack	116	C1
Coaltown of Balgonie, Fife	124	A4
Coaltown of Wemyss, Fife	124	A4
Coalville, Leics	60	C2
Coanwood, Nthumb	104	E4
Coat, Som	13	B2
Coatbridge, N Lan	116	A3
Coatdyke, N Lan	116	A3
Coate, Wilts	26	A3
Coates, Cambs	63	A3
Coates, Glouc	38	B3
Coates, Lincs	83	C4
Coates, W Suss	18	A3
Coberley, Glouc	38	B2
Cobham, Kent	31	A2
Cobham, Surrey	146	B3
Cobnash, Heref	47	C2
Cobo, Guern	145	B2
Cock Green, Essex	43	B2
Cockayne Hatley, Beds	52	C3
Cockburnspath, Border	119	C3
Cockenzie and Port Seton, E Loth	118	B2
Cockerham, Lancs	85	C2
Cockermouth, Cumb	97	E3
Cockernhoe Green, Herts	41	C1
Cockfield, Durham	99	D3
Cockfield, Suff	54	C3
Cocking Causeway, W Suss	17	C2
Cocking, W Suss	17	C3
Cocklake, Som	24	A4
Cockle Park, Nthumb	106	A2
Cockley Cley, Norf	64	B2
Cockpole Green, Berks	28	A1
Cockshutt, Shrops	69	C4
Cockthorpe, Norf	76	A3
Cockwood, Devon	6	A2
Cockyard, Derby	81	A4
Coddenham, Suff	55	A3

PLACE	PAGE	GRID
Coddington, Heref	48	B4
Coddington, Notts	73	C2
Codford St Mary, Wilts	14	D1
Codicote, Herts	42	A2
Codnor, Derby	72	B2
Codsall Wood, Staffs	58	C2
Codsall, Staffs	58	C2
Coedana, Angle	77	C4
Coedpoeth, Wrex	69	B2
Coed-y-paen, Monm	36	B4
Cogenhoe, Nhants	51	B2
Coggeshall, Essex	43	C1
Coillore, High	135	B4
Coity, Bridg	22	E1
Colaboll, High	141	B2
Colan, Corn	3	C3
Colaton Raleigh, Devon	6	B1
Colburn, N York	93	C2
Colby, I of M	145	B4
Colby, Norf	76	C4
Colchester, Essex	44	A1
Cold Ashby, Nhants	51	A1
Cold Ashton, Glouc	25	A2
Cold Aston, Glouc	38	C2
Cold Brayfield, Bucks	51	C3
Cold Hanworth, Lincs	83	D4
Cold Higham, Nhants	51	A3
Cold Kirby, N York	94	B3
Cold Norton, Essex	43	C3
Cold Overton, Leics	61	C2
Coldbackie, High	142	E2
Colden, W Yorks	87	A4
Coldharbour, Surrey	146	B4
Coldingham, Border	119	D3
Coldmeece, Staffs	70	C4
Coldred, Kent	32	C4
Coldstream, Border	111	C1
Coldwaltham, W Suss	18	A3
Coldwell, Heref	47	C4
Cole, Som	14	A1
Colebatch, Shrops	57	B4
Colebrook, Devon	12	C4
Colebrooke, Devon	11	F4
Coleby, Lincs	74	B2
Coleby, Lincs	90	A4
Coleford Water, Som	12	C1
Coleford, Devon	11	F4
Coleford, Glouc	37	A2
Coleford, Som	24	C4
Coleman's Hatch, E Suss	19	B1
Colemere, Shrops	69	C4
Colemore, Hants	17	A1
Colerne, Wilts	25	B2
Colesbourne, Glouc	38	B2
Coleshill, Bucks	41	A4
Coleshill, Oxon	39	A4
Coleshill, Warwk	60	A4
Coley, Som	24	C3
Colgate, W Suss	18	C1
Colinsburgh, Fife	124	C4
Colintraive, Argyll	114	B2
Colkirk, Norf	76	A4
Collaton St Mary, Devon	5	C4
College Town, Berks	28	B3
Collessie, Fife	124	A3
Collier Street, Kent	31	A4
Collier's End, Herts	42	B2
Collieston, Aber	134	D1
Collin, Dumf	103	E3
Collingbourne Ducis, Wilts	26	C3
Collingbourne Kingston, Wilts	26	C3
Collingham, Notts	73	C1
Collingham, W Yorks	88	B2
Collington, Heref	48	A2
Collingtree, Nhants	51	B3
Collins Green, Chesh	79	B3
Colliston, Angus	129	C4
Colliton, Devon	12	C4
Collyweston, Nhants	62	B2
Colmonell, S Ayrs	102	B2
Colmworth, Beds	52	B2
Coln Rogers, Glouc	38	C3
Coln St Aldwyns, Glouc	38	C3
Colnbrook, Berks	146	A1
Colne Engaine, Essex	43	C1
Colne, Cambs	53	A1
Colne, Lancs	86	C3
Colney Heath, Herts	42	A3
Colney, Norf	65	A2
Colpy, Aber	134	A1
Colston Bassett, Notts	73	B4
Coltfield, Moray	138	A2
Coltishall, Norf	65	B1
Colton, Cumb	91	D3
Colton, N York	89	A2
Colton, Norf	64	D2
Colton, Staffs	59	B1
Colt's Hill, Kent	30	B4
Colva, Powys	47	A3
Colvend, Dumf	97	B1
Colwall, Heref	48	B4
Colwell, Nthumb	105	C3
Colwich, Staffs	59	A1
Colwinston, Glam	22	E2
Colworth, W Suss	17	C4
Colwyn Bay, Aberc	77	F4
Colyford, Devon	7	A1
Colyton, Devon	7	A1
Combe Down, Som	25	A3
Combe Fishacre, Devon	5	C3
Combe Florey, Som	12	D1
Combe Hay, Som	25	A3
Combe Martin, Devon	22	B4
Combe St Nicholas, Som	13	A3
Combe, Berks	26	D3
Combe, Heref	47	B2
Combe, Oxon	39	C2
Comberbach, Chesh	79	C4
Comberford, Staffs	60	A2
Comberton, Cambs	53	A3
Comberton, Heref	47	D2
Combrook, Warwk	50	A3
Combs, Derby	81	B4
Combs, Suff	54	D3
Combwich, Som	23	C4
Commercial, Pemb	33	E2
Commins Coch, Powys	56	C2
Common Moor, Corn	4	A3
Commondale, N York	94	C1
Compstall, G Man	81	A3
Compton Abbas, Dorset	14	C2
Compton Abdale, Glouc	38	C2
Compton Bassett, Wilts	26	A2
Compton Beauchamp, Oxon	26	D1
Compton Bishop, Som	24	A3
Compton Chamberlayne, Wilts	14	D1
Compton Dando, Som	24	C2
Compton Dundon, Som	13	C1
Compton Durville, Som	13	B3
Compton Greenfield, Glouc	24	B1
Compton Martin, Som	24	B3
Compton Pauncefoot, Som	14	A2
Compton Valence, Dorset	7	D1
Compton, Berks	27	B1
Compton, Devon	5	C3
Compton, Staffs	58	C4
Compton, Surrey	28	B4
Compton, W Suss	17	B3
Compton, Wilts	26	B4
Comrie, Fife	117	A1
Comrie, Perth	123	A2
Conchra, High	131	A1
Concraigie, Perth	128	C4
Conderton, Worcs	49	A4
Condicote, Glouc	38	C1
Condover, Shrops	57	D2
Coney Weston, Suff	54	C1
Coneysthorpe, N York	94	C4
Congerstone, Leics	60	B2
Congham, Norf	64	A1
Congleton, Chesh	70	C1
Congresbury, Som	24	A3
Conington, Cambs	53	A2
Conington, Cambs	62	C4
Conisbrough, S York	82	C2
Conisholme, Lincs	84	C2
Coniston Cold, N York	86	C1
Coniston, Cumb	91	D2
Coniston, E R of Y	90	C3
Conistone, N York	93	A4
Connah's Quay, Flint	69	B1
Connel, Argyll	121	A1
Connor Downs, Corn	1	C1
Conon Bridge, High	137	A3
Cononley, N York	87	A2
Consall, Staffs	71	A3
Consett, Durham	99	D1
Constable Burton, N York	93	C2
Constantine, Corn	1	D2
Contin, High	136	F3
Conwy, Aberc	77	F4
Conyer's Green, Suff	54	B2
Cookbury, Devon	11	C4
Cookham Dean, Berks	28	B1
Cookham, Berks	28	B1
Cookhill, Worcs	49	B2
Cookley Green, Oxon	40	B4
Cookley, Suff	55	B1
Cookley, Worcs	58	C4
Cookney, Aber	134	C4
Cook's Green, Essex	44	C2
Cooks Green, Suff	54	C3
Cooksmill Green, Essex	43	A3
Coolham, W Suss	18	B2
Cooling, Kent	31	A1
Coombe Bissett, Wilts	15	A2
Coombe Cellars, Devon	6	A2
Coombe End, Som	12	C1
Coombe Hill, Glouc	38	A1
Coombe Keynes, Dorset	8	B1
Coombe, Glouc	37	A4
Coombe, Hants	17	A2
Cooperhill, Moray	137	D4
Coopersale Common, Essex	42	C3
Cop Street, Kent	32	C3
Copdock, Suff	54	D4
Copford Green, Essex	44	A1
Copgrove, N York	88	A1
Cople, Beds	52	B3
Copley, Durham	99	D3
Copmanthorpe, N York	89	A2
Copmere End, Staffs	70	B4
Copp, Lancs	85	B3
Coppathorne, Corn	11	B4
Coppenhall, Staffs	58	C1
Coppingford, Cambs	62	C4
Copplestone, Devon	12	A4
Coppull, Lancs	79	B1
Copsale, W Suss	18	B2
Copster Green, Lancs	86	A3
Copston Magna, Warwk	60	C4
Copt Hewick, N York	93	D4
Copt Oak, Leics	60	C2
Copthorne, Surrey	19	A1
Corbiere, Jersey	145	A2
Corbridge, Nthumb	105	C4
Corby Glen, Lincs	62	B1
Corby, Nhants	62	A4
Coreley, Shrops	48	A1
Corfe Castle, Dorset	8	C2
Corfe, Som	12	D2
Corfton, Shrops	57	D4
Corgarff, Aber	133	C3
Corhampton, Hants	16	B2
Corley Ash, Warwk	60	B4
Corley, Warwk	60	B4
Cornard Tye, Suff	54	C4
Cornforth, Durham	100	B2
Cornhill, Aber	139	B2
Cornholme, W Yorks	86	C4
Cornsay Colliery, Durham	100	A2
Cornsay, Durham	99	D2
Corntown, Glam	22	E1
Cornwell, Oxon	39	A1
Cornwood, Devon	5	A4
Cornworthy, Devon	5	C4
Corpach, High	126	E1
Corpusty, Norf	76	B4
Corrie, Dumf	104	A2
Corrie, N Ayrs	108	A1
Corringham, Essex	31	A1
Corringham, Lincs	83	C3
Corris Uchaf, Gwyn	56	B2
Corris, Gwyn	56	B2
Corscombe, Devon	11	E4
Corscombe, Dorset	13	C4
Corse Lawn, Glouc	38	A1
Corsham, Wilts	25	B2
Corsley Heath, Wilts	25	B4
Corsley, Wilts	25	B4
Corsock, Dumf	103	B3
Corston, Som	25	A2
Corston, Wilts	25	B1
Corton Denham, Som	14	A2
Corton, Wilts	14	D1
Corwen, Denb	68	D3
Coryton, Devon	4	C1
Coryton, Essex	31	A1
Cosby, Leics	61	A3
Cosgrove, Nhants	51	B4
Cosheston, Pemb	33	D3
Cossall, Notts	72	B3
Cossington, Leics	61	A2
Cossington, Som	13	B1
Costessey, Norf	65	A2
Costock, Notts	73	A4
Coston, Leics	61	C1
Coston, Norf	64	D2
Cote, Oxon	39	B3
Cotebrook, Chesh	69	D1
Cotehill, Cumb	98	C1
Cotes, Leics	61	A1
Cotesbach, Leics	61	A4
Cotgrave, Notts	73	B4
Cotham, Notts	73	C3
Cotherstone, Durham	99	C4
Cothill, Oxon	39	C3
Cotleigh, Devon	12	D4
Coton in the Elms, Derby	60	A1
Coton, Cambs	53	A2
Coton, Nhants	51	A1
Coton, Staffs	58	C1
Cott, Devon	5	C3
Cottam, Lancs	85	C3
Cottam, Notts	83	B4
Cottenham, Cambs	53	B2
Cottered, Herts	42	B1
Cotterstock, Nhants	62	B4
Cottesbrooke, Nhants	51	A1
Cottesmore, Rutland	62	A2
Cottingham, E R of Y	90	B3
Cottisford, Oxon	40	A1
Cotton, Suff	54	D2
Cotts, Devon	4	C3
Coughton, Warwk	49	B2
Coulport, Argyll	114	D1
Coulsdon, Surrey	150	B1
Coulston, Wilts	26	A3
Coulter, S Lan	109	E2
Coulton, N York	94	C4
Cound, Shrops	57	D2
Coundon, Durham	100	A3
Countersett, N York	92	D2
Countesthorpe, Leics	61	A3
Countisbury, Devon	22	C4
Coupar Angus, Perth	123	D1
Coupland, Nthumb	112	A2
Courance, Dumf	103	E2
Court Henry, Carm	34	D1
Courteenhall, Nhants	51	B3
Courtsend, Essex	44	B4
Courtway, Som	12	D1
Cousland, M Loth	118	B3
Cove, Argyll	114	D2
Cove, Border	119	C3
Cove, Devon	12	B2
Cove, Hants	28	B3
Cove, High	140	A4
Covehithe, Suff	66	B4
Coven, Staffs	58	C2
Coveney, Cambs	63	C4
Covenham St Bartholomew, Lincs	84	C3
Covenham St Mary, Lincs	84	C3
Coventry, W Mids	50	A1
Coverack Bridges, Corn	1	D2
Coverack, Corn	2	A3
Coverham, N York	93	B3
Covington, Cambs	52	A1
Cow Honeybourne, Worcs	49	B4
Cowbit, Lincs	63	A1
Cowbridge, Glam	22	E2
Cowden Station, Kent	30	A4
Cowden, Kent	19	B1
Cowdenbeath, Fife	117	B1
Cowes, I of W	16	A4
Cowesby, N York	94	A2
Cowfold, W Suss	18	C2
Cowhill, Glouc	37	B4
Cowie, Stirl	116	B1
Cowley, Devon	12	B4
Cowley, G Lon	146	A1
Cowley, Glouc	38	B2
Cowling, N York	93	C3
Cowlinge, Suff	54	A3
Cowshill, Durham	99	B2
Cowslip Green, Som	24	B3
Cowthorpe, N York	88	B2
Coxbank, Chesh	70	A3
Coxbench, Derby	72	A3
Coxford, Norf	75	E4
Coxhoe, Durham	100	B2
Coxley Wick, Som	24	B4
Coxley, Som	24	B4
Coxtie Green, Essex	43	A4
Coxwold, N York	94	B3
Coychurch, Bridg	22	E1
Coylton, S Ayrs	108	D3
Coylumbridge, High	132	E3
Coytrahen, Bridg	22	E1
Crabtree, W Suss	18	C2
Crackenthorpe, Cumb	98	D4
Crackington Haven, Corn	11	A4
Crackleybank, Shrops	58	B2
Cracoe, N York	87	A1
Craddock, Devon	12	C3
Cradley, Heref	48	B3
Cradoc, Powys	35	D1
Crafthole, Corn	4	B4
Crafton, Bucks	41	A2
Cragg Vale, W Yorks	87	A4
Craghead, Durham	100	A1
Crai, Powys	35	C1
Craig Llangiwg, Neath	35	A3
Craigbank, E Ayrs	109	A4
Craigellachie, Moray	138	C4
Craighouse, Argyll	113	D3
Craigie, Perth	128	C4
Craigie, S Ayrs	108	E2
Craignure, Argyll	120	E1
Craigo, Angus	129	C3
Craigrothie, Fife	124	B3
Craigton of Airlie, Angus	128	E4
Craigton, Angus	124	C1
Crail, Fife	124	D3
Crailing, Border	111	A3
Craiselound, Lincs	83	B2
Crakehall, N York	93	C2
Crambe, N York	94	C4
Cramlington, Nthumb	106	A3
Cranage, Chesh	70	B1
Cranberry, Staffs	70	C4
Cranborne, Dorset	15	A3
Cranbrook, Kent	20	B1
Cranfield, Beds	51	C4
Cranford St Andrew, Nhants	51	C1
Cranford St John, Nhants	51	C1
Cranford, G Lon	146	B1
Cranham, Glouc	38	A2
Crank, Mers	79	B2
Cranleigh, Surrey	18	A1
Cranmore, Som	24	C4
Cranoe, Leics	61	C3
Cransford, Suff	55	B2
Cranshaws, Border	119	B3
Crantock, Corn	3	B4
Cranwell, Lincs	74	B2
Cranwich, Norf	64	B3
Cranworth, Norf	64	C2
Crarae, Argyll	121	B4
Craswall, Heref	47	B4
Cratfield, Suff	55	B1
Crathes, Aber	134	B4
Crathie, Aber	133	C4
Crathie, High	132	B4
Craven Arms, Shrops	57	C4
Crawford, S Lan	109	D3
Crawfordjohn, S Lan	109	C3
Crawick, Dumf	109	C4
Crawley, Hants	16	A1
Crawley, Oxon	39	B2
Crawley, W Suss	18	C1
Crawshawbooth, Lancs	86	C4
Crawton, Aber	129	E1
Cray, N York	93	A3
Crayford, G Lon	30	A2
Crayke, N York	94	B4
Crays Hill, Essex	43	B4
Craze Lowman, Devon	12	B3
Creacombe, Devon	12	A2
Creaton, Nhants	51	A1
Credenhill, Heref	47	C4
Crediton, Devon	12	A4
Creekmouth, G Lon	30	A1
Creeting St Mary, Suff	54	D2
Creeton, Lincs	62	B1
Creetown, Dumf	102	E4
Cregneash, I of M	145	A4
Creigiau, Card	23	A1
Cremyll, Corn	4	C4
Cressage, Shrops	58	A2
Cressbrook, Derby	81	C4
Cresselly, Pemb	33	D3
Cresswell, Nthumb	106	B1
Cresswell, Pemb	33	D3
Cresswell, Staffs	71	A3
Creswell, Derby	82	C4
Cretingham, Suff	55	A2
Crew Green, Powys	57	B1
Crewe Green, Chesh	70	B2
Crewe, Chesh	69	C2
Crewe, Chesh	70	B2
Crewkerne, Som	13	B3
Crianlarich, Stirl	122	A2
Cribyn, Cered	45	F3
Criccieth, Gwyn	67	D3
Crick, Nhants	50	C1
Crickadarn, Powys	46	E4
Crickhowell, Powys	36	A2
Cricklade, Wilts	38	C4
Cricklewood, G Lon	147	A1
Cridling Stubbs, N York	89	A4
Crieff, Perth	123	A2
Criggion, Powys	57	B1
Crigglestone, W Yorks	82	A1
Crimond, Aber	139	F3
Crimplesham, Norf	63	D2
Crinan, Argyll	113	F1
Cringleford, Norf	65	A2
Crinow, Pemb	33	E2
Crockenhill, Kent	30	A2
Crockernwell, Devon	5	B1
Crockerton, Wilts	25	B4
Crocketford, Dumf	103	C3
Croeserw, Neath	35	B4
Croes-goch, Pemb	33	B1
Croes-lan, Cered	45	E4
Croesor, Gwyn	67	E3
Croesyceiliog, Carm	34	B2
Croft, Chesh	79	C3
Croft, Leics	61	A3
Croft, Lincs	75	B1
Croftamie, Stirl	115	B1
Crofton, W Yorks	82	A1
Crofty, Swan	34	C4
Croggan, Argyll	120	E2
Croglin, Cumb	98	C1
Cromarty, High	137	C2
Cromdale, High	133	A1
Cromer, Herts	42	A1
Cromer, Norf	76	C3
Cromford, Derby	72	A2
Cromhall, Glouc	37	C4
Cromwell, Notts	73	C1
Cronberry, E Ayrs	109	A3
Crondall, Hants	28	A4
Cronton, Mers	79	B3
Crook, Cumb	92	A2
Crook, Durham	100	A2
Crooked Holme, Cumb	104	D4
Crookham Village, Hants	28	A4
Crookham, Berks	27	B2
Crookham, Nthumb	111	C1
Cropredy, Oxon	50	B3
Cropston, Leics	61	A2
Cropthorne, Worcs	49	A3
Cropton, N York	95	A2
Cropwell Bishop, Notts	73	B4
Crosby Garret, Cumb	92	C1
Crosby Ravensworth, Cumb	98	D4
Crosby, Cumb	97	D2
Crosby, I of M	145	C3
Crosby, Mers	78	D2
Croscombe, Som	24	C2
Cross Ash, Monm	36	C2
Cross Green, Suff	54	B3
Cross Green, Suff	54	C3
Cross Hands, Carm	34	D2
Cross Houses, Shrops	57	D2
Cross in Hand, E Suss	19	C2
Cross Inn, Cered	45	E2
Cross Keys, Argyll	115	A1
Cross Lane Head, Shrops	58	B3
Cross o' th' hands, Derby	72	A3
Cross, Som	24	A3
Crossaig, Argyll	113	F4
Crossapoll, Argyll	125	A4
Cross-at-Hand, Kent	31	B4
Crosscanonby, Cumb	97	D2
Crossford, Fife	117	A1
Crossford, S Lan	109	C1
Crossgatehall, E Loth	118	B3
Crossgill, Lancs	85	C1
Crosshands, E Ayrs	108	E2
Crosshill, S Ayrs	108	D4
Crosskeys, Caer	36	A4
Crosslands, Cumb	91	D2
Crosslee, Renf	115	A3
Crossmichael, Dumf	103	B4
Crosswell, Pemb	45	C4
Crosthwaite, Cumb	91	E2
Croston, Lancs	85	C4
Crostwick, Norf	65	B1
Crouch Hill, Dorset	14	B3
Croucheston, Wilts	15	A2
Crough House Green, Kent	30	A4
Croughton, Nhants	40	A1
Crovie, Aber	139	C2
Crow Edge, S York	81	C2
Crow Hill, Heref	37	B1
Crowan, Corn	1	D2
Crowborough, E Suss	19	B1
Crowcombe, Som	12	D1
Crowdecote, Derby	71	B1
Crowell, Oxon	40	C3
Crowfield, Suff	55	A2
Crowhurst Lane End, Surrey	150	D3
Crowhurst, E Suss	20	A3
Crowhurst, Surrey	150	D3
Crowland, Lincs	63	A2
Crowland, Suff	54	D1
Crowlas, Corn	1	C2
Crowle Green, Worcs	48	C3
Crowle, Lincs	83	B1
Crowle, Worcs	48	C3
Crown Corner, Suff	55	B1
Crownpits, Surrey	146	A4
Crownthorpe, Norf	64	D2
Crows-an-Wra, Corn	1	B2
Crowthorne, Berks	28	A3
Crowton, Chesh	79	B4
Croxdale, Durham	100	A2
Croxden, Staffs	71	B3
Croxton Kerrial, Leics	73	C4
Croxton, Cambs	52	C2
Croxton, Lincs	84	A1
Croxton, Norf	64	B4
Croxton, Norf	76	A4
Croy, High	137	C3
Croy, N Lan	116	A2
Croyde, Devon	11	D1
Croydon, Cambs	53	A3
Croydon, G Lon	149	A4
Cruckmeole, Shrops	57	C2
Cruckton, Shrops	57	C2
Cruden Bay, Aber	139	F4
Crudgington, Shrops	58	A1
Crudwell, Wilts	38	B4
Crug-y-byddar, Powys	57	A4
Crumlin, Caer	36	A4
Crumplehorn, Corn	4	A4
Crundale, Kent	32	A4
Crunwear, Pemb	33	E2
Crux Easton, Hants	27	A3
Crwbin, Carm	34	C2
Cryers Hill, Bucks	41	A4
Crymmych, Pemb	45	C4
Crynant, Neath	35	B3
Crystal Palace, G Lon	149	A3
Cubert, Corn	3	B4
Cublington, Bucks	40	C1
Cublington, Heref	47	C4
Cuckfield, W Suss	18	C2
Cucklington, Som	14	B2
Cuckney, Notts	73	A1
Cuddesdon, Oxon	40	A3
Cuddington Heath, Chesh	69	D3
Cuddington, Bucks	40	C2
Cuddington, Chesh	70	A1
Cudham, G Lon	30	A3
Cudworth, S York	82	A1
Cudworth, Som	13	B3
Cuffley, Herts	42	A3
Culbokie, High	137	A2
Culcheth, Chesh	79	C3
Culford, Suff	54	B1
Culgaith, Cumb	98	D3
Culham, Oxon	40	A4
Culkein Drumbeg, High	142	A4
Culkerton, Glouc	38	B4
Cullen, Moray	139	A2
Cullingworth, W Yorks	87	B3
Culloden, High	137	B3
Cullompton, Devon	12	C3
Culm Davy, Devon	12	D3
Culmington, Shrops	57	D4
Culmstock, Devon	12	C3
Culross, Fife	116	C1
Culroy, S Ayrs	108	D4
Culsalmond, Aber	134	A1
Cultercullen, Aber	134	C1
Culverstone Green, Kent	30	B3
Culverthorpe, Lincs	74	B3
Culworth, Nhants	50	C3
Cumbernauld, N Lan	116	A2
Cumberworth, Lincs	84	D4
Cuminestown, Aber	139	C3
Cummertrees, Dumf	104	A4
Cummingston, Moray	138	B1
Cumnock, E Ayrs	109	A3
Cumnor, Oxon	39	C3
Cumrew, Cumb	98	C1
Cumwhinton, Cumb	98	B1
Cumwhitton, Cumb	98	C1
Cundall, N York	94	A4
Cupar Muir, Fife	124	B3
Cupar, Fife	124	B3
Curbar, Derby	81	C4
Curbridge, Hants	16	B3
Curbridge, Oxon	39	B3
Curdridge, Hants	16	B3
Curdworth, Warwk	60	A3
Curland, Som	13	A3
Curridge, Berks	27	A2
Currie, Edin	117	B3
Curry Mallet, Som	13	A2
Curry Rivel, Som	13	B2
Curtisden Green, Kent	20	A1
Curtisknowle, Devon	5	B4
Cury, Corn	1	D3
Cushnie, Aber	133	E2
Cusop, Heref	47	B4
Cutcombe, Som	12	B1
Cutsdean, Glouc	38	C1
Cutthorpe, Derby	82	A4
Cuxton, Kent	31	A2
Cuxwold, Lincs	84	A2
Cwm Crawnon, Powys	36	A2
Cwm Morgan, Carm	45	D4
Cwm, Denb	78	B4
Cwmafan, Neath	35	B4
Cwmaman, Rhond	35	D3
Cwmbach Llechrhyd, Powys	46	E3
Cwmbach, Carm	34	A1
Cwmbach, Powys	47	A4
Cwmbach, Rhond	35	D3
Cwmbran, Torf	36	B4
Cwmcarn, Caer	36	A4
Cwmcarvan, Monm	37	A3
Cwm-cou, Cered	45	D4
Cwmdare, Rhond	35	C3
Cwmdu, Powys	36	A1
Cwmduad, Carm	34	B1
Cwmfelin Boeth, Carm	33	E2
Cwmfelin, Bridg	35	B4
Cwmfelin, Merth	35	D3
Cwmfelinfach, Caer	36	A4
Cwmffrwd, Carm	34	B2
Cwmgiedd, Powys	35	B2
Cwmgorse, Carm	35	A3
Cwmhiraeth, Carm	45	E4
Cwm-Llinau, Powys	56	C2
Cwmllynfell, Neath	35	A2
Cwmpengraig, Carm	45	E4
Cwmsychbant, Cered	45	F3
Cwmtillery, Gwent	36	A3
Cwm-y-glo, Carm	34	D2
Cwm-y-glo, Gwyn	67	E1
Cwmystwyth, Cered	46	C1
Cwrt-newydd, Cered	45	F3
Cylibebyll, Neath	35	A3
Cymer, Neath	35	B4
Cynghordy, Carm	46	C4
Cynonville, Neath	35	B4
Cynwyd, Denb	68	D3
Cynwyl Elfed, Carm	34	B1
Dacre, Cumb	98	B3
Dacre, N York	87	C1
Daddry Shield, Durham	99	B2
Dadford, Bucks	51	A4
Dadlington, Leics	60	C3
Dagenham, G Lon	30	A1
Daglingworth, Glouc	38	B3
Dagnall, Bucks	41	B2
Dailly, S Ayrs	102	C1
Dainton, Devon	5	C3
Dairsie, Fife	124	B3
Dalbeattie, Dumf	103	C4
Dalby, N York	94	C4
Dalcapon, Perth	128	B3
Dalcrue, Perth	123	C2
Dalditch, Devon	6	B1
Dale, Derby	72	B3
Dale, Pemb	33	B3
Dalgety Bay, Fife	117	B2
Dalginross, Perth	123	A2
Dalguise, Perth	128	B4
Dalhalvaig, High	143	B2
Dalham, Suff	54	A2
Dalkeith, M Loth	118	A3
Dallas, Moray	138	B3

PLACE	PAGE	GRID
Dallinghoo, Suff	55	B3
Dallington, E Suss	19	C2
Dalmally, Argyll	121	C2
Dalmellington, E Ayrs	108	E4
Dalmeny, Edin	117	B2
Dalry, N Ayrs	114	D4
Dalrymple, E Ayrs	108	D4
Dalserf, S Lan	116	B4
Dalston, Cumb	98	B1
Dalston, G Lon	149	A1
Dalswinton, Dumf	103	D2
Dalton Piercy, Durham	100	C3
Dalton, Dumf	103	E3
Dalton, N York	93	B1
Dalton, N York	94	A3
Dalton, Nthumb	105	D3
Dalton-in-Furness, Cumb	91	C4
Dalton-le-Dale, Durham	100	C1
Dalton-on-Tees, N York	93	D1
Dalveich, Stirl	122	C2
Dalwhinnie, High	127	D1
Damerham, Hants	15	A3
Damgate, Norf	66	A2
Danbury, Essex	43	C3
Danby Wiske, N York	93	D2
Danby, N York	94	C1
Dane Street, Kent	32	A3
Danebridge, Chesh	71	A1
Danehill, E Suss	19	A2
Daresbury, Chesh	79	B4
Darfield, S York	82	B2
Dargate, Kent	32	A3
Darite, Corn	4	A3
Darley Bridge, Derby	71	C1
Darley Dale, Derby	71	C1
Darley Green, W Mids	49	C1
Darley, N York	87	C1
Darleyhall, Herts	41	C1
Darlingscott, Warwk	49	C4
Darlington, Durham	100	B4
Darowen, Powys	56	C3
Darracott, Devon	11	B3
Darracott, Devon	11	D1
Darras Hall, Nthumb	105	D3
Darrington, W Yorks	88	B4
Darsham, Suff	55	C1
Darshill, Som	24	C4
Dartford, Kent	30	A2
Dartington, Devon	5	C3
Dartmouth, Devon	5	C4
Darvel, E Ayrs	109	A2
Darwen, Lancs	86	A4
Datchet, Berks	146	A1
Datchworth, Herts	42	A2
Dauntsey Green, Wilts	26	A1
Dauntsey, Wilts	26	A1
Dava, High	138	A4
Davenham, Chesh	70	A1
Daventry, Nhants	50	C2
Davidstow, Corn	3	E1
Davington, Dumf	104	B1
Daviot, Aber	134	B1
Daviot, High	137	B4
Dawesgreen, Surrey	150	A3
Dawlish Warren, Devon	6	A2
Dawlish, Devon	6	A2
Dawn, Aberc	77	F4
Daylesford, Glouc	39	A1
Deal, Kent	32	D4
Dean Bottom, Kent	30	B2
Dean Prior, Devon	5	B3
Dean, Cumb	97	D3
Dean, Devon	5	B3
Dean, Devon	22	C4
Dean, Hants	16	A1
Dean, Hants	16	B2
Dean, Oxon	39	B1
Deanburnhaugh, Border	110	C4
Deancombe, Devon	5	B3
Deane, Hants	27	B4
Deanhead, W Yorks	81	B1
Deanland, Dorset	14	D2
Deanraw, Nthumb	105	B4
Deanscales, Cumb	97	D3
Deanshanger, Nhants	51	B4
Dearham, Cumb	97	D2
Debach, Suff	55	B3
Debden, Essex	43	A1
Debenham, Suff	55	A2
Deblin's Green, Worcs	48	C3
Deddington, Oxon	39	C1
Dedham, Essex	44	B1
Dedworth, Berks	28	B1
Deene, Nhants	62	A3
Deenethorpe, Nhants	62	A3
Deepcut, Surrey	28	B3
Deeping St Nicholas, Lincs	63	A1
Deerhurst, Glouc	38	A1
Defford, Worcs	48	C4
Defynnog, Powys	35	C1
Deganwy, Aberc	77	F4
Deighton, N York	89	B2
Deighton, N York	93	D1
Deiniolen, Gwyn	67	E1
Delabole, Corn	3	D1
Delamere, Chesh	69	D1
Dell Quay, W Suss	17	B4
Dembleby, Lincs	74	B3
Den of Lindores, Fife	124	A3
Denaby, S York	82	B2
Denbies, Surrey	146	B4
Denbigh, Denb	68	D1
Denbury, Devon	5	C3
Denby Dale, W Yorks	81	C1
Denby, Derby	72	B3
Denchworth, Oxon	39	B4
Denford, Nhants	52	A1
Dengie, Essex	44	A3
Denham Green, Bucks	41	B4
Denham, Bucks	146	A1
Denham, Suff	54	A2
Denham, Suff	55	A1
Denholm, Border	110	D3
Denholme, W Yorks	87	B3

PLACE	PAGE	GRID
Denmead, Hants	17	A3
Dennington, Suff	55	B2
Denny, Falk	116	B2
Dennyloanhead, Falk	116	B2
Densole, Kent	32	B4
Denston, Suff	54	A3
Denstone, Staffs	71	B3
Denstroude, Kent	32	A3
Dent, Cumb	92	C3
Denton, Cambs	62	C4
Denton, G Man	80	B3
Denton, Kent	32	B4
Denton, Lincs	74	A4
Denton, N York	87	B2
Denton, Nhants	51	B2
Denton, Norf	65	B4
Denver, Norf	63	D3
Denwick, Nthumb	112	C4
Deopham Green, Norf	64	D3
Deopham, Norf	64	D3
Deptford, G Lon	149	B2
Deptford, Wilts	14	D1
Derby, Derby	72	A4
Derbyhaven, I of M	145	B4
Dereham, Norf	64	C2
Deri, Caer	36	A3
Derringstone, Kent	32	B4
Derrington, Staffs	58	C1
Derry Hill, Wilts	26	A2
Dersingham, Norf	75	D4
Dervaig, Argyll	125	E4
Derwen, Denb	68	D2
Derwenlas, Powys	56	B3
Desborough, Nhants	61	C4
Desford, Leics	60	C2
Deskford, Moray	139	A2
Detling, Kent	31	B3
Devauden, Monm	37	A4
Devizes, Wilts	26	A3
Devonside, Clack	123	B4
Devoran, Corn	2	A1
Dewlish, Dorset	14	B4
Dewsbury, W Yorks	87	C4
Deytheur, Powys	57	B1
Dial Post, W Suss	18	B2
Dibden, Hants	16	A3
Dickleburgh, Norf	65	A4
Didbrook, Glouc	38	C1
Didcot, Oxon	40	A4
Diddington, Cambs	52	B2
Diddlebury, Shrops	57	D4
Didling, W Suss	17	B2
Digby, Lincs	74	B2
Diggle, G Man	81	A1
Dihewyd, Cered	45	F3
Dilham, Norf	65	B1
Dilhorne, Staffs	71	A3
Dillington, Cambs	52	B2
Dilston, Nthumb	105	C4
Dilton Marsh, Wilts	25	B4
Dilton, Wilts	25	B4
Dilwyn, Heref	47	C3
Dinas, Gwyn	67	B4
Dinas, Pemb	45	B4
Dinas-Mawddwy, Gwyn	56	C1
Dinder, Som	24	B4
Dinedor, Heref	47	D4
Dingestow, Monm	36	C3
Dingley, Nhants	61	C4
Dingwall, High	137	A2
Dinnington, S York	82	C3
Dinnington, Som	13	B3
Dinnington, Tyne	106	A3
Dinorwic, Gwyn	67	E1
Dinton, Bucks	40	C2
Dinton, Wilts	14	D1
Dinworthy, Devon	11	B3
Dippertown, Devon	4	C1
Diptford, Devon	5	B4
Dipton, Durham	100	A1
Dirleton, E Loth	119	A2
Dirt Pot, Nthumb	99	B1
Diseworth, Leics	60	C1
Dishforth, N York	93	D4
Disley, Chesh	81	A3
Diss, Norf	64	D4
Distington, Cumb	97	D3
Ditchburn, Nthumb	112	B3
Ditcheat, Som	14	A1
Ditchingham, Norf	65	B4
Ditchling, E Suss	19	A3
Ditteridge, Wilts	25	B2
Dittisham, Devon	5	C4
Ditton Green, Cambs	53	C2
Ditton Priors, Shrops	58	A4
Ditton, Kent	31	A3
Dixton, Glouc	38	B1
Dixton, Monm	37	A2
Dobcross, G Man	81	A2
Dobwalls, Corn	4	A3
Doccombe, Devon	5	C1
Docker, Lancs	92	A4
Docking, Norf	75	D4
Docklow, Heref	47	D2
Dockray, Cumb	98	B4
Doddinghurst, Essex	43	A3
Doddington, Cambs	63	B4
Doddington, Kent	31	C3
Doddington, Lincs	74	A1
Doddington, Nthumb	112	A2
Doddiscombsleigh, Devon	5	C1
Dodd's Green, Chesh	70	A3
Dodford, Nhants	50	C2
Dodford, Worcs	49	A1
Dodington, Glouc	25	A1
Dodington, Som	12	D1
Dodleston, Chesh	69	C1
Dod's Leigh, Staffs	71	A4
Dodworth, S York	82	A2
Dog Village, Devon	12	B4
Dogdyke, Lincs	74	D2
Dogmersfield, Hants	28	A3
Dolanog, Powys	56	E2
Dolbenmaen, Gwyn	67	D3

PLACE	PAGE	GRID
Dolfach, Powys	56	D3
Dolfor, Powys	56	E4
Dolgarrog, Aberc	68	A1
Dolgellau, Gwyn	56	B1
Dollar, Clack	123	B4
Dolphin, Flint	78	C4
Dolphinholme, Lancs	85	C1
Dolphinton, S Lan	109	E1
Dolton, Devon	11	E3
Dolwen, Aberc	77	F4
Dolwyddelan, Aberc	68	A2
Domgay, Powys	57	B1
Doncaster, S York	82	C2
Donhead St Andrew, Wilts	14	C2
Donhead St Mary, Wilts	14	C2
Doniford, Som	23	A4
Donington on Bain, Lincs	84	B4
Donington, Lincs	74	D4
Donisthorpe, Leics	60	B2
Donkey Town, Surrey	28	B3
Donnington, Glouc	39	A1
Donnington, Shrops	57	D2
Donyatt, Som	13	A3
Dorchester, Dorset	7	D1
Dorchester, Oxon	40	A4
Dordon, Warwk	60	A3
Dores, High	137	A4
Dorking, Surrey	146	B4
Dormington, Heref	48	A4
Dormston, Worcs	49	A2
Dorney, Bucks	28	B1
Dornie, High	131	A1
Dornoch, High	141	D4
Dornock, Dumf	104	A4
Dorridge, W Mids	49	C1
Dorrington, Lincs	74	B2
Dorrington, Shrops	57	D2
Dorrington, Shrops	70	B3
Dorsington, Warwk	49	B3
Dorstone, Heref	47	B4
Dorton, Bucks	40	B2
Douglas Water, S Lan	109	C2
Douglas, I of M	145	C4
Douglas, S Lan	109	C2
Douglastown, Angus	129	A4
Doulting, Som	24	C4
Dounby, Orkney	144	A1
Doune, Stirl	122	D4
Dousland, Devon	4	C3
Dove Holes, Derby	81	B4
Dovenby, Cumb	97	D3
Dover, Kent	32	C4
Doverdale, Worcs	48	C2
Doveridge, Derby	71	B4
Doversgreen, Surrey	150	B3
Dowally, Perth	128	B4
Dowdeswell, Glouc	38	B2
Dowland, Devon	11	E3
Down Ampney, Glouc	38	C4
Down Hatherley, Glouc	38	A1
Down St Mary, Devon	11	F4
Down Thomas, Devon	4	C4
Downderry, Corn	4	B4
Downe, G Lon	30	A3
Downend, Glouc	38	A4
Downgate, Corn	4	A3
Downgate, Corn	4	B2
Downham Market, Norf	63	D2
Downham, Cambs	63	C4
Downham, Essex	43	B4
Downham, G Lon	149	B3
Downham, Lancs	86	B2
Downhead, Som	13	C2
Downhead, Som	24	C4
Downholme, N York	93	B2
Downside, Surrey	146	B3
Downton on the Rock, Heref	47	C1
Downton, Hants	9	A1
Downton, Wilts	15	B2
Dowsby, Lincs	74	C4
Doynton, Glouc	25	A2
Draethen, Caer	23	B1
Draffan, S Lan	109	C1
Drakeholes, Notts	83	A3
Drakemyre, N Ayrs	114	D4
Drakes Broughton, Worcs	49	A3
Draughton, N York	87	A2
Draughton, Nhants	51	B1
Drax, N York	89	B4
Draycote, Warwk	50	B1
Draycott in the Clay, Staffs	71	B4
Draycott in the Moors, Staffs	71	A3
Draycott, Glouc	49	C4
Draycott, Som	24	B4
Drayton Bassett, Staffs	60	A3
Drayton Beauchamp, Bucks	41	A2
Drayton Parslow, Bucks	40	C1
Drayton, Leics	61	C3
Drayton, Norf	65	A2
Drayton, Oxon	39	C4
Drayton, Oxon	50	B4
Drayton, Som	13	B2
Drayton, Worcs	48	C1
Dreen Hill, Pemb	33	C2
Drefach, Carm	34	C2
Drefach, Carm	45	E4
Drefach, Cered	45	F3
Drellingore, Kent	21	D1
Drem, E Loth	119	A2
Drewsteignton, Devon	5	B1
Driby, Lincs	84	C4
Driffield, E R of Y	90	B1
Driffield, Glouc	38	C3
Drift, Corn	1	B2
Drigg, Cumb	91	B1
Drighlington, W Yorks	87	C4
Drimnin, High	125	F3
Drimpton, Dorset	13	B4
Drinkstone Green, Suff	54	C2
Drinkstone, Suff	54	C2
Drointon, Staffs	71	A4
Droitwich, Worcs	48	C2

PLACE	PAGE	GRID
Dron, Perth	123	D3
Dronfield, Derby	82	A4
Drongan, E Ayrs	108	E3
Dronley, Angus	124	A1
Droop, Dorset	14	B3
Droxford, Hants	16	B2
Droylsden, G Man	80	B2
Druid, Denb	68	D3
Druidston, Pemb	33	C2
Drum, Perth	123	C4
Drumbeg, High	142	A4
Drumburgh, Cumb	104	B4
Drumburn, Dumf	97	B1
Drumclog, S Lan	109	A1
Drumeldrie, Fife	124	B4
Drumelzier, Border	110	A2
Drumleaning, Cumb	98	A1
Drumlithie, Aber	129	D1
Drummuir, Moray	138	D4
Drumnadrochit, High	132	A1
Drunzie, Perth	123	D3
Dry Doddington, Lincs	74	A3
Dry Drayton, Cambs	53	A2
Drybeck, Cumb	98	D4
Drybridge, N Ayrs	108	D2
Drybrook, Glouc	37	B2
Dryburgh, Border	111	A2
Drym, Corn	1	D2
Drymen, Stirl	115	B1
Drynoch, High	130	C1
Dryton, Shrops	58	A2
Ducklington, Oxon	39	B3
Duddington, Nhants	62	B3
Duddlestone, Som	13	A2
Duddlewick, Shrops	58	A4
Duddo, Nthumb	112	A1
Duddon, Chesh	69	D1
Dudleston, Shrops	69	B3
Dudley, Tyne	106	A3
Dudley, W Mids	59	A4
Duffield, Derby	72	A3
Duffryn, Neath	35	B4
Dufftown, Moray	138	C4
Duffus, Moray	138	B2
Dufton, Cumb	98	D3
Duggleby, N York	95	B4
Duirinish, High	130	F1
Duisky, High	126	D1
Duke Street, Suff	54	D4
Dukinfield, G Man	81	A2
Dulcote, Som	24	B4
Dulford, Devon	12	C4
Dull, Perth	128	A4
Dullingham, Cambs	53	C2
Dulnain Bridge, High	132	E1
Duloe, Corn	4	A4
Dulverton, Som	12	B2
Dulwich, G Lon	149	A3
Dumbarton, Dumb	115	A2
Dumbleton, Glouc	49	A4
Dumfries, Dumf	103	D3
Dummer, Hants	27	B4
Dun, Angus	129	C3
Dunan, Argyll	114	C3
Dunan, High	130	D1
Dunbar, E Loth	119	B2
Dunbeath, High	143	D4
Dunbeg, Argyll	121	A1
Dunblane, Stirl	123	A4
Dunbog, Fife	124	A3
Duncanstone, Aber	133	E1
Dunchideock, Devon	5	C1
Dunchurch, Warwk	50	B1
Duncow, Dumf	103	D2
Duncrievie, Perth	123	D3
Duncton, W Suss	17	C3
Dundee, Dundee City	124	B1
Dundon, Som	13	C1
Dundonald, S Ayrs	108	D2
Dundonnell, High	140	D4
Dundraw, Cumb	97	E1
Dundrennan, Dumf	97	A1
Dundry, Som	24	B2
Dunecht, Aber	134	B3
Dunfermline, Fife	117	A1
Dunfield, Glouc	38	C4
Dunham Town, G Man	80	A3
Dunham, Notts	83	B4
Dunham-on-the-Hill, Chesh	79	B4
Dunhampton, Worcs	48	C2
Dunholme, Lincs	83	D4
Dunino, Fife	124	C3
Dunipace, Falk	116	B2
Dunkeld, Perth	128	C4
Dunkerton, Som	25	A3
Dunkeswell, Devon	12	D3
Dunkeswick, N York	88	A2
Dunkirk, Glouc	25	A1
Dunkirk, Kent	32	A3
Dunlappie, Angus	129	C2
Dunley, Worcs	48	B1
Dunmore, Falk	116	C1
Dunnet, High	143	D1
Dunnichen, Angus	129	B4
Dunning, Perth	123	C3
Dunnington, E R of Y	90	C2
Dunnington, N York	89	B2
Dunnockshaw, Lancs	86	C4
Dunoon, Argyll	114	C2
Dunragit, Dumf	102	B4
Duns Tew, Oxon	39	C1
Duns, Border	119	C4
Dunsby, Lincs	74	C4
Dunscore, Dumf	103	C2
Dunsdale, N York	101	A4
Dunsden Green, Oxon	28	A1
Dunsdon, Devon	11	B3
Dunsfold, Surrey	18	A1
Dunsford, Devon	5	C1
Dunshalt, Fife	124	A3
Dunsley, N York	101	D4
Dunsmore, Bucks	41	A3
Dunsop Bridge, Lancs	86	A2
Dunstable, Beds	41	B2

PLACE	PAGE	GRID
Dunstall, Staffs	60	A1
Dunstan, Nthumb	112	C3
Dunster, Som	22	E4
Dunston, Lincs	74	B1
Dunston, Norf	65	A3
Dunston, Staffs	59	A1
Dunstone, Devon	5	A4
Dunstone, Devon	5	B2
Dunswell, E R of Y	90	B3
Dunsyre, S Lan	109	E1
Dunterton, Devon	4	B2
Duntisbourne Abbots, Glouc	38	B3
Duntisbourne Rouse, Glouc	38	B3
Duntish, Dorset	14	A4
Duntocher, Dumb	115	B2
Dunton Bassett, Leics	61	A4
Dunton Green, Kent	30	A3
Dunton, Bucks	40	C1
Dunton, Norf	75	E4
Dunure, S Ayrs	108	C3
Dunvant, Swan	34	D4
Dunvegan, High	135	A3
Dunwich, Suff	55	D1
Durgan, Corn	2	A2
Durham, Durham	100	B2
Durisdeer, Dumf	109	D4
Durleigh, Som	13	A1
Durley, Hants	16	B3
Durley, Wilts	26	C3
Durlock, Kent	32	C3
Durmgley, Angus	129	A4
Durness, High	142	C1
Duror, High	126	D3
Durrington, Wilts	26	B4
Durris, Aber	134	B4
Dursley Cross, Glouc	37	C2
Dursley, Glouc	37	C4
Durston, Som	13	A2
Durweston, Dorset	14	C3
Duthil, High	132	E1
Dutton, Chesh	79	B4
Duxford, Cambs	53	B3
Duxford, Oxon	39	B3
Dwygyfylchi, Aberc	77	E4
Dwyran, Angle	67	D1
Dyce, Aberdeen City	134	C2
Dyffryn Ardudwy, Gwyn	56	A1
Dyke, Lincs	62	C1
Dyke, Moray	137	D2
Dykehead, Angus	129	A3
Dymchurch, Kent	21	B1
Dymock, Glouc	37	C1
Dyrham, Glouc	25	A2
Dyserth, Denb	78	B4
Eagland Hill, Lancs	85	B2
Eagle, Lincs	74	A1
Eaglesfield, Cumb	97	D3
Eaglesfield, Dumf	104	A3
Eaglesham, East Renf	115	C4
Eakring, Notts	73	B1
Ealand, Lincs	83	B1
Ealing, G Lon	146	B1
Eals, Nthumb	98	D1
Eamont Bridge, Cumb	98	C3
Earby, Lancs	86	C2
Eardington, Shrops	58	B4
Eardisland, Heref	47	C2
Eardisley, Heref	47	B3
Eardiston, Shrops	57	C1
Eardiston, Worcs	48	B1
Earith, Cambs	53	A1
Earl Soham, Suff	55	A2
Earl Sterndale, Derby	71	B1
Earley, Berks	28	A2
Earls Barton, Nhants	51	C2
Earls Colne, Essex	43	C1
Earls Common, Worcs	49	A2
Earl's Croome, Worcs	48	C4
Earlsferry, Fife	124	C4
Earlsfield, G Lon	147	A1
Earlston, Border	110	D1
Earlswood, Surrey	150	B3
Earlswood, W Mids	49	B1
Earnley, W Suss	17	B4
Earsdon, Nthumb	106	A1
Earsham, Norf	65	B4
Eartham, W Suss	17	C3
Easby, N York	94	B1
Easdale, Argyll	120	F3
Easebourne, W Suss	17	C2
Easenhall, Warwk	50	B1
Eashing, Surrey	28	B4
Easington Colliery, Durham	100	C2
Easington, Bucks	40	B3
Easington, Durham	100	C2
Easington, E R of Y	90	E4
Easington, N York	101	C4
Easingwold, N York	94	B4
Eassie and Nevay, Angus	128	E4
East Aberthaw, Glam	23	A2
East Allington, Devon	10	A1
East Anstey, Devon	12	A2
East Ashey, I of W	10	A1
East Ayton, N York	95	C3
East Barkwith, Lincs	84	A4
East Barming, Kent	31	A3
East Beckham, Norf	76	C3
East Bedfont, G Lon	146	B2
East Bergholt, Suff	54	D4
East Bilney, Norf	64	C1
East Boldon, Tyne	106	B4
East Boldre, Hants	15	C4
East Brent, Som	23	C4
East Bridgford, Notts	73	B3
East Buckland, Devon	11	F1
East Budleigh, Devon	6	B1
East Burnham, Bucks	28	B1
East Butterwick, Lincs	83	B1
East Calder, W Loth	117	A3
East Carleton, Norf	65	A3
East Carlton, Nhants	61	C4
East Chiltington, E Suss	19	A3
East Chisenbury, Wilts	26	B4
East Clandon, Surrey	146	A4

PLACE	PAGE	GRID
East Coker, Som	13	C3
East Compton, Som	24	C4
East Cottingwith, E R of Y	89	B2
East Cowes, I of W	16	A4
East Cowick, E R of Y	89	B4
East Cowton, N York	93	D1
East Cranmore, Som	24	C4
East Creech, Dorset	8	C2
East Dean, E Suss	19	C4
East Dean, Glouc	37	B2
East Dean, Hants	15	B2
East Dean, W Suss	17	C3
East Down, Devon	22	B4
East Drayton, Notts	83	B4
East Dulwich, G Lon	149	A3
East End, Kent	20	B1
East End, Oxon	39	C2
East Everleigh, Wilts	26	C3
East Farleigh, Kent	31	A3
East Farndon, Nhants	61	B4
East Ferry, Lincs	83	B2
East Garston, Berks	26	D1
East Goscote, Leics	61	B2
East Grafton, Wilts	26	C3
East Grimstead, Wilts	15	B2
East Grinstead, W Suss	19	A1
East Guldeford, E Suss	21	A2
East Haddon, Nhants	51	A2
East Hagbourne, Oxon	40	A4
East Halton, Lincs	90	C4
East Ham, G Lon	149	B1
East Hanney, Oxon	39	C4
East Hanningfield, Essex	43	B3
East Hardwick, W Yorks	88	B4
East Harling, Norf	64	C4
East Harlsey, N York	94	A1
East Harptree, Som	24	B3
East Harting, W Suss	17	B2
East Hatch, Wilts	14	D2
East Hatley, Cambs	52	C3
East Haven, Angus	124	D1
East Heckington, Lincs	74	C3
East Hedleyhope, Durham	99	D2
East Hendred, Oxon	39	C4
East Heslerton, N York	95	B3
East Hewish, Som	24	A2
East Hoathly, E Suss	19	B3
East Holme, Dorset	8	B1
East Horrington, Som	24	C4
East Huntspill, Som	23	C4
East Ilsley, Berks	27	A1
East Keal, Lincs	75	A1
East Kennett, Wilts	26	B2
East Keswick, W Yorks	88	A2
East Kilbride, S Lan	115	C4
East Kirkby, Lincs	75	A1
East Knighton, Dorset	8	B1
East Knoyle, Wilts	14	C1
East Kyloe, Nthumb	112	B1
East Lambrook, Som	13	B2
East Langdon, Kent	32	C4
East Lavington, W Suss	17	C3
East Layton, N York	93	C1
East Leake, Notts	73	A4
East Lockinge, Oxon	39	C4
East Lound, Lincs	83	B2
East Lulworth, Dorset	8	B2
East Lutton, N York	95	B4
East Marden, W Suss	17	B3
East Markham, Notts	83	B4
East Marton, N York	86	C2
East Meon, Hants	17	A2
East Mersea, Essex	44	B2
East Molesey, Surrey	146	B2
East Morden, Dorset	8	B1
East Morton, W Yorks	87	B2
East Ness, N York	94	C3
East Norton, Leics	61	C3
East Orchard, Dorset	14	C3
East Peckham, Kent	31	A4
East Pennard, Som	14	A1
East Portlemouth, Devon	10	A1
East Prawle, Devon	10	B2
East Preston, W Suss	18	A4
East Pulham, Dorset	14	B3
East Putford, Devon	11	C3
East Quantoxhead, Som	23	B4
East Rainton, Tyne	100	B1
East Ravendale, Lincs	84	B2
East Raynham, Norf	64	B1
East Rigton, W Yorks	88	A2
East Rudham, Norf	75	E4
East Runton, Norf	76	C3
East Ruston, Norf	76	D4
East Saltoun, E Loth	119	A3
East Sheen, G Lon	147	A3
East Shefford, Berks	26	D2
East Stockwith, Lincs	83	B3
East Stoke, Dorset	8	B1
East Stour, Dorset	14	B2
East Stowford, Devon	11	E2
East Stratton, Hants	16	B1
East Studdal, Kent	32	C4
East Taphouse, Corn	3	E3
East Thirston, Nthumb	106	A1
East Tilbury, Essex	31	A1
East Tisted, Hants	17	A1
East Torrington, Lincs	84	A4
East Tuddenham, Norf	64	D2
East Tytherley, Hants	15	C2
East Tytherton, Wilts	26	A2
East Village, Devon	12	A4
East Wall, Shrops	57	D3
East Walton, Norf	64	A1
East Week, Devon	5	B1
East Wellow, Hants	15	C2
East Wemyss, Fife	124	A4
East Wickham, G Lon	30	A1
East Williamston, Pemb	33	E3
East Winch, Norf	64	A1
East Winterslow, Wilts	15	B1
East Wittering, W Suss	17	B4
East Woodburn, Nthumb	105	B2
East Woodhay, Hants	27	A3

PLACE	PAGE	GRID
East Worldham, Hants	17	B1
East Wretham, Norf	64	C4
East Youlstone, Devon	11	B3
Eastbourne, E Suss	19	C4
Eastbridge, Suff	55	C2
Eastburn, W Yorks	87	A2
Eastbury, Berks	26	D1
Eastby, N York	87	A1
Eastchurch, Kent	31	C2
Eastcombe, Glouc	38	A3
Eastcote, Nhants	51	A3
Eastcote, W Mids	49	C1
Eastcott, Wilts	26	A3
Eastcourt, Wilts	26	C3
Eastcourt, Wilts	38	B4
Eastend, Essex	44	A4
Easter Compton, Glouc	24	B1
Easterton, Wilts	26	A3
Eastfield, N Lan	116	C3
Eastfield, N York	95	C3
Eastgate, Durham	99	C2
Eastgate, Norf	65	A1
Easthampstead, Berks	28	B2
Easthampton, Heref	47	C2
Easthope, Shrops	57	D3
Easthorpe, Essex	44	A2
Eastington, Devon	11	F3
Eastington, Glouc	37	C3
Eastington, Glouc	38	C2
Eastleach Martin, Glouc	39	A3
Eastleach Turville, Glouc	39	A3
Eastleigh, Devon	11	D2
Eastleigh, Hants	16	A2
Eastling, Kent	31	C3
Eastnor, Heref	48	B4
Eastoft, Lincs	83	B1
Easton Grey, Wilts	38	A4
Easton Maudit, Nhants	51	C2
Easton on the Hill, Nhants	62	B2
Easton Royal, Wilts	26	C3
Easton, Cambs	52	B1
Easton, Cumb	104	B4
Easton, Devon	5	B1
Easton, Dorset	7	D3
Easton, Hants	16	B1
Easton, Lincs	74	A4
Easton, Norf	65	A2
Easton, Som	24	B4
Easton, Suff	55	B2
Easton, Wilts	25	B2
Eastrea, Cambs	63	A3
Eastriggs, Dumf	104	B4
Eastrington, E R of Y	89	C4
Eastry, Kent	32	C3
Eastville, Lincs	75	A2
Eastwell, Leics	73	C4
Eastwick, Herts	42	C2
Eastwood, Notts	72	B3
Eastwood, W Yorks	87	A4
Eathorpe, Warwk	50	B1
Eaton Bray, Beds	41	B2
Eaton Green, Beds	41	B2
Eaton Hastings, Oxon	39	A4
Eaton Mascott, Shrops	57	D2
Eaton Socon, Cambs	52	B2
Eaton upon Tern, Shrops	58	A1
Eaton, Chesh	69	D1
Eaton, Chesh	70	C1
Eaton, Leics	73	C4
Eaton, Notts	83	A4
Eaton, Oxon	39	C3
Eaton, Shrops	57	D4
Ebberston, N York	95	B3
Ebbesborne Wake, Wilts	14	D2
Ebbw Vale, Gwent	36	A3
Ebchester, Durham	99	D1
Ebford, Devon	6	A1
Ebnal, Chesh	69	D3
Ebrington, Glouc	49	C4
Ebsworthy Town, Devon	4	C1
Ecchinswell, Hants	27	A3
Ecclefechan, Dumf	104	A3
Eccles, Border	111	B1
Eccles, G Man	80	A2
Eccles, Kent	31	A3
Eccleshall, Staffs	70	C4
Ecclesmachan, W Loth	117	A2
Eccleston, Chesh	69	C1
Eccleston, Lancs	79	B1
Echt, Aber	134	B3
Eckford, Border	111	B3
Eckington, Derby	82	B4
Eckington, Worcs	48	C4
Ecton, Nhants	51	B2
Edale, Derby	81	B3
Edburton, W Suss	18	C3
Edderton, High	141	C4
Eddleston, Border	110	B1
Eden Park, G Lon	149	A4
Edenbridge, Kent	30	A4
Edenfield, Lancs	86	B4
Edenhall, Cumb	98	C3
Edenham, Lincs	62	B1
Edensor, Derby	71	C1
Edenthorpe, S York	83	A2
Edern, Gwyn	67	B3
Edgcott, Bucks	40	B1
Edgcott, Som	12	A1
Edge, Glouc	38	A3
Edge, Shrops	57	C2
Edgefield Green, Norf	76	B4
Edgefield, Norf	76	B4
Edgeworth, Glouc	38	B3
Edgmond, Shrops	58	B1
Edgton, Shrops	57	C4
Edgworth, Lancs	80	A1
Edinbane, High	135	B3
Edinburgh, Edin	118	A2
Edingale, Staffs	60	A2
Edingley, Notts	73	B2
Edingthorpe Green, Norf	76	D4
Edingthorpe, Norf	76	D4
Edington Burtle, Som	24	A4
Edington, Nthumb	105	D2
Edington, Som	13	B1
Edington, Wilts	25	B3
Edingworth, Som	24	A3
Edith Weston, Rutland	62	A2
Edithmead, Som	23	C4
Edlesborough, Bucks	41	B2
Edlingham, Nthumb	112	B4
Edlington, Lincs	74	D1
Edmondsham, Dorset	15	A3
Edmondsley, Durham	100	A1
Edmondthorpe, Leics	62	A1
Edmundbyers, Durham	99	C1
Ednam, Border	111	B2
Edrom, Border	119	D4
Edstaston, Shrops	69	D4
Edstone, Warwk	49	C2
Edwinstowe, Notts	73	B1
Edworth, Beds	52	C4
Edwyn Ralph, Heref	48	A2
Edzell, Angus	129	C2
Efail Isaf, Rhond	23	A1
Efail-fach, Neath	35	B4
Efailnewydd, Gwyn	67	C4
Efailwen, Carm	33	E1
Efenechtyd, Denb	68	D2
Effingham, Surrey	146	B3
Efford, Devon	12	B4
Egerton, G Man	80	A1
Egerton, Kent	31	C4
Eggesford, Devon	11	F3
Eggington, Beds	41	A1
Egginton, Derby	71	C4
Eggleston, Durham	99	C3
Egham Wick, Surrey	146	A2
Egham, Surrey	146	A2
Egleton, Rutland	62	A2
Eglingham, Nthumb	112	B3
Egloshayle, Corn	3	D2
Egloskerry, Corn	4	A1
Eglwys Cross, Wrex	69	D3
Eglwysbach, Aberc	68	B1
Eglwyswrw, Pemb	45	C4
Egmanton, Notts	73	B1
Egremont, Cumb	91	B1
Egton Bridge, N York	95	A1
Egton, N York	95	A1
Eight Ash Green, Essex	44	A1
Elan Village, Powys	46	D2
Elberton, Glouc	37	B4
Elcombe, Wilts	26	B1
Eldersfield, Worcs	37	C1
Elderslie, Renf	115	B3
Eldon, Durham	100	A3
Elford, Staffs	60	A2
Elgin, Moray	138	B2
Elgol, High	130	D2
Elham, Kent	32	B4
Elie, Fife	124	C4
Elim, Angle	77	B3
Eling, Hants	15	C3
Elkesley, Notts	83	A4
Elkstone, Glouc	38	B2
Elland, W Yorks	87	B4
Ellary, Argyll	113	F2
Ellastone, Staffs	71	B3
Ellel, Lancs	85	C1
Ellemford, Border	119	C4
Ellenhall, Staffs	70	C4
Ellen's Green, Surrey	18	B1
Ellerbeck, N York	94	A2
Ellerby, N York	101	C4
Ellerdine Heath, Shrops	58	A1
Ellerker, E R of Y	90	A4
Ellerton, E R of Y	89	B3
Ellerton, N York	93	C2
Ellesborough, Bucks	40	C3
Ellesmere Port, Chesh	79	A4
Ellesmere, Shrops	69	C4
Ellingham, Norf	66	A3
Ellingham, Nthumb	112	C3
Ellingstring, N York	93	C3
Ellington Thorpe, Cambs	52	B1
Ellington, Cambs	52	B1
Ellington, Nthumb	106	B1
Elliots Green, Som	25	A4
Ellisfield, Hants	27	C4
Ellistown, Leics	60	C2
Ellon, Aber	134	D1
Ellonby, Cumb	98	B2
Elloughton, E R of Y	90	A4
Ellwood, Glouc	37	B3
Elm Park, G Lon	30	A1
Elm, Cambs	63	C2
Elmbridge, Worcs	48	C2
Elmdon, Essex	53	B4
Elmdon, W Mids	60	A4
Elmers End, G Lon	149	A4
Elmhurst, Staffs	59	B2
Elmley Castle, Worcs	49	A4
Elmley Lovett, Worcs	48	C1
Elmore Back, Glouc	37	C2
Elmore, Glouc	37	C2
Elmsett, Suff	54	D3
Elmstead Market, Essex	44	B1
Elmstone Hardwicke, Glouc	38	A1
Elmstone, Kent	32	C3
Elmswell, E R of Y	90	B1
Elmswell, Suff	54	C2
Elmton, Derby	82	B4
Elphin, High	140	E2
Elphinstone, E Loth	118	B3
Elrig, Dumf	96	D1
Elrington, Nthumb	105	B4
Elsdon, Nthumb	105	C1
Elsenham, Essex	42	C1
Elsfield, Oxon	40	A3
Elsham, Lincs	83	D1
Elsing, Norf	64	D1
Elslack, N York	87	A2
Elsrickle, S Lan	109	E1
Elstead, Surrey	28	B4
Elsted, W Suss	17	B2
Elsthorpe, Lincs	62	B1
Elston, Notts	73	C3
Elstone, Devon	11	F3
Elstow, Beds	52	A3
Elstree, Herts	41	C4
Elstronwick, E R of Y	90	D3
Elswick, Lancs	85	B3
Elsworth, Cambs	53	A2
Elterwater, Cumb	91	D1
Eltham, G Lon	149	B3
Eltisley, Cambs	52	C2
Elton, Cambs	62	C3
Elton, Chesh	79	A4
Elton, Derby	71	C1
Elton, Durham	100	C4
Elton, Heref	47	C1
Elton, Notts	73	C3
Eltringham, Nthumb	105	D4
Elvanfoot, S Lan	109	D3
Elvaston, Derby	72	B4
Elveden, Suff	64	B4
Elvington, Kent	32	C4
Elvington, N York	89	B2
Elwick, Durham	100	C3
Elworth, Chesh	70	B1
Elworthy, Som	12	C1
Ely, Cambs	63	C4
Emberton, Bucks	51	C3
Embleton, Nthumb	112	C3
Embo, High	141	D3
Emborough, Som	24	C3
Embsay, N York	87	A1
Emley, W Yorks	81	C1
Emmington, Oxon	40	C3
Emneth Hungate, Norf	63	C2
Emneth, Norf	63	C2
Empingham, Rutland	62	A2
Empshott, Hants	17	B1
Emsworth, Hants	17	B4
Enborne Row, Hants	27	A3
Endmoor, Cumb	92	A3
Endon, Staffs	70	D2
Enfield, G Lon	42	B4
Enford, Wilts	26	B4
Engine Common, Glouc	25	A1
Englefield Green, Surrey	146	A2
Englefield, Berks	27	C2
Englesea-brook, Chesh	70	B2
English Bicknor, Glouc	37	B2
English Frankton, Shrops	69	C4
Englishcombe, Som	25	A3
Enmore, Som	13	A1
Ennerdale Bridge, Cumb	97	D4
Ensdon, Shrops	57	C1
Ensis, Devon	11	E2
Enstone, Oxon	39	B1
Enville, Staffs	58	C4
Epney, Glouc	37	C2
Epperstone, Notts	73	B3
Epping Green, Essex	42	C3
Epping Upland, Essex	42	C3
Epping, Essex	42	C3
Eppleby, N York	100	A4
Epsom, Surrey	150	A1
Epwell, Oxon	50	A4
Epworth, Lincs	83	B2
Erbistock, Wrex	69	C3
Eridge Green, E Suss	19	C1
Eriswell, Suff	54	A1
Erith, G Lon	30	A1
Erlestoke, Wilts	26	A3
Ermington, Devon	5	A4
Erpingham, Norf	76	C4
Errogie, High	132	B2
Errol, Perth	124	A2
Erskine, Renf	115	B3
Erwarton, Suff	55	A4
Erwood, Powys	46	E4
Eryholme, N York	93	D1
Eryrys, Denb	69	A2
Escomb, Durham	100	A3
Escrick, N York	89	B2
Esgairgeiliog, Powys	56	B2
Esh Winning, Durham	100	A2
Esh, Durham	100	A2
Esher, Surrey	146	B2
Eshott, Nthumb	106	A1
Eskadale, High	136	F4
Eskdale Green, Cumb	91	C1
Eskdalemuir, Dumf	104	B1
Esprick, Lancs	85	B3
Essendine, Rutland	62	B2
Essendon, Herts	42	A3
Essington, Staffs	59	A2
Eston, N York	101	A4
Etal, Nthumb	112	A1
Etchilhampton, Wilts	26	B3
Etchingham, E Suss	20	A2
Etchinghill, Kent	21	C1
Eton Wick, Bucks	28	B1
Eton, Berks	28	B1
Ettersgill, Durham	99	B3
Ettington, Warwk	49	C3
Etton, Cambs	62	C2
Etton, E R of Y	90	B2
Ettrick, Border	110	B4
Ettrickbridge, Border	110	C3
Etwall, Derby	71	C4
Euston, Suff	54	C1
Euxton, Lancs	85	C4
Evanton, High	137	A2
Evedon, Lincs	74	C3
Evenjobb, Powys	47	B2
Evenley, Nhants	50	C4
Evenlode, Glouc	39	A1
Evercreech, Som	14	A1
Everingham, E R of Y	89	C2
Everleigh, Wilts	26	C3
Eversholt, Beds	41	B1
Evershot, Dorset	13	C4
Eversley Cross, Hants	28	A3
Eversley, Hants	28	A3
Everthorpe, E R of Y	90	A3
Everton, Beds	52	C3
Everton, Notts	83	A3
Evertown, Dumf	104	C3
Evesbatch, Heref	48	A3
Evesham, Worcs	49	A4
Ewden Village, S York	82	A2
Ewell, Surrey	150	A1
Ewelme, Oxon	40	B4
Ewen, Glouc	38	B4
Ewenny, Glam	22	E1
Ewerby, Lincs	74	C3
Ewesley, Nthumb	105	D1
Ewhurst Green, Surrey	18	B1
Ewhurst, Surrey	18	B1
Ewloe, Flint	69	B1
Eworthy, Devon	11	D4
Ewshot, Hants	28	A4
Ewyas Harold, Heref	36	C1
Exbourne, Devon	11	E4
Exbury, Hants	16	A4
Exebridge, Som	12	B2
Exelby, N York	93	D3
Exeter, Devon	6	A1
Exford, Som	12	A1
Exfordsgreen, Shrops	57	C2
Exhall, Warwk	49	B3
Exhall, Warwk	60	B4
Exlade Street, Oxon	27	C1
Exminster, Devon	6	A1
Exmouth, Devon	6	A2
Exning, Suff	53	C2
Exton, Devon	6	A1
Exton, Hants	16	B2
Exton, Rutland	62	A2
Exton, Som	12	B1
Eyam, Derby	81	C4
Eydon, Nhants	50	C3
Eye, Cambs	63	A3
Eye, Heref	47	D2
Eye, Suff	55	A1
Eyemouth, Border	119	E3
Eyeworth, Beds	52	C3
Eyhorne Street, Kent	31	B3
Eyke, Suff	55	B3
Eynsford, Kent	30	A2
Eynsham, Oxon	39	C3
Eype, Dorset	7	B1
Eythorne, Kent	32	C4
Eyton on Severn, Shrops	58	A2
Eyton upon the Weald Moors, Shrops	58	A1
Eyton, Heref	47	D2
Eyton, Shrops	57	C2
Eyton, Shrops	57	C1
Eyton, Shrops	57	C4
Faccombe, Hants	27	A3
Faceby, N York	94	A1
Fachwen, Powys	56	E1
Fadmoor, N York	94	C2
Failand, Som	24	B2
Failsworth, G Man	80	B2
Fair Oak Green, Hants	27	C3
Fairbourne, Gwyn	56	A2
Fairburn, N York	88	B4
Fairfield, Worcs	49	A1
Fairford, Glouc	38	C3
Fairgirth, Dumf	97	B1
Fairlie, N Ayrs	114	D4
Fairlight, E Suss	20	B3
Fairmile, Devon	12	C4
Fairmile, Surrey	146	B3
Fairnilee, Border	110	C2
Fairoak, Staffs	70	B4
Fairseat, Kent	30	B3
Fairstead, Essex	43	B2
Fairwarp, E Suss	19	B2
Fairy Cross, Devon	11	C2
Fakenham Magna, Suff	54	C1
Fakenham, Norf	76	A4
Fala Dam, M Loth	118	B3
Fala, M Loth	118	B3
Faldingworth, Lincs	83	D3
Faldouet, Jersey	145	B2
Falfield, Glouc	37	B4
Falkirk, Falk	116	B2
Falkenham, Suff	55	B4
Falkland, Fife	124	A3
Fallin, Stirl	116	B1
Falloden, Nthumb	112	C3
Fallowfield, Nthumb	105	C4
Falmer, E Suss	19	A3
Falmouth, Corn	2	A2
Falstone, Nthumb	105	A2
Fancott, Beds	41	B1
Fangdale Beck, N York	94	B2
Fangfoss, E R of Y	89	C1
Far End, Cumb	91	D2
Far Green, Glouc	37	C3
Far Sawrey, Cumb	91	E2
Far Thorpe, Lincs	84	B4
Farcet, Cambs	63	A3
Fareham, Hants	16	B3
Farewell, Staffs	59	B2
Faringdon, Oxon	39	B4
Farington, Lancs	85	C4
Farlam, Cumb	104	D4
Farleigh Hungerford, Som	25	A3
Farleigh Wallop, Hants	27	C4
Farlesthorpe, Lincs	84	D4
Farleton, Cumb	92	A3
Farley Green, Suff	54	A3
Farley Green, Surrey	146	A4
Farley Hill, Berks	28	A2
Farley, Staffs	71	B3
Farley, Wilts	15	B2
Farleys End, Glouc	37	C2
Farlington, N York	94	B4
Farlow, Shrops	58	A4
Farmborough, Som	24	C3
Farmcote, Glouc	38	C1
Farmers, Carm	46	A4
Farmington, Glouc	38	C2
Farmoor, Oxon	39	C3
Farnachty, Moray	138	D2
Farnborough Park, Hants	28	B3
Farnborough, Berks	27	A1
Farnborough, G Lon	30	A2
Farnborough, Hants	28	B3
Farnborough, Warwk	50	B3
Farncombe, Surrey	146	A4
Farndish, Beds	51	C2
Farndon, Chesh	69	C2
Farndon, Notts	73	C2
Farnell, Angus	129	C3
Farnham Common, Bucks	28	B1
Farnham, Essex	42	C1
Farnham, N York	88	A1
Farnham, Suff	55	C2
Farnham, Surrey	28	A4
Farnley Tyas, W Yorks	81	C1
Farnley, N York	87	C2
Farnsfield, Notts	73	B2
Farnworth, G Man	80	A2
Farr, High	142	F1
Farringdon, Devon	6	B1
Farrington Gurney, Som	24	C3
Farthing Street, G Lon	30	A3
Farthinghoe, Nhants	50	C4
Farthingstone, Nhants	50	C3
Fasnacloich, Argyll	126	D4
Fauldhouse, W Loth	116	C4
Faulkbourne, Essex	43	C2
Faulkland, Som	25	A3
Fauls, Shrops	70	A4
Faversham, Kent	32	A3
Fawdington, N York	94	A4
Fawdon, Nthumb	112	A3
Fawkham Green, Kent	30	B2
Fawler, Oxon	39	B2
Fawley, Berks	27	A1
Fawley, Bucks	28	A1
Fawley, Hants	16	A4
Faxfleet, E R of Y	90	A4
Faygate, W Suss	18	C1
Fazeley, Staffs	60	A3
Fearby, N York	93	C3
Fearnan, Perth	127	E4
Fearnmore, High	135	E2
Featherstone, Staffs	59	A2
Featherstone, W Yorks	88	B4
Feckenham, Worcs	49	A2
Feering, Essex	43	C2
Feetham, N York	93	A2
Felbrigg, Norf	76	C3
Felcourt, Surrey	150	D4
Felday, Surrey	146	B4
Felin gwm Isaf, Carm	34	C1
Felin gwm Uchaf, Carm	34	C1
Felindre Farchog, Pemb	45	C4
Felindre, Carm	34	D2
Felindre, Carm	45	E4
Felindre, Powys	57	A4
Felindre, Swan	34	D3
Felixkirk, N York	94	A3
Felixstowe Ferry, Suff	55	B4
Felixstowe, Suff	55	B4
Felling, Tyne	106	B4
Felmersham, Beds	52	A2
Felmingham, Norf	76	D4
Felsham, Suff	54	C2
Felsted, Essex	43	B2
Feltham, G Lon	146	B2
Felthamhill, Surrey	146	B2
Felthorpe, Norf	65	A1
Felton Butler, Shrops	57	C1
Felton, Heref	47	D3
Felton, Nthumb	106	A1
Feltwell, Norf	64	A4
Fen Ditton, Cambs	53	B2
Fen Drayton, Cambs	53	A1
Fen Street, Norf	64	C3
Fence, Lancs	86	C3
Fence, S York	82	B3
Fencote, N York	93	D2
Fendike Corner, Lincs	75	B2
Feniscowles, Lancs	86	A4
Feniton, Devon	12	C4
Fenny Bentley, Derby	71	C2
Fenny Bridges, Devon	12	C4
Fenny Compton, Warwk	50	B3
Fenny Drayton, Leics	60	B3
Fenstanton, Cambs	53	A1
Fenstead End, Suff	54	B3
Fenton, Cambs	53	A1
Fenton, Cumb	98	C1
Fenton, Lincs	74	A2
Fenton, Lincs	83	B4
Fenton, Notts	83	B4
Fenton, Nthumb	112	A2
Fenwick, E Ayrs	108	E1
Fenwick, Nthumb	105	D3
Fenwick, Nthumb	112	B1
Fenwick, S York	82	C1
Feock, Corn	2	A1
Ferndale, Rhond	35	C4
Fernham, Oxon	39	B4
Fernhill Heath, Worcs	48	C2
Fernhurst, W Suss	17	C2
Fernilee, Derby	81	A4
Ferrensby, N York	88	A1
Ferring, W Suss	18	B4
Ferryden, Angus	129	D3
Ferryhill, Durham	100	B3
Ferryside, Carm	34	B3
Fersfield, Norf	64	D4
Fetcham, Surrey	146	B3
Fetterangus, Aber	139	E3
Fettercairn, Aber	129	C2
Fewston, N York	87	C1
Ffair Rhos, Cered	46	B2
Ffairfach, Carm	34	D2
Ffestiniog, Gwyn	68	A3
Fforest, Carm	34	D3
Ffostrasol, Cered	45	E3
Ffrith, Flint	69	B2
Ffynnongroew, Flint	78	C4
Fickleshole, G Lon	150	D1
Fiddington, Glouc	38	A1
Fiddington, Som	12	D1
Fiddleford, Dorset	14	B3
Fiddlers Green, Corn	3	B4
Field Broughton, Cumb	91	E3
Field Dalling, Norf	76	B3
Field, Staffs	71	A4
Fifehead Neville, Dorset	14	B3
Fifehead St Quinton, Dorset	14	B3
Fifield, Berks	28	B1
Fifield, Oxon	39	A2
Figheldean, Wilts	26	B4
Filby, Norf	66	A2
Filey, N York	95	D3
Filgrave, Bucks	51	C3
Filkins, Oxon	39	A3
Filleigh, Devon	11	F2
Filleigh, Devon	11	F3
Fillingham, Lincs	83	C3
Fimber, E R of Y	90	A1
Fincham, Norf	64	A2
Finchdean, Hants	17	B3
Finchingfield, Essex	43	B1
Findern, Derby	72	A4
Findhorn, Moray	138	A2
Findochty, Moray	138	D2
Findon, Aber	134	D4
Finedon, Nhants	51	C1
Fingal Street, Suff	55	A1
Finghall, N York	93	C2
Fingringhoe, Essex	44	B2
Finmere, Oxon	40	B1
Finningham, Suff	54	D1
Finningley, S York	83	A2
Finstall, Worcs	49	A1
Finsthwaite, Cumb	91	E2
Finstock, Oxon	39	B2
Finstown, Orkney	144	A2
Fintry, Stirl	115	C1
Finzean, Aber	134	A4
Fionnphort, Argyll	120	B2
Fir Tree, Durham	99	D2
Firbank, Cumb	92	B2
Firbeck, S York	82	C3
Firby, N York	93	C3
Firby, N York	95	A4
Firsby, Lincs	75	B1
Fishbourne, I of W	10	A1
Fishburn, Durham	100	B3
Fishcross, Clack	116	C1
Fisherton de la Mere, Wilts	14	D1
Fisherton, S Ayrs	108	C3
Fishery Estate, Berks	28	B1
Fishguard, Pemb	45	A4
Fishlake, S York	83	A1
Fishtoft Drove, Lincs	75	A3
Fishtoft, Lincs	75	A3
Fiskerton, Lincs	74	B1
Fiskerton, Notts	73	C2
Fittleton, Wilts	26	B4
Fittleworth, W Suss	18	A2
Fitz, Shrops	57	C1
Fitzhead, Som	12	D2
Fitzwilliam, W Yorks	82	B1
Five Ashes, E Suss	19	C2
Five Bells, Som	23	A4
Five Oak Green, Kent	30	B4
Five Oaks, Jersey	145	B2
Fivehead, Som	13	B2
Fladbury, Worcs	49	A3
Fladdabister, Shet	144	A3
Flagg, Derby	71	B1
Flamborough, E R of Y	95	E4
Flamstead, Herts	41	B2
Flansham, W Suss	17	C4
Flasby, N York	87	A1
Flash, Staffs	71	A1
Flaunden, Herts	41	B3
Flawith, N York	94	A4
Flax Bourton, Som	24	B2
Flaxby, N York	88	B1
Flaxley, Glouc	37	B2
Flaxpool, Som	12	D1
Flaxton, N York	89	B1
Fleckney, Leics	61	B3
Flecknoe, Warwk	50	C2
Fledborough, Notts	73	C1
Fleet Hargate, Lincs	63	B1
Fleet, Hants	28	A3
Fleet, Lincs	63	B1
Fleetwood, Lancs	85	A2
Flemingston, Glam	23	A2
Flempton, Suff	54	B1
Fletcher Green, Kent	30	A4
Fletchertown, Cumb	97	E2
Fletching, E Suss	19	A2
Flexford, Surrey	28	B4
Flimby, Cumb	97	D3
Flimwell, E Suss	20	A1
Flint, Flint	78	D4
Flintham, Notts	73	C3
Flinton, E R of Y	90	D3
Flitcham, Norf	75	D4
Flitton, Beds	52	A4
Flitwick, Beds	52	A4
Flixborough, Lincs	83	C1
Flixton, N York	95	C3
Flixton, Suff	65	B4
Flockton Green, W Yorks	81	C1
Flockton, W Yorks	81	C1
Flookburgh, Cumb	91	E4
Flordon, Norf	65	A3
Flore, Nhants	51	A2
Flowton, Suff	54	D3
Flushing, Corn	2	A2
Fluxton, Devon	6	B1
Flyford Flavell, Worcs	49	A3
Fobbing, Essex	31	A1
Fochabers, Moray	138	C2
Fockerby, Lincs	89	C4
Foddington, Som	13	C1
Foel, Powys	56	D2
Foggathorpe, E R of Y	89	C3
Fogo, Border	111	B1
Fole, Staffs	71	A4
Foliejon Park, Berks	28	B2
Folke, Dorset	14	A3
Folkestone, Kent	21	C1

PLACE	PAGE	GRID
Folkingham, Lincs	74	B4
Folkington, E Suss	19	C4
Folksworth, Cambs	62	C4
Folkton, N York	95	C3
Follifoot, N York	88	A2
Folly Gate, Devon	11	E4
Fonthill Bishop, Wilts	14	D1
Fonthill Gifford, Wilts	14	C1
Fontmell Magna, Dorset	14	C3
Fontwell, W Suss	17	C3
Foolow, Derby	81	C4
Foots Cray, G Lon	30	A2
Forcett, N York	100	A4
Ford End, Essex	43	B2
Ford Street, Som	12	D2
Ford, Bucks	40	C3
Ford, Derby	82	B4
Ford, Devon	10	B1
Ford, Devon	11	C2
Ford, Glouc	38	C1
Ford, Nthumb	112	A2
Ford, Som	12	C2
Ford, Staffs	71	B2
Ford, W Suss	18	A4
Ford, Wilts	25	B2
Fordcombe, Kent	19	B1
Fordell, Fife	117	B1
Forden, Powys	57	A3
Forder Green, Devon	5	C3
Fordham, Cambs	53	C1
Fordham, Essex	44	A1
Fordham, Norf	63	D3
Fordingbridge, Hants	15	A3
Fordon, E R of Y	95	C4
Fordoun, Aber	129	D2
Fordstreet, Essex	44	A1
Fordyce, Aber	139	A2
Foremark, Derby	72	A4
Forest Becks, Lancs	86	B2
Forest Chapel, Chesh	71	A1
Forest Gate, G Lon	149	B1
Forest Green, Surrey	146	B4
Forest Hill, G Lon	149	A3
Forest Hill, Oxon	40	A3
Forest Mill, Clack	116	C1
Forest Row, E Suss	19	A1
Forestside, W Suss	17	B3
Forfar, Angus	129	A4
Forgandenny, Perth	123	C3
Forgie, Moray	138	D3
Formby, Mers	78	D1
Forncett End, Norf	65	A3
Forncett St Mary, Norf	65	A3
Forncett St Peter, Norf	65	A3
Fornham All Saints, Suff	54	B2
Fornham St Martin, Suff	54	B2
Forres, Moray	138	A2
Forsbrook, Staffs	71	A3
Fort Augustus, High	131	E3
Fort William, High	126	E2
Forteviot, Perth	123	C3
Forth, S Lan	116	C4
Forthampton, Glouc	38	A1
Fortingall, Perth	127	E4
Forton, Hants	27	A4
Forton, Lancs	85	C2
Forton, Shrops	57	C1
Forton, Som	13	A3
Forton, Staffs	58	B1
Fortrose, High	137	B3
Fortuneswell, Dorset	7	D2
Fosbury, Wilts	26	D3
Foscot, Oxon	39	A2
Fosdyke, Lincs	75	A4
Foss, Perth	128	A3
Fossebridge, Glouc	38	C2
Foston on the Wolds, E R of Y	90	C1
Foston, Derby	71	C4
Foston, Leics	61	A3
Foston, Lincs	74	A3
Foston, N York	94	C4
Fotheringhay, Nhants	62	B3
Foul End, Warwk	60	A3
Foulden, Border	119	E4
Foulridge, Lancs	86	C2
Foulsham, Norf	64	D1
Fountainhall, Border	110	C1
Four Ashes, Suff	54	C1
Four Crosses, Powys	57	B1
Four Elms, Kent	30	A4
Four Forks, Som	12	D1
Four Gotes, Cambs	63	C1
Four Lanes, Corn	1	C3
Four Marks, Hants	17	A1
Four Mile Bridge, Angle	77	A4
Four Oaks, W Mids	60	A4
Four Roads, Carm	34	C3
Four Throws, Kent	20	B1
Fovant, Wilts	14	D2
Fowey, Corn	3	E4
Fowlhall, Kent	31	A4
Fowlis Wester, Perth	123	B2
Fowlis, Angus	124	A1
Fowlmere, Cambs	53	A3
Fownhope, Heref	48	A4
Fox Corner, Surrey	28	B3
Foxcote, Som	25	A3
Foxdale, I of M	145	B3
Foxearth, Essex	54	B4
Foxfield, Cumb	91	C3
Foxhole, Corn	3	D4
Foxholes, N York	95	C4
Foxley, Norf	64	D1
Foxt, Staffs	71	A3
Foxton, Cambs	53	A3
Foxton, Leics	61	B4
Foxton, N York	94	A2
Foxwood, Shrops	48	A1
Foy, Heref	37	B1
Foyers, High	132	A2
Fraddon, Corn	3	C4
Fradley, Staffs	60	A2
Fradswell, Staffs	71	A4
Fraisthorpe, E R of Y	90	C1
Framfield, E Suss	19	B2
Framingham Earl, Norf	65	B3
Framingham Pigot, Norf	65	B2
Framlingham, Suff	55	B2
Frampton Mansell, Glouc	38	A3
Frampton on Severn, Glouc	37	C3
Frampton, Dorset	14	A4
Frampton, Lincs	75	A3
Framsden, Suff	55	A2
Frances Green, Lancs	86	A3
Frankby, Mers	78	D3
Frankley, Worcs	59	A4
Frankton, Warwk	50	B1
Frant, E Suss	19	C1
Fraserburgh, Aber	139	E2
Frating Green, Essex	44	B1
Frating, Essex	44	B1
Freathy, Corn	4	B4
Freckenham, Suff	54	A1
Freckleton, Lancs	85	B4
Freeby, Leics	61	C1
Freefolk, Hants	27	A4
Freeland, Oxon	39	C2
Freethorpe Common, Norf	66	A2
Freiston, Lincs	75	A3
Fremington, Devon	11	D1
Fremington, N York	93	B2
French Street, Kent	30	A4
Freshford, Som	25	A3
Freshwater, I of W	9	B1
Fressingfield, Suff	55	B1
Freswick, High	143	F1
Fretherne, Glouc	37	C3
Frettenham, Norf	65	B1
Freuchie, Fife	124	A4
Freystrop, Pemb	33	C2
Friday Bridge, Cambs	63	C2
Fridaythorpe, E R of Y	90	A1
Friesthorpe, Lincs	83	D4
Frieston, Lincs	74	A3
Frieth, Bucks	40	C4
Frilford, Oxon	39	C4
Frilsham, Berks	27	B2
Frimley Green, Surrey	28	B3
Frimley, Surrey	28	B3
Fring, Norf	75	D4
Fringford, Oxon	40	A1
Frinsted, Kent	31	C3
Frinton-on-Sea, Essex	44	C2
Friockheim, Angus	129	C4
Frisby on the Wreake, Leics	61	B1
Friskney, Lincs	75	B2
Friston, E Suss	19	C4
Friston, Suff	55	C2
Fritchley, Derby	72	A2
Fritham, Hants	15	B3
Frithelstock Stone, Devon	11	D2
Frithelstock, Devon	11	D2
Frithville, Lincs	75	A2
Frittenden, Kent	20	B1
Frittiscombe, Devon	10	B1
Fritton, Norf	65	A3
Fritton, Norf	66	A3
Fritwell, Oxon	40	A1
Frizington, Cumb	97	D4
Frocester, Glouc	37	C3
Frodesley, Shrops	57	D3
Frodsham, Chesh	79	B4
Frog End, Cambs	53	A3
Frog Pool, Worcs	48	B2
Froggatt, Derby	81	C4
Froghall, Staffs	71	A3
Frogmore, Devon	10	B1
Frognall, Lincs	62	C2
Frogwell, Corn	4	B3
Frolesworth, Leics	61	A4
Frome St Quintin, Dorset	14	A4
Frome, Som	25	A4
Fromes Hill, Heref	48	A3
Fron Isaf, Wrex	69	B3
Froncysyllte, Denb	69	B3
Fron-goch, Gwyn	68	C3
Frosterley, Durham	99	C2
Froxfield Green, Hants	17	A2
Froxfield, Wilts	26	D2
Fulbeck, Lincs	74	A2
Fulbourn, Cambs	53	B3
Fulbrook, Oxon	39	A2
Fulford, Som	12	D2
Fulford, Staffs	71	A3
Fulham, G Lon	147	A2
Fulking, W Suss	18	C3
Full Sutton, E R of Y	89	C1
Fuller Street, Essex	43	B2
Fulletby, Lincs	84	B4
Fullready, Warwk	50	A3
Fulmer, Bucks	146	A1
Fulnetby, Lincs	84	A4
Fulstow, Lincs	84	C2
Fulwell, Oxon	39	B1
Fundenhall, Norf	65	A3
Furley, Devon	13	A4
Furnace, Argyll	121	B4
Furness Vale, Derby	81	A4
Furneux Pelham, Herts	42	C1
Furze Platt, Berks	28	B1
Furzley, Hants	15	C3
Fyfield, Essex	43	A3
Fyfield, Hants	26	D4
Fyfield, Oxon	39	C4
Fyfield, Wilts	26	B2
Fyfield, Wilts	26	C3
Fylingthorpe, N York	95	B1
Fyning, W Suss	17	B2
Fyvie, Aber	139	C4
Gaddesby, Leics	61	B2
Gaddesden Row, Herts	41	B2
Gaer, Powys	36	A2
Gaer-llwyd, Monm	36	C4
Gaerwen, Angle	67	D1
Gailes, N Ayrs	108	D2
Gailey, Staffs	58	C2
Gainford, Durham	100	A4
Gainsborough, Lincs	83	B3
Gainsford End, Essex	54	A4
Gairloch, High	135	F1
Gairlochy, High	126	E1
Gaitsgill, Cumb	98	B1
Galashiels, Border	110	D2
Galgate, Lancs	85	C1
Galhampton, Som	14	A1
Gallowfauld, Angus	129	A4
Galmpton, Devon	10	A2
Galphay, N York	93	C4
Galston, E Ayrs	108	E2
Gamblesby, Cumb	98	D2
Gamlingay, Cambs	52	C3
Gamston, Notts	83	A4
Ganllwyd, Gwyn	56	B1
Ganstead, E R of Y	90	C3
Ganthorpe, N York	94	C4
Ganton, N York	95	C3
Garboldisham, Norf	64	C4
Gardeners Green, Berks	28	A2
Gardenstown, Aber	139	C2
Gare Hill, Wilts	14	B1
Garelochhead, Argyll	114	D1
Garford, Oxon	39	C4
Garforth, W Yorks	88	B3
Gargrave, N York	87	A1
Gargunnock, Stirl	116	A1
Garlic Street, Norf	65	A4
Garlieston, Dumf	96	E1
Garlinge Green, Kent	32	A3
Garlogie, Aber	134	B3
Garmond, Aber	139	C3
Garmouth, Moray	138	C2
Garmston, Shrops	58	A2
Garn-Dolbenmaen, Gwyn	67	D3
Garras, Corn	1	D3
Garrigill, Cumb	99	A2
Garrochtrie, Dumf	96	B2
Garsdale Head, Cumb	92	C2
Garsdon, Wilts	38	B4
Garshall Green, Staffs	71	A4
Garsington, Oxon	40	A3
Garstang, Lancs	85	C2
Garth Penrhyncoch, Cered	56	A4
Garth Row, Cumb	92	A2
Garth, Denb	69	B3
Garth, Powys	46	D3
Garthmyl, Powys	57	A3
Garthorpe, Leics	61	C1
Gartmore, Stirl	122	B4
Gartness, N Lan	116	B3
Gartness, Stirl	115	B1
Gartocharn, Dumb	115	B1
Garton, E R of Y	90	D3
Garton-on-the-Wolds, E R of Y	90	B1
Garvald, E Loth	119	B3
Garvan, High	126	D1
Garve, High	136	E2
Garvestone, Norf	64	D2
Garway, Heref	36	C1
Gasper, Wilts	14	B1
Gastard, Wilts	25	B2
Gasthorpe, Norf	64	C4
Gaston Green, Essex	42	C2
Gatcombe, I of W	9	C1
Gate Helmsley, N York	89	B1
Gateforth, N York	89	A4
Gatehouse of Fleet, Dumf	96	F1
Gatehouse, Nthumb	105	A2
Gateley, Norf	64	C1
Gatenby, N York	93	D2
Gateshead, Tyne	106	A4
Gateside, East Renf	115	B4
Gateside, Fife	123	D3
Gatley, G Man	80	B3
Gatton, Surrey	150	B2
Gaulby, Leics	61	B3
Gauldry, Fife	124	B2
Gautby, Lincs	84	A4
Gavinton, Border	119	C4
Gawcott, Bucks	40	B1
Gawsworth, Chesh	70	C1
Gawthrop, Cumb	92	B3
Gawthwaite, Cumb	91	D3
Gaydon, Warwk	50	A3
Gayhurst, Bucks	51	B3
Gayle, N York	92	D2
Gayles, N York	93	B1
Gayton le Marsh, Lincs	84	C3
Gayton Thorpe, Norf	64	A1
Gayton, Nhants	51	A3
Gayton, Norf	64	A1
Gayton, Staffs	71	A4
Gazeley, Suff	54	A2
Gedding, Suff	54	C2
Geddinge, Kent	32	C4
Geddington, Nhants	62	A4
Gedney Broadgate, Lincs	63	B1
Gedney Drove End, Lincs	75	B4
Gedney Dyke, Lincs	75	A4
Gedney Hill, Lincs	63	B2
Gedney, Lincs	63	B1
Geeston, Rutland	62	B2
Geldeston, Norf	66	A3
Gelli Gynan, Denb	69	A2
Gellifor, Denb	69	A1
Gelligaer, Caer	36	A4
Gellilydan, Gwyn	68	A3
Gellywen, Carm	34	A1
Gelston, Dumf	103	C4
Gelston, Lincs	74	A3
Gembling, E R of Y	90	C1
Gentleshaw, Staffs	59	B2
George Green, Bucks	146	A1
George Nympton, Devon	11	F2
Georgeham, Devon	11	D1
Germansweek, Devon	4	C1
Gerrards Cross, Bucks	41	B4
Gerrick, N York	101	B4
Gestingthorpe, Essex	54	B4
Geuffordd, Powys	57	A2
Gifford, E Loth	119	A3
Giggleswick, N York	86	B1
Gilcrux, Cumb	97	D2
Gildersome, W Yorks	87	C4
Gildingwells, S York	82	C3
Gileston, Glam	23	A2
Gilfach Goch, Bridg	35	C4
Gilfachrheda, Cered	45	E2
Gilgarran, Cumb	97	D3
Gillamoor, N York	94	C2
Gilling East, N York	94	B3
Gilling West, N York	93	C1
Gillingham, Dorset	14	B2
Gillingham, Kent	31	B2
Gillingham, Norf	66	A3
Gilmerton, Perth	123	A2
Gilmonby, Durham	99	C4
Gilmorton, Leics	61	A4
Gilsland, Cumb	104	E4
Gilwern, Monm	36	B2
Gimingham, Norf	76	D4
Gipping, Suff	54	D2
Gipsey Bridge, Lincs	74	D2
Girsby, N York	93	D1
Girton, Cambs	53	A2
Girton, Notts	73	C1
Girvan, S Ayrs	102	B1
Gisburn, Lancs	86	C2
Gisleham, Suff	66	B4
Gislingham, Suff	54	D1
Gissing, Norf	65	A4
Gittisham, Devon	12	D4
Gladestry, Powys	47	A3
Gladsmuir, E Loth	118	B2
Glais, Swan	35	A3
Glaisdale, N York	95	A1
Glamis, Angus	129	A4
Glanaman, Carm	35	A2
Glandford, Norf	76	B3
Glandwr, Pemb	33	E1
Glandyfi, Cered	56	B3
Glanton, Nthumb	112	B4
Glanvilles Wootton, Dorset	14	A3
Glan-y-don, Flint	78	C4
Glapthorn, Nhants	62	B4
Glasbury, Powys	47	A4
Glascwm, Powys	47	A3
Glasfryn, Aberc	68	C2
Glasgow, Glas	115	C3
Glasinfryn, Gwyn	67	E1
Glasserton, Dumf	96	D2
Glassford, S Lan	109	B1
Glasshouse, Glouc	37	C2
Glasshouses, N York	93	C4
Glasson, Cumb	104	B4
Glasson, Lancs	85	B1
Glassonby, Cumb	98	C2
Glasterlaw, Angus	129	C4
Glaston, Rutland	62	A3
Glastonbury, Som	13	C1
Glatton, Cambs	62	C4
Glazebrook, Chesh	80	A3
Glazebury, Chesh	79	C2
Glazeley, Shrops	58	B4
Gleaston, Cumb	91	D4
Gledrid, Shrops	69	B4
Glemsford, Suff	54	B3
Glen Auldyn, I of M	145	D2
Glen Maye, I of M	145	B3
Glenbarr, Argyll	107	D2
Glenboig, N Lan	116	A3
Glenborrodale, High	125	F3
Glenbuck, E Ayrs	109	B2
Glencaple, Dumf	103	D3
Glencarse, Perth	123	D2
Glencoe, High	126	E3
Glencraig, Fife	117	B1
Glendaruel, Argyll	114	B2
Glendevon, Perth	123	B4
Glendoick, Perth	123	D2
Gleneagles, Perth	123	B3
Glenelg, High	130	F2
Glenfarg, Perth	123	D3
Glenfinnan, High	126	C1
Glengolly, High	143	C1
Glenholm, Border	109	E2
Glenkindie, Aber	133	D2
Glenluce, Dumf	102	C4
Glenmavis, N Lan	116	A3
Glenmore, High	135	C4
Glenridding, Cumb	98	B4
Glenrothes, Fife	124	A4
Glentham, Lincs	83	D3
Glentrool Village, Dumf	102	D3
Glentworth, Lincs	83	C3
Glenurquhart, High	137	B2
Glenwhilly, Dumf	102	B3
Glewstone, Heref	37	A2
Glinton, Cambs	62	C2
Glooston, Leics	61	C3
Glossop, Derby	81	A3
Gloucester, Glouc	38	A2
Glusburn, N York	87	A2
Gluvian, Corn	3	C3
Glyn Ceiriog, Wrex	69	A3
Glynarthen, Cered	45	E3
Glyncorrwg, Neath	35	B3
Glynde, E Suss	19	B3
Glyndyfrdwy, Denb	69	A3
Glyn-Neath, Neath	35	B3
Glyntawe, Powys	35	B2
Glynteg, Carm	45	E4
Gnosall, Staffs	58	C1
Goadby Marwood, Leics	73	C4
Goadby, Leics	61	C3
Goatacre, Wilts	26	A1
Goathill, Dorset	14	A3
Goathland, N York	95	A1
Goathurst Common, Kent	30	A4
Goathurst, Som	13	A1
Gobowen, Shrops	69	B4
Goddard's Green, Kent	20	B1
Godmanchester, Cambs	52	C1
Godmanstone, Dorset	14	A4
Godney, Som	24	B4
Godolphin Cross, Corn	1	C2
Godre'r-graig, Neath	35	A3
Godshill, I of W	10	A2
Goetre, Monm	36	B3
Goff's Oak, Herts	42	B3
Gofilon, Monm	36	B2
Goginan, Cered	56	B4
Golan, Gwyn	67	D3
Golant, Corn	3	E4
Golberdon, Corn	4	B3
Golborne, G Man	79	C2
Goldcliff, Newport	24	A1
Golden Green, Kent	30	B4
Golden Pot, Hants	27	C4
Goldhanger, Essex	44	A3
Goldsborough, N York	88	A1
Goldsborough, N York	101	C4
Goldsithney, Corn	1	C2
Goldsworth, Surrey	146	A3
Goldthorpe, S York	82	B2
Goldworthy, Devon	11	C2
Gollanfield, High	137	C3
Golspie, High	141	D3
Gomeldon, Wilts	15	B1
Gonalston, Notts	73	B3
Good Easter, Essex	43	A2
Gooderstone, Norf	64	A3
Goodleigh, Devon	11	E1
Goodmanham, E R of Y	90	A2
Goodnestone, Kent	32	A3
Goodnestone, Kent	32	C3
Goodrich, Heref	37	A2
Goodshaw Fold, Lancs	86	B4
Goodworth Clatford, Hants	26	D4
Goole, E R of Y	89	C4
Goom's Hill, Worcs	49	A3
Goonbell, Corn	3	A4
Goonhavern, Corn	3	B4
Goonvrea, Corn	3	A4
Goose Green, Essex	44	C1
Goose Green, Essex	44	C1
Goose Green, Glouc	24	C2
Goosey, Oxon	39	B4
Goosnargh, Lancs	85	C3
Goostrey, Chesh	70	B1
Gordon, Border	111	A1
Gordonstown, Aber	139	C4
Gorebridge, M Loth	118	A3
Gores, Wilts	26	B3
Gorey, Jersey	145	B2
Goring, Oxon	27	B1
Gorran Haven, Corn	2	C1
Gorran, Corn	2	C1
Gorsedd, Flint	78	C4
Gorseinon, Swan	34	D4
Gorsgoch, Cered	45	F3
Gorslas, Carm	34	D2
Gorsley, Glouc	37	B1
Gorstello, Chesh	69	C1
Gorsty Hill, Staffs	71	B4
Gosbeck, Suff	55	A3
Gosberton, Lincs	74	D4
Gosfield, Essex	43	C1
Gosforth, Cumb	91	B1
Gosforth, Tyne	106	A4
Gospel End, Staffs	58	C3
Gosport, Hants	16	B4
Gossington, Glouc	37	C3
Gotham, Notts	73	A4
Gotherington, Glouc	38	B1
Gotton, Som	13	A2
Goudhurst, Kent	20	A1
Goulceby, Lincs	84	B4
Gourdon, Aber	129	E2
Gourock, Inverclyde	114	D2
Goveton, Devon	10	A1
Gowdall, E R of Y	89	B4
Gowerton, Swan	34	D4
Gowkhall, Fife	117	A1
Goxhill, E R of Y	90	C2
Goxhill, Lincs	90	C4
Graffham, W Suss	17	C3
Grafham, Cambs	52	B1
Grafham, Surrey	146	A4
Grafton Flyford, Worcs	49	A3
Grafton Regis, Nhants	51	B3
Grafton Underwood, Nhants	62	A4
Grafton, N York	88	B1
Grafton, Oxon	39	A3
Grafton, Shrops	57	C1
Grafton, Worcs	49	A4
Graig, Aberc	68	B1
Graig-fechan, Denb	69	A2
Grain, Kent	31	B1
Grainsby, Lincs	84	B2
Grainthorpe, Lincs	84	C2
Grampound Road, Corn	3	C4
Gramsdale, W Isle	144	A3
Granborough, Bucks	40	C1
Granby, Notts	73	C4
Grand Chemins, Jersey	145	B2
Grandborough, Warwk	50	B2
Grandes Rocques, Guern	145	B2
Grange Moor, W Yorks	81	C1
Grange Villa, Durham	100	A1
Grange, Cumb	98	A4
Grangemouth, Falk	116	C2
Grange-over-Sands, Cumb	91	E3
Gransmoor, E R of Y	90	C1
Granston, Pemb	45	A4
Grantchester, Cambs	53	B3
Grantham, Lincs	74	A4
Grantown-on-Spey, High	133	A1
Grantshouse, Border	119	C3
Grasby, Lincs	84	A2
Grasmere, Cumb	91	D1
Grasscroft, G Man	81	A2
Grassington, N York	87	A1
Grassmoor, Derby	72	B1
Grassthorpe, Notts	73	C1
Grateley, Hants	26	D4
Graveley, Cambs	52	C2
Graveley, Herts	42	A1
Graveney, Kent	32	A3
Gravesend, Kent	30	B2
Grayingham, Lincs	83	C2
Grayrigg, Cumb	92	A2
Grays, Essex	30	B1
Grayshott, Hants	17	C1
Grayswood, Surrey	17	C1
Grazeley, Berks	27	C2
Greasbrough, S York	82	B2
Greasley, Notts	72	B3
Great Addington, Nhants	51	C1
Great Alne, Warwk	49	B2
Great Altcar, Lancs	78	D2
Great Amwell, Herts	42	B2
Great Asby, Cumb	98	D4
Great Ayton, N York	101	A4
Great Badminton, Glouc	25	A1
Great Bardfield, Essex	43	B1
Great Barford, Beds	52	B3
Great Barrington, Glouc	39	A2
Great Barrow, Chesh	69	D1
Great Barton, Suff	54	C2
Great Barugh, N York	95	A3
Great Bavington, Nthumb	105	C2
Great Bealings, Suff	55	A3
Great Bedwyn, Wilts	26	C2
Great Bentley, Essex	44	B2
Great Bircham, Norf	75	D4
Great Blakenham, Suff	54	D3
Great Blencow, Cumb	98	B3
Great Bolas, Shrops	58	A1
Great Bookham, Surrey	146	B3
Great Bosullow, Corn	1	B2
Great Bourton, Oxon	50	B3
Great Bowden, Leics	61	C4
Great Bradley, Suff	54	A3
Great Braxted, Essex	43	C2
Great Bricett, Suff	54	D3
Great Brickhill, Bucks	41	A1
Great Bridgeford, Staffs	70	C4
Great Brington, Nhants	51	A2
Great Bromley, Essex	44	B1
Great Broughton, Cumb	97	D3
Great Budworth, Chesh	79	C4
Great Burdon, Durham	100	B4
Great Busby, N York	94	B1
Great Carlton, Lincs	84	C3
Great Casterton, Rutland	62	B2
Great Chart, Kent	31	C4
Great Chatfield, Wilts	25	B3
Great Chatwell, Staffs	58	B1
Great Chesterford, Essex	53	B4
Great Cheverell, Wilts	26	A3
Great Chishill, Cambs	53	A4
Great Clifton, Cumb	97	D3
Great Cowden, E R of Y	90	D2
Great Coxwell, Oxon	39	A4
Great Cransley, Nhants	51	B1
Great Cressingham, Norf	64	B3
Great Crosthwaite, Cumb	98	A3
Great Cubley, Derby	71	C3
Great Dalby, Leics	61	C2
Great Dunham, Norf	64	B1
Great Dunmow, Essex	43	A1
Great Durnford, Wilts	15	A1
Great Easton, Essex	43	A1
Great Easton, Leics	61	C3
Great Eccleston, Lancs	85	B3
Great Ellingham, Norf	64	D3
Great Elm, Som	25	A4
Great Englebourne, Devon	5	C4
Great Everdon, Nhants	50	C2
Great Eversden, Cambs	53	A3
Great Finborough, Suff	54	D2
Great Fransham, Norf	64	C2
Great Gaddesden, Herts	41	B2
Great Gidding, Cambs	62	C4
Great Givendale, E R of Y	89	C1
Great Glemham, Suff	55	B2
Great Glen, Leics	61	B3
Great Gonerby, Lincs	74	A3
Great Gransden, Cambs	52	C3
Great Green, Cambs	52	C4
Great Green, Suff	54	C2
Great Habton, N York	95	A3
Great Hale, Lincs	74	C3
Great Hallingbury, Essex	42	C2
Great Harrowden, Nhants	51	C1
Great Harwood, Lancs	86	B3
Great Haseley, Oxon	40	B3
Great Hatfield, E R of Y	90	C2
Great Haywood, Staffs	59	A1
Great Heck, N York	89	A4
Great Henny, Essex	54	B4
Great Hinton, Wilts	25	B3
Great Hockham, Norf	64	C3
Great Holland, Essex	44	C2
Great Horkesley, Essex	44	A1
Great Hormead, Herts	42	B1
Great Horwood, Bucks	40	C1
Great Houghton, Nhants	51	B2
Great Houghton, S York	82	B2
Great Hucklow, Derby	81	C4
Great Kelk, E R of Y	90	C1
Great Kimble, Bucks	40	C3
Great Kingshill, Bucks	41	A4
Great Langdale, Cumb	91	D1
Great Langton, N York	93	D2
Great Leighs, Essex	43	B2
Great Limber, Lincs	84	A1
Great Linford, Bucks	51	B4
Great Livermere, Suff	54	B1
Great Lumley, Durham	100	B1
Great Malvern, Worcs	48	B3
Great Maplestead, Essex	54	B4
Great Massingham, Norf	64	B1
Great Milton, Oxon	40	B3
Great Missenden, Bucks	41	A3
Great Mongeham, Kent	32	C4
Great Moulton, Norf	65	A4
Great Musgrave, Cumb	99	A4
Great Ness, Shrops	57	C1
Great Oak, Monm	36	C3

PLACE	PAGE	GRID
Great Oakley, Essex	44	C1
Great Offley, Herts	41	C1
Great Ormside, Cumb	99	A4
Great Orton, Cumb	98	A1
Great Ouseburn, N York	88	B1
Great Oxendon, Nhants	61	B4
Great Paxton, Cambs	52	C2
Great Plumpton, Lancs	85	B3
Great Plumstead, Norf	65	B2
Great Ponton, Lincs	74	A4
Great Preston, W Yorks	88	B4
Great Raveley, Cambs	63	A4
Great Rissington, Glouc	39	A2
Great Rollright, Oxon	39	B1
Great Ryburgh, Norf	76	A4
Great Ryle, Nthumb	112	A4
Great Ryton, Shrops	57	D2
Great Saling, Essex	43	B1
Great Salkeld, Cumb	98	C2
Great Sampford, Essex	53	C4
Great Saughall, Chesh	69	C1
Great Shefford, Berks	26	D2
Great Shelford, Cambs	53	B3
Great Smeaton, N York	93	D1
Great Snoring, Norf	76	A4
Great Somerford, Wilts	26	A1
Great Soudley, Shrops	70	B4
Great Stainton, Durham	100	B4
Great Stambridge, Essex	44	A4
Great Steeping, Lincs	75	B1
Great Strickland, Cumb	98	C3
Great Stukeley, Cambs	52	C1
Great Sturton, Lincs	84	B4
Great Swinburne, Nthumb	105	C3
Great Tew, Oxon	39	C1
Great Tey, Essex	44	A1
Great Torrington, Devon	11	D2
Great Tosson, Nthumb	105	C1
Great Totham, Essex	43	C2
Great Totham, Essex	43	C2
Great Urswick, Cumb	91	D4
Great Wakering, Essex	44	A4
Great Waldingfield, Suff	54	C4
Great Walsingham, Norf	76	A4
Great Waltham, Essex	43	B2
Great Warley, Essex	43	A4
Great Washbourne, Glouc	49	A4
Great Wenham, Suff	54	D4
Great Whittington, Nthumb	105	C3
Great Wigborough, Essex	44	A2
Great Wilbraham, Cambs	53	C2
Great Wishford, Wilts	15	A1
Great Witcombe, Glouc	38	A2
Great Wolford, Warwk	49	C4
Great Wratting, Suff	54	A3
Great Wymondley, Herts	42	A1
Great Wyrley, Staffs	59	A2
Great Yarmouth, Norf	66	B2
Great Yeldham, Essex	54	A4
Greatford, Lincs	62	C2
Greatgate, Staffs	71	B3
Greatham, Durham	100	C3
Greatham, Hants	17	B1
Greatham, W Suss	18	A3
Greatworth, Nhants	50	C4
Green End, Herts	42	B1
Green End, Herts	42	B1
Green End, Warwk	60	A4
Green Hammerton, N York	88	B1
Green Ore, Som	24	B4
Green Quarter, Cumb	91	E1
Green Street Green, G Lon	30	A3
Green Street Green, Kent	30	B2
Green Street, Herts	42	C2
Green Street, Worcs	48	C3
Green Tye, Herts	42	C2
Greenfield, Beds	52	A4
Greenfield, Flint	78	C4
Greenfield, G Man	81	A2
Greenford, G Lon	146	B1
Greengairs, N Lan	116	B3
Greenhalgh, Lancs	85	B3
Greenham, Som	12	C2
Greenhaugh, Nthumb	105	A2
Greenhill, Dumf	103	E3
Greenholm, E Ayrs	109	A2
Greenhow Hill, N York	87	B1
Greenlaw, Border	111	B1
Greenlea, Dumf	103	E3
Greenloaning, Perth	123	A3
Greenock, Inverclyde	114	D2
Greenodd, Cumb	91	D3
Greens Norton, Nhants	51	A3
Greenside, Tyne	105	D4
Greenstead Green, Essex	43	C1
Greenway, Som	13	A2
Greenwich, G Lon	149	B2
Greet, Glouc	38	B1
Greete, Shrops	47	D1
Greetham, Lincs	74	D1
Greetham, Rutland	62	A2
Greetland, W Yorks	87	B4
Greinton, Som	13	B1
Grenaby, I of M	145	B4
Grendon Underwood, Bucks	40	B2
Grendon, Nhants	51	C2
Gresford, Wrex	69	B2
Gresham, Norf	76	C3
Gressenhall Green, Norf	64	C1
Gressenhall, Norf	64	C1
Gressingham, Lancs	92	A4
Greta Bridge, Durham	99	D4
Gretna Green, Dumf	104	B4
Gretna, Dumf	104	B4
Gretton, Nhants	62	A3
Grewelthorpe, N York	93	C3
Greys Green, Oxon	27	C1
Greysouthen, Cumb	97	D3
Greystoke, Cumb	98	B3
Greystone, Angus	129	B4
Greywell, Hants	27	C4
Griff, Warwk	60	B4
Grimeford Village, Lancs	79	C1
Grimethorpe, S York	82	B1
Grimley, Worcs	48	C2
Grimoldby, Lincs	84	C3
Grimpo, Shrops	69	C4
Grimsargh, Lancs	86	A3
Grimsby, Lincs	84	B1
Grimscott, Corn	11	B3
Grimsthorpe, Lincs	62	B1
Grimston, Leics	61	B1
Grimston, Norf	64	A1
Grimstone End, Suff	54	C1
Grimstone, Dorset	7	D1
Grindale, E R of Y	95	D4
Grindleford, Derby	81	C4
Grindleton, Lancs	86	B2
Grindley Brook, Shrops	69	D3
Grindlow, Derby	81	C4
Grindon, Staffs	71	B2
Gringley on the Hill, Notts	83	B3
Grinsdale, Cumb	104	C4
Grinshill, Shrops	57	D1
Grinton, N York	93	B2
Gristhorpe, N York	95	D3
Griston, Norf	64	C3
Gritley, Orkney	144	B2
Grittenham, Wilts	26	A1
Grittleton, Wilts	25	B1
Grizebeck, Cumb	91	D3
Grizedale, Cumb	91	D2
Groby, Leics	61	A2
Groes, Aberc	68	D1
Groes-faen, Rhond	23	A1
Groesffordd Marli, Denb	78	A4
Groes-Wen, Caer	23	B1
Gronant, Flint	78	B4
Groombridge, E Suss	19	B1
Grosmont, Monm	36	C1
Grosmont, N York	95	A1
Groton, Suff	54	C4
Grouville, Jersey	145	B2
Grove Park, G Lon	149	B3
Grove, Notts	83	B4
Grove, Oxon	39	C4
Grovesend, Swan	34	D3
Grundisburgh, Suff	55	A3
Guardbridge, Fife	124	B2
Guarlford, Worcs	48	B3
Guestling Green, E Suss	20	B3
Guestwick, Norf	76	B4
Guide, Lancs	86	B4
Guilden Morden, Cambs	52	C4
Guilden Sutton, Chesh	69	C1
Guildford, Surrey	146	A4
Guildtown, Perth	123	D1
Guilsborough, Nhants	51	A1
Guilsfield, Powys	57	A2
Guisborough, N York	101	A4
Guiseley, W Yorks	87	C2
Guist, Norf	64	C1
Guiting Power, Glouc	38	C1
Gullane, E Loth	119	A2
Gulworthy, Devon	4	C2
Gumfreston, Pemb	33	E3
Gumley, Leics	61	B4
Gun Hill, E Suss	19	C3
Gunby, Lincs	62	A4
Gunby, Lincs	75	B1
Gundleton, Hants	16	B1
Gunn, Devon	11	E1
Gunnerside, N York	93	A2
Gunnerton, Nthumb	105	B3
Gunness, Lincs	83	B1
Gunnislake, Corn	4	C3
Gunthorpe, Norf	76	B4
Gunthorpe, Notts	73	B3
Gunwalloe, Corn	1	D3
Gurnard, I of W	16	A4
Gurney Slade, Som	24	C4
Gurnos, Powys	35	B3
Gussage All Saints, Dorset	14	D3
Gussage St Andrew, Dorset	14	D3
Gussage St Michael, Dorset	14	D3
Gutcher, Shet	144	A1
Guthrie, Angus	129	B4
Guyhirn, Cambs	63	B2
Guyzance, Nthumb	112	C4
Gwaenysgor, Flint	78	B4
Gwalchmai, Angle	77	B4
Gwaun-Cae-Gurwen, Carm	35	A2
Gweek, Corn	1	D2
Gwenddwr, Powys	46	E4
Gwennap, Corn	2	A1
Gwernaffield, Flint	69	A1
Gwernesney, Monm	36	C3
Gwernogle, Carm	45	F4
Gwernymynydd, Flint	69	A1
Gwespyr, Flint	78	B4
Gwithian, Corn	1	C1
Gwyddelwern, Denb	68	D3
Gwyddgrug, Carm	45	F4
Gwytherin, Aberc	68	B1
Habberley, Shrops	57	C2
Habertoft, Lincs	75	B1
Habrough, Lincs	84	A1
Hacconby, Lincs	62	C1
Haceby, Lincs	74	B4
Hacheston, Suff	55	B2
Hackbridge, G Lon	147	A4
Hackford, Norf	64	D3
Hackforth, N York	93	C2
Hackland, Orkney	144	A1
Hackleton, Nhants	51	B3
Hackness, N York	95	C2
Hackney, G Lon	149	A1
Hackthorn, Lincs	83	D4
Hackthorpe, Cumb	98	C3
Haddenham, Bucks	40	C3
Haddenham, Cambs	53	B1
Haddington, E Loth	119	A2
Haddington, Lincs	74	A1
Haddiscoe, Norf	66	A3
Haddon, Cambs	62	C3
Hadfield, Derby	81	A2
Hadleigh, Suff	54	D4
Hadley End, Staffs	59	B1
Hadley, Worcs	48	C2
Hadlow, Kent	30	B4
Hadnall, Shrops	57	D1
Hadstock, Essex	53	C4
Hadzor, Worcs	48	C2
Hafodunos, Aberc	68	B1
Haggerston, Nthumb	112	A1
Haggs, Falk	116	B2
Hagley, Heref	47	D4
Hagley, Worcs	58	C4
Hagworthingham, Lincs	75	A1
Hail Weston, Cambs	52	B2
Haile, Cumb	91	B1
Hailey, Oxon	39	B2
Hainford, Norf	65	A1
Hainton, Lincs	84	A3
Haisthorpe, E R of Y	95	D4
Halam, Notts	73	B2
Halberton, Devon	12	C3
Hale Street, Kent	31	A4
Hale, Chesh	79	B4
Hale, Cumb	92	A3
Hale, G Man	80	A3
Hale, Hants	15	B2
Hales, Norf	66	A3
Hales, Staffs	70	B4
Halesowen, W Mids	59	A4
Halesworth, Suff	55	C1
Halewood, Mers	79	A3
Halford, Devon	5	C2
Halford, Warwk	49	C3
Halfpenny Green, Shrops	58	C3
Halfway House, Shrops	57	B2
Halifax, W Yorks	87	B4
Halkirk, High	143	D2
Halkyn, Flint	69	A1
Hall Dunnerdale, Cumb	91	C2
Halland, E Suss	19	B3
Hallaton, Leics	61	C3
Hallatrow, Som	24	C3
Hallbankgate, Cumb	104	E4
Hallen, Glouc	24	B1
Hallgarth, Durham	100	B2
Hallin, High	135	A2
Halling, Kent	31	A3
Hallington, Lincs	84	B3
Hallington, Nthumb	105	C3
Halloughton, Notts	73	B2
Hall's Green, Herts	42	A1
Hallsands, Devon	10	B1
Halmore, Glouc	37	C3
Halnaker, W Suss	17	C3
Halsall, Lancs	79	A1
Halse, Nhants	50	C4
Halse, Som	12	D2
Halsetown, Corn	1	C1
Halsham, E R of Y	90	D4
Halstead, Essex	43	C1
Halstead, Leics	61	C2
Halstock, Dorset	13	C3
Halsway, Som	12	D1
Haltham, Lincs	74	D1
Halton East, N York	87	A1
Halton Gill, N York	92	D3
Halton Holegate, Lincs	75	A1
Halton Lea Gate, Nthumb	104	E4
Halton Shields, Nthumb	105	C3
Halton West, N York	86	C1
Halton, Bucks	41	A3
Halton, Lancs	92	A4
Halton, Nthumb	105	C4
Halton, Wrex	69	B3
Haltwhistle, Nthumb	105	A4
Halvergate, Norf	66	A2
Halwell, Devon	5	C4
Halwill Junction, Devon	11	D4
Halwill, Devon	11	D4
Ham Green, Worcs	49	A2
Ham, G Lon	146	B2
Ham, Glouc	37	B4
Ham, Kent	32	C3
Ham, Som	13	A2
Ham, Wilts	26	D3
Hambleden, Bucks	28	A1
Hambledon, Hants	17	A3
Hambledon, Surrey	17	C1
Hamble-le-Rice, Hants	16	A3
Hambleton, Lancs	85	B2
Hambleton, N York	89	A3
Hambridge, Som	13	B2
Hameringham, Lincs	74	D1
Hamerton, Cambs	52	B1
Hamilton, S Lan	116	A4
Hamlet, Dorset	14	A3
Hammersmith, G Lon	147	A2
Hammerwich, Staffs	59	B2
Hammoon, Dorset	14	C3
Hampden Row, Bucks	41	A3
Hampnett, Glouc	38	C2
Hampole, S York	82	C1
Hampreston, Dorset	15	A4
Hampstead Norrey's, Berks	27	B1
Hampstead, G Lon	148	A1
Hampsthwaite, N York	87	C1
Hampton Bishop, Heref	47	D4
Hampton Heath, Chesh	69	D2
Hampton in Arden, W Mids	60	A4
Hampton Lucy, Warwk	49	C2
Hampton on the Hill, Warwk	49	C2
Hampton Poyle, Oxon	39	C2
Hampton Wick, G Lon	146	B2
Hampton, G Lon	146	B2
Hampton, Wilts	39	A4
Hamptworth, Wilts	15	B2
Hamsey Green, Surrey	150	C1
Hamsey, E Suss	19	A3
Hamstall Ridware, Staffs	59	B1
Hamsterley, Durham	99	D1
Hamsterley, Durham	99	D3
Hanbury, Staffs	71	C4
Hanbury, Worcs	49	A2
Hanchurch, Staffs	70	C3
Handley, Chesh	69	D2
Handley, Derby	72	A1
Hanging Houghton, Nhants	51	B1
Hanging Langford, Wilts	14	D1
Hankelow, Chesh	70	A3
Hankerton, Wilts	38	B4
Hanley Castle, Worcs	48	C4
Hanley Child, Worcs	48	A2
Hanley Swan, Worcs	48	B4
Hanley William, Worcs	48	A2
Hanlith, N York	86	C1
Hanmer, Wrex	69	C3
Hannington Wick, Wilts	39	A4
Hannington, Hants	27	B3
Hannington, Nhants	51	B1
Hannington, Wilts	39	A4
Hanslope, Bucks	51	B3
Hanthorpe, Lincs	62	C1
Hanwell, G Lon	146	B1
Hanwell, Oxon	50	B4
Hanworth, G Lon	146	B2
Hanworth, Norf	76	C4
Happisburgh Common, Norf	76	E4
Happisburgh, Norf	76	E4
Hapsford, Chesh	79	B4
Hapton, Lancs	86	B3
Hapton, Norf	65	A3
Harberton, Devon	5	C4
Harbertonford, Devon	5	C4
Harborough Magna, Warwk	50	B1
Harbottle, Nthumb	112	A4
Harbourneford, Devon	5	B3
Harbury, Warwk	50	A2
Harby, Leics	73	C4
Harby, Notts	74	A1
Harcombe Bottom, Devon	13	A4
Harcombe, Devon	6	A2
Harden, W Yorks	87	B3
Hardgate, Dumf	103	C4
Hardham, W Suss	18	A3
Hardingham, Norf	64	D2
Hardingstone, Nhants	51	B2
Hardington Mandeville, Som	13	C3
Hardington Marsh, Som	13	C3
Hardington Moor, Som	13	C3
Hardington, Som	25	A4
Hardisworthy, Devon	11	B2
Hardley Street, Norf	66	A3
Hardley, Hants	16	A4
Hardraw, N York	92	D2
Hardstoft, Derby	72	B1
Hardway, Som	14	B1
Hardwick, Bucks	40	C2
Hardwick, Cambs	53	A2
Hardwick, Nhants	51	B1
Hardwick, Norf	65	A4
Hardwick, Oxon	39	B3
Hardwick, Oxon	40	A1
Hardwicke, Glouc	37	C2
Hardwicke, Glouc	38	A1
Hardy's Green, Essex	44	A2
Hare Croft, W Yorks	87	B3
Hare Green, Essex	44	B1
Hare Hatch, Berks	28	A1
Hare Street, Herts	42	B1
Hareby, Lincs	75	A1
Harefield, G Lon	41	B4
Harehill, Derby	71	C4
Harescombe, Glouc	38	A3
Haresfield, Glouc	37	C2
Harewood End, Heref	37	A1
Harewood, W Yorks	88	A2
Hargrave, Chesh	69	D1
Hargrave, Nhants	52	A1
Harkstead, Suff	55	A4
Harlaston, Staffs	60	A2
Harlaxton, Lincs	74	A4
Harlech, Gwyn	67	E4
Harlesden, G Lon	147	A1
Harlesthorpe, Derby	82	B4
Harleston, Devon	10	B1
Harleston, Norf	65	B4
Harleston, Suff	54	D2
Harlestone, Nhants	51	A2
Harley, S York	82	A2
Harlington, Beds	41	B1
Harlington, G Lon	146	B1
Harlington, S York	82	B2
Harlosh, High	135	B4
Harlow Hill, Nthumb	105	D4
Harlow, Essex	42	C2
Harlthorpe, E R of Y	89	C3
Harlton, Cambs	53	A3
Harlyn Bay, Corn	3	C2
Harman's Cross, Dorset	8	C2
Harmby, N York	93	B2
Harmer Hill, Shrops	57	D1
Harmondsworth, G Lon	146	A1
Harmston, Lincs	74	B1
Harnage, Shrops	57	D2
Harnhill, Glouc	38	C3
Haroldston West, Pemb	33	C2
Haroldswick, Shet	144	B1
Harome, N York	94	C3
Harpenden, Herts	41	C2
Harpford, Devon	6	B1
Harpham, E R of Y	90	C1
Harpley, Norf	64	B1
Harpley, Worcs	48	A2
Harpole, Nhants	51	A2
Harpswell, Lincs	83	C3
Harracott, Devon	11	E2
Harrietfield, Perth	123	B2
Harrietsham, Kent	31	B4
Harrington, Lincs	75	A1
Harringworth, Nhants	62	A3
Harrogate, N York	88	A1
Harrold, Beds	51	C2
Harrow on the Hill, G Lon	146	B1
Harrow, G Lon	41	C4
Harrowbarrow, Corn	4	B3
Harston, Cambs	53	A3
Harston, Leics	73	C4
Harswell, E R of Y	89	C3
Hart, Durham	100	C2
Hartburn, Nthumb	105	D2
Hartest, Suff	54	B3
Hartfield, E Suss	19	B1
Hartford End, Essex	43	B2
Hartfordbridge, Hants	28	A3
Hartforth, N York	93	C1
Harthill, Chesh	69	D2
Harthill, N Lan	116	C3
Harthill, S York	82	B4
Hartington, Derby	71	B2
Hartland, Devon	11	B2
Hartlebury, Worcs	48	C1
Hartlepool, Durham	100	C3
Hartley Wintney, Hants	28	A3
Hartley, Cumb	92	C1
Hartley, Kent	20	A1
Hartley, Kent	30	B2
Hartlip, Kent	31	B2
Harton, N York	89	B1
Hartpury, Glouc	37	C1
Hartshead, W Yorks	87	C4
Hartshill, Warwk	60	B3
Hartshorne, Derby	60	B1
Hartside, Nthumb	112	A3
Hartwell, Nhants	51	B3
Hartwith, N York	87	C1
Harvel, Kent	30	B3
Harvington, Worcs	49	B3
Harwell, Notts	83	A3
Harwell, Oxon	39	C4
Harwich, Essex	44	D1
Harwood Dale, N York	95	B2
Harworth, Notts	82	C3
Hascombe, Surrey	18	A1
Haselbeach, Nhants	51	A1
Haselbury Plucknett, Som	13	C3
Haseley, Warwk	49	C2
Haselor, Warwk	49	B2
Hasfield, Glouc	38	A1
Haskayne, Lancs	79	A1
Hasketon, Suff	55	B3
Haslemere, Surrey	17	C1
Haslingden, Lancs	86	B4
Haslingfield, Cambs	53	A3
Haslington, Chesh	70	B2
Hassingham, Norf	66	A2
Hassop, Derby	81	C4
Haster, High	143	E2
Hastingleigh, Kent	32	A4
Hastings, E Suss	20	B3
Hastingwood, Essex	42	C3
Hastoe, Herts	41	A3
Haswell Plough, Durham	100	B2
Haswell, Durham	100	B2
Hatch Beauchamp, Som	13	A2
Hatcliffe, Lincs	84	B2
Hatfield Broad Oak, Essex	43	A2
Hatfield Heath, Essex	42	C2
Hatfield Peverel, Essex	43	C2
Hatfield Woodhouse, S York	83	A1
Hatfield, Heref	48	A2
Hatfield, Herts	42	A3
Hatfield, S York	83	A1
Hatford, Oxon	39	B4
Hatherden, Hants	26	D4
Hatherleigh, Devon	11	E4
Hathern, Leics	60	C1
Hatherop, Glouc	38	C3
Hathersage Booths, Derby	81	C4
Hathersage, Derby	81	C4
Hatherton, Chesh	70	A3
Hatherton, Staffs	59	A2
Hatley St George, Cambs	52	C3
Hatt, Corn	4	B3
Hattersley, G Man	81	A3
Hatton of Fintray, Aber	134	C2
Hatton, Aber	139	F4
Hatton, Chesh	79	C4
Hatton, Derby	71	C4
Hatton, G Lon	146	B2
Hatton, Lincs	84	A4
Hatton, Shrops	57	D4
Hatton, Warwk	49	C2
Haugh of Urr, Dumf	103	C4
Haugh, E Ayrs	108	E3
Haugham, Lincs	84	C4
Haughley Green, Suff	54	D2
Haughley, Suff	54	D2
Haughton Moss, Chesh	69	D2
Haughton, Shrops	58	B2
Haughton, Shrops	69	C4
Haughton, Staffs	58	C1
Haultwick, Herts	42	B1
Hauxley, Nthumb	106	B1
Hauxton, Cambs	53	B3
Havant, Hants	17	A4
Havenstreet, I of W	10	A1
Havercroft, W Yorks	82	B1
Haverfordwest, Pemb	33	C2
Haverhill, Suff	54	A3
Haverigg, Cumb	91	C3
Haversham, Bucks	51	B4
Haverthwaite, Cumb	91	D3
Havyat, Som	24	B3
Hawarden, Flint	69	B1
Hawbush Green, Essex	43	C1
Hawen, Cered	45	E3
Hawes, N York	92	D2
Hawick, Border	110	D4
Hawkchurch, Devon	13	A4
Hawkedon, Suff	54	B3
Hawkesbury, Glouc	25	A1
Hawkley, Hants	17	B2
Hawkridge, Som	12	A1
Hawkshead Hill, Cumb	91	D2
Hawkshead, Cumb	91	E2
Hawkspur Green, Essex	43	A1
Hawkstone, Shrops	70	A4
Hawkswick, N York	93	A4
Hawksworth, Notts	73	C3
Hawksworth, W Yorks	87	C2
Hawkwell, Essex	43	C4
Hawley, Hants	28	B3
Hawling, Glouc	38	C1
Hawnby, N York	94	B2
Haworth, W Yorks	87	A3
Hawstead, Suff	54	B2
Hawthorn Hill, Berks	28	B2
Hawthorn, Durham	100	C1
Hawton, Notts	73	C2
Haxby, N York	89	A1
Haxey, Lincs	83	B2
Haxted, Surrey	150	D4
Hay Green, Norf	63	C1
Hay Street, Herts	42	B1
Haydock, Mers	79	B2
Haydon Bridge, Nthumb	105	B4
Haydon, Dorset	14	A3
Hayes End, G Lon	146	B1
Hayes, G Lon	146	B1
Hayes, G Lon	149	B4
Hayfield, Derby	81	A3
Hayle, Corn	1	C1
Hayne, Devon	5	B1
Hayne, Devon	12	B3
Hay-on-Wye, Powys	47	A4
Hayscastle Cross, Pemb	33	C1
Hayscastle, Pemb	33	C1
Hayton, Cumb	97	D2
Hayton, Cumb	104	D4
Hayton, E R of Y	89	C2
Hayton, Notts	83	A3
Haytor Vale, Devon	5	B2
Haytown, Devon	11	C3
Haywards Heath, W Suss	19	A2
Haywood, S York	82	C1
Hazel Grove, G Man	80	B3
Hazelbank, S Lan	109	C1
Hazeleigh, Essex	43	C3
Hazelwood, Derby	72	A3
Hazlerigg, Tyne	106	A3
Hazleton, Glouc	38	C2
Heacham, Norf	75	D4
Headcorn, Kent	31	B4
Headlam, Durham	100	A4
Headlesscross, N Lan	116	C4
Headley, Hants	17	B1
Headley, Hants	27	B3
Headley, Surrey	150	A2
Headon, Notts	83	B4
Heads Nook, Cumb	98	C1
Heads, S Lan	109	B1
Heage, Derby	72	A2
Healaugh, N York	88	B2
Healaugh, N York	93	A2
Heale, Som	13	A2
Heale, Som	13	B2
Healey, N York	93	C3
Healeyfield, Durham	99	D1
Healing, Lincs	84	B1
Heanor, Derby	72	B3
Heapham, Lincs	83	C3
Heasley Mill, Devon	11	F1
Heath and Reach, Beds	41	A1
Heath Green, Worcs	49	B1
Heath Hill, Shrops	58	B2
Heath, Derby	72	B1
Heath, W Yorks	88	A4
Heathcote, Derby	71	B2
Heather, Leics	60	C2
Heathfield, E Suss	19	C2
Heathfield, Som	12	D2
Heathton, Shrops	58	C3
Heatley, Chesh	80	A3
Heatley, Staffs	71	B4
Heaton, Staffs	71	A1
Heaton's Bridge, Lancs	79	A1
Heaverham, Kent	30	B3
Hebburn, Tyne	106	B4
Hebden Bridge, W Yorks	87	A4
Hebden, N York	87	A1
Hebing End, Herts	42	A1
Hebron, Carm	33	E1
Hebron, Nthumb	106	A2
Heckfield Green, Suff	55	A1
Heckfield, Hants	27	C3
Heckfordbridge, Essex	44	A2
Heckington, Lincs	74	C3
Heckmondwike, W Yorks	87	C4
Heddington, Wilts	26	A2
Hedenham, Norf	65	B3
Hedge End, Hants	16	A3
Hedgerley, Bucks	41	A4
Hedley on the Hill, Nthumb	105	D4
Hednesford, Staffs	59	A2
Hedon, E R of Y	90	C4
Hedsor, Bucks	28	B1
Heighington, Durham	100	A3
Heighington, Lincs	74	B1
Heightington, Worcs	48	B1
Heiton, Border	111	B2
Hele, Devon	12	B4
Hele, Som	12	D2
Helensburgh, Argyll	114	D2
Helford Passage, Corn	2	A2
Helford, Corn	2	A2
Helhoughton, Norf	75	E4
Helland, Corn	3	D3
Hellescott, Corn	4	A1
Hellesdon, Norf	65	A2
Hellidon, Nhants	50	C2
Hellifield, N York	86	C1
Helm, Nthumb	106	A1
Helmdon, Nhants	50	C4
Helme, W Yorks	81	B1
Helmingham, Suff	55	A2
Helmsdale, High	141	F1
Helmshore, Lancs	86	B4
Helmsley, N York	94	B3
Helperby, N York	94	A4
Helperthorpe, N York	95	B4
Helpringham, Lincs	74	C3
Helpston, Cambs	62	C2
Helsby, Chesh	79	B4
Helston, Corn	1	D2
Helstone, Corn	3	E2
Helton, Cumb	98	C4

PLACE	PAGE	GRID
Hemblington, Norf	65	B2
Hemel Hempstead, Herts	41	B3
Hemerdon, Devon	5	A4
Hemingbrough, N York	89	B3
Hemingby, Lincs	84	B4
Hemingford Abbots, Cambs	52	C1
Hemingford Grey, Cambs	52	C1
Hemingstone, Suff	55	A3
Hemington, Nhants	62	C4
Hemington, Som	25	A3
Hemley, Suff	55	B4
Hempnall, Norf	65	B3
Hempriggs, Moray	138	A2
Hempstead, Essex	53	C4
Hempstead, Norf	76	B4
Hempton, Norf	76	A4
Hempton, Oxon	39	C1
Hemsby, Norf	66	B1
Hemswell, Lincs	83	C3
Hemsworth, W Yorks	82	B1
Hemyock, Devon	12	D3
Hendy, Carm	34	D3
Hengoed, Caer	36	A4
Hengoed, Powys	47	A3
Hengrave, Suff	54	B1
Henham, Essex	43	A1
Henhurst, Kent	31	A2
Heniarth, Powys	57	A2
Henlade, Som	13	A2
Henley Park, Surrey	28	B4
Henley, Dorset	14	A4
Henley, Som	13	B1
Henley, Suff	55	A3
Henley, W Suss	17	C2
Henley-in-Arden, Warwk	49	B2
Henley-on-Thames, Oxon	28	A1
Henley's Down, E Suss	20	A3
Henllan, Cered	45	E4
Henllan, Denb	68	D1
Henllys, Torf	36	B4
Henlow, Beds	52	B4
Hennock, Devon	5	C2
Henny Street, Essex	54	B4
Henryd, Aberc	77	E4
Henry's Moat (Castell Hendre), Pemb	33	D1
Hensall, N York	89	A4
Henshaw, Nthumb	105	A4
Henstead, Suff	66	B4
Henton, Oxon	40	C3
Henton, Som	24	B4
Henwood, Corn	4	A2
Heol-y-Cyw, Bridg	22	E1
Hepple, Nthumb	105	C1
Hepscott, Nthumb	106	A2
Heptonstall, W Yorks	87	A4
Hepworth, Suff	54	C1
Hepworth, W Yorks	81	C2
Herbrandston, Pemb	33	C3
Hereford, Heref	47	D4
Hermitage, Dorset	14	A3
Hermon, Pemb	34	A1
Herne Hill, G Lon	149	A3
Herne Pound, Kent	31	A3
Herner, Devon	11	E2
Herodsfoot, Corn	4	A3
Herriard, Hants	27	C4
Herringfleet, Suff	66	B3
Herringswell, Suff	54	A1
Herrington, Tyne	100	B1
Hersden, Kent	32	B3
Hersham, Surrey	146	B3
Herston, Orkney	144	A2
Hertford Heath, Herts	42	B2
Hertford, Herts	42	B2
Hertingfordbury, Herts	42	A2
Hesket Newmarket, Cumb	98	A2
Hesketh Bank, Lancs	85	B4
Hesketh Lane, Lancs	86	A3
Hessay, N York	89	A1
Hessett, Suff	54	C2
Hessle, E R of Y	90	B4
Heston, G Lon	146	B1
Heswall, Mers	78	D4
Hethe, Oxon	40	B1
Hethersett, Norf	65	A2
Hethersgill, Cumb	104	D4
Hethpool, Nthumb	111	C2
Hetton, N York	87	A1
Heugh Head, Border	119	D3
Heugh, Nthumb	105	D3
Heveningham, Suff	55	B1
Hever, Kent	30	A4
Heversham, Cumb	92	A3
Hevingham, Norf	65	A1
Hewas Water, Corn	3	D4
Hewelsfield, Glouc	37	A3
Hewish, Som	13	B3
Hewish, Som	24	A3
Hewood, Dorset	13	B4
Hexham, Nthumb	105	C4
Hexton, Herts	41	C1
Hexworthy, Corn	4	B2
Hexworthy, Devon	5	B2
Heybridge, Essex	43	A4
Heybrook Bay, Devon	4	C4
Heydon, Cambs	53	B4
Heydon, Norf	76	B4
Heydour, Lincs	74	B3
Heysham, Lancs	85	B1
Heyshott, W Suss	17	C3
Heytesbury, Wilts	25	B4
Heythrop, Oxon	39	B1
Heywood, G Man	80	B1
Heywood, Wilts	25	B3
Hibaldstow, Lincs	83	D2
Hickleton, S York	82	B2
Hickling Green, Norf	66	A1
Hickling, Norf	66	A1
Hickling, Notts	73	B4
Hickstead, W Suss	18	C2
Hidcote Boyce, Glouc	49	C4
High Ackworth, W Yorks	82	B1
High Bankhill, Cumb	98	C2
High Beach, Essex	42	B4
High Bickington, Devon	11	E2
High Biggins, Cumb	92	B3
High Bray, Devon	11	F1
High Catton, E R of Y	89	B1
High Coniscliffe, Durham	100	A4
High Crosby, Cumb	104	C4
High Cross, Hants	17	A2
High Cross, Herts	42	B2
High Easter, Essex	43	A2
High Ellington, N York	93	C3
High Ercall, Shrops	58	A1
High Etherley, Durham	100	A3
High Garrett, Essex	43	C1
High Grantley, N York	93	C4
High Green, Norf	65	A2
High Green, Norf	65	A4
High Green, Worcs	48	C3
High Halden, Kent	21	A1
High Halstow, Kent	31	B2
High Ham, Som	13	B1
High Hatton, Shrops	58	A1
High Hawsker, N York	95	B1
High Hesket, Cumb	98	C2
High Hoyland, S York	81	C1
High Hutton, N York	95	A4
High Ireby, Cumb	97	E2
High Kilburn, N York	94	B3
High Lands, Durham	99	D3
High Lane, G Man	81	A3
High Legh, Chesh	80	A3
High Leven, N York	100	C4
High Littleton, Som	24	C3
High Lorton, Cumb	97	E3
High Marnham, Notts	73	C1
High Melton, S York	82	C2
High Mickley, Nthumb	105	D4
High Newton, Cumb	91	E3
High Nibthwaite, Cumb	91	D2
High Offley, Staffs	70	B4
High Ongar, Essex	43	A3
High Onn, Staffs	58	C1
High Roding, Essex	43	A2
High Spen, Tyne	105	D4
High Street, Corn	3	D4
High Street, Suff	55	C3
High Toynton, Lincs	74	D1
High Trewhitt, Nthumb	112	A4
High Urpeth, Durham	100	A1
High Valleyfield, Fife	116	C1
High Wray, Cumb	91	E1
High Wych, Herts	42	C2
High Wycombe, Bucks	41	A4
Higham Ferrers, Nhants	51	C2
Higham on the Hill, Leics	60	B3
Higham, Derby	72	B2
Higham, Kent	31	A2
Higham, Lancs	86	B3
Higham, S York	82	A1
Higham, Suff	54	A2
Higham, Suff	54	D4
Highampton, Devon	11	D4
Highbridge, Som	23	C4
Highbrook, W Suss	19	A1
Highburton, W Yorks	81	C1
Highbury, G Lon	149	A1
Highbury, Som	24	C4
Highclere, Hants	27	A3
Higher Ansty, Dorset	14	B4
Higher Bartle, Lancs	85	C3
Higher Combe, Som	12	B1
Higher Gabwell, Devon	6	A3
Higher Kinnerton, Flint	69	B1
Higher Town, Isles of Scilly	144	B1
Higher Walton, Chesh	79	C3
Higher Walton, Lancs	85	C4
Higher Wambrook, Som	13	A3
Higher Waterston, Dorset	14	B4
Higher Wheelton, Lancs	86	A4
Higher Whitley, Chesh	79	C4
Higher Wych, Chesh	69	D3
Highfield, Tyne	105	D4
Highgate, G Lon	148	A1
Highlane, Derby	82	B4
Highleadon, Glouc	37	C1
Highleigh, W Suss	17	B4
Highley, Shrops	58	B4
Highmoor, Oxon	27	C1
Highnam Green, Glouc	37	C2
Highnam, Glouc	37	C2
Highsted, Kent	31	C3
Highstreet Green, Surrey	18	A1
Highstreet, Kent	32	A3
Hightae, Dumf	103	E3
Hightown Green, Suff	54	C3
Hightown, Mers	78	D2
Highworth, Wilts	39	A4
Hildenborough, Kent	30	B4
Hildersham, Cambs	53	C3
Hilderstone, Staffs	71	A4
Hilfield, Dorset	14	A4
Hilgay, Norf	63	D3
Hill Brow, W Suss	17	B2
Hill Chorlton, Staffs	70	B3
Hill Common, Som	12	D2
Hill Dyke, Lincs	75	A3
Hill End, Glouc	48	C4
Hill Green, Kent	31	B3
Hill of Fearn, High	137	C1
Hill Ridware, Staffs	59	B1
Hill Side, W Yorks	81	C1
Hill Top, W Yorks	82	A1
Hill, Glouc	37	B4
Hill, Warwk	50	B2
Hillam, N York	89	A4
Hillbutts, Dorset	14	D4
Hillcliffane, Derby	72	A3
Hillcott, Wilts	26	B3
Hillend, Fife	117	B2
Hillesden, Bucks	40	B1
Hillesley, Glouc	37	C4
Hillfarrance, Som	12	D2
Hilliclay, High	143	D1
Hillingdon, G Lon	146	A1
Hillington, Norf	64	A1
Hills Town, Derby	72	B1
Hillside, Angus	129	D3
Hillstreet, Hants	15	C3
Hillswick, Shet	144	A2
Hilltown, Devon	4	C2
Hilmarton, Wilts	26	A2
Hilperton, Wilts	25	B3
Hilston, E R of Y	90	D3
Hilton, Cambs	52	C2
Hilton, Cumb	99	A4
Hilton, Derby	71	C4
Hilton, Durham	100	A4
Hilton, N York	100	C4
Hilton, Shrops	58	B3
Himbleton, Worcs	49	A2
Himley, Staffs	58	C4
Hincaster, Cumb	92	A3
Hinchley Wood, Surrey	146	B2
Hinckley, Leics	60	C3
Hinderclay, Suff	54	D1
Hinderwell, N York	101	C4
Hindhead, Surrey	17	C1
Hindley, G Man	79	C2
Hindlip, Worcs	48	C2
Hindolveston, Norf	76	B4
Hindon, Wilts	14	C1
Hindringham, Norf	76	A4
Hingham, Norf	64	D3
Hinstock, Shrops	58	A1
Hintlesham, Suff	54	D4
Hinton Blewett, Som	24	C3
Hinton Charterhouse, Som	25	A3
Hinton Martell, Dorset	14	D4
Hinton on the Green, Worcs	49	A4
Hinton Parva, Wilts	26	C1
Hinton St George, Som	13	B3
Hinton Waldrist, Oxon	39	B3
Hinton, Glouc	25	A1
Hinton, Heref	47	B4
Hinton, Shrops	57	C2
Hints, Staffs	59	B3
Hinwick, Beds	51	C2
Hinxton, Cambs	53	B4
Hinxworth, Herts	52	C4
Hipperholme, W Yorks	87	B4
Hipswell, N York	93	C2
Hirn, Aber	134	B3
Hirnant, Powys	56	E1
Hirst Courtney, N York	89	A4
Hirwaun, Rhond	35	C3
Hiscott, Devon	11	E2
Histon, Cambs	53	B2
Hitcham Causeway, Suff	54	C3
Hitcham, Suff	54	C3
Hitchin, Herts	41	C1
Hither Green, G Lon	149	B3
Hittisleigh, Devon	11	F4
Hive, E R of Y	89	C3
Hixon, Staffs	59	A1
Hoaden, Kent	32	C3
Hoarwithy, Heref	37	A1
Hoath, Kent	32	B3
Hobarris, Shrops	47	B1
Hobson, Durham	100	A1
Hoby, Leics	61	B1
Hockering, Norf	64	D2
Hockerton, Notts	73	B2
Hockley Heath, W Mids	49	B1
Hockley, Essex	43	C4
Hockliffe, Beds	41	B1
Hockwold cum Wilton, Norf	64	A4
Hockworthy, Devon	12	C2
Hoddesdon, Herts	42	B3
Hoddlesden, Lancs	86	B4
Hoddom Mains, Dumf	104	A3
Hodgeston, Pemb	33	D3
Hodnet, Shrops	70	A4
Hodsall Street, Kent	30	B3
Hodsock, Notts	82	C3
Hodson, Wilts	26	C1
Hodthorpe, Derby	82	C4
Hoe, Norf	64	C1
Hogben's Hill, Kent	32	A3
Hoggeston, Bucks	40	C1
Hoggrill's End, Warwk	60	A3
Hoghton, Lancs	86	A4
Hognaston, Derby	71	C2
Hogsthorpe, Lincs	75	B1
Holbeach Drove, Lincs	63	B2
Holbeach Hurn, Lincs	75	A4
Holbeach St Johns, Lincs	63	B1
Holbeach St Mark's, Lincs	75	A4
Holbeach St Matthew, Lincs	75	A4
Holbeach, Lincs	63	B1
Holbeck, Notts	82	C4
Holberrow Green, Worcs	49	A2
Holbeton, Devon	5	A4
Holborn, G Lon	148	B2
Holbrook, Derby	72	A3
Holbrook, Suff	55	A4
Holbury, Hants	16	A4
Holcombe Rogus, Devon	12	C2
Holcombe, Devon	6	A2
Holcombe, Som	24	C4
Holcot, Nhants	51	B1
Holden, Lancs	86	B2
Holdenby, Nhants	51	A2
Holdgate, Shrops	57	D4
Holdingham, Lincs	74	B3
Holditch, Dorset	13	A4
Hole, Devon	11	C4
Holford, Som	23	B4
Holker, Cumb	91	E3
Holkham, Norf	76	A3
Hollacombe, Devon	11	C4
Holland Fen, Lincs	74	D2
Hollandstoun, Orkney	144	B1
Hollesley, Suff	55	C4
Hollingdon, Bucks	41	A1
Hollington, Derby	71	C3
Hollington, Staffs	71	B3
Hollins Green, Chesh	80	A3
Hollinsclough, Staffs	71	B1
Hollocombe, Devon	11	E3
Holloway, Derby	72	A2
Holloway, G Lon	148	B1
Hollowell, Nhants	51	A1
Holly Green, Worcs	48	C4
Hollybush, Caer	36	A3
Hollybush, E Ayrs	108	D3
Hollybush, Heref	48	B4
Hollym, E R of Y	90	E4
Holmbridge, W Yorks	81	B2
Holmbury St Mary, Surrey	146	B4
Holme Chapel, Lancs	86	C4
Holme Green, N York	89	A2
Holme Hale, Norf	64	B2
Holme Lacy, Heref	47	D4
Holme Marsh, Heref	47	B3
Holme next the Sea, Norf	75	D3
Holme on the Wolds, E R of Y	90	A2
Holme Pierrepont, Notts	73	B3
Holme St Cuthbert, Cumb	97	D1
Holme, Cambs	62	C4
Holme, Cumb	92	A3
Holme, N York	93	D3
Holme, Notts	73	C2
Holme, W Yorks	81	B2
Holmes Chapel, Chesh	70	B1
Holmesfield, Derby	82	A4
Holmeswood, Lancs	79	A1
Holmethorpe, Surrey	150	B3
Holmewood, Derby	72	B1
Holmpton, E R of Y	90	E4
Holmrook, Cumb	91	B1
Holmwood, Surrey	146	B4
Holne, Devon	5	B3
Holnest, Dorset	14	A3
Holnicote, Som	22	E4
Holsworthy Beacon, Devon	11	C3
Holsworthy, Devon	11	C4
Holt End, Worcs	49	B1
Holt Heath, Worcs	48	C2
Holt, Dorset	14	D4
Holt, Norf	76	B3
Holt, Wilts	25	B3
Holt, Worcs	48	C2
Holt, Wrex	69	C2
Holtby, N York	89	B1
Holton cum Beckering, Lincs	84	A4
Holton le Clay, Lincs	84	B2
Holton le Moor, Lincs	83	D2
Holton St Mary, Suff	54	D4
Holton, Som	14	A2
Holton, Suff	55	C1
Holwell, Dorset	14	B3
Holwell, Herts	41	C1
Holwell, Leics	61	B1
Holwell, Oxon	39	A3
Holwick, Durham	99	B3
Holy Island, Nthumb	112	B1
Holybourne, Hants	17	A1
Holyhead, Angle	77	A4
Holymoorside, Derby	72	A1
Holyport, Berks	28	B1
Holystone, Nthumb	105	C1
Holytown, N Lan	116	A4
Holywell Lake, Som	12	C2
Holywell Row, Suff	54	A1
Holywell, Cambs	53	A1
Holywell, Corn	3	B4
Holywell, Dorset	14	A4
Holywell, Flint	78	C4
Holywood, Dumf	103	D2
Homer Green, Mers	78	D2
Homer, Shrops	58	A3
Homersfield, Suff	65	B4
Homington, Wilts	15	A2
Honey Tye, Suff	54	C4
Honeybourne, Worcs	49	B4
Honeychurch, Devon	11	E4
Honeystreet, Wilts	26	B3
Honiley, Warwk	49	C1
Honing, Norf	76	D4
Honingham, Norf	64	D2
Honington, Lincs	74	A3
Honington, Suff	54	C1
Honington, Warwk	49	C4
Honiton, Devon	12	D4
Honley, W Yorks	81	B1
Hoo Green, Chesh	80	A4
Hoo, Kent	31	B2
Hooe, E Suss	20	A3
Hook Norton, Oxon	39	B1
Hook, G Lon	146	B3
Hook, Hants	27	C3
Hook, Kent	30	B2
Hook, Pemb	33	D2
Hook, Wilts	26	B1
Hooke, Dorset	13	C4
Hookway, Devon	12	A4
Hookwood, Surrey	150	B4
Hooley, Surrey	150	B2
Hooton Levitt, S York	82	C3
Hooton Pagnell, S York	82	B1
Hooton Roberts, S York	82	B2
Hope Bowdler, Shrops	57	D3
Hope End Green, Essex	43	A2
Hope Mansell, Heref	37	B2
Hope under Dinmore, Heref	47	D3
Hope, Derby	81	C4
Hope, Devon	10	A1
Hope, Flint	69	B2
Hope, Shrops	48	A1
Hope, Staffs	71	B2
Hopeman, Moray	138	B1
Hopesay, Shrops	57	C4
Hopperton, N York	88	B1
Hopstone, Shrops	58	B3
Hopton Cangeford, Shrops	57	D4
Hopton Castle, Shrops	47	C1
Hopton on Sea, Norf	66	B3
Hopton Wafers, Shrops	48	A1
Hopton, Staffs	59	A1
Hopton, Suff	54	C1
Hoptonheath, Shrops	47	C1
Hopwas, Staffs	60	A2
Hopwood, Worcs	49	A1
Horam, E Suss	19	C3
Horbling, Lincs	74	C4
Hordley, Shrops	69	C4
Horham, Suff	55	A1
Horkesley Heath, Essex	44	A1
Horkstow, Lincs	83	D1
Horley, Oxon	50	B4
Horley, Surrey	150	B4
Hornblotton Green, Som	14	A1
Hornby, Lancs	92	B4
Hornby, N York	93	D1
Hornby, N York	93	C2
Horncastle, Lincs	74	D1
Hornchurch, G Lon	30	A1
Horncliffe, Nthumb	119	E4
Horndean, Border	111	C1
Horndean, Hants	17	A3
Horndon on the Hill, Essex	31	A1
Horndon, Devon	4	C2
Horne, Surrey	150	C4
Horner, Som	22	E4
Horning, Norf	65	B1
Horninghold, Leics	61	C3
Horningsea, Cambs	53	B2
Horningsham, Wilts	14	C1
Horningtoft, Norf	64	C1
Horns Cross, Devon	11	C2
Hornsea, E R of Y	90	D2
Hornton, Oxon	50	B3
Horrabridge, Devon	4	C3
Horridge, Devon	5	B2
Horringer, Suff	54	B2
Horrocksford, Lancs	86	B2
Horsebridge, Devon	4	B2
Horsebridge, Hants	15	C1
Horsebridge, Shrops	57	C2
Horseheath, Cambs	53	C3
Horsehouse, N York	93	A3
Horsell, Surrey	146	A3
Horseman's Green, Wrex	69	C3
Horsey, Norf	66	A1
Horsey, Som	13	A1
Horsford, Norf	65	A1
Horsham St Faith, Norf	65	A1
Horsham, W Suss	18	B1
Horsham, Worcs	48	B2
Horsington, Lincs	74	C1
Horsington, Som	14	B2
Horsley Woodhouse, Derby	72	B3
Horsley, Derby	72	A3
Horsley, Glouc	38	A4
Horsley, Nthumb	105	B1
Horsley, Nthumb	105	D4
Horsmonden, Kent	20	A1
Horspath, Oxon	40	A3
Horstead, Norf	65	B1
Horsted Keynes, W Suss	19	A2
Horton Green, Chesh	69	C2
Horton in Ribblesdale, N York	92	C4
Horton Kirby, Kent	30	B2
Horton, Berks	146	A2
Horton, Bucks	41	A2
Horton, Dorset	14	D3
Horton, G Lon	146	B3
Horton, Glouc	25	A1
Horton, Lancs	86	C2
Horton, Nhants	51	B3
Horton, Shrops	58	A1
Horton, Som	13	A3
Horton, Staffs	71	A2
Horton, Swan	22	A1
Horton, Wilts	26	B3
Horton-cum-Studley, Oxon	40	A2
Horwich, G Man	79	C1
Horwood, Devon	11	D2
Hose, Leics	73	B4
Hosey Hill, Kent	30	A3
Hosh, Perth	123	A2
Hotham, E R of Y	90	A3
Hothfield, Kent	31	C4
Hoton, Leics	61	A1
Hott, Nthumb	105	A2
Hough, Chesh	70	B2
Hougham, Lincs	74	A3
Hough-on-the-Hill, Lincs	74	A3
Houghton Conquest, Beds	52	A4
Houghton Green, E Suss	21	A2
Houghton le Spring, Tyne	100	B1
Houghton on the Hill, Leics	61	B2
Houghton St Giles, Norf	76	A4
Houghton, Cambs	52	C1
Houghton, Hants	15	C1
Houghton, Pemb	33	D3
Houghton, W Suss	18	A3
Hound Green, Hants	27	C3
Houndslow, Border	111	A1
Hounslow Green, Essex	43	A2
Hounslow, G Lon	146	B2
Houses Hill, W Yorks	81	C1
Houston, Renf	115	A3
Houton, Orkney	144	A2
Hove, E Suss	18	C4
Hoveringham, Notts	73	B3
Hoveton, Norf	65	B1
Hovingham, N York	94	C4
How Caple, Heref	37	B1
How Mill, Cumb	98	C1
Howden, E R of Y	89	C4
Howden-le-Wear, Durham	100	A3
Howe Green, Essex	43	B3
Howe Street, Essex	43	B2
Howe Street, Essex	54	A4
Howe, N York	93	D3
Howe, Norf	65	B3
Howegreen, Essex	43	C3
Howell, Lincs	74	C3
Howey, Powys	46	E2
Howgate, M Loth	118	A4
Howick, Nthumb	112	C3
Howle Hill, Heref	37	B2
Howle, Durham	99	D3
Howle, Shrops	58	B1
Howlett End, Essex	53	C4
Howley, Som	13	A3
Hownam, Border	111	B3
Howsham, Lincs	83	D2
Howsham, N York	89	B1
Howtel, Nthumb	111	C2
Howwood, Renf	115	A4
Hoxne, Suff	55	A1
Hoylake, Mers	78	C3
Hoyland Nether, S York	82	A2
Hoyland Swaine, S York	81	C2
Huby, N York	87	C2
Huby, N York	94	B4
Hucking, Kent	31	B3
Hucknall, Notts	73	A2
Huddersfield, W Yorks	81	B1
Huddington, Worcs	49	A2
Hudswell, N York	93	B1
Huggate, E R of Y	90	A1
Hugh Town, Isles of Scilly	144	A2
Hughley, Shrops	57	D3
Huish, Devon	11	D3
Huish, Wilts	26	B3
Hulberry, Kent	30	A2
Hulcott, Bucks	41	A2
Hull, E R of Y	90	C4
Hulland, Derby	71	C3
Hullavington, Wilts	25	B1
Hullbridge, Essex	43	C4
Hulme End, Staffs	71	B2
Hulme Walfield, Chesh	70	C1
Hulme, Staffs	71	A3
Hulver Street, Suff	66	A4
Hulverstone, I of W	9	C1
Humberston, Lincs	84	B2
Humbie, E Loth	118	B3
Humbleton, E R of Y	90	D3
Humby, Lincs	74	B4
Hume, Border	111	B1
Humshaugh, Nthumb	105	B3
Huncote, Leics	61	A3
Hunderthwaite, Durham	99	C4
Hundleby, Lincs	75	A1
Hundleton, Pemb	33	C3
Hundon, Suff	54	A3
Hundred End, Lancs	85	B4
Hundred House, Powys	46	E3
Hungarton, Leics	61	B2
Hungerford Newtown, Berks	26	D2
Hungerford, Berks	26	D2
Hungerford, Som	12	C1
Hungerstone, Heref	47	C4
Hunmanby, N York	95	D3
Hunningham, Warwk	50	A2
Hunsdon, Herts	42	B2
Hunsingore, N York	88	B1
Hunsonby, Cumb	98	D2
Hunstanton, Norf	75	D3
Hunstanworth, Durham	99	C1
Hunston, Suff	54	C1
Hunston, W Suss	17	C4
Hunstrete, Som	24	C3
Hunsworth, W Yorks	87	C4
Hunterston, Chesh	70	B3
Huntham, Som	13	A2
Huntingdon, Cambs	52	C1
Huntingfield, Suff	55	B1
Huntington, Chesh	69	C1
Huntington, Heref	47	B3
Huntington, Staffs	59	A2
Huntley, Glouc	37	C2
Huntly, Aber	139	A4
Hunton, Hants	16	A1
Hunton, Kent	31	A4
Hunton, N York	93	C2
Huntscott, Som	22	E4
Huntsham, Devon	12	B2
Huntshaw, Devon	11	D2
Huntspill, Som	23	C4
Huntstile, Som	13	A1
Huntworth, Som	13	A1
Hunwick, Durham	100	A3
Hunworth, Norf	76	B4
Hurdcott, Wilts	15	B1
Hurley Common, Warwk	60	A3
Hurley, Warwk	60	A3
Hurlford, E Ayrs	108	E2
Hurn, Dorset	15	A4
Hursley, Hants	16	A2
Hurst Green, E Suss	20	A2
Hurst Green, Lancs	86	A3
Hurst Green, Surrey	150	D3
Hurst, Berks	28	A2
Hurstbourne Priors, Hants	27	A4
Hurstbourne Tarrant, Hants	26	D3
Hurstley, Heref	47	C3
Hurstpierpoint, W Suss	18	C3
Hurstwood, Lancs	86	C3
Hurtmore, Surrey	28	B4
Hurworth Place, Durham	93	D1
Hurworth-on-Tees, Durham	93	D1
Husthwaite, N York	94	B4
Huttoft, Lincs	84	D4
Hutton Bonville, N York	93	D1
Hutton Buscel, N York	95	C3
Hutton Conyers, N York	93	D4
Hutton Cranswick, E R of Y	90	B2
Hutton End, Cumb	98	B2
Hutton Henry, Durham	100	C2
Hutton Lowcross, N York	101	A4
Hutton Magna, Durham	99	D4
Hutton Roof, Cumb	92	A3
Hutton Roof, Cumb	98	B2
Hutton Rudby, N York	94	A1
Hutton Sessay, N York	94	A4
Hutton Wandesley, N York	89	A2
Hutton, Border	119	D4
Hutton, E R of Y	90	B1
Hutton, Lancs	85	C4
Hutton, Som	24	A3
Hutton-le-Hole, N York	94	C2

PLACE	PAGE	GRID
Huxley, Chesh	69	D1
Hycemoor, Cumb	91	B2
Hyde Heath, Bucks	41	A3
Hyde Lea, Staffs	58	C1
Hyde, G Man	81	A3
Hyssington, Powys	57	B3
Hythe End, Berks	146	A2
Hythe, Hants	16	A3
Hythe, Kent	21	C1
Ibberton, Dorset	14	B3
Ible, Derby	71	C2
Ibsley, Hants	15	A3
Ibstock, Leics	60	C2
Ibstone, Bucks	40	C4
Ibthorpe, Hants	26	D3
Iburndale, N York	95	B1
Ibworth, Hants	27	B3
Ickburgh, Norf	64	B3
Ickenham, G Lon	146	A1
Ickford, Bucks	40	B3
Ickham, Kent	32	B3
Ickleford, Herts	41	C1
Ickleton, Cambs	53	B4
Icklingham, Suff	54	A1
Ickornshaw, N York	87	A2
Ickwell Green, Beds	52	B3
Icomb, Glouc	39	A1
Idbury, Oxon	39	A2
Iddesleigh, Devon	11	E3
Ide, Devon	6	A1
Ideford, Devon	6	A2
Iden Green, Kent	20	A1
Iden, E Suss	21	A2
Idless, Corn	2	A1
Idlicote, Warwk	50	A4
Idmiston, Wilts	15	B1
Idridgehay, Derby	72	A3
Idrigill, High	135	B2
Idstone, Oxon	26	C1
Iford, E Suss	19	A3
Ifton, Monm	37	A4
Ightfield, Shrops	70	A3
Ightham, Kent	30	B3
Iken, Suff	55	C3
Ilam, Staffs	71	B2
Ilchester, Som	13	C2
Ilderton, Nthumb	112	A3
Ilford, G Lon	30	A1
Ilford, Som	13	B3
Ilfracombe, Devon	22	A4
Ilkeston, Derby	72	B3
Ilketshall St Andrew, Suff	66	A4
Ilketshall St Margaret, Suff	65	B4
Ilkley, W Yorks	87	B2
Illand, Corn	4	A2
Illey, W Mids	59	A4
Illogan, Corn	1	D1
Illston on the Hill, Leics	61	B3
Ilmer, Bucks	40	C3
Ilmington, Warwk	49	C4
Ilminster, Som	13	B3
Ilsington, Devon	5	C2
Ilston, Swan	34	D4
Ilton, N York	93	C3
Ilton, Som	13	B3
Immingham Dock, Lincs	84	A1
Immingham, Lincs	84	A1
Ince Blundell, Mers	78	D2
Ince, Chesh	79	A4
Ince-in-Makerfield, G Man	79	C2
Inchnadamph, High	140	E1
Inchture, Perth	124	A2
Indian Queens, Corn	3	C4
Ingatestone, Essex	43	A3
Ingbirchworth, S York	81	C2
Ingestre, Staffs	59	A1
Ingham Corner, Norf	76	E4
Ingham, Lincs	83	C4
Ingham, Norf	76	E4
Ingham, Suff	54	B1
Ingleby Arncliffe, N York	94	A1
Ingleby Greenhow, N York	94	B1
Ingleby, Derby	72	A4
Ingleigh Green, Devon	11	E3
Inglesbatch, Som	25	A3
Inglesham, Wilts	39	A4
Ingleton, Durham	100	A4
Ingleton, N York	92	C4
Inglewhite, Lancs	85	C3
Ingoe, Nthumb	105	C3
Ingoldisthorpe, Norf	75	D4
Ingoldsby, Lincs	74	B4
Ingram, Nthumb	112	A3
Ingrave, Essex	43	A4
Ingst, Glouc	37	B4
Ingthorpe, Rutland	62	B2
Ingworth, Norf	76	C4
Inkberrow, Worcs	49	A2
Inkpen, Berks	26	D3
Innellan, Argyll	114	C3
Innerleithen, Border	110	B2
Innermessan, Dumf	102	B4
Innerwick, E Loth	119	C2
Insch, Aber	134	A1
Insh, High	132	D3
Inskip, Lancs	85	B3
Instow, Devon	11	D1
Inver, High	141	D4
Inver, Perth	128	C4
Inveralligin, High	135	F2
Inverallochy, Aber	139	E2
Inveran, High	141	B3
Inveraray, Argyll	121	C3
Inverasdale, High	140	A4
Inverbervie, Aber	129	E2
Inver-boyndie, Aber	139	B2
Invergarry, High	131	D3
Invergordon, High	137	B2
Invergowrie, Perth	124	A1
Inverie, High	130	F3
Inverinate, High	131	A2
Inverkeilor, Angus	129	C4
Inverkeithing, Fife	117	B2
Inverkeithny, Aber	139	B3

PLACE	PAGE	GRID
Inverkip, Inverclyde	114	D3
Inverkirkaig, High	140	C1
Invermoriston, High	131	E2
Inverness, High	137	B4
Inversanda, High	126	C3
Inveruglas, Argyll	122	A3
Inverurie, Aber	134	B2
Inwardleigh, Devon	11	E4
Inworth, Essex	43	C2
Iping, W Suss	17	C2
Ipplepen, Devon	5	C3
Ipsden, Oxon	27	C1
Ipstones, Staffs	71	A2
Ipswich, Suff	55	A4
Irby in the Marsh, Lincs	75	B1
Irby upon Humber, Lincs	84	B2
Irchester, Nhants	51	C2
Ireby, Cumb	98	A2
Ireby, Lancs	92	B4
Ireland, Beds	52	B4
Ireleth, Cumb	91	C3
Ireshopeburn, Durham	99	B2
Ireton Wood, Derby	72	A3
Irlam, G Man	80	A3
Irnham, Lincs	74	B4
Ironbridge, Shrops	58	A2
Irons Bottom, Surrey	150	A4
Ironville, Derby	72	B2
Irstead, Norf	66	A1
Irthington, Cumb	104	D4
Irthlingborough, Nhants	51	C1
Irton, N York	95	C3
Irvine, N Ayrs	108	D1
Isfield, E Suss	19	B3
Isham, Nhants	51	C1
Isington, Hants	28	A4
Isle Abbotts, Som	13	B2
Isle of Dogs, G Lon	149	B2
Isle of Whithorn, Dumf	96	E2
Isleham, Cambs	53	C1
Isleornsay, High	130	E2
Isleworth, G Lon	146	B2
Isley Walton, Leics	60	C1
Islington, G Lon	149	A1
Islip, Nhants	52	A1
Islip, Oxon	40	A2
Isombridge, Shrops	58	A2
Itchen Abbas, Hants	16	B1
Itchen Stoke, Hants	16	B1
Itchingfield, W Suss	18	B2
Itteringham, Norf	76	C4
Itton, Devon	11	F4
Itton, Monm	37	A4
Ivegill, Cumb	98	B2
Iver Heath, Bucks	146	A1
Iver, Bucks	146	A1
Iveston, Durham	99	D1
Ivinghoe Aston, Bucks	41	A2
Ivinghoe, Bucks	41	A2
Ivington Green, Heref	47	C3
Ivington, Heref	47	D3
Ivybridge, Devon	5	A4
Ivychurch, Kent	21	B2
Iwade, Kent	31	C2
Iwerne Minster, Dorset	14	C3
Ixworth Thorpe, Suff	54	C1
Ixworth, Suff	54	C1
Jack-in-the-Green, Devon	12	C4
Jackton, S Lan	115	C4
Jacobs Well, Surrey	146	A3
Jacobstow, Corn	11	B4
Jacobstowe, Devon	11	E4
Jameston, Pemb	33	D4
Jarrow, Tyne	106	B4
Jasper's Green, Essex	43	B1
Jaywick, Essex	44	C2
Jealott's Hill, Berks	28	B2
Jedburgh, Border	111	A3
Jeffreston, Pemb	33	E3
Jemimaville, High	137	B2
Jerbourg, Guern	145	B2
Jevington, E Suss	19	C4
Jockey End, Herts	41	B2
John O'Groats, High	143	F1
Johnby, Cumb	98	B3
Johnshaven, Aber	129	D2
Johnston, Pemb	33	C2
Johnstone, Renf	115	B3
Joppa, Cered	46	A2
Jordanston, Pemb	33	C1
Joyden's Wood, Kent	30	A2
Jurby, I of M	145	C2
Kaber, Cumb	99	A4
Kames, Argyll	114	B3
Kea, Corn	2	A1
Keal Cotes, Lincs	75	A1
Kearsley, G Man	80	A2
Kearsley, Nthumb	105	C3
Kearstwick, Cumb	92	B3
Kedington, Suff	54	A3
Kedleston, Derby	72	A3
Keelby, Lincs	84	A1
Keele, Staffs	70	B3
Keelham, W Yorks	87	B3
Keeston, Pemb	33	C2
Keevil, Wilts	25	B3
Kegworth, Leics	72	B4
Kehelland, Corn	1	D1
Keig, Aber	134	A2
Keighley, W Yorks	87	B3
Keir Mill, Dumf	103	C1
Keisley, Cumb	99	A3
Keiss, High	143	E2
Keith, Moray	138	D3
Keithtown, High	136	F3
Kelbrook, Lancs	86	C2
Kelby, Lincs	74	B3
Keld, N York	92	D1
Kelfield, N York	89	A3
Kelham, Notts	73	C2
Kelhead, Dumf	104	A3
Kellamergh, Lancs	85	B4
Kellas, Angus	124	B1
Kellaton, Devon	10	B1

PLACE	PAGE	GRID
Kelling, Norf	76	B3
Kellington, N York	89	A4
Kelloe, Durham	100	B2
Kelly, Devon	4	B2
Kelmarsh, Nhants	51	B1
Kelmscot, Oxon	39	A3
Kelsale, Suff	55	C2
Kelsall, Chesh	69	D1
Kelshall, Herts	53	A4
Kelsick, Cumb	97	E1
Kelso, Border	111	B2
Kelstedge, Derby	72	A1
Kelstern, Lincs	84	B3
Kelston, Som	25	A2
Kelty, Fife	117	B1
Kelvedon Hatch, Essex	43	A4
Kelvedon, Essex	43	C2
Kelynack, Corn	1	A2
Kemback, Fife	124	B3
Kemberton, Shrops	58	B2
Kemble, Glouc	38	B4
Kemerton, Worcs	49	A4
Kemeys Commander, Monm	36	B3
Kemnay, Aber	134	B2
Kempley Green, Glouc	37	B1
Kempley, Glouc	37	B1
Kempsey, Worcs	48	C3
Kempsford, Glouc	39	A4
Kempston, Beds	52	A3
Kemsing, Kent	30	B3
Kenardington, Kent	21	A1
Kenchester, Heref	47	C4
Kencot, Oxon	39	A3
Kendal, Cumb	92	A2
Kenfig, Bridg	22	D1
Kenilworth, Warwk	50	A1
Kenley, G Lon	150	C1
Kenley, Shrops	57	D3
Kenmore, Perth	128	A4
Kenn, Devon	6	A1
Kenn, Som	24	A2
Kennacraig, Argyll	113	F3
Kennerleigh, Devon	12	A3
Kennet, Clack	116	C1
Kennethmont, Aber	133	E1
Kennett, Cambs	54	A1
Kennford, Devon	6	A1
Kenninghall, Norf	64	D4
Kennington, Oxon	40	A3
Kennoway, Fife	124	B4
Kenny, Som	13	A3
Kennyhill, Suff	64	A4
Kennythorpe, N York	95	A4
Kensington, G Lon	148	A3
Kensworth, Beds	41	B2
Kentallen, High	126	D3
Kentchurch, Heref	36	C1
Kentford, Suff	54	A2
Kentisbury, Devon	22	B4
Kentish Town, G Lon	148	B1
Kentmere, Cumb	91	E1
Kenton, Devon	6	A2
Kenton, Suff	55	A2
Kent's Green, Glouc	37	C1
Kent's Oak, Hants	15	C2
Kepwick, N York	94	A2
Kerris, Corn	1	B2
Kerry, Powys	57	A4
Kerrycroy, Argyll	114	C3
Kersall, Notts	73	B1
Kersey, Suff	54	C4
Kerswell Green, Worcs	48	C3
Kessingland, Suff	66	B4
Kestle Mill, Corn	3	C4
Kestle, Corn	2	C1
Keston, G Lon	149	B4
Keswick, Cumb	98	A3
Keswick, Norf	65	A2
Ketsby, Lincs	84	C4
Kettering, Nhants	51	C1
Ketteringham, Norf	65	A2
Kettins, Angus	124	A1
Kettlebaston, Suff	54	C3
Kettleburgh, Suff	55	B2
Kettleshulme, Chesh	81	A4
Kettlesing Bottom, N York	87	C1
Kettlesing, N York	87	C1
Kettlestone, Norf	76	A4
Kettlethorpe, Lincs	83	B4
Kettlewell, N York	93	A4
Ketton, Rutland	62	B2
Kew, G Lon	146	B1
Kewstoke, Som	23	C3
Kexby, Lincs	83	C3
Kexby, N York	89	B2
Key Green, Chesh	70	C1
Key Street, Kent	31	B2
Keyham, Leics	61	B2
Keyhaven, Hants	9	B1
Keyingham, E R of Y	90	D4
Keynsham, Som	24	C2
Keysoe Row, Beds	52	B2
Keysoe, Beds	52	A2
Keyston, Cambs	52	A1
Keyworth, Notts	73	A4
Kibblesworth, Tyne	100	A1
Kibworth Beauchamp, Leics	61	B3
Kibworth Harcourt, Leics	61	B3
Kidbrooke, G Lon	149	B2
Kidderminster, Worcs	48	C1
Kidlington, Oxon	39	C2
Kidmore End, Oxon	27	C1
Kidsgrove, Staffs	70	C2
Kidwelly, Carm	34	B3
Kielder, Nthumb	104	E1
Kiells, Argyll	113	C3
Kilbarchan, Renf	115	A3
Kilberry, Argyll	113	E3
Kilbirnie, N Ayrs	115	A4
Kilburn, Derby	72	A3
Kilburn, G Lon	147	A1
Kilburn, N York	94	B3
Kilby, Leics	61	B3

PLACE	PAGE	GRID
Kilchattan, Argyll	114	C4
Kilchoan, High	125	E3
Kilchrenan, Argyll	121	B2
Kilconquhar, Fife	124	C4
Kilcot, Glouc	37	C1
Kilcreggan, Argyll	114	D2
Kildale, N York	94	B1
Kildary, High	137	B1
Kildrummy, Aber	133	E2
Kildwick, N York	87	A2
Kilfinan, Argyll	114	A2
Kilgwrrwg Common, Monm	37	A4
Kilham, E R of Y	90	B1
Kilkenneth, Argyll	125	A4
Kilkenzie, Argyll	107	D3
Kilkhampton, Corn	11	B3
Killamarsh, Derby	82	B4
Killearn, Stirl	115	B1
Killerby, Durham	100	A4
Killerton, Devon	12	B4
Killichonan, Perth	127	D3
Killiecrankie, Perth	128	B3
Killin, Stirl	122	C1
Killinghall, N York	88	A1
Killington, Cumb	92	B2
Kilmacolm, Inverclyde	115	A3
Kilmany, Fife	124	B2
Kilmarnock, E Ayrs	108	E1
Kilmartin, Argyll	120	F4
Kilmaurs, E Ayrs	108	D1
Kilmelford, Argyll	121	A3
Kilmersdon, Som	25	A4
Kilmeston, Hants	16	B2
Kilmichael, Argyll	107	D3
Kilmington Common, Wilts	14	B1
Kilmington, Devon	13	A4
Kilmington, Wilts	14	B1
Kilmorack, High	136	F4
Kilmun, Argyll	114	C2
Kiln Pit Hill, Nthumb	99	C1
Kilndown, Kent	20	A1
Kilninver, Argyll	120	F2
Kilnsea, E R of Y	84	C1
Kilnsey, N York	93	A4
Kilnwick, E R of Y	90	B2
Kilpeck, Heref	36	C1
Kilpin, E R of Y	89	C4
Kilrenny, Fife	124	C4
Kilsby, Nhants	50	C1
Kilspindie, Perth	123	D2
Kilstay, Dumf	96	B2
Kilsyth, N Lan	116	A2
Kiltarlity, High	136	F4
Kilton Thorpe, N York	101	B4
Kilton, N York	101	B4
Kilve, Som	23	B4
Kilvington, Notts	73	C3
Kilwinning, N Ayrs	108	C1
Kimberley, Norf	64	D2
Kimblesworth, Durham	100	A1
Kimbolton, Cambs	52	B2
Kimbolton, Heref	47	D2
Kimcote, Leics	61	A4
Kimmeridge, Dorset	8	B2
Kimpton, Hants	26	D4
Kimpton, Herts	41	C2
Kinbrace, High	143	A4
Kinbuck, Stirl	123	A4
Kincardine O'Neil, Aber	134	A4
Kincardine, Fife	116	C1
Kincardine, High	141	B4
Kincraig, High	132	D3
Kindallachan, Perth	128	B4
Kineton, Glouc	38	C1
Kineton, Warwk	50	A3
Kinfauns, Perth	123	D2
Kingarth, Argyll	114	C4
Kingcoed, Monm	36	C3
Kingford, Devon	11	B4
Kingham, Oxon	39	A1
Kinghorn, Fife	118	A1
Kinglassie, Fife	123	D4
Kingoldrum, Angus	128	E3
Kings Caple, Heref	37	A1
King's Cliffe, Nhants	62	B3
King's Coughton, Warwk	49	B2
Kings Langley, Herts	41	B3
King's Lynn, Norf	63	D1
Kings Meaburn, Cumb	98	D4
King's Mills, Guern	145	B2
Kings Newnham, Warwk	50	B1
King's Nympton, Devon	11	F2
King's Pyon, Heref	47	C3
Kings Ripton, Cambs	52	C1
King's Somborne, Hants	15	C1
King's Stag, Dorset	14	B3
King's Stanley, Glouc	38	A3
King's Sutton, Nhants	50	B4
King's Walden, Herts	41	C1
Kings Weston, Bristol	24	B1
Kingsand, Corn	4	C4
Kingsbarns, Fife	124	D3
Kingsbridge, Devon	10	A1
Kingsbridge, Som	12	B1
Kingsbury, Warwk	60	A3
Kingsclere, Hants	27	B3
Kingscote, Glouc	38	A4
Kingscott, Devon	11	D3
Kingsdon, Som	13	C2
Kingsdown, Kent	32	D4
Kingsdown, Wilts	25	A2
Kingseat, Fife	117	B1
Kingsey, Bucks	40	C3
Kingsfold, W Suss	18	B1
Kingshall Street, Suff	54	C2
Kingsheanton, Devon	11	E1
Kingskerswell, Devon	5	C3
Kingsland, Heref	47	C2
Kingsley Green, W Suss	17	C1
Kingsley, Chesh	79	B4
Kingsley, Hants	17	B1
Kingsley, Staffs	71	A3
Kingsmuir, Angus	129	B4
Kingsnorth, Kent	21	A1

PLACE	PAGE	GRID
Kingsthorne, Heref	37	A1
Kingston Blount, Oxon	40	C3
Kingston Lisle, Oxon	39	B4
Kingston on Soar, Notts	72	B4
Kingston on Spey, Moray	138	C2
Kingston Russell, Dorset	7	C1
Kingston Seymour, Som	24	A2
Kingston upon Thames, G Lon	146	B2
Kingston, Cambs	53	A3
Kingston, Corn	4	B2
Kingston, Devon	10	B1
Kingston, Dorset	8	C2
Kingston, Dorset	14	B3
Kingston, I of W	9	C2
Kingston, Kent	32	B4
Kingstone, Heref	47	C4
Kingstone, Som	13	B3
Kingstone, Staffs	71	B4
Kingswood, Bucks	40	B2
Kingswood, Glouc	37	C4
Kingswood, Som	12	C1
Kingswood, Surrey	150	A2
Kingswood, Warwk	49	C1
Kingthorpe, Lincs	84	A4
Kington Langley, Wilts	25	B1
Kington Magna, Dorset	14	B2
Kington St Michael, Wilts	25	B1
Kington, Glouc	37	B4
Kington, Heref	47	B3
Kington, Worcs	49	A3
Kingussie, High	132	C3
Kingweston, Som	13	C1
Kinkell Bridge, Perth	123	B3
Kinlet, Shrops	58	B4
Kinloch Hourn, High	131	A3
Kinloch Rannoch, Perth	127	E3
Kinloch, High	130	C3
Kinloch, High	142	C4
Kinloch, Perth	128	D4
Kinlochbervie, High	142	B2
Kinlocheil, High	126	D1
Kinlochewe, High	136	B2
Kinlochlaggan, High	132	A4
Kinlochleven, High	126	E3
Kinlochmoidart, High	126	A2
Kinloss, Moray	138	A2
Kinnaird, Perth	128	B3
Kinneff, Aber	129	E1
Kinnerley, Shrops	57	B1
Kinnersley, Heref	47	B3
Kinnersley, Worcs	48	C4
Kinnerton, Powys	47	B2
Kinnesswood, Perth	123	D4
Kinninvie, Durham	99	D4
Kinoulton, Notts	73	B4
Kinross, Perth	123	D4
Kinrossie, Perth	123	D1
Kinsham, Heref	47	C2
Kinsham, Worcs	49	A4
Kinsley, W Yorks	82	B1
Kintbury, Berks	26	D2
Kintessack, Moray	137	D2
Kintillo, Perth	123	D3
Kinton, Heref	47	C1
Kinton, Shrops	57	C1
Kintore, Aber	134	B2
Kintra, Argyll	120	B2
Kintraw, Argyll	120	F4
Kinver, Staffs	58	C4
Kippax, W Yorks	88	B3
Kippen, Stirl	115	C1
Kippford or Scaur, Dumf	97	B1
Kipping's Cross, Kent	19	C1
Kirbister, Orkney	144	A2
Kirby Bedon, Norf	65	B2
Kirby Bellars, Leics	61	B1
Kirby Cane, Norf	66	A3
Kirby Grindalythe, N York	95	B4
Kirby Hill, N York	93	B1
Kirby Hill, N York	94	A4
Kirby Knowle, N York	94	A3
Kirby le Soken, Essex	44	C2
Kirby Misperton, N York	95	A3
Kirby Muxloe, Leics	61	A2
Kirby Row, Norf	66	A3
Kirby Sigston, N York	94	A2
Kirby Underdale, E R of Y	89	C1
Kirby Wiske, N York	93	D3
Kirdford, W Suss	18	A2
Kirk Bramwith, S York	83	A1
Kirk Deighton, N York	88	B2
Kirk Hammerton, N York	88	B1
Kirk Ireton, Derby	71	C2
Kirk Langley, Derby	72	A3
Kirk Michael, I of M	145	C2
Kirk Sandall, S York	82	C1
Kirk Smeaton, N York	82	C1
Kirk Yetholm, Border	111	C2
Kirkabister, Shet	144	A2
Kirkandrews, Dumf	96	F1
Kirkbampton, Cumb	98	A1
Kirkbean, Dumf	103	D4
Kirkbride, Cumb	97	E1
Kirkburn, E R of Y	90	B1
Kirkburton, W Yorks	81	C1
Kirkby Fleetham, N York	93	D2
Kirkby in Ashfield, Notts	72	B2
Kirkby Lonsdale, Cumb	92	B3
Kirkby Malham, N York	86	C1
Kirkby Mallory, Leics	60	C3
Kirkby Malzeard, N York	93	C4
Kirkby on Bain, Lincs	74	D1
Kirkby Overblow, N York	88	A2
Kirkby Thore, Cumb	98	D3
Kirkby Underwood, Lincs	74	B4
Kirkby Wharf, N York	89	A3
Kirkby, Lincs	83	D3
Kirkby, Mers	79	A2
Kirkby, N York	94	B1
Kirkby-in-Furness, Cumb	91	C3
Kirkbymoorside, N York	94	C3
Kirkcaldy, Fife	118	A1
Kirkcambeck, Cumb	104	D3

PLACE	PAGE	GRID
Kirkcolm, Dumf	102	A3
Kirkconnel, Dumf	109	B4
Kirkcowan, Dumf	102	D4
Kirkcudbright, Dumf	97	A1
Kirkgunzeon, Dumf	103	C4
Kirkham, Lancs	85	B3
Kirkham, N York	95	A4
Kirkhamgate, W Yorks	88	A4
Kirkharle, Nthumb	105	C2
Kirkhaugh, Nthumb	98	D1
Kirkheaton, Nthumb	105	C3
Kirkheaton, W Yorks	81	C1
Kirkhill, High	137	A4
Kirkinner, Dumf	96	D1
Kirkintilloch, E Dun	115	C2
Kirkland, Cumb	97	D4
Kirkland, Dumf	103	C2
Kirkleatham, N York	101	A4
Kirklevington, N York	94	A1
Kirklington, N York	93	D3
Kirklington, Notts	73	B2
Kirklinton, Cumb	104	C4
Kirkliston, Edin	117	B2
Kirkmabreck, Dumf	96	E1
Kirkmaiden, Dumf	96	B2
Kirkmichael, Perth	128	C3
Kirkmichael, S Ayrs	108	D4
Kirkmuirhill, S Lan	109	C1
Kirknewton, Nthumb	111	C2
Kirknewton, W Loth	117	A3
Kirkoswald, Cumb	98	C2
Kirkoswald, S Ayrs	108	C4
Kirkpatrick Durham, Dumf	103	C3
Kirkpatrick, Dumf	103	D2
Kirkpatrick-Fleming, Dumf	104	B3
Kirksanton, Cumb	91	C3
Kirkstead, Lincs	74	C1
Kirkstile, Dumf	104	C2
Kirkthorpe, W Yorks	88	A4
Kirkton of Glenbuchat, Aber	133	D2
Kirkton of Logie Buchan, Aber	134	D1
Kirkton of Menmuir, Angus	129	B3
Kirkton of Rayne, Aber	134	B1
Kirkton of Skene, Aber	134	B3
Kirkton of Strathmartine, Angus	124	B1
Kirkton, Dumf	103	D2
Kirktown of Bourtie, Aber	134	B1
Kirkwall, Orkney	144	A2
Kirkwhelpington, Nthumb	105	C2
Kirmington, Lincs	84	A1
Kirmond le Mire, Lincs	84	A3
Kirriemuir, Angus	129	A3
Kirstead Green, Norf	65	B3
Kirtlebridge, Dumf	104	B3
Kirtling Green, Cambs	54	A3
Kirtling, Cambs	54	A2
Kirtlington, Oxon	39	C2
Kirtomy, High	142	F1
Kirton in Lindsey, Lincs	83	C2
Kirton, Aber	134	A2
Kirton, Lincs	74	D3
Kirton, Notts	73	B1
Kirton, Suff	55	B4
Kishorn, High	135	F4
Kislingbury, Nhants	51	A2
Kittisford, Som	12	C2
Kivernoll, Heref	37	A1
Knaith, Lincs	83	B3
Knaphill, Surrey	28	B3
Knaplock, Som	12	A1
Knapp, Som	13	A2
Knapton, N York	89	A2
Knapton, N York	95	B3
Knapton, Norf	76	D4
Knapwell, Cambs	53	A2
Knaresborough, N York	88	A1
Knarsdale, Nthumb	98	D1
Knayton, N York	94	A2
Knebworth, Herts	42	A2
Kneesall, Notts	73	B1
Kneesworth, Cambs	53	A4
Kneeton, Notts	73	B3
Knenhall, Staffs	70	C3
Knightcote, Warwk	50	B3
Knightley, Staffs	58	C1
Knighton, Dorset	14	A3
Knighton, Powys	47	B1
Knighton, Som	23	B4
Knighton, Staffs	70	B3
Knighton, Staffs	70	B4
Knightwick, Worcs	48	B3
Knill, Heref	47	B2
Knipton, Leics	73	C4
Kniveton, Derby	71	C2
Knock, Cumb	98	D3
Knockally, High	143	D4
Knockan, High	140	E2
Knockholt Pound, Kent	30	A3
Knockholt, Kent	30	A3
Knockin, Shrops	57	B1
Knocknain, Dumf	102	A4
Knodishall, Suff	55	C2
Knole, Som	13	C2
Knolton, Wrex	69	C3
Knook, Wilts	26	A4
Knossington, Leics	61	C2
Knott End-on-Sea, Lancs	85	B2
Knotting Green, Beds	52	A2
Knotting, Beds	52	A2
Knottingley, W Yorks	88	B4
Knowbury, Shrops	47	D1
Knowehead, Dumf	103	A2
Knowl Hill, Berks	28	A1
Knowle Green, Lancs	86	A3
Knowle Hill, Surrey	146	A2
Knowle St Giles, Som	13	A3
Knowle, Devon	6	B2
Knowle, Devon	12	A4
Knowle, Devon	12	B3
Knowle, Som	22	E4
Knowle, W Mids	49	C1

PLACE	PAGE	GRID
Knowsley, Mers	79	A2
Knowstone, Devon	12	A2
Knox Bridge, Kent	20	B1
Knucklas, Powys	47	B1
Knuston, Nhants	51	C2
Knutsford, Chesh	80	A4
Krumlin, W Yorks	81	B1
Kuggar, Corn	1	D3
Kyle of Lochalsh, High	130	F1
Kyleakin, High	130	F1
Kylerhea, High	130	F2
Kynnersley, Shrops	58	A1
Kyrewood, Worcs	48	A2
La Fontenelle, Guern	145	B2
La Greve de Lecq, Jersey	145	A1
La Rocque, Jersey	145	B2
La Villette, Guern	145	B2
Laceby, Lincs	84	B2
Lacey Green, Bucks	40	C3
Lach Dennis, Chesh	70	B1
Lackford Green, Suff	54	B1
Lackford, Suff	54	B1
Lacock, Wilts	25	B2
Ladbroke, Warwk	50	B2
Laddingford, Kent	31	A4
Ladock, Corn	3	C4
Lady Hall, Cumb	91	C3
Lady Village, Orkney	144	B1
Ladybank, Fife	124	A3
Ladykirk, Border	111	C1
Ladywood, Worcs	48	C2
Lagavulin, Argyll	107	B1
Laggan, High	132	B4
Laide, High	140	B4
Lairg, High	141	B2
Lake, Wilts	15	A1
Lakenheath, Suff	64	A4
Lakesend, Norf	63	C3
Laleham, Surrey	146	A2
Laleston, Bridg	22	D1
Lamancha, Border	117	B4
Lamas, Norf	65	B1
Lamberhurst Down, Kent	20	A1
Lamberhurst, Kent	20	A1
Lambeth, G Lon	149	A2
Lambley, Notts	73	B3
Lambley, Nthumb	104	E4
Lambourn, Berks	26	D1
Lambourne End, Essex	42	C4
Lambs Green, W Suss	18	C1
Lamerton, Devon	4	C2
Lamesley, Tyne	106	A4
Lamington, S Lan	109	D2
Lamlash, N Ayrs	108	A2
Lamonby, Cumb	98	B2
Lamorna, Corn	1	B3
Lampeter Velfrey, Pemb	33	E2
Lampeter, Cered	46	A3
Lamphey, Pemb	33	D3
Lamplugh, Cumb	97	D4
Lamport, Nhants	51	B1
Lamyatt, Som	14	A1
Lanark, S Lan	109	C1
Lancaster, Lancs	85	C1
Lanchester, Durham	100	A1
Lancing, W Suss	18	B4
Landbeach, Cambs	53	B2
Landcross, Devon	11	D2
Landimore, Swan	34	C4
Landkey Town, Devon	11	E1
Landrake, Corn	4	B3
Land's End, Corn	1	A3
Landscove, Devon	5	C3
Landulph, Corn	4	C3
Lane End Waberthwaite, Cumb	91	B2
Lane End, Bucks	40	C4
Lane Ends, Derby	71	C4
Lane Head, Durham	99	D4
Lane, Corn	3	B4
Laneast, Corn	4	A1
Laneham, Notts	83	B4
Lanehead, Durham	99	B2
Langar, Notts	73	B4
Langbank, Renf	115	A2
Langbar, N York	87	B2
Langcliffe, N York	92	D4
Langdale End, N York	95	B2
Langdyke, Fife	124	A4
Langenhoe, Essex	44	B2
Langford Budville, Som	12	C2
Langford End, Beds	52	B3
Langford, Beds	52	B4
Langford, Devon	12	C4
Langford, Essex	43	C3
Langford, Notts	73	C2
Langford, Oxon	39	A3
Langham, Essex	54	D4
Langham, Norf	76	B3
Langham, Rutland	61	C2
Langham, Suff	54	C1
Langho, Lancs	86	B3
Langholm, Dumf	104	C2
Langley Burrell, Wilts	26	A2
Langley Park, Durham	100	A2
Langley Street, Norf	66	A3
Langley Upper Green, Essex	53	B4
Langley, Berks	146	A1
Langley, Hants	16	A4
Langley, Herts	42	A1
Langley, Nthumb	105	B4
Langley, Warwk	49	C2
Langold, Notts	82	C3
Langore, Corn	4	A1
Langport, Som	13	B2
Langrick, Lincs	74	D3
Langridge, Som	25	A2
Langrigg, Cumb	97	E1
Langrish, Hants	17	A2
Langsett, S York	81	C2
Langstone, Newport	36	C4
Langthorne, N York	93	C2
Langthorpe, N York	93	D4
Langthwaite, N York	93	A1
Langtoft, E R of Y	95	C4
Langtoft, Lincs	62	C2
Langton by Wragby, Lincs	84	A4
Langton Herring, Dorset	7	D2
Langton Matravers, Dorset	8	C2
Langton, Durham	100	A4
Langton, Lincs	74	D1
Langton, Lincs	75	A1
Langton, N York	95	A4
Langtree, Devon	11	D3
Langwathby, Cumb	98	C3
Langworth, Lincs	83	D4
Lanivet, Corn	3	D3
Lank, Corn	3	E2
Lanlivery, Corn	3	E4
Lanner, Corn	1	D1
Lanreath, Corn	3	E4
Lansallos, Corn	3	E4
Lanteglos Highway, Corn	3	E4
Lanteglos, Corn	3	E2
Lanton, Border	111	A3
Lanton, Nthumb	112	A2
Lapford, Devon	11	F3
Laphroaig, Argyll	107	B1
Lapley, Staffs	58	C2
Lapworth, Warwk	49	C1
Larbert, Falk	116	B2
Largoward, Fife	124	C3
Largs, N Ayrs	114	D4
Larkhall, S Lan	116	A4
Larkhill, Wilts	26	B4
Larling, Norf	64	C4
Lartington, Durham	99	C4
Lasham, Hants	27	C4
Lask Edge, Staffs	70	C2
Lastingham, N York	94	C2
Latchingdon, Essex	43	C3
Latchley, Corn	4	B2
Latebrook, Staffs	70	C2
Lathbury, Bucks	51	C4
Latheron, High	143	D4
Latimer, Bucks	41	B3
Latteridge, Glouc	24	C1
Latton, Wilts	38	C4
Lauder, Border	110	D1
Laugharne, Carm	34	A2
Laughton, E Suss	19	B3
Laughton, Leics	61	B4
Laughton, Lincs	74	B4
Laughton, Lincs	83	B2
Laughton-en-le-Morthen, S York	82	C3
Launcells, Corn	11	B4
Launceston, Corn	4	B1
Launton, Oxon	40	A1
Laurencekirk, Aber	129	D2
Laurieston, Dumf	103	B4
Lavendon, Bucks	51	C3
Lavenham, Suff	54	C3
Lavernock, Glam	23	B2
Laversdale, Cumb	104	D4
Laverton, Glouc	49	B4
Laverton, N York	93	C4
Laverton, Som	25	A3
Lavister, Wrex	69	C2
Law, S Lan	116	B4
Lawers, Perth	122	D1
Lawford, Essex	44	B1
Lawford, Som	12	D1
Lawhitton, Corn	4	B2
Lawkland, N York	92	C4
Lawrenny, Pemb	33	D3
Lawshall, Suff	54	B3
Laxey, I of M	145	D3
Laxfield, Suff	55	B1
Laxton, E R of Y	89	C4
Laxton, Nhants	62	A3
Laxton, Notts	73	B1
Laycock, W Yorks	87	A3
Layer Breton, Essex	44	A2
Layer Marney, Essex	44	A2
Layham, Suff	54	D4
Laytham, E R of Y	89	C3
Laythes, Cumb	98	A1
Lazonby, Cumb	98	C2
Le Bourg, Guern	145	B2
Le Villocq, Guern	145	B2
Lea Marston, Warwk	60	A3
Lea, Derby	72	A2
Lea, Heref	37	B2
Lea, Lincs	83	B3
Lea, Shrops	57	C4
Lea, Wilts	26	A1
Leaden Roding, Essex	43	A2
Leadenham, Lincs	74	A2
Leadgate, Durham	99	D1
Leadhills, S Lan	109	C3
Leafield, Oxon	39	B2
Leake Common Side, Lincs	75	A2
Lealholm, N York	95	A1
Leamington Hastings, Warwk	50	B2
Leamington Spa, Warwk	50	A2
Leasgill, Cumb	92	A3
Leasingham, Lincs	74	B3
Leasingthorne, Durham	100	A3
Leatherhead, Surrey	146	B3
Leathley, N York	87	C2
Leaton, Shrops	57	D1
Leavenheath, Suff	54	C4
Leavening, N York	89	C1
Leaves Green, G Lon	150	D1
Lebberston, N York	95	C3
Lechlade, Glouc	39	A3
Leck, Lancs	92	B3
Leckford, Hants	15	C1
Leckhampstead Thicket, Berks	27	A1
Leckhampstead, Berks	27	A2
Leckhampstead, Bucks	51	A4
Leckmelm, High	140	D4
Leconfield, E R of Y	90	B2
Ledburn, Bucks	41	A2
Ledbury, Heref	48	B4
Ledgemoor, Heref	47	C3
Ledsham, W Yorks	88	B4
Ledston, W Yorks	88	B4
Ledwell, Oxon	39	C1
Lee Brockhurst, Shrops	69	D4
Lee Street, Surrey	150	B4
Lee, Devon	22	A4
Lee, G Lon	149	B3
Leebotwood, Shrops	57	D3
Leece, Cumb	91	D4
Leeds, Kent	31	B3
Leeds, W Yorks	88	A3
Leedstown, Corn	1	C2
Leek Wootton, Warwk	50	A1
Leek, Staffs	71	A2
Leeming Bar, N York	93	D2
Leeming, N York	93	D2
Lee-on-the-Solent, Hants	16	B4
Lees, Derby	71	C4
Leesthorpe, Leics	61	C2
Leeswood, Flint	69	B2
Leetown, Perth	123	D2
Legbourne, Lincs	84	C3
Legerwood, Border	111	A1
Legsby, Lincs	84	A3
Leicester, Leics	61	A2
Leigh Delamere, Wilts	25	B1
Leigh Green, Kent	21	A1
Leigh Sinton, Worcs	48	B3
Leigh upon Mendip, Som	24	C4
Leigh Woods, Som	24	B2
Leigh, Dorset	14	A3
Leigh, G Man	79	C2
Leigh, Glouc	38	A1
Leigh, Kent	30	B4
Leigh, Surrey	150	A4
Leigh, Wilts	38	C4
Leigh, Worcs	48	B3
Leighterton, Glouc	38	A4
Leighton Buzzard, Beds	41	A1
Leighton, Powys	57	B2
Leighton, Shrops	58	A2
Leinthall Earls, Heref	47	C2
Leinthall Starkes, Heref	47	C1
Leintwardine, Heref	47	C1
Leire, Leics	61	A4
Leiston, Suff	55	C2
Leitfie, Perth	128	E4
Leitholm, Border	111	B1
Lelant, Corn	1	C1
Lelley, E R of Y	90	D3
Lem Hill, Worcs	48	B1
Lenchwick, Worcs	49	A3
Lendalfoot, S Ayrs	102	B2
Lenham Heath, Kent	31	C4
Lenham, Kent	31	C4
Lennel, Border	111	C1
Lennoxtown, E Dun	115	C2
Lent, Bucks	28	B1
Lenton, Lincs	74	B4
Leochel-Cushnie, Aber	133	E3
Leominster, Heref	47	D2
Leppington, N York	89	C1
Lepton, W Yorks	81	C1
L'Eree, Guern	145	A2
Lerryn, Corn	3	E4
Lerwick, Shet	144	A2
Les Quartiers, Guern	145	B2
Les Quennevais, Jersey	145	A2
Lesbury, Nthumb	112	C4
Leslie, Aber	134	A1
Leslie, Fife	124	A4
Lesmahagow, S Lan	109	C1
Lesnewth, Corn	3	E1
Lessingham, Norf	76	E4
Lessonhall, Cumb	97	E1
Leswalt, Dumf	102	A4
L'Etacq, Jersey	145	A1
Letchworth, Herts	42	A1
Letcombe Bassett, Oxon	26	D1
Letcombe Regis, Oxon	26	D1
Letham, Angus	129	B4
Letham, Fife	124	A3
Letheringham, Suff	55	B2
Letheringsett, Norf	76	B3
Letterston, Pemb	33	C1
Letton, Heref	47	B3
Lett's Green, Kent	30	A3
Letty Green, Herts	42	A2
Letwell, S York	82	C3
Leuchars, Fife	124	B2
Levedale, Staffs	58	C1
Leven, E R of Y	90	C2
Leven, Fife	124	B4
Levens Green, Herts	42	B1
Levens, Cumb	92	A3
Leverington, Cambs	63	C2
Leverton, Lincs	75	A3
Levington, Suff	55	A4
Levisham, N York	95	A2
Lew, Oxon	39	B3
Lewannick, Corn	4	A2
Lewdown, Devon	4	C1
Lewes, E Suss	19	A3
Leweston, Pemb	33	C1
Lewknor, Oxon	40	B4
Lewson Street, Kent	31	C3
Lewtrenchard, Devon	4	C1
Lexworthy, Som	13	A1
Ley Hill, Bucks	41	B3
Leybourne, Kent	31	A3
Leyburn, N York	93	B2
Leygreen, Herts	41	C1
Leyland, Lancs	85	C4
Leys, Angus	124	A1
Leysdown-on-Sea, Kent	32	A2
Leysmill, Angus	129	C4
Leysters, Heref	47	D2
Leyton, G Lon	149	B1
Lezant, Corn	4	B2
Lezayre, I of M	145	C2
Lhanbryde, Moray	138	C2
Libanus, Powys	35	C1
Libberton, S Lan	109	D1
Lichfield, Staffs	59	B2
Lickey End, Worcs	49	A1
Lickey, Worcs	49	A1
Lickfold, W Suss	17	C2
Liddesdale, High	126	B3
Liddington, Wilts	26	C1
Lidgate, Suff	54	A2
Lidlington, Beds	52	A4
Liff, Angus	124	A1
Lifton, Devon	4	B1
Liftondown, Devon	4	B1
Lighthorne, Warwk	50	A3
Lilbourne, Nhants	50	C1
Lilleshall, Shrops	58	B1
Lilley, Herts	41	C1
Lilliesleaf, Border	110	D3
Lillingstone Dayrell, Bucks	51	A4
Lillingstone Lovell, Bucks	51	A4
Lillington, Dorset	14	A3
Lilstock, Som	23	B4
Lime Street, Worcs	38	A1
Limekilns, Fife	117	A2
Limerstone, I of W	9	C2
Limington, Som	13	C2
Limpenhoe, Norf	66	A2
Limpley Stoke, Wilts	25	A3
Limpsfield Chart, Surrey	150	D3
Limpsfield, Surrey	150	D2
Linby, Notts	73	A2
Linchmere, W Suss	17	C1
Lincoln, Lincs	74	B1
Lincomb, Worcs	48	C1
Lindal in Furness, Cumb	91	D4
Lindale, Cumb	91	E3
Lindford, Hants	17	B1
Lindley Green, N York	87	C2
Lindridge, Worcs	48	A1
Lindsell, Essex	43	A1
Lindsey Tye, Suff	54	C3
Lindsey, Suff	54	C4
Lingdale, N York	101	B4
Lingen, Heref	47	C2
Lingfield, Surrey	150	D4
Lingwood, Norf	66	A2
Linkend, Worcs	38	A1
Linkenholt, Hants	26	D3
Linkinhorne, Corn	4	B2
Linley Green, Heref	48	A3
Linley, Shrops	57	C3
Linleygreen, Shrops	58	A3
Linlithgow, W Loth	116	C2
Linstead Parva, Suff	55	B1
Linstock, Cumb	104	C4
Linthwaite, W Yorks	81	B1
Lintlaw, Border	119	D4
Lintmill, Moray	139	A2
Linton Hill, Heref	37	B1
Linton, Cambs	53	C3
Linton, Derby	60	B1
Linton, Heref	37	B1
Linton, Kent	31	A4
Linton, N York	87	A1
Linton, W Yorks	88	B2
Linton-on-Ouse, N York	88	B1
Linwood, Lincs	84	A3
Linwood, Renf	115	B3
Liphook, Hants	17	B1
Liscombe, Som	12	A1
Liskeard, Corn	4	A3
Liss, Hants	17	B2
Lissett, E R of Y	90	C1
Lissington, Lincs	84	A4
Litcham, Norf	64	B1
Litchborough, Nhants	51	A3
Litchfield, Hants	27	A3
Litlington, Cambs	52	C4
Litlington, E Suss	19	B4
Little Abington, Cambs	53	B3
Little Addington, Nhants	51	C1
Little Alne, Warwk	49	B2
Little Amwell, Herts	42	B2
Little Asby, Cumb	92	C1
Little Aston, Staffs	59	B3
Little Ayton, N York	94	B1
Little Baddow, Essex	43	C3
Little Badminton, Glouc	25	A1
Little Bampton, Cumb	98	A1
Little Bardfield, Essex	43	A1
Little Barningham, Norf	76	C4
Little Barrington, Glouc	39	A2
Little Bavington, Nthumb	105	C3
Little Bedwyn, Wilts	26	D2
Little Bentley, Essex	44	B1
Little Berkhamsted, Herts	42	A3
Little Birch, Heref	37	A1
Little Blencow, Cumb	98	B3
Little Bognor, W Suss	18	A2
Little Bolehill, Derby	72	A2
Little Bollington, Chesh	80	A3
Little Bourton, Oxon	50	B4
Little Bradley, Suff	54	A3
Little Brampton, Shrops	57	C4
Little Brechin, Angus	129	C3
Little Brickhill, Bucks	41	A1
Little Brington, Nhants	51	A2
Little Bromley, Essex	44	B1
Little Broughton, Cumb	97	D3
Little Budworth, Chesh	70	A1
Little Burstead, Essex	43	B4
Little Bytham, Lincs	62	B1
Little Casterton, Rutland	62	B2
Little Cawthorpe, Lincs	84	C4
Little Chart, Kent	31	C4
Little Chesterford, Essex	53	B4
Little Cheverell, Wilts	26	A3
Little Chishill, Cambs	53	A4
Little Clacton, Essex	44	C2
Little Clifton, Cumb	97	D3
Little Comberton, Worcs	49	A4
Little Compton, Warwk	39	A1
Little Cornard, Suff	54	C4
Little Cowarne, Heref	48	A3
Little Coxwell, Oxon	39	B4
Little Crakehall, N York	93	C2
Little Cressingham, Norf	64	B3
Little Crosby, Mers	78	D2
Little Cubley, Derby	71	C4
Little Dalby, Leics	61	C2
Little Dewchurch, Heref	37	A1
Little Ditton, Cambs	54	A2
Little Driffield, E R of Y	90	B1
Little Dunham, Norf	64	B2
Little Dunkeld, Perth	128	C4
Little Dunmow, Essex	43	A2
Little Durnford, Wilts	15	A1
Little Eaton, Derby	72	A3
Little Ellingham, Norf	64	C3
Little Everdon, Nhants	50	C2
Little Faringdon, Oxon	39	A3
Little Fencote, N York	93	D2
Little Fenton, N York	89	A3
Little Fransham, Norf	64	C2
Little Gaddesden, Herts	41	B2
Little Gorsley, Heref	37	B1
Little Gransden, Cambs	52	C3
Little Green, Som	25	A4
Little Grimsby, Lincs	84	C3
Little Hadham, Herts	42	C1
Little Hale, Lincs	74	C3
Little Hallingbury, Essex	42	C2
Little Harrowden, Nhants	51	C1
Little Haseley, Oxon	40	B3
Little Hatfield, E R of Y	90	C2
Little Haven, Pemb	33	C2
Little Hay, Staffs	59	B3
Little Haywood, Staffs	59	A1
Little Hereford, Heref	47	D1
Little Horkesley, Essex	44	A1
Little Hormead, Herts	42	B1
Little Horwood, Bucks	40	C1
Little Houghton, Nhants	51	B2
Little Houghton, S York	82	B2
Little Hucklow, Derby	81	C4
Little Hutton, N York	94	A4
Little Keyford, Som	25	A4
Little Kimble, Bucks	40	C3
Little Kineton, Warwk	50	A3
Little Kingshill, Bucks	41	A3
Little Langdale, Cumb	91	D1
Little Langford, Wilts	15	A1
Little Leigh, Chesh	79	C4
Little Lever, G Man	80	A1
Little Linford, Bucks	51	B4
Little Load, Som	13	C2
Little London, Hants	26	D4
Little London, Hants	27	C3
Little Longstone, Derby	71	C1
Little Malvern, Worcs	48	B4
Little Maplestead, Essex	54	B4
Little Marcle, Heref	48	A4
Little Marlow, Bucks	41	A4
Little Massingham, Norf	64	B1
Little Melton, Norf	65	A2
Little Mill, Monm	36	B3
Little Milton, Oxon	40	A3
Little Missenden, Bucks	41	A3
Little Musgrave, Cumb	99	A4
Little Ness, Shrops	57	C1
Little Newcastle, Pemb	33	D1
Little Newsham, Durham	99	D4
Little Norton, Som	13	C3
Little Oakley, Essex	44	C1
Little Oakley, Nhants	62	A4
Little Onn, Staffs	58	C1
Little Orton, Cumb	98	B1
Little Packington, Warwk	60	A4
Little Paxton, Cambs	52	B2
Little Petherick, Corn	3	C2
Little Plumstead, Norf	65	B2
Little Ponton, Lincs	74	A4
Little Preston, Nhants	50	C3
Little Raveley, Cambs	63	A4
Little Ribston, N York	88	A1
Little Rissington, Glouc	39	A2
Little Rollright, Oxon	39	B1
Little Ryburgh, Norf	76	A4
Little Salkeld, Cumb	98	C2
Little Sampford, Essex	53	C4
Little Saughall, Chesh	69	C1
Little Saxham, Suff	54	B2
Little Sessay, N York	94	A4
Little Singleton, Lancs	85	B3
Little Snoring, Norf	76	A4
Little Sodbury, Glouc	25	A1
Little Somerford, Wilts	26	A1
Little Soudley, Shrops	70	B4
Little Stainton, Durham	100	B4
Little Stanney, Chesh	79	A4
Little Staughton, Beds	52	B2
Little Steeping, Lincs	75	B1
Little Stonham, Suff	54	D2
Little Stretton, Leics	61	B3
Little Stretton, Shrops	57	C3
Little Strickland, Cumb	98	C4
Little Stukeley, Cambs	52	C1
Little Swinburne, Nthumb	105	C3
Little Tew, Oxon	39	B1
Little Tey, Essex	44	A1
Little Thetford, Cambs	53	B1
Little Thorpe, Durham	100	C2
Little Thurlow Green, Suff	54	A3
Little Torrington, Devon	11	D3
Little Town, Lancs	86	A3
Little Urswick, Cumb	91	D4
Little Wakering, Essex	44	A4
Little Walden, Essex	53	C4
Little Waldingfield, Suff	54	C3
Little Walsingham, Norf	76	A4
Little Weighton, E R of Y	90	B3
Little Wenham, Suff	54	D4
Little Wenlock, Shrops	58	A2
Little Whitefield, I of W	10	A1
Little Wilbraham, Cambs	53	B2
Little Witcombe, Glouc	38	A2
Little Witley, Worcs	48	B2
Little Wittenham, Oxon	40	A4
Little Wolford, Warwk	49	C4
Little Woodcote, Surrey	150	B1
Little Wymington, Beds	51	C2
Little Wymondley, Herts	42	A1
Little Wyrley, Staffs	59	A2
Little Yeldham, Essex	54	B4
Littleborough, G Man	81	A1
Littleborough, Notts	83	B4
Littlebourne, Kent	32	B3
Littlebredy, Dorset	7	D1
Littlebury Green, Essex	53	B4
Littlebury, Essex	53	B4
Littledean, Glouc	37	B2
Littleham, Devon	6	B2
Littleham, Devon	11	D2
Littlehampton, W Suss	18	A4
Littlehempston, Devon	5	C3
Littleport, Cambs	63	D4
Littlethorpe, Leics	61	A3
Littlethorpe, N York	93	D4
Littleton Drew, Wilts	25	B1
Littleton, Chesh	69	C1
Littleton, Hants	16	A1
Littleton, Som	13	C1
Littleton, Surrey	146	A4
Littleton, Surrey	146	A2
Littleton-on-Severn, Glouc	37	B4
Littletown, Durham	100	B2
Littleworth Common, Bucks	28	B1
Littleworth, Oxon	39	B4
Littleworth, Worcs	48	C3
Litton Cheney, Dorset	7	C1
Litton, Derby	81	C4
Litton, N York	92	D4
Litton, Som	24	C3
Liverpool, Mers	78	D3
Liversedge, W Yorks	87	C4
Liverton, Devon	5	C2
Liverton, N York	101	B4
Livingston Village, W Loth	117	A3
Livingston, W Loth	117	A3
Lixton, Devon	5	B4
Lixwm, Flint	69	A1
Lizard, Corn	1	D4
Llanaelhaearn, Gwyn	67	C3
Llanafan, Cered	46	B1
Llanallgo, Angle	77	C3
Llanarmon Dyffryn Ceiriog, Wrex	69	A4
Llanarmon-yn-Ial, Denb	69	A2
Llanarth, Cered	45	E2
Llanarth, Monm	36	C2
Llanarthne, Carm	34	C2
Llanasa, Flint	78	B4
Llanbadarn Fynydd, Powys	46	E1
Llanbadoc, Monm	36	C3
Llanbeder, Newport	36	C4
Llanbedr, Gwyn	67	E4
Llanbedr, Powys	36	B2
Llanbedr-Dyffryn-Clwyd, Denb	69	A2
Llanbedrgoch, Angle	77	C4
Llanbedrog, Gwyn	67	C4
Llanbedr-y-Cennin, Aberc	68	A1
Llanberis, Gwyn	67	E2
Llanbethery, Glam	23	A2
Llanbister, Powys	46	E1
Llanboidy, Carm	34	A1
Llanbradach, Caer	36	A4
Llanbrynmair, Powys	56	D3
Llancadle, Glam	23	A2
Llancarfan, Glam	23	A2
Llancloudy, Heref	37	A2
Llandanwg, Gwyn	67	E4
Llanddanielfab, Angle	67	D1
Llanddarog, Carm	34	C2
Llanddeiniol, Cered	46	A1
Llandderfel, Gwyn	68	C4
Llanddeusant, Angle	77	B3
Llanddew, Powys	35	D1
Llanddewi Brefi, Cered	46	B3
Llanddewi Rhydderch, Monm	36	C2
Llanddewi Velfrey, Pemb	33	E2
Llanddewi Ystradenni, Powys	46	E1
Llanddewi, Swan	34	C4
Llanddoget, Aberc	68	B1
Llanddona, Angle	77	D4
Llanddowror, Carm	34	A2
Llanddulas, Aberc	78	A4
Llanddwywe, Gwyn	56	A1
Llanddyfnan, Angle	77	C4
Llandefaelog-Trer-Graig, Powys	36	A1
Llandefalle, Powys	46	E4
Llandegfan, Angle	77	D4
Llandegla, Denb	69	A2
Llandegley, Powys	47	A2
Llandegveth, Monm	36	B4
Llandeilo Graban, Powys	46	E4
Llandeilo, Carm	34	D1
Llandeloy, Pemb	33	C1
Llandenny, Monm	36	C3
Llandevaud, Newport	36	C4
Llandevenny, Monm	24	A1
Llandinam, Powys	56	E4
Llandissilio, Pemb	33	E2
Llandogo, Monm	37	A3
Llandough, Glam	22	E2
Llandovery, Carm	46	B4
Llandow, Glam	22	E2
Llandre Isaf, Pemb	33	E1
Llandre, Carm	46	B4
Llandre, Cered	56	A4
Llandrillo, Denb	68	D4
Llandrindod Wells, Powys	46	E2
Llandrinio, Powys	57	B1
Llandudno Junction, Aberc	77	F4
Llandudno, Aberc	77	F4
Llandudwen, Gwyn	67	B4
Llandulas, Powys	46	C4
Llandwrog, Gwyn	67	D2
Llandybie, Carm	34	D2
Llandyfaelog, Carm	34	B2

PLACE	PAGE	GRID
Llandyfriog, Cered	45	E4
Llandygai, Gwyn	67	E1
Llandygwydd, Cered	45	D4
Llandyrnog, Denb	68	D1
Llandyssil, Powys	57	A3
Llandysul, Cered	45	E4
Llanedeyrn, Card	23	B1
Llanegryn, Gwyn	56	A2
Llanegwad, Carm	34	C2
Llaneilian, Angle	77	C3
Llanelian-yn-Rhos, Aberc	77	F4
Llanelidan, Denb	68	D2
Llanelieu, Powys	47	A4
Llanellen, Monm	36	B2
Llanelli, Carm	34	C3
Llanelltyd, Gwyn	56	B1
Llanelwedd, Powys	46	E3
Llanenddwyn, Gwyn	56	A1
Llanengan, Gwyn	67	B4
Llanerchymedd, Angle	77	B3
Llanerfyl, Powys	56	E2
Llanfachraeth, Angle	77	B4
Llanfachreth, Gwyn	56	B1
Llanfaelog, Angle	77	B4
Llanfaelrhys, Gwyn	67	B4
Llanfaethlu, Angle	77	B3
Llanfair Caereinion, Powys	56	E2
Llanfair Clydogau, Cered	46	A3
Llanfair P G, Angle	67	D1
Llanfair Talhaiarn, Aberc	68	C1
Llanfair Waterdine, Shrops	47	B1
Llanfair, Gwyn	67	E4
Llanfairfechan, Aberc	77	E4
Llanfair-is-gaer, Gwyn	67	D1
Llanfair-y-Cwmwd, Angle	67	D1
Llanfairynghornwy, Angle	77	B3
Llanfair-yn-Neubwll, Angle	77	A4
Llanfallteg West, Carm	33	E2
Llanfallteg, Carm	33	E2
Llanfarian, Cered	46	A1
Llanfechain, Powys	57	A1
Llanfechell, Angle	77	B3
Llanferres, Denb	69	A2
Llanfihangel Glyn Myfyr, Aberc	68	C2
Llanfihangel Nant Bran, Powys	46	D4
Llanfihangel Rhydithon, Powys	47	A2
Llanfihangel yn Nhowyn, Angle	77	B4
Llanfihangel-ar-Arth, Carm	45	F4
Llanfihangel-y-Creuddyn, Cered	46	B1
Llanfihangel-yng-Ngwynfa, Powys	56	E1
Llanfihangel-y-traethau, Gwyn	67	E4
Llanfilo, Powys	36	A1
Llanfoist, Monm	36	B2
Llanfor, Gwyn	68	C4
Llanfrechfa, Torf	36	B4
Llanfrynach, Powys	35	D1
Llanfwrog, Angle	77	A3
Llanfwrog, Denb	68	D2
Llanfyllin, Powys	57	A1
Llanfynydd, Carm	34	D1
Llanfynydd, Flint	69	B2
Llanfyrnach, Pemb	34	A1
Llangadfan, Powys	56	E2
Llangadog, Carm	35	A1
Llangadwaladr, Angle	67	C1
Llangaffo, Angle	67	D1
Llangammarch Wells, Powys	46	D3
Llangan, Glam	22	E1
Llangarron, Heref	37	A2
Llangathen, Carm	34	D2
Llangattock Lingoed, Monm	36	C2
Llangattock, Powys	36	A2
Llangedwyn, Powys	57	A1
Llangefni, Angle	77	C4
Llangeinor, Bridg	35	C4
Llangeitho, Cered	46	A2
Llangeler, Carm	45	E4
Llangelynin, Gwyn	56	A2
Llangendeirne, Carm	34	C2
Llangennech, Carm	34	D3
Llangennith, Swan	34	C4
Llangian, Gwyn	67	B4
Llangloffan, Pemb	33	C1
Llanglydwen, Carm	33	E1
Llangoed, Angle	77	D4
Llangollen, Denb	69	A3
Llangolman, Pemb	33	E1
Llangors, Powys	36	A1
Llangower, Gwyn	68	C4
Llangranog, Cered	45	E3
Llangristiolus, Angle	77	C4
Llangrove, Heref	37	A2
Llangunllo, Powys	47	A1
Llangunnor, Carm	34	C2
Llangurig, Powys	56	D4
Llangwm, Aberc	68	C3
Llangwm, Monm	36	C3
Llangwm, Pemb	33	D3
Llangwm-isaf, Monm	36	C3
Llangwnnadl, Gwyn	67	B4
Llangwyryfon, Cered	46	A1
Llangybi, Cered	46	A3
Llangybi, Gwyn	67	D3
Llangybi, Monm	36	C4
Llangynhafal, Denb	69	A1
Llangynidr, Powys	36	A2
Llangynin, Carm	34	A2
Llangynog, Carm	34	B2
Llangynog, Powys	68	D4
Llangynwyd, Bridg	35	B4
Llanhamlach, Powys	35	D1
Llanharan, Rhond	22	E1
Llanharry, Rhond	23	A1
Llanhennock, Monm	36	C4
Llanhilleth, Gwent	36	A3
Llanidloes, Powys	56	D4
Llaniestyn, Gwyn	67	B4
Llanigon, Powys	47	A4
Llanilid, Rhond	22	E1
Llanina, Cered	45	E2
Llanishen, Monm	37	A3
Llanllechid, Gwyn	67	E1
Llanllowell, Monm	36	C4
Llanllugan, Powys	56	E3
Llanllwch, Carm	34	B2
Llanllwni, Carm	45	F4
Llanllyfni, Gwyn	67	D2
Llanmadoc, Swan	34	C4
Llanmaes, Glam	22	E2
Llanmartin, Newport	36	C4
Llanmiloe, Carm	34	A3
Llannefydd, Aberc	68	C1
Llannon, Carm	34	C3
Llannor, Gwyn	67	C4
Llanon, Cered	45	F2
Llanover, Monm	36	B3
Llanpumsaint, Carm	34	B1
Llanrhaeadr-ym-Mochnant, Powys	69	A4
Llanrhidian, Swan	34	C4
Llanrhychwyn, Aberc	68	B1
Llanrhyddlad, Angle	77	B3
Llanrhystud, Cered	45	F1
Llanrian, Pemb	33	B1
Llanrothal, Heref	37	A2
Llanrug, Gwyn	67	D1
Llanrwst, Aberc	68	B1
Llansadurnen, Carm	34	A3
Llansadwrn, Angle	77	D4
Llansadwrn, Carm	35	A1
Llansaint, Carm	34	B3
Llansanffraid Glan Conwy, Aberc	77	F4
Llansannan, Aberc	68	C1
Llansantffraed, Powys	36	A1
Llansantffraed-Cwmdeuddwr, Powys	46	D2
Llansantffraed-in-Elvel, Powys	46	E3
Llansantffraid, Cered	45	F2
Llansantffraid-ym-Mechain, Powys	57	A1
Llansawel, Carm	46	A4
Llansilin, Powys	69	A4
Llansoy, Monm	36	C3
Llanspyddid, Powys	35	D1
Llanstadwell, Pemb	33	C3
Llansteffan, Carm	34	B2
Llanteg, Pemb	33	E3
Llanthewy Skirrid, Monm	36	B2
Llanthony, Monm	36	B1
Llantilio Pertholey, Monm	36	B2
Llantilio-Crossenny, Monm	36	C2
Llantrisant, Monm	36	C4
Llantrisant, Rhond	23	A1
Llantrithyd, Glam	23	A2
Llantwit Fardre, Rhond	23	A1
Llantwit Major, Glam	22	E2
Llanuwchllyn, Gwyn	68	B4
Llanvaches, Newport	36	C4
Llanvair Discoed, Monm	36	C4
Llanvapley, Monm	36	C2
Llanvetherine, Monm	36	C2
Llanvihangel Crucorney, Monm	36	B2
Llanwddyn, Powys	56	E1
Llanwenog, Cered	45	F3
Llanwern, Newport	36	C4
Llanwinio, Carm	34	A1
Llanwnda, Gwyn	67	D2
Llanwnda, Pemb	45	A4
Llanwnnen, Cered	45	F3
Llanwnog, Powys	56	E3
Llanwrda, Carm	35	A1
Llanwrin, Powys	56	C2
Llanwrthwl, Powys	46	D2
Llanwrtyd Wells, Powys	46	C3
Llanyblodwel, Shrops	57	B1
Llanybri, Carm	34	B2
Llanybydder, Carm	45	F4
Llanycefn, Pemb	33	E1
Llanychaer Bridge, Pemb	45	B4
Llanymawddwy, Gwyn	56	D1
Llanymynech, Powys	57	B1
Llanynghenedl, Angle	77	B4
Llanynis, Powys	46	D3
Llanynys, Denb	68	D1
Llanyre, Powys	46	E2
Llanystumdwy, Gwyn	67	D3
Llanywern, Powys	35	D1
Llawhaden, Pemb	33	D2
Llawryglyn, Powys	56	D4
Llay, Wrex	69	B2
Llechrhyd, Caer	35	D3
Llechryd, Cered	45	D4
Llechylched, Angle	77	B4
Lledrod, Cered	46	A1
Llithfaen, Gwyn	67	C3
Lloc, Flint	78	C4
Llowes, Powys	47	A4
Llwydcoed, Rhond	35	C3
Llwydiarth, Powys	56	E1
Llwyncelyn, Cered	45	F2
Llwyndafydd, Cered	45	E3
Llwyngwril, Gwyn	56	A2
Llwynmawr, Wrex	69	A4
Llwynypia, Rhond	35	C4
Llynclys, Shrops	57	B1
Llynfaes, Angle	77	B4
Llysfaen, Aberc	78	A4
Llyswen, Powys	47	A4
Llysworney, Glam	22	E2
Llys-y-fran, Pemb	33	D1
Llywel, Powys	35	B1
Loan, Falk	116	C2
Loanhead, M Loth	118	A3
Loaningfoot, Dumf	97	C1
Loans, S Ayrs	108	D2
Lochailort, High	126	B1
Lochaline, High	126	A4
Lochans, Dumf	96	A1
Locharbriggs, Dumf	103	D2
Lochawe, Argyll	121	C2
Lochboisdale, W Isle	144	A4
Lochbuie, Argyll	120	D2
Lochcarron, High	136	A4
Lochdon, Argyll	120	E1
Lochdonhead, Argyll	120	E1
Lochearnhead, Stirl	122	C2
Lochfoot, Dumf	103	D3
Lochgair, Argyll	114	A1
Lochgelly, Fife	117	B1
Lochgilphead, Argyll	114	A1
Lochgoilhead, Argyll	121	D4
Lochinver, High	140	D1
Lochmaben, Dumf	103	E2
Lochmaddy, W Isle	144	A3
Lochore, Fife	123	D4
Lochranza, N Ayrs	114	A4
Lochwinnoch, Renf	115	A4
Lockengate, Corn	3	D3
Lockerbie, Dumf	104	A2
Lockeridge, Wilts	26	B2
Locking, Som	24	A3
Lockington, E R of Y	90	B2
Locksbottom, G Lon	30	A2
Lockton, N York	95	A2
Loddington, Leics	61	C3
Loddington, Nhants	51	B1
Loddiswell, Devon	10	A1
Loddon, Norf	66	A3
Lode, Cambs	53	B2
Loders, Dorset	7	C1
Lofthouse Gate, W Yorks	88	A4
Lofthouse, W Yorks	88	A4
Loftus, N York	101	B4
Logan, E Ayrs	109	A3
Loggerheads, Staffs	70	B4
Logie Coldstone, Aber	133	D3
Logie Pert, Angus	129	C3
Logie, Fife	124	B2
Logierait, Perth	128	B4
Logierieve, Aber	134	C1
Login, Carm	33	E1
Lolworth, Cambs	53	A2
Londesborough, E R of Y	90	A2
London Apprentice, Corn	3	D4
London Colney, Herts	41	C3
London, G Lon	148	B3
Londonthorpe, Lincs	74	A3
Long Ashton, Som	24	B2
Long Bank, Worcs	48	B1
Long Bredy, Dorset	7	C1
Long Buckby, Nhants	51	A2
Long Clawson, Leics	73	B4
Long Compton, Staffs	58	C1
Long Compton, Warwk	39	B1
Long Crendon, Bucks	40	B3
Long Crichel, Dorset	14	D3
Long Ditton, Surrey	146	B2
Long Duckmanton, Derby	72	B1
Long Eaton, Derby	72	B4
Long Green, Chesh	69	D1
Long Green, Worcs	38	A1
Long Hanborough, Oxon	39	C2
Long Itchington, Warwk	50	B2
Long Marston, Herts	41	A2
Long Marston, N York	88	B2
Long Marston, Warwk	49	B3
Long Marton, Cumb	98	D3
Long Melford, Suff	54	B3
Long Newnton, Glouc	38	A4
Long Newton, E Loth	119	A3
Long Preston, N York	86	C1
Long Riston, E R of Y	90	C2
Long Stratton, Norf	65	A3
Long Street, Bucks	51	B3
Long Sutton, Hants	28	A4
Long Sutton, Lincs	63	C1
Long Sutton, Som	13	C2
Long Thurlow, Suff	54	D2
Long Waste, Shrops	58	A1
Long Whatton, Leics	60	C1
Longbenton, Tyne	106	A3
Longborough, Glouc	39	A1
Longbridge Deverill, Wilts	14	C1
Longburton, Dorset	14	A3
Longcliffe, Derby	71	C2
Longcombe, Devon	5	C4
Longcot, Oxon	39	B4
Longcross, Surrey	146	A2
Longden, Shrops	57	C2
Longdon Green, Staffs	59	B2
Longdon, Staffs	59	B2
Longdon, Worcs	48	C4
Longdown, Devon	5	C1
Longdowns, Corn	2	A2
Longfield, Kent	30	B2
Longford, Derby	71	C3
Longford, G Lon	146	A1
Longford, Glouc	38	A2
Longford, Kent	30	A3
Longford, Shrops	58	B1
Longford, Shrops	70	A4
Longforgan, Perth	124	A2
Longformacus, Border	119	B4
Longframlington, Nthumb	105	D1
Longham, Dorset	15	A4
Longham, Norf	64	C1
Longhirst, Nthumb	106	A2
Longhope, Glouc	37	B2
Longhope, Orkney	144	A2
Longhorsley, Nthumb	105	D1
Longhoughton, Nthumb	112	C3
Longley, W Yorks	87	B4
Longleys, Perth	128	E4
Longmorn, Moray	138	C2
Longnewton, Durham	100	B4
Longney, Glouc	37	C2
Longniddry, E Loth	118	B2
Longnor, Shrops	57	D3
Longparish, Hants	27	A4
Longridge, Lancs	86	A3
Longridge, W Loth	116	C3
Longriggend, N Lan	116	B3
Longrock, Corn	1	B2
Longsdon, Staffs	71	A2
Longside, Aber	139	E3
Longstanton, Cambs	53	A2
Longstock, Hants	15	C1
Longstowe, Cambs	52	C3
Longthwaite, Cumb	98	B3
Longton, Lancs	85	C4
Longtown, Cumb	104	C3
Longtown, Heref	36	B1
Longueville, Jersey	145	B2
Longwick, Bucks	40	C3
Longwitton, Nthumb	105	D2
Longworth, Oxon	39	B3
Longyester, E Loth	119	A3
Looe, Corn	4	A4
Loosley Row, Bucks	40	C3
Lopen, Som	13	B3
Loppington, Shrops	69	D4
Lornty, Perth	128	D4
Loscoe, Derby	72	B3
Lossiemouth, Moray	138	C1
Lostock Gralam, Chesh	79	C4
Lostock Green, Chesh	79	C4
Lostwithiel, Corn	3	E4
Lothersdale, N York	87	A2
Loughborough, Leics	61	A1
Loughton, Shrops	58	A4
Lound, Lincs	62	B1
Lound, Notts	83	A3
Lound, Suff	66	B3
Lount, Leics	60	B1
Louth, Lincs	84	C3
Love Clough, Lancs	86	B4
Lover, Wilts	15	B2
Loversall, S York	82	C2
Loves Green, Essex	43	A3
Loveston, Pemb	33	E3
Lovington, Som	14	A1
Low Ackworth, W Yorks	82	B1
Low Bentham, N York	92	B4
Low Borrowbridge, Cumb	92	B1
Low Bradfield, S York	81	C3
Low Bradley, N York	87	A2
Low Burnham, Lincs	83	B2
Low Crosby, Cumb	104	C4
Low Dinsdale, Durham	100	B4
Low Eggborough, N York	89	A4
Low Ellington, N York	93	C3
Low Ham, Som	13	B1
Low Hesket, Cumb	98	B1
Low Hill, Worcs	48	C1
Low Hutton, N York	95	A4
Low Marnham, Notts	73	C1
Low Mill, N York	94	C2
Low Moorsley, Tyne	100	B1
Low Mowthorpe, N York	95	B4
Low Newton, Cumb	91	E3
Low Row, Cumb	104	E4
Low Row, N York	93	A2
Low Santon, Lincs	83	C1
Low Tharston, Norf	65	A3
Low Worsall, N York	94	A1
Low Wray, Cumb	91	E1
Lowdham, Notts	73	B3
Lower Aisholt, Som	12	D1
Lower Ansty, Dorset	14	B4
Lower Apperley, Glouc	38	A1
Lower Assendon, Oxon	28	A1
Lower Beeding, W Suss	18	C2
Lower Benefield, Nhants	62	B4
Lower Bentley, Worcs	49	A2
Lower Boddington, Nhants	50	B3
Lower Brailes, Warwk	50	A4
Lower Broadheath, Worcs	48	C2
Lower Caldecote, Beds	52	B3
Lower Chapel, Powys	46	E4
Lower Chicksgrove, Wilts	14	D1
Lower Chute, Wilts	26	D3
Lower Clapton, G Lon	149	A1
Lower Cumberworth, W Yorks	81	C1
Lower Dean, Beds	52	A1
Lower Diabaig, High	135	F2
Lower Down, Shrops	57	B4
Lower Dunsforth, N York	94	A4
Lower End, Bucks	51	C4
Lower Eythorne, Kent	32	C4
Lower Failand, Som	24	B2
Lower Feltham, G Lon	146	B2
Lower Froyle, Hants	28	A4
Lower Gabwell, Devon	6	A3
Lower Gravenhurst, Beds	52	B4
Lower Hergest, Heref	47	B3
Lower Kingswood, Surrey	150	A2
Lower Langford, Som	24	A3
Lower Largo, Fife	124	B4
Lower Lydbrook, Glouc	37	B2
Lower Lye, Heref	47	C2
Lower Machen, Newport	36	A4
Lower Merridge, Som	12	D1
Lower Moor, Worcs	49	A3
Lower Morton, Glouc	37	B4
Lower Nazeing, Essex	42	B3
Lower Penn, Staffs	58	C3
Lower Peover, Chesh	80	A4
Lower Pond Street, Essex	53	B4
Lower Quinton, Warwk	49	C3
Lower Roadwater, Som	12	C1
Lower Seagry, Wilts	26	A1
Lower Shelton, Beds	52	A4
Lower Shiplake, Oxon	28	A1
Lower Shuckburgh, Warwk	50	B2
Lower Slaughter, Glouc	39	A1
Lower Stanton St Quintin, Wilts	25	B1
Lower Stoke, Kent	31	B1
Lower Stone, Glouc	37	B4
Lower Stow Bedon, Norf	64	C3
Lower Street, Dorset	14	C4
Lower Street, Norf	76	D4
Lower Street, Suff	54	D3
Lower Sundon, Beds	41	B1
Lower Swanwick, Hants	16	A3
Lower Swell, Glouc	39	A1
Lower Town, Devon	5	B2
Lower Tysoe, Warwk	50	A3
Lower Upcott, Devon	5	C2
Lower Upham, Hants	16	B2
Lower Vexford, Som	12	C1
Lower Weare, Som	24	A3
Lower Westmancote, Worcs	49	A4
Lower Whitley, Chesh	79	C4
Lower Wield, Hants	17	A1
Lower Withington, Chesh	70	C1
Lower Woodford, Wilts	15	A1
Lowesby, Leics	61	B2
Lowestoft, Suff	66	B3
Loweswater, Cumb	97	E4
Lowick Green, Cumb	91	D3
Lowick, Nhants	62	B4
Lowick, Nthumb	112	A1
Lowsonford, Warwk	49	C2
Lowther, Cumb	98	C3
Lowthorpe, E R of Y	90	B1
Lowton, Som	12	D2
Loxbeare, Devon	12	B3
Loxhill, Surrey	18	A1
Loxhore Cott, Devon	11	E1
Loxhore, Devon	11	E1
Loxley, Warwk	49	C3
Loxton, Som	24	A3
Loxwood, W Suss	18	A1
Luccombe Village, I of W	10	A2
Luccombe, Som	22	E4
Lucker, Nthumb	112	B2
Luckett, Corn	4	B2
Luckington, Wilts	25	B1
Luckwell Bridge, Som	12	B1
Lucton, Heref	47	C2
Ludborough, Lincs	84	B2
Ludbrook, Devon	5	B4
Ludchurch, Pemb	33	E2
Luddenden Foot, W Yorks	87	A4
Luddenden, W Yorks	87	A4
Luddesdown, Kent	31	A2
Luddington, Lincs	83	B1
Luddington, Warwk	49	C3
Ludford, Lincs	84	B3
Ludford, Shrops	47	D1
Ludgershall, Bucks	40	B2
Ludgershall, Wilts	26	C4
Ludgvan, Corn	1	C2
Ludham, Norf	66	A1
Ludlow, Shrops	47	D1
Ludney, Som	13	B3
Ludwell, Wilts	14	C2
Ludworth, Durham	100	B2
Luffincott, Devon	4	B1
Lugar, E Ayrs	109	A3
Lugton, E Ayrs	115	A4
Lugwardine, Heref	47	D4
Lulham, Heref	47	C4
Lullington, Derby	60	A2
Lullington, Som	25	A4
Lulsgate Bottom, Som	24	B2
Lulsley, Worcs	48	B3
Lumb, Lancs	86	C4
Lumb, W Yorks	87	A4
Lumby, N York	88	B3
Lumphanan, Aber	134	A3
Lumphinnans, Fife	117	B1
Lumsden, Aber	133	E2
Lunan, Angus	129	C4
Lunanhead, Angus	129	B4
Luncarty, Perth	123	C2
Lund, E R of Y	90	B2
Lund, N York	89	B3
Lundie, Angus	124	A1
Lunsford's Cross, E Suss	20	A3
Lunt, Mers	78	D2
Luppitt, Devon	12	D3
Lupridge, Devon	5	B4
Lupton, Cumb	92	A3
Lurgashall, W Suss	17	C2
Lurley, Devon	12	B3
Luscombe, Devon	5	C4
Luss, Argyll	115	A1
Lusta, High	135	A3
Lustleigh, Devon	5	C2
Luston, Heref	47	D2
Luthermuir, Aber	129	C2
Luthrie, Fife	124	A2
Luton, Beds	41	C2
Luton, Devon	6	A2
Luton, Devon	12	C4
Lutterworth, Leics	61	A4
Lutton, Devon	5	A4
Lutton, Devon	5	B3
Lutton, Lincs	63	C1
Lutton, Nhants	62	C4
Luxborough, Som	12	B1
Luxulyan, Corn	3	D4
Lybster, High	143	E4
Lydbury North, Shrops	57	C4
Lydd, Kent	21	B2
Lydden, Kent	32	C4
Lydden, Kent	32	C2
Lyddington, Rutland	62	A3
Lyde Green, Hants	27	C3
Lydeard St Lawrence, Som	12	D1
Lydford on Fosse, Som	13	C1
Lydford, Devon	4	C1
Lydgate, W Yorks	86	C4
Lydham, Shrops	57	B4
Lydiard Millicent, Wilts	26	B1
Lydiate Ash, Worcs	49	A1
Lydney, Glouc	37	B3
Lydstep, Pemb	33	E4
Lye Green, Warwk	49	C2
Lye's Green, Wilts	25	B4
Lyford, Oxon	39	C4
Lyme Regis, Dorset	7	A1
Lyminge, Kent	21	C1
Lymm, Chesh	79	C3
Lympne, Kent	21	B1
Lympsham, Som	23	C3
Lympstone, Devon	6	A1
Lynch Green, Norf	65	A2
Lyndhurst, Hants	15	C3
Lyndon, Rutland	62	A2
Lyne of Skene, Aber	134	B3
Lyne, Surrey	146	A2
Lyneal, Shrops	69	C4
Lyneham, Oxon	39	B2
Lyneham, Wilts	26	A1
Lyness, Orkney	144	A2
Lyng, Norf	64	D1
Lyng, Som	13	A2
Lynsted, Kent	31	C3
Lynton, Devon	22	C4
Lyon's Gate, Dorset	14	A4
Lyonshall, Heref	47	B3
Lytchett Matravers, Dorset	14	D4
Lytchett Minster, Dorset	8	C1
Lytham St Anne's, Lancs	85	A4
Lythe, N York	101	C4
Mablethorpe, Lincs	84	D3
Macclesfield, Chesh	80	B4
Macduff, Aber	139	C2
Machen, Caer	36	A4
Machrihanish, Argyll	107	D3
Machynlleth, Powys	56	B3
Mackworth, Derby	72	A4
Macmerry, E Loth	118	B3
Maddiston, Falk	116	C2
Madeley, Staffs	70	B3
Madingley, Cambs	53	A2
Madley, Heref	47	C4
Madresfield, Worcs	48	B3
Madron, Corn	1	B2
Maenclochog, Pemb	33	E1
Maendy, Glam	23	A1
Maentwrog, Gwyn	68	A3
Maen-y-groes, Cered	45	E2
Maer, Staffs	70	B3
Maerdy, Rhond	35	C4
Maesbrook, Shrops	57	B1
Maesbury Marsh, Shrops	57	B1
Maesllyn, Cered	45	E4
Maesmynis, Powys	46	E3
Maesteg, Bridg	35	B4
Maesybont, Carm	34	D2
Maesycwmmer, Caer	36	A4
Maggieknockater, Moray	138	C3
Maggots End, Essex	42	C1
Maghull, Mers	79	A2
Maiden Bradley, Wilts	14	B1
Maiden Head, Som	24	B2
Maiden Newton, Dorset	14	A4
Maiden Wells, Pemb	33	D3
Maidencombe, Devon	6	A3
Maidenhayne, Devon	13	A4
Maidenhead, Berks	28	B1
Maidens, S Ayrs	108	C4
Maidenwell, Lincs	84	C4
Maidford, Nhants	50	C3
Maidstone, Kent	31	A3
Maidwell, Nhants	51	B1
Mainsforth, Durham	100	B3
Mainsriddle, Dumf	97	C1
Mainstone, Shrops	57	B4
Maisemore, Glouc	38	A2
Makeney, Derby	72	A3
Malborough, Devon	10	A1
Malden Rushett, G Lon	146	B3
Malden, G Lon	147	A4
Maldon, Essex	43	C3
Malham, N York	86	C1
Mallaig, High	130	E4
Malltraeth, Angle	67	C1
Mallwyd, Gwyn	56	C2
Malmesbury, Wilts	26	A1
Malmsmead, Devon	22	D4
Malpas, Chesh	69	D3
Malpas, Corn	2	A1
Maltby le Marsh, Lincs	84	D4
Maltby, N York	100	C4
Maltby, S York	82	C3
Malting Green, Essex	44	A2
Maltman's Hill, Kent	31	C4
Malton, N York	95	A4
Malvern Wells, Worcs	48	B4
Mamble, Worcs	48	A1
Mamhilad, Monm	36	B3
Manaccan, Corn	2	A3
Manafon, Powys	56	E3
Manaton, Devon	5	B2
Manby, Lincs	84	C3
Mancetter, Warwk	60	B3
Manchester, G Man	80	B2
Mancot, Flint	69	B1
Manea, Cambs	63	C4
Manfield, N York	100	A4
Manley, Chesh	69	D1
Manmoel, Caer	36	A3
Manningford Bruce, Wilts	26	B3
Manningtree, Essex	44	B1
Manor Park, G Lon	149	B1
Manorbier Newton, Pemb	33	D3
Manorbier, Pemb	33	D4
Manorowen, Pemb	45	A4
Mansell Gamage, Heref	47	C4
Mansell Lacy, Heref	47	C3
Mansfield, Notts	73	A1
Manston, Dorset	14	C3
Manswood, Dorset	14	D3
Manthorpe, Lincs	62	B1
Manton, Lincs	83	C2
Manton, Rutland	62	A2
Manuden, Essex	42	C1
Maperton, Som	14	A2
Maplebeck, Notts	73	B1
Mapledurham, Oxon	27	C1
Mapledurwell, Hants	27	C4
Maplehurst, W Suss	18	B2
Maplescombe, Kent	30	B3
Mapleton, Derby	71	C3
Mapperley, Derby	72	B3
Mapperton, Dorset	13	C4
Mappleton, E R of Y	90	D2
Mapplewell, S York	82	A1

PLACE	PAGE	GRID
Mappowder, Dorset	14	B4
Marazanvose, Corn	3	B4
Marazion, Corn	1	C2
Marbury, Chesh	69	D3
March, Cambs	63	B3
Marcham, Oxon	39	C4
Marchamley, Shrops	70	A4
Marchington, Staffs	71	B4
Marchwiel, Wrex	69	C3
Marchwood, Hants	15	C3
Marcross, Glam	22	E2
Marden Thorn, Kent	31	A4
Marden, Heref	47	D3
Marden, Kent	31	A4
Marden, Wilts	26	B3
Mareham le Fen, Lincs	74	D1
Mareham on the Hill, Lincs	74	D1
Marehill, W Suss	18	A2
Maresfield, E Suss	19	B2
Marford, Wrex	69	C2
Margaret Marsh, Dorset	14	C2
Margaretting Tye, Essex	43	B3
Margaretting, Essex	43	B3
Margate, Kent	32	D2
Margnaheglish, N Ayrs	108	A2
Margrove Park, N York	101	B4
Marham, Norf	64	A2
Marhamchurch, Corn	11	B4
Marholm, Cambs	62	C3
Mariansleigh, Devon	11	F2
Maristow, Devon	4	C3
Mark Cross, E Suss	19	B3
Mark Cross, E Suss	19	C1
Mark, Dumf	102	B4
Mark, Som	24	A4
Markbeech, Kent	30	A4
Markby, Lincs	84	D4
Market Bosworth, Leics	60	C2
Market Deeping, Lincs	62	C2
Market Drayton, Shrops	70	A4
Market Harborough, Leics	61	B4
Market Lavington, Wilts	26	A3
Market Overton, Rutland	62	A1
Market Rasen, Lincs	84	A3
Market Stainton, Lincs	84	B4
Market Weighton, E R of Y	90	A2
Market Weston, Suff	54	C1
Markfield, Leics	60	C2
Markham Moor, Notts	83	A4
Markham, Caer	36	A3
Markington, N York	93	D4
Marks Tey, Essex	44	A1
Marksbury, Som	24	C3
Markyate, Herts	41	B2
Marlborough, Wilts	26	C2
Marlcliff, Warwk	49	B3
Marldon, Devon	5	C3
Marlesford, Suff	55	B2
Marlingford, Norf	65	A2
Marloes, Pemb	33	B3
Marlow, Bucks	28	A1
Marlpit Hill, Kent	30	A4
Marnhull, Dorset	14	B2
Marple, G Man	81	A3
Marr, S York	82	C2
Marrick, N York	92	B2
Marsden, W Yorks	81	B1
Marsh Baldon, Oxon	40	A3
Marsh Chapel, Lincs	84	C2
Marsh Gibbon, Bucks	40	B1
Marsh Green, Kent	30	A4
Marsh Lane, Derby	82	B4
Marsh Street, Som	22	E4
Marsham, Norf	65	A1
Marshbrook, Shrops	57	C4
Marshfield, Glouc	25	A2
Marshfield, Newport	23	C1
Marshland St James, Norf	63	C2
Marshwood, Dorset	13	B4
Marske, N York	93	B1
Marske-by-the-Sea, N York	101	B4
Marston Magna, Som	14	A2
Marston Meysey, Wilts	38	C4
Marston Moretaine, Beds	52	A4
Marston on Dove, Derby	71	C4
Marston St Lawrence, Nhants	50	C4
Marston Stannett, Heref	47	D3
Marston Trussell, Nhants	61	B4
Marston, Heref	47	C2
Marston, Lincs	74	A3
Marston, Staffs	70	C4
Marston, Wilts	26	A3
Marstow, Heref	37	A2
Marten, Wilts	26	D3
Marthall, Chesh	80	A4
Martham, Norf	66	A1
Martin, Hants	15	A2
Martin, Kent	32	C4
Martin, Lincs	74	C2
Martin, Lincs	74	D1
Martinhoe, Devon	22	C4
Martinstown, Dorset	7	D1
Martlesham, Suff	55	B3
Martletwy, Pemb	33	D2
Martley, Worcs	48	B2
Martock, Som	13	B2
Marton, Chesh	70	C1
Marton, E R of Y	90	C3
Marton, Lincs	83	B4
Marton, N York	88	B1
Marton, N York	94	C3
Marton, N York	101	A4
Marton, Shrops	57	B3
Marton, Warwk	50	B1
Marwood, Devon	11	E1
Mary Tavy, Devon	4	C2
Maryburgh, High	136	F3
Maryculter, Aber	134	C4
Marykirk, Aber	129	C2
Marylebone, G Lon	148	A2
Maryport, Cumb	97	D2
Maryport, Dumf	96	B2
Marystow, Devon	4	C2
Marywell, Aber	134	A4
Marywell, Angus	129	C4
Masham, N York	93	C3
Mastin Moor, Derby	82	B4
Matching Tye, Essex	42	C2
Matfen, Nthumb	105	C3
Mathern, Monm	37	A4
Mathon, Heref	48	B3
Mathry, Pemb	33	C1
Matlask, Norf	76	C4
Matlock, Derby	72	A2
Mattersey, Notts	83	A3
Mattishall Burgh, Norf	64	D2
Mattishall, Norf	64	D2
Mauchline, E Ayrs	108	E2
Maud, Aber	139	D3
Maufant, Jersey	145	B2
Maugersbury, Glouc	39	A1
Maughold, I of M	145	D2
Maulden, Beds	52	A4
Maulds Meaburn, Cumb	98	D4
Maunby, N York	93	D3
Maundown, Som	12	C2
Mautby, Norf	66	B2
Mavesyn Ridware, Staffs	59	B1
Mavis Enderby, Lincs	75	A1
Mawbray, Cumb	97	D1
Mawdesley, Lancs	79	B1
Mawdlam, Bridg	22	D1
Mawgan Porth, Corn	3	C3
Mawgan, Corn	1	D3
Mawla, Corn	1	D1
Mawnan Smith, Corn	2	A2
Mawnan, Corn	2	A2
Maxey, Cambs	62	C2
Maxstoke, Warwk	60	A4
Maxworthy, Corn	4	A1
Maybole, S Ayrs	108	C4
Maybury, Surrey	146	A3
Mayfield, E Suss	19	C2
Mayfield, M Loth	118	B3
Mayfield, Staffs	71	B3
Mayford, Surrey	146	A3
Maypole Green, Norf	66	A3
Maypole Green, Suff	54	C2
May's Green, Surrey	146	B3
Meadgate, Som	24	C3
Meadle, Bucks	40	C3
Meadwell, Devon	4	B2
Mealrigg, Cumb	97	E1
Meare, Som	24	A4
Mearns, East Renf	115	C4
Mears Ashby, Nhants	51	B2
Measham, Leics	60	B2
Meathop, Cumb	91	E3
Meavy, Devon	4	C3
Medbourne, Leics	61	C3
Meden Vale, Notts	73	A1
Medmenham, Bucks	28	A1
Medomsley, Durham	99	D1
Meerbrook, Staffs	71	A2
Meesden, Herts	42	C1
Meeth, Devon	11	E3
Meeting House Hill, Norf	76	D4
Meidrim, Carm	34	A2
Meifod, Powys	57	A2
Meigle, Perth	128	E4
Meikleour, Perth	123	D1
Meinciau, Carm	34	C2
Melbourn, Cambs	53	A4
Melbourne, Derby	60	B1
Melbourne, E R of Y	89	C2
Melbury Abbas, Dorset	14	C2
Melbury Bubb, Dorset	14	A4
Melbury Osmond, Dorset	13	C3
Melchbourne, Beds	52	A2
Melcombe Bingham, Dorset	14	B4
Meldon, Devon	5	A1
Meldon, Nthumb	105	D2
Meldreth, Cambs	53	A3
Melin-y-wig, Denb	68	D3
Melkinthorpe, Cumb	98	C3
Melkridge, Nthumb	105	A4
Melksham, Wilts	25	B3
Melling, Lancs	92	B4
Melling, Mers	79	A2
Mellis, Suff	54	D1
Mellor Brook, Lancs	86	A3
Mellor, G Man	81	A3
Mellor, Lancs	86	A3
Mells, Som	25	A4
Melmerby, Cumb	98	D2
Melmerby, N York	93	B3
Melmerby, N York	93	D3
Melness, High	142	E1
Melplash, Dorset	13	C4
Melrose, Border	110	D2
Melsetter, Orkney	144	A2
Melsonby, N York	93	C1
Meltham, W Yorks	81	B1
Melton Constable, Norf	76	B4
Melton Mowbray, Leics	61	C1
Melton Ross, Lincs	83	D1
Melton, E R of Y	90	B4
Melton, Suff	55	B3
Melvaig, High	140	A4
Melverley, Shrops	57	B1
Melvich, High	143	A1
Membury, Devon	13	A4
Memsie, Aber	139	E2
Memus, Angus	129	A3
Menai Bridge, Angle	67	E1
Mendham, Suff	65	B4
Mendlesham Green, Suff	54	D2
Mendlesham, Suff	54	D2
Menheniot, Corn	4	A3
Mennock, Dumf	109	C4
Menston, W Yorks	87	C2
Menstrie, Clack	123	A4
Mentmore, Bucks	41	A2
Meonstoke, Hants	16	B2
Meopham, Kent	30	B2
Mepal, Cambs	63	C4
Meppershall, Beds	52	B4
Mere Brow, Lancs	85	B4
Mere, Chesh	80	A4
Mere, Wilts	14	C1
Mereclough, Lancs	86	C3
Mereworth, Kent	30	B3
Meriden, W Mids	60	A4
Merrion, Pemb	33	C4
Merriott, Som	13	B3
Merrow, Surrey	146	A4
Merrymeet, Corn	4	A3
Merstham, Surrey	150	B2
Merther, Corn	2	B1
Merthyr Cynog, Powys	46	D4
Merthyr Mawr, Bridg	22	D1
Merthyr Tydfil, Merth	35	D3
Merthyr Vale, Merth	35	D3
Merton, Devon	11	D3
Merton, G Lon	147	A2
Merton, Norf	64	C3
Meshaw, Devon	11	F2
Messing, Essex	44	A2
Messingham, Lincs	83	C2
Metfield, Suff	65	B4
Metherell, Corn	4	B3
Metheringham, Lincs	74	B1
Methil, Fife	124	B4
Methley, W Yorks	88	B4
Methlick, Aber	139	D4
Methven, Perth	123	C2
Methwold, Norf	64	A3
Mettingham, Suff	66	A4
Metton, Norf	76	C4
Mevagissey, Corn	2	C1
Mexborough, S York	82	B2
Mey, High	143	E1
Meylteyrn, Gwyn	67	B4
Meysey Hampton, Glouc	38	C3
Miavaig, W Isle	144	A2
Michaelchurch Escley, Heref	47	B4
Michaelchurch, Heref	37	A1
Michaelstone-y-Fedw, Newport	23	C1
Michaelston-le-Pit, Glam	23	B2
Michaelstow, Corn	3	E2
Micheldever Station, Hants	27	B4
Micheldever, Hants	16	B1
Mickfield, Suff	55	A2
Mickle Trafford, Chesh	69	C1
Micklebring, S York	82	C3
Mickleby, N York	101	C4
Micklefield, W Yorks	88	B3
Mickleham, Surrey	146	B3
Mickleton, Durham	99	C3
Mickleton, Glouc	49	C4
Mickletown, W Yorks	88	B4
Mickley Square, Nthumb	105	D4
Mickley, N York	93	C3
Mid Calder, W Loth	117	A3
Mid Lavant, W Suss	17	C3
Mid Yell, Shet	144	A2
Midbea, Orkney	144	A1
Middle Aston, Oxon	39	C1
Middle Barton, Oxon	39	C1
Middle Claydon, Bucks	40	B1
Middle Duntisbourne, Glouc	38	B3
Middle Handley, Derby	82	B4
Middle Kames, Argyll	114	A1
Middle Mayfield, Staffs	71	B3
Middle Rasen, Lincs	84	A3
Middle Stoke, Kent	31	B2
Middle Town, Isles of Scilly	144	A2
Middle Tysoe, Warwk	50	A4
Middle Wallop, Hants	15	C1
Middle Winterslow, Wilts	15	B1
Middlebie, Dumf	104	A3
Middlebridge, Perth	128	A2
Middleham, N York	93	B3
Middlehill, Wilts	25	B2
Middlehope, Shrops	57	D4
Middlemarsh, Dorset	14	A3
Middlesbrough, N York	100	C4
Middleshaw, Cumb	92	A2
Middlesmoor, N York	93	B4
Middlestone, Durham	100	A3
Middlestown, W Yorks	81	C1
Middleton Cheney, Nhants	50	B4
Middleton on the Hill, Heref	47	D2
Middleton on the Wolds, E R of Y	90	A2
Middleton Scriven, Shrops	58	A4
Middleton St George, Durham	100	B4
Middleton Stoney, Oxon	40	A1
Middleton Tyas, N York	93	C1
Middleton, Derby	71	C1
Middleton, Derby	72	A2
Middleton, Essex	54	B4
Middleton, G Man	80	B2
Middleton, Hants	27	A4
Middleton, Heref	47	D1
Middleton, N York	87	B2
Middleton, N York	95	A3
Middleton, Nhants	61	C4
Middleton, Norf	64	A1
Middleton, Nthumb	105	D2
Middleton, Shrops	47	D1
Middleton, Suff	55	C2
Middleton, Swan	34	B4
Middleton, Warwk	60	A3
Middleton-in-Teesdale, Durham	99	C3
Middleton-on-Sea, W Suss	17	C4
Middletown, Powys	57	B2
Middlewich, Chesh	70	B1
Middlewood, Corn	4	A2
Middlewood, Heref	47	B4
Middlezoy, Som	13	B1
Midford, Wilts	25	A3
Midgham, Berks	27	B2
Midgley, W Yorks	81	C1
Midgley, W Yorks	87	A4
Midhopestones, S York	81	C2
Midhurst, W Suss	17	C2
Midlem, Border	110	D2
Midsomer Norton, Som	24	C3
Milborne Port, Som	14	A2
Milborne St Andrew, Dorset	14	B4
Milborne Wick, Som	14	A2
Milbourne, Nthumb	105	D3
Milbourne, Wilts	38	B4
Milburn, Cumb	98	D3
Milbury Heath, Glouc	37	B4
Milby, N York	94	A4
Milcombe, Oxon	50	B4
Milden, Suff	54	C3
Mildenhall, Suff	54	A1
Mildenhall, Wilts	26	C2
Mileham, Norf	64	C1
Milesmark, Fife	117	A1
Milfield, Nthumb	112	A2
Milford Haven, Pemb	33	C3
Milford on Sea, Hants	9	B1
Milford, Derby	72	A3
Milford, Staffs	59	A1
Milford, Surrey	28	B4
Milkwall, Glouc	37	B3
Mill Brow, G Man	81	A3
Mill End, Bucks	28	A1
Mill End, Herts	42	B1
Mill Green, Cambs	53	C3
Mill Green, Essex	43	A3
Mill Green, Lincs	63	A1
Mill Green, Suff	54	C4
Mill Green, Suff	55	A2
Mill Meece, Staffs	70	C4
Mill Street, Suff	54	D1
Milland, W Suss	17	B2
Millbrex, Aber	139	D4
Millbridge, Surrey	28	A4
Millbrook, Beds	52	A4
Millbrook, Corn	4	C4
Millbrook, Jersey	145	B2
Millcorner, E Suss	20	B2
Milldale, Staffs	71	B2
Millerhill, M Loth	118	A3
Miller's Dale, Derby	81	B4
Millhalf, Heref	47	B3
Millhouse Green, S York	81	C2
Millhouse, Argyll	114	A3
Millington, E R of Y	89	C2
Millom, Cumb	91	C3
Millport, N Ayrs	114	C4
Millthrop, Cumb	92	B2
Milltown, Devon	11	E1
Milltown, Dumf	104	A3
Milnathort, Perth	123	D4
Milngavie, Dumb	115	C2
Milnrow, G Man	80	B1
Milnthorpe, Cumb	92	A3
Milson, Shrops	48	A1
Milstead, Kent	31	C3
Milston, Wilts	26	C4
Milton Abbas, Dorset	14	B4
Milton Abbot, Devon	4	B2
Milton Bryan, Beds	41	B1
Milton Clevedon, Som	14	A1
Milton Combe, Devon	4	C3
Milton Damerel, Devon	11	C3
Milton Ernest, Beds	52	A3
Milton Green, Chesh	69	C2
Milton Hill, Oxon	39	C4
Milton Keynes, Bucks	51	C4
Milton of Balgonie, Fife	124	A4
Milton of Campsie, E Dun	115	C2
Milton on Stour, Dorset	14	B2
Milton, Cambs	53	B2
Milton, Cumb	104	D4
Milton, Derby	72	A4
Milton, Dumb	115	B2
Milton, Dumf	96	C1
Milton, Dumf	103	C3
Milton, High	137	B1
Milton, Notts	83	A4
Milton, Oxon	39	C4
Milton, Pemb	33	D3
Milton, Som	13	C2
Milton-under-Wychwood, Oxon	39	A2
Milverton, Som	12	D2
Milwich, Staffs	71	A4
Minchinhampton, Glouc	38	A3
Minehead, Som	22	E4
Minera, Wrex	69	B2
Minety, Wilts	38	B4
Minffordd, Gwyn	67	E3
Miningsby, Lincs	75	A1
Minions, Corn	4	A3
Minllyn, Gwyn	56	C2
Minnigaff, Dumf	102	D4
Minskip, N York	93	D4
Minstead, Hants	15	C3
Minsted, W Suss	17	C2
Minster Lovell, Oxon	39	B2
Minster, Kent	31	C2
Minster, Kent	32	C2
Minsterley, Shrops	57	C2
Minsterworth, Glouc	37	C2
Minterne Magna, Dorset	14	A4
Minting, Lincs	84	A4
Mintlaw, Aber	139	E3
Minto, Border	110	D3
Minton, Shrops	57	C4
Mirfield, W Yorks	87	C4
Miserden, Glouc	38	B3
Miskin, Rhond	23	A1
Misson, Notts	83	A3
Misterton, Leics	61	A4
Misterton, Notts	83	B3
Misterton, Som	13	B3
Mistley, Essex	44	B1
Mitcham, G Lon	147	A3
Mitchel Troy, Monm	37	A3
Mitcheldean, Glouc	37	B2
Mitchell, Corn	3	C4
Mitford, Nthumb	106	A2
Mithian, Corn	3	B4
Mixbury, Oxon	50	C4
Mobberley, Chesh	80	A4
Mobberley, Staffs	71	A3
Moccas, Heref	47	C4
Mochdre, Powys	56	E4
Mochrum, Dumf	96	D1
Mockbeggar, Kent	31	A4
Mockerkin, Cumb	97	D3
Modbury, Devon	5	B4
Moddershall, Staffs	70	C4
Moelfre, Angle	77	C3
Moelfre, Powys	69	A4
Moffat, Dumf	109	E4
Mogerhanger, Beds	52	B3
Moira, Leics	60	B1
Molash, Kent	32	A4
Mold, Flint	69	B1
Molehill Green, Essex	43	A1
Molland, Devon	12	A2
Mollington, Chesh	69	C1
Mollington, Oxon	50	B3
Monewden, Suff	55	B2
Moneyrow Green, Berks	28	B1
Moniaive, Dumf	103	C2
Monikie, Angus	124	C1
Monimail, Fife	124	A3
Monk Fryston, N York	89	A4
Monk Sherborne, Hants	27	B3
Monk Soham, Suff	55	A2
Monkhide, Heref	48	A4
Monkhill, Cumb	104	B4
Monkhopton, Shrops	58	A3
Monkland, Heref	47	C2
Monkleigh, Devon	11	D2
Monknash, Glam	22	E2
Monkokehampton, Devon	11	E4
Monks Eleigh, Suff	54	C3
Monks Heath, Chesh	80	B4
Monks Horton, Kent	21	B1
Monks Kirby, Warwk	60	C4
Monksilver, Som	12	C1
Monksthorpe, Lincs	75	B1
Monkswood, Monm	36	B3
Monkton Deverill, Wilts	14	C1
Monkton Farleigh, Wilts	25	A2
Monkton Wyld, Dorset	13	A4
Monkton, Kent	32	C2
Monkton, S Ayrs	108	D2
Monkwood, Hants	17	A1
Monmouth, Monm	37	A2
Monnington on Wye, Heref	47	C4
Monreith, Dumf	96	D2
Mont Saint, Guern	145	B2
Montacute, Som	13	C3
Montford, Shrops	57	C1
Montgarrie, Aber	133	E2
Montgarswood, E Ayrs	108	E2
Montgomery, Powys	57	A3
Montrose, Angus	129	D3
Monxton, Hants	26	D4
Monyash, Derby	71	B1
Monymusk, Aber	134	A2
Monzie, Perth	123	A2
Moodiesburn, N Lan	116	A3
Moor Monkton, N York	89	A1
Moorby, Lincs	74	D1
Moore, Chesh	79	B3
Moorends, S York	83	A1
Moorgreen, Notts	72	B3
Moorhouse, Cumb	98	A1
Moorhouse, Notts	73	C1
Moorlinch, Som	13	B1
Moorsholm, N York	101	B4
Moorside, Dorset	14	B2
Moorswater, Corn	4	A3
Moortown, Lincs	83	D2
Morborne, Cambs	62	C4
Morchard Bishop, Devon	11	F3
Morcombelake, Dorset	7	B1
Morcott, Rutland	62	A3
Morden, Dorset	14	C4
Morden, G Lon	147	A4
Mordiford, Heref	47	D4
Mordon, Durham	100	B3
More, Shrops	57	B3
Morebath, Devon	12	B2
Morebattle, Border	111	B3
Morecambe, Lancs	85	B1
Moreleigh, Devon	5	B4
Moresby, Cumb	97	C4
Morestead, Hants	16	B2
Moreton Corbet, Shrops	57	D1
Moreton Jeffries, Heref	48	A3
Moreton Morrell, Warwk	50	A3
Moreton Pinkney, Nhants	50	C3
Moreton Say, Shrops	70	A4
Moreton Valence, Glouc	37	C3
Moreton, Dorset	8	A1
Moreton, Essex	42	C3
Moreton, Heref	47	D2
Moreton, Oxon	40	B3
Moretonhampstead, Devon	5	B1
Moreton-in-Marsh, Glouc	39	A1
Morland, Cumb	98	D3
Morley Green, Chesh	80	B4
Morley St Botolph, Norf	64	D3
Morley, Chesh	80	B4
Morley, Derby	72	B3
Morley, W Yorks	87	C4
Morningside, N Lan	116	B4
Morpeth, Nthumb	106	A2
Morrey, Staffs	59	B1
Morston, Norf	76	B3
Mortehoe, Devon	22	A4
Morthen, S York	82	B3
Mortimer West End, Hants	27	C3
Mortimer, Berks	27	C2
Mortlake, G Lon	147	A2
Morton, Derby	72	B2
Morton, Shrops	57	B1
Morton-on-Swale, N York	93	D2
Morvah, Corn	1	B2
Morville, Shrops	58	A3
Morwenstow, Corn	11	B3
Mosborough, S York	82	B4
Moseley, Worcs	48	C2
Moss Edge, Lancs	85	B2
Moss Side, Mers	78	D1
Moss, S York	82	C1
Mossat, Aber	133	E2
Mossblown, S Ayrs	108	D3
Mossley, G Man	81	A2
Moss-side, High	137	C3
Mosstodloch, Moray	138	C2
Mossy Lea, Lancs	79	B1
Mosterton, Dorset	13	B4
Mostyn, Flint	78	C4
Motcombe, Dorset	14	C2
Mothecombe, Devon	10	B1
Motherby, Cumb	98	B3
Motherwell, N Lan	116	A4
Motspur Park, G Lon	147	A4
Mottingham, G Lon	149	B3
Mottisfont, Hants	15	C2
Mottistone, I of W	9	C1
Mottram in Longdendale, G Man	81	A2
Mottram St Andrew, Chesh	80	B4
Mouldsworth, Chesh	69	D1
Moulin, Perth	128	B3
Moulsford, Oxon	27	B1
Moulsoe, Bucks	51	C4
Moulton Chapel, Lincs	63	A1
Moulton Seas End, Lincs	75	A4
Moulton, Chesh	70	A1
Moulton, Glam	23	A2
Moulton, Lincs	63	A1
Moulton, N York	93	C1
Moulton, Nhants	51	B2
Moulton, Suff	54	A2
Mount Ambrose, Corn	1	D1
Mount Bures, Essex	44	A1
Mount Hawke, Corn	1	D1
Mount Lothian, M Loth	118	A4
Mount Pleasant, Derby	72	A3
Mount Pleasant, Suff	54	A3
Mount Tabor, W Yorks	87	B4
Mount, Corn	3	E3
Mountain Ash, Rhond	35	D3
Mountain, W Yorks	87	B3
Mountfield, E Suss	20	A2
Mountjoy, Corn	3	C4
Mountnessing, Essex	43	A4
Mounton, Monm	37	A4
Mountsorrel, Leics	61	A2
Mousehole, Corn	1	B2
Mouswald, Dumf	103	E3
Mowsley, Leics	61	B4
Moy, High	127	B1
Moy, High	137	B4
Moylgrove, Pemb	45	C4
Muasdale, Argyll	107	D1
Much Cowarne, Heref	48	A3
Much Dewchurch, Heref	37	A1
Much Hadham, Herts	42	B2
Much Hoole, Lancs	85	C4
Much Marcle, Heref	37	B1
Much Wenlock, Shrops	58	A3
Muchalls, Aber	134	C4
Muchelney Ham, Som	13	B2
Muchelney, Som	13	B2
Muchlarnick, Corn	4	A4
Mucklestone, Staffs	70	B4
Muckton, Lincs	84	C4
Muddiford, Devon	11	E1
Mudford Sock, Som	13	C2
Mudford, Som	13	C2
Mugeary, High	135	C4
Mugginton, Derby	72	A3
Muir of Fowlis, Aber	133	E2
Muir of Ord, High	136	F3
Muirdrum, Angus	124	C1
Muirhead, Angus	124	A1
Muirhead, Fife	124	A4
Muirhead, N Lan	116	A3
Muirhouses, Falk	117	A2
Muirkirk, E Ayrs	109	B2
Muirton, Perth	123	B3
Muker, N York	92	D2
Mulbarton, Norf	65	A3
Mullion Cove, Corn	1	D3
Mullion, Corn	1	D3
Mumby, Lincs	84	D4
Munderfield Row, Heref	48	A3
Mundesley, Norf	76	D4
Mundford, Norf	64	B3
Mundham, Norf	65	B3
Mundon Hill, Essex	43	C3
Mungrisdale, Cumb	98	B3
Munlochy, High	137	A3
Munsley, Heref	48	A4
Munslow, Shrops	57	D4
Murchington, Devon	5	B1
Murcott, Oxon	40	A2
Murrow, Cambs	63	B2
Mursley, Bucks	40	C1
Murthly, Perth	123	C1
Murton, Cumb	99	A4
Murton, Durham	100	B1
Murton, N York	89	B2
Murton, Nthumb	112	A1
Musbury, Devon	7	A1
Musselburgh, E Loth	118	A2
Muston, Leics	73	C3
Muston, N York	95	D3
Mustow Green, Worcs	48	C1
Mutehill, Dumf	97	A1
Mutford, Suff	66	B4
Muthill, Perth	123	A3
Mybster, High	143	D2
Myddfai, Carm	35	A1
Myddle, Shrops	57	D1
Mydroilyn, Cered	45	F3
Mylor Bridge, Corn	2	A2
Mylor, Corn	2	A2
Mynachlog ddu, Pemb	33	E1
Myndtown, Shrops	57	C4
Mynydd-bach, Monm	37	A4

PLACE	PAGE	GRID
Mytchett, Surrey	28	B3
Mytholmroyd, W Yorks	87	A4
Myton-on-Swale, N York	94	A4
Naburn, N York	89	A2
Nackington, Kent	32	B3
Nacton, Suff	55	A4
Nafferton, E R of Y	90	B1
Nailsbourne, Som	12	D2
Nailsea, Som	24	B2
Nailstone, Leics	60	C2
Nailsworth, Glouc	38	A3
Nairn, High	137	C3
Nalderswood, Surrey	150	A4
Nannerch, Flint	69	A1
Nanpantan, Leics	61	A1
Nanpean, Corn	3	C4
Nanstallon, Corn	3	D3
Nant Peris, Gwyn	67	E2
Nanternis, Cered	45	E2
Nantgaredig, Carm	34	C2
Nantglyn, Denb	68	D1
Nantmel, Powys	46	E2
Nantmor, Gwyn	67	E3
Nantwich, Chesh	70	A2
Nantyglo, Gwent	36	A3
Nant-y-moel, Bridg	35	C4
Naphill, Bucks	40	C4
Napleton, Worcs	48	C3
Napton on the Hill, Warwk	50	B2
Narberth, Pemb	33	E2
Narborough, Leics	61	A3
Narborough, Norf	64	A2
Nasareth, Gwyn	67	D2
Naseby, Nhants	51	A1
Nash, Bucks	51	B4
Nash, G Lon	150	D1
Nash, Newport	23	C1
Nash, Shrops	48	A1
Nash's Green, Hants	27	C4
Nassington, Nhants	62	B3
Nateby, Cumb	92	C1
Nateby, Lancs	85	B2
Natland, Cumb	92	A2
Naughton, Suff	54	D3
Naunton Beauchamp, Worcs	49	A3
Naunton, Glouc	38	C1
Naunton, Worcs	48	C4
Navenby, Lincs	74	B2
Navestock Side, Essex	43	A4
Navestock, Essex	42	C4
Nawton, N York	94	C3
Nayland, Suff	54	C4
Nazeing, Essex	42	B3
Near Cotton, Staffs	71	B3
Near Sawrey, Cumb	91	E2
Neasden, G Lon	147	A1
Neasham, Durham	93	D1
Neath, Neath	35	A4
Neatham, Hants	17	B1
Neatishead, Norf	65	B1
Nebo, Aberc	68	B2
Nebo, Angle	77	C3
Nebo, Cered	46	A2
Nebo, Gwyn	67	D2
Necton, Norf	64	B2
Nedd, High	142	A4
Nedging Tye, Suff	54	D3
Nedging, Suff	54	C3
Needham Market, Suff	54	D3
Needham, Norf	65	A4
Needingworth, Cambs	53	A1
Neen Savage, Shrops	48	A1
Neen Sollars, Shrops	48	A1
Neenton, Shrops	58	A4
Nefyn, Gwyn	67	B3
Neilston, East Renf	115	B4
Nelson, Caer	35	D4
Nelson, Lancs	86	C3
Nemphlar, S Lan	109	C1
Nempnett Thrubwell, Som	24	B3
Nenthead, Cumb	99	A2
Nenthorn, Border	111	A2
Nercwys, Flint	69	A1
Nesbit, Nthumb	112	A2
Nesfield, N York	87	B2
Neston, Chesh	78	D4
Neston, Wilts	25	B2
Netchwood, Shrops	58	A3
Nether Alderley, Chesh	80	B4
Nether Broughton, Leics	61	B1
Nether Cerne, Dorset	14	A4
Nether Compton, Dorset	14	A3
Nether Dallachy, Moray	138	D2
Nether Exe, Devon	12	B4
Nether Haugh, S York	82	B2
Nether Headon, Notts	83	B4
Nether Heage, Derby	72	A2
Nether Heyford, Nhants	51	A2
Nether Langwith, Notts	73	A1
Nether Moor, Derby	72	A1
Nether Padley, Derby	81	C4
Nether Poppleton, N York	89	A1
Nether Silton, N York	94	A2
Nether Stowey, Som	12	D1
Nether Wallop, Hants	15	C1
Nether Wasdale, Cumb	91	C1
Nether Whitacre, Warwk	60	A3
Nether Winchendon, Bucks	40	B2
Netheravon, Wilts	26	B4
Netherbury, Dorset	13	C4
Netherby, N York	88	A2
Netherend, Glouc	37	B3
Netherfield, E Suss	20	A2
Netherhampton, Wilts	15	A1
Netherhay, Dorset	13	B4
Netherseal, Derby	60	B2
Netherthong, W Yorks	81	B1
Netherton, Nthumb	112	A4
Netherton, Shrops	58	B4
Netherton, W Yorks	82	A1
Nethertown, Cumb	91	A1
Nethertown, Staffs	59	B1
Netherwitton, Nthumb	105	D2
Nethy Bridge, High	132	E2
Netley Marsh, Hants	15	C3
Netley, Hants	16	A3
Nettlebed, Oxon	27	C1
Nettlecombe, Dorset	13	C4
Nettleden, Herts	41	B3
Nettleham, Lincs	83	D4
Nettlestone, I of W	10	B1
Nettleton, Lincs	84	A2
Nettleton, Wilts	25	B1
Netton, Wilts	15	A1
Nevern, Pemb	45	C4
Nevill Holt, Leics	61	C3
New Abbey, Dumf	103	D4
New Aberdour, Aber	139	D2
New Addington, G Lon	150	D1
New Alresford, Hants	16	B1
New Alyth, Perth	128	E4
New Ash Green, Kent	30	B2
New Barn, Kent	30	B2
New Bewick, Nthumb	112	B3
New Bolingbroke, Lincs	74	D2
New Brancepeth, Durham	100	A2
New Buckenham, Norf	64	D4
New Crofton, W Yorks	82	A1
New Cross, G Lon	149	A2
New Cross, Som	13	B2
New Deer, Aber	139	D3
New Denham, Bucks	146	A1
New Edlington, S York	82	C2
New Ellerby, E R of Y	90	C3
New Eltham, G Lon	30	A2
New End, Worcs	49	B2
New Galloway, Dumf	103	A3
New Gilston, Fife	124	B3
New Grimsby, Isles of Scilly	144	A1
New Haw, Surrey	146	A3
New Holkham, Norf	75	E3
New Holland, Lincs	90	B4
New Houghton, Derby	72	B1
New Houghton, Norf	75	E4
New Hutton, Cumb	92	A2
New Inn, Carm	45	F4
New Lanark, S Lan	109	C1
New Leeds, Aber	139	E3
New Luce, Dumf	102	B4
New Malden, G Lon	147	A4
New Marske, N York	101	A4
New Mill, W Yorks	81	C1
New Mills, Corn	3	C4
New Mills, Derby	81	A3
New Mills, Powys	56	E3
New Milton, Hants	15	B4
New Mistley, Essex	44	C1
New Moat, Pemb	33	D1
New Pitsligo, Aber	139	D3
New Quay, Cered	45	E2
New Rackheath, Norf	65	B2
New Radnor, Powys	47	A2
New Romney, Kent	21	B2
New Scone, Perth	123	D2
New Sharlston, W Yorks	88	A4
New Stevenston, N Lan	116	A4
New Town, Dorset	14	C2
New Town, Dorset	14	D2
New Town, E Loth	118	B3
New Tredegar, Caer	36	A3
New Trows, S Lan	109	C1
New Waltham, Lincs	84	B2
New Wimpole, Cambs	53	A3
New Winton, E Loth	118	B3
New York, Lincs	74	D2
Newark, Orkney	144	B1
Newark-on-Trent, Notts	73	C2
Newarthill, N Lan	116	B4
Newbattle, M Loth	118	A3
Newbiggin, Cumb	98	C3
Newbiggin, Cumb	98	C1
Newbiggin, Cumb	98	D3
Newbiggin, Durham	99	B3
Newbiggin, N York	93	A3
Newbiggin-by-the-Sea, Nthumb	106	B2
Newbigging, Angus	124	C1
Newbigging, Angus	128	E4
Newbigging, S Lan	109	E1
Newbiggin-on-Lune, Cumb	92	C1
Newbold on Avon, Warwk	50	B1
Newbold on Stour, Warwk	49	C3
Newbold Pacey, Warwk	50	A2
Newbold Verdon, Leics	60	C2
Newborough, Angle	67	C1
Newborough, Cambs	63	A2
Newborough, Staffs	59	B1
Newbourne, Suff	55	B4
Newbridge Green, Worcs	48	C4
Newbridge on Wye, Powys	46	E2
Newbridge, Caer	36	A4
Newbridge, Corn	1	B2
Newbridge, Dumf	103	D3
Newbridge, Edin	117	B2
Newbridge, I of W	9	C1
Newbrough, Nthumb	105	B4
Newbuildings, Devon	12	A4
Newburgh Priory, N York	94	B3
Newburgh, Aber	134	D1
Newburgh, Fife	124	A3
Newburgh, Lancs	79	B1
Newbury, Berks	27	A2
Newbury, Som	25	A4
Newby Bridge, Cumb	91	E3
Newby East, Cumb	104	D4
Newby West, Cumb	98	B1
Newby Wiske, N York	93	D2
Newby, Cumb	98	D4
Newby, Lancs	86	C2
Newby, N York	92	C4
Newby, N York	101	A4
Newcastle Emlyn, Carm	45	D4
Newcastle upon Tyne, Tyne	106	A4
Newcastle, Monm	36	C2
Newcastle, Shrops	57	B4
Newcastleton, Border	104	D2
Newcastle-under-Lyme, Staffs	70	C3
Newchapel, Pemb	45	D4
Newchurch, Kent	21	B1
Newchurch, Monm	36	C4
Newchurch, Powys	47	A3
Newchurch, Staffs	59	B1
Newcraighall, Edin	118	A3
Newdigate, Surrey	146	B4
Newent, Glouc	37	C1
Newfield, Durham	100	A3
Newgale, Pemb	33	C1
Newgate Street, Herts	42	A3
Newhall, Chesh	70	A3
Newhaven, E Suss	19	B4
Newholm, N York	95	B1
Newick, E Suss	19	A2
Newington, Kent	21	C1
Newington, Kent	31	B2
Newington, Oxon	40	A4
Newland, Glouc	37	A3
Newland, N York	89	B4
Newland, Som	12	A1
Newland, Worcs	48	B3
Newlyn East, Corn	3	B4
Newlyn, Corn	1	B2
Newmains, N Lan	116	B4
Newmarket, Suff	53	C2
Newmill, Border	110	C4
Newmill, Moray	138	D3
Newmillerdam, W Yorks	82	A1
Newmills, Monm	37	A3
Newney Green, Essex	43	A3
Newnham, Glouc	37	B2
Newnham, Hants	27	C3
Newnham, Herts	52	C4
Newnham, Kent	31	C3
Newnham, Nhants	50	C2
Newnham, Worcs	48	A1
Newport Pagnell, Bucks	51	C4
Newport, E R of Y	90	A3
Newport, Essex	53	B4
Newport, Glouc	37	C4
Newport, I of W	9	C1
Newport, Newport	36	B4
Newport, Pemb	45	B4
Newport, Shrops	58	B1
Newport-on-Tay, Fife	124	B2
Newquay, Corn	3	B3
Newsham, Lancs	85	C3
Newsham, N York	93	B1
Newsholme, E R of Y	89	B4
Newstead, Border	110	D2
Newstead, Notts	73	A2
Newstead, Nthumb	112	B2
Newthorpe, N York	88	B3
Newton Abbot, Devon	5	C3
Newton Arlosh, Cumb	97	E1
Newton Aycliffe, Durham	100	A3
Newton Bewley, Durham	100	C3
Newton Blossomville, Bucks	51	C3
Newton Bromswold, Nhants	52	A2
Newton Burgoland, Leics	60	B2
Newton by Toft, Lincs	83	D3
Newton Ferrers, Corn	4	B3
Newton Ferrers, Devon	10	B1
Newton Flotman, Norf	65	A3
Newton Harcourt, Leics	61	B3
Newton Kyme, N York	88	B2
Newton Longville, Bucks	40	C1
Newton Morrell, N York	93	C1
Newton Mountain, Pemb	33	D3
Newton on Ouse, N York	89	A1
Newton on Trent, Lincs	83	B4
Newton Poppleford, Devon	6	B1
Newton Purcell, Oxon	40	B1
Newton Reigny, Cumb	98	C3
Newton Solney, Derby	60	B1
Newton St Cyres, Devon	12	A4
Newton St Faith, Norf	65	A1
Newton St Loe, Som	25	A2
Newton St Petrock, Devon	11	C3
Newton Stacey, Hants	16	A1
Newton Stewart, Dumf	102	D4
Newton Toney, Wilts	15	B1
Newton Tracey, Devon	11	D2
Newton under Roseberry, N York	101	A4
Newton upon Derwent, E R of Y	89	B2
Newton Valence, Hants	17	A1
Newton Wamphray, Dumf	103	E1
Newton with Scales, Lancs	85	B3
Newton, Beds	52	C4
Newton, Cambs	53	B3
Newton, Cambs	63	C1
Newton, Chesh	69	D2
Newton, Cumb	91	C4
Newton, Derby	72	B2
Newton, Heref	36	B1
Newton, Heref	47	D3
Newton, Lancs	86	B2
Newton, Lincs	74	B4
Newton, Nhants	62	A4
Newton, Norf	64	B1
Newton, Notts	73	B3
Newton, Nthumb	105	C4
Newton, Som	12	C1
Newton, Staffs	59	A1
Newton, Suff	54	C4
Newton, W Loth	117	A2
Newton, Warwk	50	C1
Newton-by-the-Sea, Nthumb	112	C3
Newtongrange, M Loth	118	A3
Newtonhill, Aber	134	C4
Newton-le-Willows, Mers	79	C2
Newton-le-Willows, N York	93	C2
Newtonloan, M Loth	118	A3
Newtonmore, High	132	C4
Newton-on-Rawcliffe, N York	95	A2
Newton-on-the-Moor, Nthumb	112	C4
Newtown Linford, Leics	61	A2
Newtown, Chesh	70	A3
Newtown, Cumb	97	D1
Newtown, Cumb	104	D4
Newtown, Devon	11	F2
Newtown, Devon	12	C4
Newtown, Glouc	37	B3
Newtown, Hants	16	B3
Newtown, Heref	37	A1
Newtown, I of W	9	C1
Newtown, Nthumb	112	A3
Newtown, Powys	56	E3
Newtown, Shrops	57	C1
Newtown, Shrops	69	D4
Newtown, Staffs	70	C2
Newtown, Wilts	14	C2
Newtyle, Angus	124	A1
Neyland, Pemb	33	D3
Nicholashayne, Devon	12	C3
Nicholaston, Swan	34	C4
Nidd, N York	88	A1
Nigg, High	137	C1
Nightcott, Som	12	B2
Ninebanks, Nthumb	99	A1
Nineveh, Worcs	48	A2
Ninfield, E Suss	20	A3
Ningwood, I of W	9	C1
Nisbet Hill, Border	119	C4
Nisbet, Border	111	A3
Niton, I of W	9	D2
No Man's Heath, Chesh	69	D3
No Man's Heath, Warwk	60	B2
Nocton, Lincs	74	B1
Noke, Oxon	40	A2
Nolton Haven, Pemb	33	C2
Nolton, Pemb	33	C2
Nomansland, Devon	12	A3
Nomansland, Wilts	15	B3
Noneley, Shrops	69	D4
Nonington, Kent	32	C4
Nook, Cumb	92	A3
Norbiton, G Lon	147	A4
Norbury, Chesh	69	D3
Norbury, Derby	71	B3
Norbury, G Lon	147	B3
Norbury, Shrops	57	C3
Norbury, Staffs	58	B1
Norchard, Worcs	48	C1
Nordelph, Norf	63	D3
Nordley, Shrops	58	B3
Norham, Nthumb	111	C1
Norland Town, W Yorks	87	B4
Norley, Chesh	79	B4
Norleywood, Hants	15	C4
Normanby le Wold, Lincs	84	A3
Normanby, Lincs	83	C1
Normanby, Lincs	83	D3
Normanby, N York	94	C3
Normandy, Surrey	28	B4
Norman's Green, Devon	12	C4
Normanton le Heath, Leics	60	B2
Normanton on Soar, Notts	61	A1
Normanton on Trent, Notts	73	C1
Normanton, Leics	73	C3
Normanton, Lincs	74	A3
Normanton, Notts	73	B2
Normanton, W Yorks	88	A4
North Anston, S York	82	C3
North Aston, Oxon	39	C1
North Baddesley, Hants	16	A2
North Ballachulish, High	126	D3
North Barrow, Som	14	A2
North Berwick, E Loth	119	A1
North Boarhunt, Hants	16	B3
North Bovey, Devon	5	B1
North Brentor, Devon	4	C2
North Brewham, Som	14	B1
North Buckland, Devon	11	D1
North Burlingham, Norf	66	A2
North Cadbury, Som	14	A2
North Carlton, Lincs	83	C4
North Carlton, Notts	82	C3
North Cave, E R of Y	90	A3
North Cerney, Glouc	38	B3
North Charlton, Nthumb	112	C3
North Cheam, G Lon	147	A4
North Cheriton, Som	14	A2
North Chideock, Dorset	7	B1
North Cliffe, E R of Y	90	A3
North Cockerington, Lincs	84	C3
North Common, E Suss	19	A2
North Cotes, Lincs	84	C2
North Cove, Suff	66	B4
North Cowton, N York	93	D1
North Crawley, Bucks	51	C4
North Cray, G Lon	30	A2
North Creake, Norf	75	E3
North Curry, Som	13	A2
North Dalton, E R of Y	90	A2
North Deighton, N York	88	B2
North Duffield, N York	89	B3
North Elham, Kent	32	B4
North Elmham, Norf	64	C1
North Elmsall, W Yorks	82	B1
North End, Essex	43	B2
North End, Hants	15	A3
North Erradale, High	140	A4
North Fambridge, Essex	43	C4
North Frodingham, E R of Y	90	C2
North Gorley, Hants	15	B3
North Green, Suff	55	B2
North Grimston, N York	95	A4
North Hayling, Hants	17	A4
North Hill, Corn	4	A2
North Hillingdon, G Lon	146	A1
North Huish, Devon	5	B4
North Hykeham, Lincs	74	A1
North Kelsey, Lincs	83	D2
North Kessock, High	137	B3
North Killingholme, Lincs	84	A1
North Kilvington, N York	94	A3
North Kilworth, Leics	61	A4
North Kyme, Lincs	74	C2
North Landing, E R of Y	95	E4
North Lee, Bucks	40	C3
North Leigh, Oxon	39	C2
North Lopham, Norf	64	D4
North Luffenham, Rutland	62	A2
North Marden, W Suss	17	B3
North Marston, Bucks	40	C1
North Middleton, M Loth	118	B4
North Molton, Devon	11	F1
North Moreton, Oxon	40	A4
North Muskham, Notts	73	C2
North Newbald, E R of Y	90	A3
North Newington, Oxon	50	B4
North Newnton, Wilts	26	B3
North Newton, Som	13	A1
North Nibley, Glouc	37	C4
North Ormsby, Lincs	84	B3
North Otterington, N York	93	D2
North Owersby, Lincs	83	D3
North Perrott, Som	13	C3
North Petherton, Som	13	A1
North Petherwin, Corn	4	A1
North Pickenham, Norf	64	B2
North Pool, Devon	10	B1
North Poorton, Dorset	13	C4
North Quarme, Som	12	B1
North Queensferry, Fife	117	B2
North Radworthy, Devon	11	F1
North Rauceby, Lincs	74	B3
North Reston, Lincs	84	C4
North Rigton, N York	88	A2
North Rode, Chesh	70	C1
North Scarle, Lincs	73	C1
North Shoebury, Essex	31	C1
North Side, Cambs	63	A3
North Somercotes, Lincs	84	C2
North Stainley, N York	93	D3
North Stifford, Essex	30	B1
North Stoke, Oxon	27	B1
North Stoke, Som	25	A2
North Stoke, W Suss	18	A3
North Street, Berks	27	C2
North Street, Kent	32	A3
North Sunderland, Nthumb	112	C2
North Tamerton, Corn	11	C4
North Tawton, Devon	11	F4
North Thoresby, Lincs	84	B2
North Tidworth, Wilts	26	C4
North Town, Berks	28	B1
North Town, Devon	11	D3
North Town, Som	24	B4
North Tuddenham, Norf	64	D2
North Walsham, Norf	76	D4
North Waltham, Hants	27	B4
North Weald Basset, Essex	42	C3
North Wheatley, Notts	83	B3
North Widcombe, Som	24	B3
North Willingham, Lincs	84	A3
North Wingfield, Derby	72	B1
North Witham, Lincs	62	A1
North Wootton, Dorset	14	A3
North Wootton, Norf	63	D1
North Wootton, Som	24	B4
North Wraxall, Wilts	25	B2
Northall, Bucks	41	A2
Northallerton, N York	93	D2
Northam, Devon	11	D2
Northampton, Nhants	51	B2
Northampton, Worcs	48	C2
Northaw, Herts	42	A3
Northay, Som	13	A3
Northborough, Cambs	62	C2
Northbourne, Kent	32	C4
Northchapel, W Suss	17	C2
Northcott, Devon	4	B1
Northend, Warwk	50	B3
Northill, Beds	52	B3
Northington, Hants	16	B1
Northlands, Lincs	75	A2
Northleach, Glouc	38	C2
Northleigh, Devon	12	D4
Northlew, Devon	11	D4
Northmoor, Oxon	39	C3
Northmuir, Angus	129	A3
Northolt, G Lon	146	B1
Northop Hall, Flint	69	B1
Northop, Flint	69	B1
Northorpe, Lincs	74	D4
Northorpe, Lincs	83	C2
Northowram, W Yorks	87	B4
Northrepps, Norf	76	D3
Northway, Som	12	D2
Northwich, Chesh	79	C4
Northwold, Norf	64	A3
Northwood Green, Glouc	37	C2
Northwood, Shrops	69	D4
Norton Bavant, Wilts	25	B4
Norton Bridge, Staffs	70	C4
Norton Canes, Staffs	59	A2
Norton Canon, Heref	47	C3
Norton Disney, Lincs	74	A2
Norton Fitzwarren, Som	12	D2
Norton Hawkfield, Som	24	C2
Norton Heath, Essex	43	A3
Norton in Hales, Shrops	70	B3
Norton Lindsey, Warwk	49	C2
Norton Little Green, Suff	54	C2
Norton Malreward, Som	24	C2
Norton St Philip, Som	25	A3
Norton Wood, Heref	47	C3
Norton, E Suss	19	B4
Norton, Glouc	38	A1
Norton, N York	95	A4
Norton, Nhants	50	C2
Norton, Powys	47	B2
Norton, S York	82	C1
Norton, Shrops	58	B3
Norton, Suff	54	C2
Norton, W Suss	17	C4
Norton, Wilts	25	B1
Norton, Worcs	48	C3
Norton, Worcs	49	A3
Norton-Juxta-Twycross, Leics	60	B2
Norton-le-Clay, N York	94	A4
Norwell Woodhouse, Notts	73	B1
Norwell, Notts	73	C1
Norwich, Norf	65	A2
Norwick, Shet	144	B1
Norwood Green, G Lon	146	B1
Norwood Hill, Surrey	150	A4
Noseley, Leics	61	C3
Noss Mayo, Devon	10	B1
Nosterfield, N York	93	D3
Notgrove, Glouc	38	C2
Notter, Corn	4	B3
Nottingham, Notts	73	A3
Notton, W Yorks	82	A1
Notton, Wilts	25	B2
Noutard's Green, Worcs	48	B2
Nox, Shrops	57	C2
Nuffield, Oxon	27	C1
Nun Monkton, N York	89	A1
Nunburnholme, E R of Y	89	C2
Nuneaton, Warwk	60	B3
Nunhead, G Lon	149	A3
Nunkeeling, E R of Y	90	C2
Nunney, Som	25	A4
Nunnington, N York	94	C3
Nunwick, N York	93	D4
Nuptow, Berks	28	B2
Nursling, Hants	15	C3
Nutbourne, W Suss	17	B4
Nutbourne, W Suss	18	A2
Nutfield, Surrey	150	B3
Nuthampstead, Herts	53	A4
Nuthurst, W Suss	18	B2
Nutley, E Suss	19	B2
Nyewood, W Suss	17	B2
Nymet Rowland, Devon	11	F3
Nymet Tracey, Devon	11	F4
Nympsfield, Glouc	37	C3
Oad Street, Kent	31	B3
Oadby, Leics	61	B3
Oak Cross, Devon	11	D4
Oakamoor, Staffs	71	B3
Oakdale, Caer	36	A4
Oake, Som	12	D2
Oaken, Staffs	58	C3
Oakenclough, Lancs	85	C2
Oakenshaw, Durham	100	A2
Oakenshaw, W Yorks	87	C4
Oaker Side, Derby	72	A1
Oakford, Cered	45	F2
Oakford, Devon	12	B2
Oakham, Rutland	62	A2
Oakhill, Som	24	C4
Oakington, Cambs	53	A2
Oakle Street, Glouc	37	C2
Oakley Green, Berks	28	B1
Oakley, Beds	52	A3
Oakley, Bucks	40	B2
Oakley, Fife	117	A1
Oakley, Hants	27	B4
Oakley, Suff	55	A1
Oakridge, Glouc	38	A3
Oaksey, Wilts	38	B4
Oakthorpe, Leics	60	B2
Oakwoodhill, Surrey	18	B1
Oare, Kent	32	A3
Oare, Som	22	D4
Oare, Wilts	26	B3
Oasby, Lincs	74	B3
Oath, Som	13	B2
Oathlaw, Angus	129	B3
Oatlands Park, Surrey	146	B2
Oban, Argyll	121	A2
Obley, Shrops	47	B1
Occold, Suff	55	A1
Ochiltree, E Ayrs	108	E3
Ockbrook, Derby	72	B4
Ockham, Surrey	146	A3
Ockle, High	125	F2
Ockley, Surrey	18	B1
Ocle Pychard, Heref	48	A3
Odcombe, Som	13	C3
Oddingley, Worcs	48	C2
Oddington, Oxon	40	A2
Odell, Beds	51	C2
Odiham, Hants	28	A4
Odsey, Cambs	52	C4
Odstock, Wilts	15	A2
Odstone, Leics	60	C2
Offchurch, Warwk	50	A2
Offenham, Worcs	49	B3
Offham, E Suss	19	A3
Offham, Kent	30	B3
Offord Cluny, Cambs	52	C2
Offord Darcy, Cambs	52	C2
Offton, Suff	54	D3
Offwell, Devon	12	D4
Ogbourne Maizey, Wilts	26	C2
Ogbourne St Andrew, Wilts	26	C2
Ogbourne St George, Wilts	26	C2
Ogle, Nthumb	105	D3
Oglet, Mers	79	A4
Ogmore Vale, Bridg	35	C4
Ogmore, Glam	22	D1
Ogmore-by-Sea, Glam	22	D2
Okeford Fitzpaine, Dorset	14	B3
Okehampton, Devon	11	E4
Old Alresford, Hants	16	B1
Old Basing, Hants	27	C3
Old Bewick, Nthumb	112	B3
Old Bolingbroke, Lincs	75	A1
Old Bracknell, Berks	28	B2
Old Brampton, Derby	72	A1
Old Buckenham, Norf	64	D3
Old Burghclere, Hants	27	A3
Old Byland, N York	94	B3
Old Church Stoke, Powys	57	B3
Old Cleeve, Som	23	A4
Old Clipstone, Notts	73	A1
Old Dailly, S Ayrs	102	C1
Old Dalby, Leics	61	B1
Old Deer, Aber	139	E3
Old Edlington, S York	82	C2
Old Ellerby, E R of Y	90	C3
Old Forge, Heref	37	A2
Old Grimsby, Isles of Scilly	144	A1

PLACE	PAGE	GRID
Old Hunstanton, Norf	75	D3
Old Hurst, Cambs	52	C1
Old Hutton, Cumb	92	A2
Old Kilpatrick, Dumb	115	B2
Old Langho, Lancs	86	B3
Old Leake, Lincs	75	A2
Old Malton, N York	95	A4
Old Milverton, Warwk	50	A2
Old Newton, Suff	54	D2
Old Radnor, Powys	47	B2
Old Rayne, Aber	134	A1
Old Romney, Kent	21	B2
Old Sodbury, Glouc	25	A1
Old Somerby, Lincs	74	A4
Old Stratford, Nhants	51	B4
Old Town, Cumb	92	B3
Old Town, Isles of Scilly	144	A2
Old Warden, Beds	52	B4
Old Weston, Cambs	52	B1
Old Windsor, Berks	146	A2
Old Wives Lees, Kent	32	A3
Old Woking, Surrey	146	A3
Old, Nhants	51	B1
Oldberrow, Warwk	49	B2
Oldbury on the Hill, Glouc	38	A4
Oldbury, Shrops	58	B3
Oldbury, Warwk	60	B3
Oldbury-on-Severn, Glouc	37	B4
Oldcastle, Monm	36	B1
Oldcotes, Notts	82	C3
Oldfield, Worcs	48	C2
Oldford, Som	25	A4
Oldhall Green, Suff	54	C3
Oldham, G Man	80	B2
Oldhamstocks, E Loth	119	C3
Oldmeldrum, Aber	134	B1
Oldmill, Corn	4	B2
Oldmixon, Som	23	C3
Oldstead, N York	94	B3
Oldwall, Cumb	104	D4
Oldwalls, Swan	34	C4
Ollaberry, Shet	144	A2
Ollerton, Chesh	80	A4
Ollerton, Notts	73	B1
Ollerton, Shrops	58	A1
Olney, Bucks	51	C3
Olveston, Glouc	24	C1
Ombersley, Worcs	48	C2
Ompton, Notts	73	B1
Onchan, I of M	145	C3
Onecote, Staffs	71	B2
Onibury, Shrops	47	C1
Onich, High	126	D3
Onllwyn, Neath	35	B3
Onneley, Staffs	70	B3
Onslow Village, Surrey	146	A4
Onston, Chesh	79	C4
Opinan, High	135	F1
Orby, Lincs	75	B1
Orchard Portman, Som	13	A2
Orcheston, Wilts	26	B4
Orcop Hill, Heref	37	A1
Orcop, Heref	37	A1
Ordhead, Aber	134	A3
Ordie, Aber	133	D3
Ordiequish, Moray	138	C3
Ordley, Nthumb	105	C4
Orford, Suff	55	C3
Organford, Dorset	8	C1
Orleton, Heref	47	D2
Orleton, Worcs	48	B2
Orlingbury, Nhants	51	C1
Ormesby St Margaret, Norf	66	B1
Ormesby St Michael, Norf	66	B1
Ormiston, E Loth	118	B3
Ormskirk, Lancs	79	A1
Orpington, G Lon	30	A2
Orrell, G Man	79	B2
Orsett, Essex	30	B1
Orslow, Staffs	58	B1
Orston, Notts	73	C3
Orton, Cumb	92	B1
Orton, Nhants	51	B1
Orton, Staffs	58	C3
Orton-on-the-Hill, Leics	60	B2
Orwell, Cambs	53	A3
Osbaldeston, Lancs	86	A3
Osbaston, Leics	60	C2
Osbaston, Shrops	57	B1
Osbournby, Lincs	74	B3
Oscroft, Chesh	69	D1
Osgathorpe, Leics	60	C1
Osgodby, Lincs	83	D3
Osgodby, N York	89	B3
Osgodby, N York	95	C3
Osmaston, Derby	71	C3
Osmington Mills, Dorset	8	A2
Osmington, Dorset	8	A2
Osmotherley, N York	94	A2
Ossett, W Yorks	88	A4
Ossington, Notts	73	C1
Osterley, G Lon	146	B1
Oswaldkirk, N York	94	C3
Oswaldtwistle, Lancs	86	B4
Oswestry, Shrops	69	B4
Otford, Kent	30	A3
Othery, Som	13	B1
Otley, Suff	55	A3
Otley, W Yorks	87	C2
Otter Ferry, Argyll	114	A1
Otterbourne, Hants	16	A2
Otterburn, N York	86	C1
Otterburn, Nthumb	105	B1
Otterham, Corn	3	E1
Otterhampton, Som	23	C4
Otterton, Devon	6	B1
Ottery St Mary, Devon	12	C4
Ottery, Devon	4	C2
Ottringham, E R of Y	90	D4
Oughtibridge, S York	82	A3
Oughtrington, Chesh	80	A3
Oulston, N York	94	B4
Oulton Street, Norf	76	C4
Oulton, Cumb	98	A1

PLACE	PAGE	GRID
Oulton, Norf	76	C4
Oulton, Staffs	70	C4
Oundle, Nhants	62	B4
Ousby, Cumb	98	D2
Ousden, Suff	54	A2
Ousefleet, E R of Y	89	C4
Ouston, Durham	100	A1
Out Rawcliffe, Lancs	85	B2
Outgate, Cumb	91	E1
Outhgill, Cumb	92	C1
Outhill, Warwk	49	B2
Outlane, W Yorks	81	B1
Outwell, Norf	63	C2
Outwood, Surrey	150	C4
Outwoods, Staffs	58	B1
Ouzlewell Green, W Yorks	88	A4
Over Compton, Dorset	14	A3
Over Haddon, Derby	71	C1
Over Kellet, Lancs	92	A4
Over Kiddington, Oxon	39	C2
Over Norton, Oxon	39	B1
Over Peover, Chesh	80	A4
Over Silton, N York	94	A2
Over Stowey, Som	12	D1
Over Wallop, Hants	15	C1
Over Whitacre, Warwk	60	A4
Over Worton, Oxon	39	C1
Over, Cambs	53	A1
Overbury, Worcs	49	A4
Overcombe, Dorset	8	A2
Overseal, Derby	60	B1
Oversland, Kent	32	A3
Overstone, Nhants	51	B2
Overstrand, Norf	76	D3
Overthorpe, Nhants	50	B4
Overton, Hants	27	B4
Overton, Lancs	85	B1
Overton, N York	89	A1
Overton, Shrops	47	D1
Overton, Swan	22	A1
Overton, W Yorks	81	C1
Overton, Wrex	69	C3
Overtown, Lancs	92	B4
Overtown, N Lan	116	B4
Oving, Bucks	40	C2
Oving, W Suss	17	C4
Ovingham, Nthumb	105	D4
Ovington, Durham	99	D4
Ovington, Essex	54	A4
Ovington, Hants	16	B1
Ovington, Norf	64	C3
Ovington, Nthumb	105	D4
Ower, Hants	15	C3
Owlswick, Bucks	40	C3
Owmby, Lincs	83	D2
Owmby, Lincs	83	D3
Owslebury, Hants	16	B2
Owston Ferry, Lincs	83	B2
Owston, Leics	61	C2
Owston, S York	82	C1
Owstwick, E R of Y	90	D3
Owthorne, E R of Y	90	E4
Owthorpe, Notts	73	B4
Oxborough, Norf	64	A3
Oxbridge, Dorset	13	C4
Oxcombe, Lincs	84	B4
Oxen End, Essex	43	B1
Oxen Park, Cumb	91	D3
Oxenholme, Cumb	92	A2
Oxenhope, W Yorks	87	A3
Oxenpill, Som	24	A4
Oxenton, Glouc	38	B1
Oxenwood, Wilts	26	D3
Oxford, Oxon	40	A3
Oxhill, Warwk	50	A3
Oxley Green, Essex	44	A2
Oxley's Green, E Suss	20	A2
Oxnam, Border	111	B3
Oxnead, Norf	65	A1
Oxshott, Surrey	146	B3
Oxspring, S York	81	C2
Oxted, Surrey	150	D3
Oxton, Border	119	A4
Oxton, N York	89	A2
Oxton, Notts	73	B2
Oxwich Green, Swan	22	A1
Oxwich, Swan	22	A1
Oyne, Aber	134	A1
Packington, Leics	60	B1
Padanaram, Angus	129	A4
Padbury, Bucks	40	B1
Paddington, G Lon	148	A3
Paddlesworth, Kent	21	C1
Paddlesworth, Kent	31	A3
Paddock Wood, Kent	31	A4
Padiham, Lancs	86	B3
Padside, N York	87	C1
Padstow, Corn	3	C2
Padworth, Berks	27	B2
Pagham, W Suss	17	C4
Paglesham, Essex	44	A4
Paignton, Devon	6	A3
Painscastle, Powys	47	A3
Painshawfield, Nthumb	105	D4
Painsthorpe, E R of Y	89	C1
Painswick, Glouc	38	A3
Painter's Forstal, Kent	31	C3
Paisley, Renf	115	B3
Pakenham, Suff	54	C2
Paley Street, Berks	28	B1
Palgrave, Suff	54	D1
Pallington, Dorset	8	A1
Palnackie, Dumf	103	C4
Palnure, Dumf	102	F4
Palterton, Derby	72	B1
Pamber End, Hants	27	B3
Pamber Heath, Hants	27	B3
Pamphill, Dorset	14	D4
Pampisford, Cambs	53	B3
Panbride, Angus	124	C1
Pancrasweek, Devon	11	B4
Pandy Tudur, Aberc	68	B1
Pandy, Monm	36	B1
Panfield, Essex	43	B1

PLACE	PAGE	GRID
Pangbourne, Berks	27	C1
Pangdean, W Suss	18	C3
Pannal, N York	88	A2
Pant Glas, Gwyn	67	D3
Pant, Shrops	57	B1
Pantasaph, Flint	78	C4
Pant-ffrwyth, Bridg	22	E1
Pantglas, Powys	56	C3
Panton, Lincs	84	A4
Pant-y-dwr, Powys	46	D1
Pant-y-mwyn, Flint	69	A1
Panxworth, Norf	65	B2
Papcastle, Cumb	97	D3
Papigoe, High	143	F2
Papplewick, Notts	73	A2
Papworth Everard, Cambs	52	C2
Par, Corn	3	D4
Parbold, Lancs	79	B1
Parbrook, Som	13	C1
Parc Seymour, Newport	36	C4
Parc, Gwyn	68	B4
Pardshaw, Cumb	97	D3
Parham, Suff	55	B2
Park Corner, Berks	28	B1
Park Corner, Oxon	40	B4
Park Royal, G Lon	147	A1
Park Street, Herts	41	C3
Park, Nthumb	104	E4
Parkend, Glouc	37	B3
Parkgate, Dumf	103	E2
Parkgate, Kent	30	A2
Parkgate, Surrey	150	A4
Parkham, Devon	11	C2
Parkmill, Swan	34	D4
Parr Bridge, G Man	80	A2
Parracombe, Devon	22	C4
Parson Drove, Cambs	63	B2
Partington, G Man	80	A3
Partney, Lincs	75	A1
Parton, Cumb	97	C4
Parton, Cumb	98	A1
Parton, Dumf	103	B3
Partridge Green, W Suss	18	B2
Parwich, Derby	71	C2
Paston, Norf	76	D4
Patchway, Glouc	24	C1
Pateley Bridge, N York	93	B4
Path of Condie, Perth	123	C3
Pathhead, M Loth	118	B3
Patna, E Ayrs	108	D4
Patney, Wilts	26	B3
Patrick Brompton, N York	93	C2
Patrick, I of M	145	B3
Patrington, E R of Y	90	E4
Patterdale, Cumb	98	B4
Pattingham, Staffs	58	C3
Pattishall, Nhants	51	A3
Pattiswick Green, Essex	43	C1
Paulerspury, Nhants	51	A3
Paull, E R of Y	90	C4
Paulton, Som	24	C3
Pauperhaugh, Nthumb	105	D1
Pavenham, Beds	52	A3
Pawlett, Som	23	C4
Paxford, Glouc	49	C4
Paxton, Border	119	E4
Payhembury, Devon	12	C4
Paythorne, Lancs	86	C2
Peacehaven, E Suss	19	A4
Peak Forest, Derby	81	B4
Peakirk, Cambs	62	C2
Pease Pottage, W Suss	18	C1
Peaseland Green, Norf	64	D1
Peasemore, Berks	27	A1
Peasenhall, Suff	55	C1
Peaslake, Surrey	146	B4
Peasmarsh, E Suss	20	B2
Peasmarsh, Surrey	146	A4
Peat Inn, Fife	124	B3
Peathill, Aber	139	E2
Peatling Parva, Leics	61	A4
Pebmarsh, Essex	54	B4
Pebworth, Worcs	49	B3
Pecket Well, W Yorks	87	A4
Peckforton, Chesh	69	D2
Peckham, G Lon	149	A2
Peckleton, Leics	60	C3
Pedlinge, Kent	21	C1
Pedwell, Som	13	B1
Peebles, Border	110	B1
Peel, I of M	145	B3
Peene, Kent	21	C1
Pegswood, Nthumb	106	A2
Peldon, Essex	44	A2
Pelsall, W Mids	59	A2
Pelton, Durham	100	A1
Pelynt, Corn	4	A4
Pembrey, Carm	34	C3
Pembridge, Heref	47	C2
Pembroke Dock, Pemb	33	D3
Pembroke, Pemb	33	D3
Pembury, Kent	19	C1
Pen Rhiwfawr, Neath	35	A2
Penallt, Monm	37	A2
Penally, Pemb	33	E3
Penalt, Heref	37	A1
Penarth, Glam	23	B2
Pen-bont Rhydybeddau, Cered	56	B4
Penbryn, Cered	45	D3
Pencader, Carm	45	F4
Pencaitland, E Loth	118	B3
Pencarnisiog, Angle	77	B4
Pencarreg, Carm	45	F3
Pencelli, Powys	35	D1
Penclawdd, Swan	34	D4
Pencoed, Bridg	22	E1
Pencombe, Heref	48	A3
Pencraig, Heref	37	A2
Pencraig, Powys	68	D4
Pendeen, Corn	1	A2
Penderyn, Rhond	35	C3
Pendine, Carm	34	A3
Pendlebury, G Man	80	A2

PLACE	PAGE	GRID
Pendleton, Lancs	86	B3
Pendock, Worcs	37	C1
Pendoggett, Corn	3	D2
Pendoylan, Glam	23	A1
Penegoes, Powys	56	B3
Pen-ffordd, Pemb	33	D1
Pengam, Caer	36	A4
Penge, G Lon	149	A3
Pengelly, Corn	3	D1
Pengrugla, Corn	2	C1
Penhallow, Corn	3	B4
Penhalvean, Corn	1	D1
Penhow, Newport	36	C4
Penicuik, M Loth	118	A4
Penistone, S York	81	C2
Penkridge, Staffs	59	A2
Penlean, Corn	11	B4
Penley, Wrex	69	C3
Penllyn, Glam	22	E1
Penmachno, Aberc	68	B2
Penmaenmawr, Aberc	77	E4
Penmaenpool, Gwyn	56	B1
Penmark, Glam	23	A2
Penmorfa, Gwyn	67	E3
Penmynydd, Angle	77	C4
Penn Street, Bucks	41	A4
Pennal, Gwyn	56	B3
Pennan, Aber	139	D2
Pennant, Powys	56	C3
Pennard, Swan	34	D4
Pennerley, Shrops	57	C3
Pennorth, Powys	35	D1
Penny Bridge, Cumb	91	D3
Penny Hill, Lincs	75	A4
Pennymoor, Devon	12	A3
Penparc, Cered	45	D3
Penperlleni, Monm	36	B3
Penpoll, Corn	3	E4
Penponds, Corn	1	D1
Penpont, Dumf	103	C1
Pen-rhiw, Pemb	45	D4
Penrhiwceiber, Rhond	35	D4
Penrhiwllan, Cered	45	E4
Penrhiw-pal, Cered	45	E3
Penrhos, Gwyn	67	C4
Penrhos, Monm	36	C2
Penrhyn Bay, Aberc	77	F4
Penrhyncoch, Cered	56	A4
Penrhyndeudraeth, Gwyn	67	E3
Penrice, Swan	34	C4
Penrith, Cumb	98	C3
Penrose, Corn	3	C3
Penruddock, Cumb	98	B3
Penryn, Corn	2	A2
Pensarn, Aberc	78	A4
Pensax, Worcs	48	B1
Penselwood, Som	14	B1
Pensford, Som	24	C3
Pensham, Worcs	49	A4
Penshaw, Tyne	100	B1
Penshurst Station, Kent	30	A4
Penshurst, Kent	30	A4
Pensilva, Corn	4	A3
Pentewan, Corn	2	C1
Pentir, Gwyn	67	E1
Pentlow, Essex	54	B3
Pentney, Norf	64	A2
Penton Mewsey, Hants	26	D4
Pentonbridge, Cumb	104	C3
Pentre Berw, Angle	77	C4
Pentre Hodrey, Shrops	47	B1
Pentre Llanrhaeadr, Denb	68	D1
Pentre Meyrick, Glam	22	E2
Pentre, Shrops	57	C1
Pentrebach, Merth	35	D3
Pentre-bach, Powys	35	C1
Pentre-celyn, Denb	69	A2
Pentre-celyn, Powys	56	D2
Pentre-cwrt, Carm	45	E4
Pentredwr, Denb	69	A3
Pentrefelin, Gwyn	67	D3
Pentrefoelas, Aberc	68	B2
Pentregat, Cered	45	E3
Pentre-Gwenlais, Carm	34	D2
Pentre-tafarn-y-fedw, Aberc	68	B1
Pentrich, Derby	72	A2
Pentridge Hill, Dorset	14	D3
Pen-twyn, Monm	37	A3
Pentyrch, Card	23	A1
Penwithick, Corn	3	D4
Penybanc, Carm	34	D1
Penybont, Powys	46	E2
Pen-y-bont, Powys	57	A1
Pen-y-bont-fawr, Powys	56	E1
Pen-y-bryn, Pemb	45	C4
Penycae, Wrex	69	B3
Pen-y-clawdd, Monm	36	C3
Pen-y-coedcae, Rhond	35	D4
Pen-y-cwn, Pemb	33	C1
Penyffordd, Flint	69	B1
Pen-y-Garnedd, Powys	56	E1
Pen-y-graig, Gwyn	67	B4
Penygraig, Rhond	35	C4
Penygroes, Carm	34	D2
Penygroes, Gwyn	67	D2
Pen-y-stryt, Denb	69	A2
Penywaun, Rhond	35	C3
Penzance, Corn	1	B2
Peopleton, Worcs	49	A3
Peper Harow, Surrey	28	B4
Peplow, Shrops	58	A1
Perivale, G Lon	146	B1
Perlethorpe, Notts	73	B1
Perranporth, Corn	3	B4
Perranuthnoe, Corn	1	C2
Perranwell, Corn	2	A1
Perranzabuloe, Corn	3	B4
Pershall, Staffs	70	C4
Pershore, Worcs	49	A3
Pertenhall, Beds	52	B2
Perth, Perth	123	C2
Perthy, Shrops	69	C4
Perton, Heref	48	A4

PLACE	PAGE	GRID
Perton, Staffs	58	C3
Peter Tavy, Devon	4	C2
Peterborough, Cambs	62	C3
Peterchurch, Heref	47	B4
Peterculter, Aberdeen City	134	C3
Peterhead, Aber	139	F3
Peterlee, Durham	100	C2
Peter's Green, Herts	41	C2
Peters Marland, Devon	11	D3
Petersfield, Hants	17	B2
Petersham, G Lon	146	B2
Peterstone Wentlooge, Newport	23	C1
Peterstow, Heref	37	A1
Petham, Kent	32	B4
Petherwin Gate, Corn	4	A1
Petrockstow, Devon	11	D3
Pett, E Suss	20	B3
Pettaugh, Suff	55	A2
Pettinain, S Lan	109	D1
Pettistree, Suff	55	B3
Petton, Devon	12	C2
Petts Wood, G Lon	30	A2
Petworth, W Suss	18	A2
Pevensey, E Suss	19	C4
Pewsey, Wilts	26	C3
Phepson, Worcs	49	A2
Philham, Devon	11	B2
Phillack, Corn	1	C1
Philleigh, Corn	2	B1
Philpstoun, W Loth	117	A2
Phoenix Green, Hants	28	A3
Pica, Cumb	97	D4
Pickering, N York	95	A3
Pickford, W Mids	60	B4
Pickhill, N York	93	D3
Picklescott, Shrops	57	C3
Pickmere, Chesh	79	C4
Pickney, Som	12	D2
Pickup Bank, Lancs	86	B4
Pickwell, Leics	61	C2
Pickworth, Lincs	74	B4
Pickworth, Rutland	62	B2
Picton, Chesh	69	C1
Picton, N York	94	A1
Piddinghoe, E Suss	19	B4
Piddington, Nhants	51	B3
Piddington, Oxon	40	B2
Piddlehinton, Dorset	14	B4
Piddletrenthide, Dorset	14	B4
Pidley, Cambs	53	A1
Pierowall, Orkney	144	A1
Pilham, Lincs	83	C3
Pillaton, Corn	4	B3
Pillerton Hersey, Warwk	50	A3
Pillerton Priors, Warwk	50	A3
Pilley, Hants	15	C4
Pilley, S York	82	A2
Pilling, Lancs	85	B2
Pilning, Glouc	24	B1
Pilsbury, Derby	71	B1
Pilsdon, Dorset	13	B4
Pilsley, Derby	71	C1
Pilsley, Derby	72	B1
Pilson Green, Norf	66	A2
Piltdown, E Suss	19	B2
Pilton, Nhants	62	B4
Pilton, Rutland	62	A3
Pilton, Som	14	A1
Pimperne, Dorset	14	C3
Pinchbeck, Lincs	63	A1
Pinley Green, Warwk	49	C2
Pinn, Devon	6	B1
Pinvin, Worcs	49	A3
Pinwherry, S Ayrs	102	C2
Pinxton, Derby	72	B2
Pipe and Lyde, Heref	47	D4
Pipewell, Nhants	61	C4
Pirbright Camp, Surrey	28	B3
Pirbright, Surrey	28	B3
Pirnmill, N Ayrs	107	F1
Pirton, Herts	41	C1
Pirton, Worcs	48	C3
Pishill, Oxon	40	B4
Pistyll, Gwyn	67	C3
Pitcairngreen, Perth	123	C2
Pitcaple, Aber	134	B1
Pitch Green, Bucks	40	C3
Pitch Place, Surrey	17	C1
Pitchcombe, Glouc	38	A3
Pitchcott, Bucks	40	C2
Pitchford, Shrops	57	D2
Pitcombe, Som	14	A1
Pitlessie, Fife	124	A3
Pitlochry, Perth	128	B3
Pitmedden, Aber	134	C1
Pitney, Som	13	B2
Pitscottie, Fife	124	B3
Pitsford, Nhants	51	B2
Pitt, Devon	12	C3
Pittenweem, Fife	124	C4
Pittington, Durham	100	B2
Pitton, Wilts	15	B1
Pittulie, Aber	139	E2
Pity Me, Durham	100	A1
Pixham, Surrey	146	B4
Plains, N Lan	116	B3
Plaish, Shrops	57	D3
Plaistow, Derby	72	A2
Plaistow, G Lon	149	B1
Plaistow, W Suss	18	A1
Plaitford, Hants	15	C2
Plas Cymyran, Angle	77	A4
Plastow Green, Hants	27	B3
Platt, Kent	30	B3
Plawsworth, Durham	100	A1
Plaxtol, Kent	30	B3
Play Hatch, Oxon	28	A1
Playford, Suff	55	A3
Playing Place, Corn	2	A1
Playley Green, Glouc	37	C1
Plealey, Shrops	57	C2
Plean, Stirl	116	B1
Pleasance, Fife	123	D3

PLACE	PAGE	GRID
Pleasington, Lancs	86	A4
Pleasley, Derby	72	B1
Plemstall, Chesh	69	C1
Pleshey, Essex	43	B2
Plockton, High	130	F1
Plowden, Shrops	57	C4
Ploxgreen, Shrops	57	C2
Pluckley Thorne, Kent	31	C4
Pluckley, Kent	31	C4
Plumbland, Cumb	97	E2
Plumley, Chesh	80	A4
Plumpton Green, E Suss	19	A3
Plumpton, Cumb	98	C2
Plumpton, E Suss	19	A3
Plumpton, Nhants	50	C3
Plumstead, G Lon	30	A1
Plumstead, Norf	76	C4
Plumtree, Notts	73	A4
Plungar, Leics	73	C4
Plurenden, Kent	21	A1
Plush, Dorset	14	B4
Plwmp, Cered	45	E3
Plymouth, Devon	4	C4
Plympton, Devon	5	A4
Plymtree, Devon	12	C4
Pockley, N York	94	C3
Pocklington, E R of Y	89	C2
Podimore, Som	13	C2
Podington, Beds	51	C2
Podmore, Staffs	70	B4
Pointon, Lincs	74	C4
Polbain, High	140	C2
Polbathic, Corn	4	B4
Polbeth, W Loth	117	A3
Polebrook, Nhants	62	B4
Polesworth, Warwk	60	A3
Polglass, High	140	C2
Polgooth, Corn	3	D4
Poling, W Suss	18	A4
Polkerris, Corn	3	E4
Pollington, E R of Y	89	A4
Polmassick, Corn	2	C1
Polmont, Falk	116	C2
Polnish, High	126	B1
Polperro, Corn	4	A4
Polruan, Corn	3	E4
Polstead, Suff	54	C4
Poltimore, Devon	12	B4
Polton, M Loth	118	A3
Polwarth, Border	119	C4
Polyphant, Corn	4	A2
Polzeath, Corn	3	C2
Pomathorn, M Loth	118	A4
Pondersbridge, Cambs	63	A3
Ponsanooth, Corn	2	A1
Ponsworthy, Devon	5	B2
Pont Robert, Powys	56	E2
Pontantwn, Carm	34	C2
Pontardawe, Neath	35	A3
Pontarddulais, Swan	34	D3
Pontarsais, Carm	34	C1
Pontblyddyn, Flint	69	B1
Pontefract, W Yorks	88	B4
Ponteland, Nthumb	106	A3
Ponterwyd, Cered	56	B4
Pontesbury, Shrops	57	C2
Pontesford, Shrops	57	C2
Pontfadog, Wrex	69	B3
Pontfaen, Pemb	45	B4
Pont-faen, Powys	46	D4
Pontgarreg, Cered	45	E3
Ponthenry, Carm	34	C3
Ponthir, Torf	36	B4
Ponthirwaun, Cered	45	D4
Pontllanfraith, Caer	36	A4
Pontlliw, Swan	34	D3
Pontlyfni, Gwyn	67	D2
Pont-Nedd-Fechan, Neath	35	C3
Pontrhydfendigaid, Cered	46	B2
Pont-rhyd-y-fen, Neath	35	B4
Pontrhydygroes, Cered	46	B1
Pontrilas, Heref	36	C1
Ponts Green, E Suss	20	A3
Pontshaen, Cered	45	F3
Pontshill, Heref	37	B2
Pontsticill, Merth	35	D2
Pontwelly, Carm	45	E4
Pontyates, Carm	34	C3
Pontyberem, Carm	34	C2
Pontybodkin, Flint	69	B2
Pontyclun, Rhond	23	A1
Pontycymer, Bridg	35	C4
Pont-y-pant, Aberc	68	A2
Pontypool, Torf	36	B3
Pontypridd, Rhond	35	D4
Pontywaun, Caer	36	A4
Pool of Muckhart, Clack	123	B4
Pool Street, Essex	54	A4
Pool, W Yorks	87	C2
Poole, Dorset	8	C1
Poolewe, High	140	B4
Pooley Bridge, Cumb	98	C3
Poolfold, Staffs	70	C2
Poolhill, Glouc	37	C1
Pooting's, Kent	30	A4
Popham, Hants	27	B4
Poplar, G Lon	149	B2
Porchfield, I of W	9	C1
Porkellis, Corn	1	D2
Porlock Weir, Som	22	D4
Porlock, Som	22	E4
Port Appin, Argyll	126	C4
Port Askaig, Argyll	113	C3
Port Bannatyne, Argyll	114	B3
Port Carlisle, Cumb	104	B4
Port Charlotte, Argyll	113	A4
Port Ellen, Argyll	107	A1
Port Erin, I of M	145	A4
Port Glasgow, Inverclyde	115	A2
Port Henderson, High	135	F1
Port Isaac, Corn	3	D2
Port Logan, Dumf	96	B2
Port nan Long, W Isle	144	A3
Port of Menteith, Stirl	122	C4

PLACE	PAGE	GRID
Port of Ness, W Isle	144	B1
Port Quin, Corn	3	D2
Port Ramsay, Argyll	126	C4
Port Soderick, I of M	145	C4
Port St Mary, I of M	145	B4
Port Talbot, Neath	35	A4
Port Wemyss, Argyll	113	A4
Port William, Dumf	96	D2
Portachoillan, Argyll	113	F4
Portavadie, Argyll	114	A3
Portbury, Som	24	B2
Portchester, Hants	16	B4
Portencalzie, Dumf	102	A3
Portesham, Dorset	7	D1
Portfield Gate, Pemb	33	C2
Portgate, Devon	4	B1
Portgordon, Moray	138	D2
Porth Navas, Corn	2	A2
Porth, Rhond	35	D4
Porthallow, Corn	2	A3
Porthallow, Corn	4	A4
Porthcawl, Bridg	22	D1
Porthcothan, Corn	3	C2
Porthcurno, Corn	1	A3
Porthgain, Pemb	33	B1
Porthgwarra, Corn	1	A3
Porthkerry, Glam	23	A2
Porthleven, Corn	1	D2
Porthmadog, Gwyn	67	E3
Porthoustock, Corn	2	A3
Porthpean, Corn	3	D4
Porthtowan, Corn	1	D1
Porthyrhyd, Carm	34	C2
Portington, E R of Y	89	C3
Portinscale, Cumb	98	A3
Portishead, Som	24	B2
Portknockie, Moray	139	A2
Portlethen, Aber	134	C4
Portloe, Corn	2	B1
Portmahomack, High	141	E4
Portmellon, Corn	2	C1
Portnacroish, Argyll	126	C4
Portnahaven, Argyll	113	A4
Porton, Wilts	15	B1
Portpatrick, Dumf	96	A1
Portreath, Corn	1	D1
Portree, High	135	C4
Portscatho, Corn	2	B2
Portskerra, High	143	A1
Portskewett, Monm	37	A4
Portslade-by-Sea, E Suss	18	C4
Portsmouth, Hants	17	A4
Portsoy, Aber	139	B2
Portway, Warwk	49	B1
Portwrinkle, Corn	4	B4
Poslingford, Suff	54	A3
Postbridge, Devon	5	A2
Postcombe, Oxon	40	B3
Postling, Kent	21	C1
Postwick, Norf	65	B2
Potsgrove, Beds	41	A1
Pott Shrigley, Chesh	81	A4
Potter Brompton, N York	95	C3
Potter Heigham, Norf	66	A1
Potterhanworth Booths, Lincs	74	B1
Potterhanworth, Lincs	74	B1
Potterne Wick, Wilts	26	A3
Potterne, Wilts	26	A3
Potters Bar, Herts	42	A3
Potters Crouch, Herts	41	C3
Potters Marston, Leics	60	C3
Potterspury, Nhants	51	B4
Potterton, Aber	134	D2
Potto, N York	94	A1
Potton, Beds	52	C3
Poughill, Corn	11	B3
Poughill, Devon	12	A3
Poulshot, Wilts	26	A3
Poulton, Glouc	38	C3
Poulton-le-Fylde, Lancs	85	A3
Pound Green, E Suss	19	B2
Poundffald, Swan	34	D4
Poundon, Bucks	40	B1
Poundsbridge, Kent	30	A4
Poundsgate, Devon	5	B2
Poundstock, Corn	11	B4
Povey Cross, Surrey	150	B4
Powburn, Nthumb	112	B3
Powderham, Devon	6	A1
Powfoot, Dumf	104	A4
Powhill, Cumb	98	A1
Powick, Worcs	48	C3
Powmill, Perth	123	C4
Poxwell, Dorset	8	A1
Poyle, Surrey	146	A1
Poynings, W Suss	18	C3
Poyntington, Dorset	14	A2
Poynton Green, Shrops	57	D1
Poynton, Chesh	80	B4
Poys Street, Suff	55	C1
Praa Sands, Corn	1	C2
Pratt's Bottom, Kent	30	A3
Prees Green, Shrops	69	D4
Prees, Shrops	69	D4
Preesall, Lancs	85	B2
Prendwick, Nthumb	112	A4
Pren-gwyn, Cered	45	F4
Prenteg, Gwyn	67	E3
Prescot, Mers	79	B3
Prescott, Devon	12	C3
Prestatyn, Denb	78	B4
Prestbury, Chesh	80	B4
Presteigne, Powys	47	B2
Prestleigh, Som	14	A1
Preston Bissett, Bucks	40	B1
Preston Brockhurst, Shrops	57	D1
Preston Brook, Chesh	79	B4
Preston Candover, Hants	27	B4
Preston Capes, Nhants	50	C3
Preston Gubbals, Shrops	57	D1
Preston on Stour, Warwk	49	C3
Preston on Wye, Heref	47	C4
Preston Patrick, Cumb	92	A3

PLACE	PAGE	GRID
Preston upon the Weald Moors, Shrops	58	A1
Preston Wynne, Heref	47	D3
Preston, Border	119	C4
Preston, Dorset	8	A2
Preston, E Loth	119	B2
Preston, E R of Y	90	C3
Preston, Glouc	38	B3
Preston, Herts	41	C1
Preston, Kent	32	C3
Preston, Lancs	85	C4
Preston, Nthumb	112	C3
Preston, Rutland	62	A3
Preston, Som	12	C1
Preston, Suff	54	C3
Preston, Wilts	26	D2
Prestonpans, E Loth	118	B2
Preston-under-Scar, N York	93	B2
Prestwich, G Man	80	B2
Prestwick, S Ayrs	108	D3
Prickwillow, Cambs	63	D4
Priddy, Som	24	B4
Priest Hutton, Lancs	92	A4
Priestweston, Shrops	57	B3
Primrosehill, Border	119	C4
Princes Risborough, Bucks	40	C3
Princethorpe, Warwk	50	B1
Princetown, Devon	5	A2
Priors Hardwick, Warwk	50	B3
Priors Marston, Warwk	50	B2
Priston, Som	24	C3
Privett, Hants	17	A2
Prospect, Cumb	97	D2
Prospidnick, Corn	1	D2
Prudhoe, Nthumb	105	D4
Publow, Som	24	C2
Puckeridge, Herts	42	B1
Pucklechurch, Glouc	25	A1
Puddington, Chesh	78	D4
Puddington, Devon	12	A3
Puddletown, Dorset	8	A1
Pudsey, W Yorks	87	C3
Pulborough, W Suss	18	A2
Pulford, Chesh	69	C2
Pulham Market, Norf	65	A4
Pulham St Mary, Norf	65	A4
Pulham, Dorset	14	B3
Pulloxhill, Beds	52	A4
Pumsaint, Carm	46	B4
Puncheston, Pemb	33	D1
Puncknowle, Dorset	7	C1
Purfleet, Essex	30	B1
Puriton, Som	23	C4
Purleigh, Essex	43	C3
Purley, G Lon	150	B1
Purse Caundle, Dorset	14	A3
Purtington, Som	13	B3
Purton Stoke, Wilts	38	C4
Purton, Glouc	37	B3
Purton, Glouc	37	B3
Purton, Wilts	38	C4
Pusey, Oxon	39	B4
Putley, Heref	48	A4
Putloe, Glouc	37	C3
Putney, G Lon	147	A3
Puttenham, Surrey	28	B4
Puxley, Nhants	51	B4
Puxton, Som	24	A3
Pwll, Carm	34	C3
Pwll-du, Monm	36	B2
Pwll-glas, Denb	68	D2
Pwllgloyw, Powys	46	E4
Pwllheli, Gwyn	67	C4
Pwllmeyric, Monm	37	A4
Pwll-y-glaw, Neath	35	B4
Pye Bridge, Derby	72	B2
Pye Corner, Herts	42	C2
Pyecombe, W Suss	18	C3
Pyle, Bridg	22	D1
Pyleigh, Som	12	D1
Pylle, Som	14	A1
Pymore, Cambs	63	C4
Pyrford, Surrey	146	A3
Pytchley, Nhants	51	C1
Pyworthy, Devon	11	C4
Quabbs, Shrops	57	A4
Quadring, Lincs	74	D4
Quainton, Bucks	40	C2
Quarley, Hants	26	C4
Quarndon, Derby	72	A3
Quarrington Hill, Durham	100	B2
Quarrington, Lincs	74	B3
Quarter, S Lan	116	A4
Quatford, Shrops	58	B4
Quatt, Shrops	58	B4
Quebec, Durham	100	A2
Queen Adelaide, Cambs	63	D4
Queen Camel, Som	14	A2
Queen Charlton, Som	24	C2
Queen Oak, Dorset	14	B1
Queenhill, Worcs	48	C4
Queensbury, W Yorks	87	B3
Queensferry, Flint	69	B1
Queenzieburn, N Lan	116	A2
Quendon, Essex	42	C1
Queniborough, Leics	61	B2
Quenington, Glouc	38	C3
Quethiock, Corn	4	B3
Quidenham, Norf	64	D4
Quidhampton, Wilts	15	A1
Quinton, Nhants	51	B3
Quither, Devon	4	C2
Quoditch, Devon	11	C4
Quorndon, Leics	61	A1
Quoyburray, Orkney	144	B2
Quoyloo, Orkney	144	A1
Rachub, Gwyn	67	E1
Rackenford, Devon	12	A2
Rackham, W Suss	18	A3
Rackheath, Norf	65	B1
Radbourne, Derby	72	A4
Radcliffe on Trent, Notts	73	B3
Radcliffe, G Man	80	A1
Radcliffe, Nthumb	106	A1

PLACE	PAGE	GRID
Radclive, Bucks	51	A4
Radford Semele, Warwk	50	A2
Radlett, Herts	41	C3
Radley Green, Essex	43	A3
Radley, Oxon	40	A4
Radnage, Bucks	40	C4
Radstock, Som	24	C3
Radstone, Nhants	50	C4
Radway, Warwk	50	A3
Radwell, Herts	52	C4
Radwinter, Essex	53	C4
Radyr, Card	23	B1
Rafford, Moray	138	A3
Ragdale, Leics	61	B1
Raglan, Monm	36	C3
Ragnall, Notts	83	B4
Rainford, Mers	79	B2
Rainham, G Lon	30	A1
Rainow, Chesh	81	A4
Rainton, N York	93	D4
Rainworth, Notts	73	A2
Raisthorpe, N York	90	A1
Rait, Perth	123	D2
Raithby, Lincs	75	A1
Raithby, Lincs	84	B3
Rake, W Suss	17	B2
Rame, Corn	1	D2
Rame, Corn	4	C4
Rampisham, Dorset	13	C4
Rampside, Cumb	91	D4
Rampton, Cambs	53	B2
Rampton, Notts	83	B4
Ramsbottom, G Man	80	A1
Ramsbury, Wilts	26	C2
Ramsdean, Hants	17	A2
Ramsdell, Hants	27	B3
Ramsden Bellhouse, Essex	43	B4
Ramsden, Oxon	39	B2
Ramsey Heights, Cambs	63	A4
Ramsey Island, Essex	44	A3
Ramsey Mereside, Cambs	63	A4
Ramsey St Mary's, Cambs	63	A4
Ramsey, Cambs	63	A4
Ramsey, Essex	44	C1
Ramsey, I of M	145	D2
Ramsgate, Kent	32	D2
Ramsgill, N York	93	B4
Ramshope, Nthumb	111	B4
Ramshorn, Staffs	71	B3
Ramsnest Common, Surrey	17	C1
Ranby, Lincs	84	B4
Ranby, Notts	83	A4
Rand, Lincs	84	A4
Randwick, Glouc	38	A3
Rangemore, Staffs	60	A1
Rangeworthy, Glouc	24	C1
Rankinston, E Ayrs	108	E4
Rann, Lancs	86	B4
Rannoch Station, Perth	127	B3
Ranskill, Notts	83	A3
Ranton, Staffs	58	C1
Ranworth, Norf	66	A1
Rapness, Orkney	144	B1
Rapps, Som	13	A3
Rashwood, Worcs	48	C2
Raskelf, N York	94	A4
Ratby, Leics	61	A2
Ratcliffe Culey, Leics	60	B3
Ratcliffe on Soar, Notts	72	B4
Ratcliffe on the Wreake, Leics	61	B1
Rathen, Aber	139	E2
Rathmell, N York	86	B1
Ratho, Edin	117	B3
Rathven, Moray	138	D2
Ratley, Warwk	50	A3
Ratling, Kent	32	C3
Ratlinghope, Shrops	57	C3
Rattery, Devon	5	B3
Rattlesden, Suff	54	C2
Rattray, Perth	128	D4
Raunds, Nhants	52	A1
Raven Meols, Mers	78	D2
Ravenfield, S York	82	B3
Ravenglass, Cumb	91	B2
Raveningham, Norf	66	A3
Ravenscar, N York	95	C1
Ravenscliffe, Staffs	70	C2
Ravensden, Beds	52	A3
Ravenshead, Notts	73	A2
Ravensthorpe, Nhants	51	A1
Ravenstone, Bucks	51	B3
Ravenstone, Leics	60	C2
Ravenstonedale, Cumb	92	C1
Ravensworth, N York	93	B1
Rawcliffe, E R of Y	89	B4
Rawling Street, Kent	31	C3
Rawmarsh, S York	82	B2
Rawreth, Essex	43	C4
Rawridge, Devon	12	D4
Rawtenstall, Lancs	86	D4
Raydon, Suff	54	D4
Rayleigh, Essex	43	C4
Rayne, Essex	43	B1
Raynes Park, G Lon	147	A4
Reach, Cambs	53	C2
Read, Lancs	86	B3
Reading, Berks	27	C2
Reagill, Cumb	98	D4
Rearsby, Leics	61	B2
Reay, High	143	B1
Reculver, Kent	32	B2
Red Ball, Devon	12	C3
Red Hill, Warwk	49	B3
Red Lodge, Suff	54	A1
Red Roses, Carm	34	A2
Red Wharf Bay, Angle	77	C4
Redberth, Pemb	33	E3
Redbourn, Herts	41	C2
Redbourne, Lincs	83	D2
Redbrook Street, Kent	21	A1
Redbrook, Wrex	69	D3
Redcar, N York	101	A3
Redditch, Worcs	49	A2

PLACE	PAGE	GRID
Rede, Suff	54	B3
Redenhall, Norf	65	B4
Redesmouth, Nthumb	105	B2
Redford, Angus	129	B4
Redford, W Suss	17	C2
Redgrave, Suff	54	D1
Redhill, Herts	42	A1
Redhill, Som	24	B3
Redhill, Surrey	150	B3
Redisham, Suff	66	A4
Redlingfield Green, Suff	55	A1
Redlingfield, Suff	55	A1
Redlynch, Som	14	B1
Redlynch, Wilts	15	B2
Redmarley, Worcs	48	B2
Redmarshall, Durham	100	B4
Redmile, Leics	73	C4
Redmire, N York	93	B2
Rednal, Shrops	69	C4
Redruth, Corn	1	D1
Redwick, Glouc	24	B1
Redwick, Newport	24	A1
Redworth, Durham	100	A3
Reed, Herts	53	A4
Reedham, Norf	66	A3
Reedness, E R of Y	89	C4
Reepham, Lincs	83	D4
Reepham, Norf	64	D1
Reeth, N York	93	A2
Reigate, Surrey	150	A4
Reighton, N York	95	D4
Reiss, High	143	E2
Relubbus, Corn	1	C2
Remenham, Berks	28	A1
Rempstone, Notts	61	A1
Rendcomb, Glouc	38	B3
Rendham, Suff	55	B2
Renfrew, Renf	115	B3
Renhold, Beds	52	B3
Renishaw, Derby	82	B4
Rennington, Nthumb	112	C3
Renton, Dumb	115	A2
Renwick, Cumb	98	D2
Repps, Norf	66	A1
Repton, Derby	72	A4
Rescassa, Corn	2	C1
Reskadinnick, Corn	1	D1
Resolven, Neath	35	B3
Reston, Border	119	D3
Retford, Notts	83	A4
Rettendon, Essex	43	B4
Revesby, Lincs	74	D1
Rew Street, I of W	9	C1
Rewe, Devon	12	B4
Reymerston, Norf	64	D2
Reynoldston, Swan	34	C4
Rhandirmwyn, Carm	46	C4
Rhayader, Powys	46	D2
Rhes-y-cae, Flint	69	A1
Rhewl, Denb	68	D2
Rhewl, Denb	69	A3
Rhiconich, High	142	B2
Rhigos, Rhond	35	C3
Rhiwlas, Gwyn	67	E1
Rhoden Green, Kent	31	A4
Rhodiad-y-brenin, Pemb	33	B1
Rhoose, Glam	23	A2
Rhos, Carm	45	E4
Rhos, Neath	35	A3
Rhosbeirio, Angle	77	B3
Rhoscolyn, Angle	77	A4
Rhoscrowther, Pemb	33	C3
Rhosesmor, Flint	69	A1
Rhosgoch, Powys	47	A3
Rhoshill, Pemb	45	C4
Rhoshirwaun, Gwyn	67	B4
Rhoslefain, Gwyn	56	A2
Rhosllanerchrugog, Wrex	69	B3
Rhosmeirch, Angle	77	C4
Rhosneigr, Angle	77	B4
Rhos-on-Sea, Aberc	77	F4
Rhostryfan, Gwyn	67	D2
Rhosybol, Angle	77	C3
Rhos-y-gwaliau, Gwyn	68	C4
Rhosymedre, Wrex	69	B3
Rhu, Argyll	114	D1
Rhuallt, Denb	78	B4
Rhuddlan, Denb	78	B4
Rhyd, Gwyn	67	E3
Rhydargaeau, Carm	34	C1
Rhydcymerau, Carm	46	A4
Rhydlewis, Cered	45	E3
Rhydowen, Cered	45	F4
Rhyd-uchaf, Gwyn	68	C3
Rhyd-y pennau, Cered	56	A4
Rhyd-y-clafdy, Gwyn	67	C4
Rhyd-y-foel, Aberc	78	A4
Rhydyfro, Neath	35	A3
Rhyl, Denb	78	B4
Rhymney, Caer	35	D3
Rhynd, Perth	123	D2
Rhynie, Aber	133	E1
Ribbesford, Worcs	48	B1
Ribchester, Lancs	86	A3
Riby, Lincs	84	A1
Riccall, N York	89	B3
Riccarton, Border	104	D1
Richards Castle, Heref	47	D1
Richmond, N York	93	C1
Rickham, Devon	10	A1
Rickinghall, Suff	54	D1
Rickling Green, Essex	42	C1
Rickling, Essex	42	C1
Rickmansworth, Herts	41	B4
Riddlecombe, Devon	11	E3
Ridge Green, Surrey	150	B3
Ridge Lane, Warwk	60	B3
Ridge, Herts	42	A3
Ridge, Wilts	14	D1
Ridgehill, Som	24	B3
Ridgeway, Derby	82	B4
Ridgewell, Essex	54	A4
Ridgmont, Beds	52	A4
Riding Mill, Nthumb	105	C4

PLACE	PAGE	GRID
Ridlington, Norf	76	D4
Ridlington, Rutland	61	C3
Ridsdale, Nthumb	105	B2
Rievaulx, N York	94	B3
Rigg, Dumf	104	B4
Rigsby, Lincs	84	D4
Riley Green, Lancs	86	A4
Rilla Mill, Corn	4	A2
Rillington, N York	95	B4
Rimington, Lancs	86	B2
Rimpton, Som	14	A2
Rimswell, E R of Y	90	D4
Rinaston, Pemb	33	D1
Rindleford, Shrops	58	B3
Ringford, Dumf	103	B4
Ringland, Norf	65	A2
Ringmer, E Suss	19	B3
Ringmore, Devon	6	A2
Ringmore, Devon	10	B1
Ringsfield, Suff	66	A4
Ringshall Stocks, Suff	54	D3
Ringshall, Herts	41	B2
Ringshall, Suff	54	D3
Ringstead, Nhants	52	A1
Ringstead, Norf	75	D3
Ringwood, Hants	15	A4
Ringwould, Kent	32	D4
Ripe, E Suss	19	B3
Ripley, Derby	72	B2
Ripley, Hants	15	B4
Ripley, N York	88	A1
Ripley, Surrey	146	A3
Riplington, Hants	17	A2
Ripon, N York	93	D4
Rippingale, Lincs	74	C4
Ripple, Worcs	48	C4
Ripponden, W Yorks	87	A4
Risbury, Heref	47	D3
Risby, Suff	54	B2
Risca, Caer	36	B4
Rise, E R of Y	90	C2
Risegate, Lincs	74	D4
Riseley, Beds	52	A2
Riseley, Berks	27	C3
Rishangles, Suff	55	A1
Rishton, Lancs	86	B3
Rishworth, W Yorks	81	A1
Risley, Chesh	79	C3
Risley, Derby	72	B4
Risplith, N York	93	C4
River, W Suss	17	C2
Riverhead, Kent	30	A3
Rivington, Lancs	79	C1
Road Weedon, Nhants	51	A2
Roade, Nhants	51	B3
Roadmeetings, S Lan	116	B4
Roadwater, Som	12	C1
Roberton, Border	110	C4
Roberton, S Lan	109	D2
Robertsbridge, E Suss	20	A2
Roberttown, W Yorks	87	C4
Robeston Wathen, Pemb	33	E2
Robin Hood's Bay, N York	95	B1
Roborough, Devon	11	E3
Rocester, Staffs	71	B3
Roch, Pemb	33	C2
Rochdale, G Man	80	B1
Roche, Corn	3	D4
Rochester, Kent	31	A2
Rochester, Nthumb	105	B1
Rochford, Essex	43	C4
Rochford, Worcs	48	A1
Rock, Corn	3	C2
Rock, Nthumb	112	C3
Rock, Worcs	48	B1
Rockbeare, Devon	6	B1
Rockbourne, Hants	15	A2
Rockcliffe, Cumb	104	C4
Rockcliffe, Dumf	97	B1
Rockfield, Monm	37	A2
Rockford, Devon	22	D4
Rockhampton, Glouc	37	B4
Rockhill, Shrops	47	B1
Rockland St Mary, Norf	65	B2
Rockland St Peter, Norf	64	C3
Rockley, Notts	83	A4
Rockley, Wilts	26	B2
Rockwell End, Bucks	40	C4
Rodbourne, Wilts	26	A1
Rodden, Dorset	7	D1
Rode Heath, Chesh	70	B2
Rode, Som	25	A3
Roden, Shrops	57	D1
Rodhuish, Som	12	C1
Rodington, Shrops	58	A1
Rodley, Glouc	37	C2
Rodmarton, Glouc	38	B4
Rodmell, E Suss	19	A4
Rodmersham, Kent	31	C3
Rodney Stoke, Som	24	B4
Rodsley, Derby	71	C3
Roecliffe, N York	93	D4
Roehampton, G Lon	147	A3
Rogate, W Suss	17	B2
Rogerstone, Newport	36	B4
Rogiet, Monm	36	C4
Roke, Oxon	40	B4
Rollesby, Norf	66	A1
Rolleston, Leics	61	B3
Rolleston, Staffs	71	C4
Rolston, E R of Y	90	D2
Rolvenden Layne, Kent	20	B1
Romaldkirk, Durham	99	C3
Romanno Bridge, Border	110	A1
Romansleigh, Devon	11	E2
Romford, Dorset	15	A3
Romford, G Lon	42	C4
Romiley, G Man	81	A3
Romsey, Hants	15	C2
Romsley, Shrops	58	B4
Romsley, Worcs	59	A4
Rookhope, Durham	99	C2
Rookley, I of W	10	A1
Rooks Bridge, Som	24	A4

PLACE	PAGE	GRID
Rooks Nest, Som	12	C1
Rookwith, N York	93	C3
Roos, E R of Y	90	D3
Roothams Green, Beds	52	B2
Ropley Dean, Hants	17	A1
Ropley, Hants	17	A1
Ropsley, Lincs	74	B4
Rora, Aber	139	F3
Rorrington, Shrops	57	B3
Rose Green, Suff	54	C4
Rose Green, Suff	54	C4
Rose, Corn	3	B4
Rosebush, Pemb	33	D1
Rosedale Abbey, N York	94	C2
Rosehall, High	141	A3
Rosehearty, Aber	139	E2
Rosemarket, Pemb	33	C3
Rosemarkie, High	137	B2
Rosemary Lane, Devon	12	D3
Rosenannon, Corn	3	C3
Rosewell, M Loth	118	A3
Rosgill, Cumb	98	C4
Rosley, Cumb	98	A2
Roslin, M Loth	118	A3
Rosliston, Derby	60	A1
Rosneath, Argyll	114	D2
Ross, Dumf	96	F2
Rossett, Wrex	69	C2
Rossington, S York	83	A2
Ross-on-Wye, Heref	37	B1
Rostherne, Chesh	80	A4
Rosthwaite, Cumb	98	A4
Roston, Derby	71	B3
Rosyth, Fife	117	A2
Rothbury, Nthumb	105	D1
Rotherby, Leics	61	B1
Rotherfield Peppard, Oxon	27	C1
Rotherfield, E Suss	19	C2
Rotherham, S York	82	B3
Rothersthorpe, Nhants	51	A2
Rotherwick, Hants	27	C3
Rothes, Moray	138	C3
Rothesay, Argyll	114	C3
Rothiemay, Moray	139	A3
Rothienorman, Aber	139	C4
Rothley, Leics	61	A2
Rothwell, Lincs	84	A2
Rothwell, Nhants	61	C4
Rothwell, W Yorks	88	A4
Rottingdean, E Suss	19	A4
Rottington, Cumb	97	C4
Roucan, Dumf	103	E3
Rougham, Norf	64	B1
Roughton, Lincs	74	D1
Roughton, Norf	76	C4
Roughton, Shrops	58	B3
Roundbush Green, Essex	43	A2
Roundway, Wilts	26	A3
Rous Lench, Worcs	49	A3
Rousdon, Devon	7	A1
Rousham, Oxon	39	C1
Routh, E R of Y	90	C2
Row Green, Essex	43	B2
Row Town, Surrey	146	A3
Row, Corn	3	E2
Row, Cumb	91	E2
Rowanburn, Dumf	104	C3
Rowarth, Derby	81	A3
Rowberrow, Som	24	A3
Rowde, Wilts	26	A3
Rowen, Aberc	68	A1
Rowfoot, Nthumb	104	E4
Rowington, Warwk	49	C1
Rowland, Derby	81	C4
Rowley, Durham	99	D1
Rowley, E R of Y	90	B3
Rowlstone, Heref	36	C1
Rowney Green, Worcs	49	B1
Rownhams, Hants	15	C3
Rowrah, Cumb	97	D4
Rowsham, Bucks	40	C2
Rowsley, Derby	71	C1
Rowston, Lincs	74	C2
Rowton, Chesh	69	C1
Rowton, Shrops	58	A1
Roxburgh, Border	111	B2
Roxby, Lincs	83	C1
Roxton, Beds	52	B3
Roxwell, Essex	43	A3
Roydon Hamlet, Essex	42	B3
Roydon, Essex	42	B3
Roydon, Norf	64	A1
Roydon, Norf	64	D4
Royston, Herts	53	A4
Royston, S York	82	A1
Royton, G Man	80	B1
Rozel, Jersey	145	B1
Ruabon, Wrex	69	B3
Ruaig, Argyll	125	B4
Ruan Lanihorne, Corn	2	B1
Ruan Major, Corn	1	D3
Ruan Minor, Corn	1	D3
Ruardean Hill, Glouc	37	B2
Ruardean Woodside, Glouc	37	B2
Ruardean, Glouc	37	B2
Ruckhall, Heref	47	D4
Ruckinge, Kent	21	B1
Ruckley, Shrops	57	D3
Rudby, N York	94	A1
Rudchester, Nthumb	105	D4
Ruddington, Notts	73	A4
Rudgeway, Glouc	24	C1
Rudgwick, W Suss	18	B1
Rudley Green, Essex	43	C3
Rudloe, Wilts	25	B2
Rudry, Caer	23	B1
Rudston, E R of Y	95	D4
Rudyard, Staffs	71	A2
Rufford, Lancs	79	A1
Rufforth, N York	89	A2
Rugby, Warwk	50	C1
Rugeley, Staffs	59	B1
Rumbling Bridge, Perth	123	C4
Rumburgh, Suff	65	B4

PLACE	PAGE	GRID
Rumford, Falk	116	C2
Runcorn, Chesh	79	B4
Runcton Holme, Norf	63	D2
Runcton, W Suss	17	C4
Runfold, Surrey	28	B4
Runhall, Norf	64	D2
Runham, Norf	66	A2
Runnington, Som	12	D2
Runswick, N York	101	C4
Runwell, Essex	43	B4
Rushall, Heref	48	A4
Rushall, Norf	65	A4
Rushall, Wilts	26	B3
Rushbrooke, Suff	54	C2
Rushbury, Shrops	57	D3
Rushden, Herts	42	A1
Rushden, Nhants	51	C2
Rushett Common, Surrey	146	A4
Rushford, Norf	64	C4
Rushlake Green, E Suss	19	C2
Rushmere, Suff	66	B4
Rushmoor, Surrey	17	C1
Rushock, Heref	47	B2
Rushock, Worcs	48	C1
Rushton, Chesh	70	A1
Rushton, Nhants	61	C4
Rushwick, Worcs	48	C3
Rushyford, Durham	100	B3
Ruskington, Lincs	74	C2
Rusland, Cumb	91	D2
Rusper, W Suss	18	C1
Ruspidge, Glouc	37	B2
Russ Hill, Surrey	18	C1
Russell's Water, Oxon	40	B4
Rustington, W Suss	18	A4
Ruston Parva, E R of Y	90	B1
Ruston, N York	95	B3
Ruswarp, N York	95	B1
Rutherford, Border	111	A2
Rutherglen, S Lan	115	C3
Ruthernbridge, Corn	3	D3
Ruthin, Denb	69	A2
Ruthven, Aber	139	A3
Ruthven, Angus	128	E4
Ruthvoes, Corn	3	C3
Ruthwell, Dumf	103	E4
Ruxley Corner, G Lon	30	A2
Ruyton-XI-Towns, Shrops	57	C1
Ryal, Nthumb	105	C3
Ryall, Dorset	13	B4
Ryarsh, Kent	31	A3
Rydal, Cumb	91	E1
Ryde, I of W	10	A1
Rye Street, Worcs	48	B4
Rye, E Suss	21	A2
Ryhall, Rutland	62	B2
Ryhill, W Yorks	82	A1
Ryland, Lincs	83	D4
Ryme Intrinseca, Dorset	13	D3
Ryther, N York	89	A3
Ryton, Shrops	58	B3
Ryton, Tyne	105	D4
Ryton-on-Dunsmore, Warwk	50	A1
Sabden, Lancs	86	B3
Sacombe, Herts	42	B2
Sacriston, Durham	100	A1
Sadberge, Durham	100	B4
Saddell, Argyll	107	E2
Saddington, Leics	61	B3
Saddle Bow, Norf	63	D1
Saddlescombe, W Suss	18	C3
Saffron Walden, Essex	53	B4
Sageston, Pemb	33	D3
Saham Hills, Norf	64	C2
Saham Toney, Norf	64	C3
Saighton, Chesh	69	C1
St Abbs, Border	119	D3
St Agnes, Corn	3	A4
St Albans, Herts	41	C3
St Allen, Corn	3	B4
St Andrew, Guern	145	B2
St Andrew's Major, Glam	23	B2
St Andrews, Fife	124	C3
St Ann's Chapel, Devon	10	A1
St Anthony, Corn	2	A2
St Arvans, Monm	37	A4
St Asaph, Denb	78	B4
St Athan, Glam	23	A2
St Aubin, Jersey	145	A2
St Austell, Corn	3	D4
St Bees, Cumb	97	C4
St Boswells, Border	111	A2
St Brelade, Jersey	145	A2
St Brelade's Bay, Jersey	145	A2
St Breock, Corn	3	D3
St Breward, Corn	3	E2
St Briavels, Glouc	37	A3
St Bride's Major, Glam	22	E2
St Brides super-Ely, Glam	23	A1
St Brides Wentlooge, Newport	23	C1
St Buryan, Corn	1	B2
St Catherines, Argyll	121	C3
St Chloe, Glouc	38	A3
St Clears, Carm	34	A2
St Cleer, Corn	4	A3
St Clement, Corn	2	B1
St Clement, Jersey	145	B2
St Clether, Corn	4	A1
St Columb Major, Corn	3	C3
St Combs, Aber	139	F2
St Cross South Elmham, Suff	65	B4
St Cyrus, Aber	129	D3
St David's, Pemb	33	B1
St David's, Perth	123	B2
St Day, Corn	1	D1
St Decumans, Som	23	A4
St Dennis, Corn	3	C4
St Dogmaels, Cered	45	C3
St Dominick, Corn	4	B3
St Donats, Glam	22	E2
St Endellion, Corn	3	D2
St Enoder, Corn	3	C4
St Erme, Corn	3	B4
St Erney, Corn	4	B4
St Erth Praze, Corn	1	C2
St Erth, Corn	1	C2
St Ervan, Corn	3	C3
St Ewe, Corn	2	C1
St Fagans, Card	23	B1
St Fergus, Aber	139	F3
St Fillans, Perth	122	D2
St Florence, Pemb	33	E3
St Gennys, Corn	11	A4
St George, Aberc	78	A4
St George's Hill, Surrey	146	A3
St Georges, Som	24	A3
St Giles in the Wood, Devon	11	D2
St Giles-on-the-Heath, Devon	4	B1
St Harmon, Powys	46	D1
St Helen Auckland, Durham	100	A3
St Helena, Norf	65	A1
St Helens, I of W	10	B1
St Helens, Mers	79	B2
St Helier, G Lon	147	A4
St Helier, Jersey	145	B2
St Hilary, Corn	1	C2
St Hilary, Glam	23	A2
St Ippollitts, Herts	41	C1
St Ishmael's, Pemb	33	B3
St Ive, Corn	4	B3
St Ives, Cambs	52	D1
St Ives, Corn	1	C1
St John, Corn	4	B4
St John, Jersey	145	B1
St John's Chapel, Devon	11	D1
St John's Fen End, Norf	63	C2
St John's Town of Dalry, Dumf	103	A2
St John's Wood, G Lon	148	A2
St John's, I of M	145	B3
St Johns, Kent	30	A3
St Johns, Surrey	146	A3
St Jude's, I of M	145	C2
St Just, Corn	1	A2
St Just-in-Roseland, Corn	2	A2
St Keverne, Corn	2	A3
St Kew Highway, Corn	3	D2
St Keyne, Corn	4	A3
St Lawrence, Essex	44	A3
St Lawrence, I of W	10	A2
St Lawrence, Jersey	145	B2
St Leonards, Bucks	41	A3
St Leonards, Dorset	15	A4
St Lythans, Glam	23	A2
St Mabyn, Corn	3	D2
St Margaret's at Cliffe, Kent	32	D4
St Margaret's Hope, Orkney	144	A2
St Margarets, Heref	47	C4
St Margarets, Herts	42	B2
St Marks, I of M	145	B4
St Martin, Corn	4	A4
St Martin, Guern	145	B2
St Martin, Jersey	145	B2
St Martins, Shrops	69	B4
St Mary Bourne, Hants	27	A4
St Mary Church, Glam	22	E2
St Mary Cray, G Lon	30	A2
St Mary in the Marsh, Kent	21	B2
St Mary, Jersey	145	A2
St Mary's Bay, Kent	21	B2
St Mary's Hoo, Kent	31	B1
St Mary's, Orkney	144	B2
St Maughans Green, Monm	37	A2
St Mawes, Corn	2	A2
St Mawgan, Corn	3	C3
St Mellion, Corn	4	B3
St Merryn, Corn	3	C2
St Mewan, Corn	3	D4
St Michael Caerhays, Corn	2	B1
St Michael Church, Som	13	A1
St Michael Penkevil, Corn	2	B1
St Michael South Elmham, Suff	65	B4
St Michael's on Wyre, Lancs	85	B3
St Minver, Corn	3	D2
St Monans, Fife	124	C4
St Neot, Corn	3	E3
St Neots, Cambs	52	B2
St Nicholas at Wade, Kent	32	C2
St Nicholas, Glam	23	A2
St Nicholas, Pemb	45	A4
St Olaves, Norf	66	A3
St Osyth, Essex	44	C2
St Ouen, Jersey	145	A2
St Owens Cross, Heref	37	A1
St Pauls Cray, G Lon	30	A2
St Paul's Walden, Herts	41	C1
St Peter Port, Guern	145	B2
St Peter, Jersey	145	A2
St Peter's, Guern	145	B2
St Sampson, Guern	145	B2
St Saviour, Guern	145	B2
St Saviour, Jersey	145	B2
St Stephen, Corn	3	C4
St Stephen's Coombe, Corn	3	C4
St Teath, Corn	3	D2
St Tudy, Corn	3	D2
St Twynnells, Pemb	33	C4
St Veep, Corn	3	E4
St Vigeans, Angus	129	C4
St Wenn, Corn	3	D3
St Weonards, Heref	37	A1
Saintbury, Glouc	49	B4
Salcombe, Devon	10	A1
Salcott, Essex	44	A2
Sale Green, Worcs	49	A2
Sale, G Man	80	A3
Saleby, Lincs	84	D4
Salehurst, E Suss	20	A2
Salem, Cered	56	B4
Salem, Gwyn	67	E2
Salen, Argyll	125	F4
Salford Priors, Warwk	49	B3
Salford, Beds	51	C4
Salford, G Man	80	B2
Salford, Oxon	39	B1
Salfords, Surrey	150	B4
Salhouse, Norf	65	B1
Saline, Fife	117	A1
Salisbury, Wilts	15	A1
Salkeld Dykes, Cumb	98	C2
Salle, Norf	64	D1
Salmonby, Lincs	84	C4
Salperton, Glouc	38	C2
Salsburgh, N Lan	116	B3
Salt, Staffs	71	A4
Saltash, Corn	4	C4
Saltburn, High	137	B1
Saltburn-by-the-Sea, N York	101	B4
Saltby, Leics	73	C4
Saltcoats, N Ayrs	108	C1
Salterforth, Lancs	86	C2
Salterton, Wilts	15	A1
Saltfleet, Lincs	84	D3
Saltfleetby All Saints, Lincs	84	D3
Saltfleetby St Clement, Lincs	84	D3
Saltfleetby St Peter, Lincs	84	D3
Saltford, Som	24	C2
Salthouse, Norf	76	B3
Saltmarshe, E R of Y	89	C4
Salton, N York	94	C3
Saltrens, Devon	11	D2
Salwarpe, Worcs	48	C2
Salwayash, Dorset	13	B4
Sambourne, Warwk	49	B2
Sambrook, Shrops	58	B1
Samlesbury, Lancs	86	A3
Sampford Arundel, Som	12	C2
Sampford Brett, Som	12	C1
Sampford Courtenay, Devon	11	E4
Sampford Moor, Som	12	C3
Sampford Peverell, Devon	12	C3
Sampford Spiney, Devon	4	C2
Samsonlane, Orkney	144	B1
Samuelston, E Loth	119	A3
Sanaigmore, Argyll	113	A3
Sancreed, Corn	1	B2
Sand Hills, W Yorks	88	A3
Sand Hole, E R of Y	89	C3
Sand Hutton, N York	89	B1
Sandal Magna, W Yorks	82	A1
Sandbach, Chesh	70	B1
Sandend, Aber	139	A2
Sanderstead, G Lon	150	C1
Sandford Orcas, Dorset	14	A2
Sandford St Martin, Oxon	39	C1
Sandford, Cumb	99	A4
Sandford, Hants	15	B4
Sandford, Som	24	A3
Sandhaven, Aber	139	E2
Sandhead, Dumf	96	B1
Sandhoe, Nthumb	105	C4
Sandhurst, Berks	28	A3
Sandhurst, Glouc	38	A1
Sandhurst, Kent	20	B2
Sandhutton, N York	93	D3
Sandilands, Lincs	84	D4
Sandleigh, Oxon	39	C3
Sandness, Shet	144	A2
Sandon Bank, Staffs	71	A4
Sandon, Essex	43	B3
Sandon, Herts	53	A4
Sandon, Staffs	71	A4
Sandown, I of W	10	A1
Sandplace, Corn	4	A4
Sandridge, Herts	41	C2
Sandringham, Norf	75	D4
Sandsend, N York	101	D4
Sandtoft, Lincs	83	B1
Sandway, Kent	31	C4
Sandwich, Kent	32	C3
Sandwick, Shet	144	A3
Sandwith, Cumb	97	C4
Sandy Lane, Wilts	26	A2
Sandy, Beds	52	B3
Sandygate, I of M	145	C2
Sandyhills, Dumf	97	C1
Sanquhar, Dumf	109	C4
Santon Bridge, Cumb	91	B1
Santon Downham, Suff	64	B4
Sapcote, Leics	60	C3
Sapey Common, Heref	48	B2
Sapiston, Suff	54	C1
Sapperton, Glouc	38	B3
Sapperton, Lincs	74	B4
Saracen's Head, Lincs	75	A4
Sarn, Gwyn	67	B4
Sarn, Powys	56	D3
Sarn, Powys	57	A4
Sarnau, Cered	45	E3
Sarnau, Powys	57	B1
Sarnesfield, Heref	47	C3
Saron, Carm	34	D2
Sarratt, Herts	41	B3
Sarre, Kent	32	C2
Sarsden, Oxon	39	B1
Satley, Durham	99	D2
Satterleigh, Devon	11	F2
Satterthwaite, Cumb	91	D2
Sauchen, Aber	134	B2
Saul, Glouc	37	C3
Saundby, Notts	83	B3
Saundersfoot, Pemb	33	E3
Saunderton, Bucks	40	C3
Sausthorpe, Lincs	75	A1
Sawbridge, Warwk	50	C2
Sawbridgeworth, Herts	42	C2
Sawdon, N York	95	B3
Sawley, Lancs	86	B2
Sawley, N York	93	C4
Sawston, Cambs	53	B3
Sawtry, Cambs	62	C4
Saxby All Saints, Lincs	83	D1
Saxby, Leics	61	C1
Saxby, Lincs	83	D3
Saxelbye, Leics	61	B1
Saxham Street, Suff	54	D2
Saxilby, Lincs	83	C4
Saxlingham Green, Norf	65	B3
Saxlingham Thorpe, Norf	65	A3
Saxlingham, Norf	76	B3
Saxmundham, Suff	55	C2
Saxon Street, Cambs	54	A2
Saxondale, Notts	73	B3
Saxtead Green, Suff	55	B2
Saxtead, Suff	55	B2
Saxthorpe, Norf	76	B4
Saxton, N York	88	B3
Sayers Common, W Suss	18	C2
Scackleton, N York	94	C4
Scaftworth, Notts	83	A3
Scagglethorpe, N York	95	A4
Scalasaig, Argyll	113	C1
Scalby, E R of Y	89	C4
Scalby, N York	95	C2
Scaldwell, Nhants	51	B1
Scaleby, Cumb	104	C4
Scalebyhill, Cumb	104	C4
Scales, Cumb	91	D4
Scales, Cumb	98	A3
Scalford, Leics	61	C1
Scaling, N York	101	C4
Scalloway, Shet	144	A2
Scamblesby, Lincs	84	B4
Scampston, N York	95	B4
Scampton, Lincs	83	C4
Scapegoat Hill, W Yorks	81	B1
Scarborough, N York	95	C2
Scarcewater, Corn	3	C4
Scarcliffe, Derby	72	B1
Scarcroft Hill, W Yorks	88	A3
Scargill, Durham	93	B1
Scarinish, Argyll	125	B4
Scarisbrick, Lancs	79	A1
Scarning, Norf	64	C2
Scarrington, Notts	73	B3
Scawby, Lincs	83	D2
Scawton, N York	94	B3
Scayne's Hill, W Suss	19	A2
Scethrog, Powys	35	D1
Scholes, S York	82	A2
Scholes, W Yorks	81	C1
Scissett, W Yorks	81	C1
Scleddau, Pemb	45	A4
Scofton, Notts	83	A4
Scole, Norf	55	A1
Sconser, High	130	D1
Scopwick, Lincs	74	B2
Scorborough, E R of Y	90	B2
Scorrier, Corn	1	D1
Scorton, Lancs	85	C2
Scorton, N York	93	C1
Scotby, Cumb	98	B1
Scotch Corner, N York	93	C1
Scothern, Lincs	83	D4
Scotlandwell, Perth	123	D4
Scotter, Lincs	83	C2
Scotterthorpe, Lincs	83	C2
Scotton, Lincs	83	C2
Scotton, N York	88	A1
Scotton, N York	93	C2
Scoulton, Norf	64	C3
Scourie, High	142	A3
Scrabster, High	143	C1
Scraesburgh, Border	111	A3
Scrane End, Lincs	75	A3
Scraptoft, Leics	61	B2
Scratby, Norf	66	B1
Scrayingham, N York	89	B1
Scredington, Lincs	74	C3
Scremerston, Nthumb	119	E4
Screveton, Notts	73	B3
Scriven, N York	88	A1
Scrooby, Notts	83	A3
Scropton, Derby	71	C4
Scruton, N York	93	D2
Sculthorpe, Norf	76	A4
Scunthorpe, Lincs	83	C1
Sea Palling, Norf	76	E4
Seaborough, Dorset	13	B4
Seaford, E Suss	19	B4
Seagrave, Leics	61	A1
Seaham, Durham	100	C1
Seahouses, Nthumb	112	C2
Seal, Kent	30	B3
Seale, Surrey	28	B4
Seamer, N York	94	A1
Seamer, N York	95	C3
Seamill, N Ayrs	108	C1
Searby, Lincs	83	D2
Seascale, Cumb	91	B1
Seathwaite, Cumb	91	C2
Seatoller, Cumb	98	A4
Seaton Delaval, Nthumb	106	B3
Seaton Ross, E R of Y	89	C3
Seaton, Corn	4	A4
Seaton, Cumb	97	D3
Seaton, Devon	7	A1
Seaton, E R of Y	90	C2
Seaton, Nthumb	106	B3
Seaton, Rutland	62	A3
Seatown, Dorset	7	B1
Seave Green, N York	94	B1
Seaview, I of W	10	B1
Seaville, Cumb	97	E1
Seavington St Mary, Som	13	B3
Sebergham, Cumb	98	B2
Seckington, Warwk	60	A2
Sedbergh, Cumb	92	B2
Sedbusk, N York	92	D2
Sedgeberrow, Worcs	49	A4
Sedgebrook, Lincs	74	A3
Sedgefield, Durham	100	B3
Sedgeford, Norf	75	D4
Sedgehill, Wilts	14	C2
Sedgwick, Cumb	92	A3
Sedrup, Bucks	40	C2
Seend Cleeve, Wilts	26	A3
Seer Green, Bucks	41	A4
Seething, Norf	65	B3
Sefton, Mers	79	A2
Seighford, Staffs	58	C1
Seion, Gwyn	67	E1
Seisdon, Staffs	58	C3
Selattyn, Shrops	69	B4
Selborne, Hants	17	B1
Selby, N York	89	A3
Selham, W Suss	17	C2
Selhurst, G Lon	149	A4
Selkirk, Border	110	D2
Sellack, Heref	37	A1
Sellindge, Kent	21	B1
Selling, Kent	32	A3
Sells Green, Wilts	26	A3
Selmeston, E Suss	19	B3
Selsdon, G Lon	150	C1
Selsey, W Suss	10	D1
Selside, N York	92	C4
Selston, Notts	72	B2
Selworthy, Som	22	E4
Semer, Suff	54	C3
Semington, Wilts	25	B3
Semley, Wilts	14	C2
Send Marsh, Surrey	146	A3
Send, Surrey	146	A3
Senghenydd, Caer	35	D4
Sennen Cove, Corn	1	A2
Sennen, Corn	1	A3
Sennybridge, Powys	35	C1
Sessay, N York	94	A4
Setchey, Norf	63	D2
Settle, N York	86	C1
Settrington, N York	95	A4
Seven Sisters, Neath	35	B3
Seven Wells, Glouc	49	B4
Sevenhampton, Glouc	38	B2
Sevenhampton, Wilts	39	A4
Sevenoaks Weald, Kent	30	A4
Sevenoaks, Kent	30	A3
Severn Beach, Glouc	24	B1
Severn Stoke, Worcs	48	C4
Sewards End, Essex	53	C4
Sewell, Beds	41	B1
Sewerby, E R of Y	95	E4
Seworgan, Corn	1	D2
Sewstern, Leics	62	A1
Shabbington, Bucks	40	B3
Shackerstone, Leics	60	B2
Shackleford, Surrey	28	B4
Shadforth, Durham	100	B2
Shadingfield, Suff	66	A4
Shadoxhurst, Kent	21	A1
Shadwell, Norf	64	C4
Shaftenhoe End, Herts	53	A4
Shaftesbury, Dorset	14	C2
Shafton, S York	82	B1
Shalbourne, Wilts	26	D3
Shalden, Hants	27	C4
Shalford Green, Essex	43	B1
Shalford, Essex	43	B1
Shalford, Surrey	146	A4
Shalstone, Bucks	51	A4
Shamley Green, Surrey	146	A4
Shandon, Argyll	114	D1
Shangton, Leics	61	B3
Shanklin, I of W	10	A2
Shap, Cumb	98	C4
Shapwick, Dorset	14	D4
Shapwick, Som	13	B1
Shardlow, Derby	72	B4
Shareshill, Staffs	59	A2
Sharlston, W Yorks	88	B4
Sharnbrook, Beds	52	A2
Sharnford, Leics	60	C3
Sharow, N York	93	D4
Sharpenhoe, Beds	41	B1
Sharperton, Nthumb	112	A4
Sharpness, Glouc	37	B3
Sharrington, Norf	76	B4
Shatterford, Worcs	58	B4
Shaugh Prior, Devon	4	C3
Shavington, Chesh	70	B2
Shaw Mills, N York	87	C1
Shaw, G Man	81	A1
Shaw, Wilts	25	B2
Shawbury, Shrops	57	D1
Shawell, Leics	61	A4
Shawhead, Dumf	103	C3
Shearsby, Leics	61	B4
Shearston, Som	13	A1
Shebbear, Devon	11	D3
Shebdon, Staffs	58	B1
Sheen, Staffs	71	B1
Sheepscombe, Glouc	38	A3
Sheepstor, Devon	5	A3
Sheepwash, Devon	11	D4
Sheepy Magna, Leics	60	B3
Sheering, Essex	42	C2
Sheerness, Kent	31	C2
Sheerwater, Surrey	146	A3
Sheet, Hants	17	B2
Sheffield, S York	82	A3
Shefford, Beds	52	B4
Sheinton, Shrops	58	A2
Shelderton, Shrops	47	C1
Sheldon, Derby	71	C1
Sheldon, Devon	12	D3
Sheldwich, Kent	32	A3
Shelfanger, Norf	64	D4
Shelford, Notts	73	B3
Shelley, Suff	54	D4
Shelley, W Yorks	81	C1
Shellingford, Oxon	39	B4
Shellow Bowells, Essex	43	A3
Shelsley Beauchamp, Worcs	48	B2
Shelsley Walsh, Worcs	48	B2
Shelton, Beds	52	A1
Shelton, Norf	65	A4
Shelton, Notts	73	C3
Shelve, Shrops	57	B3
Shelwick, Heref	47	D4
Shenington, Oxon	50	A4
Shenley Brook End, Bucks	51	B4
Shenley Church End, Bucks	51	B4
Shenley, Herts	41	C3
Shenmore, Heref	47	C4
Shenstone, Staffs	59	B2
Shenstone, Worcs	48	C1
Shenton, Leics	60	B3
Shepherd's Bush, G Lon	147	A2
Shepherdswell, Kent	32	C4
Shepley, W Yorks	81	C1
Shepperton Green, Surrey	146	A2
Shepperton, Surrey	146	A2
Shepreth, Cambs	53	A3
Shepshed, Leics	60	C1
Shepton Mallet, Som	24	C4
Shepton Montague, Som	14	A1
Sheraton, Durham	100	C2
Sherborne St John, Hants	27	C3
Sherborne, Dorset	14	A3
Sherborne, Glouc	39	A2
Sherborne, Som	24	C3
Sherbourne, Warwk	49	C2
Sherburn in Elmet, N York	88	B3
Sherburn, Durham	100	B2
Sherburn, N York	95	B3
Shere, Surrey	146	A4
Shereford, Norf	75	E4
Sherfield English, Hants	15	C2
Sherford, Devon	10	B1
Sherford, Dorset	8	B1
Sheriff Hutton, N York	94	C4
Sheriffhales, Shrops	58	B2
Sheringham, Norf	76	C3
Sherington, Bucks	51	C3
Shernborne, Norf	75	D4
Sherrington, Wilts	14	D1
Sherston, Wilts	25	B1
Shevington, G Man	79	B1
Sheviock, Corn	4	B4
Shibden Head, W Yorks	87	B4
Shidlaw, Nthumb	111	B1
Shiel Bridge, High	131	A2
Shieldaig, High	135	F3
Shieldhill, Falk	116	C2
Shifnal, Shrops	58	B2
Shilbottle, Nthumb	112	C4
Shildon, Durham	100	A3
Shillingford Abbot, Devon	6	A1
Shillingford St George, Devon	6	A1
Shillingford, Devon	12	B2
Shillingstone, Dorset	14	C3
Shillington, Beds	52	B4
Shilton, Oxon	39	A3
Shilton, Warwk	60	C4
Shimpling Street, Suff	54	B3
Shimpling, Norf	65	A4
Shimpling, Suff	54	B3
Shincliffe, Durham	100	B2
Shiney Row, Tyne	100	B1
Shipbourne, Kent	30	B4
Shipdham, Norf	64	C2
Shipham, Som	24	A3
Shiplake, Oxon	28	A1
Shipley, W Suss	18	B2
Shipley, W Yorks	87	B3
Shippon, Oxon	39	C4
Shipston on Stour, Warwk	49	C4
Shipton Bellinger, Hants	26	C4
Shipton Gorge, Dorset	7	C1
Shipton Green, W Suss	17	B4
Shipton Moyne, Glouc	38	A4
Shipton, Glouc	38	B2
Shipton, N York	89	A1
Shipton, Shrops	57	D3
Shipton-on-Cherwell, Oxon	39	C2
Shiptonthorpe, E R of Y	90	A2
Shipton-under-Wychwood, Oxon	39	B2
Shirburn, Oxon	40	B4
Shirdley Hill, Lancs	79	A1
Shirebrook, Derby	73	A1
Shirenewton, Monm	37	A4
Shireoaks, Notts	82	C4
Shirland, Derby	72	B2
Shirley, Derby	71	C3
Shirley, G Lon	149	A4
Shirrell Heath, Hants	16	B3
Shirwell, Devon	11	E1
Shiskine, N Ayrs	107	F2
Shobdon, Heref	47	C2
Shoby, Leics	61	B1
Shocklach, Chesh	69	C2
Shop Street, Suff	55	A1
Shop, Corn	3	C2
Shop, Corn	11	B3
Shoreditch, G Lon	149	A1
Shoreditch, Som	13	A2
Shoreham-by-Sea, W Suss	18	C4
Shorley, Hants	16	B2
Shorne, Kent	31	A2
Shortgate, E Suss	19	B3
Shortlanesend, Corn	2	A1
Shortstown, Beds	52	A3
Shorwell, I of W	9	C2
Shoscombe, Som	25	A3
Shotesham, Norf	65	B3
Shotley Bridge, Durham	99	D1
Shotley Gate, Suff	55	B4
Shotley Street, Suff	55	A4
Shotley, Suff	55	A4
Shottenden, Kent	32	A3
Shotteswell, Warwk	50	B3
Shottisham, Suff	55	B4
Shottle, Derby	72	A2
Shottlegate, Derby	72	A3
Shotts, N Lan	116	B4
Shotwick, Chesh	69	B1
Shouldham Thorpe, Norf	64	A2
Shouldham, Norf	64	A2
Shoulton, Worcs	48	C2
Shrawardine, Shrops	57	C1
Shrawley, Worcs	48	B2
Shreding Green, Bucks	146	A1
Shrewley, Warwk	49	C2
Shrewsbury, Shrops	57	D2
Shrewton, Wilts	26	B4

PLACE	PAGE	GRID
Stoke Lyne, Oxon	40	A1
Stoke Mandeville, Bucks	40	C3
Stoke Newington, G Lon	149	A1
Stoke Orchard, Glouc	38	A1
Stoke Poges, Bucks	146	A1
Stoke Prior, Heref	47	D3
Stoke Prior, Worcs	49	A2
Stoke Rivers, Devon	11	E1
Stoke Rochford, Lincs	74	A4
Stoke Row, Oxon	27	C1
Stoke St Michael, Som	24	C4
Stoke St Milborough, Shrops	57	D4
Stoke sub Hamdon, Som	13	C3
Stoke Talmage, Oxon	40	B3
Stoke Trister, Som	14	B2
Stoke upon Tern, Shrops	70	A4
Stoke Wake, Dorset	14	B4
Stoke, Devon	11	B2
Stoke, Hants	17	A4
Stoke, Hants	27	A4
Stoke, Kent	31	B2
Stoke-by-Nayland, Suff	54	C4
Stokeford, Dorset	8	B1
Stokeham, Notts	83	B4
Stokeinteignhead, Devon	6	A3
Stokenchurch, Bucks	40	C4
Stokenham, Devon	10	B1
Stoke-on-Trent, Staffs	70	C3
Stokesby, Norf	66	A2
Stokesley, N York	94	B1
Stolford, Som	12	C1
Stolford, Som	23	B4
Ston Easton, Som	24	C3
Stondon Massey, Essex	43	A3
Stone Allerton, Som	24	A4
Stone Street, Kent	30	B3
Stone Street, Suff	66	A4
Stone, Bucks	40	C2
Stone, Glouc	37	B4
Stone, Kent	21	A2
Stone, S York	82	C3
Stone, Staffs	70	C4
Stone, Worcs	48	C1
Stonebridge, Som	24	A3
Stonebridge, W Mids	60	A4
Stonebroom, Derby	72	B2
Stonecrouch, Kent	20	A1
Stonegate, E Suss	20	A2
Stonegrave, N York	94	C3
Stonehall, Worcs	48	C3
Stonehaven, Aber	129	E1
Stonehill Green, Kent	30	A2
Stonehouse, Chesh	69	D1
Stonehouse, Glouc	37	C3
Stonehouse, S Lan	109	B1
Stoneleigh, Warwk	50	A1
Stones Green, Essex	44	C1
Stonesby, Leics	61	C1
Stonesfield, Oxon	39	C2
Stoney Middleton, Derby	81	C4
Stoney Stanton, Leics	60	C3
Stoney Stoke, Som	14	B1
Stoney Stratton, Som	14	A1
Stoney Stretton, Shrops	57	C2
Stoneyburn, W Loth	116	C3
Stoneykirk, Dumf	96	B1
Stoneywood, Aberdeen City	134	C2
Stonham Aspal, Suff	55	A2
Stonor, Oxon	40	B4
Stonton Wyville, Leics	61	C3
Stony Houghton, Derby	72	B1
Stoodleigh, Devon	11	F1
Stoodleigh, Devon	12	B2
Stopham, W Suss	18	A2
Stormy Corner, Lancs	79	B1
Stornoway, W Isle	144	B2
Storrington, W Suss	18	B3
Storwood, E R of Y	89	B2
Stotfold, Beds	52	C4
Stottesdon, Shrops	58	A4
Stoughton, Leics	61	B3
Stoughton, Surrey	146	A4
Stoughton, W Suss	17	B3
Stoulton, Worcs	48	C3
Stour Provost, Dorset	14	B2
Stour Row, Dorset	14	C2
Stourbridge, W Mids	58	C4
Stourport-on-Severn, Worcs	48	C1
Stourton Caundle, Dorset	14	B3
Stourton, Staffs	58	C4
Stourton, Warwk	50	A4
Stourton, Wilts	14	B1
Stow Bardolph, Norf	63	D2
Stow Bedon, Norf	64	C3
Stow cum Quy, Cambs	53	B2
Stow Longa, Cambs	52	B1
Stow Maries, Essex	43	C3
Stow, Border	110	C1
Stow, Lincs	83	C4
Stowbridge, Norf	63	D2
Stowe by Chartley, Staffs	71	A4
Stowe, Shrops	47	B1
Stowell, Som	14	A2
Stowford, Devon	4	C1
Stowford, Devon	11	D4
Stowford, Devon	22	B4
Stowlangtoft, Suff	54	C2
Stowmarket, Suff	54	D2
Stow-on-the-Wold, Glouc	39	A1
Stowting Common, Kent	32	B4
Stowting, Kent	32	B4
Stowupland, Suff	54	D2
Strachan, Aber	134	A4
Strachur, Argyll	121	C4
Stradbroke, Suff	55	A1
Stradsett, Norf	64	A2
Stragglethorpe, Lincs	74	A2
Straiton, S Ayrs	108	D4
Straloch, Perth	128	C3
Stramshall, Staffs	71	B4
Strang, I of M	145	C3
Strangford, Heref	37	A1
Stranraer, Dumf	102	A4

PLACE	PAGE	GRID
Stratfield Saye, Hants	27	C3
Stratfield Turgis, Hants	27	C3
Stratford St Mary, Suff	54	D4
Stratford, G Lon	149	B1
Stratford-upon-Avon, Warwk	49	C3
Strath, High	135	F1
Strathaven, S Lan	109	B1
Strathblane, Stirl	115	C2
Strathcanaird, High	140	D3
Strathdon, Aber	133	D2
Strathkinness, Fife	124	B3
Strathmiglo, Fife	123	D3
Strathpeffer, High	136	F2
Strathtay, Perth	128	B3
Strathwhillan, N Ayrs	108	A2
Strathy, High	143	A1
Strathyre, Stirl	122	C3
Stratton Audley, Oxon	40	A1
Stratton St Michael, Norf	65	A3
Stratton Strawless, Norf	65	A1
Stratton, Corn	11	B4
Stratton, Dorset	7	D1
Stratton, Glouc	38	B3
Stratton-on-the-Fosse, Som	24	C4
Stream, Som	12	C1
Streat, E Suss	19	A3
Streatham, G Lon	147	B2
Streatley, Beds	41	B1
Streatley, Berks	27	B1
Street Ashton, Warwk	60	C4
Street Dinas, Shrops	69	B3
Street End, W Suss	17	C4
Street Gate, Tyne	106	A4
Street on the Fosse, Som	14	A1
Street, Som	13	C1
Streethay, Staffs	59	B2
Streetlam, N York	93	D2
Streetly End, Cambs	53	C3
Strelley, Notts	73	A3
Strensall, N York	89	B1
Strete, Devon	10	B1
Stretford, G Man	80	A3
Strethall, Essex	53	B4
Stretham, Cambs	53	B1
Stretton on Fosse, Warwk	49	C4
Stretton Sugwas, Heref	47	D4
Stretton under Fosse, Warwk	60	C4
Stretton Westwood, Shrops	58	A3
Stretton, Chesh	79	C4
Stretton, Derby	72	B1
Stretton, Rutland	62	A1
Stretton, Staffs	58	C2
Stretton, Staffs	71	C4
Stretton-on-Dunsmore, Warwk	50	B1
Strichen, Aber	139	E3
Stringston, Som	23	B4
Strixton, Nhants	51	C2
Stroat, Glouc	37	A4
Stromeferry, High	136	A4
Stromness, Orkney	144	A2
Stronachlachar, Stirl	122	A3
Strone, Argyll	114	C2
Stronmilchan, Argyll	121	C2
Strontian, High	126	B3
Strood Green, Surrey	150	A3
Stroud Green, Glouc	37	C3
Stroud, Glouc	38	A3
Stroud, Hants	17	A2
Stroude, Surrey	146	A2
Stroxton, Lincs	74	A4
Struan, High	135	B4
Struan, Perth	128	A2
Strumpshaw, Norf	65	B2
Struy, High	136	E4
Stuartfield, Aber	139	E3
Stubbington, Hants	16	B4
Stubbins, Lancs	80	A1
Stubton, Lincs	74	A3
Stud Green, Berks	28	B1
Studham, Beds	41	B2
Studholme, Cumb	98	A1
Studland, Dorset	8	C2
Studley Royal, N York	93	D4
Studley, Warwk	49	B2
Studley, Wilts	26	A2
Stuntney, Cambs	53	C1
Sturmer, Essex	54	A4
Sturminster Common, Dorset	14	B3
Sturminster Marshall, Dorset	14	D4
Sturminster Newton, Dorset	14	B3
Sturry, Kent	32	B3
Sturton by Stow, Lincs	83	C4
Sturton le Steeple, Notts	83	B4
Sturton, Lincs	83	D2
Stuston, Suff	55	A1
Stutton, N York	88	B3
Stutton, Suff	55	A4
Styal, Chesh	80	B4
Styrrup, Notts	82	C3
Suckley, Worcs	48	B3
Sudborough, Nhants	62	B4
Sudbourne, Suff	55	C3
Sudbrook, Lincs	74	B3
Sudbrook, Monm	37	A4
Sudbrooke, Lincs	83	D4
Sudbury, Derby	71	C4
Sudbury, G Lon	146	B1
Sudbury, Suff	54	B4
Suddington, Worcs	48	C2
Suffield, N York	95	C2
Suffield, Norf	76	C4
Sugnall, Staffs	70	B4
Sugwas Pool, Heref	47	C4
Sulby, I of M	145	C2
Sulgrave, Nhants	50	C4
Sulhamstead, Berks	27	C2
Summerbridge, N York	87	C1
Summercourt, Corn	3	C4
Summerfield, Norf	75	D3
Summerhouse, Durham	100	A4
Summerseat, G Man	80	A1
Sunbury, Surrey	146	B2

PLACE	PAGE	GRID
Sunderland, Cumb	97	E2
Sunderland, Lancs	85	B1
Sunderland, Tyne	106	C4
Sundridge, Kent	30	A3
Sunningdale, Berks	28	B2
Sunninghill, Berks	28	B2
Sunningwell, Oxon	39	C3
Sunniside, Durham	99	D2
Surbiton, G Lon	146	B2
Surfleet, Lincs	74	D4
Surlingham, Norf	65	B2
Sustead, Norf	76	C4
Susworth, Lincs	83	B2
Sutcombe, Devon	11	C3
Sutcombemill, Devon	11	C3
Sutterby, Lincs	84	C4
Sutterton, Lincs	74	D4
Sutton at Hone, Kent	30	B2
Sutton Bassett, Nhants	61	C4
Sutton Bonington, Notts	61	A1
Sutton Bridge, Lincs	63	C1
Sutton Cheney, Leics	60	C3
Sutton Coldfield, W Mids	59	B3
Sutton Courtenay, Oxon	40	A4
Sutton Grange, N York	93	D4
Sutton Green, Surrey	146	A3
Sutton Howgrave, N York	93	D3
Sutton Maddock, Shrops	58	B3
Sutton Mallet, Som	13	B1
Sutton Mandeville, Wilts	14	D2
Sutton Montis, Som	14	A2
Sutton on Sea, Lincs	84	D4
Sutton on the Hill, Derby	71	C4
Sutton on Trent, Notts	73	C1
Sutton Scotney, Hants	16	A1
Sutton St Edmund, Lincs	63	B2
Sutton St James, Lincs	63	B1
Sutton St Nicholas, Heref	47	D3
Sutton upon Derwent, E R of Y	89	B2
Sutton Valence, Kent	31	B4
Sutton Veny, Wilts	25	B4
Sutton Waldron, Dorset	14	C3
Sutton Weaver, Chesh	79	B4
Sutton Wick, Oxon	39	C4
Sutton Wick, Som	24	B3
Sutton, Beds	52	C3
Sutton, Cambs	53	B1
Sutton, Cambs	62	C3
Sutton, Devon	10	A1
Sutton, G Lon	150	B1
Sutton, Kent	32	C4
Sutton, N York	88	B4
Sutton, Norf	66	A1
Sutton, Notts	73	C4
Sutton, Notts	83	A3
Sutton, Shrops	58	B4
Sutton, Staffs	58	B1
Sutton, Suff	55	B3
Sutton, W Suss	18	A3
Sutton-in-Craven, N York	87	A2
Sutton-on-the-Forest, N York	94	B4
Sutton-under-Brailes, Warwk	50	A4
Sutton-under-Whitestonecliffe, N York	94	A3
Swadlincote, Derby	60	B1
Swaffham Bulbeck, Cambs	53	C2
Swaffham Prior, Cambs	53	C2
Swaffham, Norf	64	B2
Swafield, Norf	76	D4
Swainby, N York	94	A1
Swainsthorpe, Norf	65	A3
Swainswick, Som	25	A2
Swalcliffe, Oxon	50	A4
Swallow, Lincs	84	A2
Swallowcliffe, Wilts	14	D2
Swallowfield, Berks	27	C2
Swan Green, Chesh	80	A4
Swan, Swan	35	A4
Swanage, Dorset	8	C2
Swanbourne, Bucks	40	C1
Swanland, E R of Y	90	B4
Swanley, Kent	30	A2
Swanmore, Hants	16	B3
Swannington, Leics	60	C1
Swannington, Norf	65	A1
Swanton Abbot, Norf	65	B1
Swanton Morley, Norf	64	D1
Swanton Novers, Norf	76	B4
Swanwick, Derby	72	B2
Swarby, Lincs	74	B3
Swardeston, Norf	65	A3
Swarkestone, Derby	72	A4
Swarland, Nthumb	106	A1
Swarraton, Hants	16	B1
Swarthmoor, Cumb	91	D3
Swaton, Lincs	74	C4
Swavesey, Cambs	53	A1
Swayfield, Lincs	62	B1
Sweetham, Devon	12	A4
Sweethaws, E Suss	19	B2
Sweets, Corn	11	A4
Sweetshouse, Corn	3	E3
Swefling, Suff	55	B2
Swepstone, Leics	60	B2
Swerford, Oxon	39	B1
Swettenham, Chesh	70	B1
Swiftsden, E Suss	20	A2
Swilland, Suff	55	A3
Swillington, W Yorks	88	A3
Swimbridge, Devon	11	E1
Swinbrook, Oxon	39	B2
Swincliffe, N York	87	C1
Swinderby, Lincs	74	A1
Swindon, Staffs	58	C4
Swindon, Wilts	26	B1
Swine, E R of Y	90	C3
Swinefleet, E R of Y	89	C4
Swineshead, Beds	52	A2
Swineshead, Lincs	74	D3
Swinford, Leics	50	C1
Swingfield Minnis, Kent	32	B4
Swingfield Street, Kent	32	B4

PLACE	PAGE	GRID
Swingleton Green, Suff	54	C3
Swinhoe, Nthumb	112	C2
Swinithwaite, N York	93	A2
Swinside, Cumb	98	A4
Swinstead, Lincs	62	B1
Swinton, Border	111	C1
Swinton, G Man	80	A2
Swinton, N York	93	C3
Swinton, S York	82	B2
Swithland, Leics	61	A2
Swynnerton, Staffs	70	C4
Swyre, Dorset	7	C1
Sychtyn, Powys	56	D2
Syde, Glouc	38	B2
Sydenham Damerel, Devon	4	B2
Sydenham, G Lon	149	A3
Sydenham, Oxon	40	B3
Syderstone, Norf	75	E4
Sydling St Nicholas, Dorset	14	A4
Syerston, Notts	73	C3
Sykehouse, S York	83	A1
Symbister, Shet	144	A2
Symington, S Ayrs	108	D2
Symington, S Lan	109	D2
Syreford, Glouc	38	B2
Syresham, Nhants	51	A4
Syston, Leics	61	B2
Syston, Lincs	74	A3
Sywell, Nhants	51	B2
Tackley, Oxon	39	C2
Tacolneston, Norf	65	A3
Tadcaster, N York	88	B2
Taddington, Derby	71	B1
Taddington, Glouc	38	C1
Tadlow, Cambs	52	C3
Tadmarton, Oxon	50	B4
Tadworth, Surrey	150	A2
Taff's Well, Card	23	B1
Taibach, Neath	35	B4
Tain, High	141	D4
Takeley Street, Essex	43	A2
Takeley, Essex	43	A2
Talaton, Devon	12	C4
Talbenny, Pemb	33	B2
Talerddig, Powys	56	D3
Talgarreg, Cered	45	E3
Talgarth, Powys	47	A4
Taliesin, Cered	56	B3
Talkin, Cumb	104	D4
Talladale, High	136	A1
Tallarn Green, Wrex	69	C3
Tallentire, Cumb	97	D2
Talley, Carm	34	D1
Tallington, Lincs	62	C2
Talmine, High	142	E1
Talog, Carm	34	B1
Talsarn, Cered	46	A3
Talsarnau, Gwyn	67	E4
Talskiddy, Corn	3	C3
Talwrn, Angle	77	C4
Tal-y-Bont, Aberc	68	A1
Talybont, Cered	56	A4
Tal-y-bont, Gwyn	56	A1
Talybont-on-Usk, Powys	35	D1
Tal-y-coed, Monm	36	C2
Tal-y-garn, Rhond	23	A1
Talysarn, Gwyn	67	D2
Tamworth, Staffs	60	A2
Tan Office Green, Suff	54	B2
Tanfield Lea, Durham	100	A1
Tanfield, Durham	100	A1
Tangley, Hants	26	D4
Tankerness, Orkney	144	B2
Tankersley, S York	82	A2
Tannadice, Angus	129	B3
Tannington, Suff	55	B2
Tannochside, N Lan	116	A3
Tansley, Derby	72	A2
Tansor, Nhants	62	B4
Tantobie, Durham	100	A1
Tanton, N York	94	B1
Tanworth in Arden, Warwk	49	B1
Tan-y-groes, Cered	45	D3
Taplow, Bucks	28	B1
Tarbert, Argyll	113	E4
Tarbert, Argyll	114	A3
Tarbert, W Isle	144	A3
Tarbet, Argyll	122	A4
Tarbet, High	130	F4
Tarbolton, S Ayrs	108	E2
Tardebigge, Worcs	49	A1
Tarfside, Angus	129	B1
Tarland, Aber	133	E3
Tarleton, Lancs	85	B4
Tarlton, Glouc	38	B3
Tarnock, Som	24	A3
Tarporley, Chesh	69	D1
Tarr, Som	12	A1
Tarr, Som	12	C1
Tarrant Crawford, Dorset	14	C4
Tarrant Gunville, Dorset	14	C3
Tarrant Hinton, Dorset	14	D3
Tarrant Keyneston, Dorset	14	D4
Tarrant Launceston, Dorset	14	D3
Tarrant Monkton, Dorset	14	D3
Tarrant Rawston, Dorset	14	D3
Tarrant Rushton, Dorset	14	D4
Tarrington, Heref	48	A4
Tarskavaig, High	130	D3
Tarves, Aber	134	C1
Tarvin, Chesh	69	D1
Tasburgh, Norf	65	A3
Tatenhill, Staffs	60	A1
Tathwell, Lincs	84	C4
Tatsfield, Surrey	150	D2
Tattenhall, Chesh	69	D2
Tatterford, Norf	75	E4
Tattersett, Norf	75	E4
Tattershall Thorpe, Lincs	74	D2
Tattershall, Lincs	74	D2
Tattingstone, Suff	55	A4
Taunton, Som	12	D2
Taverham, Norf	65	A2
Tavernspite, Pemb	33	E2

PLACE	PAGE	GRID
Tavistock, Devon	4	C2
Taw green, Devon	11	F4
Tawstock, Devon	11	E1
Taxal, Derby	81	A4
Tayinloan, Argyll	107	D1
Taynton, Glouc	37	C1
Taynton, Oxon	39	A2
Taynuilt, Argyll	121	B1
Tayport, Fife	124	B2
Tayvallich, Argyll	113	F1
Tealby, Lincs	84	A3
Teangue, High	130	E3
Tebay, Cumb	92	B1
Tebworth, Beds	41	B1
Tedburn St Mary, Devon	5	C1
Teddington, G Lon	146	B2
Teddington, Glouc	38	B1
Tedstone Delamere, Heref	48	A2
Tedstone Wafer, Heref	48	A2
Teeton, Nhants	51	A1
Teffont Evias, Wilts	14	D1
Teffont Magna, Wilts	14	D1
Tegryn, Pemb	34	A1
Teigh, Rutland	62	A1
Teignmouth, Devon	6	A2
Telford, Shrops	58	B2
Tellisford, Som	25	A3
Templand, Dumf	103	E2
Temple Bar, Cered	45	F3
Temple Cloud, Som	24	C3
Temple Grafton, Warwk	49	B3
Temple Guiting, Glouc	38	C1
Temple Hirst, N York	89	A4
Temple Normanton, Derby	72	B1
Temple Sowerby, Cumb	98	D3
Temple, Corn	3	E2
Temple, M Loth	118	A4
Templecombe, Som	14	B2
Templeton, Devon	12	A3
Templeton, Pemb	33	E2
Tempsford, Beds	52	B3
Ten Mile Bank, Norf	63	D3
Tenby, Pemb	33	E3
Tendring, Essex	44	C1
Terling, Essex	43	B2
Ternhill, Shrops	70	A4
Terrington St Clement, Norf	63	D1
Terrington, N York	94	C4
Teston, Kent	31	A3
Tetbury, Glouc	38	A4
Tetchill, Shrops	69	C4
Tetcott, Devon	11	C4
Tetford, Lincs	84	C4
Tetney, Lincs	84	C2
Tetsworth, Oxon	40	B3
Teversal, Notts	72	B1
Teversham, Cambs	53	B2
Teviothead, Border	110	C4
Tewin, Herts	42	A2
Tewkesbury, Glouc	38	A1
Thakeham, W Suss	18	B3
Thame, Oxon	40	B3
Thames Ditton, Surrey	146	B2
Thamesmead, G Lon	30	A1
Thankerton, S Lan	109	D1
Tharston, Norf	65	A3
Thatcham, Berks	27	B2
Thaxted, Essex	43	A1
The Braes, High	135	D4
The Bungalow, I of M	145	C3
The City, Bucks	40	C4
The Den, N Ayrs	115	A4
The Forstal, Kent	21	B1
The Forstal, Kent	31	C4
The Green, Cumb	91	C3
The Green, Essex	43	B2
The Hill, Cumb	91	C3
The Holt, Berks	28	A1
The Lee, Bucks	41	A3
The Lhen, I of M	145	C1
The Mythe, Glouc	48	C4
The Sands, Surrey	28	B4
The Strand, Wilts	25	B3
Theakston, N York	93	D3
Thealby, Lincs	83	C1
Theale, Berks	27	C2
Theale, Som	24	A4
Thearne, E R of Y	90	B3
Theberton, Suff	55	C2
Theddingworth, Leics	61	B4
Theddlethorpe All Saints, Lincs	84	D3
Theddlethorpe St Helen, Lincs	84	D3
Thelnetham, Suff	54	D1
Thelveton, Norf	65	A4
Themelthorpe, Norf	64	D1
Therfield, Herts	53	A4
Thetford, Norf	64	B4
Theydon Bois, Essex	42	C3
Thickwood, Wilts	25	B2
Thimbleby, Lincs	74	D1
Thimbleby, N York	94	A2
Thirkleby, N York	94	A3
Thirlby, N York	94	A3
Thirlspot, Cumb	98	A4
Thirn, N York	93	C3
Thirsk, N York	94	A3
Thistleton, Lancs	85	B3
Thistleton, Rutland	62	A1
Thistley Green, Suff	54	A1
Thixendale, N York	89	C1
Thockrington, Nthumb	105	C3
Tholomas Drove, Cambs	63	B2
Tholthorpe, N York	94	A4
Thomastown, Aber	139	A4
Thompson, Norf	64	C3
Thong, Kent	31	A2
Thoralby, N York	93	A3
Thoresway, Lincs	84	A2
Thorganby, Lincs	84	B2
Thorganby, N York	89	B3
Thorgill, N York	94	C2
Thorington Street, Suff	54	D4

PLACE	PAGE	GRID
Thorington, Suff	55	C1
Thorlby, N York	87	A2
Thorley Street, I of W	9	B1
Thorley, Herts	42	C2
Thormanby, N York	94	A4
Thornage, Norf	76	B4
Thornborough, Bucks	40	C1
Thornborough, N York	93	D3
Thornbury, Devon	11	C3
Thornbury, Glouc	37	B4
Thornbury, Heref	48	A2
Thornby, Nhants	51	A1
Thorncliff, Staffs	71	A2
Thorncombe Street, Surrey	146	A4
Thorncombe, Dorset	13	B4
Thorndon Cross, Devon	4	C1
Thorndon, Suff	55	A1
Thorne St Margaret, Som	12	C2
Thorne, S York	83	A1
Thorner, W Yorks	88	A3
Thornes, Staffs	59	B2
Thorney, Bucks	146	A1
Thorney, Cambs	63	A2
Thorney, Notts	83	C4
Thorney, Som	13	B2
Thornfalcon, Som	13	A2
Thornford, Dorset	14	A3
Thorngrafton, Nthumb	105	A4
Thorngumbald, E R of Y	90	D4
Thornham Magna, Suff	54	D1
Thornham Parva, Suff	54	D1
Thornham, Norf	75	D3
Thornhaugh, Cambs	62	B3
Thornhill, Dumf	103	C1
Thornhill, Stirl	122	D4
Thornhill, W Yorks	87	C4
Thornholme, E R of Y	90	C1
Thornicombe, Dorset	14	C4
Thornington, Nthumb	111	C2
Thornley, Durham	99	D2
Thornley, Durham	100	B2
Thorn's Flush, Surrey	18	A1
Thorns, Suff	54	A3
Thornsett, Derby	81	A3
Thornthwaite, Cumb	97	E3
Thornthwaite, N York	87	C1
Thornton Curtis, Lincs	84	A1
Thornton Dale, N York	95	A3
Thornton Heath, G Lon	147	B3
Thornton Hough, Mers	78	D4
Thornton in Lonsdale, N York	92	B4
Thornton le Moor, Lincs	83	D2
Thornton Rust, N York	93	A2
Thornton Steward, N York	93	C3
Thornton Watlass, N York	93	C3
Thornton, Angus	129	A4
Thornton, Bucks	51	B4
Thornton, E R of Y	89	C2
Thornton, Fife	124	A4
Thornton, Lancs	85	A2
Thornton, Leics	60	C2
Thornton, Lincs	74	D1
Thornton, N York	100	C4
Thornton, Nthumb	112	A1
Thornton, W Yorks	87	B3
Thorntonhall, S Lan	115	C4
Thornton-in-Craven, N York	86	C2
Thornton-le-Beans, N York	94	A2
Thornton-le-Clay, N York	94	C4
Thornton-le-Moor, N York	94	A2
Thornton-le-Moors, Chesh	79	A4
Thornton-le-Street, N York	94	A3
Thornythwaite, Cumb	98	B3
Thoroton, Notts	73	C3
Thorp Arch, W Yorks	88	B2
Thorpe Abbotts, Norf	65	A4
Thorpe Arnold, Leics	61	C1
Thorpe Audlin, W Yorks	82	B1
Thorpe Bassett, N York	95	B4
Thorpe by Water, Rutland	62	A3
Thorpe Constantine, Staffs	60	A2
Thorpe End, Norf	65	B2
Thorpe Green, Essex	44	C1
Thorpe Green, Suff	54	C3
Thorpe Hesley, S York	82	A2
Thorpe in Balne, S York	82	C1
Thorpe in the Fallows, Lincs	83	C4
Thorpe Langton, Leics	61	C3
Thorpe le Street, E R of Y	89	C2
Thorpe Lea, Surrey	146	A2
Thorpe Malsor, Nhants	51	B1
Thorpe Mandeville, Nhants	50	C4
Thorpe Market, Norf	76	D4
Thorpe Morieux, Suff	54	C3
Thorpe on the Hill, Lincs	74	A1
Thorpe Salvin, S York	82	C4
Thorpe Satchville, Leics	61	B2
Thorpe St Peter, Lincs	75	B1
Thorpe Thewles, Durham	100	C3
Thorpe Tilney, Lincs	74	C2
Thorpe Underwood, N York	88	B1
Thorpe Willoughby, N York	89	A3
Thorpe, Derby	71	B2
Thorpe, E R of Y	90	B2
Thorpe, N York	87	A1
Thorpe, Notts	73	C2
Thorpe-le-Soken, Essex	44	C1
Thorpeness, Suff	55	D2
Thorrington, Essex	44	B2
Thorverton, Devon	12	B4
Thrandeston, Suff	54	D1
Thrapston, Nhants	52	A1
Threapwood, Chesh	69	C3
Threapwood, Staffs	71	A3
Three Cocks, Powys	47	A4
Three Cups Corner, E Suss	19	C2
Three Leg Cross, E Suss	20	A1
Three Legged Cross, Dorset	15	A4
Three Mile Cross, Berks	27	C2
Threekingham, Lincs	74	C4
Threlkeld, Cumb	98	A3
Thrigby, Norf	66	A2
Thrintoft, N York	93	D2
Thriplow, Cambs	53	B3

GAZETTEER • Thr - Ven
LI

PLACE	PAGE	GRID
Throcking, Herts	42	B1
Throckmorton, Worcs	49	A3
Throop, Dorset	8	B1
Thropton, Nthumb	105	C1
Throwleigh, Devon	5	B1
Throwley Forstal, Kent	31	C3
Thrumpton, Notts	73	A4
Thrumster, High	143	E3
Thrupp, Glouc	38	A3
Thrushesbush, Essex	42	C3
Thrussington, Leics	61	B1
Thruxton, Hants	26	D4
Thruxton, Heref	47	C4
Thulston, Derby	72	B4
Thurcaston, Leics	61	A2
Thurcroft, S York	82	B3
Thurgarton, Norf	76	C4
Thurgoland, S York	82	A2
Thurlaston, Leics	60	C3
Thurlaston, Warwk	50	B1
Thurlbear, Som	13	A2
Thurlby, Lincs	62	C1
Thurlby, Lincs	74	A1
Thurlby, Lincs	84	D4
Thurleigh, Beds	52	A2
Thurlestone, Devon	10	A1
Thurlow, Suff	54	A3
Thurlstone, S York	81	C2
Thurlton, Norf	66	A3
Thurnby, Leics	61	B2
Thurne, Norf	66	A1
Thurning, Nhants	62	C4
Thurning, Norf	76	B4
Thurnscoe, S York	82	B2
Thursby, Cumb	98	A1
Thursford, Norf	76	A4
Thursley, Surrey	17	C1
Thurso, High	143	C1
Thurstaston, Mers	78	D3
Thurston, Suff	54	C2
Thurstonland, W Yorks	81	C1
Thurton, Norf	65	B3
Thurvaston, Derby	71	C3
Thwaite Head, Cumb	91	D2
Thwaite St Mary, Norf	65	B3
Thwaite, N York	92	D2
Thwaite, Suff	54	D2
Thwing, E R of Y	95	C4
Tibbermore, Perth	123	C2
Tibberton, Glouc	37	C2
Tibberton, Shrops	58	A1
Tibberton, Worcs	48	C2
Tibenham, Norf	65	A4
Tibshelf, Derby	72	B1
Tibthorpe, E R of Y	90	A1
Tichborne, Hants	16	B1
Tickencote, Rutland	62	B2
Tickenham, Som	24	A2
Tickhill, S York	82	C3
Ticklerton, Shrops	57	D4
Ticknall, Derby	60	B1
Tickton, E R of Y	90	B2
Tidcombe, Wilts	26	D3
Tiddington, Oxon	40	B3
Tiddington, Warwk	49	C3
Tidebrook, E Suss	19	C1
Tideford, Corn	4	B4
Tidenham, Glouc	37	A4
Tideswell, Derby	81	B4
Tidmington, Warwk	49	C4
Tiers Cross, Pemb	33	C2
Tiffield, Nhants	51	A3
Tigh a Ghearraidh, W Isle	144	A3
Tighnabruaich, Argyll	114	B2
Tigley, Devon	5	B3
Tilbrook, Cambs	52	A1
Tilbury, Essex	30	B1
Tilford, Surrey	28	B4
Tilham Street, Som	13	C1
Tillicoultry, Clack	123	B4
Tillingham, Essex	44	A3
Tillington Common, Heref	47	C3
Tillington, Heref	47	D4
Tillington, W Suss	17	C2
Tillyfourie, Aber	134	A2
Tilmanstone, Kent	32	C4
Tilney All Saints, Norf	63	D1
Tilney High End, Norf	63	D1
Tilney St Lawrence, Norf	63	D2
Tilshead, Wilts	26	A4
Tilstock, Shrops	69	D3
Tilston, Chesh	69	D2
Tilsworth, Beds	41	B1
Tiltups End, Glouc	38	A4
Timberland, Lincs	74	C2
Timbersbrook, Chesh	70	C1
Timberscombe, Som	22	E4
Timble, N York	87	C1
Timsbury, Hants	15	C2
Timsbury, Som	24	C3
Timworth, Suff	54	B1
Tincleton, Dorset	8	A1
Tindale Crescent, Durham	100	A3
Tindale, Cumb	104	E4
Tingewick, Bucks	40	B1
Tingley, W Yorks	88	A4
Tingrith, Beds	41	B1
Tinhay, Devon	4	B1
Tinsley Green, W Suss	18	C1
Tintagel, Corn	3	D1
Tintern Parva, Monm	37	A3
Tintwistle, Derby	81	A2
Tinwell, Rutland	62	B2
Tippacott, Devon	22	C4
Tipp's End, Norf	63	C3
Tipton St John, Devon	6	B1
Tiptree Heath, Essex	43	C2
Tiptree, Essex	44	A2
Tirabad, Powys	46	C4
Tirley, Glouc	38	A1
Tirril, Cumb	98	C3
Tisbury, Wilts	14	D2
Tissington, Derby	71	C2
Titchfield, Hants	16	B4
Titchmarsh, Nhants	52	A1
Titchwell, Norf	75	D3
Tithby, Notts	73	B4
Titley, Heref	47	B2
Titsey, Surrey	150	D2
Tittensor, Staffs	70	C3
Tittleshall, Norf	64	C1
Titton, Worcs	48	C1
Tiverton, Chesh	69	D2
Tiverton, Devon	12	B3
Tivetshall St Margaret, Norf	65	A4
Tivington, Som	22	E4
Tixall, Staffs	59	A1
Tixover, Rutland	62	B3
Tobermory, Argyll	125	F3
Toberonochy, Argyll	120	F3
Tockenham, Wilts	26	A1
Tockholes, Lancs	86	A4
Tockington, Glouc	24	C1
Tockwith, N York	88	B2
Todber, Dorset	14	B2
Todburn, Nthumb	105	D1
Toddington, Beds	41	B1
Toddington, Glouc	38	B1
Todenham, Glouc	49	C4
Todhills, Angus	124	B1
Todhills, Cumb	104	C4
Todmorden, W Yorks	87	A4
Todwick, S York	82	B3
Toft Hill, Durham	99	D3
Toft Monks, Norf	66	A3
Toft next Newton, Lincs	83	D3
Toft, Cambs	53	A3
Toft, Lincs	62	B1
Toft, Shet	144	A2
Toftrees, Norf	76	A4
Togston, Nthumb	106	A1
Tokers Green, Oxon	27	C1
Toll Bar, S York	82	C1
Tollard Royal, Wilts	14	D3
Toller Fratrum, Dorset	13	C4
Toller Porcorum, Dorset	13	C4
Toller Whelme, Dorset	13	C4
Tollerton, N York	89	A1
Tollerton, Notts	73	A4
Tollesbury, Essex	44	A2
Tolleshunt D'Arcy, Essex	44	A2
Tolleshunt Major, Essex	44	A2
Tolpuddle, Dorset	8	A1
Tolsta, W Isle	144	B2
Tolworth, G Lon	146	B2
Tomatin, High	132	D1
Tomintoul, Moray	133	B2
Tomnavoulin, Moray	133	B1
Tonbridge, Kent	30	B4
Tondu, Brigd	22	E1
Tong Norton, Shrops	58	B2
Tong, Kent	31	C3
Tong, Shrops	58	B2
Tong, W Yorks	87	C3
Tonge, Leics	60	C1
Tongham, Surrey	28	B4
Tongland, Dumf	97	A1
Tongue, High	142	E2
Tongwynlais, Card	23	B1
Tonna, Neath	35	B4
Tonwell, Herts	42	B2
Tonypandy, Rhond	35	C4
Tonyrefail, Rhond	35	D4
Toot Hill, Essex	42	C3
Tooting Bec, G Lon	147	A2
Tooting, G Lon	147	A2
Topcliffe, N York	94	A4
Topcroft Street, Norf	65	B3
Topcroft, Norf	65	B3
Toppesfield, Essex	54	A4
Toprow, Norf	65	A3
Topsham, Devon	6	A1
Torbeg, N Ayrs	107	F2
Torbryan, Devon	5	C3
Torcross, Devon	10	B1
Tore, High	137	A3
Torksey, Lincs	83	B4
Tormarton, Glouc	25	A1
Toronto, Durham	100	A3
Torpenhow, Cumb	97	E2
Torphichen, W Loth	116	C3
Torphins, Aber	134	A3
Torpoint, Corn	4	C4
Torquay, Devon	6	A3
Torrance, E Dun	115	C2
Torridon, High	136	A3
Torrin, High	130	D2
Torryburn, Fife	117	A1
Tortan, Worcs	48	C1
Torteval, Guern	145	A2
Torthorwald, Dumf	103	E3
Tortworth, Glouc	37	C4
Torver, Cumb	91	D2
Torworth, Notts	83	A3
Toseland, Cambs	52	C2
Tosside, N York	86	B1
Tostock, Suff	54	C2
Totaig, High	135	A3
Tote, High	135	C3
Totnes, Devon	5	C3
Tottenhill, Norf	63	D2
Totternhoe, Beds	41	B2
Tottington, G Man	80	A1
Totton, Hants	15	C3
Toulton, Som	12	D1
Tow Law, Durham	99	D2
Towcester, Nhants	51	A3
Towednack, Corn	1	B1
Towersey, Oxon	40	B3
Towie, Aber	133	D2
Town End, Cumb	91	D2
Townhead, S York	81	C2
Towns End, Hants	27	B3
Townshend, Corn	1	C2
Towthorpe, N York	89	B1
Towton, N York	88	B3
Towyn, Aberc	78	A4
Toy's Hill, Kent	30	A4
Traethsaith, Cered	45	D3
Trallong, Powys	35	C1
Tranent, E Loth	118	B2
Trapp, Carm	34	D2
Traquair, Border	110	B2
Traveller's Rest, Devon	11	E2
Trawden, Lancs	86	C3
Trawsfynydd, Gwyn	68	A4
Trealaw, Rhond	35	D4
Treales, Lancs	85	B3
Trearddur Bay, Angle	77	A4
Trebarwith, Corn	3	D1
Trebetherick, Corn	3	C2
Treborough, Som	12	C1
Trebullett, Corn	4	B2
Treburley, Corn	4	B2
Trecastle, Powys	35	B1
Trecwn, Pemb	33	D1
Tredegar, Gwent	36	A3
Tredington, Glouc	38	A1
Tredington, Warwk	49	C4
Tredunhock, Monm	36	C4
Treen, Corn	1	B3
Treeton, S York	82	B3
Trefasser, Pemb	45	A4
Trefecca, Powys	36	A1
Trefeglwys, Powys	56	D4
Treffgarne Owen, Pemb	33	C1
Treffgarne, Pemb	33	C1
Trefilan, Cered	46	A2
Trefnant, Denb	68	D1
Trefonen, Shrops	69	B4
Trefor, Gwyn	67	C3
Trefrew, Corn	3	E1
Trefriw, Aberc	68	B1
Tregadillett, Corn	4	A1
Tregare, Monm	36	C3
Tregaron, Cered	46	B2
Tregarth, Gwyn	67	E1
Tregeare, Corn	4	A1
Tregeiriog, Wrex	69	A4
Tregele, Angle	77	B3
Tregidden, Corn	2	A3
Treglemais, Pemb	33	B1
Tregonce, Corn	3	C2
Tregonetha, Corn	3	C3
Tregony, Corn	2	B1
Tregoyd, Powys	47	A4
Tre-groes, Cered	45	E4
Tregynon, Powys	56	E3
Trehafod, Rhond	35	D4
Trehan, Corn	4	B4
Treharris, Merth	35	D4
Treherbert, Rhond	35	C4
Trekenner, Corn	4	B2
Treknow, Corn	3	D1
Trelawnyd, Flint	78	B4
Trelech, Carm	34	A1
Treleddyd-fawr, Pemb	33	B1
Trelights, Corn	3	D2
Trelill, Corn	3	D2
Trelleck, Monm	37	A3
Trelogan, Flint	78	B4
Trelow, Corn	3	C3
Tremadog, Gwyn	67	E3
Tremail, Corn	3	E1
Tremain, Cered	45	D3
Tremaine, Corn	4	A1
Tremar, Corn	4	A3
Trematon, Corn	4	B4
Tremeirchion, Denb	78	B4
Trenance, Corn	3	C3
Trenance, Corn	3	C3
Trencreek, Corn	11	A4
Trenear, Corn	1	D2
Treneglos, Corn	4	A1
Trent, Dorset	14	A2
Trentishoe, Devon	22	B4
Treoes, Glam	22	E1
Treorchy, Rhond	35	C4
Trequite, Corn	3	D2
Trerhyngyll, Glam	23	A1
Trerulefoot, Corn	4	B4
Trescowe, Corn	1	C2
Tresean, Corn	3	B4
Tresham, Glouc	37	C4
Tresillian, Corn	2	B1
Treskinnick Cross, Corn	11	B4
Tresmeer, Corn	4	A1
Tresparrett, Corn	3	E1
Treswell, Notts	83	B4
Trethevey, Corn	3	D1
Trethewey, Corn	1	A3
Trethurgy, Corn	3	D4
Tretire, Heref	37	A1
Tretower, Powys	36	A2
Treuddyn, Flint	69	B2
Trevague, Corn	4	A2
Trevalga, Corn	3	E1
Trevalyn, Wrex	69	C2
Trevarrian, Corn	3	C3
Treveal, Corn	3	B4
Treveighan, Corn	3	D2
Trevellas Downs, Corn	3	B4
Trevelmond, Corn	4	A3
Treverva, Corn	2	A2
Trevine, Pemb	33	B1
Treviscoe, Corn	3	C4
Trevone, Corn	3	C2
Trevor, Denb	69	B3
Trewalder, Corn	3	D2
Trewarlett, Corn	4	B2
Trewarmett, Corn	3	D1
Treween, Corn	4	A2
Trewen, Corn	3	D2
Trewint, Corn	4	A2
Trewithian, Corn	2	B1
Trewoon, Corn	3	D4
Treyford, W Suss	17	B2
Triangle, W Yorks	87	B4
Trimdon Colliery, Durham	100	B2
Trimdon Grange, Durham	100	B2
Trimdon, Durham	100	B2
Trimingham, Norf	76	D3
Trimley Heath, Suff	55	B4
Trimley, Suff	55	B4
Trimsaran, Carm	34	C3
Trimstone, Devon	22	A4
Tring, Herts	41	A2
Trinity, Angus	129	C3
Trinity, Jersey	145	B2
Triscombe, Som	12	B1
Triscombe, Som	12	D1
Trispen, Corn	3	B4
Tritlington, Nthumb	106	A1
Trochry, Perth	123	B1
Troedrhiwfuwch, Caer	36	A3
Troedyraur, Cered	45	E3
Troedyrhiw, Merth	35	D3
Troon, Corn	1	D1
Troon, S Ayrs	108	D2
Troston, Suff	54	C1
Trotshill, Worcs	48	C3
Trottiscliffe, Kent	30	B3
Troughend, Nthumb	105	B1
Troutbeck Bridge, Cumb	91	E1
Troutbeck, Cumb	91	E1
Troway, Derby	82	A4
Trowbridge, Wilts	25	B3
Trowell, Notts	72	B3
Trowse Newton, Norf	65	B2
Trudoxhill, Som	25	A4
Trull, Som	12	D2
Trumpet, Heref	48	A4
Trumpsgreen, Surrey	146	A2
Trunch, Norf	76	D4
Truro, Corn	2	A1
Trusham, Devon	5	C2
Trusley, Derby	71	C4
Trusthorpe, Lincs	84	D4
Trysull, Staffs	58	C3
Tubney, Oxon	39	C3
Tuckenhay, Devon	5	C4
Tuckhill, Shrops	58	B4
Tuddenham, Suff	54	A1
Tuddenham, Suff	55	A3
Tudeley, Kent	30	B4
Tudhoe, Durham	100	A2
Tudweiloig, Gwyn	67	B4
Tuesley, Surrey	28	B4
Tufton, Hants	27	A4
Tufton, Pemb	33	D1
Tugby, Leics	61	C3
Tugford, Shrops	57	D4
Tughall, Nthumb	112	C2
Tullibody, Clack	116	B1
Tullynessle, Aber	133	E2
Tulse Hill, G Lon	149	A3
Tumble, Carm	34	D2
Tumby Woodside, Lincs	74	D2
Tumby, Lincs	74	D2
Tummel Bridge, Perth	127	E3
Tunbridge Wells, Kent	19	C1
Tunstall, E R of Y	90	D3
Tunstall, Kent	31	C3
Tunstall, Lancs	92	B4
Tunstall, N York	93	C2
Tunstall, Norf	66	A2
Tunstall, Staffs	70	B4
Tunstall, Suff	55	C3
Tunstead, Derby	81	B4
Tunstead, Norf	65	B1
Tunworth, Hants	27	C4
Tur Langton, Leics	61	B3
Turkdean, Glouc	38	C2
Turleigh, Wilts	25	A3
Turnastone, Heref	47	C4
Turnberry, S Ayrs	108	C4
Turner's Hill, W Suss	19	A1
Turners Puddle, Dorset	8	B1
Turnworth, Dorset	14	C3
Turriff, Aber	139	C3
Turton Bottoms, Lancs	80	A1
Turves, Cambs	63	B3
Turvey, Beds	51	C3
Turville, Bucks	40	C4
Turweston, Bucks	50	C4
Tushingham cum Grindley, Chesh	69	D3
Tutbury, Staffs	71	C4
Tutshill, Glouc	37	A4
Tuttington, Norf	76	C4
Tuxford, Notts	73	C1
Twechar, E Dun	116	A2
Twelve Oaks, E Suss	20	A2
Twelveheads, Corn	2	A1
Twemlow Green, Chesh	70	B1
Twenty, Lincs	62	C1
Twickenham, G Lon	146	B2
Twigworth, Glouc	38	A1
Twineham, W Suss	18	C2
Twinstead, Essex	54	B4
Twitchen, Devon	12	A1
Two Dales, Derby	72	A1
Twycross, Leics	60	B2
Twyford, Berks	28	A1
Twyford, Bucks	40	B1
Twyford, Leics	61	B2
Twyford, Norf	64	D1
Twynholm, Dumf	97	A1
Twyning Green, Glouc	48	C4
Twyning, Glouc	48	C4
Twynllanan, Carm	35	A1
Twywell, Nhants	51	C1
Tyberton, Heref	47	C4
Tycroes, Carm	34	D2
Tycrwyn, Powys	56	E1
Tydd Gote, Lincs	63	C1
Tydd St Giles, Cambs	63	B1
Tydd St Mary, Lincs	63	C1
Tye Green, Essex	53	C4
Tyldesley, G Man	79	C2
Tyler Hill, Kent	32	B3
Tylers Green, Surrey	150	C3
Tylorstown, Rhond	35	D4
Ty-nant, Aberc	68	C3
Tyndrum, Stirl	122	A1
Ty'n-dwr, Denb	69	A3
Tynemouth, Tyne	106	B3
Tyninghame, E Loth	119	B2
Tynron, Dumf	103	C1
Tynygraig, Cered	46	B1
Ty'n-y-Groes, Aberc	68	B1
Tyringham, Bucks	51	C3
Tythegston, Brigd	22	D1
Tytherington, Glouc	37	B4
Tytherington, Wilts	14	C1
Tytherleigh, Devon	13	A4
Tytherton Lucas, Wilts	26	A2
Tywardreath, Corn	3	E4
Tywyn, Gwyn	56	A3
Ubbeston Green, Suff	55	B1
Ubley, Som	24	B3
Uckerby, N York	93	C1
Uckfield, E Suss	19	B2
Uckington, Glouc	38	A1
Uckington, Shrops	57	D2
Udimore, E Suss	20	B2
Udny Green, Aber	134	C1
Udny Station, Aber	134	C1
Uffculme, Devon	12	C3
Uffington, Oxon	39	B4
Uffington, Shrops	57	D2
Ufford, Cambs	62	C2
Ufford, Suff	55	B3
Ufton Nervet, Berks	27	C2
Ufton, Warwk	50	A2
Ugborough, Devon	5	B4
Uggeshall, Suff	66	A4
Ughill, S York	81	C3
Ugley Green, Essex	42	C1
Ugley, Essex	42	C1
Ugthorpe, N York	101	C4
Uig, High	135	C2
Ulbster, High	143	E3
Ulcat Row, Cumb	98	B3
Ulceby Skitter, Lincs	84	A1
Ulceby, Lincs	84	A1
Ulceby, Lincs	84	C4
Ulcombe, Kent	31	B4
Uldale, Cumb	98	A2
Uley, Glouc	37	C4
Ulgham, Nthumb	106	A1
Ullapool, High	140	D3
Ullenhall, Warwk	49	B2
Ulleskelf, N York	89	A3
Ullesthorpe, Leics	61	A4
Ulley, S York	82	B3
Ullingswick, Heref	48	A3
Ullock, Cumb	97	D3
Ulpha, Cumb	91	C2
Ulrome, E R of Y	90	C1
Ulsta, Shet	144	A2
Ulverston, Cumb	91	D3
Ulwell, Dorset	8	C2
Umberleigh, Devon	11	E2
Unapool, High	142	B4
Under River, Kent	30	B4
Underbarrow, Cumb	92	A2
Underwood, Notts	72	B2
Undy, Monm	24	A1
Union Mills, I of M	145	C3
Unstone, Derby	82	A4
Up Cerne, Dorset	14	A4
Up Exe, Devon	12	B4
Up Holland, Lancs	79	B2
Up Marden, W Suss	17	B3
Up Nately, Hants	27	C4
Up Somborne, Hants	16	A1
Up Sydling, Dorset	14	A4
Upavon, Wilts	26	B3
Upchurch, Kent	31	B2
Upcott, Devon	11	F2
Upcott, Som	12	B2
Updown Hill, Surrey	28	B3
Upgate, Norf	65	A1
Uphall, Dorset	13	C4
Upham, Devon	12	A3
Upham, Hants	16	B2
Uphampton, Heref	47	C2
Uphill, Som	23	C3
Uplawmoor, East Renf	115	B4
Upleadon, Glouc	37	C1
Upleatham, N York	101	B4
Uploders, Dorset	7	C1
Uplowman, Devon	12	C3
Uplyme, Devon	7	A1
Upottery, Devon	12	D3
Upper Affcot, Shrops	57	C4
Upper Arley, Worcs	58	B4
Upper Basildon, Berks	27	B1
Upper Beeding, W Suss	18	B3
Upper Benefield, Nhants	62	B4
Upper Bentley, Worcs	49	A2
Upper Bighouse, High	143	B2
Upper Boddington, Nhants	50	B3
Upper Brailes, Warwk	50	A4
Upper Broadheath, Worcs	48	B3
Upper Broughton, Notts	73	B4
Upper Bucklebury, Berks	27	B2
Upper Burgate, Hants	15	A3
Upper Caldecote, Beds	52	B3
Upper Catesby, Nhants	50	C2
Upper Chapel, Powys	46	E4
Upper Chute, Wilts	26	D3
Upper Clapton, G Lon	149	A1
Upper Coberley, Glouc	38	B2
Upper Cound, Shrops	57	D2
Upper Cumberworth, W Yorks	81	C1
Upper Dallachy, Moray	138	D2
Upper Dean, Beds	52	A2
Upper Denby, W Yorks	81	C1
Upper Dicker, E Suss	19	C3
Upper Dunsforth, N York	88	B1
Upper Eglton, Heref	48	A4
Upper Elkstone, Staffs	71	B2
Upper Ellastone, Staffs	71	B3
Upper Framilode, Glouc	37	C3
Upper Froyle, Hants	28	A4
Upper Green, Berks	26	D3
Upper Grove Common, Heref	37	A1
Upper Hambleton, Rutland	62	A2
Upper Harbledown, Kent	32	A3
Upper Hartfield, E Suss	19	B1
Upper Heaton, W Yorks	87	C4
Upper Helmsley, N York	89	B1
Upper Hergest, Heref	47	B3
Upper Heyford, Nhants	51	A2
Upper Heyford, Oxon	39	C1
Upper Hill, Heref	47	D3
Upper Hockenden, Kent	30	A2
Upper Hopton, W Yorks	87	C4
Upper Hulme, Staffs	71	A1
Upper Inglesham, Wilts	39	A4
Upper Killay, Swan	34	D4
Upper Lambourn, Berks	26	D1
Upper Landywood, Staffs	59	A2
Upper Langford, Som	24	A3
Upper Langwith, Derby	73	A1
Upper Largo, Fife	124	B4
Upper Leigh, Staffs	71	A4
Upper Lybster, High	143	E4
Upper Lydbrook, Glouc	37	B2
Upper Lye, Heref	47	C2
Upper Minety, Wilts	38	B4
Upper Norwood, W Suss	17	C3
Upper Pond Street, Essex	53	B4
Upper Poppleton, N York	89	A1
Upper Quinton, Warwk	49	C3
Upper Ratley, Hants	15	C2
Upper Sapey, Heref	48	A2
Upper Shelton, Beds	52	A4
Upper Sheringham, Norf	76	C3
Upper Slaughter, Glouc	38	C1
Upper Soudley, Glouc	37	B3
Upper Standen, Kent	21	C1
Upper Stoke, Norf	65	B3
Upper Stondon, Beds	52	B4
Upper Stowe, Nhants	51	A3
Upper Street, Hants	15	A2
Upper Street, Norf	65	B1
Upper Street, Norf	66	A1
Upper Sundon, Beds	41	B1
Upper Swell, Glouc	39	A1
Upper Tasburgh, Norf	65	A3
Upper Tean, Staffs	71	A3
Upper Town, Derby	71	C1
Upper Town, Heref	48	A3
Upper Town, Suff	54	C2
Upper Tysoe, Warwk	50	A4
Upper Wardington, Oxon	50	B3
Upper Weedon, Nhants	51	A2
Upper Wellingham, E Suss	19	B3
Upper Weybread, Suff	55	A1
Upper Wield, Hants	17	A1
Upper Winchendon, Bucks	40	C2
Upper Woodford, Wilts	15	A1
Upper Wraxall, Wilts	25	A2
Uppermill, G Man	81	A2
Upperthong, W Yorks	81	B1
Upperton, W Suss	17	C2
Uppingham, Rutland	62	A3
Uppington, Shrops	58	A2
Upsall, N York	94	A3
Upsettlington, Border	111	C1
Upshire, Essex	42	B3
Upstreet, Kent	32	B3
Upton Cheyney, Glouc	24	C2
Upton Cressett, Shrops	58	A3
Upton Cross, Corn	4	A2
Upton Grey, Hants	27	C4
Upton Hellions, Devon	12	A4
Upton Magna, Shrops	57	D2
Upton Noble, Som	14	B1
Upton Scudamore, Wilts	25	B4
Upton upon Severn, Worcs	48	C4
Upton Warren, Worcs	49	A2
Upton, Berks	146	A1
Upton, Bucks	40	C2
Upton, Cambs	52	B1
Upton, Cambs	62	C3
Upton, Corn	4	A2
Upton, Devon	10	A1
Upton, Devon	12	C4
Upton, Dorset	8	A2
Upton, Hants	15	C3
Upton, Hants	26	D3
Upton, Leics	60	B3
Upton, Lincs	83	C3
Upton, Norf	66	A2
Upton, Notts	73	C2
Upton, Notts	83	B4
Upton, Oxon	27	B1
Upton, Som	12	B2
Upton, Som	13	B2
Upton, W Yorks	82	B1
Upton, Wilts	14	C1
Upwaltham, W Suss	17	C3
Upwell, Norf	63	C3
Upwick Green, Herts	42	C1
Upwood, Cambs	63	A4
Urchfont, Wilts	26	A3
Urmston, G Man	80	A3
Urquhart, Moray	138	C2
Urra, N York	94	B1
Urray, High	136	F3
Usan, Angus	129	D3
Ushaw Moor, Durham	100	A2
Usk, Monm	36	C3
Usselby, Lincs	84	A3
Utkinton, Chesh	69	D1
Uton, Devon	12	A4
Utterby, Lincs	84	B3
Uttoxeter, Staffs	71	B4
Uxbridge, G Lon	146	A1
Uyeasound, Shet	144	A1
Uzmaston, Pemb	33	D2
Vale, Guern	145	B2
Valley End, Surrey	28	B2
Valtos, High	135	D2
Vaynor, Merth	35	D3
Velindre, Powys	47	A4
Venn Ottery, Devon	6	B1
Venngreen, Devon	11	C3
Ventnor, I of W	10	A2

PLACE	PAGE	GRID
Venton, Devon	5	A4
Vernham Dean, Hants	26	D3
Vernham Street, Hants	26	D3
Verwood, Dorset	15	A3
Veryan, Corn	2	B1
Victoria, Corn	3	D3
Vidlin, Shet	144	A2
Vigo, Kent	30	B3
Vines Cross, E Suss	19	C3
Virginstow, Devon	4	B1
Vobster, Som	25	A4
Voe, Shet	144	A2
Vowchurch, Heref	47	C4
Wackerfield, Durham	99	D3
Wacton, Norf	65	A3
Wadborough, Worcs	48	C3
Waddesdon, Bucks	40	C2
Waddingham, Lincs	83	D2
Waddington, Lancs	86	B2
Waddington, Lincs	74	B1
Waddon, Dorset	7	D1
Wadebridge, Corn	3	D2
Wadeford, Som	13	A3
Wadenhoe, Nhants	62	B4
Wadesmill, Herts	42	B2
Wadhurst, E Suss	19	C1
Wadshelf, Derby	72	A1
Wadworth, S York	82	C2
Wainfleet All Saints, Lincs	75	B2
Wainstalls, W Yorks	87	B4
Waitby, Cumb	92	C1
Waithe, Lincs	84	B2
Wakefield, W Yorks	88	A4
Wakerley, Nhants	62	A3
Wakes Colne, Essex	43	D1
Walberswick, Suff	55	D1
Walcombe, Som	24	B4
Walcot Green, Norf	65	A4
Walcot, Lincs	74	B4
Walcot, Lincs	74	C2
Walcot, Shrops	58	A2
Walcote, Leics	61	A4
Walcott, Norf	76	E4
Walden Stubbs, N York	82	C1
Walderton, W Suss	17	B3
Walditch, Dorset	7	C1
Waldridge, Durham	100	A1
Waldringfield, Suff	55	B4
Waldron, E Suss	19	C2
Wales, S York	82	B4
Walesby, Lincs	84	A3
Walesby, Notts	73	B1
Walford Heath, Shrops	57	C1
Walford, Heref	37	B2
Walford, Heref	47	C1
Walgherton, Chesh	70	B3
Walgrave, Nhants	51	B1
Walk Mill, Lancs	86	C4
Walkden, G Man	80	A2
Walkerburn, Border	110	C2
Walkeringham, Notts	83	B3
Walkerith, Lincs	83	B3
Walkern, Herts	42	A1
Walker's Green, Heref	47	D3
Walkhampton, Devon	4	C3
Walkington, E R of Y	90	B3
Wall, Nthumb	105	B3
Wall, Staffs	59	B2
Wallasey, Mers	78	D3
Wallingford, Oxon	40	A4
Wallington, G Lon	147	B4
Wallington, Herts	52	C4
Walls, Shet	144	A2
Wallsend, Tyne	106	B4
Wallyford, E Loth	118	B3
Walmer Bridge, Lancs	85	C4
Walpole Cross Keys, Norf	63	C1
Walpole Highway, Norf	63	C2
Walpole St Andrew, Norf	63	C1
Walpole St Peter, Norf	63	C1
Walpole, Suff	55	C1
Walsall, W Mids	59	A3
Walsden, W Yorks	87	A4
Walsham le Willows, Suff	54	C1
Walshaw, W Yorks	87	A3
Walshford, N York	88	B1
Walston, S Lan	109	E1
Waltham Abbey, Essex	42	B3
Waltham on the Wolds, Leics	61	C1
Waltham St Lawrence, Berks	28	A1
Waltham, Kent	32	A4
Waltham, Lincs	84	B2
Walton Card, Glouc	38	A1
Walton East, Pemb	33	D1
Walton Elm, Dorset	14	B3
Walton on the Hill, Surrey	150	A2
Walton on the Naze, Essex	44	D1
Walton on the Wolds, Leics	61	A1
Walton, Bucks	51	C4
Walton, Cumb	104	D4
Walton, Derby	72	A1
Walton, Leics	61	A4
Walton, Powys	47	B2
Walton, Shrops	58	A1
Walton, Som	13	B1
Walton, W Suss	17	B4
Walton, W Yorks	82	A1
Walton, W Yorks	88	B2
Walton-in-Gordano, Som	24	A2
Walton-on-Thames, Surrey	146	B2
Walton-on-the-Hill, Staffs	59	A1
Walton-on-Trent, Derby	60	A1
Walworth, Durham	100	A4
Walworth, G Lon	149	A2
Walwyn's Castle, Pemb	33	C2
Wambrook, Som	13	A3
Wanborough, Surrey	28	B4
Wanborough, Wilts	26	C1
Wandsworth, G Lon	147	A3
Wangford, Suff	55	C1
Wanlip, Leics	61	A2
Wanlockhead, Dumf	109	C4
Wansford, Cambs	62	B3
Wansford, E R of Y	90	B1

PLACE	PAGE	GRID
Wanshurst Green, Kent	31	A4
Wanstrow, Som	25	A4
Wanswell, Glouc	37	B3
Wantage, Oxon	39	C4
Wapley, Glouc	25	A1
Wappenham, Nhants	51	A3
Warbleton, E Suss	19	C2
Warborough, Oxon	40	A4
Warboys, Cambs	63	A4
Warbstow, Corn	4	A1
Warburton, G Man	80	A3
Warcop, Cumb	99	A4
Warden, Nthumb	105	B4
Wardington, Oxon	50	B3
Wardle, Chesh	70	A2
Wardle, G Man	80	B1
Wardley, Rutland	61	C3
Wardlow, Derby	81	C4
Wardy Hill, Cambs	63	C4
Ware, Herts	42	B2
Wareham, Dorset	8	B1
Warenford, Nthumb	112	B2
Wareside, Herts	42	B2
Waresley, Cambs	52	C3
Warfield, Berks	28	B3
Warfleet, Devon	5	C4
Wargrave, Berks	28	A1
Warham St Mary, Norf	76	A3
Wark, Nthumb	105	B3
Wark, Nthumb	111	C1
Warkton, Nhants	62	A4
Warkworth, Nhants	50	B4
Warkworth, Nthumb	112	C4
Warlaby, N York	93	D2
Warleggan, Corn	3	E3
Warlingham, Surrey	150	C2
Warmingham, Chesh	70	B1
Warmington, Nhants	62	B4
Warmington, Warwk	50	B3
Warminster, Wilts	25	B4
Warmwell, Dorset	8	A1
Warnford, Hants	17	A2
Warnham, W Suss	18	B1
Warningcamp, W Suss	18	A3
Warninglid, W Suss	18	C2
Warren Row, Berks	28	A1
Warren Street, Kent	31	C3
Warren, Chesh	70	C1
Warren, Pemb	33	C4
Warrington, Bucks	51	C3
Warrington, Chesh	79	C3
Warsash, Hants	16	A4
Warslow, Staffs	71	B2
Warsop, Notts	73	A1
Warter, E R of Y	90	A2
Warthermaske, N York	93	C3
Warthill, N York	89	B1
Wartling, E Suss	19	C3
Wartnaby, Leics	61	B1
Warton, Lancs	85	B4
Warton, Lancs	92	A4
Warton, Warwk	60	B2
Warwick, Cumb	98	C1
Warwick, Warwk	50	A2
Wasbister, Orkney	144	A1
Wasdale Head, Cumb	91	C1
Washaway, Corn	3	D3
Washbourne, Devon	5	C4
Washfield, Devon	12	B3
Washfold, N York	93	B1
Washford Pyne, Devon	12	A3
Washford, Som	12	C1
Washingborough, Lincs	74	B1
Washington, Tyne	100	B1
Washington, W Suss	18	B3
Wasperton, Warwk	49	C2
Wass, N York	94	B3
Watchet, Som	23	A4
Watchfield, Oxon	39	A4
Watchgate, Cumb	92	A2
Water Eaton, Oxon	40	A2
Water End, E R of Y	89	C3
Water End, Essex	53	C4
Water Orton, Warwk	60	A4
Water Stratford, Bucks	51	A4
Water, Devon	5	B2
Waterbeach, Cambs	53	B2
Waterbeck, Dumf	104	B3
Watercombe, Dorset	8	A1
Waterfall, Staffs	71	B2
Waterfoot, S Lan	115	C4
Waterford, Herts	42	A2
Watergate, Corn	3	E2
Waterhouses, Staffs	71	B2
Wateringbury, Kent	31	A3
Waterloo, N Lan	116	B4
Waterloo, Perth	123	C1
Watermillock, Cumb	98	B3
Waterperry, Oxon	40	B3
Waterrow, Som	12	C2
Waters Upton, Shrops	58	A1
Waterside, E Ayrs	108	E4
Waterside, E Ayrs	108	E1
Waterside, Lancs	86	B4
Waterstock, Oxon	40	B3
Waterston, Pemb	33	C3
Watford, Herts	41	C4
Watford, Nhants	50	C1
Wath, N York	93	B4
Wath, N York	93	D3
Watlington, Norf	63	D2
Watlington, Oxon	40	B4
Watten, High	143	E2
Wattisfield, Suff	54	D1
Wattisham, Suff	54	D3
Watton, E R of Y	90	B2
Watton, Norf	64	C3
Watton-at-Stone, Herts	42	A2
Wattston, N Lan	116	B3
Wattsville, Caer	36	A4
Waunfawr, Gwyn	67	D2
Wavendon, Bucks	51	C4
Waverbridge, Cumb	97	E1
Waverton, Chesh	69	C1

PLACE	PAGE	GRID
Waverton, Cumb	97	E1
Wawne, E R of Y	90	C3
Waxham, Norf	76	E4
Way Village, Devon	12	A3
Wayford, Som	13	B3
Weacombe, Som	12	C1
Weald, Oxon	39	B3
Wear Head, Durham	99	B2
Weardley, W Yorks	88	A2
Weare Giffard, Devon	11	D2
Weare, Som	24	A4
Wearne, Som	13	B2
Weasenham All Saints, Norf	64	B1
Weasenham St Peter, Norf	64	B1
Weaverham, Chesh	79	C4
Weaverthorpe, N York	95	C4
Wedhampton, Wilts	26	B3
Wedmore, Som	24	A4
Weedon, Bucks	40	C2
Weeford, Staffs	59	B2
Week St Mary, Corn	11	B4
Weekley, Nhants	62	A4
Weel, E R of Y	90	B3
Weeley Heath, Essex	44	C2
Weeley, Essex	44	C1
Weem, Perth	128	A4
Weethley, Warwk	49	B3
Weeting, Norf	64	B4
Weeton, E R of Y	90	E4
Weeton, Lancs	85	B3
Weeton, N York	88	A2
Weir Quay, Devon	4	C3
Weir, Lancs	86	C4
Welborne, Norf	64	D2
Welbourn, Lincs	74	B2
Welburn, N York	94	C4
Welbury, N York	94	A1
Welby, Lincs	74	B3
Welches Dam, Cambs	63	C4
Welcombe, Devon	11	B2
Welford, Berks	27	A2
Welford, Nhants	61	B4
Welford-on-Avon, Warwk	49	B3
Welham Green, Herts	42	A3
Welham, Leics	61	C3
Welham, Notts	83	A4
Well Head, Herts	41	C1
Well Hill, Kent	30	A3
Well, Hants	28	A4
Well, Lincs	84	D4
Well, N York	93	C3
Welland, Worcs	48	B4
Wellesbourne, Warwk	50	A3
Welling, G Lon	30	A1
Wellingborough, Nhants	51	C2
Wellingore, Lincs	74	B2
Wellington Heath, Heref	48	B4
Wellington, Cumb	91	B1
Wellington, Heref	47	D3
Wellington, Shrops	58	A2
Wellington, Som	12	D2
Wellow, I of W	9	B1
Wellow, Notts	73	B1
Wellow, Som	25	A3
Wells, Som	24	B4
Wells-next-the-sea, Norf	76	A3
Wellstye Green, Essex	43	A2
Welney, Norf	63	C3
Welsh Frankton, Shrops	69	C4
Welsh Newton, Heref	37	A2
Welshampton, Shrops	69	C4
Welshpool, Powys	57	A2
Welton le Marsh, Lincs	75	B1
Welton le Wold, Lincs	84	B3
Welton, Cumb	98	B2
Welton, E R of Y	90	A4
Welton, Nhants	50	C2
Welwick, E R of Y	90	E4
Welwyn Garden City, Herts	42	A2
Welwyn, Herts	42	A2
Wem, Shrops	69	D4
Wembdon, Som	13	A1
Wembley, G Lon	146	B1
Wembury, Devon	10	A1
Wembworthy, Devon	11	F3
Wemyss Bay, Inverclyde	114	C3
Wendens Ambo, Essex	53	B4
Wendlebury, Oxon	40	A2
Wendling, Norf	64	C2
Wendron, Corn	1	D2
Wendy, Cambs	53	A3
Wenhaston, Suff	55	C1
Wennington, Cambs	52	C1
Wennington, G Lon	30	A1
Wennington, Lancs	92	B4
Wensley, N York	93	B2
Wentbridge, W Yorks	82	B1
Wentnor, Shrops	57	C3
Wentworth, Cambs	53	B1
Wentworth, S York	82	A2
Wenvoe, Glam	23	B2
Weobley Marsh, Heref	47	C3
Weobley, Heref	47	C3
Wepham, W Suss	18	A3
Wereham, Norf	64	A3
Werrington, Corn	4	B1
Wervin, Chesh	69	C1
Wesham, Lancs	85	B3
Wessington, Derby	72	A2
West Acre, Norf	64	B1
West Alvington, Devon	10	A1
West Anstey, Devon	12	A2
West Ashby, Lincs	84	B4
West Ashton, Wilts	25	B3
West Auckland, Durham	100	A3
West Ayton, N York	95	C3
West Bagborough, Som	12	D1
West Barkwith, Lincs	84	A4
West Barnby, N York	101	C4
West Barsham, Norf	76	A4
West Bay, Dorset	7	B1
West Bedfont, Surrey	146	A2
West Bergholt, Essex	44	A1

PLACE	PAGE	GRID
West Bexington, Dorset	7	C1
West Bilney, Norf	64	A1
West Boldon, Tyne	106	B4
West Brabourne, Kent	32	A4
West Bradenham, Norf	64	C2
West Bradford, Lancs	86	B2
West Bradley, Som	13	C1
West Bretton, W Yorks	82	A1
West Bridgford, Notts	73	A4
West Bromwich, W Mids	59	A4
West Caister, Norf	66	B2
West Calder, W Loth	117	A3
West Camel, Som	13	C2
West Chaldon, Dorset	8	A2
West Challow, Oxon	39	B4
West Chevington, Nthumb	106	A1
West Coker, Som	13	C3
West Compton Abbas, Dorset	7	C1
West Compton, Som	24	C4
West Cottingwith, N York	89	B2
West Cowick, E R of Y	89	B4
West Curthwaite, Cumb	98	A1
West Dean, W Suss	17	C3
West Dean, Wilts	15	B2
West Deeping, Lincs	62	C2
West Dereham, Norf	63	D3
West Down, Devon	22	A4
West Drayton, G Lon	146	A1
West Drayton, Notts	83	A4
West Ella, E R of Y	90	B4
West End Green, Hants	27	C3
West End, Beds	52	A3
West End, Berks	28	B2
West End, Hants	16	A3
West End, Norf	66	B2
West End, Som	24	A2
West End, Surrey	146	B3
West Ewell, G Lon	150	A1
West Farleigh, Kent	31	A3
West Farndon, Nhants	50	C3
West Felton, Shrops	57	B1
West Firle, E Suss	19	B3
West Grafton, Wilts	26	C3
West Grimstead, Wilts	15	B2
West Grinstead, W Suss	18	B2
West Haddlesey, N York	89	A4
West Haddon, Nhants	51	A1
West Hagbourne, Oxon	40	A4
West Hallam, Derby	72	B3
West Halton, Lincs	90	A4
West Ham, G Lon	149	B1
West Handley, Derby	82	B4
West Hanney, Oxon	39	C4
West Hanningfield, Essex	43	B3
West Harting, W Suss	17	B2
West Hatch, Wilts	14	C2
West Heslerton, N York	95	B4
West Hewish, Som	24	A3
West Hill, Devon	6	B1
West Holme, Dorset	8	B1
West Horrington, Som	24	B4
West Horsley, Surrey	146	A3
West Hougham, Kent	21	D1
West Huntingtower, Perth	123	C2
West Huntspill, Som	23	C4
West Hythe, Kent	21	C1
West Ilsley, Berks	27	A1
West Kennett, Wilts	26	B2
West Kilbride, N Ayrs	108	C1
West Kingsdown, Kent	30	B3
West Kington, Wilts	25	A1
West Kirby, Mers	78	C3
West Knapton, N York	95	B4
West Knighton, Dorset	8	A1
West Knoyle, Wilts	14	C1
West Langdon, Kent	32	C4
West Lavington, W Suss	17	C2
West Lavington, Wilts	26	A3
West Layton, N York	93	B1
West Leake, Notts	73	A4
West Lexham, Norf	64	B1
West Lilling, N York	94	C4
West Linton, Border	117	B4
West Littleton, Glouc	25	A2
West Lockinge, Oxon	39	C4
West Lulworth, Dorset	8	B2
West Lutton, N York	95	B4
West Lydford, Som	13	C1
West Lyng, Som	13	A2
West Malvern, Worcs	48	B3
West Marden, W Suss	17	B3
West Markham, Notts	83	A4
West Marton, N York	86	C2
West Meon, Hants	17	A2
West Mersea, Essex	44	B2
West Milton, Dorset	13	C4
West Monkton, Som	13	A2
West Morden, Dorset	14	C4
West Mudford, Som	13	C2
West Ness, N York	94	C3
West Newton, E R of Y	90	D3
West Newton, Norf	75	D4
West Newton, Som	13	A2
West Norwood, G Lon	149	A3
West Ogwell, Devon	5	C3
West Orchard, Dorset	14	C3
West Overton, Wilts	26	B2
West Peckham, Kent	30	B4
West Pelton, Durham	100	A1
West Pennard, Som	13	C1
West Pentire, Corn	3	B3
West Porlock, Som	22	D4
West Pulham, Dorset	14	B3
West Putford, Devon	11	C3
West Quantoxhead, Som	23	A4
West Raddon, Devon	12	B4
West Rainton, Durham	100	B1
West Rasen, Lincs	83	D3
West Raynham, Norf	64	B1
West Rounton, N York	94	A1
West Row, Suff	54	A1
West Runton, Norf	76	C3
West Saltoun, E Loth	118	B3

PLACE	PAGE	GRID
West Sandford, Devon	12	A4
West Sandwick, Shet	144	A2
West Scrafton, N York	93	B3
West Stafford, Dorset	8	A1
West Stockwith, Notts	83	B3
West Stoke, W Suss	17	B3
West Stow, Suff	54	B1
West Stowell, Wilts	26	B3
West Tanfield, N York	93	C3
West Taphouse, Corn	3	E3
West Thorney, W Suss	17	B4
West Thorpe, Notts	61	B1
West Thurrock, Essex	30	B1
West Tilbury, Essex	31	A1
West Tisted, Hants	17	A2
West Torrington, Lincs	84	A4
West Tytherley, Hants	15	C1
West Walton Highway, Norf	63	C2
West Walton, Norf	63	C2
West Wemyss, Fife	118	A1
West Wick, Som	24	A3
West Wickham, Cambs	53	C3
West Wickham, G Lon	149	B4
West Williamston, Pemb	33	D3
West Winch, Norf	63	D1
West Winterslow, Wilts	15	B1
West Wittering, W Suss	17	B4
West Witton, N York	93	B2
West Woodburn, Nthumb	105	B2
West Woodhay, Berks	27	A3
West Worldham, Hants	17	B1
West Wratting, Cambs	53	C3
West Youlstone, Corn	11	B3
Westbere, Kent	32	B3
Westborough, Lincs	73	C3
Westbrook, Berks	27	A2
Westbury on Severn, Glouc	37	C2
Westbury, Bucks	51	A4
Westbury, Shrops	57	C2
Westbury, Wilts	25	B4
Westbury-sub-Mendip, Som	24	B4
Westby, Lancs	85	B3
Westcote, Glouc	39	A2
Westcott, Bucks	40	B2
Westcott, Devon	12	C4
Westcott, Surrey	146	B4
Westcourt, Wilts	26	C3
Westdean, E Suss	19	B4
Westdowns, Corn	3	D2
Wested, Kent	30	A2
Westerdale, High	143	D2
Westerdale, N York	94	C1
Westerfield, Suff	55	A3
Westergate, W Suss	17	C4
Westerham, Kent	30	A3
Westerland, Devon	5	C3
Westerleigh, Glouc	25	A1
Westfield, E Suss	20	B3
Westfield, Norf	64	C2
Westgate, Lincs	83	B1
Westhall, Suff	66	A4
Westham, E Suss	19	C4
Westham, Som	24	A4
Westhay, Som	24	A4
Westhide, Heref	48	A4
Westhill, Aber	134	C3
Westhope, Heref	47	C3
Westhope, Shrops	57	D4
Westhorpe, Lincs	74	D4
Westhorpe, Suff	54	D1
Westhouse, N York	92	B4
Westhumble, Surrey	146	B4
Westlake, Devon	5	A4
Westleigh, Devon	11	D2
Westleigh, Devon	12	C3
Westleton, Suff	55	C1
Westley Waterless, Cambs	53	C3
Westley, Suff	54	B2
Westlington, Bucks	40	C3
Westlinton, Cumb	104	C4
Westmarsh, Kent	32	C3
Westmeston, E Suss	19	A3
Westmill, Herts	42	B1
Westminster, G Lon	148	B3
Westmuir, Angus	129	A4
Westnewton, Cumb	97	E2
Weston Beggard, Heref	48	A4
Weston by Welland, Nhants	61	C4
Weston Colley, Hants	16	A1
Weston Colville, Cambs	53	C3
Weston Heath, Shrops	58	B2
Weston Jones, Staffs	58	B1
Weston Longville, Norf	64	D1
Weston Lullingfields, Shrops	57	C1
Weston Patrick, Hants	27	C4
Weston Rhyn, Shrops	69	B4
Weston Subedge, Glouc	49	B4
Weston under Penyard, Heref	37	B1
Weston Underwood, Bucks	51	C3
Weston Underwood, Derby	72	A3
Weston, Berks	27	A2
Weston, Chesh	70	B2
Weston, Devon	6	C1
Weston, Devon	12	D4
Weston, Hants	17	A2
Weston, Herts	42	A1
Weston, Lincs	63	A1
Weston, N York	87	C2
Weston, Nhants	50	C3
Weston, Notts	73	C1
Weston, Shrops	58	A3
Weston, Shrops	69	B4
Weston, Staffs	71	A4
Westonbirt, Glouc	38	A4
Westoning, Beds	41	B1
Weston-in-Gordano, Som	24	A2
Weston-on-the-Green, Oxon	40	A2
Weston-Super-Mare, Som	23	C3
Weston-under-Lizard, Staffs	58	B2
Weston-under-Redcastle,		

PLACE	PAGE	GRID
Shrops	69	D4
Weston-upon-Trent, Derby	72	B4
Westonzoyland, Som	13	B1
Westow, N York	95	A4
Westruther, Border	119	B4
Westry, Cambs	63	B3
Westward, Cumb	98	A2
Westwell Leacon, Kent	31	C4
Westwell, Kent	31	C4
Westwell, Oxon	39	A3
Westwick, Cambs	53	A2
Westwood, Devon	12	C4
Westwood, Kent	32	D2
Westwood, Wilts	25	A3
Westwoodside, Lincs	83	B2
Wetheral, Cumb	98	C1
Wetherby, W Yorks	88	B2
Wetherden, Suff	54	D2
Wetheringsett, Suff	55	A2
Wethersfield, Essex	43	B1
Wetherup Street, Suff	55	A2
Wetley Rocks, Staffs	71	A2
Wettenhall, Chesh	70	A1
Wetton, Staffs	71	B2
Wetwang, E R of Y	90	A1
Wexcombe, Wilts	26	C3
Wexham Street, Bucks	146	A1
Wexham, Bucks	146	A1
Weybourne, Norf	76	B3
Weybread, Suff	65	B4
Weybridge, Surrey	146	A2
Weyhill, Hants	26	D4
Weymouth, Dorset	7	D2
Whaddon, Bucks	51	B4
Whaddon, Cambs	53	A3
Whaddon, Glouc	38	A2
Whaddon, Wilts	15	B2
Whaddon, Wilts	25	B3
Whaley Bridge, Derby	81	A4
Whaley, Derby	73	A1
Whalley, Lancs	86	B3
Whalton, Nthumb	105	D2
Whaplode Drove, Lincs	63	B2
Whaplode, Lincs	63	B1
Wharf, Warwk	50	B3
Wharfe, N York	92	C4
Wharles, Lancs	85	B3
Wharncliffe Side, S York	82	A3
Wharram-le-Street, N York	95	B4
Wharton, Heref	47	D3
Whasset, Cumb	92	A3
Whatcote, Warwk	50	A4
Whateley, Warwk	60	A3
Whatfield, Suff	54	D3
Whatley, Som	13	B3
Whatley, Som	25	A4
Whatlington, E Suss	20	A2
Whatstandwell, Derby	72	A2
Whatton, Notts	73	C3
Whauphill, Dumf	96	D1
Wheatacre, Norf	66	A3
Wheathampstead, Herts	41	C2
Wheathill, Shrops	58	A4
Wheatley Hill, Durham	100	B2
Wheatley, Hants	17	B1
Wheaton Aston, Staffs	58	C2
Wheelock, Chesh	70	B2
Wheelton, Lancs	86	A4
Wheldrake, N York	89	B2
Whelford, Glouc	39	A3
Whelpley Hill, Bucks	41	B3
Whempstead, Herts	42	B2
Whenby, N York	94	C4
Whepstead, Suff	54	B2
Wherstead, Suff	55	A4
Wherwell, Hants	16	A1
Wheston, Derby	81	B4
Whetsted, Kent	31	A4
Whicham, Cumb	91	C3
Whichford, Warwk	50	A4
Whickham, Tyne	106	A4
Whigstreet, Angus	129	B4
Whilton, Nhants	51	A2
Whimple, Devon	12	C4
Whimpwell Green, Norf	76	E4
Whinburgh, Norf	64	D2
Whinnyfold, Aber	134	E1
Whippingham, I of W	10	A1
Whipsnade, Beds	41	B2
Whisby, Lincs	74	A1
Whissendine, Rutland	61	C2
Whissonsett, Norf	64	C1
Whistley Green, Berks	28	A2
Whiston, Nhants	51	B2
Whiston, Staffs	58	C2
Whiston, Staffs	71	A3
Whitbeck, Cumb	91	B3
Whitbourne, Heref	48	B2
Whitburn, Tyne	106	C4
Whitburn, W Loth	116	C3
Whitby, N York	101	D4
Whitchurch Canonicorum, Dorset	13	B4
Whitchurch Hill, Oxon	27	C1
Whitchurch, Bucks	40	C2
Whitchurch, Hants	27	A4
Whitchurch, Heref	37	A2
Whitchurch, Oxon	27	C1
Whitchurch, Pemb	33	B1
Whitchurch, Shrops	69	D3
Whitchurch, Som	24	C2
Whitcot, Shrops	57	C3
White Chapel, Lancs	85	C3
White Colne, Essex	43	C1
White Cross, Corn	1	D3
White End, Worcs	48	B4
White Lackington, Dorset	14	B4
White Ladies Aston, Worcs	48	C3
White Notley, Essex	43	C2
White Pit, Lincs	84	C4
White Roding, Essex	43	A2
White Stone, Heref	47	D4
White Waltham, Berks	28	B1
Whitebridge, High	132	A2

PLACE	PAGE	GRID
Whitebrook, Monm	37	A3
Whitechapel, G Lon	149	A2
Whitecliffe, Glouc	37	A3
Whitecraig, E Loth	118	A3
Whitefield, G Man	80	A2
Whitegate, Chesh	70	A1
Whitehall, Orkney	144	B1
Whitehaven, Cumb	97	C4
Whitehill, Hants	17	B1
Whitehills, Aber	139	B2
Whitehouse, Aber	134	A2
Whitehouse, Argyll	113	F3
Whitekirk, E Loth	119	B2
Whitelackington, Som	13	B3
Whitemoor, Corn	3	D4
Whiteparish, Wilts	15	B2
Whiterashes, Aber	134	C1
Whitestaunton, Som	13	A3
Whitestone Cross, Devon	6	A1
Whitewell, Lancs	86	A2
Whitfield, Glouc	37	B4
Whitfield, Nhants	50	C4
Whitfield, Nthumb	105	A4
Whitford, Devon	13	A4
Whitford, Flint	78	C4
Whitgift, E R of Y	89	C4
Whitgreave, Staffs	70	C4
Whithorn, Dumf	96	E2
Whiting Bay, N Ayrs	108	A3
Whitington, Norf	64	A3
Whitland, Carm	34	A2
Whitley Bay, Tyne	106	B3
Whitley Chapel, Nthumb	105	C4
Whitley Lower, W Yorks	81	C1
Whitley Row, Kent	30	A3
Whitley, N York	89	A4
Whitley, S York	82	A3
Whitley, Wilts	25	B2
Whitminster, Glouc	37	C3
Whitmore, Staffs	70	B3
Whitney-on-Wye, Heref	47	B3
Whitrigglees, Cumb	104	B4
Whitsbury, Hants	15	A2
Whitsome, Border	119	D4
Whitson, Newport	24	A1
Whitstone, Corn	11	B4
Whittingham, Nthumb	112	B4
Whittingslow, Shrops	57	C4
Whittington, Derby	82	A4
Whittington, Glouc	38	B2
Whittington, Lancs	92	B4
Whittington, Shrops	69	B4
Whittington, Staffs	58	C4
Whittington, Staffs	60	A2
Whittington, Warwk	60	B3
Whittington, Worcs	48	C3
Whittlebury, Nhants	51	A4
Whittle-le-Woods, Lancs	85	C4
Whittlesey, Cambs	63	A3
Whittlesford, Cambs	53	B3
Whitton, Durham	100	B3
Whitton, Lincs	90	A4
Whitton, Nthumb	105	D1
Whitton, Powys	47	B2
Whitton, Shrops	47	D1
Whittonstall, Nthumb	105	D4
Whitway, Hants	27	A3
Whitwell Street, Norf	64	D1
Whitwell, Herts	41	C2
Whitwell, N York	93	D2
Whitwell, Rutland	62	A2
Whitwell-on-the-Hill, N York	94	C4
Whitwick, Leics	60	C1
Whitworth, Lancs	86	C4
Whixall, Shrops	69	D4
Whixley, N York	88	B1
Whorlton, Durham	99	D4
Whyle, Heref	47	D2
Whyteleafe, Surrey	150	C2
Wibdon, Glouc	37	A4
Wibtoft, Warwk	60	C4
Wichenford, Worcs	48	B2
Wichling, Kent	31	C3
Wick St Lawrence, Som	24	A2
Wick, Glam	22	E2
Wick, Glouc	25	A2
Wick, High	143	F2
Wick, Worcs	49	A3
Wicken Bonhunt, Essex	42	C1
Wicken, Cambs	53	C1
Wicken, Nhants	51	B4
Wickenby, Lincs	84	A4
Wicker Street Green, Suff	54	C4
Wickersley, S York	82	B3
Wickford, Essex	43	B4
Wickham Bishops, Essex	43	C2
Wickham Market, Suff	55	B3
Wickham Skeith, Suff	54	D1
Wickham St Paul, Essex	54	B4
Wickham Street, Suff	54	D1
Wickham, Berks	27	A2
Wickham, Hants	16	B3
Wickhambreaux, Kent	32	B3
Wickhambrook, Suff	54	A3
Wickhamford, Worcs	49	B4
Wickhampton, Norf	66	A2
Wickmere, Norf	76	C4
Wickwar, Glouc	37	C4
Widdington, Essex	42	C1
Widdrington Station, Nthumb	106	A1
Widdrington, Nthumb	106	A1
Widecombe in the Moor, Devon	5	B2
Widegates, Corn	4	A4
Widemouth Bay, Corn	11	B4
Widford, Herts	42	B2
Widmer End, Bucks	41	A4
Widmerpool, Notts	73	B4
Widmore, G Lon	149	B4
Widnes, Chesh	79	B3
Widworthy, Devon	12	D4
Wigan, G Man	79	C2
Wiggaton, Devon	6	B1
Wiggenhall St Germans, Norf	63	D2
Wiggens Green, Essex	54	A4
Wigginton, Herts	41	A3
Wigginton, N York	89	A1
Wigginton, Oxon	39	C1
Wigginton, Staffs	60	A2
Wigglesworth, N York	86	B1
Wiggold, Glouc	38	C3
Wiggonby, Cumb	98	A1
Wighill, N York	88	B2
Wighton, Norf	76	A3
Wigley, Hants	15	C3
Wigsley, Notts	74	A1
Wigsthorpe, Nhants	62	B4
Wigston Parva, Leics	60	C4
Wigston, Leics	61	A3
Wigthorpe, Notts	82	C4
Wigtoft, Lincs	74	D4
Wigton, Cumb	98	A1
Wigtown, Dumf	96	E1
Wike, W Yorks	88	A2
Wilberfoss, E R of Y	89	B2
Wilburton, Cambs	53	B1
Wilby, Nhants	51	C2
Wilby, Norf	64	D4
Wilby, Suff	55	B1
Wilcot, Wilts	26	B3
Wilcott, Shrops	57	C1
Wildboarclough, Chesh	71	A1
Wilden, Beds	52	B3
Wilden, Worcs	48	C1
Wildmoor, Worcs	49	A1
Wildsworth, Lincs	83	B2
Wilkesley, Chesh	70	A3
Wilkieston, W Loth	117	B3
Willand, Devon	12	C3
Willaston, Chesh	70	A2
Willaston, Chesh	78	D4
Willen, Bucks	51	C4
Willerby, N York	95	C3
Willersley, Heref	47	B3
Willesden, G Lon	147	A1
Willesley, Wilts	38	A4
Willey, Shrops	58	A3
Willey, Warwk	60	C4
Willian, Herts	42	A1
Willingale, Essex	43	A3
Willingham by Stow, Lincs	83	C3
Willingham Green, Cambs	53	C3
Willingham, Cambs	53	A1
Willington, Beds	52	B3
Willington, Derby	72	A4
Willington, Durham	100	A2
Willington, Warwk	49	C4
Willitoft, E R of Y	89	C3
Willoughby Waterleys, Leics	61	A3
Willoughby, Lincs	75	B1
Willoughby, Warwk	50	C2
Willoughton, Lincs	83	C3
Willows Green, Essex	43	B2
Willtown, Som	13	B2
Wilmcote, Warwk	49	C2
Wilmington, E Suss	19	C4
Wilmington, Kent	30	A2
Wilmslow, Chesh	80	B4
Wilpshire, Lancs	86	A3
Wilsden, W Yorks	87	B3
Wilsford, Lincs	74	B3
Wilsford, Wilts	15	A1
Wilsford, Wilts	26	B3
Wilshaw, W Yorks	81	B1
Wilson, Leics	60	C1
Wilsontown, S Lan	116	C4
Wilstead, Beds	52	A4
Wilsthorpe, Lincs	62	C2
Wilstone, Herts	41	A2
Wilton, Heref	37	B1
Wilton, N York	95	B3
Wilton, N York	101	A4
Wilton, Wilts	15	A1
Wilton, Wilts	26	C3
Wimbish, Essex	53	C4
Wimbledon, G Lon	147	A3
Wimblington, Cambs	63	B3
Wimboldsley, Chesh	70	B1
Wimborne Minster, Dorset	14	D4
Wimborne St Giles, Dorset	14	D3
Wimbotsham, Norf	63	D2
Wincanton, Som	14	B2
Winchburgh, W Loth	117	A2
Winchcombe, Glouc	38	B1
Winchelsea, E Suss	21	A3
Winchester, Hants	16	A2
Winchet Hill, Kent	20	A1
Winchfield, Hants	28	A3
Wincle, Chesh	71	A1
Windermere, Cumb	91	E2
Winderton, Warwk	50	A4
Windlesham, Surrey	28	B3
Windmill Hill, Som	13	A3
Windmill, Corn	3	C2
Windrush, Glouc	39	A2
Windsor, Berks	28	B1
Windygates, Fife	124	A4
Wineham, W Suss	18	C2
Winestead, E R of Y	90	D2
Winfarthing, Norf	64	D4
Winford, Som	24	B2
Winforton, Heref	47	B3
Winfrith Newburgh, Dorset	8	A1
Wing, Bucks	41	A1
Wing, Rutland	62	A2
Wingate, Durham	100	C2
Wingerworth, Derby	72	A1
Wingfield, Beds	41	B1
Wingfield, Suff	55	A1
Wingfield, Wilts	25	B3
Wingham, Kent	32	C3
Wingmore, Kent	32	B4
Wingrave, Bucks	41	A2
Winkburn, Notts	73	B2
Winkfield Row, Berks	28	B2
Winkfield Street, Berks	28	B2
Winkfield, Berks	28	B2
Winkhill, Staffs	71	B2
Winkhurst Green, Kent	30	A4
Winkleigh, Devon	11	E3
Winksley, N York	93	C4
Winlaton, Tyne	106	A4
Winmarleigh, Lancs	85	C2
Winsford, Chesh	70	A1
Winsford, Som	12	B1
Winsham, Devon	11	D1
Winsham, Som	13	B4
Winskill, Cumb	98	C2
Winslade, Hants	27	C4
Winsley, Wilts	25	A3
Winslow, Bucks	40	C1
Winson, Glouc	38	C3
Winsor, Hants	15	C3
Winster, Cumb	91	E2
Winster, Derby	71	C2
Winston, Durham	99	D4
Winston, Suff	55	A2
Winstone, Glouc	38	B3
Winswell, Devon	11	D3
Winterborne Clenston, Dorset	14	C4
Winterborne Herringston, Dorset	7	D1
Winterborne Kingston, Dorset	14	C4
Winterborne Monkton, Dorset	7	D1
Winterborne Stickland, Dorset	14	C4
Winterborne Whitechurch, Dorset	14	C4
Winterborne Zelston, Dorset	14	C4
Winterbourne Abbas, Dorset	7	D1
Winterbourne Bassett, Wilts	26	B2
Winterbourne Dauntsey, Wilts	15	B1
Winterbourne Earls, Wilts	15	B1
Winterbourne Monkton, Wilts	26	B2
Winterbourne Steepleton, Dorset	7	D1
Winterbourne Stoke, Wilts	15	A1
Winterbourne, Berks	27	A2
Winterburn, N York	87	A1
Winteringham, Lincs	90	A4
Winterley, Chesh	70	B2
Winterslow, Wilts	15	B1
Winterton, Lincs	90	A4
Winterton-on-Sea, Norf	66	B1
Winthorpe, Notts	73	C2
Winton, Cumb	92	C1
Wintringham, N York	95	B4
Winwick, Cambs	62	C4
Winwick, Chesh	79	C3
Winwick, Nhants	51	A1
Wirksworth, Derby	72	A2
Wirswall, Chesh	69	D3
Wisbech St Mary, Cambs	63	B2
Wisbech, Cambs	63	C2
Wisborough Green, W Suss	18	A2
Wiseman's Bridge, Pemb	33	E3
Wiseton, Notts	83	A3
Wishaw, N Lan	116	B4
Wishaw, Warwk	60	A3
Wisley, Surrey	146	A3
Wispington, Lincs	74	D1
Wissett, Suff	55	C1
Wissington, Suff	44	A1
Wistanstow, Shrops	57	C4
Wistanswick, Shrops	70	A4
Wistaston, Chesh	70	A2
Wiston, Pemb	33	D2
Wiston, S Lan	109	D2
Wiston, W Suss	18	B3
Wistow, Cambs	63	A4
Wistow, N York	89	A3
Wiswell, Lancs	86	B3
Witcham, Cambs	63	C4
Witchampton, Dorset	14	D4
Witchford, Cambs	53	B1
Witham Friary, Som	25	A4
Witham on the Hill, Lincs	62	B1
Witham, Essex	43	C2
Withcall, Lincs	84	B3
Witherenden Hill, E Suss	19	C2
Witheridge, Devon	12	A3
Witherley, Leics	60	B3
Withern, Lincs	84	D4
Withernsea, E R of Y	90	E4
Withernwick, E R of Y	90	C3
Withersdale Street, Suff	65	B4
Withersfield, Suff	53	C3
Witherslack Hall, Cumb	91	E3
Witherslack, Cumb	91	E3
Withiel Florey, Som	12	B1
Withiel, Corn	3	D3
Withington, Glouc	38	B2
Withington, Heref	47	D4
Withington, Shrops	57	D2
Withington, Staffs	71	A4
Withleigh, Devon	12	B3
Withybed Green, Worcs	49	A1
Withybrook, Warwk	60	C4
Withypool, Som	12	A1
Witley, Surrey	17	C1
Witnesham, Suff	55	A3
Witney, Oxon	39	B3
Wittering, Cambs	62	B3
Wittersham, Kent	21	A2
Witton Gilbert, Durham	100	A1
Witton le Wear, Durham	99	D3
Witton Park, Durham	100	A3
Witton, Norf	65	B2
Wiveliscombe, Som	12	C2
Wivelrod, Hants	17	A1
Wivelsfield Green, E Suss	19	A2
Wivelsfield, E Suss	19	A2
Wivenhoe, Essex	44	B2
Wiveton, Norf	76	B3
Wix, Essex	44	C1
Wixford, Warwk	49	B3
Wixoe, Suff	54	A4
Woburn, Beds	41	A1
Woking, Surrey	146	A3
Wokingham, Berks	28	A2
Wold Newton, E R of Y	95	C4
Wold Newton, Lincs	84	B2
Woldingham, Surrey	150	D2
Wolferton, Norf	75	C4
Wolfhill, Perth	123	D1
Wolf's Castle, Pemb	33	C1
Wolfsdale, Pemb	33	C2
Wollaston, Nhants	51	C2
Wollaston, Shrops	57	B2
Wollerton, Shrops	70	A4
Wolseley Bridge, Staffs	59	A1
Wolsingham, Durham	99	D2
Wolston, Warwk	50	B1
Wolverhampton, W Mids	58	C3
Wolverley, Worcs	48	C1
Wolverton, Hants	27	B3
Wolverton, Warwk	49	C2
Wolvesnewton, Monm	36	C3
Wolvey, Warwk	60	C4
Wolviston, Durham	100	C3
Wombleton, N York	94	C3
Wombourne, Staffs	58	C3
Wombwell, S York	82	B2
Womenswold, Kent	32	B4
Womersley, N York	89	A4
Wonersh, Surrey	146	A4
Wood Bevington, Warwk	49	B3
Wood Dalling, Norf	76	B4
Wood End, G Lon	146	B1
Wood End, Herts	42	B1
Wood End, Warwk	49	B1
Wood Enderby, Lincs	74	D1
Wood Norton, Norf	76	B4
Wood Street, Norf	66	A1
Wood Street, Surrey	28	B4
Wood Walton, Cambs	63	A4
Woodall, S York	82	B4
Woodbastwick, Norf	65	B1
Woodborough, Notts	73	B3
Woodborough, Wilts	26	B3
Woodbridge, Devon	12	D4
Woodbridge, Suff	55	B3
Woodbury Salterton, Devon	6	B1
Woodbury, Devon	6	B1
Woodchester, Glouc	38	A3
Woodchurch, Kent	21	A1
Woodcombe, Som	22	E4
Woodcote, G Lon	150	B1
Woodcote, Oxon	27	C1
Woodcote, Shrops	58	B1
Woodeaton, Oxon	40	A2
Woodend, Nhants	50	C3
Woodend, W Suss	17	B3
Woodfalls, Wilts	15	B2
Woodford Halse, Nhants	50	C3
Woodford, G Man	80	B4
Woodford, Glouc	37	B4
Woodford, Nhants	52	A1
Woodgate, W Suss	17	C4
Woodgate, Worcs	49	A2
Woodgreen, Hants	15	B3
Woodhall Spa, Lincs	74	C1
Woodhall, N York	93	A2
Woodham Ferrers, Essex	43	C3
Woodham Mortimer, Essex	43	C3
Woodham Walter, Essex	43	C3
Woodham, Bucks	40	B2
Woodham, Surrey	146	A3
Woodhead, Aber	139	C4
Woodhill, Som	13	B2
Woodhorn, Nthumb	106	B2
Woodhouse Eaves, Leics	61	A2
Woodhouse, Leics	61	A1
Woodhurst, Cambs	53	A1
Woodkirk, W Yorks	87	C4
Woodland, Devon	5	C3
Woodland, Durham	99	D3
Woodland, Kent	32	B4
Woodlands Park, Berks	28	B1
Woodlands St Mary, Berks	26	D2
Woodlands, Hants	15	C3
Woodleigh, Devon	5	B4
Woodmancote, Glouc	38	B1
Woodmancote, Glouc	38	B3
Woodmancote, W Suss	18	C3
Woodmancott, Hants	27	B4
Woodmansey, E R of Y	90	B3
Woodmansgreen, W Suss	17	C2
Woodmansterne, Surrey	150	B1
Woodnewton, Nhants	62	B3
Woodplumpton, Lancs	85	C3
Woodrising, Norf	64	C2
Woodrow, Worcs	48	C1
Wood's Green, E Suss	19	C1
Woodseaves, Staffs	58	B1
Woodsetts, S York	82	C4
Woodside, Berks	28	B2
Woodside, Fife	124	B3
Woodside, G Lon	149	A4
Woodside, Perth	123	D1
Woodstock, Oxon	39	C2
Woodton, Norf	65	B3
Woodtown, Devon	11	C2
Woofferton, Shrops	47	D1
Wookey Hole, Som	24	B4
Wookey, Som	24	B4
Wool, Dorset	8	B1
Woolacombe, Devon	22	A4
Woolage Green, Kent	32	C4
Woolaston Common, Glouc	37	B3
Woolaston, Glouc	37	B3
Woolavington, Som	23	C4
Woolbeding, W Suss	17	C2
Wooler, Nthumb	112	A2
Woolfardisworthy, Devon	11	C2
Woolfardisworthy, Devon	12	A3
Woolhampton, Berks	27	B2
Woolhope, Heref	48	A4
Woolland, Dorset	14	B3
Woolley, Cambs	52	B1
Woolley, Som	25	A2
Woolley, W Yorks	82	A1
Woolmer Green, Herts	42	A2
Woolmere Green, Worcs	49	A2
Woolminstone, Som	13	B3
Woolpit, Suff	54	C2
Woolstaston, Shrops	57	C3
Woolsthorpe, Lincs	73	C4
Woolston, Chesh	79	C3
Woolston, Shrops	57	B1
Woolston, Shrops	57	C4
Woolston, Som	12	C1
Woolston, Som	14	A2
Woolstone, Bucks	51	C4
Woolstone, Glouc	38	B1
Woolstone, Oxon	26	D1
Woolton Hill, Hants	27	A3
Woolverstone, Suff	55	A4
Woolverton, Som	25	A3
Woolwich, G Lon	30	A1
Woore, Shrops	70	B3
Wootten Green, Suff	55	A1
Wootton Bassett, Wilts	26	B1
Wootton Bridge, I of W	10	A1
Wootton Courtenay, Som	22	E4
Wootton Rivers, Wilts	26	C3
Wootton St Lawrence, Hants	27	B3
Wootton Wawen, Warwk	49	B2
Wootton, Beds	52	A4
Wootton, Heref	47	B3
Wootton, Kent	32	B4
Wootton, Lincs	84	A1
Wootton, Nhants	51	B3
Wootton, Oxon	39	C2
Wootton, Staffs	71	B3
Worcester Park, G Lon	147	A4
Worcester, Worcs	48	C3
Worfield, Shrops	58	B3
Workington, Cumb	97	C3
Worksop, Notts	82	C4
Worlaby, Lincs	83	D1
World's End, Berks	27	A1
Worlds End, Hants	17	A3
Worleston, Chesh	70	A2
Worlingham, Suff	66	A4
Worlington, Devon	11	F3
Worlington, Suff	54	A1
Worlingworth, Suff	55	A1
Wormald Green, N York	93	D4
Wormbridge, Heref	36	C1
Wormegay, Norf	64	A2
Wormelow Tump, Heref	37	A1
Wormhill, Derby	81	B4
Wormingford, Essex	44	A1
Worminghall, Bucks	40	B3
Wormington, Glouc	49	A4
Wormit, Fife	124	B2
Wormleighton, Warwk	50	B3
Wormley, Surrey	17	C1
Wormsley, Heref	47	C3
Worplesdon, Surrey	146	A3
Worrall, S York	82	A3
Worsbrough, S York	82	A2
Worsley, G Man	80	A2
Worstead, Norf	65	B1
Worston, Devon	5	A4
Worston, Lancs	86	B2
Worth Abbey, W Suss	19	A1
Worth Matravers, Dorset	8	C2
Worth, Kent	32	C3
Worth, W Suss	18	C1
Wortham, Suff	54	D1
Worthen, Shrops	57	B2
Worthenbury, Wrex	69	C3
Worthing, Norf	64	C1
Worthing, W Suss	18	B4
Worthington, Leics	60	C1
Wortley, S York	82	A2
Worton, Wilts	26	A3
Wortwell, Norf	65	B4
Wotton Underwood, Bucks	40	B2
Wotton, Surrey	146	B4
Wotton-under-Edge, Glouc	37	C4
Woundale, Shrops	58	B3
Wrabness, Essex	44	C1
Wrafton, Devon	11	D1
Wragby, Lincs	84	A4
Wragby, W Yorks	82	B1
Wrangaton, Devon	5	B4
Wrangle, Lincs	75	A2
Wrawby, Lincs	83	D1
Wraxall, Som	14	A1
Wraxall, Som	24	B2
Wray, Lancs	92	B4
Wraysbury, Berks	146	A2
Wrayton, Lancs	92	B4
Wrea Green, Lancs	85	B3
Wreay, Cumb	98	B1
Wrelton, N York	95	A3
Wrenbury, Chesh	70	A3
Wreningham, Norf	65	A3
Wrentnall, Shrops	57	C2
Wressle, E R of Y	89	B3
Wressle, Lincs	83	D1
Wrestlingworth, Beds	52	C3
Wrexham, Wrex	69	B2
Wrinehill, Staffs	70	B3
Wrington, Som	24	B3
Wrockwardine, Shrops	58	A2
Wroot, Lincs	83	A2
Wroughton, Wilts	26	B1
Wroxall, I of W	10	A2
Wroxall, Warwk	49	C1
Wroxeter, Shrops	57	D2
Wroxham, Norf	65	B1
Wroxton, Oxon	50	B4
Wyaston, Derby	71	C3
Wyberton East, Lincs	75	A3
Wyboston, Beds	52	B2
Wybunbury, Chesh	70	B2
Wychbold, Worcs	48	C2
Wychnor, Staffs	60	A1
Wyck Rissington, Glouc	39	A2
Wyck, Hants	17	B1
Wycliffe, Durham	99	D4
Wycoller, Lancs	87	A3
Wycomb, Leics	61	C1
Wyddial, Herts	42	B1
Wye, Kent	32	A4
Wyke Champflower, Som	14	A1
Wyke, Dorset	14	B2
Wyke, Surrey	28	B4
Wykeham, N York	95	B3
Wyken, Shrops	58	B3
Wykey, Shrops	57	C1
Wylam, Nthumb	105	D4
Wylye, Wilts	14	D1
Wymeswold, Leics	61	A1
Wymington, Beds	51	C2
Wymondham, Leics	61	C1
Wymondham, Norf	64	D3
Wynford Eagle, Dorset	14	A4
Wyre Piddle, Worcs	49	A3
Wysall, Notts	73	A4
Wythall, Worcs	49	B1
Wytham, Oxon	39	C3
Wyton, E R of Y	90	C3
Wyverstone, Suff	54	D2
Y Ferwig, Cered	45	C3
Y Ffor, Gwyn	67	C3
Y Gyffylliog, Denb	68	D2
Y Maerdy, Aberc	68	D3
Y Rhiw, Gwyn	67	B4
Yafforth, N York	93	D2
Yalberton, Devon	5	C4
Yalding, Kent	31	A4
Yanwath, Cumb	98	C3
Yanworth, Glouc	38	C2
Yapham, E R of Y	89	C2
Yapton, W Suss	18	A4
Yarborough, Som	24	A3
Yarburgh, Lincs	84	C3
Yarcombe, Devon	13	A3
Yard, Devon	12	A2
Yardley Gobion, Nhants	51	B4
Yardley Hastings, Nhants	51	C2
Yarkhill, Heref	48	A4
Yarley, Som	24	B4
Yarlington, Som	14	A2
Yarm, N York	100	C4
Yarmouth, I of W	9	B1
Yarnbrook, Wilts	25	B3
Yarnscombe, Devon	11	E2
Yarnton, Oxon	39	C2
Yarpole, Heref	47	D2
Yarrowford, Border	110	C2
Yarwell, Nhants	62	B3
Yate, Glouc	25	A1
Yateley, Hants	28	A3
Yatesbury, Wilts	26	B2
Yattendon, Berks	27	B2
Yatton Keynell, Wilts	25	B1
Yatton, Heref	37	B1
Yatton, Heref	47	C2
Yatton, Som	24	A2
Yaverland, I of W	10	A1
Yaxham, Norf	64	C2
Yaxley, Cambs	62	C3
Yaxley, Suff	55	A1
Yazor, Heref	47	C3
Yeading, G Lon	146	B1
Yeadon, W Yorks	87	C3
Yealand Conyers, Lancs	92	A4
Yealand Redmayne, Lancs	92	A4
Yealmpton, Devon	5	A4
Yearsley, N York	94	B4
Yeaton, Shrops	57	C1
Yeaveley, Derby	71	C3
Yeavering, Nthumb	112	A2
Yedingham, N York	95	B3
Yelford, Oxon	39	B3
Yelling, Cambs	52	C2
Yelvertoft, Nhants	50	C1
Yelverton, Devon	4	C3
Yelverton, Norf	65	B3
Yenston, Som	14	B2
Yeoford, Devon	12	A4
Yeolmbridge, Corn	4	B1
Yeovil, Som	13	C3
Yeovilton, Som	13	C2
Yesnaby, Orkney	144	A2
Yettington, Devon	6	B1
Yetts o'Muckhart, Clack	123	B4
Yielden, Beds	52	A2
Yiewsley, G Lon	146	A1
Ynysboeth, Rhond	35	D4
Ynysddu, Caer	36	A4
Ynysybwl, Rhond	35	D4
Yockleton, Shrops	57	C2
Yokefleet, E R of Y	89	C4
York Town, Surrey	28	B3
York, N York	89	A2
Yorkletts, Kent	32	A3
Yorkley, Glouc	37	B3
Youlgreave, Derby	71	C1
Youlthorpe, E R of Y	89	C1
Youlton, N York	88	B1
Yoxall, Staffs	59	B1
Yoxford, Suff	55	C1
Ysbyty Ifan, Aberc	68	B3
Ysbyty Ystwyth, Cered	46	B1
Ysceifiog, Flint	69	A1
Ystalyfera, Neath	35	A3
Ystrad Aeron, Cered	45	F3
Ystrad Meurig, Cered	46	B2
Ystrad Mynach, Caer	36	A4
Ystrad, Rhond	35	C4
Ystradfellte, Powys	35	C2
Ystradgynlais, Powys	35	B3
Ystradowen, Glam	23	A1
Ythanwells, Aber	139	B4
Zeals, Wilts	14	B1
Zelah, Corn	3	B4
Zennor, Corn	1	B1
Zouch, Notts	60	C1

DISTANCES CHART

1 MILE = 1.6 KILOMETRES

	London	Aberdeen	Aberystwyth	Ayr	Berwick-upon-Tweed	Birmingham	Blackpool	Bournemouth	Braemar	Brighton	Bristol	Cambridge	Cardiff	Carlisle	Doncaster	Dover	Dundee	Edinburgh	Exeter	Fishguard	Fort William	Glasgow	Gloucester	Great Yarmouth	Harwich	Holyhead	Inverness	John o'Groats	Kingston upon Hull	Kyle of Lochalsh	Land's End	Leeds	Leicester	Lincoln	Liverpool	Manchester	Newcastle upon Tyne	Norwich	Nottingham	Oban	Oxford	Plymouth	Portsmouth	Sheffield	Shrewsbury	Southampton	Stranraer	Swansea	York
London		517	211	394	352	117	234	107	482	52	122	54	157	301	171	71	448	390	181	260	510	397	109	128	76	269	550	663	184	586	297	189	97	131	202	185	286	114	122	499	57	218	70	159	160	77	402	194	207
Aberdeen	517		445	183	182	420	308	564	59	573	493	471	505	221	344	588	67	125	569	504	149	145	468	517	535	439	105	232	364	189	692	327	414	383	341	340	235	496	393	178	483	615	560	360	399	547	228	507	319
Aberystwyth	211	445		317	311	114	153	207	405	253	125	214	105	224	176	292	376	320	201	56	430	320	102	294	281	111	486	601	223	499	313	169	153	199	104	129	257	276	164	412	154	237	222	159	77	201	325	73	195
Ayr	394	183	317		134	289	180	436	143	446	370	357	382	93	235	478	117	73	446	373	133	33	330	402	425	305	199	328	251	212	570	212	299	274	213	212	149	382	274	94	353	492	430	245	269	417	51	379	214
Berwick-upon-Tweed	352	182	311	134		274	181	412	148	409	362	306	368	87	184	424	113	57	428	371	190	101	318	345	372	311	215	342	185	263	552	156	252	224	219	196	64	328	221	180	324	474	401	190	265	388	170	383	148
Birmingham	117	420	114	289	274		123	147	385	163	81	100	103	196	94	194	349	292	157	170	392	292	56	180	167	148	458	574	134	471	281	113	39	90	93	80	207	166	50	384	64	203	141	76	45	128	297	119	130
Blackpool	234	308	153	180	181	123		270	281	286	204	208	209	87	94	312	239	183	282	209	296	183	174	252	275	141	348	478	127	372	405	72	140	128	49	48	129	232	111	285	187	328	264	86	98	251	188	216	96
Bournemouth	107	564	207	436	412	147	270		524	92	82	154	117	343	235	174	495	439	82	222	539	439	99	240	187	288	597	724	264	618	205	255	158	209	234	227	347	214	183	530	90	128	52	216	185	31	444	167	269
Braemar	482	59	405	143	148	385	281	524		534	477	438	483	196	310	553	52	91	550	493	125	110	443	477	504	426	75	202	327	159	665	293	389	357	318	318	201	457	353	141	465	587	547	320	371	532	194	505	285
Brighton	52	573	253	446	409	163	286	92	534		147	116	182	370	236	82	517	456	184	291	575	468	159	180	128	334	617	741	245	651	308	260	166	197	272	257	352	175	193	565	108	224	48	226	226	61	475	222	275
Bristol	122	493	125	370	362	81	204	82	477	147		169	45	277	175	202	430	373	76	154	486	373	35	275	217	206	539	668	233	552	200	194	120	183	161	161	299	252	145	465	74	122	97	161	103	76	378	85	222
Cambridge	54	471	214	357	306	100	208	154	438	116	169		190	264	116	125	406	345	249	270	479	372	123	82	67	270	505	630	139	555	374	145	68	85	194	165	241	62	83	468	83	293	144	120	159	148	379	227	165
Cardiff	157	505	105	382	368	103	209	117	483	182	45	190		289	209	238	441	385	121	112	485	385	56	284	246	216	549	680	244	564	245	232	154	208	165	183	325	262	172	477	108	167	142	194	111	121	390	41	244
Carlisle	301	221	224	93	87	196	87	343	196	370	277	264	289		142	389	152	96	353	297	206	96	247	320	336	231	262	391	158	275	477	119	206	191	120	119	57	289	194	188	260	399	348	152	176	324	101	309	121
Doncaster	171	344	176	235	184	94	94	235	310	236	175	116	209	142		242	275	219	251	247	357	249	150	167	194	181	383	507	47	432	374	29	74	39	86	61	114	147	43	346	145	297	234	18	109	209	257	232	34
Dover	71	588	292	478	424	194	312	174	553	82	202	125	238	389	242		523	462	248	331	596	488	191	185	125	360	622	747	256	671	381	260	185	202	299	276	358	174	205	585	141	300	130	245	251	143	496	274	282
Dundee	448	67	376	117	113	349	239	495	52	517	430	406	441	152	275	523		56	518	460	127	83	410	484	469	394	132	259	295	186	642	258	349	314	286	285	166	422	328	117	433	552	514	291	330	500	167	473	250
Edinburgh	390	125	320	73	57	292	183	439	91	456	373	345	385	96	219	462	56		450	399	144	44	349	386	413	333	158	285	234	216	574	202	295	258	216	215	110	366	262	123	372	496	453	235	274	438	124	412	194
Exeter	181	569	201	446	428	157	282	82	550	184	76	249	121	353	251	248	518	450		230	560	449	111	335	279	282	618	744	309	628	123	270	196	247	237	236	364	308	221	549	156	46	135	237	179	105	454	161	287
Fishguard	260	504	56	373	371	170	209	222	493	291	154	270	112	297	247	331	460	399	230		486	376	153	366	337	167	542	671	280	567	353	237	209	272	160	197	329	343	220	481	205	264	251	215	145	233	392	67	261
Fort William	510	149	430	133	190	392	296	539	125	575	486	479	485	206	357	596	127	144	560	486		101	454	527	543	438	66	195	369	79	686	329	422	399	329	329	253	504	401	49	472	595	555	348	382	541	195	496	330
Glasgow	397	145	320	33	101	292	183	439	110	468	373	372	385	96	249	488	83	44	449	376	101		346	419	432	330	166	295	254	179	573	215	314	291	216	215	148	385	293	92	356	495	448	248	272	433	84	409	217
Gloucester	109	468	102	330	318	56	174	99	443	159	35	123	56	247	150	191	410	349	111	153	454	346		225	196	191	504	628	198	528	235	174	85	159	140	126	204	110	441	52	157	119	126	77	105	343	89	189
Great Yarmouth	128	517	294	402	345	180	252	240	477	180	275	82	284	320	167	185	484	386	335	366	527	419	225		82	334	553	677	169	602	446	196	140	128	240	212	281	20	153	515	200	365	221	166	225	220	426	329	201
Harwich	76	535	281	425	372	167	275	187	504	128	217	67	246	336	194	125	469	413	279	337	543	432	196	82		349	569	693	196	611	390	223	147	155	265	228	308	73	150	524	145	309	166	187	240	164	435	267	228
Holyhead	269	439	111	305	311	148	141	288	426	334	206	270	216	231	181	360	394	333	282	167	438	330	191	334	349		474	603	231	514	405	176	190	216	102	124	272	311	185	427	238	328	311	168	113	293	338	184	204
Inverness	550	105	486	199	215	458	348	597	75	617	539	505	549	262	383	622	132	158	618	542	66	166	504	553	569	474		129	394	84	741	360	461	427	382	373	268	529	430	117	532	664	613	393	438	598	262	572	352
John o'Groats	663	232	601	328	342	574	478	724	202	741	668	630	680	391	507	747	259	285	744	671	195	295	628	677	693	603	129		518	189	868	487	588	554	511	500	395	654	557	244	656	790	737	520	567	723	379	696	479
Kingston upon Hull	184	364	223	251	185	134	127	264	327	245	233	139	244	158	47	256	295	234	309	280	369	254	198	169	196	231	394	518		445	421	55	102	44	130	95	132	149	90	346	192	355	269	65	169	256	259	264	37
Kyle of Lochalsh	586	189	499	212	263	471	372	618	159	651	552	555	564	275	432	671	186	216	628	567	79	179	528	602	611	514	84	189	445		763	394	500	476	407	406	318	582	479	128	550	674	633	427	451	618	263	594	407
Land's End	297	692	313	570	552	281	405	205	665	308	200	374	245	477	374	381	642	574	123	353	686	573	235	446	390	405	741	868	421	763		405	320	371	361	361	498	421	345	665	274	89	259	361	303	228	585	285	411
Leeds	189	327	169	212	156	113	72	255	293	260	194	145	232	119	29	260	258	202	270	237	329	215	174	196	223	176	360	487	55	394	405		95	68	75	40	92	176	70	307	168	316	257	33	109	232	220	248	24
Leicester	97	414	153	299	252	39	140	158	389	166	120	68	154	206	74	185	349	295	196	209	422	314	85	140	147	190	461	588	102	500	320	95		51	130	92	187	119	25	419	73	242	162	62	84	137	330	177	108
Lincoln	131	383	199	274	224	90	128	209	357	197	183	85	208	191	39	202	314	258	247	272	399	291	159	128	155	216	427	554	44	476	371	68	51		84	159	105	35	387	137	293	201	46	133	204	298	233	75
Liverpool	202	341	104	213	219	93	49	234	318	272	161	194	165	120	86	299	286	216	237	160	329	216	140	240	265	102	382	511	130	407	361	75	130	84		35	168	220	98	308	172	283	254	72	58	239	221	199	64
Manchester	185	340	129	212	196	80	48	227	318	257	161	165	183	119	61	276	285	215	236	197	329	215	126	212	228	124	373	500	95	406	361	40	92	159	35		132	185	73	307	144	283	236	38	69	221	220	187	64
Newcastle upon Tyne	286	235	257	149	64	207	129	347	201	352	299	241	325	57	114	358	166	110	364	329	253	148	204	281	308	272	268	395	132	318	498	92	187	105	168	132		264	157	233	260	410	337	125	201	324	158	347	84
Norwich	114	496	276	382	328	166	232	214	457	175	252	62	262	289	147	174	469	366	308	343	504	385	110	20	73	311	529	654	149	582	421	176	119	35	220	185	264		130	492	145	343	207	146	205	206	403	301	181
Nottingham	122	393	164	274	221	50	111	183	353	193	145	83	172	194	43	205	328	262	221	220	401	293	110	153	150	185	430	557	90	479	345	70	25	387	98	73	157	130		390	109	267	191	37	93	176	290	192	77
Oban	499	178	412	94	180	384	285	530	141	565	465	468	477	188	346	585	117	123	549	481	49	92	441	515	524	427	117	244	346	128	665	307	419	137	308	307	233	492	390		462	587	545	339	364	530	148	506	309
Oxford	57	483	154	353	324	64	187	90	465	108	74	83	108	260	145	141	433	372	156	205	472	356	52	200	145	238	532	656	192	550	274	168	73	293	172	144	260	145	109	462		199	77	135	106	64	379	141	181
Plymouth	218	615	237	492	474	203	328	128	587	224	122	293	167	399	297	300	552	496	46	264	595	495	157	365	309	328	664	790	355	674	89	316	242	201	283	283	410	343	267	587	199		176	283	225	151	500	206	333
Portsmouth	70	560	222	430	401	141	264	52	547	48	97	144	142	348	234	130	514	453	135	251	555	448	119	221	166	311	613	737	269	633	259	257	162	254	46	236	337	207	191	545	77	176		230	207	21	461	182	278
Sheffield	159	360	159	245	190	76	86	216	320	226	161	120	194	152	18	245	291	235	237	215	348	248	126	166	187	168	393	520	65	427	361	33	62	46	72	38	125	146	37	339	135	283	230		82	199	263	217	52
Shrewsbury	160	399	77	269	265	45	98	185	371	226	103	159	111	176	109	251	330	274	179	145	382	272	77	225	240	113	438	567	169	451	303	109	84	133	58	69	201	205	93	364	106	225	207	82		185	277	118	133
Southampton	77	547	201	417	388	128	251	31	532	61	76	148	121	324	209	143	500	438	105	233	541	433	105	220	164	293	598	723	256	618	228	232	137	204	239	221	324	206	176	530	64	151	21	199	185		445	161	258
Stranraer	402	228	325	51	170	297	188	444	194	475	378	379	390	101	257	496	167	124	454	392	195	84	343	426	435	338	262	379	259	263	585	220	330	298	221	220	158	403	290	148	379	500	461	263	277	445		417	252
Swansea	194	507	73	379	383	119	216	167	505	222	85	227	41	309	232	274	473	412	161	67	496	409	89	329	267	184	572	696	264	594	285	248	177	233	195	187	347	301	192	506	141	206	182	217	118	161	417		272
York	207	319	195	214	148	130	96	269	285	275	222	165	244	121	34	282	250	194	287	261	330	217	189	201	228	204	352	479	37	407	411	24	108	75	99	64	84	181	77	309	181	333	278	52	133	258	222	272	